COLORADO MOUNTAIN COLLEGE
Quigley Library
3000 Cty. Road 114
Glenwood Springs, CO 81601

Always in Good Taste

✦✦✦

The L. J. Minor Story

Always in Good Taste

♦♦♦

The L. J. Minor Story

♦♦♦

Authored by

Lewis J. Minor, Ph.D.

with

John B. Knight, Ed.D.

BHZ Publishing Company
P. O. Box 1584
Wilkes-Barre, PA   18711

Always in Good Taste

The L. J. Minor Story

Is Dedicated

To all the workers of the world whose God-given talents are used to maintain and improve the quality of life worldwide;

To many unsung heroes who made the L. J. Minor Corporation successful;

To the more than 700 schools here in the United States, and to others worldwide, where foodservice occupations and foodservice knowledge are taught;

Particularly, to the thousands of teachers and students at these schools, where foodservice training insures the maintenance and improvement of foodservice quality standards worldwide.

Lewis J. Minor
May, 1995

Acknowledgements

Thanks to my wife Whitney and our daughter Jackie, and sons Brad and David for their support and endless suggestions as to how to best compile the many contributions made to this text.

Of course, for their extensive writing, dedication to professionalism, love for God, family, their past employees, and the readers of this book, I thank Dr. Lewis J. and Mrs. Ruth E. Minor. You have inspired me more in life than you will ever know!

John B. Knight
August, 1995

Without the prompting, encouragement, inspiration and prayerful support of Brother Herman Zaccarelli this work would not have been undertaken or completed.

Without the support and help given by Ruth E. Minor a communication gap between Brother Herman, John Knight and me would have existed.

Without help from our daughter Ruth Ann, the photographic content of the book would be missing.

Without chapters, letters, and other testimonials from our plant executives and employees marketing, merchandising, and advertising executives, chef consultants, our CPA, Ralph Napletana, and the leaders who followed, William F. McLaughlin, and Dr. Sam Lee the narrative would be incomplete.

Lewis J. Minor, Ph.D.
August, 1995

TABLE OF CONTENTS

PART 1
L. J. MINOR: THE EARLY YEARS, 1914 - 1951
FAMILY, FAITH, AND FRIENDS

Preface

If Horatio Alger* ever wanted a rags to riches story on how strong moral character coupled with a determination to succeed brought success, he could have found no better one than the story of the life that Dr. Lewis J. Minor tells of in his book, *Always In Good Taste: The L. J. Minor Story.*

In true Alger tradition, Minor's upbringing as a child was from a home of very modest circumstances with a later struggle to earn a college degree which would qualify him to teach. After teaching for a time, he decided to go into industry where he used his knowledge in chemistry to become an expert in the identification of food flavors.

However, his ambition drove him on and he decided to start his own business which would be the manufacture of a food base that would essentially duplicate many of the fine flavors chefs build into their foods by great skill and long, arduous labor. Again, it was a struggle, but Lew Minor wisely built his business using chefs as his salespeople. It succeeded.

Still filled with the Horatio Alger desire to move on ahead, Minor entered the Food Science School of Michigan State as a doctoral candidate. Again, he succeeded and now fate, in true Horatio Alger fashion, stepped in. The School of Hotel, Restaurant, and Institutional Management needed someone to teach an overview course in food science, sanitation, and nutrition to serve as a background for those who were to enter the hospitality field. With a masterful hand, Minor not only made his courses the most popular and respected in the HRIM School, but, at the same time, he managed his business which continued to grow in the true Alger fashion.

Dr. Minor's story is not of himself alone, but also of his partner and wife, Ruth Minor, a woman of great charm, a homemaker, mother of their eight children, and a business woman, who struggled along with her husband to see him succeed.

Then there were others including hard working employees, managers, and a sales force made up of renowned culinarians, dedicated to seeing that the Minor product was the national choice of chefs for their kitchens.

But, why tell the story here? Read it! It's a fascinating story of a man who not only became a great entrepreneur and educator, but a great friend and benefactor to many as well.

Lendal H. Kotschevar, Ph.D.

* Horatio Alger (1834 - 1899) -- an American writer who wrote more than one hundred books for boys. Alger's heroes fight poverty and adversity, but gain wealth and honor. All of his works were extremely popular.

Foreword

I have been asked to write a foreword to this remarkable and true life story of Dr. Lewis and Ruth Minor. Confronting the reality of my limitations before I begin, still, I agree to the honor. I embark on this labor of love not with the high sounding words and platitudes so often found in such an effort, for in that manner I cannot speak from the heart.

I begin, instead, with a simple "fish tale." The events of this tale are true, but not, I believe, extraordinary. An ordinary fisherman and his friends go out to fish. It was their livelihood. As was the custom of their country, they fished at night. Having toiled the long evening through, they drew up their nets and headed to shore. As they approached the shore, a man they did not know appeared and said, "Friends, have you any catch?" "No," the fishermen answered. "We have toiled all night, and taken nothing." To which the man on shore replied, "Launch out into the deep, and let down your net." Consider the setting. The fishermen were tired, frustrated, and disenchanted. What would you or I have done in their place?

I think I know what Dr. and Mrs. Minor would have done. Because the story above is not really about fishing, it is about faith. The same type of faith that causes a man to "launch out into the deep" by starting a company in his garage. With a mere $6,000. Yes, the L. J. Minor Company ultimately becomes a multimillion dollar enterprise. An yes, Dr. and Mrs. Minor do indeed let down their net, ultimately drawing to themselves the hundreds of individuals whose lives they will enrich. This special couple, whose lives you are about to read, are fully aware, as Reverend Theodore M. Hesburgh, C.S.C, President Emeritus of Notre Dame University wrote, that "optimism is often thwarted, hopes dashed, and faith threatened, but we will never know what heights we can achieve unless we try." Dr. and Mrs. Minor tried, and they achieved much.

This then is the story of a couple and their family who know and lived the life of faith. Faith in their God, their values, their visions, and each other. The story of their great success will no doubt awe some who read these pages. It will inspire some, and bring a tear to the eyes of others. But it would be a mistake to see this book primarily as the chronicle of a man who achieved honor as a businessman, scientist, teacher, philanthropist, and family man. It is instead the story of a miracle.

For you see, the story of the fishermen in the "fish tale" is not, as my fundamentalist Christian friends might insist, the story of a miracle performed on shore. Nor, I am convinced, was the miracle about the nets, once cast, becoming over-flowed with fish. the miracle instead was that quite ordinary people made something extraordinary of their own lives and the lives of those that would follow, because they had the faith to do so. It has been said that "eaten bread is soon forgotten." That is true. Thus, I am sure, the fish that were caught in the true story of these fishermen were soon consumed and disappeared. But the hope and charity of those simple fishermen and the man they did not know live on today. Theirs is the story of the miracle of faith. This volume too is the story of faith, and of how quite common people, with God's help, made an extraordinary impact on those whose lives they touched. I am one of those fortunate people. After reading this book, you will be one of them also.

Perhaps you feel that thus far in life you too have "toiled all night, and taken nothing." Maybe you are a student beginning a career in the great field of Hospitality. Perhaps Dr. Minor was a friend to you, or he may instead be a man you do not yet know. I can tell you that after reading his story of faith, you too will have glimpsed a miracle.

Respectfully,

Brother Herman E. Zaccarelli, CSC

PART 1

L. J. MINOR: THE EARLY YEARS

1914 - 1951

FAMILY, FAITH, AND FRIENDS

Chapter 1

Minor Miracles: Irish Heritage and My Mother

A Blessed Baby   **Irish Ancestry and History**

A Blessed Baby

The date was October 24, 1914. My mother, Kathleen Mary Hill, and my father, Newell Wellington Minor, were living on my fraternal grandfather's farm at Forest Bay in Harbor Beach, Michigan, at the time. My birth that day was a miracle because I had the umbilical cord wound around my throat and could have been choked to death during the birth.

My dad said that I was the best looking baby he had ever seen. I weighed 10 1/2 pounds, so I was a big baby. I was christened by Father Fleming, and when I was brought home by my mother, my dad asked, "Did the Pope bless this child?" She responded, "Yes, all the way from Rome."

My father didn't like popes, because according to one of the Pope's edicts, he was born of parents from a "mixed marriage." However, he was quite tolerant when you consider everything, as he let my mother raise us children Catholics, and never complained about it. He even went to "Father and Son Nights" at St. Benedict's later when I was in grade school.

Irish Ancestry and History

At this time, my grandfather, Joseph, worked with a team of horses every day clearing stones out of the harbor in the town, which at that time was called Sand Beach, but is now known as Harbor Beach, Michigan. He and his team of horses worked a twelve-hour day clearing out stones and he got 50 cents a day for his labor and that of his horses. My mother said he would often take the money and use it to buy an orange for me to eat. He died when I was two, so I never knew him.

My grandfather served as a Captain in the Union Army Cavalry during the Civil War. After the War he farmed and did carpentry work. His tool chest was in our basement when I was a boy living in Highland Park, Michigan. My mother told me he was a philosopher. One of his sayings stuck with me all of my life.

"Since man to man is so unjust,
I hardly know which one to trust.
I've trusted many to my sorrow,
so pay today and I'll trust tomorrow."

My mother was born in a little town called Dolla in County Tipperary, Ireland, which was known as the golden vale. Her father, Patrick Hill, was a stone mason who lived with his wife, Kathleen, and their nine children on an estate that was owned by an English lord named Dunalley. As English lords went at that time, my mother said he was quite benevolent.

When my mother's father was of age, Lord Dunalley sent him to England to learn the stone mason trade. When he returned, he did a lot of building for him and, as a result of his efforts, the Lord told him he could build a special home for his family. So, my grandparents had a better home than most of their Irish neighbors. It was the one that my grandfather built.

When my mother was still a child, my grandfather went swimming with a group of friends in one of the beautiful lakes. After they came out and were going to go home, he said to his friends, "I'm going in for another dip." He was never seen again.

Dolla, where my mother spent her childhood, is a small village located at the foot of the Knockahopple Mountain, three miles from the town of Silvermines, where Dolla Catholics go to church, and seven miles from Nenagh, in County Tipperary, Ireland. Dolla's population is about 200. The cottage in which my mother was raised had three rooms and a clay floor. Historically, Dolla was a center for the uprising of the Irish Republican Army against the Black and Tans of the British.

E. H. Sheehan wrote that Dolla's origin dates back to 540 A.D. Vikings worked the silver mines in 900 A.D. The only buildings from the past left standing in Nenagh today show the influence of Norman architecture, not Celtic. With the capture of Limerick in 1650, the conquest of Ireland by Cromwell's British Army was completed.

In 1651, Courts of Justice were set up in Nenagh by the British. Many Irish patriot families, including the O'Kennedys and the O'Briens, were executed by court order. Cromwell's forces never reached the town of Silvermines, located four miles from Nenagh. Hence, Dolla village's inhabitants were spared.

A friend of mine, Maureen Rohan, sent me pictures of houses and families in Dolla today. She also sent photos of the school and church that Dolla's residents attend in Silvermines, plus books about Tipperary, Nenagh, and Silvermines. That is where this early history was obtained.

Regarding other history of Ireland, Irish (or Gaelic) was spoken and written during the early Christian period. The Vikings invaded the island between the eighth and ninth centuries. Thus, you find many Scandinavian words in modern Irish. In the twelfth century, the island was overrun with Normans who introduced French dialects. English rule began in Ireland in the seventeenth century.

3

Many uprisings were fought against the English rulers. There was constant strife for the Irish who were fighting to reclaim the land of their fathers. Some of the important dates in Irish history include:

1845-1849 - The Great Hunger Famine.
1850-1914 - The Great Emigration.
1921, 6th December - Treaty signed with Britain granting Ireland Dominion status as the Irish Free State.
1922, 7th January - The Irish Dail approves the treaty. March, Valera's Republican Society fights Irish Nationalists in a civil war.
1923, April - Civil war ends with victory of pro-treaty-forces
1948, 21st December - Irish Free State declared a Republic.
1973 - Both Northern and Southern Ireland enter the European Economic Community.

The Republic of Ireland consists of Connaught in the North, which borders Protestant Ulster, Leinster in the midlands, and Munster in the South. Ulster is a province of Great Britain. There the Catholics, organized as The Defenders in 1795, were beaten by the Protestants, who renamed their organization The Orange Order after William of Orange, and were made up of anti-Catholic vigilantes bent on burning the Catholics out of Ulster. They outnumbered the Catholics 2 to 1.

Today, Ulster is occupied by British troops. School rooms in Catholic schools are jammed beyond capacity and heavily armed. It is soldier against child. Britain's decision to keep Ulster, the Protestant part of Ireland, backfired. At the time, Ulster appeared to be the bigger prize due to its industrial makeup.

Ulstermen glorify their province where life, materially speaking, is superior to that of the Republic, or other parts of Ireland. They own the good land, while the Catholic farms are up in the rocks and heather. The Ulstermen's prosperity is the result of the industrializing of Ulster by England, which kept the remainder as a cattle ranch. In contrast to the peaceable south, Ulster lives in constant strife between the Irish Republican Army and the Royal Ulster Constabulary. The one-third Catholic minority is oppressed, depressed, harried, and desperate. Children are used in the fighting against soldiers.

People who live in the Republic want no part of the British north. The peace and prosperity they are enjoying could be lost by a union with Ulster. Meanwhile, the Ulster-Britain connection is strained to the breaking point. Hatred is inbred in Ulster with Christian against Christian.

Ireland is the island of invasions and conquests. Britain, after King Billy's conquest, took the Irish people's land, making them serfs. Thousands of Irish were put on ships that were sunk by their English appointed lords. Dogs had better lives than the Irish had under British oppression. The Orangeman's attitude is, "The only good Catholic is a dead Catholic." There is no compassion or justice for the Catholic minority. Meanwhile, wealthy

4

Ulstermen are buying up acreage in Cork. These same individuals believe that the civil war in Ulster will last for another 150 years. This is a religious war with hatred being preached from the pulpit. This fans the fires of brutality and oppression.

Today, all that a visitor would see in Dolla are two taverns, a grocery, and a cemetery. Dolla is inhabited by poor farmers. Most of them are crippled by arthritis. They wear Wellington's (knee-high rubber boots). When I visited Dolla in 1972, the people were friendly, easy going, and poor. The village dwellers lived in small cottages, but I visited Mrs. Ford, who looked after my mother when she was a little girl. Her home was nice and modern. Silvermines is where the Dolla children go to school and church today. Farming is the principal occupation. Cows are kept on the farms together with other livestock.

My grandmother's maiden name was Kathleen Mary Ryan. There are Ryans all over the county of Tipperary. A family called Ryan Scissors lives on the Knockahopple Mountain. They are so-named because they are barbers. Gleeson, Rohan, Madden, Sweeney, Ford, and Hughes are some of the dwellers.

When my grandfather drowned in 1902, my grandmother remained a widow for several years until she met a man named Ed Connell who introduced her to his cousin, Patrick Joseph Corcoran, a widower from St. Paul, Minnesota. Subsequently, she married Pat Corcoran, and went to St. Paul to live. In fact, when I was eight years old, my mother and her sister, Aunt Lill, took me to St. Paul to visit them where they lived in 1922, but that is getting ahead of my story.

In the late 1890s, my mother's uncle, Tim Hughes, sold his cow for fare to America by ship. He worked his way from Boston to Ishpeming, Michigan, where he established a successful mercantile business. Tim made annual trips back to his home in Dolla. In 1900, he took my mother's sister, Aunt May, back to Ishpeming. She met and married a railroad man. They had two daughters and lived in St. Louis, Missouri. In 1902, Tim brought back another of the Hill girls, my Aunt Lill. She also married a railroad man, settled in Dilworth, Minnesota, and had two sons and a daughter.

In 1905, he sent for my mother and paid for her passage to America. At the tender age of sixteen, she traveled from Dolla to Ishpeming alone, worked as a chambermaid at the Mather Inn, and did the same type of work, progressing from DeGuerre's Rooming House in Munising, Michigan, where she made good friends with Mrs. DeGuerre, to the Marquette Hotel in Marquette, Michigan, where she made long-time friends with Nellie Maher, and finally to a hotel in Harbor Beach, Michigan, where she met my father.

Dad came courting her on his bicycle. He lived five miles north of town at Forest Bay, Lake Huron. He had a job at the Huron Milling Company as a control chemist and first aid man. He also had fishing nets and did some commercial fishing on his own. He never found it profitable. He said, "When the fish were plentiful, I couldn't get much for them. When the catches were small, then the price was up." It was the old law of supply and demand. He was a Methodist and a Mason. They were married in 1912 by Father Fleming. Mother was a beauty when she married Dad. Aunt Winnie told me, "As a girl, Kathleen was stoop shouldered when she stood or walked. As a woman she stood tall and straight. She looked a bit like Irene Rich of movie fame, or Greer Garson."

When the immigration of the Hill family from Dolla was complete, the only Hill left in Dolla was mother's brother Tom, who never left Ireland. My uncle Jack came when he was sixteen. He worked in New York City. I remember meeting him, and watching him do the Irish Jig when I was a boy. After this visit, he went back, and two years later, we received word that he had drowned in the Hudson River while swimming with friends.

Aunt May came first with Tim Hughes, followed by Aunt Lill, my mother, then my grandmother, and Aunt Winnie. Uncle Pat was the last to come, since Tom did not leave and Uncle Jack had already arrived in America. Together they sent Uncle Pat the money for his passage. Having been a member of the IRA, Pat went to Canada.

Later, he was smuggled into this country by automobile. A relative of Pat Corcoran had a job for him at the mailing depot in St. Paul. He became a supervisor and worked there until he retired. Each year he would register at the Immigration Bureau as a citizen of Ireland. He was what Eleanor Roosevelt called, "A good alien immigrant."

Chapter 2

Uncle Pat: The Legend

Memories of Dolla   **Poetry**   **Irish Americans**

Memories of Dolla

Uncle Pat returned to Dolla quite often. His poetry and his fiddle, penny whistle, and concertina playing and singing made him welcome anywhere. People in Dolla regard Uncle Pat as a legend and talk of erecting a monument in his memory. He's survived by his son, his second wife, Sinda, and Aunt Winnie, his sister, who, at 92, resides in Mesa, Arizona, and still speaks of her childhood memories, saying, "When I was a little girl I liked to look through the iron bars at Lord Dunalley's beautiful estate. One day he told the gate keeper to let me in so I could look all around at the flowers." My mother would have the same great memories if she were alive today, but Aunt Winnie tells me many stories of bygone years, such as those of Patrick J. Hill, my uncle.

Uncle Pat, like his father before him, was sent to England to learn the stone mason trade by Lord Dunalley. After returning to Ireland, he became a captain in the IRA. This was in the 1930's when the Irish Free State was occupied by British soldiers called "Black and Tans." His troops would set up road blocks and ambush the Black and Tans when they left their trucks. They would lead them into the bogs. You could hear them screaming as they would fall into the crevasses.

One awful day, the British soldiers killed every living creature in a village. Uncle Pat and his company went to their barracks where the British soldiers were revelling. He ordered them out. They wouldn't come out. His troops burned the barracks to the ground. Horrors like this must have tormented Pat all his life, but he never talked about any of it. My mother told me that story. When I asked Aunt Winnie about it, she knew nothing, for it happened after she left Ireland. Neighbors in Dolla must have written about it to my mother.

Poetry

The following are four poems. First is "The Road Through Knockahopple," by Uncle Pat. Second is a poem about Uncle Pat written by Ed Hughes following a visit at our home. It's titled "Cousin Pat." The third is "Going Home" and the fourth "My Fight For Irish Freedom," both by Uncle Pat.

"THE ROAD THROUGH KNOCKAHOPPLE"

There is a spot in Tipperary so far across the sea,
In memory, dreams and visions, it keeps calling out to me.
It's located in the mountains, where lea and heather meet,
Where "cannovauns" are waving o'er moorlands filled with peat.
A lazy stream is flowing by the meadow's rugged edge,
Its banks all decorated with heather and with sedge.
I see it all before me, in sunshine and in rain,
That road through Knockahopple keeps winding in my brain.

I can see the Hill of Keeper clad in its robe of brown;
It is towering ever skyward o'er the famous Glen of Glown.
We climbed unto its summit on our Blessed Lady's day,
While more of our good neighbors were scaling Moher-clay.
We could see beyond the Shannon many places of renown,
And view the lovely countryside that borders Nenagh town.
To crown the grand occasion we'd enjoy a dance and tune
On the road through Knockahopple leading back to old Presoon.

I knew each house along that road. I knew the people there.
Come in, "God save you kindly, to the fire, pull up a chair.
The stranger was made welcome and invited for to stay.
The wanderer seeking shelter was never turned away.
All the local gossip was twisted, turned and spun
As the neighbors got together when their daily work was done.
There would be a game of "forty-five" as the turf fire burned bright,
On the road through Knockahopple on a chilly winter's night.

I knew each bush along that road and every field and gate,
I walked it in my boyhood when 'twas early, dark and late.
With my hound around the moorlands, I sought the wily hare,
To find where he was hiding and chase him from his lair.
With youthful chums I fished the streams in quest of speckled trout,
We'd dam the stream above the pool, the water we'd bail out.
We would take our catch and amble home to cook them with our 'tay,
On that road through Knockahopple on a lovely summer day.

That winding road was throd by some of Ireland's bravest men,
They made their plans to wreck the "tans" within the "rebel's den."
The older folks remember well when on the mountain side,

8

The bullets rained like hail stones, and Matt Ryan and Sheehy died.
There was a gloom of sadness I never will forget,
And silent vow of vengeance that perhaps is smoldering yet.
On the list of Irish heroes, they sure deserve a spot-
On the road through Knockahopple they will never be forgot.

There is a sturdy slate-roofed cottage that sits above the road.
It is not a high-class mansion, just a working man's abode.
For me it holds fond memories of a maiden young and fair,
With a healthy bloom upon her cheeks as fresh as mountain air.
Many a time and often, at a certain place we'd meet,
And the secret of our courtship made each interview more sweet.
Her glances told me stories only lovers understand-
On the road through Knockahopple where our future life was planned.

Please God, I'll soon return and walk this road once more,
And visit with the people I knew in days of yore.
I'll attend their wakes and dances from Curreeny unto Glown,
And I will be looking forward to a fair in Nenagh town.
I will dance the "Ballycommon set" to the concertina's tune,
With the local boys and girls on a Sunday afternoon.
I will feel mighty happy, my sorrows I'll unload,
When I Christmas with old friends again on Knockahopple road.

        By PATRICK J. HILL
        259 Cathedral Place
        St. Paul, Minnesota,
        U.S.A.

"COUSIN PAT"

I went to see my cousin Pat
He's down here from St. Paul.
He's staying with his sister Kate
While he visits with us all.

Not all the family members
Got to see their cousin Pat.
A bit of bad luck for them
They are some worse off for that.

For he links the generations
With his family history.
And he served the cause that changed the laws
To set old Ireland free.

But the family is prolific
and they are scattered far and wide.
Sure it'd take the Halls of Tara
To get us all inside.

But if this multitudinous family
should produce a famous man.
We'll need a family history
like the other Irish clan.

And though we're all Americans
for which we thank you God.
And forgive us for our rightful pride
that we sprung from the ol' sod.
       Cousin Ed
P.S.
One more thing dear Lord
While we're having this here chat
Please don't let the mold get broke
that you used on cousin Pat.

"GOING HOME"

Take me back to Tipperary,
To its vales and sparkling rills,
To its moorlands glens and meadows,
To its heath clod friendly hills,
To the old familiar places,
Where I roamed so long ago,
To see again the smiling faces,
Of the girls I used to know.
I'll meet the boys my loyal comrades,
who helped to formulate the plans,
To finish what our fathers started,

and defeat the Black and Tans,
To free Tipperary's tenant farmers,
from a foreign tyrants grip,
Burn down his lordly mansons,
send him on a homeward trip.

There are those who will be absent,
when a meeting I do call,
Some are far across the ocean,
some in freedoms fight did fall,
Murphy, Hughes, McGrath, and Lacken,
Tipperary's mountain fighting men,
Their deeds of valor are recorded,
"Oh" to live those days again.

In the Silvermines each Sunday morning,
early mass I will attend,
I will linger round the doorway,
for to greet each old time friend.
On the homeward trip we'll stop at Dolla,
there to have a glass of stout,
And to hear the latest gossip,
of the neighbors round about.
In the afternoon we will assemble,
all around Mountisland cross,
there will be lots of fun and banter,
and a game of pitch and toss.
To hear good concertina music,
I will wend my way to Glown,
I will be there to seek excitement,
at the fair in Nenagh Town.

I will visit all the neighbors,
I knew so well in days of yore.
I am sure the tea will be got ready,
when I step inside the door.
At night we'll sit around the table,
play a game of "forty five,"
Join the circle at the rosary,
thank the Lord to be alive.

I will build a cozy cottage,
on a fertile plot of ground.
Make my bride of some fine lady,
when shrovetide comes around.
She will have love and lots of comfort,
I'll dress her up in fashions gay,
I will settle down contented,
for I have come home to STAY.
     Just a dream
     Patrick J. Hill

"MY FIGHT FOR IRISH FREEDOM"

I am thinking of Tipperary, its hills and rushing rivers,
Its healthy robust natives, who breathe the mountain air,
God-fearing in their way of life, and very cheerful givers,
The neighbors joys and sorrows, they were ready for to share,
It was there so many years ago, that I was bred and born,
In a cottage by the roadside, as the snow came trickling down,
I first beheld the light of day on a cold December morn,
In the parish of the Silvermines, not far from Nenagh town.

I learned at an early age the wrongs and ills of Erin,
Inflicted by a tyrant, from across the Irish sea,
I longed to take an active part, to set my country free,
Nineteen sixteen in Dublin, is a year I will remember,
When patriotic Irishmen for freedom struck a blow,
Neath the banner of those heroes I soon became a member,
I swore like all my comrades, to wreck our ancient foe.

The rulers of the Empire sent a force to put us under,
The lowest kind of criminals, with no restraining bans,
Their orders were to shoot and kill, and tear our homes asunder,
They were known around the country, as the British Black and Tans,
We fought them by the roadside, we fought them on the heather,
We burned down their Barracks, with their lives we made them pay,
Sinn Fein, it was our password, like brothers all together,
We met them, and defeated them, in many a bloody fray.

Those battles now are history, old Ireland won her freedom,
The rulers of the Empire admitted their defeat,
Trusted Irish Statesmen were elected to succeed them,
To steer our ship of freedom, in a manner most discreet,
For the gallant Irish soldier, when the fighting it was over,
His outlook for the future, indeed was very bleak,
With pocket light, and heavy heart, he soon became a rover,
And sailed to far off country's, employment for to seek.

I landed in the U.S.A., way out in Minnesota,
So far from Tipperary, where our guns of freedom spoke,
As loud as Indian war whoops on the prairies of Dakota,
But we rid our mother country, of the hated saxon yoke,
The mountains now are peaceful where freedoms guns ignited,
Through many years of struggle, to break the bondage chain,
The battle now is over, our wrongs and ills are righted,
We stand before the world as a NATION ONCE AGAIN.
     By Captain Patrick Hill
     D. Company
     6th Batt
     Tipp # I Brigade
     I.R.A.
     Written in 1926

Irish Americans

By 1930, Irish Americans had passed the heavy labor jobs on to the French Canadians, Italians, Serbs and Poles. They became factory workers, tradesmen, clerks, bookkeepers, salesmen, journalists, lawyers, priests, businessmen, and employers. Now the majority are middle class but some remain in slums. Many of these will emerge to become America's noblest sons.

We Irish-Americans, a Galway man told me, are rich in dollars, while the Irish-Irish are rich in religion. By and large, the Irish in America have good homes, good jobs, and a lot of material wealth.

On Saturday, March 20, 1994 at 7:00 P.M., we attended a concert by the Chieftains who are an internationally acclaimed group that plays traditional Irish music. Twenty-five hundred people attended. Every seat in the Wharton Center Theatre, on the campus of Michigan State University was taken. The Chieftains were great and received a standing ovation.

At a brief reception held after the concert, we renewed our acquaintance with the group's leader, Paddy Maloney. Paddy plays the pipes and penny whistle. We met him 15 years ago when they performed before a much smaller audience at Lahinch, County Clare, Ireland. Paddy stayed at the Aberdeen Arms Hotel where we were staying. Seeing him again was a real pleasure. It was great to see the Chieftains' fame and that their Irish music had been accepted worldwide. Paddy said, "I'm tired of this way of life, away from home and tired out all the time. It's good for Ireland though." "Yes," I said, "You are a goodwill ambassador for Ireland, wherever you perform." Tales of Uncle Pat, his character and poetry, arise occasionally and inspire me to reflect upon my great Irish heritage.

Chapter 3

Another Legend: My Dad

Newell Wellington Minor   **His Family**   **Dad's Life**

Newell Wellington Minor

My father was born in Harbor Beach, Michigan, on October 1, 1891. He was the son of Joseph and Christina (Wood) Minor. Having been employed by the Ford Motor Company for forty years, he retired with "star man" executive status.

His Family

His brother, Louis Franklin Minor, was a corporal of Company B, Sixth Engineers, United States Army in World War I and was declared of excellent character at the time of his discharge, August 25, 1919. I knew him when I was a boy. He lived with us for two years before his death in 1926. Gas exposure during the war destroyed his health. As engineers his company prepared the way for the troops that followed them. In other words, the engineers worked in advance of the front lines.

In addition to his brother, my dad had three half sisters and a half brother from his mother's earlier marriage to Alexander Wood. His half sisters' names were Elizabeth, Fanny, and Louise. Elizabeth Wood Carter died at age 74 after serving for 25 years as principal of Beardsley School, Elkhart, Indiana.

Dad's half brother, Albert Wood, lost his life in an unbelievable storm that sank his ship, the Isaac M. Scott, on November 7, 1913, in Lake Huron, in 60 mile per hour winds and 35 foot waves. Albert Wood was captain of the Isaac M. Scott. This ore-laden vessel was making its last trip of the season when the storm hit. All hands and the captain were lost. At the time, Albert was planning to be married when this final voyage was completed. Then he would retire and live out the remainder of his life in Harbor Beach. This storm, with its high winds that lasted for nine hours, robbed him of his dream, and broke the heart of his fiancee. Altogether, there were 13 ships lost in Lake Huron during this "unbelievable storm."

My dad was named by two of his half-sisters. His grandmother lived in Aberdeen, Scotland, where his mother was born and raised. She had two daughters and a son from her first marriage to Albert Wood, and two sons, my father and his brother, Louis, from her second marriage to Joseph Minor. She was Scotch Presbyterian, and her first husband was Methodist. Being a child from a mixed marriage, Dad was tolerant about religion, except, as I said before, for the Pope, whom he always despised.

Dad's Life

Dad's boyhood was a happy one. His needs were provided. Frank Murphy, who became the Governor of Michigan and later the Governor of the Philippines, was a classmate of his in high school. Incidentally, when Murphy returned from the Philippines to Detroit, he died an untimely death. His brother George went to Detroit and brought Frank's body home to Harbor Beach for burial in Rock Falls cemetery, outside of town. I was scoutmaster at the time, and sent two of my best scouts with George. We kept an honor guard for him while he was interred at a local funeral home. On the day of Governor Murphy's burial, "Soapy" Williams, governor at that time, and an entourage of important Democrats came for the burial. My scouts handled the parking.

After marrying Mother, Dad applied for work a Coast Guard Station. A part of the examination consisted of reading complex color charts. Dad was color blind, but Mother coached him on the colors and their locations. He passed. Dad was also employed at the Huron Milling Company as a control chemist and first aid man. He also took care of his own fishing nets, as I had stated earlier. When I was three years old, he and Mother moved to Highland Park, Michigan, and Dad got a job with the Maxwell Automobile Company. It was very heavy work, handling axles. He didn't weigh much at the time, only about 120 pounds. He needed the work. My mother took in boarders. They lived on Windemere, right near Oakland Avenue. The streetcars passed nearby and men rode them going to work at the Ford Motor Company, which was located there.

My dad had the opportunity to work at Ford Motor through a friend in Harbor Beach, Captain Ludington, who had the Ludington News Company in Detroit. To improve their living standard, Dad and Mother moved to Detroit where Dad was employed at Ford Motor's Highland Park Plant in the coke oven department's control lab. His greatest contribution to the company was a system for telegraphing the gas from storage tanks to whatever location in the Rouge Plant needed it. Valves that controlled the distribution were opened and closed by turning knobs at a control desk and reading charts that showed the volumes of gas being transferred. This saved men from needing to walk gas lines in all weather to turn valves on and off.

My father was a likable man who fit in well with other managers. His boss, Newkirk, had charge of the Ford coal mines and coke ovens. Dad had charge of the coke ovens at the Rouge Ford Plant. After retiring at age 65, he was inactive for two years, playing golf daily and going to the horse races with Mother. They also played poker a lot. One day, I visited them in Detroit. Our business, the struggling L. J. Minor Corporation, at that time was in Cleveland. We gave him samples and literature and got him interested in selling our food bases. Mother went with him and wrote up the reports. He loved doing this mornings. Afternoons he played golf or went to the races. They wintered in Florida and made calls for our food bases there.

Mother and Dad lived modestly but well on his pension, their social security, and what he earned selling our bases. They enjoyed life and knew how to live with friends and relatives always around. They wintered in Ft. Lauderdale, Florida, where Dad golfed and introduced our food bases in Miami and all over Florida.

Dad always kept fit. When he and Mother married he only weighed 114 pounds. He put on more pounds as he aged, but was never fat or obese. When he was young, Dad looked like a short Charles A. Lindbergh. Later, his looks changed, and he had a strong resemblance to Dwight D. Eisenhower. My brother-in-law raised the covers on Dad's death bed, pointed to Dad's legs, and said, "What a man." He always walked enough to keep his legs in shape. They looked like those of a 20-year-old. They were wonderful parents, and we miss them, but are glad that we - my brothers, sisters and I - always respected, admired, and loved them.

Chapter 4

My Mother's Proverbs, Plus Others

From Mother   **From Me**   **From Others**

From Mother

Mother used to tell me everything, even about Ireland, and would always describe situations with proverbs. Some of these were:

"Constant dripping wears a stone." Meaning, persevere and try, try again;

"The back of one is the face of another." This meant that when I'd lose a customer on my newspaper route, not to worry, I'd soon get another;

"Don't be seeing green fields far away." In other words, be content where you are;

"Always put your best foot forward." Show self-respect. Dress properly;

"Don't be run down in the heel." Keep shoes' heels in good repair. Be sure your attire is proper;

"Don't be blowing your own horn." Be humble;

"He who goes a-borrowing goes a-sorrowing." Never try to borrow from friends or relatives;

"Always taking out of the pot, and never putting in, you soon reach the bottom." Be thrifty, don't spend foolishly;

"Your eyes are bigger than your stomach." Don't take, or order, more than you can eat;

"What you give to God you get back two-fold." Support the churches;

"Take him with you when you can. Teach him how to be a man." A subtle reminder to take care of my baby brother, and show him a good example;

18

"Show me your friends and I'll tell you what you are." This is a truism;

"The Irish were made to be boss of them all." They're doing well in the U.S.A.;

"If you don't want to be digging ditches, get a good education";

"Oh! the Crather!" Meaning the creature, spoken when she felt sorry for someone;

"He who calls his brother a fool deserves Hell's fire";

"The Bible says, the Jews will inherit the earth";

"When you eat out, butter your bread on both sides";

"The U.S.A. is the greatest country in the world";

"Cleanliness is next to godliness";

"March will starch, April will try, May will tell if you'll live or die." We had hard winters;

"God helps those who help themselves";

"Many's the time when I was in Ireland that all we had to eat was 'Hern and point.'" We would imagine that a hen hung from the ceiling and pointed at it.

She would also say:

"For beauty I sure am no star .
There are others more handsome by far.
But, my face, I don't mind it.
Because I'm behind it.
It's the people in front get the jar." But she was a beauty;

"Eaten bread is soon forgotten." This means that when you have helped out some person or cause, the help you give is often soon forgotten;

"I'm digging my grave with my teeth";

19

"I'm on my way to Long Orchard." When dying;
"Time and tide wait for no man";

"You do it right, or you do it over";

"Never put off until tomorrow what you can do today";

"Nothing is worth more than today";

"A winner never quits, and a quitter never wins";

"It is the wheel that squeaks that gets the grease."

From Me

"Live everyday as if it's your last, and one day you'll be right." (Hal Roach)

"Be honest with yourself and others."

"Punctuality should become an everyday habit."

"Always treat your employees and suppliers as well as you treat your customers."

"A leader must serve."

"There is so much good in the worst of us, and so much bad in the best of us, that it ill behooves any of us to talk about the rest of us."

Remember this, "The quality is remembered long after the price has been forgotten." And "The customer is smarter than you are."

"Be patient and consistent in reaching goals."

" Haste makes waste."

"Society's change from 'Agrarian' to 'Industrial' to 'Electronic' has been demoralizing for us Americans."

"We can be sure of three things: Death, Taxes, and Change."

Remember the Golden Rule, "Do unto others as you would have them do unto you."

From Others

Dr. T. A. Ryan said, "Things that seem bad at the time often turn out for the best."

Confucius said, "All things are difficult before they are easy."

Danny Kaye said, "Nobody is ever without a prayer."

The Bible says, "Seek and ye shall find, ask and you shall receive, knock and it shall be opened unto you."

Shakespeare said, "The evil men do lives after them, while the good is oft interred with their bones."

Dr. Chamberlain, my physics professor, said, "Whenever anything worthwhile is accomplished, there is always enough credit to go all the way around."

Dr. Fred Fabian said, "The only way a poor man can set up an estate is with insurance."

Aunt Eliza (age 90), Ishpeming, Michigan, told us, "Youth is valuable, and old age is honorable."

Tom Ryan said, "Steal my purse or steal my wife, but don't steal my vote."

George Perles (football coach) said, "Keep your mouth shut, and good things will happen."

Chapter 5

My Childhood

A Second Brush with Death   **Child's Play**

Church and Friends   **Early Jobs**   **Saving Money**

Memories of School, Home, and Family   **Historical Reflections**

Childhood
by Edgar A. Guest
(1936)

You do not know it, little man
In your summer coat of tan
And your legs bereft of hose
And your peeling sunburned nose,
With a stone bruise on your toe,
Almost limping as you go
Running on your way to play
Through another summer day.
Friend of birds and streams and trees
That your happiest days are these.

A Second Brush with Death

During my boyhood, I had a lot of sickness. Oftentimes my brother Jack would look at me and say, "What's the matter, Lewie? Do you feel pale, Red?" I became very sick when I was four years old and nearly died. This was my second brush with death. I had diphtheria and bronchial pneumonia at the same time. One day I couldn't breathe and it was below zero outside. My mother held me out the window trying to get a breath into me. One of the roomers phoned for our doctor, Dr. Dougherty. God saved me because before the call was even completed the doctor stopped by for a call. In those days, doctors made house calls. My mother challenged him as she said, "What are you going to do, let him die?" He said, "Well, there's something new called Toxin Anti-Toxin, and I'll go to the hospital and get some to inject into him ." He did that, and apparently that saved me!

During my recovery I was so weak I couldn't walk without holding on to the walls. However, by the time I was five, I was able to attend kindergarten. A girl across the street, Loretta Smith, who used to dress me up like a girl when she played with me, walked me to school. My teacher's name was Miss Quackenbush. I didn't like her at all. When I got a little pop-gun for Christmas, I told my mother I wanted to take my gun to school and use it on Miss Quackenbush.

Child's Play

During World War I, while my mother was keeping boarders, the price of butter was extremely high. One of the boarders loved to put butter on his eggs after my mother served them to him boiled. One morning she asked, "Tim, how are the eggs? Are they too soft for you?" He said, "Never mind, mum, I'll harden them with butter." So the next morning she made the eggs hard. When he came down he put just as much butter on as the day before. My mother said "What's the matter, Tim? Are the eggs too hard for you this morning?" He said, "Never mind, mum, I'll soften them with butter." So the third morning she fixed the eggs medium and he still piled the butter on and she said, "Tim, don't you know that butter is two dollars a pound?" He said, "Well, mum, good butter is worth every 'dom' cent of it." Of course, he and the other boarders then were only paying a few dollars a week for their room and board.

At the end of the war, my parents moved from Windemere to Candler between John R and Brush Streets, in Highland Park. There we lived in a four-family flat that my father bought and on which he had a $24,000 mortgage. It was right near St. Benedict's School, so that's where I went to grade school and, eventually, high school. In between, I went to public schools, including Ford School and Highland Park Junior High School.

My brother, Jack, who was named John Emmett, after the great Irish patriot, Robert Emmett, was two-and-a-half years younger than me. One day we were playing on the corner of John R and Candler Avenue where they were building a house. Jack fell into the area that was excavated for a basement. It was filled with water. He was drowning and I couldn't swim. I called for help, and one of our neighbors, an older boy, Leo McGlynn, came and pulled him out. Thank God he, did not drown.

My brother Jack had bright red hair, it was kind of an orange cast. My hair was red, but it was dark, and was more auburn or brick red. My brother Newell Junior, who was five years younger than me, had black hair and was nicknamed "Putts." Jack's nickname was "Em" and another nickname he had was "Dynamite." I don't know how he got those nicknames, but he was active. When he was four, there was a large box that lay upside down in the backyard. I do not know where it came from, but it was about eight feet square and two feet high. Jack would get up on top of this box all day long yelling, "Arreo Vish to Bo, Arreo Vish to Bo!" It meant to him "Everybody Get on Board." Everyone called me "Lewic." My brother Eddie was ten years younger than me and his nickname was "Wow."

I can remember carrying him on my shoulders to play. My mother always said, "Take him with you when you can, and teach him how to be a man." So I did this.

Nearby was Ford Park. It was just a stone's throw away and by cutting through backyards, I could be over there within minutes. It was quite a place! One part of it was an oval exactly one mile in length. It was built up so there was a running track. In the winter, it was flooded for ice skating. I used to run and skate on it and inside this huge oval was a baseball diamond and a football field. There was always a lot going on there including games on the clay tennis courts and horseshoe courts, at which I became the Jr. Horseshoe Pitching Champion at that time.

Another part of the Park, which was closer to Woodward Avenue, had swings and a children's playground, sandboxes, and tennis courts. I spent much of my boyhood in that environment. By playing at Ford Park as much as I did, I got acquainted with a man named Mr. Menolds, who was the Director of Highland Park Recreation. He asked me if I wanted to go to their summer camp up on Platte Lake in northern Michigan. I said, "Well, I can't afford to go to camp. I also have a paper route." He said, "Well, if you can find a way to go, I'll work it out so that you'll only have to pay $5.00 a week to go." I talked it over with my folks and my brother Jack. Jack said he would do my paper route if I went.

The first summer I went for a week and had a great experience. The next summer I went again, but stayed for two weeks. We learned to row and sail boats. We went on canoe trips and did a lot of overnight camping, sang a lot of songs, and got acquainted with the older fellows who were the counselors at the camp. When we were hiking along, we would be singing different songs and learning songs as we went. Some of the older boys would sing songs like "I'm Just a Prisoner of Love" and "Poor Butterfly." Of course, I memorized these songs together with others they sang and can still sing them sixty-five years later.

An accident happened to my brother Newell when we lived in the four-family flat on Candler. One of the families who lived upstairs moved and left a lot of rubbish smoldering out in the alley. They didn't put their fire out, and Newell was playing in it. We were out in the alley playing ball at the time and weren't watching the poor little fellow. We heard him screaming. He had caught on fire. His pants were burning, so we ran into the yard screaming for Mother. She ran out, got him, and rolled him up in a carpet. This put the fire out. The poor boy was burned from his hip down to his knee on his left side. It was an awful burn and left a horrible scar. Newell was such a good little fellow that he never complained and just endured everything that came his way. This handicapped him for life, with golf being one sport he could play and bowling the other.

What I saw as a boy was that the auto companies were thriving. When I walked down Woodward Avenue, from where we lived, I would go past the Lincoln showrooms and the power plant of the Highland Park Plant. The generators that made the power with their large flywheels were running. I could see them running, if I walked down Woodward Avenue to Manchester. When I went down Manchester, I would come to the Ford Store.

Many is the time my mother sent me there to buy meat and that's where my dad took us to buy shoes. It was an amazing thing. Only Ford employees were allowed to trade in that store. But they had an abundance of everything there that one would need. My mother had certain menus that she liked to fix. She often sent me to get the butt end of a smoked ham and she would use that to make a New England dinner. Another favorite was a rolled rump roast and she would always get lots of meat for the weekends.

Even in the Depression Days we lived quite well and had enough to give charity to some of the less fortunate people. All through the Depression Days, my mother would give $5.00 each week to the church. She was a very strict Catholic and brought me up that way. I tried to join the Boy Scouts and when the troop was sponsored by De Molay, the junior branch of the Masons, she found out and made me quit.

When we lived on Buena Vista, the YMCA was up at the corner of Woodward and Buena Vista, just a block away from where we lived. She would not let me join that because she said they were Protestants. She said I should not be associating with them. That was strange because she was married to a Protestant herself.

Dad was liberal and was always a good provider. During the Depression, he worked not only at Ford Motor, but also Saturday nights at the Free Press bundling Sunday newspapers. He would receive $25.00 per week for that job.

A dollar was hard to come by in those days but paved streets and alleys were being laid, sewers were being put in, electric lights and plumbing were provided in most homes, and our house had both gas and electricity. My mother cooked on a gas stove, and we had a hot air furnace that burned coke. My dad always bought coke instead of coal. He said it was more thrifty and gave better heat without a lot of smoke because the volatiles had been driven out of the coal to make the coke. That was his job, testing the products that came from the coke ovens. Ford Motor Company had a large gas-holder nearby and I could always smell gas because some of it was leaking.

Everything was fine during my childhood. It was amazing the things that we had and how reasonable taxes were in those days. Beautiful buildings were going up, like the Fisher Building and the Masonic Temple. St. Benedict's Church was a small example of what was going on, and the theaters were beautiful.

Church and Friends

When I was seven or eight I made my First Communion. My mother bought me a beautiful blue suit and I was proud of this. I went to the confectionery store, and, on the way, two of the neighbor boys, the Geislers, who were older, bullied me and pushed me down onto the pavement. Another neighbor boy who lived across the street from them, George Washer, saw what was happening and came to stop them. George and I became good friends. He had a crystal radio set that I used to listen to at his home. Great fun for anyone at that age!

There were two fine priests at St. Benedict's. The first one, Father Halle, built the church. It's a beautiful church of red brick with copper gutters and a red tile roof. The church was built at that time, back in the 20's, at a cost of $250,000. Most of it was paid for by money taken in from gambling at bazaars that they held in the old church basement. Most of it was paid for with Protestant money. Father Halle had car raffles and my father, who was a Mason, sold $500 worth of tickets at the Ford Motor Company. That doesn't seem like much these days, but it was an awful lot of money in those days. Each ticket was sold for $5.00 each, so Dad sold 100 tickets.

Father Halle was a great man, but shortly after the church was completed, he died. When the church was built, in 1924, he needed an altar and he used to pray everyday for it. He spoke to Mark Storen, one of his parishioners, who was a contractor building the freeways on Davison and other roads. Storen told him to pray and if he got the contract he was after he'd buy him the altar he wanted which would cost $25,000. He got the contract and Father Halle got the altar. Father Halle was very strict and very good. He ran the parish in a business-like manner.

Father Halle's assistant, Father Rosebrook, used to teach our catechism classes and told us that he had been a Protestant, but when he wanted to become a minister and started studying theology, he turned to Catholicism. He told us that the American Indians have one of the best religions in the world. They believe in the Happy Hunting Ground, of course, but he said they see God in all things and they're very religious people. He told how he worked his way through the seminary by loading trucks in the summertime with huge pieces of concrete that were removed from roads that had to be rebuilt. He liked to play handball with us. We had a handball court at the back of the school. The chimney gave us an extra wall. It was short but it still served as a corner that we could use when playing. Father Rosebrook was a great player. We enjoyed having him play with us.

Our next door neighbors, when I was a boy, were the Gavin family. We seldom saw the mother and father, who were working, but we did get acquainted with the children, including two boys, Ed Jr. and Jim, and one girl, Margaret. The Gavins had another house on Gerald Avenue besides the one on Candler. Mrs. Gavin would work there everyday, as it was rented to roomers. Mr. Gavin worked for the Ford Motor Company. He was a barrel chested Irishman with broad shoulders. He was a serviceman for the Ford Motor Company. I heard the story that during World War I, when Bolsheviks threatened to shut the power plant down, they would sneak into the plant and throw sand into the oil wells that lubricated the big power generators. One day Ed Gavin, the father, spotted one of these people up on a catwalk dropping the sand into the oil wells. He climbed up on the catwalk, overpowered him, and threw him down. They then took the fellows broken body and threw it into a furnace. That was the end of him.

Whether that story was true or not, the Gavins were strict Catholics. They wanted their boys to become priests. Ed Jr. went to the seminary first. When he was ready to be ordained, they gave him a two-week vacation. He spent everyday going to the movies and decided he didn't want to be a priest. The Gavins had made a tremendous financial sacrifice by sending him through the seminary, but they decided to do it again with Ed's younger brother, Jim. He also went up to the point where he was going to be ordained,

26

then left the seminary. He went to work for Chevrolet on production. Margaret Gavin, after graduating from high school, went to Washington and worked for the Federal Government. All of this taught me later in life to accept people for who they are and for what they wish to be, so the pressure is not felt unjustly by them, as felt by Ed Jr. and Jim.

Early Jobs

When I was a boy of about twelve, I got a paper route, the one on which my brother Jack helped me sometimes. At first I had a small route, but I gradually built it up. Later I bought another boy's route and then I had 124 customers. It was a tremendous task delivering these papers. I had to go from Ferris and Woodward to Six Mile and Woodward and over to Oakland Avenue; about 16 square blocks that I had to cover daily on my route. Besides delivering the papers, I had to collect for them.

In those days a daily paper cost ten cents a week delivered to the house. The papers cost us six cents, so we got four cents profit for our labors on each customer. Many times customers would run up a big bill and then move away without paying me. Those incidents were heartbreaking. The Sunday also cost ten cents at this time. It cost us seven and one half cents, so we earned two and one half cents for every Sunday paper sold. The news companies had premiums and we could win a wagon or a sled for getting new customers. I always worked hard and managed to get a wagon and a sled. I also had a savings account and put money aside as I earned it. I was always out to make a dollar any way that I could.

When I was finished delivering papers on Sundays, an older fellow, Burl Ostenfeldt, asked me to sell balloons for him. He stationed me on Woodward Avenue at Chicago Boulevard right near the Catholic Cathedral. When Mass let out, I would sell these balloons, three for a quarter. Then, after the Mass was over, he would station me on a corner at Six Mile Road and Livernois where I would work the rest of the day selling balloons. I would usually make one or two dollars commission on what I sold. Burl got the rest. That gave me an idea. I looked in the phone book for the company that sold balloons. It was on Jefferson Avenue, downtown. I found I could buy balloons for $6.00 a gross. There were 144 balloons in a gross and that included the balloon sticks to put the balloons on when they were blown up. I went into business for myself selling balloons!

My dad would take me to the corner of Seven Mile and Livernois. I would stand there all day in the hot sun blowing up balloons and selling them. Before going home, I would walk up Seven Mile to Palmer Park. I would walk into the Park and there would be groups of Armenians and other nationalities there. Once I sold the first balloon, it was easy to sell the rest. When a kid would see another with a balloon, he or she would want one. I could sell a lot of balloons in a hurry in the Park. The police would come and chase me out many times. However, by that time, I would have made fourteen or fifteen dollars on some days.

The balloons I sold went for ten cents each or three for a quarter, the same as Burl charged. The balloons had flowers on them and were all different colors. The flowers were printed in yellow on various colored backgrounds. They were pretty and sometimes they would blow up on account of the heat from the sun. Thus, I would have a certain amount of loss along with my sales. I sold balloons for quite a while and on the same corner were people selling cherries. That gave me an idea. I thought I would sell cherries too. I lost my shirt when I tried this. They were selling cherries three pounds for a quarter. To make any money, I had to sell them two pounds for a quarter. Needless to say, I could not sell mine. My dad took the remainder of the cherries back and luckily they gave him a refund on them. That ended my cherry selling episode. My dad always looked out for me. Whenever I was in trouble, he would go to bat for me!

In those days, we had streetcars and jitneys. Jitneys were automobiles like limousines that people would invest in and then take passengers down Woodward Avenue from Six Mile to downtown for a quarter. They had stops every few blocks to pick people up, and were quite inexpensive. One of our neighbors operated a jitney. Sometimes I would earn money by washing his car for him.

Saving Money

Later, when I was in high school, I took some of the money I'd earned and bought my mother a washing machine. Since my mother always worked very hard, I would help her with the washing of clothes and scrubbing of floors. I went into this store where they sold the Easy Vacuum Cup washing machine. It was $150.00 and I told the merchant I only had $105.00. He said, "I'll sell it to you for $105.00." I said, "Will you deliver it?" He said, "Yes, I'll deliver it, too." When the men came to deliver it to the two-flat that we lived in at that time on Buena Vista, having moved from Candler, my mother turned the men away. She said, "That doesn't belong here." They said, "Yes it does, it's all paid for." She finally let them bring it in. It was a complete surprise to her. It made her work a lot easier. I was always glad that I did that for her.

In those days, we had milkmen, ice men, fruit and vegetable men, and "sheenies". The milkmen, ice men, and fruit and vegetable men all had horses and wagons in those days. Later on, some of them used trucks. The sheenies were different as they came around buying up old bottles, rags, and newspapers. My mother used to save bottles, rags, and newspapers and they would buy them for a few pennies. One would not get much for them, but people were thrifty in those days. They would get whatever they could by saving things. There were even people from Italy, Germany, and other countries who went around the alleys sifting ashes to recover the coal that remained in them after the furnaces were shaken down. That is how people saved and how things were. Money was very scarce.

Memories of School, Home, and Family

The fourth grade was hard for me and I didn't do well in it. I had my problems in school. In the meantime, I studied the violin and made considerable progress. I could play the "Parade of the Wooden Soldiers." My teacher put me in St. Benedict's High School band when I was in the fourth grade. I played with the band for a performance of "Charlie's Aunt" that was put on at Highland Park High School. Baseball kept taking me away from my violin practice. My mother finally decided it was a waste of money for me to be taking the lessons. I wasn't practicing enough. I gave it up, and haven't played the violin since.

St. Benedict's School was great. We went to church every morning. We sang the Mass in Latin every day. It was a drag at the time, but now I miss it. I think it was bad when the church changed from Latin to the English form of the Mass. I guess it had to be done. Time changes everything. The Ford Motor Company moved away from Highland Park to the River Rouge, in Dearborn, where they built a huge plant and employed more than 100,000 people. My dad was transferred from Highland Park to the Rouge Plant.

When I went to the Ford School, I took manual training. I made a lamp for my mother on a lathe. Mother was always proud of that lamp and she kept it for years. I also made her a dust pan when I was in metal shop. She liked that, too. My parents worked very hard and the times were tough. When we lived on Candler, we had a coal burning furnace. It was my job to take care of the fires. I'd build the fires, shake out the clinkers, and take out the ashes. When the coke was delivered, I helped my father put it in the coal bin in the basement. I tried to do it by myself, but it was too much for me. We'd usually get about four tons at a time. For the most part, I didn't mind helping my parents with any of the work around the house.

Occasionally, I would go to a circus or to the movies when I shouldn't have, and then I'd get into trouble. I associated with older boys. They taught me all of the tricks they knew. I learned all about cigarettes, corn cob pipes, balloon sticks, and other items used for smoking. I used to go with some of them and pick up cigarette butts at the Lincoln Showroom in Highland Park. We'd go there because the people who went there were richer. They'd throw away bigger butts. They didn't smoke their cigarettes down as far as the others did. I also learned about French-Safes. In those days they were never called condoms. I heard the stories that were going around about certain girls and boys and the birds and the bees, all those things. Fortunately, I never succumbed to temptations or contracted venereal disease. That was as feared then as AIDS is now. God intended man to have only one mate so when my wife and I married, we had both abstained from sex prior to that moment and have remained faithful to one another all of our days together.

When my chores were done on Saturdays, I'd go to the movies. The entertainment industry was booming. Talking pictures came in the 30's and we would see cowboy shows like Hoot Gibson, Tom Tyler, Ken Maynard, Tom Mix, and other Western stars. I liked singers, too, like Bing Crosby, Perry Como, Maurice Chevalier, and Mario Lonzo. I would go to see all of these movies and I would learn many of the songs. I guess I was what you would call a "romantic" because I would sing these songs when I was walking home from school with my friend Fred Wilkiemeyer. We would both sing along together. Many of them were love songs. After Lindbergh flew across the ocean from New York to Paris in his plane, the Spirit of St. Louis, there was a song about Lindy. I even wrote a romantic song which went like this:

> When south winds lose their breaths in the seas,
> and gladioli swing in the breeze,
> and autumn's hand starts painting the leaves,
> I'll sing a song of you.
>
> When other eyes are watching our moon,
> and other hearts are beating our tune,
> and other lips kiss goodnight too soon,
> I'll sing a song of you.
>
> You can inspire such lasting desire
> my mind must acquire this theme.
> Someday your glow, will thrill me I know,
> but now I must go on just dreaming.
>
> At night, when heaven's galaxy shines,
> and waiters pour enchantment in wines,
> and lovers put their love on the line,
> I'll sing a song of you.

With the movie pictures, there would be serials with Jack Mullhall. Every Saturday there would be a new episode. It would cost ten cents for the movies, unless it was the Tivoli, which was twenty-five cents. I would deliver circulars for the Tivoli and get free passes. They also had an "amateur night" and I sang "In the Baggage Coach Ahead." It's a sad song with lots of verses. The MC stood beside me and kept cranking me up as I sang. I was twelve years old at the time and won the second prize. A couple sang "When the Red, Red Robin Comes Bob, Bob, Bobbing Along." They won first place.

My friends and I were excited when RKO built the Uptown Theater at Six Mile Road and Woodward. They had movies together with the legitimate stage. One time Harry Lauder, the Scottish performer, was there. Another time, The Seven Foy's were there, and so were other great acts. It cost fifty cents to go there. Needless to say, we didn't go there very often. I went to see the "Phantom of the Opera". It made such a great impression on me, with Lon Chaney's performance, that I was sick for a week with the fever afterwards. I kept seeing the couple, who were lovers, drowning.

Another movie that had a great impression on me included the song "Walking with Susie." I stayed for two shows so I could memorize the song. It went like this:

30

Every day I take a walk it's fun day,
From Monday to Sunday not one day I miss.
Every little walk that I can squeeze in this season is pleasin'.
The reason is this, I'm all aflutter,
I'm a strutter when I'm walkin' with Susie.
I'm never knowin' where I'm going when I'm walkin' with Susie.
She leads me, she feeds me, beauty and charm.
I'm woozy when Susie's holding my arm.
My heart is floppin' and a poppin' when I'm walkin' with Susie.
I hit the ceiling what a feeling, walkin' with Susie.
Although I'm choosy, Susie will do.
I'm gettin' slappy, I'm so happy walkin' with Susie.

Ice skating and roller skating were also great fun for me. One could buy a pair of roller skates made by the Union Hardware Company for three dollars. I clamped them on my shoes with a key that would tighten the clamps to the sole of my shoes. There was a strap that went over my ankles. My ice skates were clamp-ons, too, and had straps as well. Later, I thought it was great when I was able to afford a pair of shoe-mounted hockey skates. I loved to skate. When one of the roller skates wore out, I would take the good one remaining and nail half of it to the front of a four foot long two-by-four. The other half was nailed to the other end and made a scooter. An orange crate was nailed on the front. I would hold onto that. Then I pushed myself along with one foot while standing up on the two by four with the other foot. We had lots of fun with those on the concrete sidewalks when we were boys.

One time I roller skated on John R Street toward the Ambassador Theater. One of my skate wheels came off and as I sat on the curb fixing it, some people came out and got in their car and backed over my right leg. They were good people. They took me to a doctor and then they brought me home. I was laid up for two months. During this time, my cousin, Eddie Connell, peddled my papers for me.

My friends and I made our own toys. We had no money to buy things. One day, when we were off from school, some of my buddies came over and said, "Let's go frog hunting." Well, the place where the frogs were was about three miles away and they wanted to bring the frogs back with us. I asked, "How are we going to do that?" We got some paddles and buckets and then I did something that was very bad. I went into the garage and backed my father's Model T out into the alley. I drove it over to Six Mile and Dequindre where the swamp was and parked it out in the field.

We hunted frogs all day long and had pails full of the big frogs. We put them in the back seat of the car. When I tried to move the car, the wheels were stuck in the mud. We left the car and frogs there and went home on foot. I was scared to death because I had to tell my Dad about what I had done. He was great! He did not say a word. He went with me out there on foot. It was still raining and the car was bogged down in mud. I don't know how he managed to do it, but my dad found a long pole, put it under the rear axle, and moved the car wheels out to solid ground, lifted it, moved it over, and tried to start it.

The starter would not work. He checked under the hood, and saw that someone had stolen the battery. Then he cranked the car and started it. He drove us home with the pails full of frogs. They croaked all night long in the garage. My folks let me keep them for about a week, but could not stand the all-night croaking. Neither could the neighbors take the noise. We took the frogs with us and put them back into the swamp.

One time I went fishing at Palmer Park. While I enjoyed fishing with family and friends, this time I was alone and was not allowed to fish there. If the police had caught me, they would have made me stop. Anyway, I used a piece of string with a safety pin on it for a hook, and put a piece of bread on the pin and I caught a big goldfish. I carried the thing all the way home, a couple of miles. Believe it or not, it lived. I put it in my mother's washtub. Of course, she could not stand for that. She said I would have to get it out of there. We took it back and put it in the lake at Palmer Park.

Football was my game in high school. I often wish I had not played. My position was left tackle. I was the understudy for Nick Willerer who weighed 170 pounds. For some reason, Nick did not play as hard as the coach thought he should. Our coach's name was Moon Mullins. He had played for Gus Dorais, Knute Rockney's sidekick at Notre Dame. They invented the forward pass and used it for the first time against Army. Moon was University of Detroit's quarterback under the football legend, Gus Dorais. He took a liking to the way I gave everything I had to playing my position. Soon I became the team's regular left tackle. We had a so-so season, winning just half of our games.

At the end of the season, we booked a game with Highland Park High School. They were a Class A school. We were Class D. Somehow we were able to tie them. The final score was 0 to 0. I played against a fellow weighing 210 pounds. He was an All-State tackle. He just about ruined me. On every play he would cut through the line and fall on the backs of my legs. That is called "clipping." In those days, they did not penalize you for doing it. After the end of the first half, I could scarcely walk. I told the coach to take me out, and put in Nick. Nick played the rest of the game.

In high school, I continued to play softball which, in those days, was played without using gloves and the ball was pretty hard. The positions I played were pitcher, shortstop, and first baseman. I was captain of one of the teams, when I played in the Highland Park Recreation League. Besides football and baseball, I played tennis and pitched horseshoes. In fact, a friend of mine, Whitey Zabroski, and I used to play 50 ringer games. When men were coming home from the Ford factory, They'd stop and watch us. We'd top each other's ringers, with ringers of our own. Those were great times!

Other exercise that I did included swimming, golfing, and running on the track. There was also a set of rings that I would swing on at a park. There were eight rings spaced about seven feet apart. I would grasp a ring with one hand and swing to the next. Soon I could go all the way down to the end and back several times. I could also chin myself on the chinning bar about 21 times. I was able to build up my strength through these exercises. I never weighed very much when I was young. When I was thirteen years old, I weighed 110 pounds. When I got to be a senior in high school, I weighed 155 pounds.

In high school, I was taught by the sisters of St. Joseph. Courses I took were all "classical" with very little science. We had one course in physics. It did not help much. We had one course in algebra and one in plane geometry, but no trigonometry. I graduated with a B average.

When the Depression hit, my dad was forced to make a decision. He was paying off the $24,000 mortgage on our four-flat and he had it paid down to about $6,000. That was all the place was worth during the Depression. Meanwhile, he had bought a two-flat with eight rooms in each flat, having a $12,000 mortgage. This was on Buena Vista, about a mile and a half from Candler, toward downtown. He decided to sacrifice the four-flat and keep the brick duplex on Buena Vista. We moved there. That is where we lived when I went to high school, the University of Detroit, and Highland Park Community College.

Historical Reflections

Looking back now to the beginning, from the time I was born and World War I was being fought, through the time I graduated from the University, and after John F. Kennedy was killed, it is interesting to note the historical significance of this period. These were exciting times in the United States as Woodrow Wilson was President at the time of my birth, followed by Calvin Coolidge, Herbert Hoover, Franklin D. Roosevelt, Harry Truman, Dwight D. Eisenhower, and John F. Kennedy.

What was happening was that industries were being developed. The automotive industry had grown from small beginnings. The Highland Park Ford Plant was open at all times to visitors. One could see the cars being assembled. At that time, all Ford cars were black. In the 1920's my dad bought a car from Ford for $600.00. At the end of the year, the profit had been so good that Henry Ford refunded $200.00 to each of that year's purchasers. Henry Ford was a most unusual and thrifty man. His ancestors were Scotch-Irish. One must remember, in those days people weren't paying the taxes on their incomes that they are now. So when Henry Ford instituted $5.00 a day wages for factory workers, that was a great thing. That was long before unions were formed.

When the unions came, there were bitter battles. Many of the workers got hurt when strike-breakers would come in from Chicago with two-by-fours fitted with razors. Men were cut to pieces. It was a horrible time. Frank Murphy was governor of Michigan. Nobody knew what to do to put a stop to the labor difficulty caused by the formation of the UAW and CIO unions. There was a lot of talk about communists and communism.

Chapter 6

Learning Lessons: The Hard Way

First College Days   **Job Experiences**

Highland Park Junior College   **Michigan State College**

Youth
by Lewis J. Minor
(January 7, 1995)

Life's not easy when one is a youth;
One's future's a blank map and now that's the truth.
Finding one's vocation and which path to take's
A weighty decision for each youth to make.
One works for a dollar; that much youth has learned;
But taxes take another dollar for each dollar earned.
Now, here's the challenge that each youth must meet:
Find a good-paying position so your family can eat.
When we think of our needy and homeless, we say
Life's path is not easy for our youth today.
But with work, school, and teaching to provide education
Our youth'll earn its place in the world's greatest nation.

First College Days

After graduation from high school, my dad thought I would be wise to study chemical engineering, particularly since he was working at Ford Motor in the coke and gas division. I very foolishly entered the University of Detroit, where Jesuits taught me. I was in the engineering department.

My advisor was Father Schipel, who enrolled me in courses that totaled twenty one credits. I knew practically nothing about math or science at that time. I never should have taken that many credits. Fifteen credits is a full load and when one is starting a college career that is plenty. I struggled and had great difficulty getting my books. These were Depression days and the U of D bookstore would only buy a minimum of books. One would go there to buy books, but they were not available. I went through a half semester without the trigonometry book. My teacher, Clayton Pajot, had no compassion. He wrote on my papers, "You don't have a mathematical mind, Minor!" I resented that. Later I proved that he was wrong. I did have ability in mathematics and I was later able to demonstrate that.

With chemistry, physics, and mechanical drawing as classes, I was in a daze most of the time. I used to stay up and study until 2:00 AM. My high school buddy, Fred Wilkiemeyer, asked me if I would like to go out with him one St. Patrick's Night. Prohibition had been repealed and we could buy lots of beer with a little money. We went out drinking beer. Fred drove us in his father's car and I was wearing my father's overcoat. We picked up some student friends from the University of Detroit and drove to a pub on Livernois, near Six Mile Road. I had so much to drink that with those fellows sitting on my lap and all the squeezing I passed out. When we got home that night, I could not find the keyhole or put the key in the door lock. Finally, I got in by ringing the bell.

When I came upstairs, my mother and dad were playing cards with some lifelong friends in the living room. I staggered in "drunk as a skunk" wearing my father's coat. I had vomited all over it. My mother put me to bed. The next morning she asked where my ring and watch were. My ring was one that my grandfather had left me when he died. It was an emerald ring. The watch was gold and had been given to me by Aunt Winnie when I had graduated. Both were gone. My mother asked me to take a pledge that I would not drink anymore until I was 25. I did what she had asked and two years later, when she saw that I was keeping my pledge, she gave me my watch and ring back. She had taken them off and hidden them. Meanwhile, I reasoned that a passerby had roughed me up when I was alone outside of the pub.

Job Experiences

My one year experience at the University of Detroit was a total disaster. It had been all math and chemistry that I had no foundation for from high school. I failed, but learned a little about mechanical drawing. At least I learned that college demanded much more effort than high school, and more knowledge of science and math than I got from St. Benedict's High School.

When school was out in the summer, I tried to find a job, while I attended Cass Technical High School in Detroit and took trigonometry and microbiology. I did some painting around the house. Then, my cousin, Pat Ryan, the younger brother of Tom Ryan, who would play an important role in my life, called one day and asked my mother, "Does Lewie have a job yet?"

There was an opening at the Donahue Varnish Company where he was working. He offered me the job. Pat had moved from Cleveland to Detroit after being hired by a man named Peters. Together they ran the company for Mr. Donahue, the owner. One of Pat's employees said, "I would rather be on relief than do what I am doing here for $10.00 per week." He worked in the lab cleaning up steel test panels which had been sprayed with paint and had undergone weather exposure tests. They could be reused again after soaking them in solvent and scraping the paint off. He also cleaned the pebble mills. These had to be cleaned after each batch of paint was ground in them overnight.

To get to work I had to ride a streetcar to Clairmont and Woodward Avenues, then transfer on Gratiot to French Road. The Company was located near the Hudson Motor Car Company at French Road and Gratiot in East Detroit. The streetcar fare cost me over $6.00 per week, but I was glad to have the job and to get the experience. It was invaluable and rewarding to me. Pat treated me as a father would treat his own son. He saw that I learned all about paint, varnish, lacquer manufacture, and testing. Pigments, solvents, resins, gums, linseed oil (raw or heat bodied), other oils, including soybean and rapeseed, and metallic dryers all became familiar. I learned how flat paint, enamel, varnish, and lacquer were made. As a utility man, I was exposed to everything including the development and manufacturing control laboratories. I even took charge of a distillation unit that was used for reclaiming spent solvents that were used for washing equipment.

This happened because we had 50 gallon drums of solvent which had accumulated for years out on the lot. The solvent had been used for washing paint off metal surfaces and off pebbles that were used for grinding paint in the pebble mills. When you changed batches, you had to wash everything so the colors would not mix. That meant that there were a lot of drums that had been accumulated over a period of years with solvent in them. Pat Ryan got the idea of getting a still, a distillation unit, to use for recovering these solvents so they could be reused, instead of just lying in drums out in the field. After this equipment was installed, I was put in charge of operating it.

One thing we tried to do was to body, or thicken, linseed oil by heating it in the equipment. We realized that at a certain temperature there was an "exothermic" reaction and the oil would boil over and might even catch on fire. After we had this happen and had a fire, we gave up the idea. We then used the still only for recovering solvent. I would work all day taking drums of used solvent, emptying them into the still with a pump, and then creating "recovered solvent" by controlling the still's heat. The residue that was left in the still after the solvent was distilled off was used for "barn paint." It could be sold very cheap and was fine for that purpose. I was able to recover up to 1600 gallons of solvent per day.

Two of my friends at work were Dr. George Meckler and Billy Burns. Billy was a seventy year old paint and varnish chemist, for whom I worked, and George was a young Ph.D. who was learning the business. George was a brilliant mathematician. I used to go to him for tutoring in the solid geometry and trigonometry classes I eventually took. Thank goodness I knew when I needed help and could find someone to help me. If only I had learned this important lesson earlier, I might not have had such a rough first year at college. Anyway, I paid him $5.00 for each half hour tutoring. He was a great help to me in my mathematics. He taught me the mental process of doing the problems. In fact, that is one of the great values of mathematics. One needs to learn the mental process of thinking and working out problems, and nothing does this better than mathematics.

Another friend at Donahue Varnish Company was Billy Krog, an old varnish maker. He was training his son to make varnish using oil, gums, and resins. That was the way that varnish makers did it in those days. They passed their skills and trade secrets on to their sons.

Highland Park Junior College

After more than one year of working without going to school, the chemists at work encouraged me to enroll at the Highland Park Junior College, while working at Donahue Varnish Company part-time. I would ride the streetcar afternoons after finishing my classes, work, then go home to bed, exhausted. It was the fall of 1935 and during these days I would study at the McGregor Public Library in Highland Park. It was located on Woodward Avenue near Glendale. There were some sayings on the walls. As you approached the Library on the left hand side, the saying was written, "Knowledge is Proud That He Has Learned So Much, Wisdom is Humble That He Knows No More." On the right hand side was the saying, "Books are Roads to Wide New Ways." I never forgot those sayings. I was glad that the library was there so I could find the information I needed for my studies.

When Dean Altenberg at Highland Park saw my grades from the University of Detroit he said, "You've got a lot of nerve coming in here and trying to get into our School." He said, "Do you think it's any easier than the University of Detroit? What made you come here?" I said, "Well, I thought you might give me another chance. It doesn't cost as much to go to school here, and I would like to try it." He said, "Well, I will put you on probation for six months."

Two months later he called me into his office. He said, "You are failing in German!" I said, "I'm trying, but maybe I'm not going at it right." He said, "Mrs. Graves has an office upstairs in our library and she is up there all day long when she is not teaching. You can go up there and she will help you." She did. As a result, my grades in German improved and I was doing all right in my other classes. The Dean let me stay in school, thanks to Mrs. Graves, who was a mother to me like Sister Euphemia had been at St. Benedict's High School.

Because of her working with me and my dedicated work, I took German for a second year from Mrs. Graves and wrote the highest Columbia University exam of anyone in any of her classes for over six years. She thought that was wonderful since I did not come from a family that spoke German. Many of her other students did. She and I became fast friends. She became my mentor. I was very proud of her as she was the first person in the history of the University of Michigan to earn a Ph.D. in Germanic languages and dialects. It took her five years of summer school to complete this degree. It was quite an achievement because she and her husband had three children. She had to take care of them, besides teaching. So she was my hero. Out of appreciation, another student, Joe

37

Jacoby, and I gave her a testimonial dinner. It was great! There were about 50 people with students and faculty attending. It was nice to honor her that way.

(Editor's Note: L. J. Minor has been my mentor and the reason for my having the honor to work with him on this book. I was in my second year of study at Michigan State University when he was teaching a six credit course in food chemistry, production, and service. His teaching assistant unfairly gave me a C minus at the end of the semester and I was devastated. While I had not personally met with Dr. Minor during the semester, due to the large size of his class, my father recommended that I go to Dr. Minor's office and explain to him the fact that I had unfairly received a poor grade in his class. Since I was an A and B student, a six credit C would be bad for my average. My father told me to ask Dr. Minor if any person had ever taken advantage of one of his children. When I made an appointment with Dr. Minor in his office and asked him this question, he immediately told me a story of how his son had been denied the Eagle Scout badge due to the bad judgment of the Scout Leader. He asked me why I had asked him this question. When I showed him my grades for the semester and what I had done in his class, he reviewed his records, called in his secretary, and changed my grade to what we both agreed better represented my accomplishments that semester.

That day I learned that one needs to communicate feelings to make progress in this world. My father was influential in teaching me this, but Dr. Minor was kind enough to listen to my concerns and react positively. From that moment until today, Dr. Minor has been my mentor. As will be revealed throughout this book, he has motivated me, helped me to find jobs, encouraged me to write books, taught me lessons on how to raise my children, and has even taught me how to laugh and love life more. As we continue his story, all readers will gain similar insights from this great individual.)

The year was 1937 and I graduated from Highland Park Junior College with a B average. While there I had studied geometry, inorganic chemistry, qualitative analysis, and organic chemistry. I continued to work at the Donahue Varnish Company and also attended Cass Technical High School during the summer, as I stated earlier, taking trigonometry and microbiology. I had lost two years in school due to the fact that my high school courses did not fit my science program. I had to make up a lot of mathematic courses, physics, and chemistry that I did not have. By working for nearly two years at Donahue Varnish, I matured, made friends, and gained valuable business experience.

Michigan State College

My next big decision was to go to East Lansing to attend Michigan State University, which was called Michigan State College at the time. I hitchhiked there. A man named Bagaeff, who gave me a ride, told me to come and see him in downtown Detroit. He gave me a letter helping me to get a job at the Atlas Drop Forge Company in Lansing. He had some stock in it. I got paid 50 cents an hour and worked 16 hours on weekends. After a

38

few weeks, the foreman came to me and said, "You had better take out some insurance, as we have had six people killed here in the past year." I took out a $1,000 policy that cost fifty cents per week.

Meanwhile, I lived in a rooming house with 30 other fellows on Albert Street. I was elected president of the house. One of the fellows was on the football team. He was failing Spanish. He had a job at Kewpee's Cafeteria and asked me if I wanted the job. He and another fellow, Louie Jenkins, peeled 200 pounds of potatoes each day. There was a mechanical peeler, but the potatoes had to be cut, opened, and checked to see if there was any brown or black rot on the inside. If there was, we had to clean that out. After peeling the potatoes, we put them in barrels of salt water to be held for use the next day. I was glad to get this job and I left the job at Atlas Drop Forge Company. The job at Kewpee's paid $5.20 per week on a meal card, which meant that since everything that was sold there had a 100% markup, I was actually getting $2.60 per week for the work I was doing. I was working fifteen hours per week for $2.60, but was glad to be working.

When I enrolled in the Applied Science Department at Michigan State, I was in the Dean's Office and told Dean Houston's secretary what courses I wanted to take. He happened to be in the background and he interrupted and said to me, "You do not tell us what you want to take; we tell you what you have to take." I took an immediate dislike for him. I learned that he was an old "army man" and liked to run things his way entirely without any leeway. I had him as a lecturer in organic chemistry.

Occasionally, I would interrupt his lecture to ask a question. He would just stare at me, but would not give me an answer. He would just continue with his lecture. His assistant lecturer, or co-lecturer, was Professor Bruce Hartsuch. He and I became friends. He did not like Dr. Houston either, but had to work with him. When it came time for the final exam, I helped some of the other students study for their exams and wrote the highest final of 250 in the class and Houston was disgusted. He said, "Minor isn't going to get an A." So Professor Hartsuch said, "If Minor doesn't get an A, nobody gets an A." I was told that by Bob Jackson, a graduate assistant. School was very difficult for me, but I gave it everything I had. It paid off! Both Professor Bruce Hartsuch of organic chemistry and Professor Dwight Ewing of physical chemistry were father figures for me during my time at Michigan State.

I paid for my entire college education, both at Highland Park Community College and Michigan State. I'm glad that I was able to earn my way through college. Once in a while, my mother would send me $5.00. It was a great lift. Other than that, I earned all of my expenses. My room, my board, my books, my tuition--all were paid through hard work, which made me appreciate every class and made me want to work all the harder. Of course, tuition in those days was very little. It was only $35.00 per term or $105.00 for the three terms of the school year. This was not very much compared to the $10,000 it costs today, but I was earning only about $5.00 per week, and on a meal card at that!

Being so busy with work and school, I never went home except in the summertime.

One of my roommates, Clem Antonetti, worked at the Deer Head Inn on weekends. This was a roadhouse and he earned enough money to send money home to his folks in the Upper Peninsula of Michigan. I thought I would try working there and got a job as a waiter. When the customer ordered a drink, I would have to purchase the drink with my own money and then collect from the customer that amount upon serving the drink. Clem said he always got a lot of tips. One night I was serving a party of eight and I went to the table with their drinks on a tray. Somebody bumped me and I spilled the drinks all over the customers' clothes. I didn't know what to do. I panicked! I never worked there after that night. I couldn't earn any money there and I rarely got any tips. Furthermore, it was a dangerous place. There had been a murder there and they had to have a bouncer to keep order. Afterwards I found out that waiters weren't making their money by getting tips, but by over-charging their customers for their drinks.

The only way I could make out with my class work and working was to make up a schedule for every day. From seven o'clock in the morning until eight o'clock at night, I was either in school or at work. Then, from eight o'clock to ten o'clock, I would study and then at ten o'clock I would go to bed and get up in the morning at five o'clock. Then I would study until seven o'clock and my routine would begin again. The days were long, but my goals were in front of me and I had the determination to succeed.

When the application for membership in Phi Kappa Phi National Honorary Society came in the mail prior to graduation, I threw it in the wastebasket. My new bride took it out of the wastebasket and said, "What did you do that for?" I said, "Well, they want ten dollars!" She said, "That is all right. You get a dinner, your certificate, and your key for the ten dollars." So we decided to make the sacrifice and I joined after I had graduated with a 3.4 average from Michigan State in 1939. Thank goodness I had married an "Angel(l)," who would bless me all my days on this earth!

Chapter 7

Blessed by an Angel(1)

Courting   Married Life   My Ruth

The Wedding
by Edgar A. Guest
(1928)

Oh bride and groom the day is fair
And love is singing everywhere!
God bless the home that you shall build
May it with happiness be filled,
Through all that comes of grief and pain
And hurt and care may love remain.

Courting

An unbelievable encounter between two people took place over 55 years ago, in 1938. I was in my junior year between terms at Michigan State College. I had moved to another rooming house and roomed with four other fellows, on Grand River Avenue, with a Mr. and Mrs. Snell. Mr. Snell was a Michigan State Policeman. Mrs. Snell was a very kind landlady. My roommate, John Vanderpoel, and I were talking to Mrs. Snell. That night was Pal's night at Coral Gables. She asked, "Are you going to the dance tonight?" I said, "I can't for two reasons. First, I have no money for that. Second, I need a haircut." John said, "I have no money either." Mrs. Snell answered, "Well, here's 20 cents. That's all it costs. Now you can both go." It was a lucky night that I went to that dance. For, at another location, Ruth Angell, who would become my Angel and bride, was being invited to go by a group of eight, including her brother, Robert, who loved to dance.

When John got there he said to me, "You go ahead and dance; I'm going into the back room to bum a few drinks from the State Government workers. It was a dull evening. I danced a few times, but mostly watched and listened. Right at the end of the evening, I looked across the dance floor. There she sat with a wistful look. The young woman who was to be my wife and mother to our eight children. She was shy as I approached and asked her to dance.

While dancing we got acquainted. I liked her. She seemed more mature and thoughtful than the other girls I had met previously. Suddenly, I asked for her phone

41

number. She said, "I live out in the country on a farm. You wouldn't want to call me." She did write her number down for me. Then I told her that since my schoolwork would be occupying my free time, I probably wouldn't contact her for a couple of weeks.

As I have said earlier, my schedule was full. From eight to five o'clock I was in class or studying. From five to eight o'clock I was peeling potatoes at Kewpee's Cafeteria. From eight to ten o'clock I studied. From ten to five in the morning I was sleeping on the bedroom floor at Mrs. Snell's. From five to seven in the morning I studied, then had breakfast before my eight o'clock class. For me this was a regular routine.

Meanwhile, Ruth was occupied teaching country school. She taught eight grades, and fifty-five ten-minute classes a day. She had been doing this for seven years, after graduating from high school at age 15 and County Normal at age 17. In her first year of teaching she earned $40 a month. Now she was getting $80 a month. Besides teaching, she built her fires and did her own janitorial work. That wasn't all. She also played the piano at District recitals and programs.

We'd meet Friday evenings and go to the movies. When I was courting her, I wrote a song about her middle name which was Eloise. It went like this:

" Eloise, when shadows fall, our love will call you to my side.
Eloise, my loving arms may hold your charms if you decide.
Darling, when night is here and you are near, my heart is happy.
Eloise, I love you so. Please let me know that you are mine."

One icy winter evening we went with her brother, Robert and his girlfriend, Franci, to another dance at Coral Gables. As we were leaving, I helped Ruth over the ice to the car, but slipped, and we both slid under the car. Everyone laughed. Sundays, I was occasionally invited to the farm for chicken dinner. Then I met and got acquainted with her mother, father, and three brothers: Robert, whom I already knew, and Jerome and Russell. These were hard-working, God-fearing Protestant farmers.

There I was, a Catholic intruder, feeling uneasy and self-conscious. Everything was going fine until we started getting serious, and her mother was told by Ruth that I was a Catholic. Soon, summer arrived and I went home to work for the Ford Motor Company. My dad got me the job. Jobs were scarce and hard to get. Ruth and I corresponded by mail. She surprised me when she told me she was taking religious instructions from Father John Gabriels at the Resurrection Church.

When I returned to Lansing, we went to church twice some Sundays. I'd go with her to the North Presbyterian Church, and she'd attend Mass with me at Resurrection. She knew that I'd never forsake my Catholic heritage, and probably felt that she loved me so much she was willing to turn Catholic. I never asked her to do it, but I was glad she did. I knew there would be hard-sledding ahead with her mother and brothers against me. In my heart, I knew her father was tolerant and would give me a chance.

Ruth and I had planned to wed after I had graduated and started in a job. Things

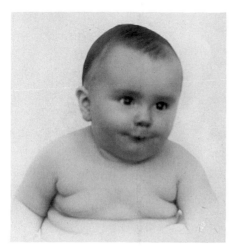

Lewis Joseph Minor.

Newell W. and Kathleen M. Minor, 1950.

Kathleen M. Hill, mother of Lewis J. Minor.

**Lewis Joseph (Lewie) Minor with brothers
John Emmett (Jack) and Newell Henry (Newell),
ages 5, 3, and 1 respectively.**

Kathleen M. Hill with sisters and brother (Back row left to right:
Lill, Pat and Winnie. Front row: May and Kathleen).

Four-Flat with Model T in front. Chandler Avenue,
Highland Park, MI where Lewis was raised.

St. Benedict's Catholic Church, Highland Park, MI.

**Lewis J. Minor (back row, middle)
with softball team.**

**Lewis J, Minor, age 18, with St. Benedict's football
team (bottom row, third from right).**

Lewis J. Minor, age 8, with parents Newell W. and Kathleen M. "Going swimming" at Belle Isle.

Newell W. Minor the golfer.

Newell W. Minor golfing.

Lewis J. Minor, high school graduation, 1933.

Robert D. Angell, age 4, and Ruth Eloise Angell, age 2.

Durfee Dewitt and Clara Bell Angell.

Ruth E. Angell with brothers Robert, Jerome and Russell.

Lewis J. and Ruth E. Angell

Minor on Wedding Day.

Ruth E. Minor holding Kathleen Mary Minor, first born, age 8 months, 1941.

Lewis J. and Ruth E. Minor's first home, 927 W. Woodruff, Toledo, OH.

Lewis J. and Ruth E. Minor with children Kathleen M., Bryan G., and Ruth Ann (held by Lewis) in front of home at 927 W. Woodruff, Toledo, OH.

Lewis J. Minor, graduation with Master's Degree from Wayne State, 1943. Holding daughter Kathleen Mary, age 3, and son Bryan Gabriel, age 2.

Lewis J. and Ruth E. Minor with family in 1949. Kathleen Mary, age 9, Bryan Gabriel, age 8, Ruth Ann, age 5, Carol Elizabeth, age 3, and Michael Lewis, age 1.

Lewis J. Minor, Scout Master, Troop 142, Harbor Beach, MI Receiving Eagle Award being pinned by Ruth E. Minor at Court of Honor.

Lewis J. Minor, mid-1940's.

Lewis J. Minor with children: Kathleen, age 10, Bryan, age 9, Ruth Ann, age 6, Carol, age 4, Michael, age 2, and number six, Josephine Eva, held by Daddy. On the steps of 149 N. 4th Street, Harbor Beach, MI.

that happened changed our plan, and cost us money. I had a $50 bet with my mother that I wouldn't marry before my 25th birthday, and lost the bet. Late in the fall of 1938, we announced our engagement. I gave Ruth the only ring I could afford, an inexpensive opal, and she liked it. In November, 1938, I wrote this proposal poem to her.

My Ruth

> There's no one in the world like my Ruth
> She's gentle, strong, and kind
> and, this is just the simple truth;
> She's always on my mind.
>
> I picture her in shining white,
> With roses at her breast.
> And when I'm fast asleep at night
> I dream of Ruth and rest.
> How many times I wonder, though,
> If there will ever be
> A home with all the happy glow
> I've planned for Ruth and me.
>
> I love Ruth, yes, and she admits
> I'm closest of her friends.
> Perhaps she'll wear a ring that fits
> Before this season ends.
>
> But circumstance and that alone
> Will help me to decide.
> If Ruth will ever be my own,
> My lovely autumn bride.
> Lewie-November 26, 1938.

Married Life

Ruth and I were married on February 11, 1939. Our Golden Wedding Anniversary was celebrated five years ago, but again, I am getting ahead of myself. After some hard fighting, me for her, and her for me, we were married on a bitter cold day. My folks came from Highland Park to the wedding Mass, given by Father John Gabriels in the Resurrection Church. Ruth's family was there, and Father John allowed a collection of lovely hymns that they wanted to be sung. Afterwards, we had a wedding breakfast at Kewpee's Cafeteria.

One of my co-workers loaned me his Model A Ford Roadster for our weekend honeymoon in Battle Creek at the Post Tavern Hotel.

> Row - row - row your boat,
> Gently down the stream.
> Merrily, merrily, merrily, merrily,
> Life is but a dream.

Yes, it was like a dream. Here we were married, with me in my senior year, and Ruth teaching in Okemos. We had a free wedding given to us by Father Gabriels. There was no prenuptial ceremony beforehand, and no expensive reception afterwards. All that we had between us and starvation were our love, devotion, health and determination to make it work. Our biggest fortune was our faith--faith in God, faith in each other, faith in finding a way to secure our future together.

Whenever I think of our wedding and celebrate its anniversary, I sing the following:

Irish Wedding Song

There they stand, hand in hand, they've exchanged, wedding bands,
Today is the day, they'll seal all their plans.
And all we, who love them, are just here to say,
Oh God, bless this couple who married today!

In good times, and bad times, in sickness and health,
May they know that riches aren't needed for wealth.
Help them with problems, they'll meet on their way,
Oh God, bless this couple who married today!
May they find peace of mind comes to all who are kind,
And may troubles ahead become triumphs behind.
God bless them with children to brighten each day,
Oh God bless this family who started today!

In good times and bad times, in sickness and health,
May they know that riches aren't needed for wealth.
Help them with problems, they'll meet on their way,
Oh God, bless this couple who married today!

As they go may they know our true love that will show,
Then as they get older may their feelings grow.
Wherever they travel, wherever they stay,
Oh God, bless this couple who married today!

44

In good times and bad times, in sickness and health,
May they know that riches aren't needed for wealth.
Help them with problems, they'll meet on their way,
Oh God bless this couple, who married today!

When we were first married, we lived in a rented room that did not have a door on it. It just had a curtain that separated us from the other rooms in the house and we only stayed there for about a week. Then we found another place where we had a room that was private and we had a three burner gas stove that we used. It was located underneath the stairway that went upstairs and was in one corner of our room. We had a wash bowl in another corner, Ruth's rug, bed, and dresser that she had bought before we were married, and a card table and chairs that we could use if needed. They would have to be set up and taken down due to space limitations.

Strangely enough, we did as much entertaining when we lived there as we ever did afterwards. At this time, milk was five cents per quart, bread was ten cents per loaf, and gasoline was fourteen gallons for $1.00. We kept a strict budget, as we did not have much income. Ruth always had envelopes. There was an envelope for the rent, and one for the food, one for recreation, and one for the automobile expense. Everything was in envelopes. Sometimes we would have to take from one to put into another to make things even out for that particular week, but somehow we always managed, with God's help through prayer.

Ruth was teaching country school and had to ride to school on a bicycle, nine miles each way over tar and gravel roads. It was a great hardship. She had a classmate from high school days, Clare Colvin, who worked for a Ford Dealership. We went to see him and he sold us a car, a used car, of course, for $35.00. This was fine until one day the piston went through the motor block and the car could not be driven any more. Then we went to see Clare again and I told him the car had gone bad. He showed us a V-8 for $100.00, but it needed tires. I said, "Well, this car needs new tires." He said, "I'll sell them to you at our cost." So he sold us four tires for $18.00. I said, "What about the other car?" He said, "I will allow you what you paid on it." So the new used car that we got was $118.00, less $35.00 for the car that went bad. Strangely enough, we drove that car for the remainder of the time that we were at Michigan State and for a year afterwards.

When I married Ruth I hit the jackpot. She has stood by me through thick and thin. She relieves me of the burden of paying bills, running the house, and keeping tax records. My well-being is always her top priority.

Whatever I have done, she has always supported my decision. We've functioned as a team in all of my endeavors. I've been blessed with the best. I'm an emotional creature, and hard to live with at times, but she never complains. We have been a perfect fit together.

Raising our children was not difficult until we became successful in business. We always worked together. But from the 60's on, Ruth bore the major burden of caring for the children. I was traveling more than I ever had before, and she was alone a lot. Whenever possible, we'd go on trips together and take the children with us. We did make a couple of trips together to Europe and especially to Ireland, but now I will try to define what the name Ruth Eloise Angell means to me after enjoying 55 years of life with her.

My Ruth

Ruth means beauty. To me, Eloise meant constancy and virtue. Angell means provident, resourceful, dependable, patient, fastidious, charitable, merciful, ever-loving, tolerant, industrious, self-sacrificing, brave, resilient, confident, contented, happy, mirthful, faithful, spiritual, and stable.

Any and all of the virtues that I lack, she possesses. That's fortunate, for I'm a troublemaker, and she's a peacemaker. She fills my life with joy and peace. When I'm ill, she nurses me. When I'm blue, she cheers me. When I'm discouraged, she encourages me. We have always worked together as a unit. Every day I thank God for giving her to me.

(Editor's Note: To give the reader some appreciation for how much Dr. Minor loves Mrs. Minor, we must return to the classroom at Michigan State University. The year was 1969 and Dr. Minor was lecturing on chemistry in the food industry. I was a student in the auditorium listening to him intently along with 150 other students. Dr. Minor began telling of his recent experiences in Cleveland where he would go regularly as founder and President of the L. J. Minor Corporation. As he related his stories one day, he was reminded in his own mind of the bus driver that had insulted Mrs. Minor somehow. The rage in Dr. Minor's voice as he told his students of this tale will not be forgotten. "No person will ever insult my wife without consequences," said Dr. Minor. I do not remember all of the details, but the lesson presented that day has helped me in my marriage significantly because he made it clear to his students that your loved ones demand respect. Dr. Minor always believed strongly in what he was saying and the love demonstrated for Mrs. Minor that day will never be forgotten by any of those students present.)

We've had a successful marriage because we've worked together at making it successful. She did her thing without interfering with me doing mine. Her care of the home, the children, the bills, our nutrition, sanitation, and nursing when there was sickness or injury was perfect. Ruth had the answers when problems arose in the family. She kept that burden away from me almost entirely. Don't get me wrong. We did a lot of things as a family. Golfing, swimming, camping, and vacation travel took place.

Scouting occupied a lot of my time. My sons, other scouts, and I attended three Scout Jamborees. Bryan, Michael, and I are all Eagle Scouts. Scouting is the greatest movement there is for World Brotherhood. My family was a source of joy and inspiration. I loved them all, equally, our eight children. We attended Mass every Sunday together when possible. Most, but not all of them, are practicing Catholics.

Ruth and I came from a different era. We were taught and trained to be abstainers, not experimenters. We had a greater fear of the consequences of illicit sexual conduct than young people have today. There is not, and never was, any safe sex. Condoms are not the answer. Thirty percent of them fail or slip off. AIDS is possible to get from French or deep-throat kissing. The HIV virus itself might even be so small that it is able to work its way through the condom's fine mesh structure. Yet, we are told half-truths by the media.

Today's education policies are not providing our children with the proper education. Respect and fear go hand-in-hand. Disrespect and permissiveness also go hand-in-hand. Girlie magazines were scarce when I was young. We got our thrills from the Sears Roebuck Catalog corset ads. Masturbation was taboo, but widely used by boys and young men in those days. Reprehensible, I suppose, depending on how you look at it. Yet, there were relatively few teen-age pregnancies or abortions then. I'm glad I was born in 1914 and not 1994. Crime, including rape, murder, robbery and burglary occur daily now. Then, you didn't have to lock your doors. The streets were safe. The real truth about sex is this, the anticipation is ten times more exciting and satisfying than the realization. Less than a minute following an orgasm, the sense of reason returns. No wonder God has spoken so clearly about sex, relationships, adultery, and lifestyles in His book, the Bible. We need to read it and put it into practice to succeed!

Ruth helped me in my schooling, work, and business. What's more, she still does. Mary Mele and Nancy Clancy, both of whom have contributed to this book, worked with Ruth and our C.P.A., Ralph Napletana, while we owned the L.J. Minor Corporation. Today, she keeps and transfers all of the records to Ralph at tax-time or whenever the IRS questions one of our returns. Thank God, this has only happened twice. We live with the knowledge that we can only be sure of three things, "death, taxes, and change."

Eric Swanson gave me some useful advice when our business was just getting started. He said, "When you're in business it's not how much you make, but what you save on taxes." Dr. Fabian said, "Lew, it takes 15 years to get a business established." He was right on the money. Bill Rapson of Rapson Electric in Harbor Beach, said, "It will take ten years before you start to make a living from your business." He was right, too. Building a business from scratch is a slow process. First, you must find out how to run a business. Then you just keep the faith, and seize opportunities as they arise. This requires a lot of costly sales activity. Until the sale is made, there's nothing. We live in a marketing society, but without a dedicated helpmate, few can succeed in this day and age.

God has a way of slowing you down when old age sets in. When I was 70, we had sold the company and retired. For 10 years after we sold the business the company continued to grow. Then in March, 1994, I received a letter from Sam Lee that Nestle had then relegated the company to the status of a division of FIDCO, Food Ingredient Sales Company (FISC). Looking back, I see that the children's tale of the Spider and the Fly applies to the Minor Corporation. Tom Ryan used to say that, "The big fish eat the little fish." It's true, but we must accept and live with change.

Nevertheless, we had our day. It was a happy one for us and our employees. We were a team, a family, that worked together and prospered. Our image was that of a well-run successful small business. Time changes all things, but we who were the Minor Corporation in the 70's can look back now and say, "We had our day, and proved that the quality will be remembered long after we're all forgotten." We had our day in the sun. Ruth and I are happy in the knowledge that together we did it right, despite all odds. But I am, again, getting ahead of myself, so let us return to those building years.

Chapter 8

School, Work, and Family

Back to Michigan State   **New Horizons**   **Early Family**

Activity
by French Jenkins
(1940)

I'm neither an optimist
nor a pessimist.
I'm an activist!

On Flattery
by French Jenkins
(1941)

Flattery is worse than a buzzard.
A buzzard eats you after you're dead.
But flattery eats you while you are still alive!

Back to Michigan State

After graduating, Professor Hartsuch, who was my hero, asked me if I would like to get a graduate assistantship in organic chemistry. I told him I would. So he put in an application for me. During the summer following graduation, I got a letter from the Michigan Department of Agriculture telling me that I had been appointed to a graduate assistantship in the organic chemistry department. I returned to Michigan State. We rented an apartment on the upper floor of what had been a barn, but which had been made into an apartment. The floors were wide boards with big cracks between them. There was a gas heater and we managed all right. We were happy there. As I had indicated earlier, we did quite a bit of entertaining while we were there. During the summer following graduation, I went job hunting.

Jobs were scarce in those days. I put in an application at the Reichold Chemical Company, where Pat Ryan now worked, for their pilot plant. Then I took the phone book and decided I would like to go into the food business because people always have to eat.

49

My dad thought that might be a good idea as well.

LaChoy Chinese Foods were listed and I called to speak with the general manager. My guardian angel must have been standing on my shoulder because the general manager actually spoke with me. His name was French Jenkins. He told me to come for an interview. I went there, and he said, "Well, we are not ready to hire anybody just now, but give me your application and write me a letter when you get back to school and I will let you know." I also put an application in to the Ford Motor Company for their soybean plant.

That summer we rented a teacher's furnished apartment on Dexter Avenue in Detroit. I worked at Ford Motor Company on production. We went to Kelly Furniture Company as it was going out of business in Highland Park. We bought a beautiful living room set, upholstered in red mohair and trimmed in walnut. We still have it in our apartment in Cleveland. We also bought a dinette set. The top was covered with white porcelain. There were four chairs with it. We also bought a nice baby buggy and high chair. The whole lot cost us only $150.00. We had it sent to Lansing and installed in our barn apartment.

New Horizons

In the Fall term at Michigan State, I taught organic chemistry in the laboratory and at the end of the term I received a letter from LaChoy and was offered a job to work for them in their Detroit plant on Schoolcraft. Mr. Jenkins had sent for me to become the technical director for LaChoy. I started at $35.00 per week and he wanted me to set up a research and quality control system for LaChoy. He also became father-in-business for me, giving me carte blanche to do my own thing for the company.

We set up a quality control system for checking everything we made. For testing, we used methods of the Association of Official Agricultural Chemists. We purchased a pH meter, Orsat apparatus, moisture tester, fat tester, Kjeldahl protein apparatus, standard drained-weight screens, micrometer, glassware, including distillation apparatus. Control cards were made up for keeping daily records of manufacturing performance.

We lived in an apartment next door to my folks in the upstairs of a house owned by the Wagners. It was a couple of miles from the house to LaChoy. After I had set-up the quality controls requested of me, and they were working for all products, I started experimenting with bean sprouting.

Bean sprouts were a real problem with the company because every once in a while we would get a lot of spoilage in the sprout tanks. My experimenting led me to believe that we needed humidity control in the room between waterings. We watered the sprouts every four hours, so if we kept the beds drier, we would not have the problem that we were having. I told Dr. Fabian about this and he said it didn't make any sense. He said, If you are watering, what good is it going to do to be drying out the beds?" I said, "The reason is that in the wintertime when the beds do dry out and we have heat in the building, we do not have the spoilage. It is in the spring and the fall that the spoilage occurs. What happened in the beds to cause spoilage was that the bean sprouts take in oxygen and give off carbon dioxide. When the bed is dry the carbon dioxide goes down the drain. When the bed retains water, the carbon dioxide and water react to form carbonic acid. This changes the pH, and lactic acid forms. Then the bed rots, contaminating the entire room. The rotted sprouts have to be removed and the room thoroughly cleaned."

We got a bid from the Surface Combustion Company to install a unit that would meet the specifications that I had set. Unknown to me, the plant superintendent allowed the specs I had worked out to be changed and the humidity was consequently higher than it should have been. Thus, spoilage was occurring. He allowed this change just to save a few thousand dollars. I had to go in there and stay night and day to monitor the system myself and salvage the investment. We discovered that by raising the temperature of the room, we could lower the humidity. The sprouts that used to take five days to grow were growing in just two days. Thus, what could have been a disaster, the large investment we had made in the lithium chloride system for removing the moisture from the air, turned out to be beneficial and profitable. The only problem was that when the sprouts grew faster, they had tails on them. However, they were healthy and we were able to get much higher yields. Our customers did not object, but our competitor's bean sprouts were fatter and had no tail-roots on them.

My next project was to contact the United States Department of Agriculture's Division of Plant Exploration and Introduction so that we could get strains of mung beans that could be grown domestically instead of bringing our beans in from China and Manchuria as we were doing. Thus we would not have to pay to have them stored in chilled warehouses under federal control. This was an expensive proposition and many times the beans were infested with weevils, resulting in considerable losses. We needed a system for separating the good from the bad beans. Ferry Morris Seed Company in Detroit had a machine with a vibrating table for separating good seeds from the bad. We bought one and it worked well.

We tried to interest several American seed companies in growing mung beans domestically. Paramount Seed Company in California became one source, and Cornell Seed Company in St. Louis another. We experimented with growing these beans in different locations and were successful in Illinois. Beans grown in Michigan also did well, but as these experiments were progressing, World War II began.

LaChoy decided to give up the plant in Detroit and move to Archbold, Ohio. There they could produce a new product that we had developed called Vegamato Juice Cocktail. This was a take-off of the product V-8, but used yellow tomatoes instead of red initially. It had a milder, more pleasant flavor, and had ten components instead of eight, as V-8 had. Later we changed to red tomatoes for better quality control and availability reasons.

French Jenkins wanted a "Magic Touch" seasoning that we developed, but never marketed due to the World War II interruption of our plant caused by tinplate shortages. I was able to get LaChoy the fermentation process French Jenkins wanted for soy sauce. We got this from Archer Daniels Midland in Minneapolis. They had developed the process, but never used it. When I asked them for it, in exchange for using their soy protein, they gave it to us.

When I joined the Institute of Food Technologists in 1940, Ruth and I went to the meeting in Pittsburgh. We had a harrowing night's drive through stony underpasses labeled "Jesus Saves." This meeting was great. The Institute was new. I met Al Fonyo of Striange Seasoning Company, Chicago, and Dr. I. J. Hutchings of Grocery Store Products Company, West Chester, Pennsylvania, and others who became lifelong friends. We purchased our mushrooms from Grocery Store Products. Our plant manager, Ed Neel, and I visited the caves where mushrooms were grown. We were fascinated by the beautiful green stone homes and buildings built with green stone indigenous to that region.

French Jenkins always took me along when attending the National Canners Convention or the Can Company Laboratories. To check things out, I would go to the literature, look up patents in the Patent Gazette, and keep up with new developments by reading the *Food Technology Journal, Food Engineering, Food Science, Chemical Engineering News, Food Industry Magazine*, and other pertinent journals. Many weekends and nights were spent at the Detroit Public Library, Technical Library.

I learned much in the library. For example our chop suey in cans was chunky and not fluid when removed from the can. A literature search revealed that a seaweed derivative, sodium alginate, was being used as a stabilizer in chocolate milk, ice cream, and other foods. We could make our chop suey pour freely by adding a small amount into the cooked mixture with the starch. We were allowed to use it in our vegetable chop suey and chow mein, but not in our beef products that came under meat inspection.

When the plant moved to Archbold, LaChoy let the salesmen go. French Jenkins called me in and told me I should plan to leave, too, because it would take a year or two to get the plant built and operating.

One of French Jenkins friends was Dr. C. Olin Ball of legendary fame in the canning industry. He had developed the mathematical methods for determining heat processing times and temperatures for canning. He invited me to visit the American Can Laboratories at Oakwood, Illinois, near Chicago, and French Jenkins and I went there together.

Some months later, through wise investigation, I learned that Dr. Ball, who had been with American Can, had joined Owens-Illinois in Toledo, Ohio, and was in charge of experimentation for their can division. At that time, they made metal containers as well as glass containers. I learned that they wanted someone in their laboratory. I learned this by going to the Engineering Society of Detroit, which was located downtown near the public library, and looked in their employment catalogue. I found a listing of a lab job in Toledo, Ohio. By putting two and two together, I concluded that this was the opening that Dr. Ball needed someone to fill at Owens-Illinois.

French Jenkins verified this by a call to Dr. Ball. They interviewed me in the glass block building on Dorr Avenue. The interview was conducted by a man named Herb Barnaby who kept his office ice cold. He was a very "cold fish" himself. During the interview, he asked me what I expected to be paid. I told him $300.00 per month. He took his slide rule, then said, "That does not figure out even by the week." He said there are 4 1/3 weeks in a month.

When we got stuck on that point of $300.00 per month, he said, "I am going to M.I.T. next week to interview a couple of fellows." Just then, Jim Harris, who was Dr. Ball's assistant, came in to see how the interview was progressing. Herb Barnaby told him he was going to interview some people at M.I.T. Harris said, "I don't want anyone from M.I.T., I want Minor." Then Barnaby asked me how, in just two years, my pay had been increased from $35.00 per week to $55.00 per week at LaChoy. I said, "I was being compensated for achievement." He answered, "Well, they don't give out raises like that these days." These were just early post-Depression days.

Anyway, after Jim Harris talked to Barnaby, I was hired. I got $300.00 per month. I didn't think it was such a big deal. Later, I learned that very capable research men who had been there at Owens-Illinois for six years or longer were getting $55.00 per week. This fact made me feel contrite and humble. Still, I needed the money for my family and I felt that I earned it while I was there. One time, Dr. Ball said to me, "Don't try to invent things that are already invented." That statement encouraged me to visit the libraries all the more to insure that the work I was doing was the best.

While at Owens-Illinois, I canned pumpkin and sauerkraut for test packs. We had a whole assortment of canned vegetables put up in substitute tinplate containers. One of the individuals I met at work was an old Greek gentleman. He told me, "You have to be master of your own destiny." I never forgot his words.

During World War II, I put in an application to the Navy. The only openings were for deck officers. After they received my application, they turned me down saying, "Due to your basic civilian qualifications, we can't take you." As luck would have it, at that time Tom Donofrio of McKay-Davis Company in Toledo called. I went for an interview. Tom wanted me to develop bouillon powder for K rations for their use. McKay-Davis had been packaging this, and their packaging machinery was being fouled up by screw drivers, wrenches, and even rubber boots. They packaged it in ten gram aluminum-printed envelopes for the U. S. Army Quartermaster Depot, Chicago.

Tom said, "We're packaging a product for the Army called bouillon powder." When asked if I could develop the formula for him and his brothers, who ran the Company, I told him I could. He said, "You can begin the experimenting evenings in our plant. He asked, "How long will it take you?" I said, "Probably a couple of weeks." He asked, "How much do you want to be paid for this?" I answered, "We need a downstairs bathroom in our house and we can't get the materials for it because of the War." He said, "Well, we are a defense industry here and we can get it done for you."

We agreed on this. I worked out a formula in exchange for our bathroom. I worked with Tom's brother, John Donofrio, at their plant. There was a lab there. The building was strongly built with brick walls four feet thick. In about two weeks, Tom went to Chicago with samples of my work. Captain Wright of the U. S. Quartermaster Corps rejected the product saying, "I need soluble spices, not natural spices in it." He didn't want the specks in the solution when the bouillon was dissolved.

Then I went to Basic Vegetable Products in Cleveland. I got soluble spices from them. After mixing the ingredients, we would tray the powder, dry it overnight in an oven, and granulate it by screening it through a granulator. In another two weeks, I had new samples for Tom. He went back to Chicago and got a contract for thirty thousand pounds. These contracts ran for three months. The second contract was for eighty thousand pounds. Contracts kept getting bigger and bigger. Some were for two hundred fifty thousand and some for three hundred thousand pounds. This kept our plant humming. We made the product they wanted and eliminated our competition one-by-one. Finally, just before the War ended, we got a contract for six hundred thousand pounds. This became our last contract, the first one having been awarded three years earlier. At that time, I was paid $100.00 per week. We were given all of the bouillon powder business because of our quality. Colonel Isker sent me a certificate from the U. S. Army Quartermaster Corp for my civilian services in the War effort!

When the war ended, they decided to go into the seasoning business. We worked on products for different companies including Chun King and did a quarter of a million dollars in sales the first year. This pleased the three Donofrio brothers, Tom, Tony, and John. Meanwhile, they went into the aspirin business. McKay-Davis used the oven mixer and granulator for a product like Alka-Seltzer which they sold under the brand name of "Briolina." This was a formula developed in Italy by the three brothers. On his death bed, their father made the brothers promise to stick together and carry on as before. They had made a lot of money by packaging for the Signal Corps during the War.

They started investing this money into a plant to make the new product. It was located in Rossford, Ohio. This was an ill-fated venture. After two years, they were in financial difficulty. They were using my connections to buy monosodium glutamate and hydrogenated vegetable shortening, which they would sell on the black market to make a profit. They were not paying their bills to the suppliers from whom they were buying the glutamate and shortening. I was a Vice President, but not an Executive Vice President. I soon started to receive letters from friends who were helping me get these materials for them. When I found out they were not paying their bills, I turned in my resignation. I had worked in Toledo for six years between Owens-Illinois and McKay-Davis.

Upon returning home, as I decorated the house, I got the idea to call George Ross whom I knew at the Huron Milling Company to ask if they had an opening that I might fill. He told me to come to New York for an interview. I rode the train there, but I could not sleep in the Pullman. All night I kept thinking about my interview. The next day I was hired. I was to be located in Harbor Beach, Michigan, where I had been born. Thus, I was working where my dad had worked thirty years earlier.

Beginning in the laboratory, I experimented with monosodium glutamate and hydrolyzed vegetable protein. I was Technical Director at the plant office and laboratory.

Huron Milling Company was the largest wheat starch manufacturer in the United States and was owned by the Jenk's family. Jerry Jenks, Research Director, was my boss. Product development and working with the salesmen to solve customer problems and promote sales were my main jobs. This required quite a bit of travel. Jack Scranton, Vice President asked at a board meeting, "Why do we give all of Minor's products away? Why don't we market them ourselves?" His mother, Mrs. Scranton, was a nice elderly woman and she enjoyed visiting with us.

Jerry Jenks and Al Redfield, who handled company sales for the plant, were nice fellows to travel with and to know. On a trip to a Corn Product Research Meeting held at Oyster Bay, Massachusetts, Jerry Jenks ran out of white shirts, so I lent him two of mine. Later, they hired a man named Bob Farr who had been president of Diamond Crystal Salt. He was a real pusher and came to add more sales pizzazz. He told us, "No one can work for me unless he works, works, works." When he hired the wrong fellow, in my opinion, from General Mills, and put him over me as my boss, I decided to depart. My pleasant years had ended with the death of Mr. Scranton, so when I was adamant about leaving, even though Farr didn't want me to leave, he said, "We'll give you six months severance pay." That was a great help in supporting my growing family, now that I was starting my own business in Cleveland.

Early Family

For five years, from 1945 to 1950, I had success with Huron in new product development and technical sales. During this time I was Scoutmaster in Harbor Beach. Never having been a boy scout, I decided to become an Eagle Scout.

After receiving my Eagle Scout, I also became a member of the Order of the Arrow. I attended three Jamborees--two at Valley Forge and one at the Johnson Ranch near Colorado Springs and Pike's Peak. Ours was the town's service troop. Being commissioner of parks on the city council, I used my troop to keep the parks clean, and for community Easter Service ushering. I also enjoyed being a member of the men's chorus.

As the years progressed so did our family and the homes we enjoyed. Our first baby arrived in 1940 and we named her Kathleen Mary Minor after my mother. Bryan Gabriel arrived in 1941. Ruth Ann, whom Mrs. Scranton called Roxanne, was our third baby and arrived while we lived in Toledo, Ohio. By 1949, our family had grown by three more with Carol Elizabeth, Michael Lewis, and Josephine Eva being born in Harbor Beach, Michigan.

PART 2

L. J. MINOR: THE REMARKABLE YEARS

1951 - 1983

FOUNDER, FATHER, AND PROFESSOR

Chapter 9

The L. J. Minor
Corporation is Founded

A Gamble   **The Beginning**   **Building a Sales Force**

Success
by Edgar A. Guest
(1928)

Success is doing something well,
It's winning faith and trust,
It's keeping honest, when you meet
An easy chance to play the cheat.
But who with any trust does less
Will never be a real success.

Work
by Unknown Author
(Contributed by Ruth Minor)

Let me but do my work
   from day to day
In field or forest
   at the desk or loom
In roaring market place
   or tranquil room
Let me but find it in my heart to say
When vagrant wishes beckon me astray
This is my work, my blessing,
   not my doom
Of all who live, I am the one
   by whom this work can best be done
   in the right way

Then shall I cheerful greet
      the laboring hours
And cheerful turn when the long
      shadows fall at even-tide
To play, and love, and rest
Because I know for me
      my work is best.

A Gamble

The first thought of starting my own business came from my second cousin, Tom Ryan. He was a gifted Irishman who could charm the shoes off of any leprechaun. In fact, he was born in Dolla, Tipperary, Ireland, the little town in which my mother was born. Their house was two miles away from Mother's. I had asked him to give a talk at the St. Clair Inn to the Food Technology meeting. I was program chairman of the Great Lakes Section of this organization. He was a great hit.

Afterwards he came to Harbor Beach and stayed with us for a few days. When he was visiting us he asked, "What are you going to do when you retire, sit on the front porch and throw rocks into the lake? Why don't you come to Cleveland and start a business there?" How could I refuse? He said, "Vernon Stouffer lives in Cleveland and owns a Prince of Wales yacht." I was 36 years old and was told that "it takes fifteen years to establish a business. If it lasts for seven years, it may become successful."

At the time I had been experimenting with food bases for Custom Foods, and had improved the existing products on the market. We thought this might be a good venture to consider, so I took Tom up on his suggestion. With our six children, we moved from Harbor Beach to Cleveland. I had rolled the dice, but what would our future hold?

The Beginning

The first assignment Tom gave me was to look around for a food seasoning business for sale. Of course, there were none available. After going all over the city chasing leads I had obtained from the phone book, I became acquainted with Cleveland and Clevelanders. I liked those that I met, the city shoreway, the airport, and rapid transit system. All were as appealing to me as were the cultural attraction Cleveland had to offer.

At first, I experimented with chicken base in an office adjacent to Tom's law office. I had a very simple set-up working on a desk. We needed a plant in which to get started, but that was more difficult to find than I anticipated. My problems were solved when I met Joseph Bertman, a Russian Ukrainian, who was a General Foods distributor on East 76th Street in Cleveland. I heard about Joe from another Joe, Joe Hoffman, who was with Beatrice Foods and was a close friend of Tom Ryan's junior law partner, Bob Weinstein.

58

Weinstein heard of my problem, and provided me with an opportunity to solve it which I did by convincing Joe Bertman that I'd deliver on what I promised him. I will have to give Bertman credit. He took time from his busy hands and schedule to sit in his office and listen to my story of what I could do. Without Bertman's help, the L. J. Minor Corporation may never have come into being.

Bertman had a room 18 x 20 feet, with eight foot high ceilings, constructed for me inside his pickle and mustard plant. It had a window-type air conditioner and the complete rent was $100 per month, although he did charge me an extra $25 per month for waste removal. I gave him a far better price on soup bases made and packed under the Bertman label. Thus, we had a deal. That is where the L. J. Minor Corporation had its beginnings.

With a total of $6,000 invested three ways between myself, Thomas Aloysius Ryan, and Joseph Bertman, the L. J. Minor Corporation was founded in 1951.

At that time, Cleveland was advertised to be "the best location in the nation." Having worked for LaChoy Chinese Food Company in Detroit, Michigan, for two years; Owens-Illinois Can Division in Toledo, Ohio, for two years; McKay-Davis in Toledo, Ohio, for three years; and the Huron Milling Company, Harbor Beach, Michigan, for three years; I knew food was my game and food seasoning and flavor were my specialty. I was ready to plunge into deep water and swim with my own company.

Joe did all that he said he would do and I lived up to my end of the bargain. He would let me use his packing tables, warehouse space for my jars and caps, and even allowed me space in his cooler. Setting up the plant in the little room was simple. All it took was an old Hobart mixer with 80 quart bowls that, incidentally, had to be re-tinned regularly. An exact weight scale for weighing the jars which contained one pound of base, a platform scale for weighing-in dry ingredients, a labeler, scoops for weighing, and ice cream scoops for filling the jars were all that I needed to do business. Labels had to be ordered together with raw materials, and packaging materials.

We used canned breast meat of chicken to start. Beef was purchased fresh locally. Jars, caps, and shipping cartons could also be ordered locally together with plastic liners for 10 pound, 25 pound, and 50 pound fiber drums which we obtained in small lots from Continental Can Company. Dry ingredients were ordered from Corn Products, Morton Salt and Huron Milling. Spices came from Woolson Spice Company in Toledo, Ohio. We also used McCormick in Baltimore for spices, and Joseph Adams Company in Cleveland for soluble pepper and celery. Because I was known by most of my suppliers, they gave me a line of credit.

Joseph Adams, President of the Joseph Adams Company, had been a long time friend. He had been chief chemist at William J. Stange, a Chicago seasoning manufacturer. Now he had his own business and started about when I did. We would get together and weep on each other's shoulder. Joe would prepare an entire year's supply of oleoresin of pepper and celery, and store them for use as needed at no additional cost to us. He told us about Givaudon mushroom flavor and set up a Moyno pump for us that would pump the base out of the mixing bowl and into a stainless steel batch-size funnel to make filling containers easier. Later, he would come to the plant and taste our Chicken Base. We always wanted more flavor and he said, "You should be using fresh chickens." We did this immediately. Older birds had been what we were using, in fact, old roosters and hens to be exact. The hens were juicier, but did not yield as much meat. One of our salespeople, Ernie Koves, came into the plant one day and after seeing the size birds we were using, his mouth flew open and he said, "Those birds look like turkeys!" Joe was of great help to us.

Tom Ryan's secretary, Mary Mele, placed orders, handled billing, and collections. We kept it all simple and workable with a minimum of overhead and labor. At first, most of what we made and packaged was the economy grade soup base. Our goal was not to make soup bases, but food bases, which command a better price and out-perform all cheaper bases.

After all, we knew that prior to World War II nearly every professional kitchen had a stock pot to provide the stocks that were necessary to make soup, gravy, sauces, and entrees that met the standards of the great French Chef, Auguste Escoffier, the father of the modern kitchen and classical cooking.

Escoffier, who died in the '30s, stated that "Stock is everything in cooking, at least, in all good and well-flavored cooking. When one's stock is good, the rest of the work is easy. When it is not, nothing worth while is accomplished."

This, then, was the challenge I wanted to meet. That is, to produce food bases that would make the stock pot, with all of its short comings, obsolete. To do this would meet a need brought on by changes in meat distribution called, "portion control." This began after the end of World War II. Prior to then, chefs would order bones to be used to make stock. There would be enough meat on the bones that the excess could be removed and used to make hamburger. Enough meat would remain to flavor the stock pot ingredients consisting of vegetable trimmings, egg shells, and other kitchen remnants. The pots were extremely heavy and required a lot of fuel to keep them hot. Bones that chefs could get post World War II were then, and are now, stripped bare with the last vestige of meat gone.

Now, however, with food bases available, the stock pot is almost obsolete. A few die-hards still stick with it despite its shortcomings. I designed a product with meat, meat juices, bone stock, and seasoning. Complete! All that the user needed to do was add one pound of base to five gallons of boiling water. The result was 640 ounces or 100 servings of broth. Soup could readily be made by adding noodles, rice, or vegetables. It was simple, easy, quick, economical, and a real improvement over adding a soup base, seasoning, to the stock pot. The product could be basted on meat, poultry, or fish or added to entrees which then required no additional salt.

The development of the L. J. Minor Corporation was slow. Early in the game, though, I eliminated my partners after hearing that "the only partner to have in business is the one you sleep with." Tom Ryan did not like the idea of selling me his one-third interest, but he did so with the understanding that if the business succeeded he would be properly rewarded, and he was.

The first two years in business were hard. Many times I felt like it would not succeed. Faith and determination helped me. Fortunately, I had a consulting job with International Mineral and Chemicals Company that lasted for a year and a half. That, plus six months terminal pay that I had received from the Huron Milling Company, kept bread on our table. Fortuitously, when Toby Bishop, President of International Mineral Company heard that I was leaving Huron, he started calling and trying to hire me. When I insisted that I was starting my own business, he said, "If you promise you will not compete with us, we will give you a $500 per month consulting fee to work with Bob Cocroft in developing a protein derivative by-product at our Rossford, Ohio, plant and lab." These, too, were pennies from heaven, and were a big help when we went into business. My consulting time was just two days per month.

Salespeople at that time, were getting $12,000 per year, plus a car, and commission. Years before, when I was with Huron Milling, a steamboat chef, Mark Zimmer, whom I had met at the St. Claire Inn in St. Claire, Michigan, told me, "You need a chef to sell your product. A salesperson is standing on just one foot when he or she is trying to sell the chef." I told Joe Bertman this when we were together at lunch one day. He said, "August Erb just retired from the Hollenden Hotel. Why not call him?" I did, and August sold a few accounts, but the orders were small. August was our first chef.

Building a Sales Force

My own sales efforts had been with local distributors. They bore little fruit. I had a food broker, whose wife was a dietitian, for a customer in Boston, and another broker in New York named Johnny Hayes. Our sales in 1951 were just $30,000. In 1952, we did $60,000. In 1953, we were at $80,000.

Meanwhile, pursuing the "chefsalesman:" tactic, I went to Detroit. A caterer there, George Roumell, used chefs for large parties. I met him and said, "I need a retired chef to sell my food bases." He said, "I have just the man for you. His name is Jean Caubet, and he is preparing a meal for 600 this evening at the Latin Quarter at Grand Boulevard near Woodward. Go and see him." Before going in, I said a rosary. My guardian angel must have been on my shoulder.

Handing Chef Caubet two one pound jars of Chicken Base with the Dietitian brand label, I told him I wanted him to introduce the product to the Detroit market. God was with me. Caubet said, "I am not a salesman. I am a chef! See, I have six cooks here and the salad girls. We are serving 600 people 'chicken fricassee' tonight. I will try them out!" After the meal was served, he received many compliments. Having a little of the base left, he took it home. The next day he made chicken soup for his daughters. They said, "Daddy, this is good chicken soup!" That did it. Caubet then knew how good the base was. He met with our distributor, Delsoy, and they gave him a kit of samples of our Beef and Chicken Bases, together with our price list and literature.

When I first met with Jean Caubet, I did not realize what credentials, status, and influence he had. Caubet had been president of the cooks union for forty years. He was also a founder of the Chef's 100 Club. We brought August Erb to Detroit to work with him. Chef Erb was astonished when Jean would go into a hotel like the Statler, get the head chef, sous chef, and food manager together and say, "We make up the chicken broth", and walk out with a fifteen case order after they tasted it.

Our company office address was Tom Ryan's law office. He took care of that end of the business. Tom soon became aware of the L. J. Minor Corporation potential, and helped me find other chef representatives.

Tom Ryan and I regarded ourselves as talent scouts. We were always looking for people who would help us with sales. That meant that we kept getting more and more chefs who were retired and wanted to affiliate with us. They were our salespeople, and each worked on commission.

One salesperson, Frank Sigmund, was not a chef, but he was still paid only for what he sold, after we got paid. He was a fancy grocery salesperson. He introduced us to the famous Maître d'hotel, Peter Gust Economou, who learned the business from the great Statler himself of hotel fame. Tom wanted Sigmund to sell for us on commission. He finally did after Tom upset him by telling him that the night before he had dreamed about "Flotsam and Jetsam." When Sigmund asked Tom what that was he said, "It's offal floating down the river." Frank got us some great accounts in Buffalo, Wisconsin, and Minnesota. That was his territory. We would fill the accounts for him and hold his commissions until the accounts were paid. Frank became a close friend. He would stop in at Tom's office, and come by the plant whenever he passed through Cleveland. We loved him and it was mutual. Tom was asked to give Frank's epitaph when Frank died.

Later on, as the business grew, Tom started to make deals with salespeople. He would put them on a draw where they would get so much per week against commissions from what they sold.

Sometimes these people would be on a draw for three or four years before they would be able to go off the draw and be on their own without our underwriting part of their income. However, it was fortunate that we could do this, because we were able to get some very professional salespeople, like Frank Aicardi and Frank Szabo, who had both worked for a competitor and knew how to sell bases.

Aicardi, an Italian American, was located in Boston. Szabo, a Hungarian American, lived in Ohio. The strange thing about Frank Szabo was that while he was working for LeGout, he was also selling Minor's Bases in certain areas of West Virginia. When the sales manager at LeGout called him in and confronted him about selling our bases he said, "Well, I'm only selling Minor's in a territory that I don't have for LeGout, and I intend to go on doing it!" So they let him get away with it.

Later on, Ernie Koves, our New York chef salesperson whom I mentioned earlier, got a hospital manager, in Philadelphia, named Howard Schatz, to sell for us. He built his sales up to over two million dollars per year. We had Otto Denkinger in Seattle, a club-chef, selling for us. He worked as a salesperson and a distributor, storing the bases in his own home. He delivered with his car. Later, Otto established accounts for us in Hawaii and Alaska at his own expense.

Another chef to assist us was Al Mahlke who lived in St. Paul and worked as executive chef at Charlie's Cafe Exceptional in Minneapolis, Minnesota. Harry Bazaan was in California. It spread like a chain letter. We just kept adding sales representatives as we slowly grew in size. It was like the song, "Give me some men who are stout hearted men, and I'll soon get you ten thousand more."

Our charisma grew quickly and interest in our company was increasing all the time. Chef John Secter joined us and after five years we were moving along toward bigger and better things. We got rid of the Dietitian label when a dietitian at a food show held in the Carter Hotel in Cleveland (where we shared a booth with A Lo Presti and Sons) asked, "Are you putting dietitians in a jar?"

Gus Lo Presti and I traveled together to Columbus where we sold Kuenning's restaurant, the leading hotel, and also to the state penitentiary. We went to Cincinnati where we sold to Marzetti's restaurant, famous for their salad dressing, and others. Gus and I became close friends. He had the Mills Restaurant chain for an account and others. We worked well together and helped each other.

Chapter 10

Expansion

A New Plant   A New Customer   New Opportunities

A Guiding Force
(Irish Humor by Hal Roach)

Father Murphy was working on his Sunday sermon. All at once he looks down and there is water up to his knees. He didn't realize it, but the dam in the village had broken. Just then, a boat came by and those in it said:

"Father, get into the boat and save yourself."

He says:

"No, I'm just fine!"

So pretty soon, the water comes up higher and he is on the second floor still writing his sermon. Another boat comes by and those in it say:

"Father, for God's sake, get into the boat and save yourself."

He says:

"No, the good Lord will take care of me!"

Then he winds up in the belfry tower. Another boat comes by and those in it say:

"Father, this is your last chance, get into the boat."

Well, the flood engulfed the village and Father Murphy ended up looking at St. Peter and Father Murphy says:

"I don't know why God did that to me. He never did that to me before."

St. Peter says:

"We did send three boats, you know."

(Editor's Note: God's voice speaks continuously to man. Unfortunately, man forgets to ask "What is God saying to me?" Dr. Minor frequently gave credit to his guardian angel for his successes and prayed for guidance and direction. When life's opportunities and challenges arrive, don't end up like Father Murphy when God sends three boats to the rescue. "Trust in the Lord with all your heart, and don't lean on your own understanding. In all your ways, acknowledge Him, and He will direct your paths." [Proverbs 3: 5-6])

A New Plant

After two years, we moved from Bertman's warehouse to a concrete block building on West 115th Street that at one time had been a horse barn. We then had about 1,000 square feet of manufacturing space. We stored our glass and caps upstairs. We would buy glass by the truck load and put it in through an upstairs window.

Salt and other ingredients were stored downstairs. We kept chicken fat, hams, and butter in a reach-in cooler. We had a newer Hobart with six stainless steel 120-quart bowls. We used home-style electric roasters for cooking the beef and continued using canned breast meat for our chicken base. We bought special hickory smoked ham for our ham base.

Our plant was always clean and passed Cleveland City and Federal Food and Drug Inspection. We coated the cement blocks with Mechanics Enamel (white). We had a taped joint, painted plaster board ceiling that met federal inspection standards. The sink was a wall type with a porcelain splash back, small but adequate for washing our utensils. We used a hose for the mixing bowls. The floor was asbestos tile with one floor drain. We had foot-pedal operated valves for water. It was all simple and adequate.

Shipping and receiving were no problem. We had access to both doors, front and rear. Trucks could pass in our cinder-covered yard and drive. We kept everything simple. Our packing tables and material handling tubs were stainless steel. Everything was on wheels or movable except the Hobart mixer. Things were going well. I took care of filling the orders with my small task force. I also designed the label which now said simply, "MINOR'S." The name was in a red curved banner and printed in white. I wrote up the orders and sent the shipment statements to Mary Mele, who then did the billing. She now had Nancy Clancy working with her. Mary and Nancy were close friends, but when they worked together, there was no talking. We ran a tight ship.

By using "Manpower" as a labor source, we did not add any worker to our regular payroll until the individual worked out to our satisfaction while still in Manpower's employ. After I knew enough about the person's individual and work habits, I hired them.

Another one of my tasks was working out the label ingredient statements. Tom and I wrote up the ads which appeared in the National Culinary Review. We had the Review's seal of approval, and we were the first to have colored ads in that journal.

A New Customer

By now I had five women and a man helping me with making and packing the bases. For years I had called on Stouffer's, but could not get past the purchasing agent, named Mallman. He would always say that Stouffer's would never use anything like our product.

Then one day a Durkee salesperson named Boswell stopped into our plant on 115th Street and told us that Mrs. Mitchell was having trouble making *au jus* for a beef tenderloin they were developing. She was Vernon Stouffer's assistant and was in charge of their restaurants. I told him how Mrs. Minor always basted beef roasts with our beef base, collected the juices that were co-mingled with the beef juices, removed the fat, and made the gravy from this. He asked me to get the recipe and I did.

Mrs. Mitchell tried it on their tenderloins and it produced a good result. She called me and said, "You have a product you can be proud of. We want to use it." Our beef base solved their problem and ours. We now began selling the Stouffer chain. This account helped us open needed distributors in many cities. That was not all. I asked her if they ever used any chicken base. She said, "Yes, we've been using a product from your competitor for about eleven years." I asked if she would be willing to test our product. She put it on their taste panel. Later, she reported that out of thirteen people on the panel who tasted the two products side by side, they picked ours 12 to 1 over what they had been using.

From then on our business with Stouffer's started to really grow. Mrs. Mitchell soon asked me to develop a turkey base. Then she wanted a ham base. We developed that, too. Next was a clam base for clam chowder. Later, she asked for mushroom base.

As time went on, our product line grew and we were able to sell these products to our other customers besides Stouffer's. Our business with Stouffer grew especially fast when they built the frozen food plant. Their purchases accounted for about 25% of our sales.

In the meantime, our sales to other customers kept growing. The business was maturing and soon we sold onion, garlic, fish, lobster, shrimp, and veal bases, dry roux, chicken supreme sauce, glace de viande, gravy prep in chicken, beef, pork and turkey flavors, liquid Consommé, brown gravy sauce, and others.

We would get orders from their restaurants in various parts of the courntry, like Pittsburgh, Chicago and New York. We would ship them ten pound drums by mail. Every day I would go to the post office with a stack of ten pound drums for various Stouffer units. As time went on, we were able to get distributors in these locations, and their sales to the Stouffer account helped us to keep these distributors. Tom Ryan did a wonderful job of managing the business through these years.

New Opportunities

Tom found an excellent portrait of Escoffier. We used this in our ads along with his classic statement about stock. We had pencils made up with our motto which said, "Minor's -- Always in Good Taste."

We had a station wagon that I used for Boy Scouting activity and for making deliveries. Tom and I took trips together in it, too. He liked night driving because he could see the lights on other cars. We would take turns driving, and we had a mattress in the back to rest on while the other drove.

Sometimes, Tom and I would visit Cornell and would send our chefs in to put on demonstations for their students using our bases. *(Editor's Note: While Dr. Minor tells of his travels to Cornell, he never would forget the little people either. For example, his chefs visited each of the smaller schools at which I directed hotel and foodservice programs. He did this across the country, in fact. At great expense paid for by the L. J. Minor Corporation, the chefs would speak to the students and then demonstrate the full product line offering sample jars to all present at the lectures. I, for one, will never forget the impact these chefs had on our students' lives and how much the lectures and demos meant to me as an instructor attempting to provide the highest quality education to my students.)* Tom and I went to Buffalo where we stayed at the Park Lane Apartment Hotel. Frank Sigmund lived there. We also traveled to New York City where we would stay at the Lexington Hotel that Arthur Godfrey made famous.

Peterson and Owens, a highly reputable meat distributor, agreed to handle the Minor line. Through them we met Ernest Koves, an eminent Hungarian chef, who was at a small residential hotel near Hunter College. At one time, he was head chef at the Astor Hotel, and had 200 other cooks with him in their big kitchen. Ernie knew New York City and was a powerful personality. We liked him because he was eager about coming with us and his quality meant a lot to Tom and me.

He joined us after testing our bases for six months and finding out that they were all we claimed them to be. Ernie called it a marriage. Our chefs were overcome by his authoritative manner. He was consultant for the Culinary Review and this is how we were able to make a historical and profitable association with this journal when it first began.

(Editor's Note: Shortly after I arrived at Michigan State as an undergraduate student, Dr. Minor invited me to fly to and stay in New York City by myself to meet Dr. Koves. Dr. Minor provided exquisite accommodations for me at one of the new mega hotels and I spent a number of days testing the Minor line with Dr. Koves. I will never forget him, his apartment in which he worked and had his labs, or my stay as a guest of the L. J. Minor Corporation. Was this trip given to me because I was an honors college student? Was it because I took an interest in what Dr. Minor said and did? My answer is that God was directing my paths in a fashion similar to how He always led Dr. Minor. Looking to Him, I received the blessings early and continue to receive them through Dr. and Mrs. Minor today.)

God works in strange ways. Tom Ryan and I were both in Fairview Hospital in 1957, the seventh year of the Minor Corporation, having our gall bladders removed. That was a tough operation in those days. While I was lying on my back recovering, I told Ruth, "I'm either going to be a doctor or a teacher." She decided for me that I couldn't handle the pressure of being a doctor, but could become a teacher.

Tom used to say, "Things that seem bad at the time usually turn out for the best." While recuperating, I attended night school at Baldwin Wallace in Berea, got my Teaching Ceftificate in 1959, and taught chemistry half days for one year at Rocky River High School.

Tom had his own network of professionals whom we could hire part-time at low cost. Also, borrowing money was a phobia of mine. Tom knew that, so all changes or needed improvements had to come from profits. I had trained Audrey Chubbs to make batches, do the packaging, shipping, and other chores. She could write up the orders, receive, and store raw materials; in short, take over for me. We used Manpower for getting other extra help.

Meanwhile, I had my own network of workers and handy men who would work for us by the hour and get needed materials at low cost. We put a small addition on the 115th Street plant. This provided a restroom with a cot for the women. We few men had our own restroom.

For many years I handled inventory and purchasing. Tom took care of building the sales structure which I began, together with prices to distributors, discounts, and freight. Our original terms were 20% to distributors, 10% to the sales force, and 5% for sales promotion. Terms were "2%-10 days, net 11," meaning two percent discount for payment withn ten days, full payment on the eleventh day. Manufacturers, like Weight Watchers and Stouffers, were house accounts with no sales commission paid on either.

About 1958 I called the Food Agricultural and Tobacco Division of the CIO and told them we would like to join. I did this for two reasons. The first reason was that we needed the Union Seal for our label. The second was that I wanted to show the women employees, who thought they were missing something, that they were not.

Jackie Presser, the son of the notorious Teamster boss, William Presser, drove up to our plant with one of his organizers. I was just returning from making a delivery to two of Stouffer's downtown stores. When I walked in, Jackie said, "You stand in good with your help, and you are the first man that ever called and asked to join our union." He invited me to an evening meeting. I went and he liked that. He said, "Minor, I'm giving you a break. You only need to have your part-time employees join. You can use the check-off system and have the company pay the dues." After that, we did as we were asked and never had any trouble with them. I figured if you can't lick them, you had better join them. Besides, all the restaurant workers belonged. Our employees learned that we were treating them better, and paying them more than the union required us to pay.

Two important organizations invited us to become members. These were the U. S. Quartermaster Corps Procurement Agency in Natick, Massachusetts, and the Glutamate Manufacturers Committee. Each wanted a prohibitive amount for us to join, which we couldn't afford. I wrote to each of them and offered to pay a much smaller amount to join. Both accepted.

For more than 25 years, I served on the Quartermaster Committee with food scientists from Campbell, Heinz, and other huge companies. Later, I had my former student, Mike Zelski, take over for me. I enjoyed the competitive fellowship I had at these meeetings. It kept us abreast of irradiated foods and other developments that were being worked on by the government. Also all new happenings in the monosodium use saga that still exist in the use of this efficacious ingredient, which has been condemned unjustly by consumer panic-button pushers. Fortunately, the USDA food scientists recognize its safety, food flavor enhancing value, and purity.

Another of my tasks was to keep up with all new developments pertaining to our field. We were soon purchasing beef bone stock from Hormel, powdered whey from Monsanto Chemical Company, hydrolyzed cereal solids from Corn Products, Co. and alginate stabilizer from Kelco. Huron Milling supplied our dry and liquid hydrolyzed wheat proteins. We also bought monosodium glutamate (MSG) from them and the Accent people. A new product, Disodium Inosynate and Disodium Guanylate, derived from yeast, was reported at a food technology meeting that I attended. By using 5% of this with 95% glutamate, a stronger flavor enhancer than MSG alone resulted.

We were a small company with big competitors, but we found our own niche in the foodservice field. We were building a franchise on a solid foundation of chef consultants. Tom Ryan used to say, "Big companies make big mistakes." We had a policy that if any person wanted to visit our plant, he or she had to be a government inspector. We discouraged plant visitations. Visitors were not allowed in our plant, and I refused all invitations to visit other facilities. Sometimes, I would send one of my employees to check on equipment they were using, but only by invitation.

One night, after getting home from the West 115th Street plant, Joe Dwyer, night production manager for Stouffer's Frozen Food Plant, called me at home. I had just come in the door. He said, "We need 200 pounds of chicken base for our night shift." Mrs. Minor and I went back to the plant together. I made up the batches, packed the product in four 50 pound plastic lined fiber drums, put them in our station wagon, and Mrs. Minor delivered them to Stouffer's at the East Side Market plant. Then she came back and helped me clean up and get ready for the next day. We reached home at midnight after working five hours.

Chapter 11

Insuring Success

Philosophies at Work   **Forty Plus Suggestions**

Let There Be Light
(Irish Humor by Hal Roach)

One morning in church, prior to the flood taking place (as recorded in Chapter 10 of this text, Father Murphy said:

"What the church needs is a chandelier."

So they had a meeting of the committee and Doolin, who was the chair, went to see Father Murphy after the meeting and says:

"You may not have the chandelier for three reasons."

The priest says:

"Well, what are they?"

He says:

"No one in town can spell it. No one in town can play it, and what the church needs most is more light!"

(Editor's Note: In this chapter, Dr. Minor offers words of wisdom on insuring success. It is interesting to note that no mention of "work by committee" is given, except for the above reference to the committee formed by poor Father Murphy. The following tale proceeds Dr. Minor's words of advice and, again, demonstrates what the real business world can be like with its many temptations and opportunities to do what is wrong! But remember that Dr. Minor founded his business on the precepts of honesty, integrity, perseverance, commitment to quality, respect for fellow employees, and teamwork, as stated in his "Business Aims" written in 1951.)

Building a Fountain in Dublin
(Irish Humor by Hal Roach)

The city of Dublin was trying to install a new fountain and the city fathers advertised in the newspaper, and sent out for bids with over 150 coming in. From those, the fathers selected three: one from a contractor in Galway, another from a contractor in Mayo, and the third from the cute contractor, Dugan, in County Cork.

So when they came to give their bids, the fellow from Galway went in first and the clerk said:

"How much to build the fountain?"

The fellow from Galway replied:

"Three thousand pounds."

The clerk asked him to break that down and he said:
   "One thousand pounds for materials, one thousand pounds for the men and
      labor, and one thousand pounds for me."

The clerk said wait outside. The next to come in was the contractor from Mayo and the clerk said:

"How much to build the fountain?"

The contractor from Mayo responded:

   "Six thousand pounds. Two thousand pounds for materials, two thousand
      pounds for the men and labor, and two thousand pounds for me."

The clerk said wait outside. The next to come in was Dugan, the cute contractor from County Cork. The clerk says:

"How much to build the fountain?"

Dugan says:

"Nine thousand pounds."

The clerk asks Dugan to break that down. Dugan says:

"Three thousand pounds for you, three thousand pounds for me, and we'll give the job to the fellow from Galway!"

Philosophies at Work

Three philosophies motivated me at this time. The first came from French Jenkins, who said, "It is always better to shoot at the eagle than it is to aim at the rat." His second philosophy that greatly affected me was, "Always remember that the line of demarcation between recreation and dissipation rapidly becomes indistinct." That is why we never had hospitality suites at shows when other companies did. The third, which was quoted earlier, was, "Always remember that flattery is worse than a buzzard. A buzzard eats you when you are dead, but flattery eats you while you are still alive."

In 1952 I first stated for publication my "Business Aims," and we practiced them unfailingly during the years I owned the company. They will be noted throughout this text and are presented here in full for the reader:

"I believe that honesty, integrity, accuracy, punctuality, courtesy, kindness, friendliness, helpfulness, and cleanliness are the tenets upon which my business shall be built;

I will endeavor always to be fair and helpful, not only to employees, my management team, and stockholders, but also to customers, government agencies, and competitors;

My experience in the food industry indicates there will always be room for a company that will sell quality products that are constantly controlled to insure uniformity at a fair price that will result in a normal profit;

Service will be the keynote of our business and every effort will be put forth to give the customer exactly the product that he specifies."

Forty Plus Suggestions

1. **Look for a window of opportunity.**
   What's that? It's a product, service, or process that's needed. This can be something new or an improvement on what already exists.
2. **Be your own person.**
   You don't want any partners. Sharing profit is okay, but don't give stock. Have a sole proprietorship.
3. **Ask the man or woman.**

What does this mean?

Whenever you need something -- it can be knowledge, skill, legal advice, a line of credit, help with solving a problem, or whatever -- try to determine whom you should call on for assistance. Contact that person, state your need, and ask for the help you want. Explain why, and determine what the cost will be.

4. **Start small with used, rented, or borrowed space and equipment.**

   Don't go in debt or try to have everything as you'd wish it to be.

5. **Expand out of profits.**

   Don't try to borrow. The only time a bank will lend you money is when you don't need it. Don't ask friends, relatives, or acquaintances for loans. Sell what you have or use that as collateral, if you have to. But try to avoid it.

6. **Keep your liquidation high.**

   This is the ratio of what you have to what you owe. For example: it is your inventory, accounts receivable, and bank account balance vs. your accounts payable or other debts.

7. **Live and conduct your business wisely.**

   My grandfather's philosophy was this: "Since man to man is so unjust, I hardly know which one to trust. I've trusted many to my sorrow, so pay today and I'll trust tomorrow."

8. **Run a tight ship.**

   Keep overhead down. Control expenses including labor, taxes, maintenance, power and water cost, travel expense, office, legal, insurance, inventory, accounts receivable, and accounts payable. Minimize your cost of doing business. Your CDB. The overhead is called "the nut." Keep it easy to crack at all times.

9. **Hiring.**

   Hire only super people. Seek loyal, honest, punctual, team-oriented, conscientious, empathetic, and trustworthy employees. Good grooming and dress habits are important. These denote self-respect. Others won't respect you, unless you respect yourself.

10. **Suppliers.**

    Your suppliers are just as important to you as your customers. Pay your bills promptly. Treat them as you would want to be treated.

11. **Customers.**

    Always remember, "The customer is smarter than you are." Never sell a customer any products other than those he orders and expects. Make prompt delivery. Cooperate with customers. Keep them informed whenever price changes or other changes are going to be made.

12. **Competitors.**

    Be friendly with competitors, and not combative. Henry Ford said,

"Competition is the life blood of business." We need competition to give us the incentive to improve and stay ahead.

13. **Inspectors.**

Always be friendly with inspectors. To me, government inspectors were guardians of quality who helped keep standards high. They protect both the customer and the manufacturer. They were like another plant manager who safeguarded our products and our business. They were our friends.

14. **Law Suits.**

Avoid legal entanglements. A great lawyer once said to me, "Watch yourself. Don't be getting into law suits. No one ever wins in a fight except the courts and attorneys." Press coverage of disputes can cost you customers and ruin a business.

15. **Dunn and Bradstreet.**

Don't tell them anything. Let them guess. You'll get a better rating from them this way. Their reports can be useful in a way, but their accuracy is doubtful.

16. **Unions.**

Unions are not all bad. We had a union just because our employees wanted us to have one. So did some of our customers. We never had any trouble with the union in thirty years. I brought it in myself and belonged to it. Employees' rights counted for more with us than executive rule and greed. We found it better to give all we could to our employees, rather than to shortchange them. That way their spirits were always high, and the plant people loved Mrs. Minor and me. They knew we were all family. Ignorance rules the minds of greedy executives. In any business, the government takes half of the profit. To increase profit at the expense of labor, wages, and benefits in order to pay higher executive salaries for showing a better *bottom line* on the annual profit is ruthless, improvident, ignorant and predatory. And invites employees to *strike*.

17. **Little people.**

Take care of the little people. One time, a speaker I heard in our high school auditorium referred to production workers, miners, stevedores, and all laborers as "automatons." His point was that you should aim higher than being an individual who did the same routine task day after day. Be an executive; that's what he meant. Another speaker addressing supervisors said, "Give them praise and encouragement, help them. Let them know you care about them, and they'll form a platform under you and lift you up." One day, when our business had just started to get going, our son, Bryan, said, "Dad, don't ever forget the little people." I never did. When we eventually sold the business, we took care of the little people. We gave them two million of the thirteen million we got for the business. We gave the U.S. Treasury $3 million instead of the $4 million we'd have paid the IRS had we not given $2 million to our "little people." What did it do for the "little people?" Many bought houses. Some used it for education, others for travel. We bought a house for a woman who got our products made and shipped when I had my gall bladder operation and couldn't work for several weeks. In two years we got the bank to put the mortgage in her name. She was happy, for she once said to me, "Mr. Minor, I would never have been able to buy a house if it weren't for you." No other manufacturer ever did these things, and none may ever do them again.

We always tip waiters and waitresses more than others of our means do. I learned that from Tom Ryan and Frank Sigmund. Frank's father told him, "You're a gentleman, and people will greet you when you come into their restaurant or club with, 'Hello, Mr. Sigmund, we're happy to see you.'" It's true. Everyone likes to be asked, "What's your name?" and then be treated royally. We're all God's creatures. "Do unto others as you'd want them to do unto you." Three hundred years ago a man said, "The more I gave away, the more I had." Remember the "little people." Look out for them, and they'll look out for you.

18. **Profit sharing.**

Profit sharing is much better than selling stock options. Employees love to achieve and attain reasonable goals.

19. **Sanitation.**

The L.J. Minor Corporation was always a model plant. Federal Inspectors told us ours was the cleanest plant they ever inspected. "Cleanliness is next to Godliness." My philosophy was that we spend a major part of our life at work. Good lighting, safety, floors so clean you could eat off them, tile, stainless steel, floor cleaning, not with a mop, but with a wet-dry vacuum that picks up all the dirt instead of leaving it in cracks or seams and painting dirt on the base of walls with a mop. A woman using a toothbrush and detergent to sanitize the corners the machine couldn't reach. These are all attainable goals. Soap with iodine antiseptic in it for hand washing. Clean uniforms for employees. Air conditioning, and heating for comfort and process control. "It's better to aim for the eagle than shoot at the rat." You can't start that way, but you can reach these standards later. We did!

20. **Business Hazards.**

Any business can be wiped out anytime by financial failure, fire, explosion, loss of life by an employee, law suits, adverse publicity, strikes. All of my life I've been running scared as:

- a newsboy scared of customers moving and not paying.
- a student scared of exams and excessive homework loads, of some

teachers.

- a God-fearing man scared of Hell, purgatory, limbo, sacrilegious behavior.
- a production worker scared of machinery, heat-treating furnaces, cyanide baths, exposure to solvent vapors, fire, explosion, fatal accident, maiming accident.
- a football player scared of crippling injury, the coach.
- a businessman scared of government inspectors, accounts payable being non-collectible, accidents, lawsuits, strikes. Scared of not being able to meet the payroll. Scared of owing money to the bank.
- an investor scared of losing money. The only investments I made that paid off were my wonderful, happy, successful marriage, our family, the L.J. Minor Corporation, my education, and Scudder Managed Municipal bonds.
- a retiree scared of the economy, inflation, dilution of savings, and the depreciation of real estate values.
- one who will die. "I don't fear death, but I do love life" as French Jenkins would say. Everyone's life is a race against time. Brother Herman Zaccarelli (who is a Holy Cross Brother and educator for cooks at Catholic institutions, and so close to the Minor family that Ruth and I refer to him as our "adopted son") encouraged me to write the L. J. Minor Corporation story, and although my candle is burning low now, I have succeeded in getting it done for him, thanks be to God.

21. **Discipline.**

People want discipline that improves them and increases their potential. Always temper discipline with praise.

22. **Temper and Grudges.**

Tom Ryan said, "Minor has a temper. He'll rant and rave over something he doesn't agree with. But, when his anger subsides, he cools off, and it's over. He never holds a grudge against anyone, and you'll never find a better friend." Temper is a bad, a dangerous handicap for anyone to possess. In a moment of rage, a friendship can be lost, an injury can be done to an innocent person. It upsets everyone present. Whenever I get angry, and lose my temper, huge drops of perspiration start falling from my armpits, which, at such times, give off a strong onion-garlic kind or odor. Deodorant doesn't prevent it either. "Hold your pivot." Don't let your temper master you. Self-control must be learned. Don't hold grudges. When an argument or dispute is over, forget it, and move forward.

23. **Patience.**

Patience is a great virtue. French Jenkins of LaChoy said, "Anything of mushroom proportions will usually have mushroom consequences." This means businesses that enjoy quick success often suffer quick failure. Growth and development of a company takes time. Usually, a business that makes it for seven years will endure.

24. **Minority Hiring.**

Government regulations force the hiring of minorities. L.J. Minor Corporation is like the United Nations. We have Japanese-Americans, Korean-Americans, Russian-Americans, Ukrainian-Americans, Polish-Americans, Hungarian-Americans, Spanish-Americans, Afro-Americans, Cuban-Americans, Mexican-Americans, Irish-Americans, German-Americans, French-Americans, Yugoslavian-Americans, Czechoslovakian-Americans, British Americans, Australian-Americans, Canadian-Americans, and others.

25. **Employee Benefits.**

Social Security, health care, vacation time, bonuses, retirement, education, and other benefits are possibilities depending on the company's status.

26. **Government Relations.**

The U.S. Government is a 50/50 partner with every U.S. business. Employers must pay Social Security, Workmen's Compensation, and withholding taxes for all employees. Give your employees all that you can instead of giving it away in taxes or needless expenses on trips and entertainment.

27. **Risk Taking.**

Anyone in business is taking risks. Try to minimize the risks you're taking. Fire prevention, sanitation, theft and burglary prevention, safety guards on equipment, avoidance of unnecessary expansion and borrowing are ways of minimizing risks.

Banks consider themselves "risk-takers," but from my experience, the only time a bank will lend money is when your assets are greater than the amount they're offering to lend you. Paying interest on loans can break a company's back. Expand out of profits, not by borrowing.

28. **Charter your company.**

Dr. Ryan obtained a Delaware Charter for our company. The Delaware Charter or license has been the best for corporations and continues to be so in my opinion.

29. **Directors.**

Always have an uneven number on the board of directors to try to preclude stalemates in voting. A board with a minimum of three members or 5, 7, 9, etc. is the recommendation that Dr. Thomas A. Ryan made to me.

30. **Don't quit.**

You never know how close you are. Success may be near when it seems so far. Stick to the fight when you're hardest hit. It's when things seem worse

77

that you must not quit.

31. **"Laissez Faire."**

    My experience is that a "Laissez Faire" policy works. Give people the training they need, then let them do the job. Emerson said, "The best governed are the least governed."

32. **Machines don't hurt people, employment-wise.**

    The L.J. Minor Corporation is mechanized as completely as any manufacturing company. Whenever a worker is displaced by a machine, another job is found for that person. In 43 years of business not one job was lost due to mechanization.

33. **Multiple job training.**

    At the L.J. Minor Corporation production workers do not work on just one job. All workers get multiple job training. Supervisors work closely with foremen and workers in training all employees.

34. **Flex time.**

    Flex time is given to employees who need time off to fulfill family needs or all situations that require it.

35. **You can't win them all.**

    From time to time setbacks may occur. Machines break down. Power shortages occur. Deaths require correct burial. Weddings, births, and special anniversaries must be observed. Days in months vary affecting sales. Weather may affect attendance. Theft and burglary may occur. Auto-truck accidents occur. Government regulations and taxes may cause adverse changes. Finally, there is Murphy's Law which states that, "Anything that can happen will happen."

36. **Cut down on errors.**

    Don't rush into buying machinery. Run tests on machines before investing in them or you may have a warehouse full of "white elephant" relics. Don't buy property until "Zoning status" of the property is determined. Tom Ryan would say, "Let's roll it around a few days. We'll sleep on it, and consider all the angles." Measure carefully, check weights of raw material deliveries. Be as accurate as possible in weighing finished product. We always gave away 1/8 oz. per 1 lb. jar, 1 oz. per 10 lb. drum, and 1/4 lb. per 25 lb. drum or 50 lb. drum. Never shortchange a customer, employee, supplier, the government, or even competitors.

37. **Quality.**

    What does quality mean? It's the value of anything. For example, two suits of clothes may look identical hanging on a rack, but the one that is a perfect fit is worth far more than the other. Two products may have different prices, but the one that performs best is the one you'll choose.

Joseph Wechsberg, one of my favorite authors, says this about Quality: "The Bohemian Tailor is a symbol of quality. He's known all over the world like the Italian tenor, the Russian ballerina, the Swiss watchmaker, the Hungarian gypsy primas, the French chef.

"Imitations always show up, but these are a long way from the original article: Italianized tenors with a double chin but without "bel conto" training; French chefs from Sicily or Bucharest; Russian ballerinas born in Nebraska and Idaho; and naturally, Bohemian tailors who never saw Bohemia."

John Ruskin wrote, "There is nothing that someone cannot make a little cheaper, but not as good as the genuine article of top quality. Those who patronize him are their own victims."

(Editor's Note: One of Dr. Minor's favorite sayings remembered by all who ever met him has been "Quality is remembered long after the price is forgotten.")

38. **"Caveat Emptor."**

Caveat Emptor means let the purchaser beware. If in his judgment one article is a better buy than another, that may not be what he wanted but according to law he has no course of redress. It was his decision, and he's stuck with it.

39. **Service.**

Service is a very important part of satisfying a customer. Delivery, alterations to suit the customers needs, advice and help to the customer are fundamental reasons for preferring one manufacturer to another. Delivery by air is expensive, but may save money in the long run.

40. **Packaging.**

A suitable package can make all the difference between acceptance or rejection of a product. Packaging experts should be consulted in attacking and solving packaging problems.

41. **Advertising.**

Advertising is costly, but is essential to the growth and development of a business. You can't hide your head in a bushel and hope to grow as fast as you can by advertising.

Smart Advertising.

You don't need a page when one-eighth of a page can be a good, productive ad if it's well located and properly worded. Color advertising outperforms black and white, but is costly. Free advertising can be obtained when introducing new items. Journals devote special sections for new products and processes.

42. **Naming a business.**

    Your name might be long and hard to pronounce, but the consumer will trust a product with the manufacturer's name more than one with a contrived name. For example, Munchhauserr Beer is a better name than Starlight Beer.

43. **Know your customers.**

    Visit your customers. Get their reaction toward your product, and any suggestions for improvement they may offer.

44. **Adapt to change.**

    Consumers are becoming conscious of the functional advantages one product may have over another, e.g., anti-lock brakes compared to disc brakes.

Chapter 12

Quality Control

What is Quality?   **How May Quality Be Achieved?**

What is a Cook?   **Quality Food Standards**

Summary and Conclusion   **Twelve Things To Remember**

Ice Cream Scorecard

What Makes a Good Cook?
by Lewis J. Minor
(1973)

1 -   A love of fellow-man and his well-being.
2 -   A knowledge and appreciation of good food and good drink.
3 -   A desire to learn more.
4 -   Attention to details.
5 -   Keen perception of subtle differences.
6 -   Knowledge that the customer is smarter than you are and is the final judge and jury.
7 -   An ability to smell and taste.
8 -   An appreciation of hygiene and sanitation.
9 -   Patience and forbearance.
10 -   A sense of timing.
11 -   An awareness of what others are doing.
12-   A desire to improve with a cheerful manner and an enthusiasm for the most noble of occupations shared with the world's greatest chefs and homemakers who serve mankind 24 hours a day, 365 days a year.

What is Quality?

Quality may be defined as character with respect to grade or excellence. The term implies surpassing a median standard or average.

E.G.   Prime Beef, U.S. Fresh Fancy Eggs, Grade A Poultry, 92 Score Butter.

Remember that simple food, well prepared, can be the very best. When is quality food served?

- A. Desire
    - 1. It starts by introspection
    - 2. In the heart and mind
- B. Expression in the menu
    - 1. Consistently pleasing
    - 2. But not stereotyped
- C. Authenticity
    - 1. Strawberry shortcake
    - 2. French onion soup
    - 3. Clam chowder
    - 4. Coffee
    - 5. Tea
    - 6. Orange juice
- D. Appealing
    - 1. To the eye
    - 2. To the nose (Escoffier)
    - 3. To the touch - consistency
    - 4. To the taste
        - a. Temperature
        - b. Salt, sugar, acid, spices and herbs

"Happiness is dependent on the taste and not on things. It is by having what we like that we are happy, not by having what others think desirable."
-Duc De La Francois Rochefoucault (1830-1880)

How May Quality Be Achieved?

- A. Philosophy - Desire - Honesty
    - 1. Establishing and maintaining standards
    - 2. Resisting changes that lower standards
- B. Accuracy
    - 1. Measuring and weighing
    - 2. Time and temperature control
    - 3. Testing and re-testing recipes
    - 4. Comparison with a standard
- C. Hygiene and Sanitation
    - 1. Personal
        - a. Grooming and clothes
        - b. Smoking taboo
        - c. Hand-washing
        - d. Physically well
        - e. Tests and control

      2.   Environmental

a.	Air (ventilation)	c.	Coolers, freezers, storage rooms <u>T&RH</u>
b.	Equipment	d.	Wet-dry vacuum sanitizers

D.   Efficient requisitioning and stock rotation
      1.   Anticipate needs
      2.   Control ordering and inventory
      3.   Control receiving

E.   Control factors affecting raw materials
      1.   Light
      2.   Oxygen
      3.   Relative humidity
      4.   Temperature

F.   Control selection, pre-preparation, combining, processing of ingredients

G.   Use garniture to up-grade
      1.   Flavor   e.g., Bouquet garni
      2.   Color   e.g., Parsley, chives, peppers
      3.   Fresh with canned or frozen
          a.   Peas (frozen)
          b.   Fruit salad

H.   Equipment

I.   Control presentation or service
      1.   Maintain temperatures 40-140 degrees F
      2.   Stagger preparation
          a.   Make and serve fresh
          b.   Avoid overexposure
          c.   A good dinner - perfect coffee - salad vegetables

J.   Strive for perfection

"If a man will be sensible and one fine morning while he is lying in bed count at the tips of his fingers how many things in this life truly give enjoyment, invariably he will find food is the first one."   -Lin Yutang

What is a cook?

A.   Escoffier's team
Sous chef, rotisseur, entremetier, saucier, potager, patissier

B.   Your team
"There is not a person we employ who does not, like ourselves, desire

recognition, praise, gentleness, forbearance, patience." Give them praise.

C.   Importance of the cook
1.   Guardian of health
2.   Inventor of better ways
3.   Artist
4.   Economist
5.   Friend to man
6.   A gentleman

"Cookery has become an art, a noble science; cooks are gentlemen."
    -Robert Burton
"We may live without poetry, music and art;
We may live without conscience and live without heart;
We may live without friends; we may live without books;
But civilized man cannot live without cooks.
He may live without books--what is knowledge but grieving?
He may live without hope--what is hope but deceiving?
He may live without love--what is passion but pining?
But where is the man that can live without dining?"
    -Edward George Bulwer-Lytton (1803-1873)

Quality Food Standards

A.   Definition of "Quality Food"
Dietitians -   "We are convinced that every one of us has a somewhat different standard. A single composite definition seems as impossible to obtain as a sunrise on a foggy morning."

B.   Measurement of Food Standards
1.   Nutritive value
2.   Flavor
3.   Appearance

C.   Ultimate goal is palatability

Appearance	Color	Consistency
Arrangement	Portion size	Shape or form
Palatability	Temperature	Flavor
Seasoning	Texture	Odor
Degree of doneness		

D.   Palatability Control
1.   Freshness
2.   Preparation skill
3.   Proper method of preparation

E. Standardized Recipes
    1. Quantity food production requires accuracy
    2. Control size and type of equipment
    3. Ascertain acceptability and cost
F. Food Specifications
    1. Determine and specify your needs
    2. Define standards for each ingredient
    3. Include:
        a. Product name and number code
        b. Weight or volume
        c. Federal grade or brand
        d. Unit to be priced
        e. Desired characteristics of the food ingredient
G. Advantages of the standardized recipe
    1. Cost and quality control
    2. Accurate portion control
    3. Aid to purchasing and production
    4. Better employee training and development
    5. Speedier food service
    6. Deviations from standard can be checked

Summary and Conclusion

A. Quality surpasses a median standard
B. Starts in the heart and mind
C. Achieved by controlling
    1. Personnel
    2. Equipment
    3. Sanitation
    4. External factors
    5. Raw materials
    6. Processing
    7. Presentation and service
D. Implementation of the standardized recipe

Twelve Things To Remember

1. The value of time.
2. The success of perseverance.
3. The pleasure of working.
4. The dignity of simplicity.

5. The worth of character.
6. The power of kindness.
7. The influence of example.
8. The obligation of duty.
9. The wisdom of economy.
10. The virtue of patience.
11. The improvement of talent.
12. The joy of originating.

Ice Cream Scorecard

Item	Perfect Score
Flavor	45
Body & texture	30
Bacteria	15
Color & package	5
Melting quality	5
TOTAL	100

Chapter 13

Quality as an Economic Force in the Food Service Industry

Food: Nutrition, Flavor, Appearance

Personnel and Equipment

(Editor's Note: Quality as an Economic Force in the Food Service Industry was originally conceived by Dr. Minor in the 1950s. Upon publication in The Cornell HRA Quarterly, the article was noted for its excellent content and is reprinted here in full.)

Quality
by Lewis J. Minor
(January 16, 1995)

Quality's a term often misunderstood;
We've been led by the media to believe something is good
Whereas quality doesn't mean that at all.
For a product's true character may rise or may fall;
It's flavor, color, and purity may vary a lot
And God still controls the result that we get.
Man uses "Quality Control" it is true
But then there's a limit to what he can do.
The weather, the soil, land the process define
What vintners proclaim is a vintage year wine.
Quality varies from high down to low
And God helps decide where quality standards may go.

An Excellent Repast
by Henry James
(1843-1916)

"I had an excellent repast - the best repast possible - which consisted simply of boiled eggs and bread and butter. It was the quality of these simple ingredients that made the occasion memorable. The eggs were so good that I am ashamed to say how many of them I consumed...it might seem that an egg which has succeeded in being fresh has done all that can be reasonably expected of it. But there was a bloom of punctuality, so to speak, about those eggs of Bourg, as if it had been the intention of the very hens themselves that they should be promptly served."

With its connotation of superiority and excellence, the word "Quality" commands attention. The quality of a given product is measured in relation to a set standard for that particular item; thus, a product may lie anywhere along a quality spectrum, depending upon how well its characteristics reflect our notion of desirable qualities.

When I was a boy, the "Louisville Slugger" bat and the "Flexible Flyer" sled were considered the epitome of quality products - the "slugger" for its balance, grip, and durability, and the sled for its strength, light weight, and steering. Other products--gems, foodstuffs, automobiles - are judged on the basis of different criteria.

What constitutes quality in foodservice? Varying with the nature of the operation, numerous components of the dining-out experience, including menu variety, prompt service, food preparation techniques, and ambiance, are deemed indications of quality. To provide quality, the restaurateur must establish standards for personnel, equipment, sanitation, raw materials, food preparation, and presentation, and service.

Consumers are willing to pay for quality, but they are also cost-conscious. If a restaurateur pays whatever price is necessary to achieve the highest quality in his or her operation - by securing the best possible personnel, equipment, and raw materials - quality will be assured, but profits will not. Because competition and economic conditions limit the price that can be charged for quality, the operator must balance considerations of quality and those of cost to maintain good customer value.

The restaurant operator may institute a number of procedures to improve quality and still maintain value. Streamlining the menu, for example, can improve the ratio of productivity to wages. Other ways to provide variety and high quality at lower cost include the use of pre-prepared foods and new equipment systems.

Food: Nutrition, Flavor, Appearance

Food itself is probably the most important single component of the customer's perception of the dining experience. Quality in food is a combination of nutritional value, flavor, and appearance. Raw materials used must be the freshest available. the strictest purchasing, receiving, storage, and sanitation standards must be maintained. Arranged attractively on a plate of appropriate size and design, served at the proper temperature, food should appeal to all the senses. The use of garnishing, for example, indicates management's interest in pleasing the patron's eye.

The combination of food items on the menu must also be chosen with care. Patrons must have a sufficiently broad selection of items from which to choose, but too diverse a menu places a burden on the operation itself, which may result in lower quality in the food delivered to the patron.

The foodservice operator must also aim for consistency. The patron must be confident that when he or she orders a particular item, it will be the same item served when he or she ordered it on an earlier occasion. Standards must be established and maintained for each raw material, recipe, and finished menu item, including garnishing and mode of service. Obviously, preparation procedures must be standardized to include control of time, temperature, pressure, agitation, and all other factors that may influence the finished product.

Another consideration is portion size. Many operations simply serve too much food - and the result is an inordinate amount of plate waste, rather than satisfied customers. The restaurateur must decide what constitutes a reasonable portion - enough food to satiate the guest's hunger, but not overwhelm him or her - and may ultimately wish to offer a choice of portion sizes. In the long run, it is far better to serve rather modest portions of excellent food than it is to serve large helpings of mediocre food.

Quantity food production demands accuracy - thus, standardized recipes are a necessity, facilitating purchasing and production efficiency, cost and quality control, portion control, employee training, and speedy food service.

Although consistency is an important goal, management must also regularly consider innovations in product, preparation techniques, and service. Various technological advances may be used with great success, and the operator should keep abreast of new developments in such areas as ingredients, machinery, packaging, and processing. A food item rarely requested may be dropped from the menu, and a new one substituted. The customer will surely notice the restaurateur's commitment to providing exactly what patrons want.

The operator must also consider the tastes and nutritional concerns of his or her patrons when developing the menu. Because consumers have grown increasingly nutrition-conscious in recent years, the restaurateur who wishes to satisfy them may be called upon to provide wholesome food without excessive caloric content. One example of this trend is the popularity of Guerard's cuisine minceur, a cuisine that minimizes calories and cholesterol while utilizing the natural juices resulting from the cooking process (thus maximizing nutritional content).

Personnel and Equipment

Personnel selection and training are the most important aspects of quality control. Even if the food served is outstanding, a server who is something less than pleasant can spoil the patron's dining experience - while courteous service cannot compensate for food poorly prepared by the cook. Every worker in the operation is a vital part of the organization - and must be made to feel so. As Vince Lombardi said, "Individual commitment to a group effort - that is what makes a team work, a company work, a society work, a civilization work." Instilling a sense of pride in the operation and the desire to achieve high standards is crucial. It must be impressed upon restaurant employees that whenever a patron is pleased with the operation, the credit belongs to every worker.

Ideally, the restaurant's staff should consist of quality-conscious workers with a genuine, self-motivated desire to provide excellent food and elicit customer approval. Their commitment to quality should be evident in every aspect of their behavior and appearance - from the honest pleasure they show at a patron's arrival to their immaculate fingernails and well-kept attire.

Management must indicate to staff members its genuine interest in each of them, their working conditions, and their performance. When excellent performance is recognized and rewarded, all members of the organization are likely to strive for excellence in their own work.

The manager plays the role of the team captain. He must choose each of his "players" with care, assigning them all to the positions in which their unique talents may best be used. The individual's ability to meet or surpass performance standards should be the basis of remuneration.

Unfortunately, wages in the foodservice industry lag behind those in many other industries. As a result, many foodservice positions are filled by the undereducated and underskilled - a situation that poses a problem for the quality-minded restaurant operator. Profit-sharing, career-ladders, multiple-job training, advancement incentives, and company-financed retirement benefits are among the lures that can aid in attracting and retaining quality personnel.

Without the proper equipment and personnel well versed in its operation, no foodservice establishment can produce a quality product. Equipment must be suited to the requirements of the menu and the abilities of personnel. When new machinery is procured, employees should be trained thoroughly in its proper use and care. They must be taught preventive maintenance techniques to insure maximum performance efficiency and longevity. It is also wise to purchase equipment from a reliable manufacturer who can provide service on short notice when emergencies demanding immediate attention arise, because the breakdown of an important piece of machinery can spell disaster.

Take a look at your own operation with the impartial eyes of a patron. Is the dining area tastefully decorated and functionally designed? Is it immaculate, well ventilated, and appropriately lighted? Is the food nutritious and outstanding in both flavor and appearance? Is there a sufficiently broad selection of menu items? Is the service staff well groomed and courteous? Is the food served with reasonable speed? If you can answer "yes" to these queries, you have quality at work for you, exerting the positive economic force it has held since time immemorial.

Chapter 14

Tom Ryan and Other Stars Insured Company Success

Dr. Thomas Aloysius Ryan   **How Great He Was**

Other Company Stars   **Tom and Babe's Colonial Tudor Home**

Tom and Babe as Santa and Wife

Appearances
by Tom Ryan

Always put your best foot forward
and dress like you don't need the job.
Keep your shoes shined, and
don't look run down at the heel.
Find a good Chinese laundry, and
have your shirts done there.

Secrets of the Successful
by Lewis J. Minor

They risk change and are challenged by the unknown.
They are deeply committed to their work.
They see failure as a learning experience.
Their sense of humor keeps small problems in perspective.
They believe that they will achieve their goals even when it is unclear how they
    will do it.
Their intimate relationships are top priority.
They keep themselves free to complete tasks and thoughts.
They take responsibility for their problems and admit it when they are wrong.
They note stress and act to reduce it.
They forgive themselves and others for not doing all of the above, all of the
    time.

Quote from Dr. Lewis J. Minor

"Live one day at a time. Today is that day. For we have no control
over what happened yesterday or what may happen tomorrow."

Dr. Thomas Aloysius Ryan

Tom Ryan and I were second cousins, his mother being my grandmother's sister. Tom's father and mother came from a family known as "Scissors" Ryan. Some of his forebears were barbers. They lived on the side of the Knockahopple Mountain beside Dolla in County Tipperary, which is two miles from Ireland's famous "Silver" mines and seven miles down from a town called Nenagh. Tom's mother, Florence, and father, Pat left Ireland together, after being married, moving to Grand Rapids, Michigan. Later, they moved to Cleveland, Ohio where Tom was reared. He attended St. Ignatius High School and John Carrol University. There were five children, Tom being the oldest.

Tom's dad was killed in an explosion at the Union Carbide plant where he worked. Tom was twelve at the time. St. Ignatius High School has the best tradition, reputation, and standards of any Cleveland high school. Teachers are Jesuits. After his father's untimely death, his brother, Will Ryan, became the breadwinner for the family. He was employed by a meat distributor, the firm later becoming the Will Ryan Provision Company which is still operated by his widow and two sons.

Tom continued in school as Will and his mother asked him to do. He would work selling straw hats, and later cemetery wreaths. He was a fast learner and gifted persuader, even as a youth. Later on, during the Depression years, Tom worked for the Cleveland Retailers Association and sold memberships. He was a true salesperson.

How Great He Was

Tom wanted to finish high school and work full time to help support his mother, his younger brother, Pat, and two sisters, June and Florence. He knew the value of time, which Thomas Edison said is our most valued possession.

Accordingly, Tom went into the principal's office and asked if there were any way for him to graduate in three rather than the usual four years. The headmaster said, "No one graduates from St. Ignatius in three years. You may find it difficult to make your degree in four years. Many of our students are unable to do so." Tom Ryan was not easily rebuked.

After reading Benjamin Franklin's Autobiography, he discovered Franklin's quotation, "If a person does you a favor once, no matter how small, they cannot help doing it again." With this in mind, Tom went to the 5 and 10 cent store and purchased the cheapest rosary he could find. He waited for a chance to put it on the Principal's desk when the office was crowded with students. He elbowed his way through the crowd, laid the rosary on the desk and said, " Here, Father, bless this when you have time." Then he left.

Tom said, "I knew the rosary was wearing a hole in his pocket, and every time I saw him I'd duck up a stairway and disappear. One day, he came into our literature class and stayed until the class was over. He confronted me then saying, 'Here, Thomas, is your rosary. Come to my office and we'll discuss that other matter.'"

At their meeting the priest said, "Thomas there is a young priest on the faculty. I told him to help you after school. This way you can graduate in three years with the extra time and tutoring. If there is any problem in dealing with him come in and tell me. Then we will take care of it." Tom told me he knew that the principal had learned the story of his widowed mother and the family's need. He did graduate in three years, although it required extra effort.

After graduating in three years from St. Ignatius High, Tom sold funeral wreaths to earn money to attend John Carrol University in Cleveland. He aimed to become a lawyer. He was 22 at the time he graduated.

His brother Will was supporting the family with his meat packing and distributing job. Prior to getting his Law Degree, Tom was at Sunday Mass with his mother. He spotted an attractive blonde sitting with her parents in the front row. He pointed her out to his mother and said, "Ma, I'm going to marry her." Her name was Elizabeth Arth, but Tom always called her "Babe." Her father owned the Arth Brass Company in Cleveland.

After Mass, Tom waited outside the church for her. When she came out, he asked if he could take her to the movies. She accepted. Several months later, in 1929, they married. They spent their honeymoon in the Cleveland Public Library, reading all day, until his brother Will got off work. Then Will took them out to dinner.

Tom got his first job with the Cleveland Retailers Association where he was employed several years, gaining valuable acquaintances and experience. Meanwhile, Tom and Babe were blessed with a son, Tom Jr., whom they called Tommy. He was killed in the "Battle of the Bulge" while serving as a Glider Pilot. Tommy got the "Purple Heart" medal posthumously. When he tried to save a comrade who had been shot, the Germans killed him.

Babe's life was wrapped tightly around Tommy. Tom had little time available for his wife or son. His Jesuit teachers told the law students that if they wished to amount to anything in their professions their families would not hardly know them. Practicing law was a night and day occupation for Tom. He was now a divorce lawyer having left the Cleveland Retailers Association.

One of Tom's partners, Bob Weinstein, confided to me early on that Tom had a need and a desire to get into business. In practicing divorce law, Tom would take one divorcee and Bob Weinstein the other. That's how it worked. Tom's client was usually the wife. He was a talented counselor and comforter for these poor unfortunates. The law firm's name was Ryan, Tinscher, Brideau, and Weinstein. Tinscher was a handwriting expert, Brideau handled civil law suits, and Weinstein worked with Tom and managed the office supply needs. Weinstein would save on towels and soap by washing his hands when he got to the place where he would be eating lunch. This way, over a period of time, he saved about $50. He told Tom and Tom said, "Fine, we will have a little party with the money."

Tom and I met when I was 21, attending the wedding in Cleveland of his brother Pat, who they called "Packie." Tom Ryan was slender, standing straight as an arrow and 6'4" tall. He always wore a hat, a sign of royalty, that made him close to 7" tall. He immediately commanded attention and respect. His regal bearing always made him stand out in a crowd. There was a sort of "Charismatic Charm" about him. Handsome in appearance, too, he had an executive, or nearly "Kingly" manner about him. His chin jutted out like he owned the world. When you tried to walk beside him, you couldn't. He would always take big strides and if you were trying to tell him something, you would be talking to his back and not to his face saying, "Wait up, Dr. Ryan, what's your hurry." Sometimes I would do the same thing when others were walking with me. He was unforgettable.

A few years later, after our initial meeting in Cleveland, Tom had packed on some weight. His stomach protruded due to an emergency appendectomy he'd had that nearly caused his death from peritonitis that developed after his appendix ruptured. The incision was long, and after the stitches were pulled out, he was left with just a thin layer of skin holding his stomach together. When he got into bed at night he would support it with a pillow underneath.

When his younger brother Packie hired me to work at Donahue Varnish Company, we became friends. Shortly after we were married, Ruth and I would visit Pat and his wife, Eileen. They were great companions and we meshed well together. Pat once told my mother, "Lewis is the only person I know of who could ever tell Tom what to do, and get him to do it." When I asked him to look after things, whenever I was away, Tom did it efficiently.

Speaking of that, Tom was the most efficient person I ever witnessed using the phone. He always planned ahead the message he wanted to get across. So with him it was like this, "This is Tom Ryan at L. J. Minor, we need a truck load of glass jars next week," then he would put the phone down, and make the next call the same way. He figured his time was valuable and he was working for L. J. Minor, and not the phone company.

One time, Tom and I, at the request of Mike Jacobs who was one of our chef representatives, called on Railton Company, Chicago, one of the largest foodservice distributors. They handled everything including other bases, but wanted to do more with ours.

The meeting was attended by their head purchasing agent, sales manager, president, Tom, Mike Jacobs, and me. Mr. Brown, the president, asked, "Minor, tell me about your company." Before I could say anything, Tom said, "Minor has the toughest terms in the world and if you are not paid up in 15 days he will call you on the phone and tell you that you may not have any more product." Everyone was shocked.

Two weeks later at a food show, Tom ran into the purchasing agent who said, "Ryan, if I live to be 100, I will never forget what you said. If there is anyone in the United States that pays on time and takes their discounts, it's Railton!"

We would get into a lot of heated discussions, because he was my sounding-board whenever I wanted to do something. We would discuss all aspects and try to find the hole in the doughnut, if there were one. No matter what came up, we always got along and remained best friends, even though he could be abrupt at times.

Speaking of his abrupt and unusual style, I recall one evening when a group of our chefs, Tom, and General McLaughlin were in New York City. He took all of them to dinner at a restaurant with a floor show. General McLaughlin said everyone was having an enjoyable evening when Tom began pounding the table with his wooden cane. The maitre'd came running and asked, "Is there something wrong sir?" Tom shouted, "We're not going to sit here and listen to a singer who wears plaid slacks with a striped jacket. Bring me the check. We're leaving."

Tom Ryan and I always kept our consciences clear. For example: A man whose business interfered with ours was bugging us by letting his customers park in our company's driveway so that trucks couldn't get in.

When I told an acquaintance about it, he asked, "Do you want him burned out? I can handle it for you in a hell of a hurry." We told him, "forget it. We don't operate that way." We lived as Christians should and never hurt anyone; employee, competitor, inspector, customer, no one. We had friends. They were our employees, suppliers, customers, and even competitors. Our policy was, "Live and let live." We compromised with our neighbor to cure the problem.

Pat told me of Tom's exceptional speaking abilities and how he was able to "spellbind" an audience with his humorous folksy approach combined with his serious conclusions. Tom was pragmatic, visionary, charismatic, charming, and on-target at all times. When he spoke to the Great Lakes Section of the Institute of Food Technologists, at my request, the audience swarmed around him asking questions when he finished.

As you know by now, Tom was my mentor, confidante, and friend from when we started the L. J. Minor Corporation, in 1951, until his death in 1975. For 25 years, we were together. From 1960, until his untimely death, this man took the tiny seeds of production, sales, quality control, federal inspection, and land acquisition that I had planted, and which had barely sprouted, and brought them to fruition. True, we did it together, but Dr. Ryan was the one who did it, and deserves full credit for it.

While I attended Michigan State and earned a Ph.D. in Food Science, he ran the business from 1961 to 1964. When I began teaching in 1964, he remained as manager until his death. Together, we hired all the key personnel, many of whom are briefly introduced here.

Other Company Stars

Quote from Sammy Davis Jr.

"Mental peace is achieved through recognition of the good in people."

Jack Seibert, a handsome, pleasant, personable young friend from Harbor Beach, where his parents operated a drug store, joined me in Cleveland when the business began. He and his wife only stayed a short time, then they went back to Harbor Beach. Jack never confided in me concerning his plans and actions, so I really don't know what happened, but I do recognize his original contributions in helping to get the business started.

Audrey Chubbs, who I called, "My Girl Friday," was from Cleveland. She took over the production management when I had my gallbladder out in the late 1950s, and was with us until the late 1970s when Mike Zelski took over at the plant. Other women, including **Helen Crites, Rose Wilson, Pearl Geiss** and **Ruth Ann Minor Fields**, assisted Audrey in meeting production needs between 1951 and 1962. They looked after our every need.

Joe Gilbert, was with us from 1958 to 1966 and did a creditable job running the plant during those years. One morning, in May, 1958, a knock came at the front door of our plant. A young man looking for work was there. I interviewed him, and learned that he was a high school graduate with two years work experience at a packaging company in Elyria. I hired him, on a trial basis, had him make batches, and observed his personal habits. He was handsome, medium tall fellow with black wavy hair, and was married. He was a Catholic.

Tom Ryan was just getting clear of some bad investment entanglements and starting to take an active role in the business. After three months on the job, I suggested that Joe Gilbert might have potential to operate the plant when I was gone on trips. Tom said, "I want to meet him, and get acquainted. Let's get together with him." As a result of this meeting, we made Joe Gilbert the plant manager. When I left to attend Michigan State, in 1961, he was on his own. Fortunately, Ruth Ann, our daughter, was working for us then, and watching out for things. I trained him for production, but he had a lot of mechanical ability.

After my Ph.D. program was completed in 1964, I observed all of my students while teaching in the hotel school. When Michael Zelski graduated in 1967, Tom Ryan and I met with him at the Downtowner Motel and hired him to be our plant manager. I told Joe Gilbert we wanted him to stay and train Mike Zelski . After turning over the plant supervision to Mike Zelski, Joe Gilbert became plant development engineer.

To our amazement, the following morning he came in early, left his keys on the front desk with a note saying, "I quit." He didn't even discuss his feelings with us, but went with

Stouffer's and only lasted two months there. He and his wife had two children. He left them, and took up with a young woman who we had recently let go. We never heard from him again. We were shocked to say the least.

Mike Zelski, a native of Lansing, Michigan was a student in my first class at Michigan State University. He was there on the GI Bill of Rights Program and had worked for Win Schuler, Marshall, Michigan. He was the one I picked for plant manager. Tom Ryan and I got him to come with us.

He started with us in 1968, stayed with the company until it was sold in 1983, and remained two years longer with the new owners. Mike fitted into the plant personnel management role perfectly. He had a genuine care for the people and they felt it. He was great, and just the person we needed to take over as plant manager.

During the nearly 18 years from 1968 to 1985 while Mike ran the plant his job requirements grew to include property acquisition, plant growth needs, quality control supervision, and more, including zoning. He hired George Hvizd, a capable young assistant.

Bob Herron, food purchasing manager, Michigan State University, called Mike "the best manager of the cleanest, most efficient, and best managed plant with the highest employee morale that I ever visited during my 30 years at the University."

Mike resigned in 1985 and was given one year terminal pay for the fine job he had done. Kellogg Company hired him for one of their plants in Chicago, which was later bought by CPC International.

Mike was like a son to us. He was a great human being. The workers respected him, and whatever I asked him to do was like having money in the bank. He loved Tom Ryan, Mrs. Minor, and me, and our children who worked under him, including Ruth Ann, Michael, Josephine, and Mary. In fact, Mike and Ruth Ann were like a brother and sister to him. Our other two children at the company, Bryan and Carol, had worked as quality control checkers. We all still love him and always will.

George Hvizd, proved to be a valuable assistant to Mike Zelski. He assumed a large part of Mike's role and was with us from 1970 until the business was sold in 1983. He left in 1984.

From the Stouffer's organization came four professional women who contributed much to our Corporation. Tom Ryan, once again, gets the credit for being the talent scout as he hired each of the following.

Ruth Engler, who together with Wally Blankenship, established the Stouffer's Frozen Food Plant, joined us and set up our job classification and procedure specifications. She did a lot for quality control needs, too. She was with us for several years before we sold the company.

Jan Williams came with us from Stouffer's at Mrs. Engler's recommendation. She was great and stayed with the business until 1993 when she took voluntary retirement. To sum up her contributions is not easy for they were so far-reaching.

Jan set up a quality control program, controlled label declarations, developed specifications for all products, prepared product description bulletins, conducted our expert taste panels, worked with our son, Mike Minor, and me in developing new products, developed the line of low MSG and low sodium bases that Nestle's now owns. She is great and has done so much more for us through the years.

Beverly Delaney came after Jan. She worked with Jan and took over raw material specifications, working with Mike Zelski and Bart Katuscak on purchasing. Her value to the business was also great. She is still with Nestle's which proves her great value.

Lavere Vokt was the fourth woman who came from Stouffer's. Her forte was quality control. she did a great job, working on our night shift, and was with Nestle until after 1990. She did a lot for the business.

Ruth Ann Minor Fields Egan, our daughter, safeguarded the plant operation and quality control of the products, working with Mike Zelski, George Hvizd, government inspectors, and the people she supervised in the plant. She worked long hours most days. When she retired in 1989, Ruth Ann had up to 70 production workers and 6 supervisors under her direction, and they loved her.

Michael Lewis Minor didn't come with us until 1977 when we decided we could not get along any longer without him.

Mike, working with Mike Zelski, learned the business from the ground up. He started out making batches. He developed new products, improved packaging, mixing, cooking, and waste disposal. He continues to work for Minor's as Vice President, Culinary Services under the Nestle's banner, and we are so proud of him But there are many other success stories I need to tell the reader before relating Mike's success.

Tom and Babe's Colonial Tudor Home

George Forbes, a west-side Realtor who handled fine homes, sold Tom and Babe a lovely Colonial Tudor home located in Cleveland's finest "west side" subdivision, Rocky River. They hired a gardener to keep the grounds for them.

At this time, Thomas Aloysius Ryan, Jr. was taken in the draft. After his untimely death in battle, Babe would sit looking at the Gold Star Flag hanging in their front window. These were sent by the War Department to parents of servicemen who served their country and gave their lives doing it. Every day when he came home, Tom would see Babe sitting, thinking of the wonderful times she and Tommy had while Tom worked.

This somber pall that hung over Babe upset Tom. He couldn't bear thinking of her, alone every day, pining for their lost son. Finally, he told Babe she should move to a hotel where she would be with other people. He contacted George Forbes saying, "I want you to sell the house this weekend for me." He answered, "Tom, if I do that, you'll take a huge loss." Tom said, "I do not care. Do it!" Forbes sold their home.

Naturally, this rash act of Tom's upset Babe. Instead of going to a hotel, she contacted a lifelong friend, Gladys, who owned the duplex I later lived in with them when I first came alone to Cleveland from Harbor Beach. Later, Babe purchased the upstairs half of the duplex from Gladys. She had her own money that she got when her parents, who had the Arth Brass Company, passed on. Their money was split between her and her only sibling, a sister. She left Tom and lived alone with Gladys.

Tom spent much of his free time with his sister June, who lived in Cleveland. His other sister, Florence, and brother Will were now dead. Only he, June, and his brother, "Packie," who lived with his wife and two daughters in Tuscaloosa, Alabama, where he managed a Phenol plant owned by Reichold Chemicals, Royal Oak, Michigan, remained. Now, he was frequenting his sister June's home in Lakewood. June's husband, Eddie Morgan, worked for the Retail Credit Man's Association in Cleveland, as Tom had years before. Since Eddie was able to close deals with difficult clients, they kept him on the payroll. June and Eddie had two sons, Bill and Eddie Junior, and four daughters, Mary Ann, Joyce, Flora and Rose.

June was the principal breadwinner for their family. She ran the office for Fisher foods, a large chain of stores, supermarkets that sold groceries, meat, and produce in various neighborhoods in Cleveland and its suburbs. The firm had two huge warehouses or storage facilities, one for groceries consisting of canned, dried, and frozen, where June was employed, and another for meats. A "punch card" system was used for keeping records. June handled this system, and later on the computers which replaced the punch cards. She was a brilliant person and a great manager for years at the Fisher Food Chain's office.

During the time they were separated, about six years, Tom would call on Babe. He loved to bring gifts to her. Suddenly, Tom was stricken by the aforementioned "ruptured appendix." He nearly died, as I stated earlier, hovering between life and death for several days. He sent for Babe who stayed with him comforting and praying for him. After Tom survived, he moved back in with Babe and was with her until his death.

Tom and Babe as Santa and Wife

In the fall of 1950, as we moved from Harbor Beach to our "dream house" in Fairview Park, Christmas would have bleak for our six children had it not been for Tom and Babe. Babe took the children with her to see the Christmas decorations in downtown Cleveland. Lights festooned Cleveland's Public Square. The department stores, May Company, Higbee's, Halle's, and Sterling Lindner-Davis all had displays. Each had a Santa's helper, except for Halle's who had Mr. "Jing-a-Ling." The children loved this excursion with Babe. Ruth stayed home unpacking and arranging our things.

Totally unexpected, after we had attended Mass Christmas morning, Tom and Babe drove up in Tom's Lincoln sedan. Tom preferred Lincolns, but Babe like Packards and Cadillacs. The back of Tom's car was filled with gifts for our six children and their nieces and nephews whom they visited later that day. I still remember one of their gifts. It was two pogo sticks which we still have.

Tom had a great time with the children. A mutual love was quickly generated between him and them. Suddenly, he asked Bryan to get him the broom from the kitchen. Believe it or not, Tom held the broom handle between his two hands and jumped over the handle without releasing it. It shook the house. That did not matter.

Tom had many hidden talents. Besides jumping over broom handles, he could sit like an Indian on the floor while pulling his feet under him. He used to watch TV that way. He and Babe each had their own TV. His was in one corner and hers in the opposite corner of their living room. Tom took lots of naps, and read all of the important magazines including *Time* and *The New Yorker*. He loved New York City and wanted to live there.

When in New York he liked to have dinner at Mama Leone's or go to different hotel dining rooms and restaurants with our Chef, Ernest Koves, alias Dr. Koves. Tom's favorite entertainment was to go to see the floor show at the Latin Quarter, but number one for him was the Cotton Club of Duke Ellington fame. Their talented, agile, lively dancers charmed him. We used to go there together when we went to the annual Hotel Show which is always held there. One night Tom took Koves and his wife Irene there with us. We all had a fine time, although I do not think Irene was fond of "girlie" shows.

Tom had a fetish for beautiful, unusual home furnishings. We have a gorgeous mirror in our Cleveland apartment hallway which he gave us. This greets whoever walks into the apartment. It's ornate frame is attractive. He loved gift-giving. When we owned the business, Tom would give our chefs nice useful gifts which they could give their wives. We gave gifts but never money to our customers. Many would tell us, "With products of the quality we get from you, you are already helping our business. You do not have to give us gifts." We always gave small gifts to truck drivers who picked up at our plant. Whatever we gave had to be good quality. That was our trademark, "Quality."

(Editor's note: I remember picking Dr. Minor up at the airport in Boston one year. This was not an easy task for I lived some two hours away, yet I would never forego a chance to see him. On the way back to the airport, Dr. Minor asked me what time I had. My watch had recently broken and I told him so. About two weeks later, a new Hamilton watch arrived in the mail for me. It was from Dr. Minor. When I took it to the repair shop some years later, the owner would not even open the back of the watch because of its high quality. He was not familiar with that kind of watch and recommended that I return it to Hamilton for repair since he would not wish to damage it. I never had such a fancy watch prior to knowing Dr. Minor and I have never purchased one since. Later, I realized that he had given to me one of those

unusual gifts normally reserved for only his best clients or employees.)

Tom's motto was, "It's the sizzle that sells the steak." The pens we gave out were Papermate, not brands for which one could not find refills, costing half as much. They were the "sizzle" needed to sell our quality Bases! We have been out of the business now for nearly fifteen years, and still run into friends who are using the pens given. It's true. "The quality is remembered long after the price has been forgotten." We learned that from our fabulous salesperson, Frank Sigmund. Another motto of ours, "Minor's Always in Good Taste" was provided by a broker of ours in Boston, Bob Buntin, who I got to represent us in the early '50s.

Tom Ryan used Machiavellian methods for bringing people into the business. He would meet them at lunch or sometimes breakfast or dinner, break bread with them, tell them about our company and products. He always credited me with unbelievable achievements and business policies. For example, he would say, "Minor has certain non-profit items, that are difficult to manufacture, like our liquid consommé."

From those earliest days, it was a moving, uplifting, and learning experience to be so close to this great man, Tom Ryan. His guidance and support were crucial in getting the business started. His secretary, Mary Mele, was a Godsend, too. Tom got her from Miss Jenny at the May Company after learning how capable, dependable, and efficient Mary was. She was on loan for two weeks. But, when Miss Jenny called Tom and asked when Mary would be returning, he said, "She won't be."

Mary, of course, liked the excitement of being with Tom. His charm and charisma were hard to match. These traits combined with super intelligence were captivating. Other women who would bring gifts or kept calling on Tom always troubled Mary. Her allegiances were to God first, her family second, and L. J. Minor Corporation third. Soon after meeting Margaret Mitchell, Vernon Stouffer's assistant mentioned earlier in the text, Tom had her portrait hanging on the wall behind his huge mahogany desk. He was an imposing and compelling personality, sitting behind that huge desk in an upholstered swivel chair. He kept Mary with him until she passed-on in 1974. She was loyal, dutiful, obedient, and effective.

Just prior to her death, we came out with our Espagnole Base. This was the one in which we used air-dried tomatoes. One of our great chefs, Emil Burgermeister, experimented with this and recommended it to all the chefs he knew. Tom gave Emil the nickname "Espagnole" Burgermeister.

When Tom and I were on our way to the cemetery, where Mary was interred, Tom said, "You're a lucky guy." I asked, "Why?" He answered, "Mary has been training Nancy Clancy for the past nine years." She had been working with us at her home. Nancy came with us full-time three years prior to Mary's passing. Eventually, she would assume Mary's role as the Mother of the Minor Corporation, but that was later.

Tom was the master of his destiny, and all who came under his influence. He would tell me, "Always keep yourself free to do your own thing." He said, "You need a separate bank account so you can surprise your wife with a nice gift now and then." At the end of the business year, he would say to Herman Taber, our tax man, and Ralph Napletana, our CPA, "Minor has to take a bonus to avoid taxes!" I would put this, or part of it, in an account I opened at the Central National Bank, across the street from our office in the Bulkley Building.

When Tom and Mary came with the L. J. Minor Corporation, we left the National City Bank Building where Tom had been for years. It was right across from the Hollenden Hotel and the famous Theatrical Grill on Short Vincent Street. That's where the Police Commissioner and Mafia head met for lunch. They had all the meat they wanted, and the very best during war-time rationing. This gave them a leg-up over other Cleveland restaurateurs.

Tom Ryan found our new office in 436 Bulkley Building. He told the manager that someday we would be renting the entire 4th floor from them. We worked well together. Yet, Tom used to occasionally frustrate me by getting himself into business deals with Friden, of Gulf States Lumber Company, and Godes, of Godes Homes. When he had a difficult time, his clients, Ruth and I lost money. But for the most part, I would ask about doing this or that and he would say, "Well, let's roll it around for a day or two." Looking back, it appeared like a master plan for the business baby, which was now at the crawling stage.

As a final note of celebration, Dr. Thomas Aloysius Ryan received posthumously, at the Academy of Chefs Dinner in New York City, membership into the American Academy of Chefs Hall of Fame for Distinguished Services to the Culinary Profession. He was inducted by Richard Bosnjak, Chairman of the Academy of Chefs. Thus, he is now on the Honor Roll at the ACF Headquarters in St. Augustine, Florida, along with Emil Burgermeister, General McLaughlin, and me.

Chapter 15

Mrs. Minor, Family, and Recipes

Ruth Eloise Minor　　　　　**Family**　　　　　**The Recipes**

Eloise
By Lewis J. Minor
(June, 1938)

Eloise, when shadows fall
Our love will call you to my side.
Eloise, my loving arms
May hold your charms
If you decide.
Darling, when night is here,
And you are near,
My heart is happy.
Eloise, I love you so
Please let me know that
You are mine.

Love
By Lewis J. Minor
to Ruth
(February 14, 1993)

What is love? What is love?
We wonder what love can be
To some it's a dream to others it's just a game.
What is love? What is love?
We call it life's mystery, but when I'm with
　　　you, here's what love can mean to me.
When I look into your eyes, you make me
　　　realize what love is.
And, when I hold your hand you make me
　　　understand what love is.

Such a tender felling suddenly comes stealing
　　way down to my toes.
My pulse is beating stronger. Can't wait
　　any longer.
The tension just grows and grows.
Then the pressure of your lips can set
　　my fingertips to burning.
While deep within my heart, the tide of
　　love will start returning.
So - it's no mystery that what you bring
To me is love both tender and true.
Now, I guess I know what love is
It's anytime when I'm with you.

Ruth Eloise Minor

Fortunately, I had a wife who went along and let me do what I had to do. She never burdened me with any of the domestic problems and worries. She had been using a used Plymouth for shopping and taking the children to lessons. Of our eight children at the time, our oldest boy, Bryan, was in college, and our first born, Kathleen, had graduated from Michigan State University.

Family

Saturdays, Mrs. Minor would bring the children in to pack samples. Samples took a great deal of time. We packed one ounce jars with a spoon. By God' saving grace and providence, one Saturday, Father Osborne, one of the St. Angela Parish Priests, visited us. What he wanted was a sign, "Keep of the Grass," and asked me to cut a stencil for him.

When Father noticed the laborious effort needed to fill the small jars, he asked, "Why don't you go to a Baker's Supply and get a cake decorating bag with nozzles. Then you simply need to fill up the canvas bag with the base, and squeeze it into the jars. Then no spoons are needed." I got some of these, and the following Saturday the children filled up both packing tables with samples. All were filled and labelled.

Monday, when my girl Friday, Audrey Chubbs, walked in, she and Helen Crites, who took care of my label cabinet, said, "My heavens, look what Dr. Minor's children can do. At this rate we won't have to put up any more samples."

The Recipes

While taking care of the family needs, Mrs. Minor perfected recipes at home, some using the Bases. Many a guest, including the editor of this text, have enjoyed a home cook meal by Mrs. Minor, and asked for the recipe. The following are just a few of the initial recipes Mrs. Minor has used to entertain the clients and giants Dr. Minor brings home to meet his impressive family.

Beef Pot Roast
by Ruth Minor

English cut, chuck, or top round of beef. Heat roasting pan on medium. Brown meat on both sides. Use 1/2 teaspoon Minor's Beef Base per pound of meat. Spread on sides of roast that have been browned. Slice medium sized onion. Place onion slices on top of roast. Cover roasting pan and place in 350 degree oven. For a 3 pound pot roast cook for an hour per pound. For a larger roast of up to 6 pounds, cook for 3/4 hours per pound. When the juices in roaster cook down, add a small amount of water to prevent burning. Add water as needed to prevent burning.

One-half hour before serving, pour juices into saucepan. Cool by setting pan in cold water. When grease comes to the top of the juice and becomes hard, remove fat, then bring juice to boil, and thicken with cornstarch. When gravy is cooked, taste. If it doesn't have enough beef flavor, add a little Beef Base. Season with Beef Base to suit your taste.

If you wish to cook carrots or potatoes, or any vegetables with the roast, place them in the roasting pan with the meat an hour before serving.

Cheese Soup
by Ruth Minor

1/2 cup diced carrots
1/2 cup diced celery
1/4 cup diced green pepper
1/4 cup diced onion
1 cup grated cheddar cheese
2 cups milk
1/4 cup beer (if desired)
2 cups water
1 teaspoon Minor's Chicken Base

Place vegetables and Chicken Base in water.

Bring to boil. Let simmer until vegetables are tender.

1/4 cup Minor's Chicken Supreme Sauce
1/2 cup warm water

Add Supreme Sauce to 1/2 cup of warm water. Blend until smooth.

Add Supreme Sauce mixture to cooked vegetables. Bring to boil and stir until thickened.

Add grated cheese and stir.

Add milk and stir.

Add beer and keep hot until ready to serve.

Cherry Pie with Lattice Top
by Ruth Minor

<u>Crust</u>

1 1/2 cups all-purpose flour
1/8 teaspoon salt
1/2 cup corn oil or some cooking oil
1/4 cup cold water

Mix ingredients together with fork to make a soft ball.

Place 2/3 of dough on floured waxed paper. Put a little flour on top of dough and place another piece of waxed paper on top. Roll to make bottom crust of pie. When rolled, place in pie pan.

1 quart fresh or frozen cherries. To the cherries add
3/4 cup sugar
2 tablespoons minute tapioca
1 tablespoon lemon juice

Combine above ingredients. Pour into pie shell.

Roll remaining pie dough and cut into strips. Place on top of cherries making the lattice look.

Place in 425 degree oven for ten minutes. Reduce heat to 350 degrees and bake 45 minutes longer. Remove from oven and place on cooling rack.

Chocolate Cake
by Ruth Minor

1/2 cup margarine (room temperature)
1 1/2 cups sugar
2 eggs (room temperature)
2 squares unsweetened chocolate (melted)
2 cups cake flour
1 cup sour milk (room temperature)
1 tablespoon vinegar
1 teaspoon baking soda
1 teaspoon vanilla

Cream together margarine and sugar. Add one egg. Beat until creamy. Add other egg and beat well.

Add melted chocolate. Blend.

Add 1/3 of flour. Blend.

Add 1/2 cup of milk. Blend.

Add 1/3 of flour. Blend.

Add remainder of milk. Blend.

Add remainder of flour. Blend.

Put vinegar in cup and add baking soda.

Add to other ingredients. Add Vanilla

Blend.

Makes 2 doz. cupcakes or 1-2 layer 8 inch cake.

Chocolate Frosting
by Ruth Minor

2 squares unsweetened chocolate
1 tablespoon butter
2 tablespoons milk
2 cups confectioners sugar
1 teaspoon vanilla

Melt chocolate and butter in top of double boiler.

When melted, add milk and confectioners sugar. Stir until smooth. (May need a little more milk to make frosting spreadable)

Add vanilla. Keep hot in double boiler until ready to put on cake.

(Enough icing for 2 dozen cupcakes or 1-2 layer cake.)

Apple Pie
by Ruth Minor

<u>One Crust Pie</u>

1 cup flour
1/16 teaspoon salt
1/3 cup corn oil or other cooking oil
1/6 cup of cold water

10 medium apples (recommend Macintosh)
3/4 cup brown sugar
1/8 teaspoon cinnamon

Stir ingredients with fork until you can form a soft ball.

To roll - Place dough on piece of waxed paper that you have put flour on to keep it from sticking.

Put more flour on top of dough and place another sheet of waxed paper on top.

Roll to make the crust.

Peel and slice about 10 medium apples (Macintosh are good).

Place apples in greased baking dish.

Add 3/4 cup sugar and sprinkle on a little cinnamon.

Place crust on top of apples. Put in 425 degree oven for 10 minutes, reduce heat to 350 degrees, and bake about 45 minutes.

Remove from oven and place on cooling rack.

Fruit Cake
by Ruth Minor

2 cups boiling water
2 cups sugar
1 tablespoon cooking oil (Mazola)
2 teaspoons cinnamon
1 teaspoon cloves
2 cups raisins
2 cups currants

Combine ingredients in sauce pan. Bring to boil. Boil 6 minutes. Let cool.

When cold, add 2 cups all-purpose flour, one cup chopped walnuts, and 1 teaspoon baking soda.

Bake in well greased 9" x 13" cake pan.

Bake in 325 degree oven for about an hour.

Chapter 16

People and Land:
A Huge Family

by Ralph A. Napletana
(1955-Present)

Acquisition 1   **Acquisition 2**   **Acquisition 3**

Acquisition 4   **Acquisition 5**   **Acquisition 6**   **Acquisition 7**

On Real Estate

by Don A. Lutz
(1960-Present)

Quote from Socrates

"Limit the course of your studies to those of real utility."

Meeting Men
by Edgar A. Guest
(1916)

Did you ever sit down and talk with men
In a serious sort of way,
On their views of life and ponder them
On all they have to say?
If not, you should in some quiet hour;
It's a glorious thing to do;
For you'll find that back of the pomp and power
Most men have a goal in view
And back of the gold and back of the fame
And back of the selfish strife,
In most men's breasts you'll find the flame
Of the nobler things of life.

Confucius says:

All things are difficult before they are easy.

Can't
by Edgar A. Guest
(1916)

Can't is the word that is foe to ambition
An enemy ambush to shatter your will;
It's prey is forever the man with a mission
And bows but to courage and patience and skill.
Hate it with hatred that's deep and undying,
For once it's welcomed 'twill break any may;
Whatever the goal you are seeking, keep trying
And answer the demon by saying "I can."

(Foreword by Dr. Minor: After all of my 12 early years of manufacturing, product development, quality control, government inspection, government procurement, purchasing, microbiological control, batch dating on labels, sanitation, humidity control, personnel management, food law, and nutrition data, I could handle whatever the business needed except for legal matters, taxes, and employee compensation laws. Tom, Ralph Napletana, and Herman Taber, took care of these last three items in fine fashion.)

A Huge Family
by Ralph A. Napletana

Lewis J. and Ruth Minor are an innocent sounding pair of people from an Irish-American background. People and more people is really this entire story, yet I am no more a teller of stories now than Herman Taber, the great L. J. Minor Corporation lawyer, said I was or am.

The Minors are dreamers of many things. First, of family, since without it, L. J. and Ruth could not and would not exist. Second, of children, since most can tell of the pride in their eyes when they see children, marriages; grandchildren, marriages; and now many great grandchildren, and more marriages, no doubt.

Family and friends need only remember the 55th wedding anniversary which happened just recently to have a reminder of the depth of family meaning to the Minors. It even goes to the adoption of two of the finest sons of old Ireland, Brother Herman

113

Zaccarelli and myself, Ralph Napletana, via Italy, of course, into the Minor clan. When L.J., who could barely stand or speak at the celebration due to illness, announced that the adoption was now final, the Irish roar filled Kellogg Center where the party was being held.

Desire to achieve, never say Can't, and through determination benefit all involved: the result is the L. J. Minor Corporation legacy. Everyone who was at all apart of it would be direct and indirect beneficiaries of everything that would accrue. It was never a written policy of any kind, but the strong driving force of L. J. The strong will of Ruth was there to temper him. The theory that people and their families always come first is the motto by which L. J. and Ruth lived, then and now.

The third dream of the Minors was their desire to surround themselves with wonderful, difficult, hard-to-always-control "thinkers," who were the innovators toward success. The dream did not involve money, for they had none. Wealth was not even a part of their dream or ultimate destination. The beginning was the year 1951.

Thomas A. Ryan, a practicing lawyer and L. J.'s second cousin, with his ability to convince people to listen and hear him out, became sales manager and the operating leader in almost every phase of the business except manufacturing and research. After becoming general manager, he started his primary mission in life: to acquire remarkable people.

The acquisition of internationally known chefs by both Minor and Ryan has been well documented and is again better known by others. It obviously was not my field, even though I was involved in almost every phase of company operations.

Acquisition 1

Acquisition 1 was my Girl Friday, Mary Mele. She was the office manager and gave secretarial support to the operating plant. She had been a totally devoted legal secretary to Thomas A. Ryan. She never really stopped being his legal secretary because he continued his law practice. He needed to house and feed Babe Ryan, another devoted wife and backer, while he managed the L. J. Minor Corporation in his own law offices in the National City Bank Building at 629 Euclid Avenue, Cleveland, Ohio.

Mary Mele ran both businesses by herself. She truly did, including purchasing and checking of incoming shipments, all billing and credit references, payment of invoices on discount days, all payroll matters, commission payments for sales, hiring and firing, and much more. What a lady! She was a wonderful, tough lady! Whew! She knew only one line: straight! It included L. J. and Tom Ryan.

Acquisition 2

Acquisition 2 was Herman Taber who joined the Corporation around 1955 after Tom Ryan, a friend already for 25 years, convinced him to become corporate lawyer and tax lawyer without payment of any kind. Friendship and more friendship helped to bring the corporate structure together. Herman was not afraid to say exactly what was on his mind whether it pleased anyone or not, including L. J. and Tom Ryan. A little known fact was that Herman Taber was fired three times and quit once to the utter dismay of everyone, including myself. He was normally gentle, yet the toughest hard man one would ever wish to meet when he was convinced that he was right.

A case in point was his absolute refusal to write, hear, or go along with the proposed sale of the L. J. Minor Corporation to Litton Industries. The price as proposed was wonderful and included the sale of Stouffer Family corporate stock also to Litton Industries. The "restricted" Litton stock sale was absolutely valueless in Herman Taber's mind. No money, no sale!

One week after no sale, Litton stock went from 90 to 115 and Herman Taber resigned because of the explosion heard everywhere. Still no money in the deal, and one year later, Herman resigned again, but for only one day this time. The Litton stock was selling on the New York Stock Exchange for $6.50 per share, not $90. Both Herman Taber and myself, as accountant, received a substantial bonus!

Herman Taber was a great human being and just plain loved people. When Tom Ryan needed Herman Taber, he responded instantly. His friendship where the Minors and their family were concerned was and is proof enough. Herman Taber was the finest man and friend that Rose and I had, or ever could have had!

Acquisition 3

Acquisition 3 was Ralph A. Napletana of which too much has already been said. Tom Ryan and I belonged to the Cleveland Knights of Columbus and I was already doing the Club's auditing. In 1955, it was suggested that I assist their accountant in preparation of all tax returns without pay, which went on through 1957. In 1958, the former accountant retired and my office did all the corporate records and record keeping as well as all tax work. Two very successful audits were done with the IRS. No tax consequences and none later were ever seen through my work. I was a member of the five-man group that literally ran the L. J. Minor Corporation, including L. J. Minor, Herman Taber, Thomas A. Ryan General John McLaughlin (who replaced Tom after Tom's death in 1975), and Michael Zelski.

This showed the single mindedness of L. J. Minor in creating successful family oriented corporation with each man having one and only one vote, including L. J. Minor. Success came because each employee was totally responsible for his own area of expertise; however, the main actions came from the five-man group.

Acquisition 4

Acquisition 4 was Nancy Clancy, who loved all people and was loyal, honorable, and totally capable. She came to help and assist Mary Mele and became the chief of almost anything that needed to be done.

115

L. J. and Ruth had implicit faith, very well placed, in Nancy. The old story of an iron fist with a velvet glove is what she basically was and is. Do your job and she was wonderful. Don't do your job and "ouch!"

She was responsible for bank accounts, accounts receivable, accounts payable, payrolls, hiring, and firing. She taught everyone their various jobs and skills. She encouraged employees to go to school and to learn how to help the L. J. Minor Corporation. She taught loyalty and brought loyalty to her own job. She computed and paid all commissions. She checked all travel vouchers. She prepared all records for the accountants and made their job simpler because the records were complete at all times. She was and is a priceless and lovely lady, one whom I love as does everyone else.

Acquisition 5

Acquisition 5 was General John McLaughlin who brought a different viewpoint when he replaced Thomas Ryan as the head of sales. As one of the managing group of five, he came to learn the family orientation of the company.

Acquisition 6

Acquisition 6 was a gem strike, Michael Zelski. As a student of L. J. Minor at Michigan State University, he came aboard and became the superintendent of the plant. He was in charge and actively engaged in all phases of manufacturing, including purchasing of equipment and facilities expansion.

His other responsibilities included the purchasing of all raw materials, including huge purchases of lobster, shrimp, and clams. He was involved with quality control encompassing all phases of the manufacturing process, including labels. Manufacturing, plant office, product and development and quality control, and employees were all Mike Zelski's direct responsibility.

He eventually proved to be what L. J. Minor and Tom Ryan predicted he would be. They said he would be a top notch superintendent and plant manager. He was also one of the five managers of the company.

Acquisition 7

Acquisition 7 was Walt Nicholes, who proved to be as important as any other named thus far. He filled the void in advertising know-how and direction.

This missing link was filled first by Walter Nicholes as a consultant. He later became head of all advertising and promotional literature and brochures for magazines, seminars, and food show exhibits.

His ability to put forth ideas to reach chefs and food operators in the food industry was incredible. Priceless is an overused word, but he brought organization and total product awareness to the industry in the United States and Canada.

In total, what I said initially about being a member of the family, teamwork, and the uncanny ability of L. J. and Ruth Minor to pick people, has held true. The story of the L. J. Minor Corporation is still people -- a huge family of fine people and more people! I am proud to say that I have been and continue to be a part of that family!

On Real Estate
by Don A. Lutz

The time that I spent with Tom Ryan was always pleasurable and brings back a lot of fond memories.

The first time that I met Tom was when he offered to buy my two parcels of property on Pearl Court. These were the two largest parcels on that street, which were needed for the expansion of the L. J. Minor Corporation. He and Mary Mele met me at the houses and he was more than satisfied with my price on the properties. These properties were to be the first acquisitions at the onset of the company's expansion program. Chicago Title conducted the transfer and the rest of the paper work was done in Tom's office at the Bulkley Building on Euclid Avenue. We shook hands on the deal and I thought this would be my first and last encounter with him.

A couple of months later, I received a call from Tom and he told me that he had approached another property owner on Pearl Court in regards to purchasing a parcel. They asked an exorbitant amount because they knew that he represented the company. When he asked me if I would be willing to buy the property in my name and transfer it to the company, I said that would be all right. I then purchased the property for $10,000 instead of the $35,000 that they had asked from him. Chicago Title again handled the sale and Herman Taber, company attorney, handled the transfer to the L. J. Minor Corporation. This was the beginning of a very meaningful relationship with the company for me. I purchased further property in the same fashion and managed to always get the property for no more than $15,000 (except for the Durkee Building, which was acquired for $60,000).

After purchasing an apartment property, the company rented the units out to low income tenants for a most reasonable amount of rent. I collected the rents weekly, with the utilities included in the rent. Utilities were included due to the fact that during the first winter that the company owned the property, a bad experience, with a tenant losing his gas service caused pipes to freeze. This ended up costing about $2,000 in repairs. With utilities included, this never happened again. Andy Gibbel was the company plumber who handled the repairs.

The rents were turned in every Monday to Mary Mele. This caused me to have direct contact with her every week. She was a very strict supervisor who ran a very tight ship. She worked on the average of 12-14 hours per day. When she became ill with cancer, I would accompany her to University Hospital for her treatments. She never wanted any of her employees to know how really sick she was. She maintained this rigorous schedule up until about one week prior to her passing. She used to go to Tom's office and take a short nap in the afternoons. She was a very devoted employee who taught everything she knew to a part-time employee at that time, Nancy Clancy. By the grace of God, she came on the scene and was in turn able to take over where Mary left off and seemed to get more done with sweetness and sincerity than Mary did by exercising a firm hand. Not to take away from either, they both were most efficient and loyal employees. The L. J. Minor Corporation was a very lucky company to have had these types of people in its employ. (Two weeks ago I attended a retirement party for Nancy and was pleased to see some of Dr. Minor's children there.)

The company is still using the same policy that was instituted by Tom Ryan in the '70s. They just recently bought two pieces of property from me on Potter Court which were needed for more parking area. They paid me a fair price for the property and also gave the current tenants sufficient notice to relocate. They were given the last month free rent, plus a bonus of $500 to vacate the premises within the allotted time. By using this policy, the company never had to do a legal eviction on anybody. The tenants cooperated since they knew they were being treated fairly.

The years of my association with the L. J. Minor Corporation were some of the most rewarding for me. I have always been impressed with the way it does business which reflects upon the high business ethics of L. J. Minor himself!

Chapter 17

Success in the Early 1960s

Our Own Building   **Back to School, Again**   **A New Home**

An Unforgettable Person
by Phyllis Markioli
(April 16, 1961)

Mrs. Walther's French Class
Translation
French II

I believe that the most unforgettable person that I know is Mr. Minor, the teacher of chemistry in our high school. I shall always remember him because he is very intelligent and interesting. In his class I learn not only chemistry but many other important things. Mr. Minor tells us his experiences in college. His past experiences are very useful to me, because I shall go to college this fall. Also Mr. Minor has humor sometimes; he is very funny. He is a good philosopher and gives us much to think about. To me, he is an unforgettable person!

Time
by Thomas Edison

When interviewed at age 80, Thomas Edison was asked the question, "What do you consider to be the most valuable thing in life?" Edison's answer was, "Time is the most valuable thing in life, for you cannot buy one minute no matter how much wealth you have."

Our Own Building

For about three years, we had been pondering how to get our own building. Then one evening I found the West Side news on the porch, read the ads, and saw a blind ad for a car wash at 2621 West 25th Street.

Before we could buy it, the zoning had to be checked out at the zoning office in City Hall. I went there and learned that a freeway was soon being built near the property. It turned out that it was more than a block away. Our business was in the light industry class, and we qualified in that regard.

We bought the place since it included a five-apartment building in front of the car wash. When we moved to West 25th Street, I obtained a map with the homes on the two adjacent streets and owners shown. Herman Taber and Ralph Napletana advised us to purchase as many as we could. The plan was to tear the houses down and use the property for future expansion needs. We were to do this through the years and rent out the houses that we did not need immediately.

The owner was in trouble with the IRS. He had not been paying the withholding taxes for his employees. His business included the installation of the flight schedule board at the Cleveland Hopkins Airport, and he employed electricians. The purchase was what Tom Ryan called "a sleeper." The man's wife held the purse strings and controlled its sale. Their asking price was $60,000. We got a loan from Parma Savings, a Polish bank recommended by Tom's City Hall friend and Brother Knight of the Cleveland Council Knights of Columbus.

We found a painter named Mr. Semenyok for the interior of our home in Fairview Park, a west-side Cleveland suburb. He knew a talented carpenter named Joe Vokulich who fixed a shaky wooden banister for us. He became my private contract carpenter for the five family apartment which had several city code violations that had also deterred the property's sale. God was looking after the infant L. J. Minor Corporation in His own way.

Our modus operandi in the plant was as simple and neat as anyone could ever imagine. Equipment was kept to an absolute minimum. It was all easily disassembled and cleaned. I preferred Hobart machinery which we used with an inexpensive service contract with the Cleveland Hobart Branch. All we needed at first were the Hobart Mixers and Food Cutter, a Toledo platform scale, X-Act weight scales, a semi-automatic labeler, raw materials, stainless steel storage bins from Southern Equipment Company, and aluminum dry material scoops and ice-cream scoops used to fill jars.

We used mainly one pound jars with screw caps, packed twelve jars to a case. We had fibre drums in 10-pound, 25-pound, and 50-pound sizes. Plastic bag liners of different sizes were used inside the drums that were then taped shut. We also had a stencil cutter with cardboard stencil cards, thirty inches by six inches, and a stencil brush and ink. All was kept simple so maintenance was minimal, and employees could be trained to do it all.

People were trying to help us. We represented "The American Dream." It was just the beginning. One day our original partner, Joe Bertman, visited the West 25th Street plant and said to me, "You two fellows have done one beautiful job with this company." He was right. We first exhibited at the Ohio Restaurant Shows and Ohio Dietitians Conventions. As Tom said, "We're in the picture." By doing this I got acquainted with a Mr. Manners who had a chain of restaurants in Cleveland. He said to me, "Minor, why do you hide your head in a basket? Why don't you advertise like we do?" I knew why. We were not ready, able, or willing to advertise at that stage. But in time that changed when my plant manager, and former student, Michael Zelski, met Walt Nicholes. We brought him on board and he got us a lot of free advertising by promising the leading food service newspapers and periodicals future business.

Back to School, Again

As the reader will recall, I had returned to school after having my gallbladder removed. I enrolled at Baldwin Wallace College in Berea, taking my teaching credits. I went to school nights, continued to work in the plant, and after about a year, completed my classwork. I started practice teaching at Rocky River High School which meant that I was there everyday for a half day in the morning for one year teaching chemistry.

After getting my Teaching Certificate, Tom Ryan took over as Sales Manager and General Manager of the Minor Corporation, so that I could be gone for three years (1961-1964) to earn a Ph.D. degree, with a thesis on The Chicken Flavor of Old vs. Young Birds, from Michigan State's Food Science Department.

Our son, Bryan, was attending Michigan State at the time, and he insisted that if I went there that he wanted to live with me. In the meantime, Tom Ryan told me that some of the relatives were talking, telling what a dirty guy I was to leave my family and go to school as I was planning to do. I rented an apartment in "married housing," at Michigan State on Cherry Lane. Bryan and I painted it.

Bryan would invite his girl friend over for dinner quite often. I had a steady boarder besides Bryan. What bothered me was that she was in a lower grade than he was. She was always asking him to help her with her work. That was detracting from his scholastic achievement, but I was proud of him. As a freshman, for example, he was chosen the "Outstanding Cadet" in the Army's Reserve Officer Training Program (ROTC) at Michigan State. He later became Captain of the Pershing Rifles, a drill team that traveled around to other ROTC schools and competed against their rifle drill teams.

He thought he was in love with the girl he was dating so I asked if he had any money in the bank. He said he did. I told him he should buy a ring and give it to her. I told him that the "Cardy Jewelry" was going out of business. He went there and picked out a ring that he thought she would like and gave it to her. She lived in upstate New York. When he started hearing wedding bells in his head, he began to panic and decided that he did not want to get married after all.

As time proceeded, I was glad that I had a good foundation from Highland Park Junior College to help me in my chemistry and mathematics courses. One day I was in the microbiology laboratory that was run by Dr. Costilow, Dr. Fabian's successor. Dr. Fabian came into the lab and spotted me. He asked me, "Lew, what are you doing here?" I said, "I am working on a Ph.D., Fred." He said, "What in?" I said, "Chicken flavor." He said, "Chicken flavor? Don't you know what the country needs is a good contraceptive!"

In my flavor work we were able to show that old chickens have more flavor than young chickens. We used different methods like gas chromatography, and thin layer chromatography. To get the samples for gas chromatography I had to use a distillation apparatus and distill the volatiles out of the old and young chickens and collect them for analysis. One afternoon my glass distillation equipment exploded. Fortunately, I instinctively raised my arms to cover my eyes. Once again, my guardian angel protected me and must have warned me to do this. A fellow student, Ed McCabe, took me to the hospital to have pieces of glass removed from my arms. Thank God, there were no permanent harmful effects from this accident.

We also used paper chromatography to help identify the different components in the chicken flavor volatiles. A man named Pippen had done most of the work on chicken flavor that was reported in the literature. He was with one of the U. S. Department of Agriculture experimental laboratories. His work was on carbonyls. Mine was on sulfur compounds. When I published my thesis, Pippen wrote to Dr. Schweigert, head of the Food Science Department, and told him that my work was the most significant that he had seen in several years, especially in the knowledge of chicken flavor. Again, the good Lord was kind to me as I worked hard.

Getting my Ph.D. when I was fifty years old was a real challenge. My hardest courses were in physical and biochemistry, calculus, and electron, and nuclear physics. Dr. Al Pearson was my advisor. He was a meat flavor research specialist. We hit it off well most of the time, although there was one occasion that I remember when we were at odds.

When I was doing gas chromatography analysis of chicken volatiles from old and young birds, I was up night and day. One morning after a hard night of analytical work, Dr. Pearson looked the charts over and told me, "Do them again." I should not have said it, but I told him, "Do it yourself!" Most of the time I continued to learn and make contacts by attending every class, meeting and clinic I could.

When my oral final exam was over and I passed, Dr. Schweigert invited me to lunch. This was customary for all Food Science grads. He said, "Lew, you took longer than anyone to answer the examining committee's questions. I take it that this was part of your strategy." I answered, "You are darn right." Then he told me I was one of only two people he ever knew in all his years in higher education who ever came back to school to complete a Ph.D. program in Food Science. He used to say, "No one knows the cross that the other person is bearing." I guess he was referring to me. I graduated in June 1964 in three years!

My dissertation reported the importance of sulfur compounds in chicken flavor. We were able to use the information I got in our business, and the chickens we made our base from were the heavy birds, the mamas and the papas of the broilers, since broilers had very little flavor.

In fact, a masseur that I had in Kansas City at the YMCA said chicken today is nothing but a fugitive from the shell. He was right because the broilers were so young that they had no chance to develop flavor. The hens and roosters that we used were two years old. We got a higher meat yield from the roosters than we did from the hens, so we used them, mostly. The hens had more liquid in them. The flavor was equally good from one or the other sex, and what amazed Dr. Koves when he came into our plant one day was the size of the chickens. Many of them weighed 14 or 15 pounds. We could not get them that size all the time. Some of them ranged down as light as five or six pounds. The supply was not super-abundant. In fact, as our business grew, we were using most of the available birds of that size that were on the market. They came mainly from Alabama, Georgia, and other southern regions.

Our bases were made by the standards that Escoffier, the great French chef, set. In his cookbook he states that, "Stock is everything in cooking, at least in all good and well flavored cooking. When one's stock is good the rest of the work is easy. And when it is not, nothing worthwhile can be accomplished." He went on to say that, "The older species of poultry, beef, and other meats have the most flavor." So in our beef base we used shoulder clod from older animals. Later on we confined our use to the inner rounds, with low fat content, obtained from older animals.

Dr. Pearson decided, without mentioning it to me, that he wanted me to teach. He wrote letters to MIT, the University of Massachusetts, and other schools recommending me. Again , fate intervened. After I finished my Ph.D. at Michigan State, someone was needed to teach in the Hotel School. The students were having difficulty in the chemistry department and the course they were taking was not food-related. It was no help when they got into their Quantity Foods course with Dr. Lendal H. Kotschevar, the most renowned, prolific, and sought after lecturer, teacher, and writer of foodservice texts. He would talk about gelatinized starch and denatured protein and other subjects in class. They did not know what he was talking about. There were many other topics like fermentation that they did not understand. He asked me to help him out. He said, "We've been sending our Hotel School students to the chemistry department and they learn no food chemistry. Would you consider teaching a foodservice science course in our school?" I said, "Let me think about it." I told Dr. Pearson, my Food Science Ph.D. advisor, about Kotschevar's situation.

Dr. Pearson said, "Lew, that is the job for you. The students could profit from your knowledge and experience out in the field." He had Dr. Schweigert call Professor Barbour, the head of the Hotel School.

When Barbour interviewed me, I said, "I would like to set up my own course. First, I will visit your alma mater, Cornell, and find out what is being taught to their students." I went, and met Dean Lattin who introduced me to Laura Lee Smith, their chemistry professor. She invited me to sit in on her classes. Soon, I became acquainted with Dean Beck of the School of Hotel Administration and Professor Vance Christian. Also Helen Recknagle, the editor of *The Cornell HRA Quarterly* and Jerry Wanderstock, the meats specialist. Also Marshall McLennon who was developing recipes to Escoffier standards. These were printed in color and bound into *The Cornell HRA Quarterly* on index cards. Soon, the recipes included our food bases, too.

After a discussion with my Board of Directors at the company, we decided that I should seize this opportunity. So I began teaching Food Service Science (HRI 245) at Michigan State University. All of the philosophy that I had accumulated from my parents, father figures, religious teaching, and study were passed on to my students, together with accounts of my "odyssey" in the business world.

My teaching efforts were recognized and praised by Dr. Robert Bloomstrom, who succeeded Henry Ogden Barbour as the head of the Hotel, Restaurant, and Institutional Management School at Michigan State University. Dr. Kotschevar resigned shortly after Barbour's departure to go to the University of Nevada at Las Vegas (UNLV). It was a dilemma until Bloomstrom called a faculty meeting at which my colleagues decided that I should take over Kotschevar's Quantity Food Lectures and Labs. Another course I taught for many years was Food Flavor Evaluation which the students loved. In addition, I taught a wine course.

(Editor's Note: As a Michigan State Hotel School graduate, I had the pleasure of taking all of Dr. Minor's courses. As previously noted, he was my mentor and confidante throughout my college career. While each class afforded the student new insights into the industry, I particularly enjoyed the food he introduced me to while in his laboratories. Realizing that most students could not afford the finer things in life, I remember him buying with his own funds, steak, lobster, and other delicacies so that we were all intelligent on the quality of these items. While I did not know he was spending his own money on our course, I did learn later of his willingness to provide the best for his students. What a professor!)

My teaching appointments in the Hotel School, by mutual agreement, were for Spring and Fall terms only. That left me free for the winter and summer to finish the Food Service Science text I was co-authoring with Laura Lee Smith of Cornell. What I envisioned was the adoption of my type program by the two original Hotel Schools. Dean Meek started Cornell's five years before Michigan State's was initiated. Unfortunately, this did not happen. Even though she only contributed one chapter to the entire volume, and did the index, she put her name first. I said, "That is all right; the age of chivalry is not dead yet."

With my program the students learned about air, water, solutions, detergents, paints and varnishes, fats, proteins, carbohydrates, and food additives. These were all topics they could use as managers. There was also a chapter on meats. That was the one Laura Lee contributed. The book was published by a friend of mine, Dr. Donald Tressler, founder and owner of AVI Publishing in Westport, Connecticut. They specialized in Food Science texts.

Dr. Tressler was also a prominent Food Scientist. Many of the chapters were written by my guest lecturers, including Don Anderson of Wyandotte Chemicals, Harry Lawson of Proctor and Gamble, Joe Rakosky of Central Soy Company and Mark Wolf of Dow Chemical Company on such topics as detergents, fats and oils, soy protein products, and food additives.

In class, I would bring low and high temperature pocket thermometers, hydrometers, a hygrometer, a pocket refractometer, and other instruments about which managers should know. It was my hope and vision that all hotel courses would provide this knowledge to their students. That still has not happened, although the Culinary Institute of America in

Hyde Park, New York, adopted some of the material in their programs.

Food science majors would often enroll in my course. One of them, Kenneth Fox, wrote a letter to Dr. Schweigert stating that "All Food Science majors should be required to take Dr. Minor's course." Dr. Schweigert didn't like the letter and lost no time telling me off. Since the student's letter was spontaneous, and was written conscientiously, I had no qualms about its consequences. In other words, no one put him up to it.

Getting back now to what I was saying: Dr. Bloomstrom said to me, "Lew, you saved us by taking on Len's teaching load in addition to your own." I told him that I was glad to help out and pleased that my peers had recommended me for the task. I enjoyed the students and the experience. Gary Shingler, an ex-football player, was my lab assistant. Being 6'4" tall and weighing 275 pounds, he had no trouble getting the students to keep their lab places clean and tidy.

After two years, Don Bell was hired to teach the lecture and lab. He later added a wine course to his area of expertise. He had graduated from MSU and worked for Holiday Inn as a manager. While at MSU, he went on to get a Ph.D. in Food Science as did Dr. Ronald F. Cichy, present head of the school.

Soon after that, Don left and joined a former acting head of the school and friend of mine, Dr. Frank Borsenik, at UNLV. Dr. Bloomstrom retired in 1980 and was succeeded by the flamboyant ex-restaurateur, Don Smith, who was in turn succeeded by the school's computer authority, Michael Kasavana, who in turn was succeeded by Dr. Cichy in 1988. He has remained in the leadership position doing an excellent job.

Not to get ahead of myself, but when Dr. Bell left for UNLV, I was able to get Don Smith to hire Chef Robert Nelson, one of the L. J. Minor Chefs to replace him. After 13 years of service, and never having been tardy or absent a single day, Chef Nelson told Dr. Cichy that his wife had passed. Dr. Cichy gave him a week off to recoup his good-humor and the equanimity that charms and pleases the students so much.

Chef Nelson was the right man at the right time to improve and increase our students' knowledge about foodservice from the all-important hands-on aspects of the kitchen, "The Heart of the House" not "Back of the House," as it was historically called.

The kitchen is not a "back house" or "privy," so I introduced the term "Heart of the House." That is what it is if one will reflect on the functions, the purpose, and potential of a well-run kitchen to a successful hospitality operation.

But getting back to my story, Dr. Kotschevar and I were close friends. Dr. Ryan also became a close friend of Len Kotschevar. We conducted seminars for Brother Herman Zaccarelli at his request and all worked well together. We put both Kotschevar and Brother Herman on a token retainer. The same was true for others.

Teaching was easy for me. With my firsthand experience in the food processing field, I had a lot of good advice for my classes. Whenever I knew of someone who would be better, I would get them. Some came from government agencies, some from industry, and some from the Food Science and Human Nutrition Department.

Chefs were brought in for food lab demonstrations. When a guest speaker or chef came three or more times, they received an Honorary Professor Award, framed. These were nice for them to hang in their offices.

Following his wife Margaret's untimely death in a car accident, Dr. Kotschevar went from UNLV to teach at Florida International University.

After spending the summer at their beautiful cedar log home on Lindbergh Lake in Montana, about 80 miles from Missoula where he at one time taught at the University of Montana, they each took a car and headed for UNLV for Len's winter teaching. Margaret probably had a heart attack.

Her car went into the river. The luggage floated downstream and that is how the State Police found her. She was a dear friend of ours. Mrs. Minor and I loved her Irish charm. She was as perfect a partner for Lendal as Ruth has been for me.

We had visited them with Rosalie and Mary, our youngest daughters. Len took us fishing at another mountain fed lake. We went through brush, two miles up the mountain, where we fished for brook trout. We caught a lot of these and had them for dinner. Rosalie stood up to her knees in that ice-cold water for an hour.

Len also took us to Glacier National Park where we enjoyed a bottle of white wine with our lunch. Afterwards, he took the girls with him and hid the bottle. They then repeated the process and hid a new bottle, but we haven't been back since Margaret's passing.

For several years after Margaret's death, Lendal has had concerts on the lake at night in her memory. We attended two of these. Their bedrooms were all taken by the singers and musicians so we obtained a room for the night at the Lindbergh ranch across the lake with the help of Len's daughter Julie. Margaret's death crushed Len, but Julie's new baby, a boy, is Grandpa's pride and joy. She will get everything Len owns when he passes, and he has already given her some money and property. She has always been his "little darling" and "the apple of his eye." She was the graduate assistant for my "Food Flavor Evaluation" class, and proved to be very well trained by the Human Nutrition School from which she graduated.

Every year we used to see Len at the National Institute for the Foodservice Industries (NIFI) luncheon at the National Restaurant Association (NRA) Show. We still meet him annually at the Golden Toque meeting. Both of us are Honorary Members.

A New Home

When Ruth's mother and dad were gone from this world, her dad's farm went to her three brothers and her. For her share she took the farmhouse with two outbuildings, a shed, and milk house. We decided to move there in Lansing, Michigan, from Cleveland. Our younger son, Michael Lewis, came to live with us in this old family farmhouse that had been in the Angell family for 50 years.

We modernized the house. The roof was raised. We started with a three bedroom, one bath, one dining room, and one kitchen house. We finished with three possible living rooms, two dining rooms, plus a dinette, a large recreation room, front and back stairs, and a three-car garage with space heater and a ceiling high enough for an inside basketball court. We finished off the basement with a small air raid shelter for storage, new fieldstone walls (re-mortared), and a terrazzo floor over the entire recreation room area.

For the roof-raising, we brought Joe Vokulich from Cleveland. Ruth's cousin, Jim Siegrist, was a skilled tile man. We made him the contractor on a percentage basis. He supervised the plaster and wood work and did the tile and terrazzo himself. He also did the concrete walks. Spartan asphalt put in a 600-foot asphalt driveway. Siegrist paved the garage with concrete. The heated three-car garage was Tom's idea.

Ruth owned the entire place including fenced in yard and three 1,000 gallon septic tank system. We bought a 1/3 acre lot at the south side of the drive from Ruth's brother, Bob Angell, who lived next door in a brick bungalow he had built for him and his wife, Frances, and their sons, Bill and Richard. Although he was head purchasing agent for the university and a Brigadier General in the Michigan National Guard, he still kept the farm with beef cattle (Black Angus). At one time our children had as many as six horses to ride. Bob sold us hay for them and let them pasture in his field.

Chapter 18

Food Flavor

by Lewis J. Minor, Ph.D.

Summary   **The Importance of Flavor**   **What is Flavor?**

Taste   **Odor**   **Practical Use of Flavor Research Developments**

Meat Substitutes   **Literature Cited**

On Doing More
by Lewis J. Minor

It's all right to be contented, but not to be satisfied.
You can always do better.
Be contented with what you've done,
but not satisfied.
You can always do more.

Scientists
by Lewis J. Minor
(January 6, 1995)

The Scientists are destined to work all alone,
Seeking solutions to problems but just on their own.
Finding answers to problems both great and small
Their minds meditating on these one and all.
In the libraries many long hours do they spend
Doing research that often appears without end.
Seeking leads that were followed by others before
Men searched just as they do now, but in days of yore.
Then often no matter how great their resolve
A problem may face them that's too hard to solve.
New plans of action will be taken then
And library searches will start once again.

Summary

Dr. Lewis J. Minor received his B.S. in Organic Chemistry from Michigan State University (1939), his M.S. in Analytical Chemistry from Wayne State University (1944), and his Ph.D. in Food Science from Michigan State University (1964).He has served the La Choy Food Co. as technical director for product control, process development and new product research (1939-1942); Owens-Illinois as research associate in their research center (1942-1944); McKay-Davis as vice president and research director (1944-1946); and the Huron Milling Co. as technical service director (1946-1952). Since 1952 Dr. Minor has been president of the L. J. Minor Corporation, manufacturer of food seasonings, bases, and sauces. He also teaches courses in Food Chemistry and Food Flavor Evaluation in Michigan State University's School of Hotel, Restaurant, and Institutional Management, where he is a visiting assistant professor.

(Editor's Note: Dr. Schweigert, Head of Food Science at Michigan State, asked each Ph.D. candidate, including Dr. Minor, to publish at least one article from their thesis in an accredited scientific journal. Dr. Minor had five published. Later, he had articles on both Food Production Systems and Flavor, both of which are reprinted in this text. The Flavor article is presented here and is a classic with over seventy references.)

In closing the world's protein gap, flavor control is a vital factor. Food primarily must be nutritious to sustain life, but unless the flavor is acceptable to the human palate, it may not be eaten. Today, new ways are being found to upgrade natural foods lacking flavor and to add flavor in new man-made meat substances having a high nutritive content.

Flavor chemistry is the newest branch of food chemistry in the United States. Gas chromatography, whereby food flavor volatiles can be separated into their manifold chemical components, is being perfected. Other physicochemical techniques are also being used to identify these chemicals, but with the help of the human nose and brain which are more sensitive than mechanical devices.

New and improved synthetic fruit flavors have already been developed as there are not enough natural fruits grown to meet the demand for these flavors in foods. Similarly, beef extract is being replaced with flavor potentiators: MSG (monosodium glutamate); HVP (hydrolyzed plant proteins); and the flavor nucleotides - 5' IMP (inosine 5' monophosphate) that occurs in meat and fish muscle, and 5' GMP (Guanosine 5' monophosphate), which is produced biochemically from yeast and yeast derivatives. Progress has been made with meat substitutes. Natural flavorings derived from beef, chicken and ham have been combined with soy, yeast or algae protein to make simulated meats.

The Importance of Flavor

Food may be nutritious and possess maximum eye appeal. But when flavor is lacking, the food is neither acceptable nor marketable. Nature itself provides many interesting examples. Apples having a beautiful, lustrous red color may be discarded after one bite if they are dry and pithy. It is a rare treat to taste a really good melon. Green fruits shipped to market and then ripened are seldom tasty. Some meat can look tempting when you purchase it, but no matter how you cook it the toughness remains. Chicken breast meat or lobster meat with eye appeal may be tasteless, dry and tough after preparation for the table.

Research and quality control have been helpful in combating either quirks of nature or a combination of handling, storage, and cooking variables. Yet, within limits, products still vary. Generally we must admit that nature provides her best and most nutritive product when the fruit, vegetable, meat, poultry or fish has attained its ripest, most tender and most succulent stage. Accordingly, tenderometers are applied to representative samples of fruits and vegetables prior to harvest in order to check their maturity. Meats and poultry are tested with shear meters. Many other physical and chemical methods are employed in upgrading and safeguarding the yield, nutrition and flavor of our food production. Research and quality control have been helpful in combating either quirks of nature or a combination of handling, storage, and cooking variables. Yet, within limits, products still vary.

Ecologically speaking, the simple relationship between food and man is better appreciated than the interrelationship of food nutrition, food flavor, and man. Perhaps one of the most memorable instances of this neglect of flavor occurred during World War II with respect to the Army's canned C-rations (meat and vegetable stew, meat and vegetable hash, meat and beans, etc.). These rations were models of nutritional balance. But they were found unpalatable by the soldiers due to a combination of factors, including effects of canning and storage as well as the lack of added flavoring or enhancers.

Proof of this flavor inadequacy was obtained by a fortuitous circumstance. Hungry soldiers wouldn't eat their rations: indeed Caul[1] reported that soldiers stationed in the Arctic region preferred hunger to unpleasant-tasting though nutritive foods. Then, the soldiers by experimentation learned that the bouillon powder contained in their K-rations could be used to flavor the C-rations and thus improve palatability.

Another valuable lesson was learned at a later date in connection with the Marshall Plan program of feeding Europe after the war. Grain, vegetable oil, and milk powder combinations were formulated with and without added monosodium glutamate, hydrolyzed plant proteins, and spices for flavoring. Since the flavor additives increased cost about 5 percent, the procurement officers decided that flavoring was unnecessary. They maintained that the primary object was to provide calories and protein, not flavor. When General Lucius D. Clay attempted to feed these ersatz products without seasoning to the hungry masses of Europe, they were rejected. Eventually General Clay issued the order to dump millions of pounds of this unpalatable food into the ocean.

Daily thousands of kitchens in the United States prepare food items that are either partly or entirely rejected at the table. Garbage cans and disposals are frequently filled with discarded or uneaten protein foods. This wanton waste could be eliminated by intelligent leadership in the foodservice industries. For example, by giving proper recognition to the importance of flavor in food preparation. Chef-less food preparation in a quantity kitchen for a captive pensioner audience should be as acceptable as chef-prepared-to-order food for a millionaire.

The renowned American food scientist I. J. Hutchings[2] stated that: "Food must be made not only nutritious but more appealing to the consumer. Food scientists have been negligent in the area of developing or creating food flavors." In a similar vein, the eminent nutritionist and late president of Wisconsin University C. A. Elvehjem[3] predicted: "Just as individual nutrients such as vitamins were identified, isolated, synthesized, and then used for enriching foods, so a similar attack will be made on flavors and aromas present in foods and food products. By 1980, foods combined to meet specific nutritional requirements may be enriched with these factors just as we now enrich with vitamins."

What Is Flavor?

Flavor may be described as consisting of three fundamental parts: 1) *taste* or the non-volatile constituents including sweetness, saltiness, sourness, bitterness and monosodium or nucleotide enhancing effects (which emphasize taste bud sensitizing and mouth feel in protein foods); 2) *odor* consisting of the volatile constituents of fruits and spices and of cooked meat, poultry, fish, vegetables, eggs, etc.; and 3) *kinesthetic factors* - such as texture and other physical qualities - that may affect the senses of sight, touch or hearing.

Numerous definitions of flavor could be given, but the one chosen is that of Kazeniac[4] who used four designations as proposed by Sjostrom and Cairncross.[5] The first was taste, consisting of saltiness, sweetness, sourness and bitterness, to which Moncrieff[6] has recently added metallic. The second was aroma, which described odor sensations. The third was body, which referred to the texture or sensation caused by chewing, but had nothing to do with taste or aroma. The fourth was mouth satisfaction, which implied salivary stimulation, blending and pleasantness. Thus defined, flavor is an interaction of these four basic sensations.

Taste, smell and feel are our chemical senses.[7] By realizing that all matter is electrical in nature and that temperature affects reaction rates, we may conclude that our chemical senses are affected by both electrochemical and thermochemical phenomena. Salivary enzymes (protein catalysts) often cause chemical changes to occur within the food even while it is being chewed. Furthermore, texture must be considered in any overall concept of taste. Tactile sensations (which affect the sense of touch) and also the responses resulting from seeing or hearing (as in the case of water-chestnuts or popcorn when they are being chewed) the food are useful in evaluating its physical characteristics. Hence, both kinds of taste effects - chemical and kinesthetic or physical - are important.

Since the two chief parts of flavor are taste and odor, separate discussions on each follow. Taste will be considered first.

Taste

Taste is a relatively simple physical sensation which originates in the mouth's taste buds. The taste buds are stimulated by the food's chemical make-up, its temperature, pH (relative acidity) and the interplay of other senses: smell, touch (biting, chewing, tongue feel, swallowing), eye-appeal, and so on. Taste and odor work together, reaching the taste buds with or without other sensory side effects such as sight and hearing. The brain combines these sensory reactions into the complex response called flavor.

Taste Physiology. Taste is one of our simpler senses. There are only five principal dimensions in taste as compared to countless varieties of odors. Yet the innovation of taste is more complex than that of smell.[7]

Taste receptors are called taste buds. They are located on moist body surfaces, i.e. in the mouth cavity of human beings, on the gills of fish, and on the feet of butterflies. Our taste buds are embedded in the covering of papillae, which are minute projections located mostly on the tongue but also found on the inside surface of the cheek and on the epiglottis. There are about 245 taste buds in each papilla and approximately 9,000 taste buds in all.

Taste buds consist of sensory cells in the mouth surface tissue (epithelium) that are motivated by nerve endings. Taste occurs when a chemical compound in solution or dissolved in the saliva seeps into the taste bud and stimulates the nerve ending which transmits an electrical impulse to the brain. Tasting doesn't always require ingestion of the compound directly into the mouth. For instance, when an antibiotic is injected into the arm or thigh of a medical patient, the patient may experience a bitter taste almost instantly via the bloodstream as the taste-buds absorb it from the blood.[8]

The tongue is the principal instrument of taste and can differentiate between two separate stimuli occurring simultaneously only five one-hundredths of an inch apart.[9] Tasting is a rapid reaction. Experimental results show that the papillae of the rat will respond to the taste of a sodium chloride solution within five one-hundredths of a second.[19]

According to Kazeniac, sweetness is detected mainly at the tip of the tongue, saltiness at the frontal edges, sourness at the sides, and bitterness at the back of the tongue.[4] Taste perception zones shown by Crocker (see Figure 1) deviate appreciably from those ascribed to the tongue by Kazeniac. However, as will be clarified later under the heading "Taste Theories," this appraisal of taste bud functions with respect to location may be passé. Taste buds have been known to migrate with age. Sweet-sensitive buds located in the cheeks of infants and small children disappear as the children grow older.

Dysautonomic patients (persons with malfunctioning autonomic nervous systems) are unable to perceive taste or discriminate between tastes.[11] But in most people tasting ability is taken for granted, although it can be dulled or sharpened. Smokers and heavy coffee or liquor drinkers sustain a fatiguing effect on their taste buds. One distinguished epicurean club called Quando Manducamus ("When Do We Eat?")[12] has placed a taboo on smoking until after dining is completed and coffee has been served. A glass of sherry and a cup of consommé preceding the meal serve to attune the diner's taste mechanism by stimulating the flow of gastric juices. Tobacco chewers as distinguished from smokers are often proficient tasters. So one might assume that constant mastication stimulates the salivary gland and cleanses the taste buds.

A series of classical experiments concerned with the salt, sour, sweet and bitter tastes were reported by Moncrieff.[13, 14, 15, 16] Later, this same worker showed that bitterness in chemical compounds increases in direct proportion to the molecular weight.[17]

Taste Theories. Recently, Von Bekesky[18] proposed a "duplexity theory" of taste. First he studied the relationships between warm and cold stimuli and the four basic taste stimuli-sweet, salty, sour and bitter. Then he separated the tongue sensations into two general groupings: 1) bitter, warm and sweet; 2) sour, cold and salty. He also concluded that sour and salty tastes merge together at the center of the tongue, whereas sweet and sour tastes do not.

The newest concept of taste bud action is based on studies of electron micrographs of taste buds. Two cell types exist, one light and the other dark. The light-colored cells are compared to bricks in building, and the darker cells are likened to the mortar as they serve to bind the lighter cells together. Dark cells absorb the chemical osmium, but light cells do not. Both kinds of cells, together with a hair-like nerve cell that transmits taste responses to the brain, are present in taste buds. Taste buds vary in shape, and their position in the epithelium (mouth's surface tissue) may undergo change. Accordingly, experimental evidence indicates that the nature of the taste bud may be that of a migratory lymph cell.[19]

Taste Psychology. Historically, taste classification is based on phenomenological evidence. The Swedish botanist Carolus Linnaeus (1707-1778) enumerated eleven tastes: sweet, sour, salty, fatty, bitter, aqueous, viscous, astringent, nauseous, sharp, and insipid. Wilhelm Wundt (1832-1920), founder of the first experimental psychology laboratory, reduced the number of tastes to six: sweet, sour, salty, bitter, alkaline and metallic. Later, Wundt held to the basic four consisting of sweet, sour, salty and bitter as proposed by Crocker.[20] General acceptance of this four-dimensional characterization of the taste phenomenon led Henning[21] to develop the taste tetrahedron concept. Now, Moncrieff[6] holds that it is necessary to add metallic to the four primaries of Crocker.[20]

A psychophysical scale that measures gustatory values of different foods has been devised by Beebe-Center and Waddell.[22] Since taste is synonymous with the term "gustation," a unit of taste called the "gust" was devised. The "gust" is based on the taste of a one percent sugar solution. On the scale, undiluted lime, lemon or pickle juice has a rating of over one hundred gusts. Acceptable foods rarely exceed fifty gusts, and the average limit of tolerance is about one hundred gusts. Therefore, we usually serve foodstuffs that occupy positions near the middle of the scale.

Off-tastes can profoundly influence likes or dislikes for food. Tomato juice or other fruit or vegetable juices from a can may have a fishy or metallic taste due to the reaction between the acid in the juice and the metals in the container. Packing in glass or in drawn metal cans having acid-resisting enameled surfaces corrects this problem. Orange juice served warm and coffee served cold have objectionable tastes. Foods that should be sweet but taste salty or vice versa are highly unacceptable. Too much monosodium glutamate (MSG)* is not good either.

In foodservice a common fault is leaving onion soup or consommé on the steam table too long before tasting it to see if evaporation has caused too high a salt concentration. Adding the correct amount of water is a simple antidote, but this is often overlooked. Food should always be tasted prior to serving and checked at frequent intervals whenever it is held hot. A good cook, according to Escoffier,[23] uses the freshest and finest ingredients, exercises utmost care in meal preparation, and uses both his nose and his tongue to test the food.

Sometimes our sense of taste can warn us that the food we are eating may be harmful to our health. For example, medical researchers found that burned fat volatiles deposited on charcoal broiled steaks contain benzopyrene, the cancer-causing chemical found in cigarette smoke.[24] Charred meat may cause cancer to start in the intestinal tract[25]; and spent fat from the potato chip industry, when added to chicken rations, caused breast cancer in the chickens.[26] For meats, other than pork, cooking time and temperature should be held to a minimum whenever possible.[25] A diner is warned of the presence of this harmful chemical by the charred or burned taste of fat in the food.

Taste blending is important. Salt enhances sweetness and masks sourness. Monosodium glutamate (MSG) reduces earthiness and/or bitterness in potatoes, onions and bean sprouts. Nucleotides ** and monosodium glutamate act synergistically*** to reduce bitterness and disguise other bizarre notes in vegetable products such as onions. In short, these so-called flavor potentiators[27] can make a vegetable dish tolerable to a meat eater by improving the flavor profile.[28]

Often two similar products can be combined to form a single superior product. Tomato juice from the West Coast is added to tomato juice from the Midwest to reduce the acidity and improve the color of the Midwestern product. Likewise Niagara and Concord grape wines of the East and Midwest are blended with California wines because the fruits from California are sweeter and less acidic than those from the eastern United States and yield wines of higher alcohol content.

Our food patterns and tastes are in a constant state of flux. For example, pickles are milder, ham is less salty, and wieners are seasoned with MSG, as are soups and baby foods. Within the past twenty-five years food scientists have learned to make these and many other changes in order to increase consumer acceptance.

Taste Control. Taste may be controlled within the limits of natural variance by taste-testing together with careful grading, weighing, processing and handling of foods. Taste-testing may be done directly by the organoleptic methods of feeling, smelling and tasting or indirectly by chemical and instrumental testing. Taste-testing in the manufacturing of foods requires stringent control of the seasoning profile and careful consideration of the kinesthetic and

134

chemical factors in taste.[29] The influence of processing (chlorination, washing, heating-cooling, freezing-thawing, etc.) on sensory properties of food must likewise be controlled to insure taste acceptance.

Quality. Consumer preference, detection of difference, difference-preference, selection of the best sample or process, and determination of grade or quality level may be studied by taste panels.[30] The attributes of quality included under taste are texture, temperature, appearance, sweetness, bitterness and metalicness. Glutamate and nucleotide effects should also be considered whenever these seasonings are added to protein foods. Fiber, moisture, fat, protein, carbohydrate and ash are determined by chemical procedures.[30] The attributes of quality included under taste are texture, temperature, appearance, sweetness, bitterness and metalicness. Minerals such as sodium, potassium, arsenic and lead are assayed by spectrographic, polarographic and X-ray diffraction or chemical techniques.[31]

Texture. Characteristics of texture as related to touch and taste are measured directly by sight and by mouth or finger feel. Texture can further be determined by instrument testing: firmness and juiciness are tested by compression, chewiness by shear-pressure, fibrousness by comminution (cutting fine), and stickiness by tensile strength. Grittiness is measured by comminution, sedimentation and elution (separation of material by washing). Mealiness is measured by starch or gum analysis. Color measurements have also proved useful in the realm of kinesthetic factors.[32] Temperature is tested directly by feel and indirectly by either a thermometer or a potentiometer.

Taste Chemicals. The chemical tastes may be easy or difficult to measure depending on their nature. Sugar, salt, pH (relative acidity of the food), monosodium glutamate and the 5' nucleotides usually occur in natural or prepared foods at concentrations that permit either chemical or biochemical and physicochemical measurements. The Glutamate Manufacturers Technical Committee has published methods for determining the monosodium glutamate content of foods, and Pabst Laboratories has perfected techniques for the 5' nucleotides. Constituents of food that impart bitter notes are difficult to assay due to their complex chemical nature.

Taste Stimuli. According to Sharon,[33] taste stimuli may cause both direct and indirect reactions. When food is put into the mouth, we have a direct response to it. Salivary and gastric stimulation may also result from seeing food which we have learned to like. This indirect response to taste stimuli can measurably increase pancreatic secretion when the food is being digested in the intestine later on.

    There are other responses to eating besides the stimulation of the taste buds and the stomach. When lumps of meat are chewed, the soft palate tissue, tooth membranes, muscles and joints are stimulated. Thus more gastric juice elicits from eating stew than from eating hash.[34]

Continuing research is essential in the taste area of food science. Currently, however, the emphasis is being placed on food odor analysis. The problems involved in first analyzing and then synthesizing or biochemically producing food odors is a timely challenge that food scientists have accepted.

Odor. Odor has been termed the most important sensory component of flavor by Moncrieff.[7] Evidence of the importance of olfaction can be obtained readily by holding the nose and tasting first an apple and then a potato. If you hold your nose when you are blindfolded, you cannot tell the difference between the apple and the potato. Moncrieff says, "gustation is to taste as olfaction is to smell."

Odor is a complex physiological response occurring at specific chemical receptor loci known as the hairs of the olfactory cell, and due to electrochemical, thermochemical and kinesthetic reactions at those specific sites. Whenever smell with or without superimposed feeling contacts the receptor site concomitantly, the brain computes the overall effect of the complex response known as odor.

Odor Physiology. By comparing the chemical senses of taste and smell, Moncrieff[6] found that the brain is capable of recognizing more than 200,000 different odors, and that while the palate and tongue have thousands of taste receptors, the nasal cleft has millions of olfactory receptors. These olfactory receptors are embedded in the small patch of mucous membrane situated on each wall of the nasal cleft, which is a narrow space in the uppermost compartment of the nose.

According to Von Frisch,[35] rabbits, dogs, and eels possess many more olfactory receptors than man. The olfactory bulb of the rabbit contains 100,000,000 receptor cells with 6 to 12 hairs per cell. Man's total is 50,000,000 glomeruli receptors served by 45,000 secondary neurons connected to the olfactory brain.[36] The rabbit has only 25,000 of the secondary neurons leading to the cortex of the brain.

In a series of classical experiments, Gesteland and Lettvin[37] measured the electrical responses of individual olfactory nerve cells in the olfactory organ of the frog. (Frogs are the species most frequently chosen for olfaction experiments because their neural anatomy resembles that of man.) These workers connected microelectrodes to the individual cells, and their experiments demonstrated that specific cells react selectively with specific odors. Eight kinds of odor receptors were identified in the frog, and five of these receptor-types reacted with the seven primary odors which Amoore[38] described. Thus, Gesteland and Lettvin's experiments give support to the stereochemical theory of odor (see "Odor Theories"), proposed by Amoore, Johnston and Rubin.[39] These workers have been successful in establishing the fact that the sense of smell is governed by an electrical process that originates in the olfactory nerve whenever a whiff of odor hits the lining of the nose.

The human nose is an instrument of remarkable sensitivity and precision. Even though the sensitivity to odors varies between individuals, most people can detect vanillin at a concentration of one part in ten million. Odor thresholds also vary according to the

136

chemical compound that is being smelled. For example, ethyl mercaptan-the active ingredient in skunk odor-may be smelled at a concentration as low as 0.000000000000071 ounce (7 x 10^{-14} ounces). Yet this is equivalent to more than 19 billion (19 x 10^9) molecules of ethyl mercaptan.[40] Odor sensitivity is about 10 thousand times that of taste sensitivity,[20] and as will be discussed later, ordinary chemical methods are often impractical in the study of food odors.

Odor Theories. More than 2,000 years ago the Roman poet Lucretius postulated that the palate contains small pores of various sizes and shapes.[39] Odor perception was attributed by Lucretius to the specific shapes of the odorous molecules together with their capabilities of fitting particular pores in the palate.

In 1949, Moncrieff[41] proposed a so-called new theory of odor remarkably similar to the ancient one of Lucretius, but based on modern scientific evidence. According to Moncrieff's deductions, the odorant must be volatile and has to possess a molecular configuration complementary to that of a specific site on the olfactory receptor. He stated that olfaction occurs in six stages: 1) odorant molecules pervade the air; 2) odor-containing air is inspired by the subject and sniffed into the nasal cleft; 3) molecules lodge themselves on sites of suitable receptors; 4) lodgment may cause an energy change, such as a reduction in surface tension; 5) the energy shift in the receptors sends discrete electrical messages up the olfactory nerve to the brain; and 6) the brain processes and computes the smell.

About fifteen years later, after more than a decade of classical experimentation with hundreds of organic odor compounds,[38] Amoore and co-workers [39] proposed the stereochemical theory of odor. While there are three primary colors of sight, these workers chose seven primary odors: camphoraceous, musky, floral, pepperminty, ethereal, pungent and putrid. The first five of these seven primary odors are complementary to the seven primary receptor sites, which resemble cavities and slots.[39] According to Amoore, each of these five primary odors can be identified by the size and shape of its moleculism, and particular odors fit into specific openings. Pungent and putrid odors are distinguished by electrical charge rather than by shape. Thus, these workers propose a complex odor spectrum for smell that resembles the simpler color spectrum for sight.

Experimental evidence substantiates the stereochemical theory of odor -- the first direct support of the Amoore theory is Gesteland and Lettvin's experimental discovery of differentiated receptor sites in the olfactory organ of the frog. Obviously, Amoore's theory is of great value, although it may prove to be an oversimplified explanation of the complex phenomenon of odor. Further studies will place the stereochemical theory of odor in proper perspective.

Instruments. So far man has devised no instrument to equal the performance of the human nose and brain. Work is being done to develop better instruments for detecting odors. In making such efforts, scientists are learning more about the way the human nose functions.

According to Moncrieff,[42] the smell stimulus is a physicochemical adsorptive process, and the chemical molecules responsible for a particular flavor lend themselves to instrumentation.[43] His mechanical nose is made up of a thermostat coated with a peanut protein film and a glass enclosed thermistor having a resistance capacity of 2 thousand ohms, with a drop in resistance of 60 ohms per degree Centigrade rise in temperature. When an odorant vapor in air is passed over the coated thermostat at a controlled rate of one liter of air per minute, a temperature rise occurs which unbalances the Wheatstone bridge resistance circuit. This device, while more sensitive to acetone than the human nose, is inferior to the nose in detecting vanilla or musk odors.

Quite recently, investigations on the sense of smell were begun at Honeywell Research Center, Hopkins, Minnesota.[44] The ultimate goal of this research effort is to develop electronic sensors capable of detecting and identifying odors. The research team consists of director H. E. Heist, D.J. Landis and B. D. Mulvaney. They have already been successful in separating individual olfactory cells, and in making electron micrographs of the cell parts that are suspected of being odor receptors and/or transmitters.

Rabbit cells have been separated and maintained as single cells for weeks at a time and have been subjected to various odor and visual tests. Prior to electron microscopy, the cells are embedded individually in an epoxy resin block for sectioning. An ultramicrotome is used to prepare sections of 500 Angstrom thickness (about 25 millionths of an inch) for subsequent tests. Correlated studies using light microscopy are made with thicker sections averaging one micron in thickness (about 5 ten-thousandths of an inch).

Results indicate that the hairs and olfactory vesicles hold the greatest promise for future studies. Heist, Landis, and Mulvaney have noted that each rabbit olfactory cell averages 6 to 12 olfactory hairs. These cells resemble those of other animals by displaying the conventional 9-plus-2 pattern of fibers at their proximal ends.

Odor Psychology. Both good and bad odors exert remarkable psychological influence on our lives. Food appetites and personal performance can be whetted or dulled by the odors in the air we breathe.[45] Emotional effects of odors can also profoundly affect food sales.[40]

A pleasant feeling and salivary stimulation can result from inhaling food aromas. Consider for example: the fragrant essence of freshly picked tree-ripened oranges, apples, peaches, pears, or bananas; the yeasty aroma of homemade bread baking; the smell of beef roasting, corn popping, coffee percolating, cheese curing, hops brewing, or fudge cooling on a marble slab. These fragrances can cause us to recollect childhood smelling experiences and to reminisce. In contrast, the lachrymatory effects of peeled onions cause tears to flow; the sickening gassy smell of sour milk, spoiled meat or fermented fruits and vegetables turns the stomach and upsets the entire central nervous system.

Hazardous odors serve as a warning mechanism with the aid of our chemical senses.[7] Gas leaks are identified by means of the mercaptan stench that is added to natural-gas supplies. Burned fat and heavy smoke odors warn us of the formation of carcinogens (cancer producing chemicals) during improper charbroiling or smoking of meats, poultry or fish. The application of excessive heat to fat when frying potato chips or other foods causes the release of these same polynuclear hydrocarbons that the nose may detect.[24, 25] Hence, our chemical warning system protects us today as it did primitive man many thousands of years ago.

Odor transfer problems have plagued engineers for many years. Design engineering is needed to minimize problems of odor transfers in apartment buildings, refrigerators and food packages. Tests prove that fatty or oily materials are especially receptive to certain odors.[46] Butter or chocolate can be ruined by exposure to paint and varnish fumes. Or if butter is cut with a knife that hasn't been cleaned after being used on fish, onions, or garlic, the butter flavor may be spoiled. Within a refrigerator, butter should not be exposed to raw fish, smoked ham, onion, garlic, sauerkraut or limburger cheese volatiles. Chefs, on the other hand, sometimes use odor transfer advantageously. For example, they produce a lobster butter by incorporating cooked lobster essence into creamery butter.

Odor Analysis. Odor has been called the principal part of flavor. Consequently. the problem of odor analysis is being attacked with ever-increasing vigor by food scientists in all parts of the world. Taste analysis is comparatively simple -- the taste or non-volatile portions of flavor are fewer in number and occur naturally in foods at high enough concentrations to permit either direct chemical or microbiological analysis. Odor analysis is much more difficult. The odor or volatile parts of flavor are low in concentration to start with. And as the many individual components are separated for subsequent analysis, further reduction in sample size occurs. Accordingly sophisticated chemical and/or instrumental methods of analysis are being developed to cope with the situation. Some of these will be described later.

There is a growing awareness that determining what chemicals constitute an odor may be the simplest part of solving an odor problem. For, beyond this, it is essential to determine the relative concentrations of all the chemicals constituting the odor. Since it is not uncommon for a food odor to contain more than one or two hundred different chemicals at varying concentrations, the tasks of analyzing a particular food odor and then matching it by synthesis are apparently extremely difficult both chemically and mathematically speaking.

Even this concept of food odor analysis is oversimplified, however, for food is living matter that is in a constant state of flux. Fruit enzymes, for instance, are constantly forming esters from acids and alcohols present in the fruit. Meanwhile other enzymes are hydrolyzing esters to form alcohols and acids. Many other chemical changes are concomitantly occurring. These changes happen even while an apple, orange or banana is being eaten. Analysis showed that crushed fresh strawberries contain one part in 2 million of the alcohol hexene 2-ol, whereas none of this particular alcohol was present in the whole fresh fruit.[47] Mere crushing, a physical effect, thus changes the chemical nature of the strawberries and alters their flavor.

In applying modern research instruments to the study of flavor, scientists are continually discovering more complexity in the natural flavors of all foods, although there

139

are a few common-denominator type factors. Many of the same chemical compounds have been found in different foods at varying levels of concentration. Thus it has been established that there may be some qualitative chemical similarities accompanied by both qualitative and quantitative chemical differences between foods.[48]

Gas chromatographic methods for separating flavor volatiles are complex and expensive. It is safe to estimate that the rate of improvement in gas chromatographs during the past five years has been at least five times as great as the rate of change in automobile models. Constant development and refinement of gas chromatographs is still going on.

For example, the results of a gas chromatographic study of cooked chicken volatiles by Minor et al. was published in 1965.[49] A total of less than thirty peaks representing at least that many chemical entities was obtained on each of the chromatograms for breast and leg muscle using a packed column and temperature programming. During the two-year interim from the start of the study to the publication of the results, gas chromatographs equipped with electron capture detectors and capillary column fractionators resulted in the separation of about two hundred peaks indicative of that number of individual compounds in cooked chicken aroma. However, separation has proved to be much easier than the subsequent identification of the peaks, each of which may represent either one discrete entity or several chemical entities combined. In other words, the more peaks one separates by gas chromatography the more involved their identification may become.

Separating the volatiles is only the first step in analyzing a particular food odor. Samples of odorous materials injected into a gas chromatograph average about 1 or 2 milliliters of concentrated flavor volatiles. Fractionation - ideally - involves separation of this small amount of flavor compounds into one hundred or more discrete and minute component fractions. Subsequent identification of these fractions requires sensitive instruments. For example, a combination of the human nose, mass spectrometry, nuclear magnetic resonance, and infrared and ultraviolet spectrophotometry is being used by Day in studies on the analysis of cheese volatiles.[50]

As stated before, chemical methods of identification require much higher concentrations of food volatiles than one obtains by using gas chromatographic separations of odorous constituents. Accordingly, Hoff and Feit[51] devised an ingenious syringe technique for functional group analysis by microchemical methods followed by gas chromatography. Solubility classification, functional group analysis, derivative preparation, gas chromatography, and organoleptic (taste and odor) tests have been used in combination by Minor et al.[49] in making a series of studies on chicken flavor.[49 52 53] The uses and limitations of gas chromatography in flavor research have been reported by Burr.[54] Progress is being made in analysis of food odors by applying organoleptic tests, chemical tests, instrumentation and other physicochemical methods together with physiological studies.

Food flavor research is progressing on bread, wine, red meats, poultry, fish, milk, cultured dairy products, cheese, potato, onion, hops, peaches, pears and other fruits, coffee, and flavor potentiators such as monosodium glutamate and the sodium salts of the 5' nucleotides.[6]

Practical Use of Flavor Research Developments

For centuries we've relied on the addition of salt, sugar, spices, and wood smoke to the natural flavors that occur in foods. These additives lend savory richness to certain dishes. Soya sauce as a flavoring and monosodium glutamate as a seasoning and flavor potentiator have been developed in the Orient to make vegetable protein foods tolerable to a meat eater.

Soya sauce with vinegar and spices is the base for Worcestershire sauce. Prime quality soya sauce is made from wheat and soy beans by a slow fermentation process. MSG occurs naturally in wheat, meat, poultry and other foods, and since the early 1900's it has been manufactured by several methods.[55] Today it is being produced by microbiological or enzyme action from low cost sources.[58]

Vanilla bean extract is another flavoring of antique origin. Other extracts such as oil of wintergreen, spice oils, oleoresinous extracts from spices, and natural fruit extracts have also been used as food flavorings for decades. Hydrolyzed plant proteins from grain and yeast sources, and the sodium salts of the 5' nucleotides from Japan represent more recent developments that are being applied to complement or replace beef extract which is oftentimes expensive and in short supply.

A list totaling 1,023 flavoring ingredients was compiled recently.[57] We may wonder why so many flavoring materials - both synthetic and natural - are needed. But, let us consider one small facet of the total fruit flavor picture - strawberry flavor. Based on the annual consumption of strawberry flavoring (imitation) and the average annual production of strawberries in the United States, it has been calculated that the entire strawberry crop, if used only to provide a natural flavor extract, would yield only enough to satisfy the annual needs of a city the size of Pittsburgh. That would leave none for the rest of the United States. So synthetic flavorings are useful and necessary supplements to our natural fruit flavor supplies.

Fruit flavors have been worked on for several decades by organic chemists. Synthetic strawberry, raspberry and cherry flavors have been used in candies and gelatin desserts for three decades or longer. Recently it was stated in an article by Moncrieff that the best flavors are still the natural ones, although much progress has been achieved in the synthetic flavor field.[17] This advancement in synthetic flavors is partly due to the complete analysis (chromatographic and spectrographic) of complex mixtures of natural products: for example, raspberry flavoring constituents. One key advantage of these synthetics is their stability toward oxygen in the air.

Synthetic flavors today are better than ever before. Still we have not succeeded in duplicating even the simplest one of the true natural flavors. Qualitative and quantitative factors combine to magnify the problem to computer proportions and perhaps beyond that. As with infinity in mathematics, we may find that we can approach nature's flavor handiwork but never quite attain it. Thus, flavor chemistry may offer the food scientist a never-ending challenge.

It is easiest to synthesize imitations of fruit flavors. Vegetable flavors are harder, and butter and cheese flavors harder still to imitate, although biochemists are producing useful cheese essences. Most difficult of all flavors to simulate are those for meat, fish and poultry. Research on meat flavor began nearly two centuries ago when chemistry was in its infancy in Europe. At that time scientists had begun studying the chemical composition of meat extract.

Beef extract, hydrolyzed vegetable proteins,[58] casein digests, and yeast autolysate extracts are flavorings that have characteristic amino acid, peptide, protein, nucleotide, and "browning reaction"* flavors. Each hydrolyzed plant protein is different than the other; the protein source and the manufacturing process chosen are responsible for flavor differences. Yet these products are compatible or synergistic with one another and/or with certain meats or meat and vegetable mixtures. In short, these are meat and vegetable flavor synergists that work with meat flavor to enrich or supplement it. Occurring as by-products of glutamate manufactured from plant protein hydrolysates, they are related to monosodium glutamate as molasses is to sugar. In other words, they are the compounds present in the mother liquor from which MSG is isolated by chemically controlled crystallization.

Pure chemical compounds that are likewise synergistic with the flavorings described above, with meat, and with each other are MSG, DSG, and DSI.** Their primary function is to provide flavor enrichment by blending flavors synergistically and additively.[56,60,61,62] The secret of flavor development according to Sjostrom and Cairneross is "blended flavor."[5] Of all the condiments, however, meat extract provides the truest resemblance to the mouth satisfaction indigenous to freshly prepared meat stock. In fact, there is no flavor substitute that matches real meat taste and aroma.

* The "browning reaction" or "Maillard synthesis" occurs in foods when either amino acids, peptides, or proteins react with reducing sugars to form brown colored reaction products having individualistic flavors.

** DSG and DSI are abbreviations for the sodium slats of the 5' nucleotides, disodium guanylate, and disodium inosinate.

Meat Substitutes

Liebig's classical meat extract preparation and analysis was prompted by meat shortages in Europe resulting from the Napoleonic wars.[63] Today there are about 3.2 billion people on our planet with 550 million consuming over 90 percent of the world's meat supply.[64]

In the search for ways to close the ever-widening protein versus population gap, the Japanese have turned to fishing. A Frenchman, Champagnat,[65] has succeeded in producing protein from crude petroleum by developing strains of yeast that can subsist on petroleum hydrocarbons. A soy protein matrix perfected by Boyer[66] is flavored with beef-like, ham-like, bacon-like, and chicken-like flavors.[67] A Purdue research team has recently announced development of a Lysine-rich mutant strain of corn in their efforts to alleviate Kwashiorkor (protein deficiency disease) among infants in underfed countries.[68] Furthermore, lysine and most of the other essential amino acids* are now produced by synthesis or microbiologically. But in their present stages, none of these developments or any combination of them can go far toward alleviating protein shortages.

* Essential amino acids are those not synthesized by the body's enzymes that must be provided in the diet to maintain health.

Man improves the biological efficiency of grain proteins by feeding them to ruminants, thus converting them to animal protein of relatively high biological value. However, it takes 7 calories of plant carbohydrate to produce 1 calorie of beef protein and 3 1/2 calories of plant carbohydrate to produce 1 calorie of chicken protein. Meanwhile, the natural resource holding the most serious threat to our food supply and living standard is water.[69] About 330 gallons of water are required to provide enough wheat for one person to subsist on for one day; whereas 4200 gallons are needed to produce only one pound of beef.

We must look to the Orient for guidance in making practical substitutions of vegetables for meat and in flavoring these substitute foods. Bean sprouts produced from either soy or mung beans are highly nutritious and flavorful. Furthermore, the Chinese have discovered that a combination of green soybeans with Chinese cabbage provides a complete and balanced spectrum of the essential amino acids in adequate amounts to support growth and maintenance of the human body.

Flavor satisfaction is achieved by adding soya sauce, monosodium glutamate, and the sodium salts of the 5' nucleotides to the bland vegetables and rice that make up their main diet. For centuries the Japanese have used sea tangle for its glutamate effect and dried bonito for its nucleotide effect in seasoning their meals.[61]

It was reported by Ikeda that the principal flavor component of sea table extract is monosodium glutamate (MSG).[70, 71] Today most of the MSG is produced by direct fermentation processes. The world's supply, which was recently reported to be 150 million pounds per year valued at about $80 million, comes mainly from Japan.[72] Production in the United States is less than one-fourth of the total amount produced. When one considers that monosodium glutamate usage is at a level of one-tenth the concentration of salt used in food, and its use is restricted to protein foods, we begin to appreciate the impact of this Oriental seasoning on our American food habits. We're seasoning about 30 billion pounds of protein foods annually (about 150 lbs. per person per year) with MSG and the use is increasing.

The 5' nucleotides may also be used to flavor meat substitutes. Inosinic acid, an important 5' nucleotide, was first isolated from beef muscle in 1847 by Liebig, who named it after the Greek word meaning muscle.[61] This nucleic acid, upon neutralizing with mild alkali, yields the flavor nucleotide disodium inosinate (DSI). It is interesting to note that this flavor is a constituent of ribonucleic acid which is present in the muscle and brain of mammals and fish.

Ribonucleic acid (RNA) is present in every living cell. There are several types of RNA and one type transmits information within a cell. When RNA from the brains of trained rats was injected into the brains of untrained rats the latter responded immediately at the learning level of the trained rats. The precursor of RNA, desoxyribonucleic acid (DNA), is the key compound in genetic modification. Some day RNA may be used to determine human behavioral characteristics.[73]

Apparently then, there are key relationships between flavor and life. It is interesting to note that the compounds which contribute to life processes occurring in nature may also be isolated, purified, and neutralized to serve as food flavor potentiators.

First of all there is MSG, the monosodium salt of glutamic acid, which is a building block of protein and is the most widely occurring amino acid found in natural proteins. Next, there is the nucleotide disodium inosinate (DSI), which occurs in the RNA of muscle and may be derived directly from RNA by acid hydrolysis followed by neutralization with sodium hydroxide, or by enzyme action. DSI contributes an amazing synergistic action to the flavor accentuating powers of MSG and the hydrolyzed plant proteins. Disodium guanylate (DSG), another nucleotide, is derived from yeast cells and is about 20 times as effective as DSI, but in a little different manner.

The nucleotides are effective in seasoning protein foods at concentrations in the range of one-twentieth of the level of MSG or less. A blend of nucleotides consisting of 50% DIS and 50% DSG is being marketed in the United States. This product is imported from Japan and sells for $25 per pound - the price is dropping. At present its main use is to partially replace beef extract.* By modifying and improving hydrolyzed plant protein flavors, the nucleotides achieve a meatier connotation of flavor than is possible with MSG alone. Scientists have proved that inosinic acid, the precursor of the flavor nucleotide, is one of the major active ingredients in natural beef, chicken, and fish muscle, present in the non-volatile flavor fraction of cooked meat.

* A 100 lb. formula useful in replacing 50% of the beef extract in a flavor formulation contains: 2 lbs. nucleotide blend (50% DIS and 50% DSG), 48 lbs. yeast extract, 48 lbs. glucose, and 2 lbs. caramel.

As Borgstrom says,[64] we live on a hungry planet where the protein gap may soon challenge our existence. He warns that complacency will spell our doom. Perhaps this is true, but man's mind has unlocked many God-given secrets, and more will be discovered. Studies of the organic chemicals in sea water may reveal untapped nutritional wealth.[74] Fertilizers offer quick results for more food.[75] A sensible solution to the fresh water problem has been suggested by Maxwell.[69] According to Dr. Robert H. Burris,[76] nitrogen fixation is a key biochemical process for feeding the hungry planet. A leader in the development of synthetic rubber, Dr. Archibald T. McPherson of the Institute for Applied Technology, National Bureau of Standards, believes that proteins, amino acids and vitamins can be produced synthetically to ease the world's growing problem of hunger.[77]

Scientific research and development may one day close the protein gap by applying known biochemical principles to the conversion of air, water, and carbohydrate or carbon to protein. This kind of protein when available will have to be modified in texture, appearance, taste and aroma. For unless the synthetic product is acceptable in both nutrition and flavor, it will not be eaten.

Our flavor heritage and the current pace of flavor research augur well for the future. Flavor chemistry activity in the field of food science is destined to increase several-fold within the next two or three decades. Scientists will press on toward the seemingly infinite goal of matching natural flavors with synthetic or enzyme produced replacements as the protein gap is being closed.

Research effort in diverse fields of science may one day result in food production capabilities that will cope with the emergencies created by burgeoning population pressures. Nutrition and flavor together will then triumph over world hunger when a balance between birth-rate and death-rate on this planet is made to conform with man's total resources and his food production capabilities.

Literature Cited

1. Caul, J.F. 1958. Food acceptance, in *Encyclopedia of Chemistry* (Supplement). Reinhold Publishing Corp., New York, pp 130-33.

2. Hutchings, I. J. 1961. An introductory thought for food, *Stanford Research Institute Journal*. 5:2-3.

3. Newell, Gordon W. 1961. *Future trends in American diet. Ibid.* 5:30-36.

4. Kazeniac, S. J. 1961. Chicken flavor, in *Proceedings Flavor Chemistry Symposium-1961.* Campbell Soup Company. Camden, New Jersey. pp. 37-56.

5. Sjostrom, L. B. and S. E. Cairncross. 1950. Flavor profiles - a new approach to flavor problems. *Food Technology.* 8:308.

6. Moncrieff, R. W. 1965. Introduction to the symposium. *Symposium on Foods: the Chemistry and Physiology of Flavors.* Meeting held at Dept. of Food Science and Technology, Oregon State University. Corvallis, Oregon, September 8-10. Sponsored by the National Institutes of Health. Proceedings to be published by the AVI Publishing Company, Inc., Westport, Connecticut.

7. Moncrieff, R. W. 1944. *The Chemical Senses.* John Wiley and Sons, Inc., New York.

8. Beidler, L.M. 1958. The physiological basis of taste in *Flavor Research and Food Acceptance.* Arthur D. Little Inc., Reinhold Publishing Corp., New York. pp. 3-28.

9. Langley, L. L. and E. Cheraskin, 1951. *The physiological foundation of dental practice.* C. V. Mosby Co., St. Louis.

10. Kramer, A. 1964, Definition of texture and its measurement in vegetables products. Food *Technology.* 18(3): 46-49.
11. Smith, A., A. Farman and J. Davies. 1965. Absence of taste-bud papillae in familiam dysautonomia. *Science,* 146:1040-1.
12. Barthel, Joan, 1966. Quando Manducamus. *Status.* 2(1):47-50.
13. Moncrieff, R.W. 1950. The salt taste. *Perfumery Essential Oil Record.* 41:367-71.
14. Moncrieff, R.W. 1950. The sour taste. Ibid. 415-19.
15. Moncrieff, R.W. 1951. The sweet taste. Ibid. 42:25-30.
16. Moncrieff, R.W. 1952. The bitter taste. Ibid. 51-5.
17. Moncrieff, R.W. 1955. Taste, smell and molecular weight. *Chemical Products.* 18:131-3.
18. Von Bekesy, G. 1964. Duplexity theory of taste. *Science.* 145:834-5.
19. Farbman, A. I. 1965. Structure of chemoreceptors. *Symposium on Foods: the Chemistry and Physiology of Flavors.* Meeting. Oregon State U. Sept. 8-10.
20. Crocker, E. C. 1945. *Flavor.* McGraw-Hill, New York. p 7.
21. Henning, H. 1924. *Der Geruch,* Barth, Leipzig.
22. Beebe-Center, J. G. and D. Waddell, 1948. A general psychology of taste. *Journal of Psychology.* 26:517.
23. Escoffier, August. 1941. *The Escoffier Cook Book.* Crown Publishing Co., New York.
24. Lijinsky, W. and P. Shubik. 1964. Benzo (aopyrene) and other polynuclear hydrocarbons in charcoal-broiled meat. *Science.* 145:53-55.
25. Anonymous. 1959. "Charcoal-flavored" steaks without charcoal present - a real menace to consumers' health. *Consumer Bulletin.* 42(4):24-26.
26. Brew, W.B., J.B. Dore, J.H. Benedict, G.C. Potter and E. Sipos, 1959. Characterization of unidentified compound producing edema in chicks. *Journal of the Association of Official Agricultural Chemists.* 42:120.
27. Meyer, Lillian Hoagland, 1960. *Food Chemistry.* Reinhold Publishing Corp., New York. p. 160.
28. Caul, J.F. 1957. The profile method of analysis, in *Advances in Food Research.* 7:1-40.
29. Rietz, Carl A. and Jeremiah J. Wanderstock. 1965. *A Guide to the Selection, Combination, and Cooking of Foods.* The AVI Publishing Co., Inc. Westport, Conn.
30. Kramer, Amihud and Bernard A. Twigg. 1962. *Fundamentals of Quality Control for the Food Industry.* The AVI Publishing Co., Westport, Conn. pp 105-36.
31. Association of Official Agricultural Chemists. 1960. *Official Methods of Analysis of the Association of Official Agricultural Chemists.* Washington, D.C.
32. Kramer, A. 1965. The effective use of operations of research and EVOP in quality control. *Food Technology.* 19(1) 37-39.
33. Sharon, Irving M. 1965. Sensory properties of food and their function during feeding. Ibid. 35-6.

34. Janowitz, H.D., F. Hollander, D. Orringer, M.H. Levy, A. Winkelstein, R. Kaufman, and S.G. Margolin, 1950. A quantitative study of the gastric secretory response to sham feeding in a human subject. *Gastroenterology.* 16:104.

35. Von Frisch, Karl. 1964. Smell, sex, and survival in animals. Science *Digest.* 53:65-72.

36. Deving, K.B. 1965. Physiological basis of odor. *Symposium on Foods: The Chemistry and Physiology of Flavors.* Meeting. Oregon State U. Sept. 8-10.

37. Gesteland, R.C. and J.Y. Lettvin. 1964. Smell governed by electrical process. *Science News Letter.* 86:328.

38. Amoore, J.E. 1952. Stereochemical specificities of human olfactory receptors. *Perfumery Essential Oil Record.* 43:321-23.

39. Amoore, John E., James W. Johnston, Jr., and Martin Rubin. 1964. The stereochemical theory of odor. *Scientific American.* 210(2):42-49.

40. Hicks, Clifford B. 1965. Your mysterious nose. *Today's Health.* October: 35.

41. Moncrieff, R.W. 1949. A new theory of odor. *Perfumery Essential Oil Record.* 40:279-85.

42. Moncrieff, R.W. 1957. Stimulus for smell. *Perfumery Essential Oil Record.* 48:34-58.

43. Moncrieff, R.W. 1961. An instrument for classifying odors. *Journal of Applied Physiology.* 16:742-49.

44. Honeywell. 1965. An investigation of the sense of smell through examination of individual olfactory cells. *Scientific American.* 213(6):1.

45. Laird, Donald A. and Eleanor C. Laird. 1961. *The Dynamics of Personal Efficiency.* Harper & Brothers Publication, New York. pp 81-85.

46. McKinley, Russell W. 1958. Odor- and taste-transfer testing, in *Flavor Research and Food Acceptance.* Reinhold Publishing Co. New York. pp 94-96.

47. Moncrieff, R.W. 1964. Progress and problems in flavors, *Manufacturing Chemist.* 35(9):63-5.

48. Hornstein, Irwin. 1965. Flavor of red meats. *Symposium on Foods: The Chemistry and Physiology of Flavors.* Meeting. Oregon State U. Sept. 8-10.

49. Minor, L.J., A.M. Pearson, L.E. Dawson, and B.S. Schweigert. 1965. Chicken flavor: the identification of some chemical components and the importance of sulfur compounds in the volatile fraction. *Journal of Food Science.* 30(4):686-96.

50. Day, E.A. 1965. Flavor of cheese. *Symposium on Foods: The Chemistry and Physiology of Flavors.* Meeting, Oregon State U. Sept. 8-10.

51. Hoff, J.D. and E.D. Feit. 1963. Functional group analysis in gas chromatography with the syringe reaction technique. *Analytical Chemistry.* 5:1298.

52. Minor, L.J., A.M. Pearson, L.E. Dawson and B.S. Schweigert. 1964. Gas chromatographic analysis of volatile constituents from cooked carcasses of old and young chickens. *Poultry Science.* 44(2):535-43.

53. Minor, L.J., A.M. Pearson, L.E. Dawson and B.S. Schweigert, 1965. Separation and identification of carbonyl and sulfur compounds in the volatile fraction of cooked chicken. *Journal of Agricultural and Food Chemistry.* *13:298*-300.

54.   Burr, H.K. 1964. Gas chromatography in flavor research. *Food Technology.* 18(12):60-62.

55.   Marshall, A.E. 1948. History of glutamate manufacture. *Symposium on Monosodium Glutamate.* 1:4-14.

56.   Kuminaka, Akira. 1965. Flavor potentiators. *Symposium on Foods: The Chemistry and Physiology of Flavors.* Meeting, Oregon State University. Sept. 8-10.

57.   Hall, Richard L. and Bernard L. Oser. 1965. Recent progress in the consideration of flavoring ingredients under the food additives amendment. III. Gras Substances. *Food Technology. 19*(2) part 2:151-97.

58.   Hall, L.A. 1948. Protein hydrolysates as a source of glutamate flavors. *Symposium on Monosodium Glutamate.* 1:53-61.

59.   Caul, J.F. and S.A. Raymond. 1964. Home-use test by consumers of the flavor effects of disodium inosinate in dried soups. *Food Technology.* 18(3):95-99.

60.   Toi, B., S. Maeda, S. Ikeda and H. Furnkawa. 1963. Flavoring and preparation thereof. U.S. Pat. No. 3, 109, 741.

61.   Kuninaka, A., M. Kibi, and K. Sakaguchi. 1964. History and development of flavor nucleotides. *Food Technology.* 13(3):29-35.

62.   Kurtzman, C.H. and L.B. Sjostrom. 1963. The flavor modifying properties of disodium inosinate. Program 23rd Annual Meeting of Institute of Food Technologists. Paper 110.

63.   Liebig, J. 1847. Ober die Bestandtheile der Flossigkeiten des Fleisches. *Annalen der Chemie and Pharmacic.* 62:257.

64.   Borgstrom, Georg. 1965. *The Hungry Planet.* The Macmillan Company, New York.

65.   Champagnat, Albert. 1965. Protein from petroleum. *Scientific American.* 213(4):13-17.

66.   Boyer, Robert A. 1956. Method of preparing imitation meat products (pH control). U.S. Pat. No. 2,730,448.

67.   Minor, L.J., L.E. Dawson and A.M. Pearson. 1964. Flavor its factors and significance. *Poultry Meat.* 12:26-32.

68.   Anonymous. 1965. In brief. *The Sciences (New York Academy of Sciences)* .5(40):27.

69.   Maxwell, John C. 1965. Will there be enough water? *American Scientist.* 53(1):97-104.

70.   Ikeda, Kikunae. 1908. Japanese Patent 14805.

71.   Ikeda, Kikunae. 1909. On a new seasoning. *Journal Tokyo Chemical Society.* 30:820.

72.   Nagle, J.J. 1965. Big gains are made by food seasoning. *New York Sunday Times -* Market Section - Sunday Nov. 10. p 9, col. 4.

73.   Byerrum, R.U. 1965. The Scientific revolution. Address given to graduate students, College of Natural Science, Michigan State U., Sept. 29. pp 5-7.

74.   Wangersky, P.J. 1965. The organic chemistry of sea water. *American Scientist.* 53(3):357-74.

75.   Pratt, Christopher J. 1965. Chemical fertilizers. *Scientific American.* 212(6):62-76.

76.   Burris, Robert H. 1965. Snatch nitrogen from air. *Science News Letter.* 87:68.

77.   Misc. & Savory. 1965. Synthetic foods forecast from coal, gas, petroleum. *Food Technology*. 19(1):60.

Chapter 19

Helping Students, Again

A Les Gourmet Dinner   **Harry Friedman**   **A Grand Affair**

On Being Evasive
(Irish Humor by Hal Roach)

The Irish people's middle name is evasive. Murphy got a new car and Casey borrowed it to go to the dance. He did not get back until two o'clock in the morning and Murphy said:

> "How did it go?"

He said:

> "Oh, we had a great time. We had a little trouble with the car as we got some water in the carburetor."

Murphy said:

> "Well, where is my car?"

Casey said:

> "In the river."

Scout Motto

Be prepared!

Scout Pledge

On my honor, I'll do my best to
    help other people at all times,
    to obey the Scout Law,
    and keep myself physically strong,
    mentally awake, and morally straight.

A Les Gourmet Dinner

One afternoon while I was in my office at Kellogg Center on the campus of Michigan State University (I had offices there and also at Eppley Center), Bill Stafford came to see me. He had charge of the annual Les Gourmet dinner put on by the students to show alumni and backers how proficient they were in foodservice.

Since the school was always on display on these annual occasions, and the dinners were held at Kellogg Center, the reputations of both places were on the line. This year, however, the dinner was to be held at the International Center since the students decided to do a Thailand meal. This was to include the ambiance of dining in Thailand. The decor and recipes must both be truly representative of Thai dining.

As usual, I called Tom Ryan and told him the situation. Tom said, "I will contact Helen Recknagle and hear what she recommends." He called back and said: "Two of Cornell's friends and benefactors of the School of Hotel Administration (SHA), Harry Friedman and his wife, Dottie, have menus and costumes and cookware from all over the world. They have just returned from Thailand after a six month trip there. Call him and seek his support." His business address was Miami, Florida, and he had his office in his home there right on the bay and the water.

Harry Friedman

Upon calling him, I introduced myself as follows: "This is Dr. Minor at the Hotel School at Michigan State University. Our students want to use Thailand as the theme for their annual Les Gourmet dinner this year. They know nothing about where they can obtain authentic menus, dress, and decor for the dinner."

Friedman was all business. He said, "I've helped Cornell put on some of their Ezra Cornell Weekend dinners and have given donations for their students' benefit. I would have to visit with your students beforehand to discuss our plans." The time for the dinner was March, 1966.

Friedman arrived on schedule, met with the student committee, and made his plans with them. Harry said, "I promised to do this for you and we will proceed with our plans. You see I brought Dottie with me, as promised, and we will make the costumes and take care of the decor for the students."

We had rooms for them reserved at the Kellogg Center when they arrived Monday to prepare for the Thai dinner to be served Saturday night at the International Center. Harry said, "We need elephant tusks for an entrance portal. Can your props department furnish these?" They could not, so we found a plastics company in the phone directory, called them, and visited the manager.

Harry explained how these were to be fabricated from Styrofoam. Then he sketched a free-hand pattern of them and their 7' lengths. The L. J. Minor Corporation bought them,

151

and after the dinner we shipped them to our plant on West 115th Street in Cleveland. They were never used again and eventually we discarded them.

The next thing Harry wanted was some decorations that could be fastened to the tusks. We went downtown for these, and as good fortune would have it, we spotted a Thai woman figure in the window of Cardy's Jewelry Store. It had costume jewelry hanging from its multiple arms. Harry and I asked the manager if it could be borrowed for the dinner. We guaranteed to return it "as-is." A courtesy card with their store's name on it would be furnished. After some hesitation, the manager told us we could take it.

Next, Harry needed some low stands for flower vases and plume-type long-stem artificial flowers for each side of the elephant tusk entrance-arch. These he made up himself of wood, with a shellac coating and red, yellow, green, and black enamel hand-painted Thai-style decoration. Harry painted these himself. His sleeves were not rolled-up because he was wearing short sleeves. Harry was a real trooper, moving fast as he walked, and not concerned that he was in snow up to his ankles. He wore no rubbers, but charged ahead like a moose with a purpose.

He had purchased some round trip air tickets for the student committee to visit Miami following the dinner. He wanted them to see the hotel kitchens he had installed, the dining rooms he had developed unique "ambiance's" for, and how he had accomplished these things in his small home office with the support and help of his beautiful wife, Dottie. Unfortunately, only two of the six committee members were able to make the trip, including the cook, Don Weaving, and Christine Prager, who helped Dottie make the servers' costumes.

Like a Hollywood movie director, Harry knew exactly what he wanted to do, and pulled out all of the stops to get it done. He called Cres-Cor, Crescent Metal Products, Cleveland, and ordered several large stainless steel hot and cold holding cabinets he wanted for serving "hors d'oeuvres and desserts." He also requested them to send four men to take care of the service to guests. We arranged for MSU's Food Stores to receive the shipment from Cres-Cor and truck the equipment to the International Center when it arrived.

Harry proceeded to do everything he promised and planned to do and kept all of his promises. He was a tall man, about 6'3" and he walked with his head forward like a football fullback going into a line behind blockers.

Harry had tremendous confidence in his personal knowledge and value. His motivation and concentration were obvious. He was a charger, and always moved forward. Bill Stafford worked with him and got other students, besides those on the committee, to help him and Dottie.

The students had a rich learning experience as Harry and Dottie were both geniuses. With all of the information Harry and Dottie gathered from all over the world, it was easy for them to create the desired effect.

A Grand Affair

The day of the affair, Harry worked swiftly with deft fingers putting butterflies, green beetles, flowers, and leaves on the elephant tusks. Then he had a student help him string the yellow crepe-paper ribbon he used as part of the decor. The Thai artifact we obtained from Cardy's Jewelers was set on a decorated display table, surrounded by flowers, with its multiple arms festooned with costume jewelry.

Harry and Dottie had the dining room decorated and the waiters in Thai-style jackets as the 600 guests started arriving. George E., the son of George T. Baggott, the owner of Crescent Metal Products, was in charge of the four men who helped serve hors d'oeuvres and desserts to the guests.

Henry Barbour arrived with an entourage of special guests he had invited to the dinner. I felt that Henry never gave Harry the credit due to him, yet Harry and Dottie were pleased with the job they had done and the affair turned out successfully.

With the event over, it brought home to me the naiveté of the students and the need for better guidance and counseling by their teachers before letting them plan these dinners on their own.

Certainly, a dinner menu must be compatible with what the kitchen equipment and staff is able to produce for a sitting of several hundred guests. Hot soup, for example, is difficult to keep hot when serving a lot of guests. To do this, more waiters, serving stations, and temperature control are needed than for Gazpacho or cold Vichyssoise. Steak, served correctly, is impossible to prepare and serve to 600 guests all at the same time.

Time has to be carefully controlled so that everyone can be served on schedule. Otherwise, the meal will be strung out for four hours. I have seen it happen even when professional chefs, who know better, make the mistake of estimating that they can overcome the limitations of the kitchen and the cooks and salad people. When this happens, the patrons who pay for the dining experience may not complain, but they never return. You lose the guest's respect and good will and never recapture the lost reputation. Word about "faux pas" of this sort spreads like wildfire to other clients.

Henry Barbour, when I challenged him concerning the students' capabilities and experience needed to plan the Les Gourmet dinners, said, "When I was at Cornell, after being an Army cook, we did a good job with the Ezra Cornell dinners. We students did it all ourselves without faculty help or the advice of a professional chef."

Tom Ryan would attend these dinners in order to present the "Senior of the Year" check from the L. J. Minor Corporation. After some were over, he would go to Bill Knapp's for an edible meal. Then he would pour this on me saying, "Are the Hotel School people crazy? Don't they know that when they sell a poor dinner to people who are well-traveled and knowledgeable about what good cuisine has to be, that the Hotel School name is 'mud?' Then when it is held at Kellogg Center, it is a reflection on their reputation, too."

Finally, when Robert Bloomstrom became Director of the School, he authorized my suggestion to have the students meet with one of the L. J. Minor chefs -- it was usually

George Marchand -- to plan the Les Gourmet dinner each year. This produced the desired results. The students' knowledge increased, and the customers' opinions of the Hotel School and Kellogg Center improved. We needed the chef to supervise these dinners and teach the students and I knew that the L. J. Minor Corporation was again helping students!

Chapter 20

A Meeting of Minds

The "Hospitality Business"   At the Farm   Chefs and Their Art

Quote from Julian Bond

"I rest best when my mind and body are busy."

Family Celebration
(Irish Humor by Hal Roach)

When they have a wake in the Conamara Mountains, what they do is lay the corpse out on the kitchen table, on a satin sheet, with a satin pillow on it. Such a man laying there is O'Shaunessy. While the wake is going on in the parlor, Murphy and Casey are with the corpse out in the kitchen. All at once, the legs to the kitchen table break and O'Shaunessy goes rolling on the floor. So Casey says:

"What are we going to do now?"

Murphy says:

"I have an idea."

He says:

"We'll put a chair under his head, We'll put another under his feet, and We'll put one in the middle and level him up."

Casey says:

"It is a good idea!"

Murphy says:

"Leave it to me. I'll get the chairs."

So he goes in the room where they are having the wake and he says:

"Can I have three chairs for the corpse?"

Everybody stands up and yells:

"Hip, Hip, Hoo-ray! !"

The "Hospitality Business"

There's a lot to learn about the "Hospitality" business. Harry Friedman said to me, "Minor, don't just be a manufacturer serving the foodservice field. Get yourself immersed in the entire picture. Learn about foodservice machinery, appliances, serving and holding cabinets. Understand ovens of all kinds, including convection, microwave, gas and electric ranges, and baking ovens.

Know pastry and confectionery equipment. Know about aluminum, stainless steel and copper bottom utensils including pots, frying pans, kettles, with Teflon and Silverstone. Know about mixers and blenders and microwave cookware. Lenox China, Wedgewood China from England and Lemoge China from France, glazed pottery having approval of the American Pottery Association that prohibits use of poisonous glazes. Know about glassware from Owens Corning, Waterford, Cavan and Belleek from Ireland, and other varieties from Italy, Czechoslovakia, France, Poland, and other nations. Know about silverware from Oneida, Community and William Rogers. Also Sheffield from England, Solygen from Germany, and other countries including France, Italy, and Czechoslovakia. Know about table linens from England, Ireland, the Philippines, Guatemala, China, Switzerland, France, and Germany."

Harry said, "You must also know all about wines, liquors, and liqueurs." This led me to the teaching of my "Beverage Class," and invitations to Grossman, author of the best selling book on wine and spirits, Harry Green of Seagram's, and to the Budweiser people to lecture to our students. I also invited speakers from Wearever Aluminum, the makers of Silverstone and Revere Ware. In addition, I had speakers from Wyandotte Chemical Company and Economic Laboratories of St. Paul, Minnesota to lecture on laundry, dish, and glassware detergents. There was a lot for me and my students to learn.

In the meantime, everyone seemed anxious to have our venture succeed. Once a customer used the Minor Food Bases, they would reorder. Our accounts receivable were nearly always paid up. Our sales reps were good collectors. Tom saw to that.

A solid foundation was forming for us within the hospitality business. We had more chefs working with us than any other company. The leading hospitality schools were on our side including Cornell and Michigan State University, the Culinary Institute of America, Johnson & Wales University, Chadsey High School in Detroit, Washburn Institute in

Chicago, Sullivan County Community College in New York, and Paul Smith College, also in New York. The American Culinary Federation was behind us, too.

Jack Sullivan, a pugnacious Irish American chef at Disneyland in Anaheim, California, was the chef impresario at the National Restaurant Show for many years. He had a cadre of chefs ice carving, decorating, and cooking in conjunction with the annual Culinary Art Exhibition. His efforts gave valuable publicity for the culinary profession. We met him and soon Tom had Jack's wife for a sales agent in California.

This would happen again and again. Then Mrs. Minor and I would become friends with our salespeople and our big family of quality relationships would grow and grow. In the case of Mrs. Sullivan, she came from the Orient, we became good friends and she gave Mrs. Minor dolls for her collection

At the Farm

When we moved from Cleveland to Lansing, because I was teaching at Michigan State, Tom Ryan brought our chefs Jean Caubet, John Secter, Otto Denkinger, Harry Bazaan, Herman Breithaupt, Michael Palmer, Pierre Bach, and Ernest Koves to the remodeled and enlarged Angell Centennial Farmhouse that was our new home.

Our eight-year-old daughter, Rosalie, mingled with the chefs during a meeting break and afterwards came to her mother and said, "Each one of the chefs thinks that he's the greatest." My father, who worked for the Ford Motor Company for forty years and was now selling our bases in Detroit and Miami, heard this comment as well.

Also present at the meeting were Tom Ryan and Eric Swanson, co-founder of Delsoy Whipped Topping and our Detroit distributor. Eric had been brought up in the dairy industry in Chicago. When he met Bob Smith, the chemist who developed soybean product for Henry Ford, they formed Delsoy together. He announced that he was leaving Delsoy and becoming a partner with Jean Caubet. Jean had Wayne County and Eric had Oakland County and outstate Michigan.

Eric told me when I first met him, "Remember this: it's not how much profit you make that counts in business, it's how much you can save on taxes." The government was taking fifty cents of every dollar we earned. That was the Federal government, economic stats but we also paid city, county and regional taxes, withholding for our employees, social security and workman's compensation to the state, plus unemployment tax. Eric was right and he saw a great opportunity in selling our bases.

When he learned that Herman Breithaupt had cooked in hotels in Iowa, Minnesota, Wisconsin, and Illinois, he envisioned a franchise that he could develop for him, his wife, Hazel, and his son, David. We told him to go ahead. We needed distributors in all these states. Eric paid Breithaupt to go with him and put on demos for customers and distributor's salespeople.

Eric heard that Colonel Sanders was looking for someone to make gravy for his chicken. Later, Tom and I went to Louisville, met the Colonel, and made gravy with him in his own kitchen. Unfortunately, his grandson did not support the Colonel when telling me, "What he does to every one of his suppliers is this. He gets them coming his way, then demands a better price." I was to learn that truth the hard way.

The Colonel's gravy exemplified one of Tom's favorite statements, "It's the sizzle that sells the steak." What the Colonel used to make as gravy was what he called "cracklings." Cracklings consisted of the burned breading that went to the bottom of the fryer as the breaded chicken cooked. He would cook this 'carcinogenic' substance with flour and water. The thickened mixture was the Colonel's gravy.

What he wanted us to make for him was a fluid gravy in cans printed with his face on them in red and white. To produce this gravy we needed a new piece of equipment, namely, a horizontal mixer heated on the bottom of the mixing bowl with gas jets. A special extra-soft wheat flour was needed for this. Tom located an Ohio flour mill that could provide the kind we needed. The formula was flour, water, and cooking oil. This made a nice gravy.

We needed a can sealer for the cans. We were supplied with 30,000 lithographed cans. Colonel Sanders' Kentucky Fried Chicken unit in Indianapolis was the Colonel's test store. The manager liked the product. We didn't because we were selling it at a break-even figure with no profit.

When the Colonel asked for a lower price we refused the business. Tom made a deal with the Colonel to use up the remaining cans. That ended this venture. However, it got us into the "gravy-prep" business under the Minor label. We developed Minor's Chicken Supreme Sauce. This was ideal for cream-style restaurant dishes. One of our best customers reported it to be the best product we had. We also made chicken, beef, turkey and pork gravy preps, pea soup with ham, and clam chowder. So, again, as Tom often said, "Things that seem bad at the time often turn out for the best."

Another blessing from God came to us quite unexpectedly. Just when we had split with Colonel Sanders and started making our own gravy preps and dry soup preps, I came across an interesting patent on a flour toaster that employed a vacuum. Bob Cocroft, with whom I had worked in Rossford, Ohio, at International Mineral and Chemicals Company, went into business publishing Food Abstracts. We subscribed to these. It was in one of them that I discovered this patent. The patentee was located in Cincinnati. When I told Tom about this, he became fascinated and contacted the old German engineer named Frondorf.

Tom arranged for us to meet with him and his wife at a Catholic hospital where he had been employed as boiler and maintenance engineer for many years. He and his wife used his toaster-oven for producing toasted flour under their own brand label. We made a deal with him to install a machine for us at our 115th Street plant. It worked well after we combined it with a flour sifter of the kind we used at the Huron Milling Company. Later on, Tom brought him back to construct and install a larger one, called Big Tom, at the West 25th Street plant. Tom said, "We had better get him to do it before he dies."

158

This machine together with the special soft flour from the Ohio Flour Mill enabled us to produce a beautiful Chicken Supreme Sauce, Roux, gravies, and dry soup preps. Knowing the hazards of flour processing by witnessing explosions while with Huron, I purchased a separate building with a blow-out front. Huron used corrugated galvanized sheet metal walls that blow out whenever an explosion occurred. We had the machines grounded and fortunately avoided an explosion by using brass utensils that were spark-free. We did not toast the flour to a hazelnut brown color, but instead made it match a canary yellow color standard.

We kept records of every batch of gravy prep produced on dated quality control cards. Tests on flavor, color, salt, viscosity, solubility, appearance, and microbiology, and other tests were done as needed. Samples of batches were labeled and held for six months under refrigeration so we could check on any complaint or claim made. Since meat, poultry, seafood, and fish were blended into the bases together with juices and bone stock, refrigeration was required upon receipt of the bases by distributors or bulk users. We shipped by common carrier, non-refrigerated by necessity, shipments were nearly all LTL (less than truckload). We did have shipments to West Coast Warehouses that were sent in refrigerated trucks.

Getting back to the subject of the meeting with the L. J. Minor chefs at the farm: Eric Swanson and others were sharing their experiences that they'd had selling and developing new uses for Minor Food Bases.

Jean Caubet was first. Jean said, "I come from the Pyrenees Mountains of France that are close to Spain. After apprenticing at age 14 to a small restaurateur, I worked in some of the best restaurants and hotels in France. Then I went to Canada first, and then to Detroit where I opened the Book Cadillac Hotel. After World War II, I was head chef during the Depression at the Detroit City Club. That's where I learned, from listening to the members talk, how to make money in the stock market. Those who made the most bought low and sold high, but not at the peak, they would sell before the peak was reached, then after that the stock went down. Doing this with Chrysler stock I was able to buy three houses and make three trips to France with my wife, Claire, and my daughters Claudette, and Irene. When I retired from being a full-time chef, I joined George Rommel Catering Company, and put on parties for him, but this was part-time."

He continued, "Now, I am a salesperson, for the first time, for the L. J. Minor Corporation. We work together building the business in Detroit and out-state Michigan at the resorts up north. We are getting lots of distributors. They want the Minor Bases because we sell them to their customers who are using other kinds. I am still with George Rommel, and I use a lot of Minor Consommé, Chicken and Beef Bases at these parties. Now, your Dad and Eric Swanson are with me. Our sales are good and will improve as we get more distributors. No one gets an exclusive right to be a Master Distributor over the others, but some have asked for this."

Jean and I made calls together in Northern Michigan and we opened a distributor in Charlevoix. Jean's meat distributor, Stanny-Morris-Livingston, gave us a list of their accounts in this vacationland and we were calling on every one of them. One night we shared a bed and room at Dam Site Inn to save the $6.00 an additional room would have cost us.

John Secter said, "I am a French Chef. I come from a village located near Lyons, France. I became an apprentice at age 14 to a very good French chef. When I came to the United States, I became head chef at the Baltimore and Ohio, or so-called "Chessie" railroad. They owned the famous Greenbrier Resort at White Sulphur Springs, West Virginia. That's where I was for several years. Then I had my own restaurant in Cincinnati until I retired, and became a consultant. Tom Ryan asked me to sell food bases, and I enjoy demonstrating the product that Dr. Minor has developed for the chefs. They make the kitchen work so much easier for them. I enjoy the trips I make alone or the visits to Cornell and Michigan State with other chefs. It is the life for me now." Tom always used John Secter for demos, shows, and workshops with Brother Herman in Canada.

Otto Denkinger said, "I came to this country from Cologne, Germany, where I was an apprentice to a chef when I was fourteen. My wife and I love Seattle where I run the Yacht Club. Whenever the board changes managers, they ask me who I think they should hire. My son is with Northwest Airlines and I can get passes to Alaska and Hawaii where I am also introducing our bases. Then, too, I sell to the U. S. Army base in Tacoma."

Otto Denkinger is a great personality. He is endowed with great vigor, energy, and enthusiasm. His wife is quite a business woman in her own right. They both drive Mercedes sedans. Otto was his own distributor.

Our price list was based on 20% off for the distributor, then 10% for the salesperson, and 5% for sales promotion. This totals 35%. Terms were 2% 10 days - net 11, and all freight was prepaid. This meant that we paid considerably more for shipping to the West Coast. But Otto was getting 33% on his sales, compared to 13% for the chefs who worked with distributors. That was the 10% sales and 5% sales promotion or advertising allotment. This also did not preclude Otto from getting other distributors with the 13% sales commission.

Harry Bazaan said, "I am living, working, using, and selling Minor Bases in Orange County and Disneyland Park. The Orange County American Culinary Federation (ACF) Chapter has just named me their Chef of the Year."

Herman Breithaupt said, "I was born in Alsace Lorraine at a town located on the banks of the Rhine, and right on the German border. I started Chadsey High's Commercial Foods Department 40 years ago with nothing but an idea and a two-cent stamp. I used it to send my idea to the Detroit School Board who accepted my appeal for a cooking school. We have over 100 students in cooking, baking, and meat-cutting classes. Dr. Minor's son, Bryan, graduated summa cum laude. Students take their regular high school classes besides those taught in our department. Bryan was also in ROTC, and worked for me one summer at our resort on Walloon Lake."

Michael Palmer said, "After retiring from Proctor and Gamble's Technical Sales

Department last year, I joined the L. J. Minor Corporation. I hope to be helpful by continuing to make demonstrations to schools as I have for the past 25 years."

Pierre Bach said, "Jean Caubet and I have been friends since we were boys in the same town. He sent me Minor's chicken and beef to try. Dr. Minor's parents visited me at the Americana Hotel in Miami. I told them I wanted their son to become King of the Bases.

Ernest Koves said, "I am Food Editor for the *Culinary Review,* the approved ACF Journal, and we have their seal of approval for our bases. No other company has that. The quality is the reason. I came from Budapest, Hungary, and have worked in many of New York City's greatest hotels, including the Astor. We had 200 men in white in the kitchen. I joined Minor's after testing the bases for six months. They are very good, and I believe in them. However, my expenses run high for everything I do in New York City."

During the New York World's Fair a fortuitous event took place. Of the three apartments Koves owned, the first floor unit was vacated. Tom told him the company wanted to rent it so that employees, guests, and customers could use it. Our daughter, Carol, stayed there when she attended the Fair in 1966.

To cap the meeting, we made plans to have Tom Ryan, John Secter, Emil Burgermeister, George Marchand, Herman Breithaupt, and Ernest Koves attend the 1968 Culinary Olympics in Frankfurt, Germany. This would be the first of several for us. We were just learning by observing on this first visit to the German sponsored event, "The International Kochung Ausstellung," which in English means "The International Cooking Exhibition." This is attended by cooks from all over the world who compete against each other for gold, silver, and bronze medals. Each chef plans and prepares six hot and six cold dishes. Teams of five individuals compete against others of equal size, then the committee of the IKA judges each individual's efforts. Teams from 24 countries competed in 1968.

Chefs and Their Art

Someone once said, "Chefs are prima donnas." I cannot agree with that statement. What I have learned is that they are honest, sincere, dedicated, and trustworthy human beings. Their knowledge of food selection, preparation, and cooking far transcends that of any other human being. That is, with the possible exception of cooks who are widely traveled, well-read, and devoted completely to cooking such as James Beard and Julia Child who built on the limited knowledge of food selection, preparation, and cooking that they learned at schools such as the "Cordon Bleu" Cooking School in Paris. There, a chef demonstrates each day the preparation of one particular dish. Then the students go to their own kitchens, at home or in rented apartments, and practice making that same dish themselves.

In contrast, at a culinary school, the students observe the chef preparing consommé, Filet de Boeuf, Chicken a la King, Lobster Thermidor, Beef Tenderloin with Champignons,

Vichyssoise, Bouillabaisse, Crepe Suzettes, Peach Melba, Grand Marnier Soufflé and so on. After each is prepared, every student does the same thing as the chef step-by-step.

They learn the "Mis en Place," or having every ingredient, the cookware, cutlery, whatever is needed for the dish ready before the procedure begins. They learn menu planning, purchasing, judging, and creativity. Someone said, "Creating a new dish is more important to man than finding a new star in the heavens."

Besides cooking, the executive chef must learn baking, pastry making, confectionery making, ice cream making, decorating, and the many nuances accompanying each of these skills.

Further, to become an executive chef, the cook, baker, or pastry maker must apprentice him or herself to a great culinarian such as Carême or Auguste Escoffier in days past, or a present day Hermann Rusch, Hans Bueschkens, John Secter, Joseph Amendola or Charles Camerano. Then he or she must rise through the ranks until achieving the status of a "sous chef" or chief assistant to the head chef.

Someone once said, "I could eat my own grandfather if I had the right sauce to put on him." An extreme and indelicate expression, but one having impact. An executive chef must also have the ability to control food and labor costs, work with the catering manager in big places to plan wedding receptions, Bar Mitzvahs, parties, banquets, funeral breakfasts, receptions, and other events involving hundreds or even thousands of guests; some lasting for several days. To do this, costs must be estimated closely. Food and labor costs for each item on the menu must be known as well as overhead including energy, taxes, insurance, possible legal costs, equipment requirements, and the knowledge of how limitations in labor or equipment and service limitations may result in necessary changes in certain menu items.

The question comes to mind: "How does the knowledge, experience, and training - or practical vs. academic credentials - compare?" A Ph.D. gets the degree in three to seven years after the Bachelor Degree. The Ph.D. includes getting a Master's Degree, which usually takes two years. The Ph.D. also completes high school, whereas, an executive chef may not. So, a Ph.D., including three years of high school, four years of college as an undergraduate, and five to seven years of college as a post-graduate student, spends twelve to fourteen years learning what is known in his or her field.

In contrast, an executive chef, on an average, spends four or five years in culinary school, or that many years as an apprentice in a kitchen. Then, he or she will spend an additional 10 to 15 years learning the academic knowledge of mathematics, nutrition, food science, sanitation, law, and labor management. Thus, the chef will require fourteen to seventeen years, on an average, to get his or her training. If the chef were trained in the best places or by working under the masters of the culinary arts, I would give him or her the edge of knowledge, human relations, and management skill over the Ph.D.

Now, this should make the academicians, trustees, and presidents of American universities think about the intellectual aristocracy they have created by requiring anyone who wants to teach in their schools to have a Ph.D. degree. I have taught in the universities of Michigan State, Cornell, University of Nevada Las Vegas, and Purdue, and I have my

Ph.D. in Food Sciences. I have stated many times with honesty and sincerity that the executive chefs whom I know and respect, who have worked or consulted for the L. J. Minor Corporation, each have more knowledge about food selection, blending, and preparation in their little finger than I, or any Ph.D. I know, has in his or her entire body.

It is ludicrous for our great universities to discriminate, exclude, and ignore qualified persons without Ph.D.'s who can teach the students more about specialized subjects like business, culinary arts, engineering, entrepreneurship, art, music, and science than any Ph.D. could ever teach the students.

Newman's philosophy of higher education embraced all fields of learning. Why do academic oriented administrators of our bureaucratic big universities exclude teaching by practitioners who our society recognize as more valuable than the members of the exclusive fraternity of Ph.D.'s who are pampered, protected, and nourished by them. Are they fulfilling the school's obligations to society, or are they depriving, cheating, and defrauding the people who support them and the sons and daughters they send to them to be taught? We should think about this, and act to correct this caste system that exists in our universities.

Chapter 21

My Years with The
L. J. Minor Corporation

by Michael S. Zelski
(1968-1985)

An Anniversary Celebration   The Beginning   A Dream Come True

Growing with the Company   Plant and People   A Major Turning Point

Under New Management   A Time of Rejoicing   Conclusions

A Thought
by Lewis J. Minor

When George Ross, President of Huron Milling Company, hired me, he said, "You may not fly as high with us, but you won't fall as far either." That comment pleased me, and made me feel welcome in my new position with them.

Meditative Thoughts
by Lewis J. Minor

I believe that we all need the help of God in pursuing our goals in life. In time of need, prayer always helps. Whenever I've been sick or injured, I look to God for He says, "And you shall serve the Lord your God, and He shall bless your bread and your water; and I will take sickness away from the midst of you" (Exodus 23:25). I pray every day for the benefit of my family, others, and the L. J. Minor Corporation. Before I went for my Ph.D. exams, I spent two hours on my knees at the Newman Student Center on campus. Never underestimate the power of prayer, as the Bible says, "The fervent prayer of a righteous man can accomplish much" (James 5:16).

Quote from Terence Cardinal Cooke

"There is simply no better way to make our pressures bearable
than taking ourselves and our problems to our Heavenly Father in prayer."

Quote from Norman Vincent Peale

"Peace of mind is entirely possible through
a committed relationship with Christ and God."

Quote from Harmon Killebrew

"Pray as if everything depended on God; work as if everything depended on you."

An Anniversary Celebration

The date was April 16, 1994. Dr. and Mrs. Minor were celebrating their 55th wedding anniversary. It seemed like old times. My wife, Maxine, and I were there along with the Minor children, their spouses and grandchildren, relatives, MSU colleagues, close friends, and past employees. While Dr. Minor was not feeling well, he still managed to introduce everyone with a personal touch, sang special songs to Mrs. Minor, and even danced!

A sit down luncheon ensued. The afternoon was a revival of joyous, wonderful memories I have of many other Minor gatherings for anniversaries, weddings, holidays, key employee and chef testimonials. The Minor Corporation was a happy family frequently bonded together with family type reunions. For a few brief hours that afternoon, I mingled and celebrated time with beloved individuals and colleagues from the past, in the Kellogg Center on the campus of Michigan State University, where it all started for me in 1965, reliving my ultimate employment experience of a life time with the L. J. Minor Corporation from 1968 to 1985.

The Beginning

Lansing, Michigan was my birthplace on July 31, 1940. Through pure coincidence, Dr. Minor's wife, Ruth E. Minor, was a native of Lansing also, and one of their daughters, Josephine, was born on July 31st, my birthday.

After high school and four years in the U. S. Air Force, I was influenced to enter Michigan State's Hotel, Restaurant, and Institutional Management (HRIM) School in 1964 by my first cousin's husband, Robert Greiner. He had graduated from HRIM at MSU and was pursuing a successful career with Marriott, opening and managing new hotels.

The decision to major in HRIM was the right one because I enthusiastically enjoyed the studies, my eventual career path, and the hundreds of personal friendships and contacts developed, which is especially unique to the hospitality, foodservice industry.

In the fall of 1966, my junior year, I was required to take a food product technology course that only one professor, Dr. Lewis J. Minor, taught. The way to graduate was through him. It was a high-credit hour class, and many upper classmen warned me that the homework load was heavy. I entered his classroom the first day, in Berkey Hall, with great apprehension expecting to meet a very demanding, heartless professor. I found the homework was heavy, but meaningful, and a professor that was firm, but fair, knowledgeable and sincere about what he taught.

It was a dynamic learning experience as course material was made more enjoyable through his teaching style, guest speakers, and renowned chefs presenting the subject matter. I was intrigued that this man also owned a food corporation in Cleveland, Ohio.

In the beginning our professor-student relationship was slightly strained because Dr. Minor was a strong anti-smoker advocate and found out that I was a smoker. In class, he lectured us about the health hazards of cigarette smoking, non-smokers rights, and the fact that restaurants and hotels must designate no smoking sections and rooms. He convinced me to stop smoking for which I will always be grateful.

Eventually, Dr. Minor became one of the two most outstanding and influential professors I had. (The other being Lendal H. Kotschevar.) As our professor and student relationship grew closer my senior year, I volunteered to assist an L. J. Minor chef, George Marchand, in class. I was amazed at his talents, as this was my first encounter with a professional chef.

As impressive to me were the Minor Food Bases which were being used in my production lab classes and in the dorm kitchens on campus. Reconstituting one pound of base in water conveniently made five gallons of delicious, quality stock for soups like magic. I often thought I would love to make these products.

A Dream Come True

A few weeks before graduation, December, 1967, I was ready to accept a job offer from Stouffer's Frozen Foods when Dr. Minor extended to me a very honored invitation to join Dr. and Mrs. Minor's family owned corporation. I toured the West 25th Street plant, in Cleveland, and realized the growth potential for food bases, the quality of the L. J. Minor Corporation, and the promising career opportunity that was before me.

A few weeks later, Maxine and I were interviewed in the 436 Bulkley Building headquarters by Dr. and Mrs. Minor, and Tom Ryan. They displayed a genuine, personal touch, and by noon I was hired. I did not think I would last long, though, because as we all left together to go to lunch, we got onto the elevator and I accidentally leaned back and pushed all the buttons causing the elevator to stop on every floor. Dr. and Mrs. Minor smiled and kindly said, "That's okay, Michael." Tom Ryan, on the other hand, was somewhat intimidating to me at the time and gave a stern look as if to say what did we get ourselves into hiring this chap?

Dr. and Mrs. Minor were in Europe when I started working for the L. J. Minor Corporation. I was greeted with the following telegram:

```
MR MICHAEL ZELSKI
C/O LJ MINOR CORP
436 BULKLEY BLDG CLEVELAND
GREETINGS MICHAEL WE'RE
HAPPY YOU'RE WITH US BEST
REGARDS
        MR AND MRS LJ MINOR
```

The original objective of my job position was to learn manufacturing plant operations, assist in establishing production efficiencies, and formalize organizational policies as the company continued to grow. After a few months, a vacancy occurred and I was appointed plant manager. Ruth Fields, Dr. and Mrs. Minor's daughter, assisted and guided me through that early period of control procedures. George Henderson, Gaye Taylor, Audrey Chubbs, Helen Crites, Pearl Geiss, Angelo De Jesus, Rose Wilson, Catherine Calhoun, Margie Stanley, Marie Brown, Terry Clancy, Adam Young, and Tom Mele worked in plant operations with me. All were immediately supportive and key to my training and management effort to oversee two shifts.

Tom Ryan and Mary Mele, who were located downtown in the Bulkley Building, also gave me optimum support. This unique mix of dedicated super people was the winning team allowing Dr. Minor the freedom to run his business from a distance and teach at MSU. I quickly fell in love with my work and the nature of this company.

Growing with the Company

The years ahead were to give me a unique, gratifying, rewarding, comprehensive business experience that only a very few individuals are fortunate to ever encounter. The company was seventeen years old when I started in 1968. It was a small business with annual sales at a few million dollars. Fifteen years later, sales had grown about eight times.

In the spring of 1969, Ruth Ann Fields suddenly had to take temporary leave of her full time position as production scheduler and supervisor when her husband, Dorsey Fields, got seriously ill and passed away several months later. Dorsey was very qualified to maintain the plant and equipment and I missed his talents and constant encouragement to me to "Hang in there."

With their absences, I was darned determined to keep plant operations running smoothly. My previous mechanical experience installing home heating and air conditioning systems with my father during summer breaks helped in the gas and electrical areas.

Audrey Chubbs assisted with production scheduling and I will always be grateful to Gaye Taylor who worked second shift packaging line and was extremely reliable, good natured, hard working, and optimistic. She filled Dorsey's shoes in the sense of constant encouragement for me.

The employee staff was spread thin so I depended upon every employee's super work effort. Major lessons were learned by me about how to manage people such as delegating responsibility, giving employees clear guidance, work standard expectations, sincere respect, enthusiastic appreciation and credit for good work done, treatment with dignity, name recognition, a smile, and listening to and implementing some of their ideas for improvement. In return, the work staff gave back good communications, respect, cooperation, and a winning work team spirit.

Dr. Minor came to my rescue when he hand-picked Paula Neese, one of his graduating students from HRIM. She developed into a tremendous asset for the plant and super work partner for me. While she eventually had to resign, Ruth Fields was able to return to work and fill the vacancy in the same capable, responsible manner.

As time progressed, production volume grew and equipment needed to be mechanized in uncharted waters. Food base manufacturing was specialized and no company designed buildings and equipment exclusively for food base production. Equipment used in the baking, meat, candy, and foodservice industries had to be acquired, converted, and modified.

Flexibility to quickly rearrange and convert the configuration of tables, food pumps, and filling equipment necessitated all equipment being on casters. High standards of housekeeping and sanitation were ways of life. Make-up air and humidity-controlled environments became all important issues. Many food ingredients were very dry, hygroscopic powders. If exposed to moisture, they became sticky, caked, lumped, or solid, thus, unusable.

We exhausted a lot of warm air from cooking equipment and that had to be replaced with heated and cooled make-up air to prevent negative air pressure which could cause dusty outside air to be sucked in through cracks, open doors, and exhaust stacks. Employee hygiene practices were another challenge.

To be plant manager of the L. J. Minor Corporation, I needed the knowledge of many vocations which I had to learn and apply. I thoroughly enjoyed it and eventually was involved with virtually all manufacturing functions including receiving, storage, production, quality control, packaging, shipping, purchasing, product development, maintenance, personnel administration, communications with in-plant USDA meat/poultry inspectors, downtown management, and Dr. Minor. There was never a moment of boredom because the business was like painting a faster and faster moving train. The challenge was absolutely thrilling, and I was given more and more freedom to make major decisions.

Sales growth from 1968 to 1974 was steady but single digit. Amazingly, word of mouth through field sales personnel, chefs, and friends on the street and at trade shows were the major means of growth with minimal advertising in foodservice publications.

Tom Ryan had a brilliant sales mind and charm to go with it. He sought and drew other talented, admiring, and influential foodservice leaders and chefs to him such as Brother Herman Zaccarelli and Chef Ernest Koves. When presenting the bases, Brother Herman would often speak with fresh fruit props on the lectern likening them to natural food bases. Chef Koves was effective in New York City using his small test kitchen to demonstrate grand results to visiting and prospective clients.

The sales philosophy was to stay close to the customer through 20 high commissioned sales brokers almost totally dedicated to representing L. J. Minor. Customers' strong product demand pulled products through the foodservice distributor. This marketing approach fueled production growth and the constant need for increased production capacity.

Dr. Minor would only distribute the product line through those willing and able to refrigerate the bases. They had such an excellent flavor and only because of their high quality. They were unique because of their meat first for flavor predominance. Refrigeration insured stabilized color, appearance, and flavor attributes.

In 1981, we convened a lot of the sales force at a conference at Michigan State.

Plant and People

The plant was two miles from downtown Cleveland at 2621 West 25th Street, zoned commercial and surrounded by approximately twenty-five low cost homes and apartments, zoned residential. Trucks could pick up product, deliver materials, and the area was within a vast labor market. Our long term plan was to maintain neighborhood public relations, negotiate the purchase of residential homes as they became available, and rezone the property for future commercial development and expansion. This prevented the plant from being land-locked.

Don Lutz was the master housing purchasing negotiator, maintenance upkeep manager, and rent collector. Eventually, Tom Ryan delegated the overall housing responsibility to me which became like playing a living Monopoly Game!

As business grew, the main plant lacked sufficient office space and packaging storage capacity. Some of the company owned neighborhood houses and apartment buildings were converted into production facilities to provide emergency and temporary relief for offices and warehousing.

Two previously used 35 foot refrigerated trailers were parked adjacent to the plant. They innovatively doubled as storage for finished packaged bases and shipping dock when trucks backed up to the side doors to load.

Dr. Minor was always frugal around the plant. As his mother taught him, "Those who go a borrowing, go a sorrowing." The bankers in Cleveland were always frustrated because they always paid interest to the Minor Corporation rather than the other way around. We operated on an austerity budget, never purchasing anything, unless we had the funds to pay.

Going to trade shows was difficult because I could only look at new processing equipment. After a few years of delayed gratification, spending money on new equipment was fun because we saw immediate productivity efficiencies from our purchases. For example, a semi-automated food pump/auger filler accurately metered amounts of bases into containers quickly replacing a slow, inaccurate food pump for soft bases, ice cream scoops for dense bases, and hand squeezed pastry bags used for sample jars.

By 1977, adequate warehousing for dry raw materials and packaging became a pressing issue as anticipated. Robert Herron, Director of Michigan State's Food Stores, was hired to design and build with us a 5400 sq. ft. warehouse that could absolutely house all of our needs.

One of my most exhilarating, then embarrassing, and then jubilant experiences with the company occurred during the growth years when all the construction was taking place. I call this episode "The Machine."

After researching and pilot plant-testing a huge cutter/mixer to upgrade the processing volume and efficiency of food bases, Mike Minor and I saw the exact machine on the floor of a trade show for $120,000, not $160,000, the list price. We called Dr. Minor with the good news, and he approved the purchase. It was shipped to Cleveland but needed to be stored for about six months until the new processing room was finished for its installation.

Dr. Minor came to Cleveland for a plant visit and asked to see the new machine. I told him it was in storage. He was taken back and could not believe a huge monetary investment wasn't operational. I immediately realized that we had not made it clear to him during our presentation that it would not be operational for some months.

Dr. Minor was not too happy about this, but once the machine was operational, he smiled often admiring the powerful processing and improved product quality benefits of "The Machine." A few years later we got another one that was even larger, but timed to be purchased, delivered, and installed after site construction was completed!

Superior plant and product quality practices were insisted upon by Dr. and Mrs. Minor. One time, Joe Thomas, quality control supervisor, walked around with the Minors when Dr. Minor said, "That is my name on the label and that means every product must leave this plant with consistent high quality and never substandard!"

Dr. and Mrs. Minor visited monthly. Employees felt good about their visits because they were often addressed by name, made to feel appreciated, and in conversation Dr. Minor would share some pearl of wisdom to either work or live by. If deserving a reprimand, we all understood his meaning and never left with animosity lingering between us.

All employees were considered major assets. Dr. Minor lived that philosophy and employees always felt appreciated, and experienced his generosity. They received competitive industry wages, annual merit increases, semi-annual profit sharing bonuses, very good health and pension benefits, ham and turkey gifts at Christmas, New Years, and Easter.

Ruth Engler also played a major role giving sound quality control advice. She had retired from Stouffer's after forty years and started with us in a consulting capacity. She did some new product development work helping to establish a bonafide product development department. She introduced me to Jan Williams, another former Stouffer's employee, who began part-time, but who also eventually filled the full time position of product development director throughout the '70s and '80s.

Mike Abramovich was a very active resident who promoted the welfare of the local neighborhood and became a valuable source for employees. He recommended George Hvizd, the first person I ever hired, a 16 year old part-time clean up boy after school who developed and eventually worked up to assistant plant manager, operations manager, and vice president of logistics over a seventeen year span. He also recommended Blanca Nieves who started as a housekeeper and developed into a dedicated, conscientious quality assurance assistant.

Dr. Minor had established Ed Lossman as the plumbing and heating contractor. Though his prices were astronomical, his quality workmanship was well worth it. I looked up to him because he gave me sound plumbing, equipment and building expansion advice. He would send one of his employees, Frank Katuscak to work on plant repairs and installations. Two employees joined us through Frank including his wife, Gloria, and their son, Bart. Gloria packaged product on the evening shift, while Bart worked in shipping, and later, in material and supply procurement. Bart eventually married the plant secretary, Diana Nieves, the daughter of Blanca, who worked in quality assurance. One can see that we were all one big, happy family!

As General Manager, Tom Ryan was a controlled, firm but gentle, charismatic, humorous, peace-maker, and witty business leader. He possessed great ability for seeking talented people. He surrounded himself with dedicated employees and culinarians and was the spark plug of the L. J. Minor Corporation. He loved his Irish heritage and shared it. Several dozen friends annually received green colored carnations in celebration of Saint Patrick's Day.

Over the phone, Tom sternly told Minor sales brokers, "Dr. Minor has some of the toughest customer payment terms in the industry. If you fail to pay within those terms, expect a phone call." He would wink his eye at me while talking, but he meant business, and good cash flow for our business was the result.

Tom was a gift-giver to customers, friends, and key business associates all year round. Clocks, watches, small appliances, glassware, and jewelry were his favorites, although copper pans and other more expensive gifts were not unusual at Christmas time. He even presented my parents gifts at dinner one evening, handing Mom a pearl necklace and Dad a wallet. He loved to make people feel important, proud, and good about themselves.

We got along famously together. Both he and Dr. Minor gave me broad responsibility, authority, and trust to manage the plant, expand departments, improve facilities, upgrade processing equipment, and maintain personnel harmony through hiring and training people. They made me feel a partner in the business, if not an owner. Both led me quickly from a young supervisor into a responsible manager of the plant.

Dr. Minor provided constant encouragement, coaching, teaching, communications, and inclusion in all business affairs. Tom, on the other hand, told me bluntly one day when I was whining, just once, about a disrespectful plant employee, "If you can't handle the heat, get out of the kitchen." I learned quickly about the art of resolving problems in my area of responsibility.

In the summer of 1974, Tom Ryan and I were attending the Tri-State Restaurant Convention in Cincinnati, Ohio with other Minor sales representatives. Before dinner we were all enjoying a cocktail in his hotel suite, when he shocked us by bravely announcing the fact that he was 74 years old with emphysema leading to cancer, and we would soon have to carry on the work of the L. J. Minor Corporation without him. We all told him that he would be fine, but actually were trying to convince ourselves that what he said was not true. The thought of him not being there was unthinkable and frightening, because he was always there to lead and shelter our well-being.

A Major Turning Point

In October of 1974, the L. J. Minor Corporation exhibited in the American Dietetic Association convention in Philadelphia. Tom Ryan and I were traveling together when he informed me that I would be meeting Lt. Gen. John D. McLaughlin, a retired three star general, as a possible candidate to join us. In the military, I had once met a one star general, so this made me excited and anxious.

As I arrived at the hotel's front desk, I was tired, casually dressed, and needed to take care of some personal hygiene after a long journey. I had driven the portable booth there in the company van and slipped into a rear door hoping not to run into anyone important prior to getting to my room. As chance would have it, the lobby elevator door opened and out came Tom Ryan, neatly dressed as usual. He looked at me, strolled over, and introduced the person ahead of me as The General!

The next time I met him was at the 1974 annual American Culinary Federation convention at which I was privileged to witness the professional status birth of the American chef. As Chef Louis Szathmary made a famous speech declaring "We are not domestics," referring to the U. S. Department of Labor's recognition of the chef as a "domestic." He said there was one individual in the room that could lead the chefs in their efforts in having the U. S. Department of Labor upgrade its classification of executive chef in its Dictionary of Occupational Titles from "domestics" to "professionals" and that would be General McLaughlin. Dr. Minor, through Tom Ryan, immediately stated that the Minor Corporation would monetarily support the General by paying all of his expenses in this endeavor which was accomplished in 1977.

Tom Ryan passed in January, 1975, just after Mary Mele shocked us with her illness and passed away in December of 1974. Nancy Clancy took over as executive secretary, mother, hub, and heart of the L. J. Minor Corporation. She continued to implement the Irish traditions of Tom Ryan with Dr. Minor's sole support. The General was made head of sales and I became head of operations as Dr. Minor took on a more active management role.

Gen. McLaughlin was the Commanding General of the United States Theater Army Support Command, Europe administering the logistics of billions of dollars worth of military supplies to include food, when he retired, in July, 1974. Among other assignments, he was

172

Commandant of the U. S. Army Quartermaster School and Commander of Fort Lee, Virginia. Among his awards, he was given the renowned Silver Plate Award from the International Foodservice Manufacturers Association for his work in improving the Army's foodservice.

He did fantastic networking within the foodservice industry and I admired his untiring work ethic and his capability to recall civilian and war stories with exacting detail. In conversation, he wove in descriptive phrases such as "soul searching," "role up your sleeves," "get a good grip on the situation," and many more. His leadership philosophy was "you cannot lead until you have learned how to take orders." I felt very honored to work with him and learned many new methods of administrative management from him.

Under New Management

Having selected to work for the smaller Minor Corporation, General McLaughlin turned down several opportunities to head huge foodservice related corporations. We met frequently together in a small room in the Bulkley Building known as "The War Room." There, we could use the walls to tape up topics, projects, graphs, labels, advertising and promotion literature and visual aids for in-depth analysis and planning.

In one session, we looked at the booming anticipated growth of the foodservice industry and determined that, given the same 6% to 8% real annual growth that the industry had been experiencing, the L. J. Minor Corporation would realistically double its size in the next five years. It was amazing, but frightening, although Dr. Minor chuckled with perhaps some skepticism about achieving such an optimistic goal.

Business growth was to be stimulated by many significant advertising, marketing and sales campaigns, and management appointments. I commissioned Walter Nicholes, head of his own small independent advertising agency, to work with us and the General listened to what he had to say. When handed a life-size plastic lobster and told by the General to improve sluggish Lobster Base sales, Walter developed a Lobster Base Recipe Booklet and a publication ad to promote it. The plan worked and Walter went on to develop ads for food publications, product flyers, brochures, product container labels, food base application recipes, and more, creating great awareness and product demand in all foodservice markets. His campaign was a key marketing factor in the continued growth of the L. J. Minor Corporation.

In order to generate more company awareness and product exposure, the General and I discussed and got permission to exhibit at the National Restaurant Show in Chicago. From our initial location downstairs to a better location the next year, the Show generated terrific customer awareness and response each successive year. We exhibited in most of the major national and regional trade shows thereafter.

F. David Swanson was appointed Vice President of Institutional Sales and John "Jack" Cassidy was appointed Vice President of Industrial Sales. This organization and team expanded the sales, chef consultant, and dietitian consultant staff resulting in business growth exceeding 20% annually for the remainder of the '70s and early '80s.

Operations needed to keep pace with growth so I had real challenges on my hands as we were about to grow at a frenzied rate. In 1976, I was blessed to be introduced to polyethylene and polypropylene plastic cups and bulk containers. Unlike the glass jars we were using, the plastic cups were nestable, label preprinted, could be machine filled, check weighed, sealed, and lidded. Dr. Minor enthusiastically supported the conversion. We were the first base company to replace the old glass containers in the kitchen and this applied to the larger fiber drums as well. Filling operation efficiencies increased and the food bases had a new container look.

The sales projections that General McLaughlin and I originally plotted were exceeded beyond our expectations. The company was doubling sales every three years from the late '70s. Construction needs became multi-million dollar projects. Layout, design, and construction of these building additions were challenging, knowledge gaining, extremely gratifying, and fun.

Personnel were developed into key supervisory and management positions. George Hvizd was admirably assisting me in directing, organizing, and coordinating manufacturing along with Ruth Fields. Nancy Clancy was the keeper of the corporate-soul managing the front office staff, handling customer services, payroll, and customer and corporate accounting functions.

Nancy was one of the most jovial, happy, easy going, congenial, and competent persons I have ever known. She was the main communication link within the company, for sales brokers and customers. Everyone loved her.

Another asset to the company was Dr. Minor's son, Chef Michael L. Minor, who joined after reaping the benefits of working for a few other companies. He also experienced a culinary education at The Greenbrier in White Sulphur Springs, West Virginia. He became our on-site chef in the Cleveland plant in 1977 working most every position. He has a magnetic personality, warmth toward people, enthusiasm, high energy level, positive attitude, and creativity. We always got along well together and he became my colleague, confidante, and friend.

Mike became a significant contributor to production and cooking efficiency and mechanization. Being a people-person and motivator, he helped train and keep employee morale and production output high. Mike also brought youth to the ranks of aging Minor Corporation demonstration chefs.

One of Mike's most useful, dedicated, and fun-loving demo chefs was Chef Frank Scherer who had retired from the Oakwood Country Club, Cleveland Heights, Ohio, where he had used Minor Bases in the kitchen. I was very fond of other people in the company including Herman Taber and Ralph Napletana. Dr. Minor always said, "Herman was the smartest man he ever knew," and both men were present at most all activities held by the L. J. Minor Corporation including national sales conferences, testimonial dinners, weddings, and anniversaries.

Ralph commanded a lot of respect because of his excellent accounting skills. Herman was continually telling jokes and said, "Don't take life too seriously. Have a sense of humor and enjoy it." He would go to lunch with top management and Mrs. Minor would often be the only woman present. Herman would refer to her as "One of the boys." Both of these gentlemen were tremendous influences and business friends in my life and did much to positively influence the L. J. Minor Corporation.

Modern age technology brought pocket size digital calculators to the Minor Corporation in the early '70s. By the mid '70s we were being provided with our first computerized printed stock status reports, but receiving the information historically after a week or more had passed.

Soon payroll was computerized and current stock status information became available in the early '80s when we purchased an IBM personal computer for the plant. Ingolf Nitsch, another graduating student of Dr. Minor's, arrived in 1980 and was trained in all aspects of plant operations and eventually supervised production scheduling. Upon his recommendation, Norbert Urban was hired to assist Ingolf and, along with Josephine Minor, all admirably maintained and advanced the Minor Corporation into a new age of computerized information systems.

A Time of Rejoicing

With the plant in good hands, I was able to travel more. One very memorable trip came in 1975 when I went to the Orient. Chef Jean Caubet joined me at Dr. Minor's wish and we presented seminars for Hotel Inter-Continental which specified Minor Bases worldwide. We visited Hong Kong, Singapore, Bangkok, Tokyo, Hawaii and San Francisco. Chef Caubet was a great traveling companion, always saying, "I am a chef, not a salesman," but then his voice would begin trembling with excitement and emotion when talking about and demonstrating Minor Bases to anyone!

Another extraordinary trip was attending the 1976 International Culinary Olympics, held every four years, in Frankfurt, Germany, to see some of the world's best professional chefs from 28 countries compete. Others from the company attended and some of us, including Maxine, took a side trip to Rome prior to the Olympics. Brother Herman Zaccarelli arranged for us to meet Sister Mary Alma who worked at the Vatican. After many personalized tours in the non-public areas, we were invited to hear the Pope in the Basilica and had great seats. What a blessing!

The Culinary Olympics was the first of its type that I had ever seen. Observing teams of four chefs representing their countries in the hot foods competition, working in glass-fronted display kitchens, turning out "native" meals of 200-each of four separate creations sold to spectators over two successive days, was a glance at high-level professionalism. The cold food display categories were no less spectacular. Just like the Olympic athletes, these talented chefs skillfully and with precision put it all on the line demonstrating their professional knowledge of food preparation, art, nutritional composition, originality, taste, and teamwork abilities. I gained eye opening appreciation for the culinary profession, the skills it embraces, and the eventual overflow contributions of the culinary event to the foodservice industry.

In 1980, I witnessed a spectacular self-confidence transformation in Mike Minor when Dr. Minor encouraged him to participate in the prestigious International Culinary Competition, in Frankfurt, Germany. The pressure was on to gather a team of chefs and prepare his own culinary display.

Mike expressed some anxiety at the magnitude of displaying with the top, professional chefs in the world. This tremendous undertaking was planned, organized, and rehearsed incredibly well, and Mike proudly brought the team back with three gold medals, including one for himself, four silver, and one bronze. Plus, a gold medal titled "House of Minor" was presented to the Corporation for outstanding displays.

Mike's level of confidence in himself multiplied ten-fold. After four years, in 1984, he captained Minor's International team of eight chefs in the same event capturing seven gold medals, one silver medal, and the "Grand Gold." These achievements further advanced the L. J. Minor Corporation's professional image of being the highest quality food base manufacturer in the foodservice industry.

Mike and I would return often to provide demos to students in Dr. Minor's classes studying HRIM. These were special moments for me as we would sometimes dine with the students in exclusive restaurant settings, just as he had done with me when I was a student. On one of these occasions, I met Dr. Minor's special guest, Chef Hans J. Bueschkens from Windsor, Canada. Chef Bueschkens became renowned with chefs worldwide and eventually became the Minor Corporation's Vice President for International Operations.

Conclusions

Minor growth continued such that by late 1982, I was in the process of finding yet another building in which we might expand. Taking a phrase from Dr. Minor, my finding a refrigerated, finished product warehouse in Brecksville, Ohio was like "A jewel in the desert."

Cleveland treated me well as did all of the Minor family. Maxine and I came from small cities in Michigan and took advantage of all that Cleveland had to offer. We were able to own a beautiful home and start a family. In fact, on a personal note, Dr. Minor and Tom Ryan's written character reference of me to St. Vincent DePaul resulted in the adoption of our first two sons, Steven and Tom. Though Maxine and I were reportedly unable to have children, the third boy, Michael, came along shortly after adopting Tom.

Dr. Minor's daughter, Ruth, loved children and we will never forget the thoughtful gifts she constantly gave to our boys. We developed golden, life-long friendships with several couples. Mike Minor and his wife, Eddie, were extremely hospitable people in their home to relatives, friends, and associates. Mike and Eddie's three daughters were close in age to my three sons, and we had a lot of family fun together. Cleveland was good to us, and we loved it.

Many companies that have long life often lack historical documentation about the founding fathers and some of the past supporting cast during the growth years. The period of time from 1968 to 1983 with the family owned L. J. Minor Corporation was filled with the most unique, self esteem building, gratifying, happy, rewarding, and fulfilling employment experience of my life and I am thankful to Dr. and Mrs. Minor for the opportunity to be one of their family team workers. I am grateful to my wife, Maxine, who never complained about long hours, stuck by me through thick and thin, was my best friend and loyal companion. I am indebted to the Minor children, Ruth, Mike, and Josephine, and all employees who loyally supported me. I am appreciative for the opportunity to write about it.

(Editor's Note: For those readers who know Michael S. Zelski, this chapter has said it all. For those who have not had the pleasure to meet him, may I simply state that from the first day I met him, Mike has been one of my favorite people in life. Although we do not see each other frequently, he is in the same status as the other two gentlemen that Dr. Minor considers adopted sons. In fact, at the Minor's 55th wedding anniversary, Dr. Minor introduced Mike and Maxine as an "adopted son and daughter." They are special people and Mike's contribution to this text was one of the finest chapters received, in my opinion. To Mike, I say thanks for a great job done and sorry that I was unable to use every detail of every page that was so beautifully written. You are the greatest!)

Chapter 22

Building the Business

Pioneers in Industry   **After the 1972 Culinary Olympics**

The Customer
by Lewis J. Minor
(January 9, 1995)

The customer's smarter than you
Know's better what your product can do
For him, and his needs are what he knows best;
He'll see if your product measures up to his test.
Confidence in your product has to be earned;
When faith in its quality consistency is learned.
Controlling the quality requires special care
Paying-off when the repeat order is there.
Consistent quality's a primary need
To earn customer confidence and really succeed.

A Willingness to Lend a Hand
(Irish Humor by Hal Roach)

An old lady is waiting at a bus stop when she says to Muldoon:

"Can you see me across the street?"

Muldoon says:

"Stand right here and I'll go across and have a look!"

Pioneers in Industry

Now, my hopes for a larger business that would be able to compensate the employees better with health and retirement benefits were materializing. As soon as possible, I

178

arranged through my insurance man, William Mayer of Manufacturers Life, a well-known Canadian firm, for employee pension benefits. Tom got us Blue Cross coverage for all. The wife of a fellow K of C Knight, Walter Marnell, managed Blue Cross' Cleveland office. She always took care of us. Tom liked what we were doing. Our sales in 1968 were up over three million dollars a year, just after being in business 17 years. This was a lot for a small new seasoning business.

With Tom Ryan as General Manager, I said, "Thou art Thomas and on this rock I shall build the Minor Corporation," just as Jesus Christ said, "Thou art Peter, and on this rock I shall build my church." Dr. Thomas Aloysius Ryan was my rock. Like a father, he looked after me and my family while I got ready for the future scientific needs of the company. Many times he would tell me, "I want you to become a millionaire." Eventually, after his death, by building on the foundation that Tom and I had constructed, with the help of our chefs and Mrs. Minor, I became a multimillionaire.

We already had eight highly qualified chefs with us. Many more would follow in their footsteps, for each one of them was a disciple and missionary who would convince cooks that Minor's was the best base available. Then distributors would want to handle our product in order to satisfy their customers.

LeGout and Custom Foods in the Chicago area both listed chicken and beef bases with meat as the first ingredient, but they evidently did not feature them as food bases. Most of what they were selling after the War was what they had sold before World War II; that is, soup bases for flavoring, not making stock. Their pricing for these products, which were accompanied on their price lists by several lower priced bases with less or no meat, did give us a clue on what we should charge for our food bases.

We were pioneers in using the "Food Base" title for complete stock bases. With them, customers could make five gallons of stock instantly, simply by suspending the one pound of base in five gallons of boiling water.

When Jean Caubet and I made our historic sales trip visiting resorts in Northern Michigan, we came across a major competitor's chicken base, with meat as the first ingredient, that had turned from yellow to black after being on the shelf during the winter months. This told me that we should specify that our food bases be kept under refrigeration by the distributor and customer.

Now, I did not have to do everything myself. We had finally put a strong team together. Our quality control worked well and our plant sanitation brought praise from inspectors who visited meat and poultry plants all over the United States. The Minor name had become synonymous with quality, uniformity, value, and customer service that outstripped our competition.

We kept things simple, orderly, clean, and tidy. Stainless steel was used in all of our equipment. Plant improvements and growth were paid for out of profits. We owed nothing to banks or persons. Dunn & Bradstreet was kept in the dark so no one knew just how prosperous our business had become because we did not want the big companies to invade our field. Later, however, they did.

When you are on top of the world, or doing well, keep it to yourself. Do not invite ruthless or unfair competition. Always be good to your employees and pay them as much as you can. Pay your suppliers on time and maintain good relations with them. Be courteous and cooperative with inspectors, whether federal, state, or local. Be friendly with competitors, but do not tell them your secrets.

When we broadened our product line with Supreme Sauce, Ham Base, Mushroom Base, Clam Base, Turkey Base, Consommé Base, Magic Sauce, Brown Gravy Sauce, Lobster Base, Onion And Garlic Bases, and later on Shrimp Base, Fish Base, and others, we had truly earned our position and reputation as the Food Base people.

Suddenly, I knew that like, a painter, sculptor, composer, or inventor, we had created a kind of masterpiece as a jewel that was unequalled in beauty or value. It was the L. J. Minor Corporation. But, in addition, we had developed new and essential courses for Hospitality Schools with my Food Service Science text and course, and Food Production Systems addition to the Quantity Foods course. What a wonderful world! My Food Flavor Evaluation course was a classic. Students loved it.

My classes were going well, the months went by quickly during the Fall and Spring terms. Then winter and summer I could help build the business, and develop new teaching aids for my classes that would benefit our business.

My guest speakers and Food Science professor friends often helped if needed. All I had to do was ask. We had a problem with fat separating out of our chicken base and going to the top. Then, some of the fat would leak out of the plastic bag liner we used inside the 10 pound, 25 pound, and 50 pound fiber drums. This fat stained the containers by penetrating through the fiber. Harry Lawson of Proctor and Gamble told me a method to stabilize the fat in the base like that which is done in peanut butter and the problem was solved, greatly improving the appearance of our Chicken base.

We needed a special starch for our Supreme Sauce. My guest speaker from the National Starch Company solved our problem with one of their modified starches. Dr. Dawson, Head Poultry Science Professor in MSU's Food Science Department helped us get the birds and rendered chicken fat we needed. Our government inspectors helped us too. They would inform us of food choppers from Germany, called Schnell Kutters that revolutionized our processing.

On the other hand, when new inspectors were assigned to our plant, from time to time one would have a question on a label statement. Once an inspector claimed that we didn't have carmel color listed on our beef base label. Since we weren't using carmel coloring but instead carmelizing sugar (a method used in the manufacture of candy) as a natural coloring, we shouldn't have to divide it out of the sugar listed. I talked to the head of label standards in Washington. He gave approval to keep our label "as is".

Strangely, a new inspector came into the plant and declared that the beef base label we had used for years was not in compliance with the Meat Inspection Department's labeling standards. I went to Washington to see Head Meat Inspector Steele. When the MID trained new inspectors, they would send them into plants all over the country. Finally, they would show them ours to demonstrate how clean and up to standards a processing plant could be.

Steele didn't want to go against the inspector's claim concerning our beef label. He called in an assistant. We went around and around. I claimed that beef meant anything from the animal as it stood in the field. That was beef. They disagreed. Finally, I asked, "Well, if we cannot label it beef, what do you suggest?" They said, "You can call it 'Beef Soup Concentrate (Roasted Beef, and Concentrated Beef Stock)'". A few years later we changed it to 'Beef (Roasted Beef and Concentrated Beef Stock)'. This let us state beef three times as the first ingredient instead of once as before.

Tom Ryan would call me to Cleveland if I were teaching and we needed a new meat product label sent in for approval. Walter Pietrascz was the inspector assigned to our plant in that era. After I would discuss the label he would give his approval.

During the time we first received meat and poultry inspection, we had an inspector named Emil Kralik. He loved our small enterprise, and helped stamp shipping cartons with the government inspector seal when we were busy packing and labeling, getting ready for a truck pick up. After he retired from the inspection service, he came to work for us.

Inspectors did not even accept a free lunch. Tom established a close relationship with Dr. Romine, Chief of the Cleveland inspection operation. Inspectors were at Stouffer's and several local meat packing houses and sausage manufacturing facilities. Two of Tom's favorite descriptive terms were "Schnozzy" for a Cadillac or Mercedes car, and "Hinky Dink" for a person he did not like. He got an artist to make up a crest and banner for Minor cartons and had some embroidered patches with this trademark for our chefs jackets. We also developed a trademark of a chef with a palette of colors called Minor's Bases, "Artistry in Flavor."

Now we had everything needed to compete with the numerous other companies in soup base manufacturing. I always knew our products were the best, and God, as usual, was providential. A fortuitous event occurred that gave us Federal Poultry inspection.

When I heard that Dr. Willey, Head of U. S. D. A. Poultry Inspection Department was visiting Stouffer's Frozen Food facility, which was new and enlarged, I sent word to him that I would like to meet him. Again, God and my Guardian Angel were at work. After he checked us out, I asked if we could qualify for Federal Inspection. He said, "I will approve your setup for inspection by having you cross-licensed by the Meat Inspection Department." That meant we would have to pay for the inspector who had to be present when we were manufacturing. This was an added expense, but it was the best advertising in the world for us to have the U. S. D. A. inspection seal on our chicken and turkey bases. Then, too, the transition to both meat and poultry inspection was made easier.

Before we moved into the building at 2621 West 25th Street, formerly a car wash, we needed to make a lot of changes in order to meet U. S. D. A. Meat Inspection requirements. A plaster board ceiling with taped joints painted white was needed. Plumbing standards for floor drains and restrooms needed to be met. Wisely, we put light green tile on the processing room, control lab, and women's restroom walls. Air conditioning was also provided in the processing area. By personal preference, based on experience in the West 115th Street facility, we installed a green flecked, white asbestos tile floor over the concrete. Individual pedal operated stainless steel sinks were also installed. A separate washer and washroom was made for washing mixing bowls.

By now we had three 120-quart Hobart Mixers with three stainless steel bowls for each mixer. We were now able to get a stainless steel food cutter from Hobart which was a new item I had requested. We ordered some additional stainless steel work tables from Koch in Kansas City.

Approval was granted by the U. S. D. A.'s plant inspection office in Washington, D.C. I drew up a crude schematic mechanical drawing of the new plant, and took my drawing to Mr. Hagman, the Head of Inspection. He checked it over, finding no fault except for the asbestos tile floor laid over concrete. I assured him that we used this type floor successfully in the smaller plant. He then took a red pencil and labeled the floor conditionally approved. He then pointed to a stack of prints of plans that were awaiting his approval, and said, "See these? It will be six months before they can all be checked." How fortuitous it was that I could leave with the approved plan, and all without paying an architect and waiting for many months for approval. I said to myself, "Thank God and my Irish mother who taught me that 'time and tide wait for no man'." If you want anything to be done, do it yourself.

Surely, the power of persuasion coupled with Hagman's empathy for a struggling newcomer influenced his decision. Definitely the prayers I said while waiting for it helped, too. "Ask the Man!" That was my policy as the Bible says, "Ask, and it shall be given to you; seek, and you shall find; knock, and it shall be opened to you (Matthew 7:7)."

When John Hannah, President of Michigan State University, asked me, "How are you able to teach here and run a business in Cleveland?" I said, "With good people looking after the store." Hannah said, "Yes, that's what's needed , good people." Tom Ryan used to say, "You go ahead, and do your thing, I'll look after the store."

Everything needed to be the best quality. Our chefs and sales representatives, office and plant personnel, equipment, raw material, packages, labels, and customer service all were the best we could get. Our raw material sources and materials were also the finest.

Our fundamental philosophy was to treat our suppliers, customers, and employees fairly. We operated like Thomas Edison. He put the accounts payable on one spindle and the accounts due on another. That was it. What are the accounts payable, the accounts due and what is the value of the inventory? We did not keep much reserve capital. Not by choice, of course, but by necessity. My mother taught me that, "He who goes a-borrowing, goes a sorrowing." Bankers only lend you money when you do not need it. Seldom or never when you do.

Tom and I heard about a great chef, Chef Sidoli, at the Drake Hotel in Philadelphia. We went to see him, and my son, Bryan, who worked for him one summer. This fine hotel was located on Rittenhouse Square and was a Mecca for wealthy connoisseurs. Sidoli's menu and preparation met their exceptionally high standards. His sous-chef and cooks were mainly Spaniards who spoke little English. Sidoli was king at the Drake. His reputation preceded him wherever he chose to work. As usual, Tom charmed him by his audacious manner and authoritative conversation.

Tom Ryan would frequently travel with John Secter who was probably our greatest chef, until John died of cancer. My father said that John Secter had as good an executive manner about him as anyone he had ever met at the Ford Motor Company or Western Golf and Country Club where he and Mother were members.

Tom, John Secter, Ernie Koves, and I visited the Culinary Institute of America (CIA) in Hyde Park, New York, when it was under reconstruction. It had been a Catholic Monastery. Brother Herman Zaccarelli, a Holy Cross Brother and educator for cooks in Catholic institutions, found this facility an ideal location for the CIA, as it was called.

This famous training ground for cooks, including pastry chefs, was started in a small store front by an attorney, Frances Roth. Under her auspices and influence, the school grew like "topsy." She had a board made up of representatives from Campbell Soup, Heinz, International Minerals, Chemicals Company, Syracuse China Company, Seagrams, Christian Brothers, Gallo Wineries, and others.

At one of her fund-raising meetings, my friend and sponsor, the dapper Toby Bishop, who named monosodium glutamate (MSG) "Accent," piped up and said, "Ladies and Gentlemen, we are giving $50,000 to help get this school going. What are each of you going to do?" Of course, they were all stunned. Toby Bishop, like Tom Ryan, never went in with a "pea shooter". He used a cannon.

Joe Amendola, the great pastry chef whose text on this subject was the best available, was in charge of renovation work. So with Joe Amendola and Brother Herman Zaccarelli, a strong Italian-American team leading the way, the Culinary Institute of America as it is today was started.

Joe Amendola later sent us two of our best chefs when they retired from teaching at the Institute. They were Art Jones, who represented us in California, and Jean Simon, who settled in St. Augustine, Florida, which later became the location for the American Culinary Federation. Hence, the Minor Corporation was in on the ground floor when the CIA's historic rise to national and world renown began in the '70s.

Actually, professionals like Frances Roth, founder, Jake Rosenthal, president, and Walter Luftman, chairman of the board, spearheaded the Institute's growth.

Today, Ferdinand Metz is president. He was hired from H. J. Heinz product development department. His influence in the American Culinary Federation, and leadership in getting stronger financial backing for the U. S. Culinary Olympic teams, bore fruit mainly through the efforts of the L. J. Minor Corporation and General John D. McLaughlin.

As stated earlier, we also had a close friendship with Johnson & Wales College, which later became Johnson & Wales University. We set up "Student Loan Funds" there in memory of John Secter and Herman Breithraupt. This enabled us to meet Morris Gaebe, its president, and other staff members. Thus, we were in solid as a company with two nationally established culinary arts schools. We also had a close liaison with Chadsey High School's Programs and others. Many of these relationships were established through the "Loan Funds" as well. We would often get good PR, such as the following, with each Fund established.

(Editor's Note: Even today, Dr. and Mrs. Minor are still establishing these Funds or contributing to them. Our Hotel, Restaurant, and Tourism Management Program at Indiana University and Purdue University at Fort Wayne has been the recipient of $12,000 in the past two years. It was established in memory of Dr. Minor's mother and is titled the "Kathleen Mary Minor Student Loan Fund." What a blessing it has been to the students who have needed the money in times of crisis!)

L. J. Minor Corporation Establishes
Student Emergency Loan Fund

The L. J. Minor Corporation has donated $1000 to establish a self-perpetuating student emergency loan fund at Grand Valley State College in Allendale, Michigan.

The award was made by Dr. and Mrs. Lewis J. Minor to Gary Page, Director of Hospitality and Tourism Management. Dr. Minor is Board Chairman and Chief Executive Officer of the L. J. Minor Corporation, a producer of premium quality Natural Food Bases and convenience preps and mixes used by the commercial institutional and processing foodservice industries.

The fund is similar to several others established by the Minor Corporation in various U.S. culinary schools to aid students in need and to help preserve the memory of famous deceased American chefs who worked for the Minor Corporation as chef consultants.

Persons or firms who wish to contribute to the new student loan fund should contact Gary Page, Director, Hospitality and Tourism Management, Grand Valley State College, Allendale, Michigan 49401. Or phone him at 616-895-6611.

Our business prospered when Eisenhower, Johnson, and Nixon were Presidents. However, when the Jimmy Carter regime took over, inflation became rampant. Interest rates climbed rapidly from 6% to 18% for bank loans. This change shook up the entire foodservice industry. We got caught with higher raw material and CDB (cost of doing business) costs. Room rates doubled or tripled, travel costs rose rapidly, and we were caught sleeping.

During this time, Hobart Manufacturing had to hire 36 new accountants to adjust their pricing on new equipment made. Our bases increased in price by only five cents per pound, which was equal to no improvement at all. We used a pricing formula of 3 to 1 based on our costs. Now we needed 4 to 1 or even 5 to 1 on certain products. At this time we sustained losses for two years.

After the 1972 Culinary Olympics

Following the 1972 Olympics, our attendees each had two weeks free to do as they pleased. Our five chefs went to the Strasbourg's Cooking School, which was the only one in the world at that time making movies in color of fine cuisine preparation and cooking procedures for all the classical dishes . I wanted these for my classes, but I wanted some that compared the time and labor cost of the classical methods of Escoffier with the newly developed Minor method.

Tom and I met with our four French chefs - John Secter, Jean Caubet, George Marchand, and Emil Burgermeister - to plan this movie about classical dishes for viewing by our customers, chef chapters around the United States, and my students. Our dear friend, Charles Camerano, of pulled and blown sugar artistry, Herman Breithaupt, and others were indirectly involved as they attended the Culinary Olympics with us.

Emil Burgermeister's home village was only 11 miles from Strasbourg. When he suggested that it would be a good idea for him to visit the school and make advance preparations, we immediately concurred.

They made colored movies of Lobster Americaine, Chicken a la King, Beef a la Deutsch, Medallions of Veal, and Poulet Supreme. Our chefs used the Minor method. The school's chefs used Escoffier's "classical" method. The time and labor comparisons were made together with a taste panel evaluation by all the chefs. While all agreed that dishes made by the Minor method were equal in taste to those they made by the classical method, the time and labor costs with the Minor method were a fraction of what they were with Escoffier's classical method.

These films were perfect for my classes at Michigan State and for sales promotion by the L. J. Minor Corporation. They meant a lot to us for demonstrating, with authentic endorsements by some of the world's greatest chefs, that using our food bases was both economical and produced results unsurpassed by the classical method. They also helped make sales to key accounts such as hotel chains, fine restaurant chains, fine clubs, resorts, and hospitals with high foodservice standards.

Later, in making a movie showing how our bases could be beneficial in the preparation of world-class cuisine, I called again upon Harry Friedman since he had the necessary menus and costumes. We had chef John Secter prepare the dishes. Dotty Friedman provided the costumes and called upon the young men and women from Dade County Community College to be the actors and actresses to serve and be the guests. Included in the movie were menus from the U. S. A., France, Italy, Spain, Germany, Hungary, Turkey, and Japan.

Harry Friedman was producer, director and prop man all in one. He built a little Japanese Teahouse, used brass cookware from Asia and got a Fry-top table that's used for Japanese cooking by the Benihana Restaurant chain, all of which were used in making the movie. The set was his estate in Miami. His grounds were covered with green-colored statues and there was a huge white porcelain serving table. Some of the girls did a "Belly Dance." Harry produced a one-and-one-half-hour long masterpiece. He earned a great deal of respect from Chef Secter and the L. J. Minor Corporation's personnel, and expanded respect for our food bases. Everyone was skeptical about our products before using them. Afterwards, they did not want to cook without them.

Tom called the bases the Alpha and the Omega. They would outperform all other food bases and soup bases as well. Although soup bases were cheaper, they had no true beef or chicken flavor. So a chef could use less of the Minor base and get a better result, while paying no more in the end by using the higher priced food base.

Chapter 23

Further Successes

Accolades Received   **Traveling Abroad**

Victor Ceserani **A Cabin in New Brunswick** **Other Journeys**

A Quick Trip
(Irish Humor by Hal Roach)

Flanagan called Shannon Airport and asked:

"How long does it take for the jumbo jet to go from Shannon to New York?"

The operator said:

"Just a minute."

Flanagan put down the phone and said:

"That's fantastic!"

Friends
by Edgar A. Guest
(1936)

Be a friend you don't need money.
Just a disposition sunny,
Just the wish to help another
Get along some way or other;
Just a kindly hand extended
Out to one who's unbefriended;
Just the will to give or lend,
This will make you someone's friend.

Accolades Received

One time at the National Restaurant Show in Chicago, the father of one of my students whom I had never even met, came up to me and kissed me saying, "I would not even have a business if it were not for you!"

Another day when I was working with Jean Caubet and Eric Swanson, I stopped in to see Dad and Mother. They were watching Arthur Godfrey on TV. Dad had recently retired from the Ford Motor Company. I put him to work helping Chef Caubet and Eric sell our bases around Detroit. A few months later, they came to Cleveland to visit us. As he stepped out of the car, Dad said to me, "You do not know what a fine product you have. When I call on the women who are using them, they put their arms around me and thank me for introducing it to them."

Dad and Mother were a good sales team for us. Dad made calls and Mother wrote up his reports for us. In the winters they went to Florida and met Pierre Bach, Jean Caubet's lifelong friend, who was called "King of the Beach" in Miami. He opened the Fontaine Bleu and Eden Roc, Miami's finest. He used our bases and liked them so much that he said to my parents, as previously told about the chefs meeting at the farm, "I want your son to be 'King of the Bases' someday.

When he retired, he moved to San Francisco. I went around with him there opening accounts, and met the fabulous Paul Debes. Chef Debes had his own frozen food plant producing special meals for the airlines. His wife's professional name was Penny Prudence, as she had a nationally syndicated foods column. We became such close friends that we even visited Paul's hometown, Colemar in Alsace Lorraine, France, and hired a driver who took us around. We tasted onion rolls, drank the seven-wine drink called "The Hemmel's Leiter," and bought a fruity Alsation white wine from a vintner whose family business had endured for more than 600 years. We loved the small shops where pastries, meats including wild game, confections, and fruits and vegetables were sold just as they had been sold for hundreds of years.

Traveling Abroad

Tom booked us into the finest hotels in Europe when Ruth and I went to the Culinary Olympics in 1968. In truth, the small villages in Alsace, Salzburg , Austria, and Nazaré in Portugal were like fairy tale lands to us. Others such as Dundee, Scotland, and Lahinch, Ennistymon, and Ennis in County Clare, Ireland had the same impression on us.

When Ruth and I visited the hotel schools of Lausanne, Switzerland; Brussels, Belgium; Strasbourg in Alsace Lorraine, and Ealing College of Higher Education in London, I learned a lot. We also visited one in Vienna, Austria.

Henry Barbour, Director of the Hotel School, had just made a similar trip so Tom and I felt that I should do the same thing. Henry stated, "Brussel's school was the finest." I agreed with him. They offer two programs. The first teaches the nuances and skills of cooking, baking, and pastry-making. The second goes further into business and property ownership and management.

In 1970, Tom contacted a travel agent in East Lansing, Michigan, and had her arrange another memorable trip for Ruth and me. We flew into Orly Airport on Air France, visited the Arc de Triomphe and walked along the side of the River Seine where artists exhibit their work. We stopped at Notre Dame Cathedral, returned to Orly Airport, and went to Zurich by train to see the famous Uli Prager who had a daughter, Christine Prager, in my classes. Dr. Kotschevar had helped her get into the Hotel School at Michigan State.

When we arrived in Zurich, we learned that Uli had had a bad ski accident and was at the Cantonspital, or hospital. We went there and found him lying in traction, flat on his back, with four telephones at his bedside. This was how he carried on the business while being incapacitated. Uli was glad we came to visit him, and to learn that Christine was doing great in our Hotel School. She made up costumes for a Swiss dinner put on by our Les Gourmets student club.

Uli invited us to visit his manager and have lunch at the Zurich Movenpick restaurant. Movenpick meant move along and pick out what you want. Uli got the idea from a trip he made to the United States. It caught on well. Later he changed the Movenpick restaurants into full-service dining, but carried on the original concept in the Kiegelbaum chain of fast-food operations that he owned. We did enjoy our meal. While in this area, Tom had us booked into a picturesque inn, located in Luzerne, on a hill overlooking a small lake full of swans, ducks, and geese.

Eating at the local train station was inexpensive and pleasant. We would take the elevator down the hill and walk to the station. Bratwurst and roasting potatoes were our favorite lunch. Roasting potatoes are made by first baking the potato and then slicing and frying it. They are so-o-o-o-o good, as is the wonderful veal bratwurst you can only get there where calves are plentiful. The beautiful brown Swiss cows that graze on mountain pastures produce so much milk and cream that it is their principal export product. Enough calves are available for slaughter to provide milk-fed pure white veal bratwurst, our favorite sausage.

At Geneva, Tom had us booked into a luxurious hotel, the President. Strangely, though, when I asked to cash a $100 check, the desk clerk would not do it. Here we were paying $5 for an egg and $5 for a peach, and they failed to cash my check.

Down the street was the Hilton International Hotel. Helen Recknagel of Cornell had told me about Max Blouet, the greatest hotelier in Europe and perhaps in the whole world. When I called him, he invited us over and immediately cashed my check. Ruth and I were welcomed by Max Blouet. We dined with him and for the next 20 years received a beautiful Christmas card from him wherever he was. Ten years later, I had lunch with him at the London Hilton on the Park. As soon as we met and shook hands, he asked, "Where's Ruth?" He had just finished playing tennis with his son.

What a genial host Max was! Joking with me, he asked if I knew his brother Louie

Blouet at the London Hilton. I did not, but when I visited Chef Sylvino Trompetto at the Savoy Hotel in London, the chef proudly told me that he lived next door to Louie Blouet.

Trompetto had 200 cooks in white in his kitchen. To me, he was the greatest active European chef I ever met. I gave him a Kennedy half dollar. I took 25 with me in 1970 to pass out. In scouting, we always did this. Trompetto asked where I was headed after we parted. I said, "I am going to visit the French chef at the Claridge." He asked, "How would you like to come back afterward, at 2:00 PM, and have lunch with me?" What a wonderful opportunity to visit with this great man. I felt so lucky. God was looking after me again!

Oh what a lunch we had! Soufflé of Salmon, baby green beans stacked on a two-inch diameter mushroom, rissole potatoes, asparagus with a chicken supreme dressing, all finished off with fresh peach halves in Pouilly Fuisse Latour white wine. Sylvino said, "For me, it's the only wine!" When I walked out after thanking the chef, I had stars in my eyes. What a rich experience. By any measure it had to be one of the finest repasts anyone could have. Chef Trompetto told me how he came to be such a great chef at one of the world's finest hotels, the Savoy in London.

(Editor's Note: Interestingly enough, in looking back at Dr. and Mrs. Minor's trip, a few years later Dr. Minor was willing to afford me the same trip as he took and experienced. In my case, I was sending one of my community college students to Europe for one year. The Council on Hotel, Restaurant, and Institutional Education (CHRIE) asked if I would establish the International Hospitality Exchange Program (IHEP) to allow students an opportunity to study abroad. I agreed and traveled, Dutch treat, with one of my students, John Philip French, now president of Heart Smart International nearly 20 years later, as he looked at European hospitality schools in which he might study. Dr. Minor arranged for a private meeting for us with each of the renowned chefs, industry leaders, and educators he himself met and knew in Europe.

The reader should now begin to understand why a student-professor relationship is one of the most valuable to be established in life. Because I was willing to step into Dr. Minor's office and seek his advice and understanding, he was willing to be a mentor to me and share life's finest with me. In fact, he would be the one to find my first three jobs for me, and be influential in helping me to secure all jobs I took in life! Need I say more to those of you who are students and are shy about talking with your professor or instructor?)

Victor Ceserani

During this trip I also visited Chef Victor Ceserani at the Ealing College of Higher Education's Catering School. Together, Victor Ceserani and Ronnie Hinton published an excellent catering text that was used at the School. The School's Director wanted Ceserani to get a Master's degree at Cornell's Hotel School. After I had an opportunity to speak with the Director of our School, Henry Barbour, Ceserani, who was a polished speaker and fine teacher, ended up securing his Master's Degree from Michigan State using his status and experience from being executive chef at London's oldest club, The Boodle Club. He taught quantity foods cooking for two years, took his classes, and graduated by the skin of his teeth.

His problems were intensified one day as Ruth took some hoteliers to the on-campus medical center, Olin. We had three Irish hoteliers come as guests to our School. One morning I came to Kellogg Center and had Ruth along to make a coffee demonstration to my Food Flavor Evaluation class. As we walked in the door, Michael Vaughan, who ran the Aberdeen Arms Hotel in Lahinch County Clare, came running saying that Victor Ceserani was all gray looking and had nearly passed out. Victor had come to take the three Irishmen to Oakland Community College for a morning visit.

Ruth took him in our car to Olin Health Center. Luckily an orderly saw Victor's grayness when Ruth brought him into the Center. The orderly put him in a wheel chair and took him right in to the doctor. Ceserani was told that open-heart surgery was needed. Victor asked the doctor to treat him so that he could finish out the term before having his operation.

Between terms, Victor had his surgery without missing a single class. He was a man of God, a Catholic, didn't worry about a thing, prayed and left it all in the Lord's hands. Five surgeons worked on him. It must be true what they say that "too many cooks will spoil the broth." Victor's arteries plugged right up again. They failed to prescribe the blood thinners needed, so he went through the ordeal again between the next two terms. This time he was given blood thinner and he still lives in Jersey, a London suburb, and is doing well.

Later, Victor became the Director of the Ealing College of Higher Education's Catering School and was knighted by Queen Elizabeth for his services to England. He wrote two books, UNDERSTANDING COOKING and UNDERSTANDING FOODS with Lendal Kotschevar (these were English versions of Lendal's best sellers as the terms used in catering instruction in England, such as metric units for weights and measures, are in considerable variance with the ones used in the United States), and a volume about his life and experiences as a cook. He sent me an English volume titled "The Master Chefs", which I used for my Food Flavor Evaluation class.

Ruth undoubtedly deserves credit for saving Victor Ceserani's life, permitting him to enjoy the most fruitful and happiest years of his illustrious career as a chef and catering educator. I am glad that I met him, sponsored him at Michigan State where he earned his Master's Degree in Business, and introduced him to Professor Kotschevar who collaborated with him on the English texts.

A Cabin in New Brunswick

One afternoon prior to Professor Kotschevar leaving Michigan State where he had an office next to mine, he said, "Lew, I'm in trouble. I would like to help Brother Herman Zaccarelli with his workshops for Catholic nuns and brothers who work in foodservice for Catholic institutions in the United States and Canada."

Now the Minor Corporation had assisted Brother Herman in his workshops previously. In fact, two were unforgettable. The first was at Memrans Cooke near Moncton in the Maritimes. Nuns attended from institutional kitchens in several locations.

After we arrived, we met with Brother Herman and Tom Ryan. George Marchand was there, too, so I went with him to a fine family restaurant I knew. At dinner, George told me that his first job after leaving his home in Normandy, France, was at the New Brunswick Hotel in Moncton.

All of a sudden there was a violent thunderstorm that sent a bolt of lightning through the restaurant. It hit the transformer and deep fat fryer. Everything was pitch black as George and I returned to the convent at 11:00 PM. We entered through a door on the opposite side of the building from that where we had departed earlier that afternoon. We could not see the room numbers and entered one with two nuns in it. We dashed from their room as we discovered our error.

The second workshop was at Laval University, Quebec. Our three French-speaking chefs were there with us: John Secter, George Marchand, and Emil Burgermeister. Nothing but French was spoken there. When a nun came to me in the morning, Tom said, "Say 'Bonjour.'" So I did, since I knew no "Cum Si or Cum Sa" or "Comment allez-vous."

Upon returning home to Cleveland, I took a French class at Baldwin Wallace, Berea, Ohio. It was a 4th year class, and I got in over my head. Of course, I failed the first exam, but kept with the course.

By diligent study while locked in a bedroom at home, and by hiring the best woman student in the class who tutored me following each class session, I was able to surprise our professor. I was first in the class to finish the final. He graded it at once and said, "I don't know how you were able to do it, but you passed my 4th year French reading class."

Considering Kotschevar's latest request to assist Brother Herman, I called Tom Ryan and he said, "We will play with him," and how we did! I went to Zaccarelli's workshop, this time in Toronto, where we took chefs Secter, Marchand, and Burgermeister. Tom also invited MSU's kitchen planner, Gladys Knight, and Matthew Bernatsky of Cornell, all at no cost to Brother Herman. The Minor Corporation paid the tab except for food and lodging. We paid for all instructional personnel, for special cookbooks for the nuns, and roses and champagne for all which Tom insisted upon. Tom never went off half-cocked but did things in an unforgettably effective and grand manner.

We had a dress code for all of our sales representatives. Tom told George Marchand that the sport jacket he was wearing was not up to L. J. Minor Corporation standards. So after the first day's session, he took our chefs and Matthew Bernatsky to the leading haberdashery in Toronto to purchase clothing representative of the Minor dress code. Tom's demonstrative performance taught them all a lesson. They had better dress up when they were not teaching in their white chef uniforms.

Brother Herman repaid us for the support given him by helping to get the food base account at Notre Dame where he trained as a Holy Cross brother. He also helped us with sales to several Ivy League universities.

Mrs. Minor was with me, and Mrs. Helen Bernatsky with Matthew. Helen and Ruth got along so well that we bought their property on the Miramichi River in Blackville, New Brunswick from them.

Tom encouraged this purchase. He went and checked things out for us. We built a Lindahl cedar-siding home there of U. S. cedar from Oregon. Later we had a livable cabin built of 12 inch logs for our chefs. This was constructed from plans that we had for building one in Michigan. It took four days to get to the place from Lansing. We took our grandsons and a granddaughter there with us. Our daughters, Ruth Ann (mother of two of the children) and Josephine visited us there. George and Henrietta Marchand, John and Betty McLaughlin, our daughter Kathleen and her husband, Jim Swanson, David Swanson and his family and others spent time there with us.

Since it was so far away and we watched a two hour TV show titled, "Yankee Go Home" on a Canadian network we decided to sell the place after four years for less than half of what we had in it or just $50,000. It was a lot of work keeping the place up to our standards.

We had it beautifully furnished, including a fine, regulation-size pool table and an upright piano. We went mackerel and lobster fishing, and cemented relations with the New Brunswick lobster packer from whom we got our lobster supplies for our lobster base. We would often buy a dozen one-pound lobsters and cook them. The smaller ones are the best. The Shediac packer even had sea water indoor holding tanks for keeping live lobsters fresh for shipping.

Once we sold the 600 feet of river frontage and 100 acres of forest and nice cedar home and log cabin, we never missed them. We had better salmon fishing in Michigan than they had on the Miramichi. At one time it had been the best lobster fishing anywhere on the East coast. Shediac was called the Lobster Capital of the world.

Eventually, the business relationships we developed with the New Brunswick governmental officials helped our company get the lobster needed to make our lobster base and meet the demand. Lobster fishing was limited in both Nova Scotia and New Brunswick to about ten weeks per year.

Other Journeys

When the Ceserani's asked to visit the Maritime province of Canada with Ruth and me, we decided to go together. We first took them to the Laurentian Mountains and stayed at LaSapien where the chef had been recommended to us by one of our employees, Hans Bueschkens. We visited the chef's home and were amazed to learn that his wife and the wife of our dear guest lecturer friend, Milos Cihelka, of Golden Mushroom Restaurant fame, were sisters. It really is a small world when occasions of this sort arise.

Victor and I enjoyed a nice game of tennis there and he beat me. We stayed at the New Brunswick Hotel in Moncton and at the Nova Scotia in Halifax. We even stayed overnight at the Keltic Lodge in Ingonish, Nova Scotia, and visited Alexander Graham Bell's estate museum in Bedeck.

We also visited Keltic College in Bedeck which is famous for its Scottish dancing and bagpipe instruction taught by teachers brought over specially from Scotland each summer. Our daughters, Rosalie and Mary, and our grandson, Dorsey, all went to Keltic College for a couple of weeks one summer.

Wherever we took the Ceserani's, we visited the chefs. And if they were unable to join us for dinner, we would invite their wives to join us. At the Keltic Lodge, the chef liked us so much that he complimented not only our meals there but our lodging as well. Of course, he knew Hans Bueschkens had sent us there.

Ceserani had a lot of class and readily impressed the chefs he met. His calm, confidential, and pleasant demeanor added up to Italian charm, although his Irish wife and he were completely Anglicized and loved old England and London where they lived.

He was a man who came up from the crowd and I was happy that I could help him accomplish this. We will always be friends and Ruth and I will always treasure the sweaters his wife, Betty, knitted for us. In fact, we looked after his teen-aged sons, John and Michael, now men, when he first came to East Lansing. They are doing well in London and stay close to their parents.

On another trip Ruth and I took John and Betty McLaughlin around the Maritimes and used our station wagon. Betty loved it, and since it was a company car, I gave it to them for their use.

From our summer home in Blackville, we went to Fredericton to show them the tidal bore, and then drove to Truro, the hub of the Maritimes from which you can go to Prince Edward Island and Nova Scotia, or Newfoundland, the other three Maritime Provinces. On this trip we went to Bedeck first and visited Bell's estate and the Keltic College. Then we went on to Duck Cove Bay Motel. While there, we visited Elizabeth Laforte's Barn Studio.

Betty liked a painting of cherry trees in blossom. This was not an oil or water color painting, but one made from colored threads that Elizabeth Laforte blended together on a loom. First, she started with plain white cotton thread, and then dyed it to the different shades needed to produce a picture exactly the same as that seen on a color photo that she copied in her own ingenious way. The one Betty chose cost $400 and she placed it in her home in Colonial Heights, Virginia. It was lovely.

Ruth and I also bought a painting from Elizabeth Laforte that is now hung in our family room. It is in color showing a deer and two fawns watering in a forest stream. It measures 30 x 24 inches. We also purchased a beautiful portrait of Pope John for Brother Herman that measured three by four feet.

We all celebrated John and Betty's anniversary together that evening at dinner. Betty appreciated having an opportunity to be with John in a relaxed atmosphere since he had been away in the service for so long in Wurms, Germany, and she was at home alone. Besides going to the Maritimes with us, we went to Hawaii and Isle Royale in Lake Superior with them. These trips allowed us all to enjoy one another's company.

194

Chapter 24

Today's Food Production Systems

by Lewis J. Minor, Ph.D.
School of Hotel, Restaurant, and Institutional Management
Michigan State University

Introduction

Demands of a Growing Market

Coping with Low Kitchen Productivity

Where the Food Service Dollar Goes

Hotels and Restaurants

Food Production Systems

New Directions for a Food Service Company
Fred Sanders, Detroit Michigan

Highly Mechanized Central Food Preparation
Ford Motor Company
Dearborn, Michigan

Bill Knapp's
Battle Creek, Michigan

AGS Chilled Food
Greenville, South Carolina

Fairfield Farms Kitchen
Silver Springs, Maryland

Marriott's Highly Automated Fairfield Farms Kitchen

Proceeding Systematically
by Lewis J. Minor

Things of mushroom proportions will usually have mushroom consequences. In other words, when a business comes up quickly, it usually folds fast. Many restaurants start beautifully. Then management cuts service and food costs to enhance profit and the restaurant folds.

This article is based on an address delivered by Dr. Lewis J. Minor at Stage X: Food Systems of the Future, held at the School of Hotel Administration, Cornell University. Dr. Minor was an acting professor in the School of Hotel, Restaurant, and Institutional Management at Michigan State University where he taught courses in food science.

Introduction

Many experiences led me to write the following article for Helen Recknagel who, as editor of *The Cornell HRA Quarterly*, first used it for publication in her magazine (May, 1972 issue). My knowledge came from commissary operations such as the Ford Motor kitchens where meals were processed daily for thousands of workers. I knew the manager, John Zureki, who graduated from our Hotel School.

Bill Knapp's kitchens in Battle Creek, Michigan, provided me with experience dealing with thousands of chickens cooked, deboned, halved or quartered, and hundreds of pounds of ground round steak made up in hamburger patties for daily shipment in refrigerated trucks to their own restaurants in Michigan, Indiana, and Illinois.

Marriott's huge central kitchens in Washington, D.C. also provided me with an outstanding understanding of today's food production systems. It was on that trip with Dr. Kotschevar that John Secter was with us and we visited the great chef and dear friend of ours, Walter Haller, who worked for Kennedy and Johnson, and was cooking for the Nixons at the time of our visit. He and his sous chef visited with us over a bottle of the President's favorite wine from the Rhone Valley in Germany. It was a lovely medium dry white wine.

Chef Haller wrote the Minor Corporation a testimonial letter that he sent to Brother Herman stating that Minor's bases were used exclusively in his kitchen at the White House, not just every day, but on all special occasions, when dinner receptions using gold table service were prepared. We posted this letter in the plant to provide employees with justifiable pride in the jobs they were doing.

Here, then, is the article as it appeared in Cornell's publication.

Many landmarks of fine cuisine are closing their doors today. Those preparing food in the manner of Escoffier, with kitchens manned by expert chefs and specialized cooks, find that payroll and other costs have soared beyond the revenue obtainable. Lack of steady patronage, particularly for dinner in city business districts, is given as the reason for their demise.

Although their menu prices are pegged high, the cost of maintaining the multi-station French kitchen cannot be recaptured unless there is a steady flow of customers. As Gene Carvello, Jr., president of New York's Colony restaurant said: "I was losing money just to work there every day."

Some fine restaurants are seeking dinner volume by selling banquets. Others, such as El Morocco, have sold club memberships to assure that fixed costs are covered. Meanwhile, both city and country clubs find that it is increasingly difficult to make their food services self-sustaining. Bar business and banquets help bail them out.

The solution seen in Paris where a similar situation prevails (Newsweek, March 13, 1972) is for skilled young chefs to operate their own small restaurants. The chef as owner-operator has incentive, according to the article, to serve fine cuisine to a small group of patrons and doesn't encounter the payroll and quality control problems of a place like Maxim's. *Fortune* magazine of March 1972 ("Restaurants Need Some New Recipes for Survival") foresees the same solution, that fine restaurants in America may become mom-pop-and-son places.

Because sales volume is stressed in all of these instances, it would seem that only large hotels of the luxury type with a great deal of regular business supplemented with conventions and banquets can afford a chef-run kitchen. Chefs are also required by food manufacturers such as Heinz, Sara Lee, Marriott, Armour and others to create new dishes and oversee their development.

Demands of a Growing Market

Yet there is growing demand for food service in the marketplace. More people than ever before are eating away from home. In 1970 the figure was one out of five meals; by 1980 the estimate is that it will be one out of three. Why then the failure of places serving the very finest food?

The demand, of course, is for moderate-priced food, prepared with a minimum of high-priced services. The great growth in food eaten away from home is at such food service establishments as schools and colleges, hospitals and nursing homes, industrial plants and offices.

There is also the meal eaten out or taken home, because so many married women work and have little time to cook. And there are meals eaten on the road as more people travel for pleasure and recreation during weekends, holidays, vacations. Add them all up, though, and the market is for food at prices that aren't too much higher than a "convenience food" meal can be gotten together at home.

Another significant trend is the change in food tastes and eating habits, the growing tendency to snack at any hour. This is partly due to diet-consciousness and partly due to

197

the informality of home meals. Everyone seems too busy to eat a full meal around the family dining table. Despite the tremendous sale of gourmet cookbooks, they may be opened only on weekends or holidays.

Coping With Low Kitchen Productivity

Having thus covered the nature of the market demand, let us take a look at how food service establishments are coping with the need to produce moderate-priced meals with minimum kitchen payroll. Five years ago, it was estimated that the average kitchen worker's output was about $10,000 annually. Due to inflation and higher menu prices, this figure — assuming the same production methods are used — would be over $12,000 annually today, or scarcely enough to cover wage increases and benefits given to workers during the same period. But the food service organizations which are prospering, despite the squeeze between menu prices and rising costs, are those that obtain better than four to ten times this figure of worker-to-sales volume productivity.

Most of these food service organizations are multiple unit, either chain or franchise companies, with a systematic approach to hold down food production costs. The chains often centralize major steps in food production in a highly mechanized commissary and transport prepared products to service outlets.

The franchised fast food place, independently owned, emphasizes standard quality for limited menu, priced lower than neighborhood restaurants. Food products are purchased semi-prepared and some fully prepared, often through a centralized franchise supply system. Centralized purchasing in quantity can cut costs and assure standard quality.

Because of technically developed cooking equipment — fryers, pressure cookers, ovens, grills — no highly paid skilled cook is needed at the fast food unit. A semi-skilled worker can put menu items together in jig time. High sales volume produces a profit even though food cost as a percentage of sales may be higher than at a traditional restaurant. Non-productive payroll is kept to an absolute minimum through careful worker scheduling. Customer self-service is emphasized.

Specialty restaurants operate on pretty much the same principle, volume sales for a popular limited menu. Because they serve higher grade food and provide more service and atmosphere, the specialty restaurants command a higher check average. But their operating costs are higher.

Provision is made in most productive food service establishments to have basic food preparation chores, sometimes even major steps, separated from the service outlet. This may be done in a commissary which produces fresh food and delivers it chilled to service outlets. Or it may be done in a central facility which freezes major food items for transport over relatively long distances while fresh products are purchased by the service outlet. Schools, hospitals, colleges, airlines may purchase processed food from multiple commercial sources and confine most efforts on the premises to assembling meals.

In the commissary and factory, highly paid chefs, cooks, dietitians, and food technologists utilize their services to mass-produce food, thereby lowering their payroll cost per unit. When coupled with new types of equipment and technology, the productivity figure for all workers is high.

Moreover, the commissary or factory is located away from high rent districts and where a supply of capable workers can be found. The service outlet, on the other hand, is located in heavily trafficked areas, where rent and labor costs are usually high. The disadvantage of the centralized food production system is that of distribution. Transporting food products in the frozen or chilled state is expensive and rigid controls are required to conform to public health regulations.

Where the Food Service Dollar Goes

A 5-year two phase cooperative survey conducted by the marketing economics division of USDA, and co-sponsored by the International Food Service Manufacturers Association, revealed that the retail value of food and non-alcoholic beverages moving through the over-all food service industry approximated $35 billion in 1969 vs. $28 billion in 1966. Food service operators paid $16 billion for these foods and non-alcoholic beverages purchased in 1969 resulting in a ratio of about 2 1/4 to 1 for sales revenue versus food cost. About half of all foods purchased in 1969 was by outlets with annual gross food sales of $100,000 or more, and representing 14 percent of the total number of establishments. Outlets with sales of less than $20,000 annually represented 38 percent of the total number surveyed, but only 14 percent of the total food purchased.

Commissaries and other company owned facilities grew from an insignificant figure in the 1966 survey to 6 percent of the total foods purchased in 1969. Thus, it appears that company-owned central production kitchens are primarily high volume operations. According to the USDA this source of supply will probably grow significantly in the years ahead.

Data was based on the values of individual foods and food product groups received during a seven day period in 1969 by a national sample from about 3,000 food service operators in 48 states.

Hotels and Restaurants

But, you may well ask, what about hotels and fine restaurants? What use are they making of this technology? In many of them, kitchen union restrictions preclude bringing in prepared food. In these establishments, also, the customers expect a higher level of food quality than they do in the plant cafeteria or at the fast food outlet.

Three studies will be of interest. The first, which was made by the U.S. Department of Agriculture, shows food purchases for a representative sample of the food service industry. Note that fully prepared foods, baked goods, and soups, sauces, and gravies came only to a little over 11% of the total. Of course, a portion of dairy products and "ices" would raise this figure a little.

Next, let us consider a survey published in *Frozen Food Age* of November 1971 as to the market penetration of frozen products. It showed that 77.5% of food service operators purchased some type of frozen products. But in only 1.4% of the establishments did frozen dishes provide over 75% of the menu offerings; and in another 1.5% of those surveyed frozen dishes provided 51-75% of menu offerings. The products listed, in order of their sales volume, were: frozen seafood; entrees; dessert pies, cakes, and pastries; bread and rolls; hors d'oeuvres; ethnic items; soups; and, at the end of the list, complete dinners.

The greatest use, the study found, was made of table-ready foods by schools and colleges - 92% used some products. Only 57.1% of fast food places use any. Cafeterias use more than restaurants. Companies with multiple and diversified outlets - cafeterias and restaurants, restaurants and inplant feeding - and the airlines make the widest use of frozen prepared foods.

A third report is given by Michael Warfel, vice president of food and beverage for I.T.T.-Sheraton in the May 1970 issue of *The Cornell Hotel & Restaurant Administration Quarterly*. Warfel reports that frozen entrees do not yet have reliable quality for hotel service and that the price of quality products is far too high. He also points out that most frozen entrees are sauced items, which don't appeal to today's diet-conscious patrons. Only 8% of the food served in this large hotel chain is comprised of frozen entrees.

Warfel states, however, that many convenience foods are purchased at varying stages of preparation, from those in the initial stage - salad greens, pared vegetables, precut portioned meats, etc. - through stages where items are frozen or canned, on to the most advanced stage, table-ready or "chef-ready."

One solution to the food quality-high payroll dilemma would be for hotel kitchens to mass-produce their own food specialties during kitchen slack time and hold them either frozen or chilled for future service over a fairly short time period. This concept was developed by the late H. Alexander MacLennan in his Ready Foods Program. Hotels already have master chefs, skilled cooks, and mass-production techniques for their banquet facilities. This concept, however, has won the largest acceptance overseas where commercial products are not abundantly available.

Several large hospitals are following this practice, particularly for diet foods. The AGS concept, described later in this article, produces pasteurized cooked food in a central commissary and holds it chilled at 30 to 32 degrees Fahrenheit for delivery to hospitals in three neighboring cities.

There is no dearth of commercial frozen entrees on the American market. The American Hotel & Motel Association annually publishes a *Directory of Frozen Entrees* which are commercially available. The most recent issue lists some 900 frozen entrees of which about 350 are different products. Customer preferences, frozen entree costs and quality, and union resistance are the factors Warfel cites as to why hotels and restaurants use frozen entrees only to round out simplified menus built around steaks, roasts, and chops, which require little cooking time and skill.

Yet the principle of table-ready foods is not new. The frozen meal dates back to the 1940's when the late Bernie Proctor first developed the TV dinner for the Armed Forces. During the same decade, the H. J. Heinz Company introduced their canned soup display kitchens - standup bars where individual canned servings of soup, stew, pork and beans, and other items were heated and served at a low price. Both types of heat-and-serve meals are still on the market.

The progress which has been made in the last thirty years is that both canned and frozen foods have become broader in variety and their quality has been upgraded. Processing to preserve food quality now involves the use of modified starches and other weather-control agents, antioxidants, sequestrates, and similar additives. New techniques have evolved for baking, cooking, freezing, packaging, warming foods. Far more food than ever before is now processed in one or more stages toward being table-ready, reducing the need for preliminary food preparation at the point of service.

But the food tastes of the customer who goes to a commercial establishment to buy his meal are such that he does not choose the frozen-cooked dish to any great extent. Where he has little choice, he eats what is given to him, or he "snacks" and eats at home.

Food Production Systems

The systems used by five large food service organizations are described in this article. The first three - Fred Sanders, Ford Motor Company, and Bill Knapp's, all located in Michigan, - use conventional food preparation methods with highly productive equipment to mass-produce food in commissaries. From the commissaries, the fresh food is trucked chilled to satellite service units.

The AGS system, developed by Col. Ambrose T. McGukian for the Andersonville-Greenville-Spartanburg (South Carolina) hospitals goes two steps further. The food is partially prepared in the conventional manner and then packaged in portions, pasteurized, and held chilled just above the freezing point until the hospitals requisition it from storage. The food is produced to meet a three-week menu cycle. At the hospitals, the food needs only reheating in a hot water bath or, when plated, in a microwave oven. The food does not undergo the strains of freezing and thawing, which makes it easier to retain quality and less expensive than freezing methods. But rigid controls of sanitation and inventory-dating must be maintained.

The fifth - Marriott's Fairfield Farms - is an all-product food factory which prepares convenience foods of different types to match quality specifications of hotels, restaurants, hospitals and airlines to which the company caters. The most sophisticated cooking, baking, and freezing technology is used, along with mass-production equipment which is food factory in type, not commercial kitchen.

Considerable progress has been made in the technological production of food of acceptable quality. As yet, however, nothing has been developed to equal the talents of an expert chef.

New Directions for a Food Service Company
Fred Sanders
Detroit, Michigan

This company has been in business for over 100 years. It sells food through company-owned stores; baked goods and candies in separate supermarket departments; and candies in drug stores and department stores located in Michigan, Ohio, and Indiana. Sales volume for 1970 was $29 million.

Sanders' Detroit plant was built in 1941 and employs 900 workers. Another 900 people work in Sanders retail outlets. Harry Wilson is the plant manager and Edward Maeder is the chef. Plant employees work 40 hours per week in two shifts.

Because union wage scales and taxes are high in Detroit, Sanders now farms out its food production to non-union kitchens in other areas and concentrates its plant facilities on producing baked items, candies, and ice cream. Sanders' lunch-counter food has declined in quality despite good specifications. For years, their urban stores averaged $1 million annually in sales; today, four stores are needed to sell the same volume. Better locations must constantly be sought. The outlook is that the company may concentrate on producing confectionery items with marketing handled by other organizations.

Highly Mechanized Central Food Preparation
Ford Motor Co.
Dearborn, Michigan

Ford's highly mechanized commissary, which prepares food for 25,000 company employees at 12 locations within a 15-mile radius, is fully described in the May 1968 issue of this magazine. Director of food service is Richard Mather, who, with an office-supervisory staff of four, oversees the food production of 25 employees working in three shifts, Monday through Friday. Unionized food workers receive wages and fringe benefits of better than $5 per hour, necessitating high productivity. Meal prices at the satellite service units are set low by company-union agreement. Even so, commissary workers produce $52,000 worth of food annually per worker.

All food, except for some meat items, is prepared fresh a day ahead of service and kept chilled for delivery by refrigerator trucks. To keep the meat department busy, some items are frozen for storage, but delivered thawed to service units. Satellite service units have finishing kitchens with grills, fryers, and ovens, but have refrigerators large enough only to hold daily food needs. Menus are planned on a six-week cycle. Orders from each unit are tabulated in advance at the commissary. Recipe quantities are machine-calculated and carefully measured in an ingredient room before production begins.

Food processing performed in the commissary is as follows:

• Braised meat entrees, such as Swiss steak or short-ribs, are completely cooked,

202

refrigerated, and transported to satellite units for reheating and serving;

• Ground meat entrees, such as meat balls and meat loaf, are also fully prepared and trucked to the satellites for reheating before service;

• Short-order grilled or broiled entrees are prefabricated and trucked either chilled or frozen to the satellite where they are cooked to order;

• Soups, chili, gravies, and sauces are fully prepared and shipped chilled to the satellite for reheating;

• Creamed, scalloped, and au gratin vegetables are fully prepared from raw products and only reheated at the satellite;

• Fresh vegetables and fruits are cleaned, cut, and bagged and sent chilled to the satellite for assembly and service. Potatoes are French fried in the finishing kitchens;

• Pastries, pies, cakes and some rolls are produced in the bake shop (bread is purchased) and readied for shipment;

• Gelatin desserts and salads are first mixed and then poured into 1.25 gallon pans; they are portioned before delivery. Ice cream and sherbet are purchased from a supplier.

Bill Knapp's
Battle Creek, Michigan

Bill Knapp was a salesman for Standard Brands before he started his first moderate-priced restaurant in Battle Creek in 1948. In 1956, when he had four restaurants grossing a total of $250,000 annually, he built his first commissary. Today his company operates 25 restaurants, 18 of them in Michigan and the other 17 in northern Indiana and Ohio, with total sales for 1970 of $12 million to 7 million customers. A second commissary and five more restaurants are planned for 1972. Growth rate has been over 25% annually. In design, Knapp's restaurant resemble a red brick New England town hall. Each free-standing store costs about $360,000 for land, building, equipment and parking area. They are located on busy highways near industrial and shopping centers and suburban residential areas. Managers are high school graduates selected and trained for several years by Knapp.

Menus feature fresh food, trucked to stores in refrigerated trucks (only the potatoes au gratin come frozen). The present commissary employs 100 workers (one fourth of them part-time) who work 40 hours weekly on two shifts. Sales revenue produced by the food prepared in the commissary averages well over $120,000 per worker.

How much food the commissary should produce for delivery the next morning to each restaurant is forecast by computer, which has 77 items programmed into it. To make the forecast, the computer compared food sold in each restaurant on a particular day. Friday for example - with that of four preceding Fridays and that of a corresponding Friday one year earlier. Adjustments are made for weather, events, and the year's increase in volume.

Food, which has been stored in refrigerator coolers is trucked in refrigerated carts to restaurant locations. Each truck serves four restaurants. At the restaurant the food receives final heating and assembly. Soup, a major menu item, merely needs reheating.

AGS Chilled Food
Greenville, South Carolina

This 10,000 sq. ft. commissary cooks and pasteurizes food in vacuum-packaged bags holding one to twenty portions, quick-chills it for storage at near the freezing point and delivers it by refrigerated truck to hospitals located in Anderson, Greenville, and Spartanburg (AGS), South Carolina. At the hospitals, pantry workers reheat the food either in the package in a hot water bath set for 160 degrees to 170 degrees Fahrenheit, or, after the food is plated, in a microwave oven.

The concept, which resembles Sweden's NACKA system, was developed by Col. Ambrose T. McGukian (U.S.A., ret.), who was formerly in charge of army food service. Colonel McGukian is president of AGS. The vice president is Cdr. Ezra Ferris (U.S.N., ret.) who was in naval hospital food service.

The commissary produces 3 million pounds of food annually, on a three-week menu cycle, using a single 40-hour weekly shift. The equipment needed costs about half that for a frozen food plant that would produce the same quantity of food. Hospitals using this system find they can reduce their own dietary staffs by 50% and have high-quality food available in their refrigerators day and night.

Food at the commissary is processed only to the nearly-done stage, with the remainder of the cooking completed during reheating at the hospital. Products which must be partially cooked before the cooking-pasteurizing stage are conventionally prepared. Raw vegetables are also prepared before cooking them.

In a separate room, to avoid contamination, products are machine-portioned into bags. (Items too large to go through the automatic filler such as sliced roast beef, ham, or chicken, are portioned manually.) Packages are vacuum-sealed in a high-vacuum cabinet before they are cooked-pasteurized.   After pasteurization, packages are quick-chilled and then stored in refrigerators especially designed to hold the food at 28 degrees - 30 degrees Fahrenheit, just above the food's freezing point. Separate refrigerators are needed for mostly-meat items and for vegetable items. Food is delivered to the hospitals by refrigerated trucks on the tray-carts used to hold it in storage.   Rigorous sanitary methods are required to avoid food contamination. Food in storage is labeled and dated to assure freshness, although tests have shown it will keep twice as long as the three-week cycle used.

Fairfield Farms Kitchen
Silver Springs, Maryland

Marriott Corporation is the nation's largest company-controlled food service organization. The company also has a hotel division, a franchised inn division, restaurants both company-controlled and franchised, and hospital and airline catering divisions. For 1971, Marriott's revenue from its different food service operations was over $510 million. Of course, not all food sold was produced by Fairfield Farms.

Marriott's decision to build and operate its own commissary was made in 1965. First, however, a chef-run pilot plant was operated to prove the project's feasibility in producing high quality food economically. In 1968, Fairfield Farms was completed.

Fairfield Farms is a huge, all-purpose commissary that occupies a 7-acre tract on the outskirts of Washington, D.C., the corporate headquarters. The receiving dock in back of the plant has a railroad spur leading up to it so that freight cars carrying raw products can be unloaded and refrigerated cars reloaded for shipment. The plant also maintains its own fleet of refrigerator-freezer trucks for product delivery.

The commissary's range of products include baked goods, ice cream, precut and oven-ready meat and poultry items, meat patties, and frozen cooked entrees. The most advanced, large-scale food processing equipment is utilized. Freezing technologies used - or experimented with - include plate and blast freezers, liquid nitrogen and Freon systems. The plant has a large freezer warehouse to store products ready for shipment, and several refrigerated coolers.

Considerable automation is used within the plant; automated trolleys which travel on a cog-track, conveyor belts, and pump lines. Thermometer control boards monitor food in process and in storage. Ingredient weighing for large formulations is done automatically. Containers are filled and weighed by controlled automation.

Processed items are shipped in cartons via refrigerated cars and trucks. Some fresh items are shipped chilled to Marriott's nearby units. Until recently, Fairfield Farm products were made for Marriott's own operations and catering divisions but some are now offered to the general institutional market.

Marriott's Highly Automated Fairfield Farms Kitchen

Dr. Robert Jackson is Fairfield Farm's general manager and Dr. Duane G. DeWeese is director of product improvement. These two food scientists are assisted by a staff of food technologists, a dietitian, a chef, and production supervisors. Federal food inspectors are constantly on duty to certify products for interstate shipment.

Chapter 25

General John D. McLaughlin

Our First Meeting   **God is Good!**   **Splendid Achievements**

Business Practices   **Sweet Dreams**

Who's Who in America (1988-1989)

Grit
by Edgar A. Guest
(1917)

How much grit do you think you've got?
Don't boast of your grit till you've tried it out.
For it's easy enough to retain a grin
In the face of a fight there's a chance to win.
But the sort of grit that is good to own
Is the stuff you need when you're all alone.

Quote from General Douglas MacArthur

"Old soldiers never die; they just fade away."

Quote from Joan Baez

"Being honest with yourself is more relevant than peace of mind."

Our First Meeting

I first met General McLaughlin at Fort Lee, Virginia, at the U. S. Army Quartermaster School in early 1972. Dr. Ryan was with me. My feeling when I shook hands with the General was one of awe, respect, and patriotism. I caught my breath as I looked into the face and eyes of this great American. At that time he was a two-star general. He was cheerful, friendly, hospitable, and inquisitive.

Earlier, in 1970, John Secter told Tom about the ineptitude of the Army chefs who tried to compete in culinary arts shows. As one of the judges, John knew that they needed help. So Tom called Colonel James Moore, Director of the U. S. Army Quartermaster School which General McLaughlin headed as Quartermaster General.

With the help of our chefs and that of our dear friend and colleague, Charles Camerano, who was the world's greatest living master of pulled and blown sugar creations, the Army chefs returned proudly to Fort Lee with gold, silver, and bronze medals. As a result, Tom received a nice letter of appreciation from the General.

His appreciation for the help that our great chefs John Secter and Charles Camerano had given his army chefs in their competitive cooking and display pieces was evident, however. His questions were about commissary or central kitchen food preparation. Having visited the central kitchens at Ford Motor Co., Bill Knapps, Marriott and Stouffer's, I was familiar with all of these operations.

He asked at once if I could go to Tacoma, Washington, where the CAFE (Central Army Feeding Experiment), under Dr. Livingston's guidance was underway. Of course I could, and I was there the next two weeks.

It was in appreciation that Gen. McLaughlin sent me a Meritorious Service Award from the United States Army Quartermaster School, Fort Lee, Virginia, Feb. 9, 1973. Another service recognition award had been given to me on Dec. 18, 1972.

Two citation letters, dated Feb. 5, 1973 and Feb. 9, 1973, were also sent to me by Gen. McLaughlin. These awards were connected with the article previously presented in this text, "Today's Food Production Systems," published in *The HRA Cornell Quarterly*, Vol. 13, No. 1.

On a subsequent trip in the fall of 1972, Dr. Robert Bloomstrom, Director of Michigan State University's Hotel, Restaurant and Institutional Management School, and I visited Gen. McLaughlin and Col. James Moore at the United States Army Quartermaster School to learn about the curricula offered to U.S. Army personnel. We learned about their many officer training programs and their cooking and baking school. We visited the Quartermaster Museum and saw pictures of all of the Quartermaster Generals who served the Army, including the picture of Gen. McLaughlin.

You can see that we knew Gen. McLaughlin before he retired in 1974 after getting his third star and commanding 70,000 troops in Wurms, Germany. At the time, I frequently thought of White Christmas, a movie starring Bing Crosby, Danny Kaye, and Rosemary Clooney which featured a song titled, "What Do You Do With A General When A General Retires?" The song tells about all the generals who are unemployed and I was thinking about Gen. McLaughlin's future after he would retire.

When I first met Gen. McLaughlin with Dr. Ryan, word was sent from his office that his back, which had been injured in a parachute jump, was troubling him. When I met him that afternoon, I no sooner said hello than I asked him if I could see him privately. He said,

"Sure, come into my office and tell me what you want."

My thoughts turned away from the L. J. Minor Corporation as I said, "Our son, Bryan, has just been sent to Korea. He was recently divorced by his wife who maintained custody of their children. Could you contact a chaplain in Korea, where Bryan is stationed, and have the chaplain talk to him?" McLaughlin said, "I will contact his chaplain at once and have him talk to Bryan. We are friends as he was stationed here in Fort Lee prior to going to Korea."

As I stood with Gen. McLaughlin that first day, the thought crossed my mind, "Wouldn't it be something if someday he was with the L. J. Minor Corp?" A man with such impeccable credentials earned by years of patriotic service, whose speaking capabilities were hard to match, whose manners were perfect, whose grooming and personal care habits were apparent from viewing his clean and glistening fingernails, his easy and confident manner of speaking without any traces of crudity in diction, his ramrod straight military bearing, his ready smile and sense of humor, his shoes, spit and polished to perfection. Everything about him shouted to me: "Here's a great man. Get him for the company if you can!"

God is Good!

At the American Culinary Federation (ACF) annual meeting, at the Cleveland Hotel in June, 1974, there he was, recently retired, and looking for a job. Gen. John D. McLaughlin, who I admired and had a good friendly relationship with, talking to Dr. Thomas Aloysius Ryan. He asked Tom to find him a job with a big company as export sales manager. Tom was excited while telling me this, then I said, "What's wrong with the Minor Corporation?" Tom said, "He would not care to come with us as we are too small."

Shortly after Mary Mele's death, Tom Ryan had started to talk about dying, saying, "God stands between me and harm. But if I am taken, you should consider Frank Aicardi for sales." My thoughts were along the line of Gen. McLaughlin becoming Tom's successor instead of Frank. His polite manner, convincing and interesting speaking manner, and ability to tell stories about his experiences, and his ready humor gave me the gut-feeling that maybe he was the right man to succeed Tom.

Of course, he would never be considered for Tom's position as long as Tom Ryan lived. No one could ever do what Tom was capable of, at least in my mind.

Returning now to the ACF meeting: Tom and Gen. McLaughlin were discussing the problem of getting chefs reclassified by the U.S. Labor Department from "domestics" to "professionals." Dr. Koves, Dr. Ryan and I had often talked about this problem and how it might be solved.

Dr. Ryan asked me to join the conversation. Chef Louis Szathimary was making an impassioned, Hungarian-accented speech on the subject in the general session. Tom Ryan and I sensed that now was the moment to support Gen. McLaughlin to do the task.

Tom asked me, "Will the L. J. Minor Corporation pay the General's expenses to accomplish this?" I replied, "Yes, we will." Then Tom spoke up in the general session, saying, "While the ACF has a $5,000 fund set aside for this purpose, we don't want you to use any of its money. The L. J. Minor Corporation will take care of the General's expenses in accomplishing this task!" After John made a lot of trips to Washington, he accomplished the task, which took nearly three years and a $50,000 budget. This finally was accomplished by Gen. McLaughlin with the help of the L. J. Minor Corporation in 1977. Sadly, Tom did not live to witness it, as he died two years before.

In November, 1974, Dr. Ryan called my office at Eppley Center at Michigan State University. He sounded excited, saying, "Gen. McLaughlin wants to come with us. I took him to a demonstration of our food bases in New Orleans. Afterwards he decided to join us." I said, "This is great news. He can help make the business grow faster." I knew of Tom's illness at this point, and felt that by having him involved in identifying this new member of the Minor team, he would rest more comfortably knowing our company would be in good hands.

Tom's next move was to convince Gen. McLaughlin completely that joining us would provide him with a great business opportunity. The General loved to plan ahead and have every day filled with more than he could finish. He'd skip meals, and take cat naps on a leather davenport in his office.

I met the General in New York City and we drove together in a rented car to the Culinary Institute of America for a meeting of the board. We got acquainted. He said I only want to work for one boss. I said, "That will be me." I went on to say that we wanted him to manage our sales groups of chefs and salesmen.

In explaining our pricing, commission, discount, and freight policy, I stated, "Starting with the suggested retail price list, the distributor's discount is 20%. The salesman gets 10% after the distributor's 20% is subtracted from the retail price. Then after the sales commission, there's 5% for sales promotion, thus, 20-10 and 5 is our policy, and this totals 33%. Distributors receive an additional 2% for payment in 10 days. After that it's net. He absorbed it all.

That same month, Tom Ryan took Mike Zelski, Carl Richter, who was our newest chef, Hans Bueschkens, and Gen. McLaughlin to our school in Chef Ernest Koves' demonstration kitchen in New York City to learn more about the Food Base line and its uses by foodservice customers. They also visited Peterson-Owens, a leading meat purveyor who distributed our food bases in Manhattan.

In December, Tom Ryan went into Lakewood Hospital. He was diagnosed as incurable and released. A hospital bed was put in their apartment, and his wife, Babe, nursed him until he died in January, 1975. While Tom lay dying, Mike Zelski, Gen. McLaughlin and I visited him. He was as alert and sharp as ever, and told us to keep up our appearance.

Herman Taber and Ralph Napletana also visited him. Tom said to Herman, "Look after Lewie, when I'm gone as he'll be all alone." Recently, Ralph Napletana reminded me of this.

Herman did what Tom asked. On several occasions he reminded everyone, "This is not our company, it's Dr. Minor's." Three unauthorized projects cost the company huge sums of money after Tom's passing. Herman noted on three other, separate occasions that such ill-fated entrepreneurial pursuits could sap our resources, and discouraged such pursuits.

Gen. McLaughlin did the L. J. Minor Corporation a lot of good, but he would say to Herman Taber and me, "I don't want to be hobbled." We never could hobble him, but we did slow him down. I knew that one of John's principal motivations was to help his family, as we would all wish to do. I also have no doubt that had any of the unauthorized projects been profitable, that I would have shared in those profits.

Gen. McLaughlin, Walt Nicholes, our advertising man, Mike Zelski, Mike Minor, Ruth Ann Fields, and Jan Williams were a great team. The business was doing well, and we brought our grandson, Dorsey Fields, into the company at this time when he was in high school. Now, in 1995, he is a sales executive with the company in Dallas.

John called me his Irish brother. He kept the American flag on the right hand side of his desk, and the Irish flag on the left. We traveled to Ireland together and I believe it was one of the highlights of his life as he would often ask when we were going again.

Splendid Achievements

When Tom died in January, 1975, we saw Gen. McLaughlin's finest humanitarian hours with the L. J. Minor Corporation. He drove one of our station wagons to the airport, took people from the airport to their hotels, the funeral parlor, and funeral breakfast and back. He carried bags and organized the entire operation and involved his former Army Aide, Colonel Jim Moore, in all matters. He carried people's bags and completely submerged himself in helping others during this dark hour.

Gen. John D. McLaughlin's most positive achievements came when he established a symbiotic relationship between the L. J. Minor Corp. and the American Culinary Federation (ACF), the Culinary Institute of America, Johnson and Wales University, Cornell University, and Michigan State University. It is also fair to say that Dr. Thomas Aloysius Ryan and I pointed him in these directions to build on the foundation Tom and I had already established.

Gen. McLaughlin was on the Boards of Directors of the Culinary Institute of America, the International Food Manufacturers Association, the National Institute for the Food Industries, and the Food Service Executive Association. His influence was greatest with the American Culinary Federation.

His interest in the chefs profession began when our L. J. Minor chefs, John Secter and Charles Camerano, worked with Col. James Moore, Director of the United States Army Quartermaster School, to raise the skill levels of Army cooks who were competing in national and regional culinary art competitions and demonstrations. The improvement in

Army cooks' skills brought recognition to the School.

Gen. McLaughlin's interest in this activity was enhanced. Of course, Chef Secter's professional appearance and enthusiastic conversational manner, and Dr. Ryan's charming brilliance, made him realize that here was an important facet of the U.S. Army Quartermasters School that could bring honor and recognition to the School's reputation.

This interest was manifested when, after retirement from the Army, he came to the 1974 ACF meeting in Cleveland and accepted the challenge to change the status of the executive chef from "domestic" to "professional" rank. We knew that if he achieved this goal, as he did in January, 1977, that a symbiotic relationship between the L. J. Minor Corp and the chefs of America would be a reality. That is exactly what happened.

Concomitantly, when Gen. McLaughlin's appeal was made to the head of the United States Department of Labor for the chef's status to be changed from "domestic" to "professional," the Department gave the ACF a grant of $500,000 over a period of six years to develop an apprentice program for cooks and chefs. This program gave impetus to the growth of the ACF. Six regions were designated and six executive chefs appointed to carry out this program.

Gen. McLaughlin had three things he loved besides his wife and family--letter writing, travel, and meetings. He loved to work with others to both improve and avoid the "status quo."

When the L. J. Minor Corp. first began participating in the "Internationalle Kochung Ausstellung" (the international cooking exhibition), or what we Americans have named "The Culinary Olympics," there was only one food company sponsoring the team. They gave the American team of chefs who competed every four years in Frankfurt, Germany, against the chefs of the world, $50,000 to participate. A film was then produced depicting the results of the competition that was used in sales promotion. This film was privately held and not available without special permission.

Gen. McLaughlin worked with the ACF to bring other food company sponsors into the program, and brought the team's financial backing from $50,000 to $1,000,000. The ACF team backing is now on a par with the Canadians. Not only that, Gen. McLaughlin helped the American team by serving as team manager every four years from 1980 for as long as he lived. He also got help for the team from the local Army commander in Germany.

Furthermore, he used the resources of the L. J. Minor Corporation to help other teams who wanted to compete in the Culinary Olympics, and who asked our company for financial backing. The General and his son, William F. McLaughlin, have both made noteworthy gifts to the Culinary Institute and Johnson and Wales. They are both members of the elite chef society, The Order of the Golden Toque. The General is also inshrined in the American Academy of Chefs Hall of Fame at the ACF Headquartersin St. Augustine, Florida, along with Dr. Ryan, Chef Emil Burgermeister of the L. J. Minor Corp., and myself.

Gen. McLaughlin and his son, William, started the L. J. Minor Recipe Contest and the Professional Chef of the Year Award in 1988. Gen. McLaughlin died in 1992 and is buried in Arlington Cemetery with other great Americans. I respected him as friend and regular fellow. I really liked him. He would write me a friendly Thank-You note, now and then, and sign it, "Your Irish Brother, John."

But with his driving, challenging and ambitious hurry-up manner, I couldn't relax as I did in the personal and business relationship that I had with Tom Ryan whom I referred to as my "Business Dad." No one could ever replace Tom Ryan or be the confidante and mentor he was to me.

As Jackie Gleason would say, "How sweet it is." That's how I felt with Tom Ryan managing the company. I always trusted him completely and followed his advice, too, on most occasions.

With Gen. McLaughlin I felt entirely different. His forte was finance and personnel management. He lacked the legal and street smart mind that made Tom so helpful and valuable to me and the L. J. Minor Corporation. Tom found Herman Taber, who he called the leading expert on tax laws in the state of Ohio. Tom's CPA partner, Ralph Napletana, and Herman worked in the Internal Revenue for many years before establishing their tax and estate planning partnership.

Herman, Ralph and the General worked out the General's salary together. I never knew or cared what his salary was. I was confident he would earn it and would help to advance the business.

Ralph and Herman were with us from 1955 to 1983 when the business was sold. Now, Ruth and I retain Ralph as our tax agent. Herman died two years ago but was retained by us after we sold the company until his death.

Gen. McLaughlin was a great American soldier and businessman whose legendary accomplishments, like those of his predecessor, Thomas A. Ryan, will live on so long as the L. J. Minor Corporation endures.

Today, I love and miss my two great Irish associates. Dr. Thomas Aloysius Ryan, who was my second cousin, and Gen. John D. McLaughlin, who built a large company on the foundation that was laid by Dr. Ryan and me. Thank God! Life is beautiful.

Business Practices

Gen. McLaughlin liked to write letters. Tom Ryan and I avoided writing letters. You never know when a letter will come back to haunt you. Herman and Ralph had a meeting with him and he stopped doing it. I know that before he died, Tom told them to look after me and the business. I'm glad that he did. Sailing into the sea of business with a Gen. was like sailing in uncharted waters.

As I mentioned earlier, the General was always meticulously dressed. His speaking ability was exceptional, every word perfectly pronounced and clearly enunciated. Conversationally, John was a great story-teller. He could go on for hours reciting his experiences in the army. He knew McArthur, Patton, Eisenhower, Clark, and many others.

In our business, a good sense of smell and taste is essential. Thus, we were forced to exclude Tom Ryan and John McLaughlin from our taste panel tests. Both men were taste-blind.

In conversation, the General was an expert, a collector of incidents he had related before with positive reception by the listener. Tom Ryan also had this capacity. His tonal inflection, gestures, and movement always fit and lent emphasis to his theme. Both men had excellent memories.

Unlike Tom Ryan, John F. Kennedy, and myself, the General never uttered a blasphemous word or even a crudity of diction. He was the soul of dignity in appearance, grooming, speech, and table manners at ease with everyone including business executives, government officials, diplomats, company presidents, multimillionaires, university deans, professors, and presidents. In fact, anyone. His work with the Boy Scouts of America earned him the highest award a volunteer can get, the Order of the Buffalo, and like me, he was an Eagle Scout, as were Walt Nicholes and our son, Michael.

John loved meetings, travel, and letter writing as stated earlier. I was proud to have him with us to organize the business.

His knowledge of computers was nil. I asked Dr. Michael Kasavana, my colleague and computer training specialist from MSU, to spend a Saturday at our plant office to get us started using computers. Herman Taber and Ralph Napletana said we didn't need it, but I didn't want us to miss out on any new development that might be profitable and helpful.

Mike Zelski and his assistant, George Hvizd, met with Kasavana, John and me. Michael Kasavana told us that the computer was an outgrowth of the key punch procedure that had been used by business for payroll and inventory control for many years. Today, machines and processes are all computer controlled, after programs have been perfected for doing it. Labels once printed by Oxford Press are now printed on in-house computers.

If at first you don't succeed, try, try again. It's called grit! That's how we finally overcame the computer-inertia that, at first, almost discouraged us. All that we needed was the right person with the knowledge of how to do it. Today, the computer is a vital part of the business that is now owned by Nestle's.

John McLaughlin loved to travel and meet people. He would travel around the world just to attend a meeting. No one I ever knew enjoyed meetings like John did. When I was called in to set up a Quality Improvement Program, instead of going to the Cleveland Athletic Club for lunch, as we did when the company was ours, John had a caterer bring food to the office. We would then gather around desks, or balance the plate on our knee, and set the cup on the floor. This was to save time while having our meeting.

Like Thomas Edison, John didn't waste a precious minute or want anyone else to do so. Go-go-go! Press forward! Don't stop! Continue until you're weary! He would take a quick nap on a leather sofa he put in his office and then carry on.

His business practice resembled that of Gen. Patton leading his troops pell-mell through Germany as he moved on to Berlin. The orders he received to let the Russians take the city frustrated and angered Patton.

John had all of his plans ready for the following day, firmly fixed in his mind before going to bed. He was a high achiever and a long-range planner.

John was an easy mark for "con men" though. Finding the hole in the doughnut was hard for him.

Despite the mistakes he made, I still loved him, but not in the same way I loved Tom Ryan. John did us a lot of good and we appreciate it. His respect and admiration for me was apparent. John always looked out for me after the business was sold. Now I miss him and pray for him as I do for Tom Ryan, every day.

Sweet Dreams

One last story about my first trip with Gen. McLaughlin was when we met in New York City to visit a restaurant that served nothing but soup. There were nine different soups on the menu. It was in January, 1975, just a couple of weeks after Tom Ryan's burial. The three of us, Gen. McLaughlin, his wife, Betty, and I knelt before the altar in St. Patrick's Cathedral and prayed for Tom Ryan, who we knew must be in heaven. Afterwards, the General said, "Tom Ryan was a great man."

We drove together to the Culinary Institute in Hyde Park, New York. On the way, I told the General about the travails and problems of the L. J. Minor Corporation. Having worked for several years at San Francisco's Bank of America before going into the service, John readily grasped any figures that were thrown at him. He had the memory of an elephant for all that you'd tell him.

When I told him that his total sales budget for the year 1977 would be just $50,000, he was perplexed. So I explained. I said, "We're in financial straits due to the ineptness we had in not raising our prices in conformity with increased raw material and other manufacturing costs. Inflation caught us napping. Our selling prices for our food bases were too low." Gen. McLaughlin immediately laid plans for price adjustments in each individual product. He was the right man to straighten out our pricing. That was his "cup of tea" so to speak, and it saved our company.

In less than a year, we were making a profit again. From then on we grew and profits increased apace. In 1975, our sales were $4 million and by 1983 when the company was sold, our sales were $18 million.

In 1978, I took Gen. McLaughlin and his son John, now with the L. J. Minor Corporation, with me to the annual meeting and product exhibition of the Institute of Food Technologists in Philadelphia. Gen. McLaughlin was enraptured with the potential for our business that this exhibition promised. He had a quick mind for grasping business opportunities that would increase our sales.

At this meeting, I met the General's other son, William F. McLaughlin, who at that time was enrolled at Harvard. He was married and had a two year old son. He married a lovely young woman, Diane, from West Virginia.

William F. McLaughlin became president of the Minor Corporation in 1984, and served in that capacity for nearly 10 years.

After becoming an Executive Vice President in the Nestle U.S.A. Foodservice Division, of which the L. J. Minor Corporation is a member, William F. McLaughlin recently resigned from Nestle's and is now a top executive at Sweetheart Paper Cups.

He should do well and go far with Sweetheart Paper Cups Company. He has it all together including health, vigor, personality, and business acumen.

Bill completed his MBA degree at Syracuse University in 1979 and also taught U.S. Army business trainees at Purdue University before joining his dad at Minor's. I'm glad that Michael and Dorsey are close to him and have his confidence and good will. I only wish that my relationship with him was as good as that which I enjoyed with his father. I guess it wasn't meant to be.

But like his father before him, Bill was and continues to be a sharp and able businessman. Throughout his time with Minor's, he carried on his father's historic role with the American Culinary Federation, The Culinary Institute of America, Johnson and Wales University, Cornell's Hotel School, International Food Manufacturers Association, and Educational Foundation of National Restaurant Association.

Edsel, Henry Ford's son, lived in the shadow of his father. To please and impress his father, Edsel had a new coke oven built at the Rouge plant, Dearborn, Michigan. When it was done, he showed it to his father. The next day, Henry Ford had it dismantled, so it was never used.

Shortly after having received the NIFI Diplomate Award, I was pleased to hear from President Metz of the CIA. He wrote me the following letter:

The Culinary Institute of America
Hyde Park, New York 12538 - (914) 452-9600
Office of the President

July 28, 1983

Dr. Lewis J. Minor
Chairman
L. J. Minor Corporation
436 Bulkley Building
Cleveland, Ohio 44115

Dear Dr. Minor:

We are so pleased to see that you have recently been inducted into the College of Diplomates of the National Institute for Foodservice Industry and are glad that this organization has recognized your lifelong dedication and support of the foodservice industry in general.

On behalf of the American Culinary Federation, as well as the Culinary Institute of America, I'd like to congratulate you for displaying this kind of leadership; and we are extremely proud that we all have an association with you personally.

Please give our best regard to Mrs. Minor. We missed you at the recent ACF meeting, but we look forward to seeing you again soon.

Sincerely,
Ferdinand E. Metz
President

Regarding the Award the following appeared in *NATION'S RESTAURANT NEWS*, May 23, 1983.

NRA SHOW PREVIEW
NIFI to honor Royal, Ferguson, Minor, Stratton at Brunch

CHICAGO-Four industry leaders who have made significant contributions to foodservice education will be honored at the 10th annual Diplomates Brunch May 22 at 11 a.m. in the Palmer House. The champagne brunch and awards ceremony is sponsored by the National Institute for the Foodservice Industry.

Approximately 400 people will honor James Ferguson, chairman of the board of General Foods Corp. of White Plains, N.Y.; Dr. Lewis J. Minor, chairman of the L. J. Minor Corp. of Cleveland; Ernest H. Royal, president of Royal's Hearthside Restaurant of Rutland, VT., and William G. Stratton, the vice-president of corporate relations for Canteen Corp., Chicago. Stratton is a former governor of Illinois and ex-NIFI president.

"At this tenth annual brunch, the College of Diplomates will again pay tribute to outstanding individuals whose long-term active support has contributed significantly to upgrading professional management standards in the food-services industry," said Richard J. Hauer, NIFI executive vice-president.

Ferguson is being honored for his foodservice education leadership throughout the United States and Canada,

216

particularly in the era of consumer nutrition. He has directed an innovative public education program on nutrition, stressing balance, variety and moderation.

Ferguson's efforts, General Foods has contributed management services and support to the foodservice educational activities of NIFI, the International Foodservice Manufacturer's Association, the Culinary Institute of America, and such universities as Cornell, Michigan State, New York, and Guelph.

Minor has an extensive record of accomplishment in foodservice education. Over the years, he has assisted both students and restaurant operators. Minor has provided scholarships and loan funds for students of foodservice education at colleges and culinary schools.

A visiting professor at Michigan State's School of Hotel, Restaurant and Institutional Management, Minor has emphasized the need for and benefits of high standards of quality and service. As the author of numerous scientific journal articles and through research and active participation in industry conferences, Minor has increased the product knowledge of restaurateurs. Minor also rendered important service to the U.S. Army Quartermaster Corps during World War II.

During his business life, Royal has encouraged young people to seek hospitality industry careers. In a special 18 week, external work-study curriculum operated through his restaurant, he has regularly provided employment for students.

Royal has promoted "Career Ladders" for progressive achievement in the foodservice industry and in his restaurant. As chairman of the NRA Human Resources Committee, Royal has long been involved with employment opportunities for the handicapped and the mentally ill. A member of the CIA board of trustees, he has helped to publicize and shape educational policy for the foodservice industry.

As governor of Illinois and an officer and director of several national and state foodservice organizations, Stratton played a leadership role in promoting professionalism in hospitality industry education. During his two-year term as NIFI president, he assisted in broadening NIFI's cooperative working relationship with educational institutions and industry associates.

Another letter sent in tribute to this award and presented here was treasured by me. It was written by the famed restaurateur Peter Gust Economou, Buffalo Park Lane.

June 1st, 1983

Dr. Lewis Minor - 1501 Euclid Ave., Cleveland, Ohio

Dear Dr. Minor:

You are Terrific - You are dynamic - You are Fantastic! - You are wonderful!

You are a beautiful humble humane being and our Lord has blessed you abundantly. Especially with a very lovely family + Plus.

Really you stole the show at this years NIFI Champagne Sunday Luncheon May-22d/83. You surprised everybody who was fortunate to attend the party with a terrific sense of humor, and an excellent singing voice as well! I was indeed highly honored to have you take the time to introduce me to your lovely family - your charming wife Ruth - to dear son Michael and the three daughters and many other friends!

Your speech was tops, the great standing ovation you received speaks for itself.

The next day, Monday May 23d, Brother Herman Zaccarelli was attending the IFMA Awards dinner at the Conrad Hilton Hotel, and had a short visit. I had to attend because as you know I was a recipient of the Gold Plate award since 1958 - and a number of people that night who know you well were very much surprised with your many talents - I wish Tom Ryan was alive to see and hear your praises.

The party of NIFI's this year will remain a historical event. Many, many thanks Dr. Minor. I cherish your friendship with much love-respect and admiration - and pray our Lord and Savior bless you, and all your dear family through life, as only He can.

Affectionately, Peter Gust

Long after the company was sold in 1989, Gen. McLaughlin invited us to Cleveland and surprised me by dedicating the Lewis J. Minor Technical Center which is located at the plant. Cleveland's Mayor George Voinovich and two members of the Cleveland Council were present as Mrs. Minor and I cut the ribbon at the opening ceremony.

We would meet at the annual L. J. Minor Corporation Awards Dinner, and sit together at the Annual IFMA Awards Banquet at the NRA Show where we would also attend The Golden Toque Luncheon together.

John had the laudable goal in all of his work to have his wife, Betty, and their children - John, Jr., Bill, and his daughter, Susan - provided for when the company was sold to Nestle. John was a good practical Catholic who attended Mass and Holy Communion regularly.

After selling the business, I missed his fellowship. He was a meticulous man with great self-respect. His fingernails were always carefully manicured, his hair styled, his shoes shined, suit pressed, shirt collar and cuffs starched.

His attire was well chosen. He had a perfect physique, pleasant countenance, good sense of humor, intense motivation. He was a financial wizard, a people-person, a great persuader, and a likable man.

After the sale of the company, when we met at the dedication of the most recent plant addition in 1990, I asked "How are things, John?" He smiled and answered, "The sky's the limit, we're just getting started with building the sales of Minor Food Bases."

John called me two weeks before he died in January 1992. He was his usual ebullient self, and told me he had just become a member of the U.S. Army Quartermaster Hall of Fame. I congratulated him, and told him it was a well-deserved and hard-earned honor.

John said to me, "Why don't you and Mrs. Minor come and visit us in our new big home in Richmond?" I said, "We don't get around much anymore, John. I guess we're just settling-in now for old age." He sounded just as up-beat and enthusiastic as ever. When we got word two weeks later that John had died I was shocked and saddened.

Now, when I say my prayers every day, I include him in the appeal I make to help the L. J. Minor Corporation remain strong, healthy, and prosperous. I ask that John McLaughlin be with Him in heaven. He did a lot of good in his life.

Who's Who in America (1988-1989)

The following profile of Gen. John D. McLaughlin is from *Who's Who in America* 1988-1989.

John D. McLaughlin, food manufacturing company executive, retired army officer. Born, San Francisco, December 24, 1917. Married Susan Stumper July 11, 1946. Children: John D., William F., and Susan C.

Education: George Washington University graduate Armed Forces Staff College, 1956; National War College, 1959; Advanced Management Program, Harvard University, 1963; Ph.D. (Hon.) Johnson and Wales College, 1980; advanced through the grades to become 2nd Lt. in the U.S. Army in 1942 and became Lt. General Staff Assistant in the Office of Sec. Defense 1960-61; Executive Officer of Defense Supply Agency 1961-63. Assistant

Commander U.S. Army Quartermaster School, 1963-65; Chief of Staff U.S. Army, Viet Nam, 1965-66; Director Supply U.S. Army General Staff 1966-67; Asst. Chief of Staff for logistics Pacific Command 1967-69. Commanding General Quartermaster Center, U.S. Army Quartermaster School, Fort Lee, VA 1969-73; Commander, U.S. Theater Army Support Command, Europe 1973-74; Vice President L. J. Minor Corporation 1974-79; President L. J. Minor Corporation 1979-83; President L. J. Minor International 1987; Executive Council Richmond, VA, Boy Scouts; Advancement Board Educational Institute of American Culinary Federation; Trustee Culinary Institute of America; President, U.S. Culinary Team Foundation; Vice President Quartermaster Memorial Foundation. Served with U.S. Army 1934-74. Decorated Distinguished with Oak Leaf Cluster, Legion of Merit with four oak leaf clusters. Bronze Star medal with two oak leaf clusters; Air medal Distinguished Service medal Greece; Recipient Silver Plate Award, International Food Service Manufacturers Association, 1973;

Others: Member Quartermaster Association, President Washington Chapter 1969-70; Harvard Business School Alumni Association; American Culinary Federation Gold and Silver Plate Awards; Society of American Academy of Chefs (life honors); American Legion, VFW; Military Order World Wars; Honorable Order of the Golden Toque.

Clubs: Kiwanis of Petersburg (past director); Harvard of Virginia Petersburg Country, Army-Navy country; Commonwealth (Richmond, VA); Died, December 1992. Buried in Arlington Cemetery with full dress military honors and 21 gun salute.

Gen. McLaughlin's motto: "Always take the time, no matter how busy you are, to assist, guide, and/or counsel people who come to you with their problems. Your support as a leader increases a thousand fold for each time you take time to listen, provide understanding, and help those in need."

Chapter 26

Expansion, Again

Our Advertising Man

Surprise! A Branch Office

International Prospects

Back Home with My Son

The General Becomes President

**Do Your Best
by Lewis J. Minor**

You can't stand still.
You'll either move forward
or slide backward!

Living
(Irish Humor by Hal Roach)
"Live every day as if it's your last, and one day you'll be right."

**Never Quit
by Edgar A. Guest**
(1916)

No one is beat till he quits,
No one is through till he stops,
No matter how hard failure hits;
No matter how often he drops,
A fellow's not down till he lies
In the dust and refuses to rise.

Quote from Schiller

"There are three words of strength: hope, faith, and love."

Our Advertising Man

In 1975, Michael Zelski, L. J. Minor Corporation plant manager for 18 years, met a local advertising man, Walt Nicholes. Mike and Gen. McLaughlin made a deal with him to work for us as a private contractor, and not on our payroll. Walter would visit me, and ask me questions that would give him the insight into our products, how they are made, why they are better than our competitors, special reasons why prospective customers should purchase them, how dishes could be improved by seasoning them with our bases. He also wanted to know our business aims and policy statement.

Then, he would make up ads with pictures of the bases and submit them to journals and periodicals including *Institutions Magazine, The Restaurant News, Food and Equipment News, The Journal of Food Technology*, and others. He would request that they announce the availability of this new line of food bases and include the availability, on request, of samples brochures, technical advice and service to anyone interested by calling or writing our office in the Bulkley Building, Euclid Avenue, Cleveland, Ohio. These were "freebies" for which we promised paid advertising in future issues.

Fortunately, sales began increasing at a more rapid rate after Walt Nicholes' ad campaign was launched. Tom Ryan and I established a sound selling organization consisting of a blend of chefs and salesmen working with an increasing number of distributors, and Walt Nicholes Advertising built on that. Our industrial accounts, including Stouffer's, Weight Watchers, ARA Catering, and a host of others were becoming a major factor added to our "Foodservice" accounts business. Michael Zelski was also a major contributor. John McLaughlin inherited a "Bonanza." He didn't create it, but he did manage it effectively. We grew quickly with his expertise.

By 1975, when Dr. Ryan died, sales had grown to $6,000,000 per year. When Gen. McLaughlin came on board, there was a national, consumer-motivated campaign for natural foods. He jumped on this bandwagon at once and advertised our Food Bases as all natural.

As a food chemist, I could find no fault in it, for all food is made up of chemicals. I believe that the ultimate achievement of food chemists will be reached when they are able to match natural flavors with artificial ones having the same identical composition and concentration as those in the food flavor they are matching. Givaudan and International Flavors and Fragrances are companies whose flavor chemists are engaged in identifying and matching beef, chicken, lobster, fish, mushroom, and other natural flavors.

When this is accomplished, it will be possible to maintain uniformity in these flavors and also to fortify that in the foods whose flavor has been matched. Then more intense and satisfying meat, chicken, lobster and fish flavor will be available for our added enjoyment in dining and cooking. Of course, these flavors will have the approval of the United States Department of Agriculture Agencies (USDA), Meat Inspection Department (MID) [Today these agencies are: Food Safety Inspection Service (FSIS), Inspection Operations (IO).], and the Food and Drug Administration (FDA).

Gen. McLaughlin said to me, "I want to know all about this business. I intend to get

222

right down to the bowels of the business." I said, "We don't intend to hide anything from you, but we're going to continue doing things the way that have proven successful. Don't try to start changing things. We don't want to grow too fast. Rather, we'd like to grow at a slower and more assimilable rate. Production should be maintained without paying for a lot of overtime."

His army experience taught him to take command and tell you what was done later. This type of action would upset me because, as owner, I was interested in all activities of the business. One of our best salesmen said, "The General would make a good mushroom grower. His policy was to keep them in the dark and feed them plenty of redolent horse manure." He was right. John would tell people, "Don't tell Dr. Minor." My loyal employees often tipped me off about a change he made or something he purchased.

Surprise! A Branch Office

The General and his wife invited Mrs. Minor and me to visit them again at their Colonial Heights home. When we arrived he said he had a surprise for us. He had set up an L. J. Minor Corporation Export Branch in Colonial Heights.

He took us to visit a site that he and Betty purchased as an investment. The property included a building that had been a doctor's office. It cost them $30,000. They purchased an L. J. Minor Corporation sign and had already mounted it in front. When we entered, a display of the General's multitudinous army awards and decorations greeted us. Many were sitting on a large library table that John's mother gave him. This action was taken before board approval.

After much pro and con discussion, the approval was given, based on the belief that McLaughlin would be able to increase sales enough to make it an insignificant matter. Now that we were in the export business, sales did increase. Herman Taber said, "The General could sell ice cubes to Eskimos."

International Prospects

In 1978 Gen. McLaughlin got all excited about the U.S. government program for increasing export of U.S.A. food and food products. He reserved rooms for us at the Cunard Hotel in London, together with a booth in the Exhibitions Hall. John took care of visitors to our display booth. All I was scheduled for was to give a talk and demonstration of our food bases.

It thrilled me when my friend, the great master chef Sylvino Trompetto, came to hear me speak. We met years before when I visited Ceserani and Ealing College of Higher Education. I thanked him for coming and he said, "Listen, Dr. Minor, I came to see and hear you. Otherwise, I'd never leave my kitchen at the Savoy or would I ever set foot in a crummy hotel like this."

After the exhibition was over, John and I had a dinner for our friends. I invited

Victor and Betty Ceserani. He invited the Cunard's manager and his wife and three British Army Officers he knew and their wives. We enjoyed reminiscing.

We visited Max Blouet, the great hotelier who was now at the new Hilton Hotel on the Park. As soon as we met and shook hands, Max asked me, "Where's Ruth?" General McLaughlin and Max got on famously. They discussed the war with Hitler during which Max operated a luxury hotel that the Germans occupied.

When we left Max Blouet after enjoying an excellent lunch and a bottle of vintage red wine, I winced at the thought that I might never see my dear friend again in this world. We exchanged Christmas cards for several years but never enjoyed another repast together.

Nostalgia seized me, and on such occasions I was comforted by the belief that we would meet again in heaven. I never met a nicer man, and would always feel indebted to Helen Recknagel for introducing me to him.

As the reader will recall, she helped me by publishing my articles - a total of seven on different foodservice relevant topics - and introduced me to Marshall McLennon, who was developing recipes in small quantities for publication in the Cornell Quarterly. These recipes were made to Escoffier standards by Chef Mueller.

When McLennon learned that our food bases met Escoffier standards, he used them in many of the entree recipes. Mrs. Recknagle was a friend to Tom Ryan, to me and the L. J. Minor Corporation. She was always ready to help us, all we needed to do was call her. She never failed us.

How fortunate we were to have the goodwill and support of Cornell and Michigan State, the two leading hospitality schools in America, and the Culinary Institute of America, and Johnson and Wales University, the leading catering or culinary schools. In addition, our food bases had the Seal of Approval of the American Culinary Federation.

After visiting Max Blouet, John and I had lunch in the Queen Mary room at the Ealing College of Higher Education's Catering School. Everything in this historic dining room is served by students who are supervised by staff members. Mr. Lillicrap was the maître d', and Andrew MacIntosh was his assistant. They each wore white shirts, gray ascots, black swan-tail coats, and narrow striped gray and black trousers. Their black shoes were so brightly shined that they were like mirrors.

When a young lady student served us, she placed the plates with the entree on the side of the plate opposite us instead of directly in front and adjacent to us. Andrew raised an index finger, she came, and he told her to adjust the plates. After she left, he said to us, "Everybody needs a little prompting now and then."

We spent two days at Hyde Park, famous for its "soap box" orators. These individuals are very entertaining, and some so humorous that I was rolling in the grass laughing. Some were discussing international politics. Others were commenting on current events. But the most humorous were two who were debating whose sexual prowess was greater.

They spoke from adjacent wooden stepladders. One was Australian, and the other Canadian. The Australian vehemently argued that he could seduce any woman better than the Canadian. The Canadian maintained that he knew more ways of getting women than the Australian did.

They argued back and forth. A young woman in the audience that had gathered around them piped up; "I don't think Canadians are as good at sex as Australians are." This irritated the Canadian speaker so much that he assaulted her stating, "Listen to her. She thinks that the entire solar system revolves around her body."

For years the General had carried so much responsibility that he had forgotten how to laugh. Now he was enjoying himself so much that it showed on his countenance. He was "loose as a goose."

We had a luncheon appointment with Harry Bricker, former Colonel and Head of the British Army Catering Corps. After retirement he became Catering Manager for the Bank of London in charge of 50 catering managers at branch banks. Our appointment was at 12:00 noon.

McLaughlin always set his watch two minutes fast so he'd always be on time. That day we had train transfer problems with a gate person who was taking transfers. I had lost mine, and the man was giving me a bad time. He wouldn't let me pass. I told him to move aside. I had paid my fare and I passed him. John had to wait for me to catch up.

At noon we were rounding the street corner that the bank was on. John McLaughlin broke into a run after glancing at his watch. Then I saw him dashing up the steps of the bank. Colonel Bricker had left his office at noon and had come to the top of the steps. He said to John, "You're two minutes late."

Bricker was a tall, rotund individual. He told me he was from Luxembourg and considered himself to be the world's leading catering manager. He said, "I purchase 59,000 bottles of vintage wine each year." When I told him that our food bases were the world's finest, he doubted me as did all chefs who hadn't tried them.

At lunch, he informed us that he would be retiring the following year. I told Gen. McLaughlin to hire him to get our food bases entrenched in London while he still had the influence he did in his current position. He could have put our bases in all of their 50 catering units. McLaughlin didn't think that was ethical, although all of our active chefs in the USA were doing it.

After Bricker retired, McLaughlin hired him. His power was gone and the results he produced in England and Ireland didn't amount to much. He hired a Protestant to sell in Ireland, and that fellow was as popular as a leper with the oppressed Irish Catholics. We poured a lot of our hard-earned dollars into Bricker's operation and sustained losses as long as he remained with us. McLaughlin wanted me to visit the British Army Catering Corps at Aldershott so we took a train there.

That day the Army cooks were making consommé. The instructor put the procedure on the blackboard for the cooks to follow. I was impressed with the training that the British cooks were getting and with the philosophy of the British Army for feeding in the field compared to that of the U.S. Army.

Our army provides nutritious ration items, principally dehydrated. Their army wanted the soldiers to have fresh fruit, vegetables, poultry, meat, fish, seafood and dairy products.

The object was to give their men cooking as close to "Home Cooking" as possible. Fresh flavor is what they wanted. Their belief concurred with mine that the combatants' morale and physical capabilities would benefit from the enjoyment of good meals.

Dehydrated food is lacking, even objectionable, in flavor. Civilians don't accept it in restaurants, but some items that are dehydrated are used by hospitals. White and toasted onion powder, white and toasted onion slices, celery flakes, and green and red peppers are being used. Freeze-dried foods are being perfected. They can't compare with fresh, but are better than other dehydrated products. Air-dried and vacuum-dried foods are also being experimented with. I always told my students that "Nothing is improved by freezing, not even ice cream."

On our journeys, I told Gen. McLaughlin that it would be a good idea for his son, John, whom I had just given a job, to spend six months or a year at the British Army Catering School, Ealing College of Higher Education's Catering School, or at the Culinary Institute or Johnson & Wales.

Before joining Minor's, John Jr. was a professional clown with Ringling Brothers Circus and enjoyed that experience more than business. I like John Jr. and thought he would do well, in time, selling our food bases. His personality appealed to me as being ideally suited to sales. He was enthusiastically interested in helping build the business. He wasn't "budget-oriented" like his brother, Bill, who became president of Minor's after the company was sold in 1983.

Gen. McLaughlin helped us with his knowledge of business management. Bill was trained in business by the Army as his dad before him had been. They kept the business on course by concentrating on the bottom line. Gen. McLaughlin had worked for the Bank of America as a young man. After joining the Army he took business courses, including a short course at the Harvard School of Business. This knowledge, which was used in Army purchasing and personnel management, helped us as did his "window-dressing" with the American Culinary Federation (ACF), International Food Manufacturers Association (IFMA), National Institute of the Food Industries, Food Services Executives Association, and his position as trustee for the Culinary Institute of America (CIA). His activity in all of these organizations was expensive, but necessary, and helped our image as a manufacturer as well as my personal "charisma" as seen by the public.

Neither Gen. McLaughlin, his son Bill, or Tom Ryan for that matter, played a part in the development of our food base formulas, quality control program, manufacturing processes, or label statement of ingredients. That was all in my realm of expertise gained from years of experience, study, literature research, and intuition. Our son, Michael, has carried on in these aspects of the business.

Getting back to our prospects for international business and our trip to London, we visited a friend, Derek Gladwell, in Sheffield, England. He had come to the U.S. on a Rhodes Scholarship to study our foodservice industry and report on it.

Helen Recknagel, our close friend at Cornell, told Derek to contact our office. Tom met him and told him to use our Cleveland office as a clearing house. While in San

Francisco, where he was to meet his wife, Sheila, Derek stepped off a curb and sprained his ankle. They went to New York City after visiting Cornell's Hotel School and stayed in the Koves apartment we rented.

Tom called Ernie Koves and told him to entertain the Gladwells. Ernie took them to the Latin Quarter one evening and told the manager his guest was in a wheel chair. The manager told Ernie to take Derek to the stage entrance. When they passed through, Derek said, "I never saw so many beautiful girls before in my life." They had a great time.

Now, when I told Derek that the General and I wished to visit him, he invited us to lunch at their home. Sheila fixed a wonderful meal. Afterward, Derek saw us off on our train back to London from Sheffield.

Gen. McLaughlin's father's forebears migrated from Ireland to San Francisco. His father was the Fire Chief in the city with the Golden Bridge. John had never been to Ireland until I took him there.

It was February and the Shamrocks were in bloom, and the General picked one. We hired a car and driver after arriving at the Shannon Airport. I asked the driver to take us to the Aberdeen Arms Hotel in Lahinch, County Clare.

We arrived in the afternoon and had a nice visit with our friends Michael and Philomena Vaughn. We enjoyed a repast of champagne and sliced smoked salmon, with scones that Philomena had just removed from the oven, topped with fresh unsalted butter and some of her homemade currant and raspberry jelly. They suggested that we go to Bunratty Castle and enjoy the evening of entertainment, consisting of Irish music and play-acting, that accompanied dinner there. We went.

We entered the Castle, were shown through it, and brought into the great hall to dine. It was a cold, damp evening and we partook of mulled wine that was ready to enjoy. After drinking the wine and conversing with other guests, we were seated for dinner. Our places were near a door that was opened and closed as the food was brought to the feast board.

After dinner, when the entertainment was about to commence, one of the beautiful ladies who were dressed in bejeweled velvet gowns asked me, "Are you all right?" I answered her, "No, my arse is cold." With that, she took the General and me by the hand and seated us at the fireplace which was located right by the stage. She said, "Here now, you can warm your arses." We thanked her, relaxed, and enjoyed the music and play-acting.

We spent the night at Fitzpatrick's Motel nearby. It had marvelous steaks and hamburgers, the best in Ireland, made of U.S. Inspected beef that was shipped in to the Shannon airport just minutes away.

The next day we went on to Dublin and stayed at the Burlington Hotel, one of the Doyle Hotel Group. I immediately called Pat O'Laughlin, Ireland's leading processor of chickens, and also an egg distributor. We arranged a dinner meeting for six o'clock at the Burlington. I wanted Gen. McLaughlin to meet him, and get his input on how we should proceed with his sale of our food bases in Ireland.

We entered the dining room at 6:00 p.m. At 6:30, Pat O'Laughlin called to tell us it would be eight o'clock before he would arrive. At 8:00 p.m. we went back into the dining room, waited, and at 8:30 received another call from Patrick saying he couldn't make it until 9:00. He walked in at 9:30, and before I could greet him he said, "What is wrong with you, Minor. You're no spring chicken yourself. And who's this 'old goat' with you? Don't you know that young men, not old men, run businesses. Don't you have any young executives?" I said, "We do, but they're back in Cleveland."

Then I introduced the General. O'Laughlin wasn't impressed. When McLaughlin told him he wanted Colonel Bricker to sell for us in England and Ireland, Pat said, "Don't send an Englishman in here. We've had trouble with them for 600 years. I can get you an Irish representative if you want me to."

Pat excused his lateness by explaining how he had worked all day, before meeting us, wrapping up a deal which made him the leading egg distributor in Ireland. We parted amicably as friends, but never met again or took advantage of his offer to help us if we decided to set up a food base manufacturing plant in Ireland. McLaughlin and I took O'Laughlin's admonition concerning young executives to heart.

We next visited the village of Cong in the Connemara Mountains where John Ford made the classic movie, The Quiet Man, with John Wayne, Maureen O'Hara, Barry Fitzgerald, and Victor McLaglen. This was John Ford's dream come true to film this story which he bought years before for $100. He won an Oscar as director, and other Oscars were awarded to the film and members of the cast.

Ashford Castle is where the film company stayed during the filming. We stayed there too. The Guinness family spent $13 million restoring Ashford Castle. During the Depression, they sold it to Noel Huggard who in turn sold it to an Irish millionaire.

We enjoyed a Guinness Ale at Cohans Pub which the film company frequented when they were there. I went into a small shop to buy a newspaper. The lady, thinking she knew me, said, "Is it yourself?" I answered, "It is." She said, "It's me, too. What did you want?" I said, "I want the newspaper." She said, "Do you want today's paper or yesterday's?" I said, "I want today's paper." She said, "Well, then you'll have to come back tomorrow."

We went to Galway in County Mayo and at a gift shop, John and I each bought beautiful "Waterford Crystal" bud vases to bring home to our wives. Unfortunately, his broke inside his luggage. Betty asked him to get her another at an Irish import store. He did.

Each morning the Irish people greet you this way. "It's a beautiful day, thank God!" If it's raining they say, "It's fresh isn't it? Thank God!" Ireland is the only place in the world where the people thank God for life each day. You enjoy hearing this when you arrive in Ireland, and miss it after you're gone. A poor country, God bless us, with annual average incomes of $1200. Tourism is the country's principal source of revenue.

An Irish comedian, Hal Roach, says, "You'll love the 30 shades of green and Irish humor. We laugh at ourselves. Ireland's the only place in the world where you wake up and hear the birds coughing. A Californian came to Dublin for rheumatism, and he got it

228

in 60 days." The following chapter is dedicated to more of his Irish humor.

McLaughlin loved the brown Irish bran bread and jams, and fresh churned pure creamery butter. We enjoyed some classically cooked meals in Dublin as guests of CERT (The Council for Education Recruitment and Training), whose purpose is to train cooks, waiters, bartenders and maids for the Irish Tourism Board's placement in hotels and restaurants.

Ireland's foodservice standards have improved steadily in the last 25 years. There were two Irish chefs who led the Canadian Team to victory over all countries in the 1992 Culinary Olympics in Frankfurt, Germany. There are catering schools at the Shannon Airport and Galway for training cooks, bakers, maître d's, and hoteliers.

When we flew from Ireland back to London, we stayed at the Westbury Hotel on Bond Street and saw a movie featuring Charles Bronson. We enjoyed it. During our trip, John remarked how outspoken I was about anything I didn't approve of in life. He simply confronted me with it all. When we went to Heathrow to return home, we checked in at British Airways. John had a huge box with fourteen suits and a top coat that he got at Dunn & Company in London. He always knew how to dress properly.

As we checked-in, the General maintained that a plane's thrust on takeoff is so powerful that excess baggage weight doesn't matter. When the ticket agent asked John to put his bags and the box on the scale, she said his bags and box were overweight and that it would cost him 69 British pounds more for his ticket due to excess baggage weight. John went into a dither.

During our entire three-week trip he had been the soul of equanimity. Now he outdid any complaining or criticism that I had demonstrated on the trip. He vowed that he wasn't going to pay 69 pounds more for his ticket. She said, "Suit yourself." Then he proceeded to every other airline in an attempt to avoid the charge, without success. He finally returned to British Airways after spending most of two hours arguing, and barely made the plane a minute before the jetway closed.

All the way home we were concerned about customs. McLaughlin had far more to declare than I did, but he got through in Washington without paying anything. I wasn't as lucky and paid $28.00 to U.S. Customs.

John McLaughlin loved our trip to London and Ireland and kept asking me when we were going back. But we never went together again. He took Betty to Ireland and a trip on the famous luxury train, the Orient Express, which went through Hungary, Poland and other communist countries. He loved to travel anywhere, anytime.

Back Home with My Son

When we got home I sent for Mike Minor to resign his job as Executive Chef for Deering-Milliken Textiles in South Carolina. When he told Mr. Milliken that his father needed him in the Cleveland manufacturing plant, Roger Milliken said, "My Dad sent for me the same way when I was still in college." He thanked Mike and wished him a bright and happy future with the L. J. Minor Corporation.

Mike started in making batches. He learned each operation in our manufacturing processes. Soon, he was working closely with Mike Zelski. They made a great team and were like two loving brothers who had deep respect for each other.

Mike Minor's nine years of hands-on experience in the kitchen provided us with valuable processing improvements. He also had a knack for developing better meat-chopping and batch-making, and got a new packaging machine that speeded up the packing of one-pound containers while putting a tamper proof seal on the mouth of the container. Mike developed a fish base, dry roux, and hundreds of recipes for base usage.

Meanwhile, Mike Zelski revolutionized our one-pound containers by converting from glass to plastic with the Minor logo, ingredient statement, and net weight lithographed on the packages. Of course, doing this meant ordering greater numbers of containers, to get the resulting price advantage, and advance ordering from the container supplier to give them the required time to make up the containers for us. Sales were increasing rapidly, and customers loved the plastic containers which precluded breakage of glass.

McLaughlin always wanted to have a meeting in the office out at the plant on 25th Street or a meeting with our sales personnel. The day after we returned from our three-week trip, John scheduled a sales meeting at Kellogg Center at Michigan State University, East Lansing.

This was convenient for me, and it was the first sales meeting since Dr. Ryan's death. McLaughlin stated new rules governing the salesperson's expense vouchers and proclaimed new procedures for reporting sales calls. Accounts receivable that were past due were the salesperson's responsibility to collect or have deducted from commissions.

After these announcements by the General, Chef Harry Bazaan from California stood up and proclaimed, "At last the L. J. Minor Corporation will stop flying by the seat of its pants. It is now on a sound business basis."

Later, after the business was sold, John got rid of our sales force and appointed brokers to sell our bases. He said, "By appointing brokers to replace the sales personnel, we have 600 national sales people instead of 100, and they're costing us half as much. They work on 6% commission." I answered, "They are not sales representatives. They are order takers. You still need people to sell the products and get orders for them." He said, "We're using the chefs for that." He was right. The chefs do the selling for the brokers.

Tom Ryan always told me that my son, Mike, has a better personality than I have. He may have been right, but looking back on my career, I find that I could ask people for help with the business or my classes, and was never refused by anyone. My friendships lasted for years and still endure. Hence, I conclude that although my personality isn't equal to Mike's, it was adequate with God's help, and our happiest days in business were those when we were building the Minor Corporation and when I was developing my courses for Michigan State's hospitality students.

At that sales meeting, Mike Minor started his talk this way: "You fellows are lucky. You got jobs with L. J. Minor's immediately when you were chosen. I had to wait nine years because my Dad wanted me to become a professional chef after I trained for six years with Chef Hermann Rusch at the Greenbrier. That was so, in case anything happened to destroy the business, I could always get gainful employment as a pastry chef or executive chef."

Mike Minor hired a brilliant young engineer, Tom Arthur, from the electrical contractor we used. Tom Arthur computerized production for Nestle's after the business was sold for the second time.

The General Becomes President

In 1980, I decided to make Gen. McLaughlin president. He was overjoyed and called Betty immediately. He had built his charisma on working with the chefs of America, and through his affiliations with the Foodservice Executives Association, National Institute for the Food Industries, International Food Manufacturers Association, and memberships that he valued, like sitting on the Board of Trustees of the Culinary Institute of America.

Ruth and I were invited to Colonial Heights to attend Sunday Mass at their tiny Catholic church. There were very few Catholics in the South. This didn't trouble me. My father did me a great favor in the fields of business and education that ruled my life. He was a lifetime Mason, and whenever I had to deal with a WASP (White Anglo Saxon Protestant) I would mention that fact. Then they would look at me a little differently than they had when I told them I was Catholic. Presbyterians, Methodists, Baptists, Episcopalians, and Congregationalists were not a problem for me.

Lutherans were another matter until I would tell them the story about the rare book collector who called on O'Reily in County Clare. When the collector asked O'Reily, "Do you have any old books?" O'Reily said, "We did have an old Bible that started with the letters GU. I don't remember the rest." The collector said, "My God, was it a Gutenberg?" O'Reily said, "That's it." Then he said to O'Reily, "An original Gutenberg would fetch 150 million pounds. Where is it?" O'Reily said, "We threw it out. Some guy named Martin Luther scribbled all over the pages." Then they would double-over with laughter.

John said, "After Sunday Mass we'll all visit our neighbor who invited us for breakfast. John Jr. has been good to her, helping her with problems she has been having. He painted for her and replaced some rotted timbers underneath the house. She is giving her house and the estate to John Jr. when she dies." We had breakfast with her after we attended Sunday Mass.

The lady had a large linen-covered Feast-Board set up with elegant silver and crystal and a myriad of goodies including gingerbread, macaroons with strawberry jam, puff pastry, muffins, jams of strawberry, grape, raspberry and cherry flavor together with orange marmalade. There was an assortment of fresh fruit, peaches, oranges, apples, grapes, and Kiwi from New Zealand. Breakfast with her was a nice experience. John was proud and happy. It pleased me to be able to inspire him, and accept him as a business friend. That was when we invited him and Betty to go with us to Isle Royale, in Lake Superior, and they

231

accepted.

The following week, in Cleveland, we had our Board meeting, and I announced to Mike Zelski, Herman Taber, and Ralph Napletana that I had made Gen. McLaughlin President of L. J. Minor Corporation. My new title was Chairman of the Board. John announced that he was calling for a meeting of all of our chef-salesmen and other salesmen and their wives to be held at Williamsburg's convention center at Williamsburg, Virginia. Ruth and I were at the meeting, and received special honors that John planned for us.

Herman acted to protect me. This is what Tom Ryan told him to do. "Look after Lew Minor when I'm gone. Let him always keep the business a sole proprietorship. I want him to be a rich man like Vernon Stouffer. See to this after I'm gone."

In 1981, we had a number of large companies contacting me and trying to buy our business. I told Joe Adams, my oleoresin manufacturing friend about this. Joe said, "Watch out; they'll offer you a bag of shells. Don't accept stock; if you decide to accept an offer, insist on getting cash.

Joe and I used to meet regularly for coffee and talk chemistry and business. He was a genius and had constructed his own processing facility for making oleoresin spice extracts. He used solvents to extract the oil-resin combination from the spices which he comminuted in a Fitzpatrick machine that was called a "Fitz Mill."

He installed a phone hook-up to the still and pumps so that when a batch needed to be distilled at 2:00 a.m. all he did, instead of getting up and going to the plant, was pick up the phone and dial his code number. He told me about a fresh-tasting dry tomato product from Italy. This was air-dried in a gravity tower. The reader might recall that it was used wonderfully in our liquid Consommé and Glace de Viande.

When Joe divorced his first wife, she let Joe have custody of their son, Patrick. Joe and I would go to the Cleveland Barons hockey games together with our sons.

He always did anything I ever asked him to do for me or our family. We used to get peppercorns from him. He loved our family, and was a great admirer of me as I was of him. We would attend the Institute of Food Technologists' conventions with our wives after he remarried. I never knew his precise heritage but always appreciated everything he did for me. He was a good man, and is now with God in Heaven.

232

Chapter 27

On the Lighter Side

Irish Humor by Hal Roach

(Editor's Note: Dr. Minor knows more jokes than anyone I have ever met. It is not unusual to have dinner with him and Mrs. Minor and not be able to eat your food due to all of the laughter. While I believe Mrs. Minor has heard some of these jokes before, she faithfully sits, each time Dr. Minor tells a joke, with a slight smile on her face until the punch line. Then she roars with everyone as they wipe their eyes dry from laughing tears. As the Bible says, "A merry heart does good like medicine, but a broken spirit dries the bone." (Proverbs 17:22). I have no doubt that a considerable amount of credit for Dr. and Mrs. Minor's success in life is due to their marvelous sense of humor I dedicate this chapter to them as these jokes have each been individually told, by Dr. Minor to me, and have been such a blessing to my family!)

Reflections

There was a new pub in Donegal and it had mirrors all around the perimeter of it, from the floor to the ceiling. Casey and Murphy went in. They were having a few drinks. At about eleven o'clock at night, they forgot about the mirrors being on the walls and Casey looked across the room and said to Murphy:

"The fellow over there is the spitting image of you, Murphy!"

So Murphy looked over and says:

"There is a fellow sitting next to him that looks just like you! Let's go over and buy them a drink." He stands up.

Casey says:

"Sit down, I think they are coming over!"

Slight of Hearing

There was an explosion at a construction sight where Casey and Murphy were working. Murphy had lost his ear. All the workmen stopped working and looked for Murphy's ear,

233

but they couldn't find it! Suddenly, Casey cried out:

"Murphy, come here! I just found your ear!"

Murphy took a look and said:

"It's not mine."

Casey said:

"How do you know?"

Murphy said:

"Mine had a pencil in it"

Murphy Needs a Dog

Murphy was in London one night at four o'clock in the morning standing in the subway station about to descend on the escalator. There was a sign there,

DOGS MUST BE CARRIED ON THE ESCALATOR

Murphy says to himself:

"Where am I going to find a dog at this time in the morning?"

Natives

Casey and Murphy were standing in front of the kangaroo cage at the zoo. The sign read:

NATIVE OF AUSTRALIA

Murphy said:

"To think, my sister married one of them."

The Music of Love

Marriage is like a violin. After the beautiful music is over, the strings are still attached.

A Talking Bird

Danaher purchased a bird and tried to make it say its name, Joey. For hours every day he would say to the parrot:

"Joey, Joey, Your name is Joey."

This went on for weeks. Again, one day he said to the parrot:

"Joey, Joey, My name is Joey."

The parrot said:

"That's funny, so is mine!"

Golfing with Flanagan

Casey and Flanagan were having a round of golf. During the round Flanagan became ill and Casey had to carry him back to the club house where the pro said:

"That took some doing."

Casey said:

"It was not his weight that bothered me. It was lifting him and setting him down before and after each shot that was tough."

Casey Buys a Motorcycle

Casey bought a big motorcycle. It cost him 5,000 pounds. He was in this little village and he said to Murphy:

"Get on the back of my bike and we'll go for a little spin."

Murphy gets on and they go about two miles when Murphy starts yelling:

"Stop the bike! Stop the bike! The wind is cutting the chest out of me!"

Casey says it is very simple:

"What you do is turn your jacket around back to front, button it up, then the wind can't get at you!"

They go along for another two miles. Casey looks around and Murphy's not there. He is missing. So Casey turns the bike around and he goes back and he sees a bunch of farmers around this fellow laying in the middle of the road. He stops the bike and he says to the farmer:

"Is he all right?"

The farmer replies:

"Well, sir, he was all right, until we turned his head around the right way, but he hasn't spoken since."

Standing Alone

Up in heaven, there are two big signs. The one sign says,

ALL THE MEN WHO ARE HEN PECKED
BY THEIR WIVES STAND OVER HERE

There are thousands of men standing there. Another sign says:

ALL THE MEN WHO ARE NOT HEN
PECKED BY THEIR WIVES STAND OVER HERE

No one is standing there except Flanagan. St. Peter says:

"Why are you standing there on your own, Flanagan?"

Flanagan says:

"My wife told me to stand here!"

A Call for Heaven

Father Riley is making a sick call up in the mountains of Conamara. It is after curfew time when he leaves to go back home. On the way he passes a little thatch covered pub and he hears voices inside, so he goes in. He says:

> "This is what is wrong with the world today! There is too much wine, women, and song, and people are not living their lives the right way. You all forgot about God."

So he says to Flaherty, who is standing at the bar:

> "Flaherty, do you want to go to heaven?"

Flaherty responds:

> "I do, Father."

Father Riley says:

> "Right, come and stand over here."

Next, he says to Muldoon, who is at the bar:

> "Do you want to go to heaven?"

Muldoon says:

> "God knows I do, Father!"

Father says:

> "Come stand over here."

So Murphy is sitting at the bar with a pint of Guinness in each hand. He thinks that's the recipe for a balanced diet. So Father Riley says to Murphy:

> "Do you want to go to heaven?"

Murphy says:

"Not me, Father."

Father says:

"You mean to tell me that when you die you do not want to go to heaven?"

He says:

"When I die, yes, but I thought you were going right now!"

The Wrong Room

Dugan got a job as a first mate on a cruise ship. One morning the Captain says:

"Dugan, go to cabin 32 and have the occupant who died during the night buried at sea."

He said:

"Yes, Captain!"

Two hours later, Dugan meets the Captain and he says:

"Sir, I went to cabin 22 and had the occupant buried at sea."

The Captain says:

"My God, I said 32. Who was in 22?"

Dugan replies:

"A fellow from Kerry named Malony."

The Captain says:

"Was he dead?"

He says:

"No!"

The Captain says:

"Well, what did you do?"

He says:

"I buried him at sea. You know those Kerry men are terrible liars."

A Lump of Lead

O'Malley had a horse and no matter what race he entered him in, the horse would always win. The trouble was that just before it got to the finish post, it would bear to the right and run out into the field. So he says to Danaher, the vet:

"I'm losing a fortune on this horse!"

The vet says:

"I am very familiar with that affliction and there is a cure for it."

O'Malley says:

"What is it?"

The vet says:

"You get a little lump of lead and put it in the horse's left ear."

O'Malley says:

"How do I do that?"

The vet says:

"With a gun!"

Celebration Time

Donovan was elected the mayor of Ennis and they had a big celebration. He had a few drinks and it got to be midnight. He heard the band start playing and suddenly had the urge to dance. He looked across the floor, saw a beautiful vision in red, sauntered over, and said:

"Would the lovely lady in red care to dance with me?"

The figure said:

"Well, I cannot dance with you for three reasons. First, I don't dance. Second, that is not dance music the band is playing, it is the national anthem, and third, I'm not your lovely lady in red. I am the Bishop of Galway!"

Standing Tall

One Sunday morning Father Murphy started to say Mass and when he started his sermon he said:

"You know, the end of the world is coming any time now and we have to be ready for it. All those in the church who want to go to heaven stand up!"

Of course, we all stood up. Now he said:

"Sit down. Anyone in the church that wishes to go to hell, now stand up."

No one stood up except for Doolin in the middle of the church. Father Murphy said:

"Doolin, do you want to go to hell?"

Doolin responded:

"No, Father, but I just didn't want to see you standing there on your own."

Housekeepers and Priests

The housekeepers for the priests in Ireland have a reputation for being very tough on the priests and most of them are called Bridget. Bridget ran Father O'Shea's life. She told him what to wear, what time to go to bed, what to eat, she told him everything. So he went away to a retreat in Dublin and the subject of the retreat was that too much power has been given to the housekeepers of the priests in Ireland. Housekeepers should remember that the priest is the boss. So when Father O'Shea went home, he rang the bell. Bridget came to the door, and said:

"Go around to the back! Your feet are dirty."

Father O'Shea said:

"I will not go around to the back. I am coming in right here. Furthermore, you are not going to tell me what to wear, you are not going to tell me when I have to go to bed, and if I want a little drinkie before I go to bed, I am going to have it! What do you say to that?"

Bridget said:

"That's the last retreat that you are going to!"

Children Stories

Children stories are very humorous. One day the teacher asked Johnny:

"What is a cannibal?"

Johnny says:

"I don't know."

The teacher says:

"What would you be if you ate your father and your mother?"

He replied:

"An orphan."

Always in Good Taste

A Matter of Choice

Murphy went to his fiancee's house and told the father that he wanted to marry his daughter. The girl's father said:

"Well, have you seen her mother?"

Murphy said:

"Well, yes, but I would prefer to marry your daughter."

A Long Winter's Night

Muldoon was very fond of the game of football. So one day, he told his wife:

"I'm going to the game now."

He did not come back until five years later. He came to the door, and his wife said:

"What happened?"

He said:

"We lost!"

She said:

"Well, go into the kitchen and sit down, now, but don't blame me if your tea is cold."

A Cottage in County Kerry

Riley and his wife rented a cottage in County Kerry which was all falling apart. The worst thing about it was the fact it was beside a railroad track. Every night at two o'clock, the train would come by and knock them out of bed. So Riley's wife called the landlord to come over and when he arrived she said:

"It is terrible."

The landlord responded saying:

"It cannot be as bad as you say."

She says:

"There is going to be a train by here any minute. Lie here on the bed along side of me, and you can experience it for yourself."

Just then Riley walks in and says:

"What is going on here?"

The landlord says:

"You aren't going to believe this, but we are waiting for a train."

A Good Night's Sleep in Donegal

A fellow went into Donegal (a town so small that if you plug in your electric razor it would dim the street lights). He was looking for a room for the night and the landlord said:

"I do not have a thing. The only thing I might have is a room with a double bed in it, but if you went there, the man that sleeps there snores like a bull and you would be awake all night."

The fellow replied:

"I have to have something, so I'll take it."

The next morning the fellow came down all bright eyed and bushy tailed and the landlord said:

"You look great. Were you able to sleep?"

The fellow says:

"I did!"

The landlord says:

"How did you manage that?"

The fellow says:

"When I went into the room he was sitting on the bed reading and I went over to him and kissed him. He stayed awake all night watching me."

Smog and Worst

Ireland's the only country in the world where you can wake-up in the morning, hearing the birds coughing. A man from Los Angeles came to Ireland for arthritis and got it in two days.

Meeting of Brothers

I met a fellow at Shannon Airport who was there to meet his brother who hadn't been home for 45 years. I said:

"Will you know him?"

He said:

"No, I haven't even got a photograph of him."

I said:

"Will he know you?"

He said:

"Of course he will know me. I haven't been away."

A Matter of Time

Casey and Murphy have been working in Australia for three years. Casey had a telegram telling him that his wife had just had a new baby boy. So he said to Murphy:

"We'll have to go out tonight and celebrate."

Murphy said:

"What for? We've been away for three years."

Casey said:

"Three years isn't a lot. I am sure there was five years between my brother and me.

The Phone Call

Muldoon's wife was in the hospital expecting a baby. Muldoon called to ask how his wife was getting on. The nurse told him:

"She's doing fine, it could be any minute. By the way, is this her first baby?"

Muldoon answered:

"No, it's her husband."

A Kiss

"A kiss is a funny thing," Doolin said to Fitzgibbons.

"It is given to a small boy. A teenage boy has to beg for it. An old man has to buy it. It's a baby's right, the wife's hope and the old maid's charity."

Addition and Subtraction

Murphy, Casey, and Flanagan applied for a position. The personnel manager asked Murphy:

"What's 3 plus 3?"

Murphy answered:

"247"

He then asked Casey:

"What is 3 plus 3?"

Casey said:

"It is Wednesday."

He then asked Flanagan:

"What is 3 plus 3?"

Flanagan said:

"6!"

The manager said:

"That's the right answer. How did you get it?"

Flanagan said:

"I simply subtracted 247 from Wednesday."

Criminals

The New York police sent a photograph to the Dublin Police of the most wanted criminals. The picture was the front view and two side views. Two weeks later the Dublin Police telegraphed New York and said:

"We caught the one in the middle, but we are still looking for the other two."

Lost and Found

Murphy wrote the following letter to the editor of the New York Times:

"Dear Sir, Last week I lost my gold watch, so yesterday I put an advertisement in your lost and found column. Last night I found the watch in the trousers of my other suit. God bless your newspaper."

The Seasons

Murphy and his wife were strolling in the art museum one summer. Murphy stopped at a painting of a beautiful woman covered only with a few leaves. As he stood there, his wife nudged him and said:

"Come on let's go. We cannot wait here until autumn!"

The Good Life

Murphy was 80 years old and went to the doctor and said:

"I am going to marry a 36 year old widow."

The doctor said:

"At your age, Murphy, that could prove fatal."

Murphy says:

"Well, if she dies, she dies!"

Prosperity

A thought:

"Prosperity is buying things that you do not need, with money that you do not have, to impress people that you do not like!"

Home

Another thought:

"Home is a place where most men go when they are tired of being nice to people."

Appearances

Another thought:

"A good front does not last long without some backing."

Lost Dog

Hennessy:

"I lost my dog."

Casey:

"Why not put an ad in the paper?"

Hennessy:

"Don't be stupid. The dog can't read!"

Proposing Marriage

After courting Maggie for twenty years, Casey decided to pop the question:

"Maggie, how would you like to put your shoes under my bed?"

Maggie replied, blushing:

"Whatever can you mean?

He then said:

"What I mean is how would you like to be buried with my people?"
Romantic proposals, aren't they?

Take Your Medicine

Danaher went to the doctor and he came home looking sad. His wife said:

"What is the matter?"

Danaher said:

"The doctor has told me that I must take a pill every day for the rest of my life."

His wife responded:

"What's wrong with that? Many people have to take pills for the rest of their life."

Danaher said:

"Yes, I know, but he only gave me four pills."

A Costume Party

Danaher and his wife were invited to a swanky Halloween Party. So the wife got costumes for them both. On the night of the party she got a terrible headache and told her husband that he would have to go without her. He protested but she said that she was going to take a couple of aspirin and go to bed. She said:

"You go and enjoy yourself!"

So he got into the costume and off he went. His wife woke up after one hour, was feeling fine, decided to go to the party, put on her costume, and off she went. In as much as her husband did not know what kind of costume she was in, she decided to slip into the party and observe how he would act not knowing she was around. This she did and as soon as she joined the party the first one she saw was her husband cavorting around the dance floor, dancing with all of the best looking women. So the wife sidled up to him, and being a rather attractive woman herself, he dropped the woman with whom he was dancing and he devoted all of his attention to her.

Later they went for a little kiss and cuddle, etc. Just before midnight, the unmasking time, she slipped away home and got into bed, wondering what kind of explanation her husband would make as to his behavior. He got home about 1:30 a.m. and slipped into bed. She was sitting up in bed reading and said:

"What kind of time did you have?"

He said:

"You know, the same old thing. You know I never have a good time when you are not there."

She said:

"Did you dance much?"

He said:

"Well, I never danced a dance. When I got there Casey, Flanagan, and some other fellow were stag too. So we just sat back and played poker. But I will tell you one thing. The fellow I loaned my costume to sure had a good time!"

Divorce Settlement

Doolin was in court and charged with not supporting his wife. The judge said:

"Doolin, after a long deliberation, I have decided to award your wile 56 pounds per week."

Doolin replied:

"God bless you, Your Honor, and I will try to send her a few pounds myself."

A Lesson on Sex

Doolin was the last speaker to speak on sex and the chairman asked him to make it brief. So Doolin stood up and said:

"It gives me great pleasure . . ."

Then he sat down.

A Matter of Age

Flanagan found a way to show his wife how to drive more carefully. He reminded her that if she had an accident, the papers would print her age.

Being Tired

O'Toole and his wife were celebrating their golden wedding anniversary. She had weathered the years well, but she was a little deaf. When every one was gone, he said to her:

"Maggie, I am proud of you."

She responded:

"That's all right, I am tired of you, too."

The Value of Land

Mary Kate said to her husband:

"What has happened to our marriage? Before we wed, you said to my father you worshipped the ground I walked on."

He responded:

"Yes, I thought he owned it."

Out of Gas

Father O'Shea ran out of petrol while driving down a country lane. He did not know what to do, because he had no petrol can. He finally got a kid's potty that he had kept from a family outing from the trunk of his car. He walked to the nearest garage and got the potty filled with petrol. He came back to the car, pouring it into the tank, when a passing motorist shouted out:

"Hey Father, you have more faith than I have!"

Early Alarm

The switchboard operator at a local hotel in County Galway was making her morning alarm calls. At 6:00 a.m. she rang room 206, but just as a sleepy voice answered, she glanced at her list again, and saw that the call for room 206 was for 8:00 a.m.. She said as sweetly as she could:

"Good morning, sir, you have two more hours to sleep."

Working Nights

Mrs. O'Toole went to the doctor for a check-up. She is 65 years old. At the examination the doctor told her that she is expecting. She said:

"I cannot be expecting; I am 65 years old."

Doctor said:

"You are."

She said:

"May I call my husband to tell him?"

He said:

"Yes."

She dialed the number and said:

"Doolin, I'm expecting!"

He said:

"Who's speaking?"

Quoting Shakespeare

Little Michael's mother was very angry with him for using bad language.

"Shakespeare uses it!"

replied Michael. The mother said:

"Then, you will just have to stop playing with him."

Getting His Money Back

Maggie said to Pat:

"Here is your ring back. I cannot marry you because I love someone else."

Pat said:

"Who is he?"

Maggie said nervously:

"You are not going to kill him?"

Pat said:

"No, not at all, but I will try to sell him the ring."

Marching Orders

A five-year-old County Cork boy came home from school in tears and told his Mother:

"The teacher asked us to raise our hand if we wanted to go to Heaven"

The Mother said:

"You raised your hand, didn't you?"

The sobbing boy said:

"No, you told me to be sure and come straight home."

Pure Thoughts

Mrs. Hennessy says to Mrs. O'Shaunessy:

"I hope you do not mind my mentioning it, but your daughter is busy knitting baby clothes."

253

Mrs. O'Shaunessy says:

"I told her to do anything that would take her mind off boys."

Running Out of Time

Mrs. O'Brien is at her husband's wake when Mrs. O'Riley says:

"Doesn't he look wonderful."

Mrs. O'Brien says:

"He should. He had been running 20 miles every day!"

Say Cheese

People were surprised to see Flanagan's corpse after he had been struck by lightning and killed. He was smiling. Everyone asked why he was smiling. His wife said:

"He thought it was a flash photo that was happening to him."

Ordering Pies

Murphy went into a cafe and there was a sign on the wall that said:

TWO PIES SIXTY PENCE

He said to the waitress:

"How much is one pie?"

She said:

"Forty pence."

Murphy said:

"Right, I'll have the other one."

The Octogenarians

Shawn and Mary Kate are in the living room, in rocking chairs, one evening when Mary Kate says:

"Shawn, I'd like some vanilla ice cream."

Shawn says:

"I'll bring it to you."

Mary Kate says:

"You had better write it down."

Shawn answers:

"I don't have to write it down. You want vanilla ice cream. I'll bring it to you."

But, says Mary Kate:

"I want chocolate syrup on it too. You had better write it down."

No, says Shawn:

"You want vanilla ice cream with chocolate syrup!"

But, Mary Kate says :

"I want nuts on it too. For goodness sake, please write it down!"

No, Shawn replies:

"You want vanilla ice cream with chocolate syrup and nuts. I'll be right back."

Twenty minutes later, Shawn appears with a tray of bacon and eggs.

Mary Kate says:

"I told you, you should have written it down."

Shawn asks:

"What is wrong?"

She replies:

"You forgot the toast!"

Chapter 28

Employees First

Employee Benefits   **Some of the Best**

More Exciting Journeys

A Twenty Pound Job
(Irish Humor by Hal Roach)

A fellow came along one day and he said to Riley:
"I'll do any kind of a job, if you will pay me twenty pounds."

Riley replies:
"Why not, you can paint my porch."

Four hours later the fellow says to Riley:
"I am finished painting, but you are a comedian!"

Riley says:
"What do you mean?"

The fellow says:
"It wasn't a Porsche, it was a Mercedes!"

Necessities
by Father Coughlin
(1931)

The necessities for life that we work for are:
food, clothing, shelter, and fuel.
Labor is the one thing that can be bought, sold, stolen, or cheated upon.

Divine Benefits
(Irish Humor by Hal Roach)

The sign on the church bulletin board said:

**WORK FOR THE LORD
THE PAY IS NOT GOOD
BUT THE RETIREMENT BENEFITS
ARE OUT OF THIS WORLD**

Employee Benefits

Sales were good, and for the first time we had million-dollar-a-year sales from several of our men. This bothered John who said to me, "They're making more than you are." I answered, "Yes, but after you deduct their expenses from their commission they aren't and besides I'm happy to learn that after years of patience and personal sacrifice they're doing well." I wanted all of our employees to earn a good living by helping us build the business.

Our hourly employees were getting $8 per hour on an average plus sharing in profits at the end of the year. Their health and dental insurance was paid by the company and we had a retirement benefit program for them to supplement Social Security benefits following retirement. Their retirement benefits were vested after giving 10 years service to the company. Employee morale was always high.

We also paid them their regular pay rate for any injury recovery time that they needed. Turkeys were given to them at Thanksgiving and Christmas, and at Easter we gave each one a ten to twelve pound ham. We hired temporary employees from Manpower and they stayed on Manpower's payroll until we were certain we wanted them on our team.

Our employees received eight paid holidays a year. After the first year, the employee received a one week vacation. After two years, they had two weeks. After five years, three weeks. Ten years, four weeks. And fifteen years, five weeks. Workmen's Compensation was also paid for the hourly employees as well as their union dues. Free samples were also available to all employees for home use. Executives were given cars and some had gasoline and service credit cards.

Life insurance for hourly employees was $10,000, and executives got $25,000 to $100,000 in coverage. Business travel expenses were paid, also. Overtime pay was double for Sunday or holidays, and time-and-a-half for weekdays. Any hourly employee working for us felt like he died and went to Heaven, compared to what they experienced in other places they had worked.

All employees were trained to do all jobs. When their regular job was done, they would do other jobs where needed. Utility helpers were also provided, one per shift. We worked three shifts of eight hours. They got two fifteen-minute and one half-hour break per eight-hour shift.

Each and every food handler had to have a food handler's permit. Chest X-rays were required every two years, and a tine test if the employee refused the X-ray test. Our company retained a physician for treating any employee who required first aid or other treatment. Supervisors all had to be certified First Aid specialists trained by Red Cross.

Women could lift up to 50 pounds. Ear plugs were furnished for employees working in a noisy environment. Each employee was given one pair of safety shoes with steel toes per year for working in dry areas. Workers in wet areas got one pair of shoes and one pair of boots per year. If more shoes or boots were needed, the employee paid half and the company paid half.

Insulated jackets were provided for employees who worked in cold rooms, coolers, or freezers. Gloves (plastic) were provided for all food handlers. Meat-cutters wore disposable knit gloves to protect them when using knives.

Head covers had to be worn and these were also furnished by the company. Hard hats had to be worn when operating tow motor trucks. White laundered uniforms were given free to employees five times a week. Aprons were also provided daily. No jewelry with gem settings were allowed and no perfume could be worn. Beards were not allowed. The L. J. Minor Corporation paid for all of these incidentals.

Furnishing aprons and uniforms and safety shoes meant that employees had to spend very little for clothing, dry cleaning, or laundry when employed by us.

During the 32 years we had the company, there were only four serious accidents:

- A woman lost tips of two fingers operating a pail sealing machine.
- An 80-gallon steam-jacketed kettle exploded, damaging the building but without serious injury.
- A meat cutter with a 300-pound capacity stainless steel bowl was damaged when an employee left a wrench in the huge machine. The machine, walls, and floor were damaged. A courageous supervisor, Dan Mullen, crawled under the machine with pieces of metal flying all around him and turned the machine off. Thank God his Guardian Angel was busy protecting him. He could have been killed or badly injured. Two men were cleaning the machine and each thought the other took the wrench out.
- Mary Mele's brother, Tom, came from the flour building and got crushed between a truck and a steel post that protected the building he was going to. At the precise instant he reached the post, the driver released the brakes of the truck. Tom thought there was no driver in the truck or he wouldn't have passed that way in an attempt to avoid having to walk around the truck. His vital organs were crushed. He missed a few months of work after spending one month in the hospital. Thank God, Tom wasn't killed, but he was never the same as before the accident. He collected Workmen's Compensation. Tom had been an assistant pro at Pepper Pike, the swankiest country club in

the Cleveland area. After his accident, Tom could never play golf again.

Mike Zelski used a metal fabricating shop down the street from the plant to make parts or small machinery we needed and safety guards for our equipment. One day as Margie Stanley stepped over an auger driven filling machine, the auger grabbed her slacks panty hose and pulled them right off. Luckily the only injury she sustained was to her dignity. We immediately got the metal fabricator to put a guard over the exposed auger.

Our employee policy was simple: Treat each person as you would want to be treated. As His Word states, "Therefore whatever you want others to do for you, do so for them, for this is the Law of the Prophets" (Matthew 7:12). Make them know that they are working for some of the best people in the world.

Before he died, one of our greatest chefs, Carl Richter, told his wife, "I worked for companies in four different countries and no one I worked for ever treated me as well as Dr. and Mrs. Minor did."

He was a talented artist and gave us two beautiful oil paintings. The one was a bouquet of roses in a vase. They were red, pink and white. He said when he gave it to us, "This is my masterpiece. I want you to have it." We keep it in our Cleveland apartment on the living room wall. It's beautiful.

Some of the Best

Mike Zelski saved the Bill Knapp account for us. When they complained that we had weakened the flavor strength of our base, Mike visited their plant in Battle Creek and discovered that the problem was not with our bases, but was caused by a change their purchasing agent made in their tomato puree. He had bought a cheaper brand with more water in it that was diluting the flavor strength of their vegetable-beef soup.

Mike also got the Weight Watchers account for us, and strengthened our ties with Stouffer's Frozen Foods. His keen ability to test new equipment before purchasing it was a great help in preventing production problems. We never bought any new equipment without testing it to see if it would perform the task we wanted it to do for us. We also checked on the safety, electrical requirements, or gas requisites to know that we could add the required amount of capacity needed with regard to electricity or natural gas.

Our plant's electrical, gas, and plumbing needs grew apace with the rapid expansion that Gen. McLaughlin's sales demand required. Somehow, the two Mikes - Mike Zelski and Mike Minor - were always able to come up with the right answers without spending so much that we needed to borrow from the bank.

Mike Minor knew all about the entire scope of the business, and by 1980, became an important cog in the wheel. Gen. McLaughlin, Herman Taber, Ralph Napletana, and I all appreciated his ability and achievements. His raises came from the General and Herman Taber. Mike is still with Nestle and doing a great job for them in 1995. His job title now is Chef and Vice President in charge of Professional Services.

It's not possible for me anymore to name all of the individuals who helped out in the plant or with sales. At the time the business was sold they totaled more than 100 in the plant and nearly 200 in sales. All of them, together, did a fantastic job of growing the business. We were all family at the time the company was sold in 1983.

Some of the contributions of important employees through the years follow.

Ruth Ann Minor Fields served the company for 30 years until she retired, voluntarily, following her marriage to Bill Egan. No matter who was named plant manager, as long as she was there, she was the custodian of the L. J. Minor plant at West 25th Street. Her total influence is beyond description.

Gen. McLaughlin was immediately impressed with Ruth Ann's abilities and value to the plant operation including manufacturing, quality control, process and product development, cooperation with government inspectors, managing personnel and the entire plant. She spent long hours there each day.

Ruth Ann has great admiration for her son Dorsey's achievements. Fortunately, they were recognized by General and Bill McLaughlin. Bill took him to Solon, and had him groomed for sales. Dorsey, Ruth Ann, and Mike all have Key Employee Status in the company. Dorsey is now working out of Dallas, Texas and is in charge of Southwest Sales.

Mike Minor's accomplishments in product development, plant improvement, and sales promotion are now legendary. His work ethic is unmatched, I'm sure. Mike is also editor of the Golden Toque Cookbook.

Josephine Minor put in 10 years in quality control and computer management at the plant. She retired voluntarily in 1988 due to eye trouble from computer-watching. Her ability to memorize is unique and often proved valuable to the McLaughlins, Ingolf Nitsch, and the company. Now Josephine earns her living in retail sales.

Mary Minor worked at the plant doing packaging but left to finish her schooling. She now has her own business.

Carol Minor Walker worked for 8 years under Jan Williams supervision checking on the quality control checkers by examining samples sent to her home.

Dorsey Fields started out making boxes and breaking apart frozen chicken. He did nearly every job in manufacturing operations, and helped his mother and Ingolf Nitsch with plant scheduling and inventory control. His appointment to Key Employee Status, and graduation with a business degree from Baldwin Wallace College by using a company-employee education program, made a big impression on the McLaughlins. Bill likes him and has proven his appreciation of Dorsey's dedication to the company by providing him with the sales opportunity he is now enjoying.

      We all have heroes who help to improve our status in life. The following is a list of my heroes.

Mother - Kathleen Mary Minor
Father - Newell Wellington Minor
Wife - Ruth Eloise (Angell) Minor
"Steamer" Horning - coach
Thomas Aloysius Ryan - Business associate and 2nd cousin
Kathleen Swanson - daughter, teacher
Bryan Gabriel Minor - son
Ruth Ann Fields - daughter, plant superintendent
Carol Minor - daughter
Michael Minor - son
Josephine Minor - daughter
Rosalie Minor - daughter
Mary Minor - daughter
Sister Euphemia - H.S. teacher
Sister Mary Michael - H.S. teacher
Sister Rita - H.S. teacher
Patrick Ryan - 2nd cousin
Mrs., Dr., Marie Graves - teacher
Mr. Carl Malloy - teacher
Dean Altenburg - teacher
Dr. Fred Fabian - teacher
Professor Bruce Hartsuch
French Jenkins - employer
C. Olin Gull - employer
Tom Donofrio - employer
John Donofrio - employer
George Ross - employer
Dr. Vincent Hegarty - nutritionist
Monsignor James Murray - priest
Monsignor John Gabriels - priest
Jerry Jenks - employer
Joe Bertman - partner
Jean Caubet - chef, friend
John Sector - chef, friend
Ernest Koves - chef, friend
George Marchand - chef, friend
Hermann Rusch - chef, friend

Hans Bueschkens - chef, friend
Michael Zelski - student and plant manager
Margaret Mitchell - business associate
Brother Herman Zaccarelli - educator, friend
General McLaughlin - associate
Doctor Jamieson - osteopath
Doctor Grecius - osteopath
Dr. Lyne - osteopath
Mr. Ingolf Nitsch - protegé & manufacturer
Mr. Herman Taber - lawyer
Mr. Ralph Napletana - CPA
Dr. Schweigert - educator
Dr. Pearson - educator
Dr. Stine - educator
Dr. Trout - educator
Dr. Dawson - educator
Dr. Kotschevar - colleague
Mr. Robert Herron - friend
Mr. Pete Eckel - author
Dr. R. F. Cichy - protegé and educator
Dr. John B. Knight - protegé and educator
Mr. Harry Lawson - engineer
Mr. Worth Weed - flavorist
Dr. Joseph Rakosky - food scientist

There were others too numerous to mention who helped me succeed. God bless them all.

More Exciting Journeys

One of the General's joys were his frequent travels. So to treat him, as well a few other employees, in 1977 we went to Hawaii with John and Betty. We embarked by plane from John's hometown, San Francisco. There was a critical water shortage there, and a stench from sewage permeated the atmosphere just as it does in India and China. To conserve water, bricks were put into the toilet tanks to cut down the quantity of flush water. Car washing was done with pails of water.

In San Francisco, John took us around the outskirts of the city, and at the zoo we saw a group of three - two men and one woman - lying in the grass at the entrance.

John told us that the Hawaiians call Americans "Howlies". At military headquarters, he showed us the driveway that was lined with Royal Palms. He knew all about the Pearl

Harbor bombing by the Japanese and told us a lot of interesting but sad tales to us about it.

Mike Minor and I played golf with Tony Bartoletta, Sexton Foods chef, at the military course used for Army officers. Our son Mike and his wife Edwina were there with us. Early mornings Mike, Wolfgang Bierer, Carl Eberly and Ferdinand Metz played tennis.

We stayed at the Sheraton, but to save money, Mike ate at McDonald's and bought beer in a store and took it to his room. Socrates Inonog of Johnson & Wales was there, too.

The General had a friend there whose son became our Hawaii sales rep. Otto Denkinger was already selling most of the big hotels so the new rep started with a solid base from which to work.

On the trip home, we got word of my mother's death. We had plans to stop off at Missoula, Montana, rent a car, and drive to Dr. Kotschevar's for the annual tribute to his deceased wife, Margaret, at Lindbergh Lake at night. He invited us, and since we both loved Margaret, we attended. Julie found a room for us at the Lindbergh Ranch. Julie loved her Dad dearly and never missed the opportunity of spending summers with him at the log lodge on Lindbergh Lake.

Mother's funeral Mass was said at her parish church. Nancy and Terry Clancy sent a green vestment and gold chalice for the mass. The priest used them for the service and kept them. Mother was 88 and Dad had passed on four years earlier. At his death bedside, she bent over, kissed Dad, and said, "I'll be with you soon, Pa."

My parents worked hard until Dad retired after 40 years of service to Ford Motor Company. Dad played golf, and both Dad and Mother played poker and attended the horse races.

Whenever a race meet was on at Hazel Park track, Mother always studied the form sheet. She often picked the jockey, not the horse, and won most of the time. Dad always bet on the favorite but made a side bet after learning the horse Mother had her money on.

Dad wore out a lot of shoe leather and used his car to sell Minor Food Bases during his retirement. Mother wrote up Dad's sales reports. His sales were all made in Jean Caubet's territory and in Florida in the winter. They cooperated on a friendly basis. Jean attended both funerals of my parents.

When Jean Caubet purchased a cottage at Horseshoe Lake up north, Tom Ryan told me, "Jean's getting sporty in his old age." Without his help, the L. J. Minor Corporation would never have gotten off the ground. We owe a lot of our early success to Chef Caubet. Jean died in December, 1996.

Our next trip was to Ireland and benefited other employees including Terry and Nancy Clancy, their sons Marty and Terry Jr., and their daughters, Charlotte and Colette, Michael and Maxine Zelski, Ruth Ann and her children, Dorsey, Sallie and Kristin. Mike Minor went along to do demonstrations and had his wife Edwina with him.

Mike put on demonstrations of our Food Bases in Dublin to the CERT students and faculty, and in London at Ealing College of Higher Education's Catering School. Michael has always been popular with the Irish chefs. He is friendly and helpful to everyone including competitors.

Michael Vaughan got us a bus with a driver, a Jarvey, to take us to the Burren*. The Burren is a limestone mountain in County Clare about 35 miles east of Lahinch and the Aberdeen Arms where we all stayed with our genial, friendly and helpful host, the innkeeper Michael Vaughan and his charming and talented wife, Philomena, who is an expert baking and pastry chef. They had twin sons - John, with red hair, and Michael Jr., with black hair - and three daughters: Aileen, Marie, and Brede, who was room clerk at the Burlington Hotel where we stayed when we all went to Dublin.

(* Note: The Burren is called "a place without enough wood to hang a man, enough water to drown him or enough earth to bury him.")

From there we went to Limerick by train. We had fun, good fellowship, sight-seeing at the Cliffs of Moher, in Caves at the Burren, and viewing the pastures and farms, eating huge blackberries that we found on bushes growing beside the road on stone walls that separated the road from the green fields. "Thirty shades of green" the comedian, Hal Roach, would say in describing Ireland's landscape. To the Irish people, Ireland is a little bit of heaven that fell from the sky one day! This seems strange, that a land so poor can conjure up such love for it and its heritage. We were told that animals which grazed on the Burren's pastures had steel-like bones due to the lime in their diets.

One day Michael's (Mehaul's) brother Brendan, who taught school, took Ruth and me to the Burren on a holiday. Orchids, violets, and a myriad of other blooms were shown to us. He also showed us where monks chose that location for their chapel and dwelling place 600 years earlier in the 13th century. We were blessed with beautiful weather and the pleasure of learning about the Burren from a brilliant, pleasant, and eloquent guide who knew the history. He told us about the "Cairns'." The Cairns' are heaps of stones that were created as a result of battles. Each stone was put there to represent an Irishman who died in the defense of his homeland.

Handball was invented in Ireland. The farmers put up stone walls in their field, and leveled the ground to make a handball court. You can see these 16-foot high stone walls standing alone in the fields in many parts of Ireland.

Hurling is Ireland's National Sport as baseball is ours in the U.S. In the western counties of Mayo, especially in the Kinomere Mountain region, you see boys playing on a "pitch" which is what the Irish call a field on which football and hurling are played. A native of the village, Liscanor, County Clare, invented the submarine.

Hurling is played with a stick about the same length as a baseball bat, or about three feet long. The end of the stick has a curved flat surface about eight inches in length. A hard ball resembling a baseball is used. The field has goals on both ends. Each team has a center, two forwards, two guards and a goalie. My mother used to tell about her uncle Paddy Ryan, goalie for the championship Tipperary team, who had all his teeth knocked out

265

playing the game.

The object of the game is to pass the ball and keep moving toward the opponent's goal The opponents try to steal the ball and attack your goal. It is a game of skill and speed like lacrosse or ice hockey. What amazed me was how the hurling players could pick the ball up with their stick, toss it in the air, and swing at it, sending it to another teammate while running at top speed. Swinging sticks in each other's faces and around their heads you would think they would all be strewn dead on the pitch, but somehow they miraculously avoided being hit.

Each goal counted one point and the team that scored the most goals won. The pitch had its boundaries marked, and if a team hit the ball out, the other team got it to put back in play. An umpire and two referees called fouls like grabbing or tripping an opponent. It's a great spectator game, and in Ireland, it's not unusual to have 100,000 spectators at a championship game between two teams such as Mayo and Tipperary.

When I was a teenager, a team from Ireland and a Detroit team had a hurling match at the University of Detroit stadium. My mother got tickets and took me. I played baseball, football, and a little bit of soccer but the skill of the hurling teams with their speed, courage, and competitive spirit won my applause and admiration. It was far more exciting to watch than any game I ever watched before with the possible exception of Jai Lai.

Our bus driver took us to Lisdonvarna after we left the Burren. Here is where matchmaking takes place each Spring. The "Chalkolans" or matchmakers gather to find partners for their clients.

Willy Daley from Lahinch area had an American gentleman who offered Willy $20,000 if Willy could find him the right match. Willy came up with a fine looking Irish woman that his American client fancied, but she wouldn't go for it. Then Willy told her if she would go for it, he'd give her $10,000 of the $20,000 the American agreed to pay him. She still refused, and said, "I don't love him." Willy said, "That doesn't make any difference. Marry him anyway. Then divorce him in three months and keep the money."

Lisdonvarna was famous as a health center or sanitarium. Rooms and meals were available for guests who bathed in the hot mineral springs, sat in the sun, and drank the mineral water. An odor reminiscent of rotten eggs was redolent in the air you breathe there. It is the same odor you get when you drive past Mt. Clemens in Michigan. Hydrogen sulfide, a deadly poisonous gas, causes the smell. When you drink the water you swallow this gas. Patients are either killed or cured there, I guess.

Our last stop before arriving back at our hotel, the Aberdeen Arms, was in Kinsale, a coastal resort. That evening the Chieftains, a world traveled group of six Irish musicians featuring traditional historic music, put on a great performance. The violinist was from Ennistymon located ten miles east of Lahinch.

Their leader, Paddy Maloney, and his family booked-in at the Aberdeen Arms where Mrs. Minor and I had a nice friendly visit with Paddy. As the reader will recall, a concert by Paddy was given in the Wharton Center for the Performing Arts at Michigan State University recently. We renewed our acquaintance with Paddy Maloney, and realized his

266

group is now world famous.

Doolin is a tiny village ten miles northwest of Lahinch. Evenings we would go there to sing and listen to the fiddler, harpist, drummer, flutist and concertina player. The only pay they got were drinks which customers purchased for them. Their main purpose for being there was to play together and improve their musicianship and entertain. They were great, and a friendly, cheerful group of local Irish "Tipplers" sang and visited. We enjoyed all of them. Some were farmers and others fishermen.

From Lahinch we went to Dublin and as I said, we took the train to Limerick which is just a few miles from the Shannon Airport. Going to the airport from Limerick we had a ride of sheer terror. The driver's name was Shamus O'Shaunessey. Every red light we came to, he drove right through without stopping. I tapped him on the shoulder and said, "Surely you're supposed to stop for red lights." He said, "I never stop at them, they're a nuisance, and I have a brother in Limerick with seven cabs who never stops at them either." On we went. Suddenly, we came to a green light. He jammed on the brakes so hard we nearly went through the windshield. I asked, "Why are you stopping at the green light?" He said, "I must be careful, you know, my brother might be coming from the other way."

In 1983, Mrs. Minor and I made our last trip to Ireland and took our grandson, Patrick Lee Brewer, with us. We went in June and as usual stayed at the Aberdeen Arms, Lahinch, County Clare, with our friends, Michael Vaughan, the innkeeper, and Philomena Vaughan, the baker, and Michael's wife. Ireland at Lahinch was cold and rainy.

Mrs. Minor got sick, and wasn't improving with the ministrations of local doctors. Michael Vaughan helped us get home. He changed our tickets on Northwest Airlines from tourist to first class and helped us through customs.

Northwest had an agent meet us in Boston. Our grandson, Pat, did all he could to help get his Grandma home. He was great. When we got to Lansing, she went immediately to Lansing General Hospital. Our daughter, Carol, Pat's mom, made all of the pre-arrangements.

Dr. Tilden took a large tumor out of her and Dr. Williams prescribed radiation afterwards. That nearly killed her. Fortunately, I got her to the Cleveland Clinic where Dr. Weakley saved her. Now, 11 years later, she's doing well. Thanks be to God and the prayers raised on her behalf.

At the same time, I was fainting, my fingers were white, and shriveled on the ends, and when I went into Dr. Jamieson's office, I fainted. When they brought me to, he sent me over to Lansing General Hospital. They put me on a heart monitor, and ran tests on my blood count. They told me I needed a pacemaker, and Dr. Mercer put one in.

My body iron was so low that Dr. Dalinn had a nurse watch for anaphylactic shock while one liter of colloidal iron went into my bloodstream. This amount still didn't bring the count up high enough, and another liter was given to me to get the iron count up where it should be.

Dr. Dalinn told Dr. Jamieson that I couldn't absorb iron from food, and would have to be brought in as an outpatient. Dr. Jamieson said, "We can give him shots every week at the office." He had the nurse do this for seven years.

From these injections, I got large lumps on both hips. Dr. DeCalo, a Caribbean doctor practicing on St. Martins Island, told me to put magnets on the lumps. We did, and the size was decreased. The lumps were also softened by using these magnets. Now, I still get shots, but only once a month, instead of four times. My blood iron count remains okay.

When all is said and done, I know it has been prayers guiding the doctors' hands which have returned Mrs. Minor and me to good health. Three classes of elementary children have prayed for me in my time of illness. Brother Herman has had King's College priests and brothers, where he works, pray for me. Our friends, Bob and Eileen Emerson, have had four Masses said for me. Our health has been carried on a wave of prayer. As the Bible says: "And you shall serve the Lord your God, and he shall bless your bread, and your water; and I will take sickness away from you." (Exodus 23:25) Also, "Bless the Lord, O my soul, and forget not all His benefits: Who forgives all your wrong doings; who heals all your diseases" (Psalm 103:2-3).

So much for our last trip to Ireland, although fond memories of our prior trips yet linger in both Mrs. Minor's and my minds, especially when we look at some of our pictures like the one we took with the Ambassador to Ireland in 1980.

We now plan to vacation every February in St. Martins Island until the saints come marching in, and do we enjoy ourselves? Yes!

Chapter 29

Lewis J. Minor: The Man, The Legend

by John B. Knight and Ronald F. Cichy

In The Beginning	**The Move To Cleveland**
The Road To Success	**Educator, Mentor, And Author**
Minor's Students Remember	**Philanthropist And Patriarch**
The Meaning of a Smile	

This article tells the story of the man and his teaching and business better than I can tell it. It provides a concise, accurate summation of my life's work, and I'm indebted to these former students of mine for doing this for posterity.

The L. J. Minor Profile was published in the February 1994 *Cornell HRA Quarterly*:

On December 12, 1951, Lewis J. Minor stated the business aims of the L. J. Minor Corporation when he said, "The tenets upon which I shall build my business will be honesty, integrity, accuracy, kindness, punctuality, courtesy, friendliness, helpfulness, and cleanliness." He went on to say, "I will endeavor always to be fair and helpful, not only to employees, my management team, and stockholders, but also to customers, government agencies, and competitors."

Anyone who has met and known Lewis J. Minor knows that those words sum up his philosophy of life and have been the basis for his success, not only as an individual, but as an entrepreneur, and educator, a mentor, and author, a philanthropist, and a patriarch.

In The Beginning

Lewis Joseph Minor was born in Harbor Beach, Michigan, on October 24, 1914. After graduating from high school, he went to work for the Donahue Varnish Company, where he took charge of the manufacture of lacquer solvents and helped paint and varnish research chemists develop new and improved products.

In September 1933, Minor enrolled at the University of Detroit to study engineering, but several months later he returned to the Donahue Varnish Company to oversee the construction and installation of a thousand-gallon distillation unit that was used for various industrial processes, including reclaiming spent solvents used to clean centrifuges, pebble mills, stone mills, and other equipment used in paint manufacture.

With an initial understanding of solid business practices and an interest in chemistry, Minor enrolled at Highland Park Junior College in 1935, graduating with honors in 1937 and continuing that same year to study chemistry at Michigan State College, from which he graduated with a Bachelor of Science degree in chemistry in June 1939 and where he was a member of Phi Kappa Phi, a national honor society.

During the summers of 1937, 1938, and 1939 Minor worked for the Ford Motor Company. Later that same year, the Michigan State Board of Agriculture appointed Minor a graduate assistant in chemistry at Michigan State College. He completed one term of work toward a Master of Science degree and left Michigan State College in January 1940 to become technical director of LaChoy Food Products Company, in Detroit.

During his two years at LaChoy, Minor improved the company's bean-sprouting process and doubled the yield of sprouts per pound of beans planted, while shortening sprouting time from five days to three days. He also developed a soy-sauce-manufacturing process for LaChoy, developed a seasoning called Magic Touch and a beverage called Vegamato Juice Cocktail, and found domestic sources of mung beans and water chestnuts. He established quality controls for all LaChoy's Chinese-food products. When he had completed that task, he took a position with the research group in the can division at Owens-Illinois in Toledo, Ohio.

He spent between two and three years at Owens-Illinois, working for Olin Ball, research director for the can division. Minor's job was to evaluate the performance of electrolytic tinplate and enamel-coated containers developed to replace hot-dipped tinplate. At the same time, he worked part-time evenings at McKay-Davis Company to develop bouillon powder for the U. S. Army.

After receiving a Master of Science degree in analytical chemistry from Wayne State University in 1944, Minor joined McKay-Davis full-time, where his bouillon product became the forerunner of the soup and gravy food bases Minor later developed to replace bouillon powder. Minor was appointed a vice president of McKay-Davis in 1946 and introduced a line of seasonings and other products for food manufacturers' use.

In March 1947, Minor left McKay-Davis and joined Huron Milling Company in Harbor Beach, Michigan - his home town - as technical director. At first Minor was to work on the development of new products aimed at increasing sales of wheat starch and wheat gluten. In June 1949 he joined the sales department to help increase the sales of both monosodium glutamate (MSG) and hydrolyzed vegetable protein.

At the same time, Minor was an active member of his neighborhood community; he was the scoutmaster of Harbor Beach (population 2,500), a member of the men's chorus, and a councilman for Parks and Buildings. He was also program chairman of the Great Lakes section of the Institute of Food Technologists, a role that indirectly influenced him to start his own business.

He resigned from Huron Milling in the fall of 1950 to start making plans for his own business. Nevertheless he remained on the company's payroll for six months after leaving. Meanwhile, Toby Bishop of International Minerals & Chemicals - manufacturers of Accent - offered him a technical position. Minor turned down this opportunity, so Bishop hired him as a consultant instead, to work with their food scientists developing new products. Minor received a monthly retainer from International Minerals & Chemicals for two years.

The Move To Cleveland

When Minor invited his second cousin, Thomas A. Ryan, to give a speech on his views on food to the Institute of Food Technologists, Ryan challenged Minor to sell his house, move to Cleveland, and start a business. He predicted that in Cleveland Minor could become as famous in the food industry as Vernon E. Stouffer.

So it was that, after selling their house, the Minor family moved to Cleveland and Minor founded the L. J. Minor Corporation in September 1951. At 37 years of age, Minor was in business for himself, starting with a lot of faith, $6,000, a borrowed Hobart mixer, and an air-conditioned rented room. The cash represented the equal investments of Minor; Joe Bertman, Cleveland's General Foods distributor and the first distributor of Minor's products there; and Tom Ryan, a lawyer who remained as a participant in the venture until his death in 1975.

Minor's plan was to make food bases (chicken and beef) that would improve on and, eventually, replace soup bases. For the first time in history, chefs would be able to use instant stocks to make foods that met the quality standards of "classical cooking" established by Auguste Escoffier. "From my experience in the food industry," Minor recalls, "I knew there would always be room for a company that sells quality products consistently controlled to ensure uniformity at a fair price. Service must be a keynote. Every effort must be put forth to give the customer exactly the product he or she specifies. If one does that, one must be proud to name the company after himself or herself."

"After World War II," explains Minor, "the foodservice industry needed food bases that could be the foundation for stocks, soups, sauces, and gravies." Rising meat costs and portion-controlled meats had eliminated the supply of meaty bones once available for making stocks. And chefs who were trained in the classic stockpot method were scarce. Instead of using meatless soup bases, it made sense to use bases that included meat and could be the foundation for more than just soup.

Minor developed concentrates of freshly cooked meat and poultry, and later of seafood and vegetables, that made it easier and more economical to prepare stock because they saved time, labor, equipment, and fuel in the kitchen. Moreover, quantity soups, sauces, gravies, and entrees could be enriched with natural flavors.

The first bases, made of chicken and beef, were sold under the ill-conceived "Dietitian" brand name. At first Minor did the manufacturing, packaging, and selling himself. He did not have the funds to hire a salesperson, and no one could be found who would work on a straight commission. Minor sold a few accounts in Cleveland but says he realized his "ineptness as a salesman."

On a trip to Boston, Minor enticed Bob Buntin, a broker, to carry his line in that city. Eventually, Buntin gave Minor the motto for Minor's bases: "Always in good taste." Next, Minor hired Johnny Hayes, the Olympic marathon champion in 1912, who had been selling olives, to sell Minor's food bases in New York City. When Minor was asked at a dietitians' convention if he was putting dietitians in jars, he changed the name on the label to "Minor's." But still not much business was being done.

Minor heard of a caterer in Detroit name George Rommel. He went to Rommel and told him that he needed a chef to represent the product line and sell bases. Rommel suggested Jean Caubet, who was preparing a meal that night for several hundred people. Minor proposed to Caubet that he sell the product line. Caubet said: "I am not a salesman. I am a chef. But I will try it tonight in my chicken fricassee."

"Well," Minor exclaims, upon recalling that episode, "My guardian angel must have been on my shoulder, because Chef Caubet received compliments on the fricassee and took the leftover food bases home with him and made soup for his daughters, who opined, "Daddy, this is good soup."

The rest is history. Chef Caubet represented the Minor's brand in Detroit, and in partnership with a salesman, Eric Swanson, Minor's business grew to over $2 million in sales a year in Michigan. But we are getting ahead of the story.

The Road To Success

Minor had to be frugal with funds. He tells of the trip he went on with Chef Caubet to northern Michigan to call on resorts. "One night we slept together in the same bed at the Dam-Site Inn. The room cost us just six dollars, but we had to save every dollar we could."

In 1952, Minor bought out his partners, Ryan and Bertman, by taking out a second mortgage on his house and borrowing against an insurance policy. Ryan remained active with Minor's, however, and became sales manager of the firm and eventually general manager. A great persuader, Ryan was also a gifted talent scout who brought outstanding people into the business. He had intuition and was a seasoned judge of human character. Minor considered Ryan the greatest human being he ever knew and, as Minor reports, at the time Minor thought to himself, "Thou art Thomas, and on this rock I shall build my business." Today, 22 years after Ryan's death, Minor says his convictions about Ryan are just as strong.

Plants and samples. Minor's first plant was a 18-by-20-foot room, with an air conditioner, in Bertman's pickle plant. The second was in an old horse barn, built in the 1890's in a former coal yard. After a 1957 renovation, the plant passed federal inspection. The third plant, which had been a car wash, was renovated to meet plant standards set by the Meat Inspection Department of the United States.

Samples were a necessity from the beginning. On Saturdays the Minor family would visit the plant and make up one-ounce and four-ounce samples in glass jars, using a small spoon to fill the jars. One Saturday the Minors' parish priest happened to stop by and, upon seeing the tedious assembly line, suggested that the Minor family use cake-decorating bags and nozzles. That one suggestion revolutionized sample packing.

In 1959, Stouffer became Minor's first chain and industrial account. Bases were sold to their restaurants and frozen-food plants. New bases were developed, including clam, ham, mushroom, and turkey; later, lobster, onion, and garlic bases were added.

From the earliest moments of the company, Minor realized that the people who would appreciate the value of his product line were retired executive chefs. "Each chef was an outstanding, respected professional with extensive kitchen experiences and impressive culinary credentials," says Minor.

Three of the best-known chefs to assist the company were John Sector, Jean Caubet, and Ernest Koves (who established a school in his house in New York City for teaching others how to use Minor's bases). Carl Richter, Michael Minor, Hans Bueschkens, and more than 50 chefs who had trained and worked all over the world joined the Minor Corporation in Cleveland.

Others became the corporation's most-effective salespeople and workers, including John Secter, Herman Breithaupt, George Marchand, Michael Palmer, Otto Denkinger, Emil Burgermeister, Pierre Bach, and Harry Bazaan. Brother Herman Zaccarelli, Matthew Bernatsky, Frank Sigmund, Peter Gust Economou, and Ruth E. Minor (Lewis' wife) and the rest of Minor's family also had influential roles. Mrs. Minor in particular helped by joining Minor at night filling emergency orders and making the deliveries while Minor stayed behind to clean up. Perhaps Mrs. Minor's biggest contribution came when Stouffer's needed a sauce for beef tenderloin. Mrs. Minor's gravy saved the day and led to a closer relationship with Margaret Mitchell, who was executive assistant to Vernon Stouffer and in charge of quality control and product development for all Stouffer restaurants.

The Cornell Hotel and Restaurant Administration Quarterly also promoted Minor's bases in many of its "tested quantity recipes" that appeared in the magazine in the 1960s and 1970s. Ryan and Minor spent a good deal of time at Cornell and had close relationships with many of its faculty members and administrators, all of whom became valuable friends of Minor's. Those Cornell connections helped Minor build the business, and the influence of *The Cornell Quarterly* gave his company an aura of class and distinction that was mutually advantageous to the development of the business and the education of Minor's students when Minor was teaching.

In 1961 Minor returned to school. "I went back to school and enrolled in Michigan State's food science department," Minor recalls, "to verify scientifically Escoffier's contention that older animals have more flavor than younger ones of the same species and thus provide better soup and gravy stocks." In 1964 he earned his Ph.D. in food science. His thesis topic was "The identification of Some Chemical Components of Chicken Flavor - Comparing That of Young and Old Birds."

With his doctorate in hand, the recently graduated Minor became an assistant professor in the School of Hotel, Restaurant and Institutional Management at Michigan State University, where he taught half-time for 20 years and became a full professor. Among many other things, Minor taught his students about the harm of smoking long before the topic was fashionable, and predicted as early as 1965 that some day restaurants would have "no smoking sections" and hotels and motels, "no smoking rooms", for their guests.

One day the university's president, John A. Hannah, asked Minor how he could teach at MSU while owning the Minor Corporation in Cleveland at the same time. Minor replied simply, "Because I have good people there." Hannah concurred by saying, "That's what it takes, good people, isn't it?"

Educator, Mentor, And Author

Minor's entry into teaching in 1964 was due, in part, to an invitation by well-known hospitality educator Lendal Kotschevar, who was teaching at Michigan State University at the time. In his new position as visiting professor at the School of Hotel, Restaurant and Institutional Management, Minor taught foodservice science during the fall and spring quarters and shaped the school's foodservice and food-science curriculum until 1984. For nine years, starting in 1975, his classes included one in food-flavor evaluation.

During his 20 years at Michigan State University, Minor touched the lives of over 1,000 present-day leaders in international hospitality with his high standards of excellence. Statements he made 20 and 30 years ago in his classes are as important today as they were then. For example, one of Minor's favorite slogans is, "Quality is remembered long after the price is forgotten." He taught students to "aim for the eagle rather than shoot at the rat," and quoted his mother as saying, "Eaten bread is soon forgotten" and his father as noting, "Accuracy is the key to success." In other words, do your best today and then repeat that outstanding performance every day of your life. He also emphasized Irish comedian Hal Roach's entreaty, "Remember to live every day as if it's your last, because one day you'll be right."

On September 10, 1993, Minor received the outstanding alumnus award from Michigan State University's Department of Food Science and Human Nutrition alumni association.

Ruth. Minor taught the importance of one's spouse in business and life. Without hesitation he credits his choice of marriage partner as the smartest decision he ever made and boasts to those close to him that of all the triumphs in his life, he is proudest of his relationship with her.

Lewis and Ruth Minor's relationship is a prefect example of marriage as a partnership. Ruth Eloise Angell, a native of Lansing, Michigan, graduated from Clinton County Teacher's College in 1933 and thereafter taught eight grades of students in one-room schools for six years. Lewis and Ruth married in February 1939, after which she focused on raising their eight children. In 1951 she took on the additional duties of helping Minor establish the L. J. Minor Corporation. Says Minor, "The success of the business and the man can be attributed to her unfailing support in good times and bad."

Minor's Students Remember

Richard Brooks, vice president of rooms management for Stouffer/Renaissance Hotels and Resorts, recalls that Minor brought "a high standard of excellence to the classroom. Perhaps most important, he had a sense of identification with his students that was communicated every day. He brought reality to the classroom and shared his experiences freely."

Houston Striggow, general manager of Top of the Triangle restaurant, says that by bringing chefs into the classroom, Minor "provided his students with an appreciation for food and the foodservice industry."

Michael Zelski, director of technical development for CPC International, remembers how Minor "taught with a mix of theory and real-world experience that led to better understanding."

Bennett Schwartz, vice president of Harper and Associates, says that Minor "taught because he enjoyed it, and I enjoyed learning because of him."

Kotschevar, now a professor at Florida International University, wrote this about Minor in 1992: "He is a great teacher and gives liberally from his broad knowledge. All students who came in contact with him enriched their lives and gained valuable information from which they could better perform in their professions."

John Zehnder, food and beverage director for Zehnder's, Inc., says: "When my time finally came to take a course taught by Minor, I approached it not unlike a primitive youth about to begin the rites of passage into adulthood. Fear, excitement, and curiosity - all those emotions stirred within me. The classroom was respectfully quiet as he entered through the door on the first day of class, and there he was - Lewis J. Minor - the legend. No one knew what to expect. We had all heard stories. And oh, the lessons that we learned.

"We were taught that smoking wasn't healthy, at a time when smoking was still the thing to do. We were often reminded that as college students we didn't have all the answers, even though we thought we did. We were lectured on responsibility and accountability, in an era of rebellion. Minor taught us more than management principles; he taught us lessons in life. He taught us to be professionals. He taught us that ethics are more important than most business people realize."

Robert Brymer, a professor of hospitality administration at Florida State University, says, "I will never forget the great open-house parties at [the Minors'] home. As a graduate student and assistant to Minor, this warmth and congeniality was most appreciated. I will always appreciate the tremendous personal interest Minor took in his students. He truly cared about each and every one of us."

M.A. Bossler, executive manager of the Detroit Athletic Club, sums up the feelings of Minor's former students when he says, "I learned from Minor that in life great deeds are never done alone. There is always someone to thank. Thank you, Doctor Minor."

Minor has authored, co-authored, and edited over 12 textbooks and has written several articles on topics covering food quality, flavor, and production systems in refereed journals and trade magazines.[1]

[1] For example, L. J. Minor is an author with six citations in the 34-year history of *The Cornell Hotel and Restaurant Administration Quarterly*. See: "Food Flavor", Vol. 7, No. 3 (November, 1966); "Views on Pollution in Science Press: and "Eliminating Warmed-Over Flavor in Precooked Food", Vol. 11, No. 2 (August, 1970);' "Today's Food-Production Systems", Vol. 13, No. 1 (May, 1972); "Nutrition", Vol. 15, No. 1 (May, 1974); and "Quality as an Economic Force in the Food-Service Industry", Vol. 18, No. 2 (August, 1977).

Philanthropist And Patriarch

From his earliest teaching days Minor brought chefs to the classroom at his own expense, and each term for the past ten years he has donated food supplies for his laboratory food classes. In the fall of 1993 he made a $2.5 million gift to Michigan State University to benefit both its School of Hotel, Restaurant and Institutional Management and the food science department. Two-million dollars of that gift was for the School of Hotel, Restaurant and Institutional Management to establish the MSU-HRIM Michael L. Minor Master of Science in Foodservice Management, a fifth-year post-baccalaureate program designed to prepare culinary professionals for careers leading to fast-track positions as executive chefs and foodservice entrepreneurs. That business-focused program was launched during the fall semester of 1994.

Minor has also given to the American Culinary Federation, the Cleveland Clinic, Cornell University's School of Hotel Administration (in honor of Thomas A Ryan), the Culinary Institute of America, the William F. Harrah College of Hotel Administration at the

---

[1]For example, L. J. Minor is an author with six citations in the 34-year history of *The Cornell Hotel and Restaurant Administration Quarterly*. See: "Food Flavor," Vol. 7, No. 3 (November 1966); "Views on Pollution in Science Press" and "Eliminating Warmed-Over Flavor in Precooked Food," Vol. 11, No. 2 (August 1970); "Today's Food-Production Systems," Vol. 13, No. 1 (May 1972); "Nutrition," Vol. 15, No. 1 (May 1974); and "Quality as an Economic Force in the Food-Service Industry," Vol. 18, No. 2 (August 1977).

University of Nevada at Las Vegas, Johnson and Wales University (in honor of Hermann Rusch), the Purdue University Restaurant, Hotel, Institutional, and Tourism Management School (in honor of Minor's father, Newell W. Minor), the University of Rochester, the Ryerson Institute, and Sullivan County Community College. Also, Lewis and Ruth Minor recently established the Kathleen Mary Minor Student Loan Fund at Indiana University-Purdue University Fort Wayne, in memory of Minor's mother.

In 1980 the Minors were catalysts in bringing a certified executive chef, Robert Nelson, who was a former L. J. Minor Corporation chef, to Michigan State University to be *Chef de cuisine* at the School of Hotel, Restaurant and Institutional Management. Nelson thus became the first chef in the world appointed to the faculty of a hospitality program in a college of business. Later the Minors pledged to endow a chair at Michigan State University, to be called the Dr. Lewis J. and Mrs. Ruth E. Minor School of HRIM Chef de Cuisine.

As head of the Minor family, mentor to industry leaders, professor emeritus of Michigan State University's School of Hotel, Restaurant and Institutional Management, and founder of the L. J. Minor Corporation, Lewis J. Minor is indeed one of Hospitality's benefactors.

The Meaning of a Smile

Minor professed that laughter is the relief valve for life, and his philosophy regarding the meaning of a smile he attributes to Hal Roach:

It costs nothing, but it creates much.
It happens in a flash, but the memory of
it sometimes lasts forever.
There are none so rich that they can get
along without it, and none so poor but
are richer from its benefits.
It brings rest to the weary, comfort to the
sad, hope to the discouraged, and
is the countersign of friends.
It fosters good will in business and
happiness in the home.
It is something that cannot be begged,
bought, borrowed, or stolen, but it is of
no earthly good to anyone until it is
given away.
So if in the course of the day your friends
are too tired to give you a smile, why
don't you give them one of yours?

For nobody needs a smile more than
those who have none left to give. Smile!

Chapter 30

From the Beginning
To the End

by Ruth Ann Minor Fields
(1953-1989)

Through the Eyes of a Child   **In My Teen Years**

Young Adulthood   **Accidents**   **New Procedures**

Cooking Processes   **Sanitation and Clean-up**   **Great Benefits**

(Editor's Note: As I reviewed this chapter, the first of numerous contributed by the Minor children, I was inspired by the blessing a man and woman receive when they raise their children correctly. The Bible says, "Train up a child in the way he might go, even when he is old he will not depart from it" (Proverbs 22:6). For forty plus years, considering the early Saturdays spent at the plant, Ruth Ann Fields was a blessing to her parents. Furthermore, God has blessed her richly because of it.

On a personal note, I would like to thank her for all of her help in putting this book together. She worked long and hard in assembling the many pictures seen and wrote the captions for them all. The book would not have been the same without her superb attention to detail. The material she contributed regarding her own story was excellent also. Thank you, Ruth Ann, for a job well done!)

I Was Always There to Guide and Direct You!
(Irish Humor by Hal Roach)

A balloonist is passing over Ireland. He has lost his way. Casey is down on the field plowing, so he lowers his balloon within 20 feet of Casey and he yells down:
"Where am I?"

Casey looks up and says:
"You can't fool me! You're up there in that little basket!"

Quote from Anna Eleanor Roosevelt

"It seemed to me stupid to have the gift of life
and not to use it to the utmost of one's ability."

Through the Eyes of a Child

Reflecting back to when I first aspired to work for my parents at the L. J. Minor Corporation, my memory wanders to the Saturday Dad took me with him to get some painting accomplished on West 115th Street. As I recall, the edifice was originally a horse barn; then it was used for storing coal!

As young as I was, about eight, perhaps nine, I would watch Daddy (some help, eh?) painting the walls white after trying to clean the dirt off of them, and would think, how in the world will this ever be clean? But he did it!

What a bright, clean tidy place it was to move his already established business into and it was really big, too . . . so we thought. Comparatively speaking, it was a definite improvement from the small room he worked out of at Bertman Foods, and it was a place Mother and Dad could "call their own."

Even then, in my heart, I must have sensed my destiny. I took such pride watching Daddy working so diligently and painstakingly to get the place suitable for food manufacturing. It was there I remember our family spending time on weekends helping our parents (as much as we could) with various tasks.

As I grew a little older, having acquired the technique and proper way of sample packaging, I looked forward to going in on my weekends and helping out. After all, where else in that day in age could I go to work? Not to mention make a little money!

Of course, as I recall, nothing came easy, as early on I was taught that part of the process was cleaning up after yourself. One way to get smart in a BIG hurry was not to make any more of a mess than absolutely necessary. I was a learner in that regard.

As for the money, I do not clearly remember what the original amount was . . . something like one cent per every jar. It was not until we "graduated" and moved to the West 25th Street facility that we were into the big bucks . . . approximately $.50 per hour, providing we completed a specified number of jars, be it one or four ounce.

Actually, the four-ounce were simpler from the cleaning and labeling standpoint but packing them was a real killer. Once samples got to be big business, we began using pastry bags to pack with, at someone's suggestion from our parish.

It was simpler than using the messy spoon method, but pity the poor kid who got some "stiff" product to squeeze. By the end of the work day, your hands and arms would be so-o-o sore! Some of the products could not be packaged any other way than by the "spoon" method, such as ham base, as they were too dense.

We used to discuss (argue was more like it) who would do the spooning and who

280

would do the squeezing. Keep in mind we were getting paid by the number of pieces put out! Obviously, once I was put in charge that was resolved. We would collectively work on one product until it was completed, then move on to the next. Needless to say the demand for implements increased!

During the time the company was located at its 115th Street, I learned several things, primarily having to do with the packaging operation. This learning process took place during summer vacation and time off from school for winter and spring breaks. My weekends were earmarked for sample packing.

When I first learned how to package, the product line was small. Seems to me that the products were limited to chicken, beef, ham, and possibly consommé and mushroom bases. Since Minor's customer base was small, one might say we were "custom making" products.

Package sizes varied from one pound glass jars to 10, 25, and 50 pound fiber drums. Liquids were offered in one pint (amber glass) bottles and later in one gallon sizes too.

Besides my dad, women who worked for him--namely Audrey Chubbs, Rose Wilson, and Helen Crites -- taught me how to package. They sure had the technique on how to use ice cream scoops. Audrey especially knew the packaging business. Years later, she and I would have timed "contests" to see who could pack the most jars accurately in the time allotted. I swear, you could see the sparks coming out of Audrey's scoop while she was packing!

It was all in the way you held and operated the scoop and jar as to how quickly it could be done. Oh yes, judgment capabilities helped also. Keep in mind, too, the job had to be done neatly, as the standard set was nothing short of impeccable, which included not only quality product but appearance of packaged product and shipping container as well.

Also, I learned early on the fundamentals on how to "set up" orders, make up Bills of Lading (documents required by truck lines), and load product onto trucks. I helped unload incoming raw materials and packaging materials. This was all done by hand in those days.

As an example, the cases of empty glass used for packing product came in hundreds at a time. We unloaded them one at a time originally. Another example was salt as it came in 100 pound bags at that time and each one was unloaded by hand and stacked onto pallets.

Naturally, in my younger years I did not help with heavier items since Dad would not allow it. But as I got older and wiser and Dad was not around to see, I did help with those deliveries . . . against the advice of Audrey, who was in charge when Dad was not there.

Funny when you are young how invincible you feel, like you are never going to get old and all the dumb things you do while you are young will not come back to haunt you! 'Tis like yesterday, I would hear one of the women say "You are going to wish you had never done this as you get older." But, like your parents, what did these gals know? I can only say, "I should have listened." Too late!

When raw materials came in, Dad would check each item for quality from standards set. Audrey had this responsibility when Dad was not there. One of her favorite gigs was to have the "new kid on the block" taste test a teaspoon full of oleoresin black pepper (if she could get away with it).

Most people would fall for it, but not yours truly, thank goodness (hot stuff)! Why? By that stage in my life, I had been taught to smell something before tasting it. Great habit to have, not to mention it is the correct way to evaluate a product.

Taste testing was one of the first things each of us children learned once Dad was in the flavor business. He would bring products home at night so we could "evaluate" them. This was done prior to meal time so our taste buds would be acute. Often the products Dad and Mother wanted evaluated would be our dinner!

They believed, and still do, that children have the most acute, discerning taste buds and honest straight-forward opinions. Thus, the Minor Corporation's original "taste panel" was headed up by, none other than, our dear Mother!

This may not be the place to interject the following, but speaking of black pepper, our supplier for that and various other flavorings was The Joseph Adams Company. This company was owned and operated by Joseph Adams, "a man amongst men," a prince, just like my dad. There was nothing Mr. Adams would not do to accommodate our needs.

He was a great business man, a great help in making recommendations when Dad would be in the developmental stage of a product. Also, if we ran low or out of one of his products, it was just a phone call away from being where we needed it! What service. Both Mother and Dad had a gift of drawing nice people to them.

To this day, when I count my blessings, Mr. Adams is one of them. It was an honor, a privilege to have had him as a part of our organization. He truly made a difference during, not only the formative years, but through time.

Again, Dad and Mother had a knack for drawing great people to them, be it suppliers, customers, sales people, service people, personnel, acquaintances, friends, not to mention relations, especially children (just kidding). Of course, my uncle, Tom Ryan, who helped Dad get started and, until his death, helped to run the business, also had the same "gift."

He, like my dad, was a great man, a true leader. He trusted those working under him to do their jobs without "looking over their shoulder" all the time. He was a real confidence builder and a delegator.

If Uncle Tom needed something done and thought you could do it (despite the fact you might not have much or any experience with whatever he would assign), he expected you to do it. Great expectations make things happen.

He was very supportive in our efforts at the plant, also. Even though he worked out of an office in downtown Cleveland and did a lot of traveling (along with Dad), he stayed in tune with the day to day happenings in operations. He would be there if and when you needed him.

Uncle Tom seemed to have a lot of confidence in my worth, for which I credit a lot of my success. He offered great support, but no greater than what my folks afforded me.

They would lead by example. They were nurturing, positive, loving, caring, yet lighthearted.

When I consider how they led, I think of a poem that starts out, "Things grow best in a happy place, where they quickly spread from face to face." I think of the poem Dad has often recited, "The Meaning of a Smile."

The Minor Corporation was a happy place when my parents started it and through time. That is how a work environment should be if the business is to withstand the course of time. I guess if you want to start a business, there are basic fundamentals, principles you must establish and upon which you must build.

Quality, be it people, product, work ethic, facility and grounds, machinery, raw materials and supplies, service, or whatever, must be at the very core from which you operate. That was the standard set, quality uppermost and foremost, from the beginning.

While other companies were out there figuring out ways to do things at a cheaper cost, and increase their profit margin, Dad was always trying to find ways to improve his products, methods, facility, employee talent, compensation, and, in general, the overall business. Cost was always the last item to be considered.

For this, someone once said Dad lacked in business skills. I, for one, did not agree! Looking back on life, I dare say my parents ran their business very much the same way they took care of their family and their home. They were, and still are, very frugal people.

Yet, nothing was spared when it came to quality of life. The finer things were always there. They wanted things done thoroughly, correctly, in a timely manner, professionally, always. After all, right is, and will always be, right! I might add, between my parents, Uncle Tom, the original employees, and other leaders that came with the company at a later date, I had quality skills instilled in me early on that helped me in what would turn out to be a career, my livelihood. For this I was, and still am, forever grateful.

Getting back to the product line, we offered a few types of chicken and beef base. Yes, even back in the late '50s our standard line was called Dietitian Brand. The beef base contained beef as its main ingredient, and the chicken contained chicken as its main ingredient.

The consistency of these products was paste-like. (Somewhat more fluid than peanut butter) These were, by far, the easiest in the line to pack. Naturally, being the top of the line, they were the highest priced, but the best value as well. Years later, we ran tests on these products where water was added to dilute them more than the recommended amount, and the flavor was still predominant.

There were people who chose not to buy our standard line products, so we offered three other types. Quality/Choice was the next best quality at a slightly lower cost. It was a blend of our standard product and Godfrey base and was only being used by City Hospital to my knowledge. Caterer Brand and Godfrey Brand were our least expensive products. Caterer Brand was somewhat dry, crumbly, and hard. Godfrey Brand, on the other hand, was fluffy and easy to pack, unless, of course, it was too full of air resulting in a product too hard to pack because it was difficult to fit the required weight into the package!

The standard ham base was another product difficult to pack due to the fact it was very viscous, especially if it had been refrigerated. That procedure definitely separated the men from the boys.

Besides packing, weighing, "topping" those products warranting that procedure, cleaning off the inside lip of the glass jar, placing the lid on the jar and tightening it with all of your might, each jar had to be labeled. Guess who got that job which seemed to be THE job no one wanted? That's correct, me, the "low guy on the totem pole!"

To perfect that job was a great undertaking. I mastered it over the course of time through trial and error and mainly downright determination. We used a Labelette labeling machine (the simplest one they produced), which many years later, after acquiring their newest model, I personally would have given my eye teeth to have back. It was easier to clean. There is something to be said for simplicity!

Our customer base expanded to surrounding states quickly, so the necessity of acquiring federal inspection came sooner than anticipated. Both Dr. Romine and Inspector Emil Kralik were working with us and I know we had a workable relationship with the federal government early on, something not all processing plants are able to say.

Our standards were high, far above those set by the federal government, and we had already been working with the city inspector, Gene Kurka, who helped us in setting acceptable guidelines for food production. Both overall appearance and cleanliness of the facility were important as well as those of the employees.

In fact, at that time, each employee had to obtain a food handler's permit, requiring a chest x-ray to be taken. Later, this test was replaced with a T.B. tine test which we did in-house with a registered nurse to save employee's time.

Eventually, we had two federal inspectors, one for meat, Inspector Kralik, and one for poultry, Dr. David Fenoy. Our first assigned inspector was Bill, but I do not remember his last name and am sorry for that. We were compatible with the inspection process and for that I am thankful. Many other plants in the area had told me of their nightmares which we never experienced. Incidentally, after his retirement from the government, Emil Kralik worked part-time for the Minor Corporation.

As I leave the discussion of my tender, initial years working, I must say that one of the "fetes" that I mastered, while working with Audrey and Rose, was to eat a pork steak sandwich . . . bone in! I did not even know what a pork steak was, let alone that it could be devoured in sandwich form. I preferred mine, unlike theirs, without the strawberry jam!

In My Teen Years

When the plant at West 115th moved to its current location, I remember washing walls and floors with Sal Soda, recommended by Elmer Roper, the best tile man in town. They needed to be scrubbed until picture perfect.

One of the gals opened one of the label cabinets in search of a specific label. What a mess . . . since labels were stored in cabinets with dividers wide enough for labels to fit in, someone had the brainstorm they could move it "as is." Have you ever heard of 52 pick-up? Well, this was 5,200!

The Norris Brother Company moved all of the larger equipment and made it look simple. A lot of smaller items were taken over in car loads by Robbie, an older fellow hired by Dad to run errands. He used the company Jeep and was so helpful and accommodating. What a gem!

When we saw the new facility, we could not believe the size and space we had. As you will read elsewhere, it was not long before the first addition had to be built. Since the building did not have refrigeration, Dad bought a used cooler and had it installed on the north side of the existing building.

Also, a refrigcrated trailer was used to store packaged product in and set up outgoing orders. John Zsori, an older gentleman, was hired to do this shipping function, and what a job he did. That had been the job I set my sights on once I started full time with the company, but Dad had greater expectations for me!

At some point in my schooling, I was assigned a paper on what I wanted to be when I grew up. I wrote about being a policewoman or physical education teacher. By my teen years, I was offered an opportunity to make some money in a different field than either of the above.

Since I had the knowledge of sample packing, and Dad needed someone who would not only work with, but organize and oversee a group of neighborhood children and my siblings to package one and four ounce samples on weekends, I was hired. The position was a challenge, but I enjoyed my job.

After all, how many teenagers do you know who can boss their brother, sister, and neighbor kids around and get paid for it? I was a working supervisor who expected all to keep pace with me as the more samples we completed, the more money we would be paid. Aside from ignoring the wailing of my counterparts because their hands and feet were hurting and because they were always hungry, I was a great boss, as you would have guessed.

My sister, Carol, and her pal, Gerry O'Malley, would attest, no doubt, to my skill level. They are still talking about their work experience at Minor's. Being a teenager, I had my sights set on getting the job done correctly and getting out, so there was no time for nonsense, like breaks and such. We must proceed and that we did!

By the time I graduated from high school, I looked forward to working full time. When that arrived in September of 1962, I was taught to do anything and everything I had not previously learned. My main job function, though, was packager.

By this time, Minor's had a new plant manager, Ronald (Joe) Gilbert. Also there were a couple new employees like Pearl Geiss, who was responsible for chopping meats and poultry. She came from an employment service, Manpower, and then we hired her as she worked out for us. Both the men and women working at the plant at this time were superior workers, sticklers for detail, meticulous, and thorough.

Although I do know when it happened, probably in the early '60s, something took place that would significantly change my destiny with the company. Audrey phoned in to report she had broken a limb. She would not be able to work for a few weeks.

Joe asked me to take over her duties in her absence. Holy mackerel! What didn't Audrey do? I must admit, I did offer to help Joe! Now came the help from Joe and greater guidance from God, plus moral support from my parents, Uncle Tom, Mary Mele (his secretary), and Nancy Clancy. I resolved myself to the realization that this would be no easy task, but through team work, we could do it!

At first, I looked at unfilled orders. I did this at home since daily duties were too plentiful at work. The stack seemed endless as I tried to prioritize them and there were some two weeks back logged. Each specified the date the order was received, and date a customer wanted product to be shipped or received, and an itemized list of product size and quantity.

After a concentrated effort to organize all, I realized why these orders had been put on the back burner. On them were products not routinely made, were time consuming to pack, or contained raw materials needing to be ordered. Seeing Audrey was also our purchasing agent, guess what else, besides production and packaging, that I had to do?

It took two weeks of hard labor, plus overtime, to get caught up . . . but we did it through trial and error and a lots of prayers. Another facet of the business, which I had already had some experience in required my attention also. That was Quality Control (Q. C.). Incoming raw materials, final blend batches, weights, and packages, all needed to be checked, or at least spot-checked. Batch cards needed to be completed for each product, and each batch of product as well as measuring or weighing control products (C. P.'s).

The batchmakers weighed and handled the larger quantity raw materials, but it was Q. C.'s responsibility to take care of C. P.'s. That ought to give a clearer picture of what Audrey did in the course of a day. In her spare time she helped out in packaging which was my area of responsibility. Accordingly, I continued to do my job there in the normal working hours and complete what I could of Audrey's responsibilities during breaks, lunch time, and after hours.

By the time she returned to work, I had learned a lot and was exhausted. Everyone had helped me, including suppliers and customers, but I was better educated and knew more about the business than ever!

Young Adulthood

When Audrey returned, I was sent to our West 115th Street facility, which Dad had the foresight to keep, to manufacture Colonel Sander's chicken gravy. The operation was a one person job, once organized, but the deal fell through after a few months and I was back to the business at hand.

After my marriage to Dorsey Benton Fields, Dorsey Michael was born to us on July 23, 1964. After attempting to return to work too soon, I had a set back and started again in the fall of that year.

While at work, I hired Gaye Taylor to baby-sit our little guy. She lived in an apartment in front of the plant, eventually known as the "Taylor" building, which was very convenient. Unfortunately, Gaye broke her arm a few months later and was no longer able to help me.

With her armed healed, Gaye decided to work for the L. J. Minor Corporation in packaging. By 1967, she was team leader on the second shift. About the same time, Tom Mele, Mary Mele's brother, started to work and in the early '70s was made packaging supervisor on the second shift.

My husband, Dorsey, became a supervisor in the company, successfully handling the people who picked chicken (deboners), chopped it, and did the final blending of product. He also kept equipment running and was in the process of helping select a new packaging pump when God had a different plan. He passed away in 1969.

Besides our son, we were blessed with two lovely daughters, Sallie in August, 1966, and Kristin in September, 1969. Unfortunately, Dorsey did not live long enough to see his last bundle of joy, yet he truly loved his children, just as I have. Incidentally, God blessed me once again in December of 1984 with one more child to love, Patrick Ryan!

Margie Stanley was one of the deboners in Dorsey's original crew. She recently retired after 25 years of service to the company doing diverse fast-paced jobs including being team leader in packaging on the first shift. I have to commend her for a job well done.

George Henderson is another employee who started with us in the '60s, 1964 to be exact, and is still with the company today. He was another workaholic and eventually was in supervision.

As you will recall, Pearl Geiss worked in chopping. At first she used one tabletop Hobart chopper for grinding meats, poultry, and mushrooms. Soon she needed three choppers. Then the Hobart "Schnell" cutter was acquired.

Unlike the tabletops that were open, the new chopper had a lid on it which, once it was locked down, the blades would operate. You would turn a handle on top to force the product being chopped into the blades. This was a much safer piece of equipment and had a sliding door on top through which you could view the product. This opening also allowed for heat to escape as meat items often came right from the ovens for chopping.

There were procedures in place as to the amount and time the chopping would take. Poultry was changed with the new cutter to include salt and fat during the chopping. This helped with getting the meat finer and made an emulsification so the final product would be better blended and less apt to separate. Pearl eventually needed additional part-time help as the process became more difficult.

Some of my fonder memories involved two men who came in on our newly established second shift to process chicken base. Adam Young worked days as a delivery man for Kaufman container, who supplied us our packaging materials, and part-time with us chopping poultry products.

As important, Terry Clancy, Nancy's husband, was a Cleveland policeman by day and made final batches at night. From their first day on the job, I marveled at the productivity of these fellows after having been on another job all day! They were always happy and fun loving. Terry even brought in fellow policemen to work for him if he had to trade shifts on his full time job.

Speaking of special people, Michael Zelski, arrived on the job just as we needed him. Everyone liked and respected Mike as he had many qualities and was a people person. He thought nothing was impossible and would roll up his sleeves to help out. You could not say no to him.

Mike Zelski was a great team player and organizer. He was an educator, explaining anything you did not understand. He was a researcher, studying machinery, packaging and raw materials, room design, or whatever needed to be known prior to a decision being made. He arrived in 1968 and accomplished what he did at Minor's through his work efforts and nurturing of his peoples' work efforts.

He got a lot of support from another Mike, none other than my brother, Mike Minor. He joined the company in 1975 and they made a super team together and with everyone else. He was and still is well liked by all. His special quality that he instills in others is that he likes to have fun when he works, yet, there is no one who has ever worked harder in the company than Mike. What a guy!

One last reason that both Mikes worked so well with people is the fact that both are fair and honest. They showed little favoritism and were true to their word. What's more, they were innovative, creative, and uncommonly clairvoyant.

They both were experts when it came to picking out equipment. I remember the huge chopper Mike Minor assisted in purchasing. A Minor (major) breakthrough occurred when he realized you could not only use it for chopping meats, poultry, vegetables, or seafood, but the entire batch could be made in this one piece of equipment!

This presented a few fixable problems as it shifted a portion of the final blend to the chopper area. We split the team in dry blend and had them do the premixes together on part of their shift. The premixes were the weighing and combining of dry ingredients. We referred to these as plant products (P. P.'s). These P. P.'s were then mixed together on the Hobart vertical mixers. Then one of the two man teams would go into the chopper area to help with final blend for the remainder of the shift.

The sauces for the beef base, for example, were measured out by the person doing the chopping. On first shift, Anni Fleig worked in this capacity. I hated it if she called in sick, as I might have to take her place!

The beef stock used in making these sauces was very viscous and difficult to handle. Your arms would become so sore by the end of this procedure, so I really respected what Anni had to do day in and day out!

When my sister, Josephine, who worked at the company also, asked if she could help me one day, I jokingly sent her in to measure these ingredients. She really struggled, but I went in to help. She worked in Q. C. and offered to help because she knew production was in a pinch. Later, Josephine worked for Ingolf in inventory control and did well since she knew how to work with both production and packaging employees.

As the business grew, a day came when an even larger piece of equipment was needed for production. The new chopper was able to handle about two and one-half times more product!

Accidents

Incidentally, one of the major accidents we experienced occurred in that first chopper. I had reached the position of plant manager with two supervisors reporting to me during each shift. Dan Mullen, who started in 1978, was first shift production supervisor.

The location where I was when the "news" hit shall never be forgotten. Mrs. Ruth Engler, a retiree of the Stouffer Corporation, had come on board in the early '70s to help write procedures for sanitation, job descriptions for manufacturing, and to develop a formal taste panel.

As a selected member of the original taste panelists, an honor given to a choice few, I was in a tasting session when Dan came in and motioned that he needed to speak with me privately. From the look on his face, I had this eerie sensation that I was not going to like what he was about to tell me. I was correct!

Two of the people from the final blend/chopper area, men used to doing the heavy lifting and volume, had completed their scheduled work and had begun to clean. Unfortunately, one hand did not know what the other hand was doing, and a huge metal wrench, used to loosen chopper blades, was left in the giant stainless steel chopper bowl.

While the bowl was being filled with water for cleaning, the fellow who had forgotten the wrench left the room. When the other fellow saw the soapy water reach the top of the bowl, he shut the lid and turned the chopper on, totally unaware that the wrench was in the bowl.

By that time both people were in the room, the first figuring the other one had seen the wrench and removed it. Needless to say, bullet-like fragments of metal were shooting out at them throughout the entire room. Seeing what was happening, Dan entered the room, slid on his stomach, and "basic training style" made it over to the machine to turn it off.

God was looking after us as no one was hurt. The machine was damaged beyond belief, but the amazing metal fabricators repaired it later like new. Unfortunately, the lost time without the chopper was about one week and gave us a new appreciation for its worth.

In the meantime we had to use the old "Schnell" cutter once again, which had been moved to grind flour for our dry gravy products. Arthur Tubbs, who had been hired in the early '60s, was our designated flour toaster.

The building used for toasting was different from the plant. It was done with a machine custom made for that unique function. After toasting, the flour would be ground to assure all lumps were removed, but to be doubly certain it was then sifted through an "automatic" sifter. Through this entire process Q. C. would test the flour for proper viscosity and flavor.

We were always taught to make the best of everything. Subsequently, many good things emerged from what seemed at the time to be strictly a disaster. Following the "big" accident, new procedures were adopted regarding cleaning, tools, and the entire process of running the chopper. To say the least, at no time were tools permitted to be in the room at the same time the chopper would be running, and thus, they were locked in a custom made stainless steel cabinet only a supervisor or above could open.

Another major accident in the company's history happened due to malfunctioning steam pressure relief valves in one of our 80-gallon steam-jacketed kettles. Upon exploding, the kettle launched like a rocket. We used to joke with Tom, long after the incident, that it was a staged test to make certain that he could handle life-threatening situations.

The detailed accounting of this should come from Tom Arthur as he was our newly hired head of maintenance on his third day when it happened. I had just walked through the hallway that went between what then was Cookrooms 1-3, which had been numbered in the order in which they were built, and the deboning room when the "blast" hit.

The impact thrust the swinging doors at the east end of the corridor open and shut. I walked back through to see what had happened and saw my son, Dorsey, helping one of our female employees back to her feet. He himself had been knocked down. He had been working in Cookroom 3 at the time cooking beef.

Cookroom 3 was diagonally across the corridor from Cookroom 2, where the kettles were situated. Needless to say, once Tom cleared my thinking, he had me and the supervisors vacate the building as quickly as possible since we were all in imminent danger.

Since Tom was new and still familiarizing himself with the facility, he was trying to locate the main gas shut off valve to secure everyone's safety. That way we could get back to business. I was amazed and impressed with the way Tom handled the entire situation. We were all shaken, but he had us all back in operation in a very timely manner.

Another time, on second shift, Gloria Katuscak, was putting lids on plastic pails. At the time we had an air activated lidder. You simply placed the pail under this mechanism and after activating buttons with a hand on either side of the machine, a solid steel disc would snap down to seal the pail.

The buttons were no doubt there for safety reasons, but on this particular occasion, Gloria had just finished the last pail and evidently had her hand resting on the sealed pail lid when one of the packaging assistants disconnected the air. Down came the steel plate on Gloria's fingers and she lost a couple of finger tips in a matter of seconds.

This was another case of carelessness that might have been avoided with a little thought, consideration, and caution.

While Tom Mele was second shift supervisor, he had a really bad accident of which Dad has already spoken in one of his chapters. He had just finished loading an outgoing order, when he, I, and the driver of the truck were chatting. I just happened to be in shipping to get some information.

Tom stepped outside for a moment and the driver walked out to get into his truck. At the same moment as Tom was behind the truck, the driver released his air brakes, the truck rolled back , and Tom was pinned against the pilaster or post placed there to protect the building from damage. He had no escape and ended up with extensive injuries including a broken pelvic bone and kidney damage.

A couple of years after the company relocated to West 25th Street, a young man started working there in packaging. One day he was asked to plug in the pump and as he started to do so, flames shot out and ran right up his arm. I always thought his arm must have been wet, but he maintained it was not.

In the shape that his arm was, there was no way to confirm or deny it. It was sickening as it looked like a marshmallow looks after you have burned it on an open flame. The poor man was in a great deal of pain.

Then in the early '80s, our infamous chicken cooker, Mario Quinones, almost had the "big one, one day." At that point in time, the cook teams, at best had a bad situation. Namely, these fellows would remove cooked chickens from the Cleveland Range steamers in a room that was well over 100 degrees. Once the next cooking was put on, they would go in the cooler, kept between 35 and 40 degrees.

As a company, we recognized the potential danger of human beings subjected to this type of drastic temperature change and would allow them to sit in the lunch room between procedures for a few minutes. One hot summer this was not enough as Mario started turning purple and going into convulsion-like shaking.

Ingolf recognized it as hyperthermia and had him lie on a table while we were waiting for the ambulance. As luck would have it, he was all right. At the time this happened, research was being done on the new Cookrooms.

New Procedures

Accidents brought on the advent of many more procedures adapted and used in operations. Team work was encouraged to develop these policies and procedures with both employees and management working together.

The Golden Rule, respect for others, management by example, all of these principles working together suggested that all most people want is to be treated like they count for something and that their presence is important.

We were good listeners, including both Mikes. If an employee had something to say, I wanted to hear it, and do whatever was humanly possible to help. After all we were all in this together! Some days I went home totally exhausted, but never too tired to take a phone call if a question needed answering.

The feeling of accomplishment, proud of the work we were all doing, gave me an excitement about each new day at work. I know this is how the majority of people felt back in those "Golden Years." Each day was charmed with a new adventure, a new challenge, with a diversified group of people who, for the most part, had no problems co-existing. It was like a labor of love.

Sometime during the early to mid '70s, when I was first shift production supervisor, I also scheduled production! I was like a mad scientist at times asking for the impossible to get it all done. I was asked at one point by Mike Zelski to head up Q. C., but my response was to cry as I saw that as a "fate worse than death."

My love was in manufacturing, so he agreed when I promised to be supportive of Q. C.'s efforts along with my people. Other areas in which Mike asked me to take responsibility beyond my basic duties included U. S. D. A. transmittals. This meant Mike would fill the label transmittals out and I would present them to inspectors, since I had established such good relations with them, for approval and signature.

Another form that had to be submitted to the government was a schedule of hours the plant would be opened for processing, packaging, cleanup, etc. Boy, was that fun to complete! I also helped rewrite the formula books which included proof-reading, correcting, and changing as necessary, each and every formula and procedure. Working with Research and Development (R. & D.), Quality Control (Q. C.), management, and personnel, this undertaking took me almost one full year!

When Mike hired school kids to clean between shifts in packaging around the late '70s, every one of them, all boys, came to work for us upon graduating from high school. One of them, George Hvizd, was taught how to schedule and was given the job. Later, he developed into a full time assistant to Mike and departed the company in 1985, just prior to Mike's departure.

Shortly after these boys were hired, Mike and I allowed my son, Dorsey, to come in on weekends to assist in making boxes. We saw no risk in Dorsey working at such a young age as we instructed him on how the job should be done. He started on Saturdays and soon other young people were hired to help him. The volume of boxes being made was increasing substantially because a decision was made to put an outer casing over the 25 and 50 pound plastic pails to prevent them from getting filthy in shipment due to static electricity.

A woman named Georgeanne Mahon had come to work in packaging and her son, Richard, was anxious to assist in box making also. Like Dorsey, he is still with the company. The Clancy brothers also joined in at this time as did Reynoldo (Cookie) Massa, son of a hard working lady named Confi, who has been in packaging longer than I can remember. Cookie originally worked under Tom Mele in second shift packaging and is still at Minor's! These fellows could really pump out some good work!

After two years of college, Dorsey came to work full time for Minor's and has worked in various jobs at various levels through the years. Our daughter, Sallie, worked with the company during her teen years, also. She worked mainly in production wherever she might be most useful . . . like labeling! But, like her parents, she did not complain, and was grateful to have the opportunity to make some money. She was very ambitious and was a very hard worker.

My sister, Mary Minor, was fresh out of school when she first worked with us in the plant. She **had** great expectations about what a job should be. Many days I encouraged her to go in and **make** it through the day; yet, this never affected the outstanding job she would do. She learned to enjoy her job since she liked everyone working at the plant so much.

As a teenager and young adult, my older brother, Bryan, would help out when time permitted. Bryan became a doctor and assisted in Q. C. when possible. At some point he became too busy to test samples of product batches as volume increased and my sister, Carol, became involved.

She took over product testing and became involved in Q. C. She worked closely with Janet Williams who was heading up R. & D. at the time. Carol became quite a valued expert in product taste testing and giving detailed opinions on her findings.

By 1980 I had moved from production manager and was placed over up to 70 people as plant manager. I had six supervisors, a weekend team leader, each of their employees, and the part-time people. The support system I had made it all possible.

One, Ingolf Nitsch who headed scheduling and inventory control, was a systems whiz. He had been my dad's student and had super organizational skills. Norbert Urban contributed part-time at first and later full time to perfect our computer system, which had been originally set up by George Hvizd.

Blanca Nieves, working with Josephine Minor, was in charge of Q. C. and always did whatever she could to be timely and accommodating. Everyone liked working with Josephine because she was always witty and had a joke or two to relieve stress.

From the time Mrs. Engler started in R. & D., the department became better due to her procedures. When Janet Williams came in 1975, she was extremely helpful to operations.

Maureen Barendt Beyer, a true friend, was a great asset while in R. & D. If you ever needed a smile in your day, Nancy Clancy was the one to call in Customer Service. She could right any problem, no matter what the size, and between both of us, we put in plenty of overtime. The ladies working with her were great, too, including Judy Ward, Rose C., Nancy Jr., Ceil, and Mary. Bridget, Nancy's daughter, did a super job in payroll. She was a chip off the old block and as accommodating!

Tom Arthur rose to be maintenance manager after co-owning, with his brother Al, G & B Electric, which was our first electrical company when Henry Kondrat owned it. If good things are worth waiting for, then our wait for Tom was well worth it. He totally developed the maintenance department and did one great job, even as he continues to do today.

In total, the support received by all of these people and their departments was like a conductor with an orchestra. One member was as important as the next and did we ever play some fine music together!

Of course, proper training played an important role in developing appropriate work skills at this time. Our super training program had supervisors working in every area of operations for two weeks to learn every facet of operations for a total of six months!

This worked out great, for when a production supervisor was off, the packaging supervisor on that shift would take care of both areas. When Mike Minor and I were both managers, we would help out as needed. I would spend time, too, with new hourly employees, especially those working with formulas, to go over proper sanitation and good manufacturing procedures.

Team leaders were elected that would work alongside these new employees to instill correct habits in them. Training was done by supervisors to insure bad habits did not get out of hand. I always thought someone who had less job experience was better to hire since we could then bring them up correctly. That worked for me, leading by example.

Cooking Processes

As mentioned, the chickens were cooked in Cleveland Range steamers. Each steamer had three compartments, each compartment held two pans of "birds." Periodically during each cooking cycle, steam was released from the steamers to keep pressure at correct levels.

Once chickens were cooked, each pan was removed from the steamer, juices were drained from the pan, and pans were placed on a rack for a few minutes to cool. The deboners needed to be able to handle the product.

All pans from that cooking, which would be as many as 42, were placed on a large stainless steel table and, with that volume, four people would pick meat off the bones, and skin and veins out of the meat. After each "table of birds" had been picked through, the skin and veins were discarded.

They were held in a refrigerated room, designed expressly for refuse, until a rendering company picked them up. In time, the rendering company had pick-ups two to three times daily. These people, the deboners or "chicken pickers" had their work cut out for them, but Minor's had the best little chicken pickers in the good old U. S. A. What a team!

When volume increased, there were two four-person teams. The deboners' duties became more diversified with master schedule changes. They opened canned products including seafood and mushrooms. They picked lobster, clams, and sometimes a ham product we were using. They opened hams. They cleaned offices, lockers and restrooms, and the lunch room. At times, they helped in packaging and in the sample room. They were extremely versatile.

Beef was cooked in CresCor ovens. Back in the '60s, we panned meat on racks that were inside the pans, covered the meat with aluminum foil, placed it in the oven, and roasted it. Procedures were set on all cooking methods, including temperatures, cooking times, and yield recording.

There were records kept for each cooking monitored by Q. C. Newer ovens were purchased and a new cookroom (Cookroom 3) had to be added to accommodate the expansion. We had two of the older models, using them around the clock, before the newer model was purchased. About this time, we stopped using foil and started using cooking bags.

Juices, "sauces," and stocks used in various products were reduced (concentrated) originally in roasting pans. The majority of the roasters were Westinghouse. Later we invested in a steam jacketed kettle which was eventually replaced by one with an 80-gallon capacity.

What a time, energy, and labor saver that larger model was! As volumes increased even more, another kettle was purchased. Although we had been totally satisfied with the operation of the original kettle, management decided to invest in a different, less expensive kettle. Funds were tight and you definitely get what you pay for, as the saying goes.

In terms of operating, the less expensive kettle had an outside surface that would become very hot while in use. We found ourselves devising all kinds of safety handling procedures in operating this equipment to assure no one would get burned.

Even later, a third kettle like the original one was purchased. The two similar kettles were placed in Cookroom 2 where all chicken cooking took place. Chicken fat was rendered in those kettles as well as natural chicken juices from the cooked chickens, concentrated.

We purposely placed them in this cook room since they were faster and, more importantly, safer to work with and around. The third kettle was installed in Cookroom 1, where beef was cooked. It was basically used to make sauces for beef and concentrate bone (beef) stock, not only for our beef base, but for our low sodium product, Glace de Viande.

A few of our manufactured products, like Consommé, were made in the kettles also. As was the case with other equipment, you could see how fine tuned and precise scheduling became as the years passed and production/packaging increased to assure equipment would be available when time and employees were!

Another function that was done in Cookroom 1 was sugar carmelization. This was a very unique operation. It was a job that needed baby sitting from start to finish. Once product was ready, Q. C. used a spectrometer to test the darkness.

Sanitation and Clean-up

Sanitation and personal hygiene were "a way of life." The standard set from the company's beginning was that nothing should come in the way of perfection in these areas. Skimping was totally unacceptable.

People could lose their jobs over not following the proper sanitation standards set, if it became apparent they were frequent offenders and refused to conform. When giving people their orientation, sanitation and personal hygiene were first and foremost in terms of priority. Once booklets were developed by Mike Zelski and Mrs. Engler, employees were given one at orientation prior to starting work. Speaking for myself, I did not just hand the pamphlet out, I went over it with an incoming employee to emphasize the importance of both cleanliness and sanitation. After all, we were in the food business.

Also, if I was not the person doing the initial orientation, cleanliness and sanitation, plus safety, would be the first thing I would go over with employees. If someone started out with bad habits, there was no teaching them the right way later.

Repetition was the best teacher for this subject. I was amazed at the number of people who came into the organization without that quality instilled in them as a child.

Equipment cleanup was big business, from a small spoon to the largest piece. They needed washing, rinsing, sanitizing, and drying after each use. By the time the company moved to its current location, a person designated to specifically clean pots and pans, small items, and the facility was hired. This person had his work cut out for him from day one.

As time went on, that person working in the "pan room" had all he could do to keep up with that responsibility. Those people working in a specific room were responsible for its clean up at the shifts end. Basically, that is how it remained during the time I was there. The thought being, people worked cleaner if they knew they had to clean-up after themselves.

Clean equipment was stored in covered containers. Larger equipment had lids that we had fabricated out of stainless steel. As time went on a room was built specifically for storing clean equipment. Unfortunately, this room was sometimes a nightmare in itself, as inevitably, the item you needed was buried.

In terms of the facility clean up, floors and lower walls were done on a daily basis. Actually, floors were done mid-shifts with scrubbing taking place at the end of the shift. Of any one task, I am not certain scrubbing was ever truly perfected.

The reason for this was that mops would be used and if someone thought they could get away with it, without someone seeing them, they would bring out the hose instead. You just could not get it through some individuals' heads that plain water from a hose would not clean anything.

Also, mops were extremely difficult to keep clean and free of bacteria. We would actually wash, sanitize, and dry them. Later we started changing "heads" on them daily!

As for scrubbers, we had them all. The ones you would hold onto and move around would splash the dirty water all over the base of the walls. Then we would have those to wash. The larger ones that you would walk behind would only get the places over which it moved.

In the end, we all did the best we could and did a great job at that. We worked hard keeping operations clean and always deserved any breaks we took!

Great Benefits

The others with whom I worked through the years were numerous, and it would be impossible to name them all. Minor's attracted and retained good employees because the pay was outstanding, almost twice minimum wage.

The compensation package was twice as good, too. Benefits included medical, profit sharing, and a pension plan after one year. Vacations were given to first-year employees with the schedule being one year, one week, 2-5 years, two weeks, 6-10 years, three weeks, 11-15 years, four weeks, and 16-20 years, five weeks of paid vacation.

Paid days off were given beyond paid vacation. Double pay on holidays and time and a half was paid for over 40 hours worked. Minor's paid into Workman's Compensation and, as any reputable company would, we paid someone with short term disability.

Employees would receive paid days for jury duty and, if an employee left in good standing to serve our great country, they were guaranteed a job if honorably discharged. The classic "attendance bonus" we initiated came in the early '80s to give employees even better compensation.

If an employee were on time for and at work every scheduled day for a three month period, they had a choice of taking a company designated day off with pay, an option of between 5-7 specified dates, or $100 cash!

Bonuses above and beyond profit sharing were given at Christmas time and Dad initiated them for every June as well. Once or twice we even received bonuses for energies saved over the course of a few months!

At Thanksgiving and Christmas, all were given a choice of either a turkey or boneless ham, and, at Easter, everyone got a ham. A can of nuts was also given to everyone at Christmas.

Other benefits that most took for granted included furnished uniforms, safety equipment such as ear, eye, hand, and head protection, and safety shoes. First-aid programs, including CPR., were given, and as mentioned previously, T. B. tine testing for food handlers was done in-house on company time.

Speakers from the fire department, sanitation department, and others would address us from time to time. These were beneficial discussions for the home as well as for the job. The number one speaker people looked forward to hearing and seeing was the owner himself, Dad! He periodically gave hand-washing demonstrations.

People treasured time spent with him, his presence being a sure pick-me upper! One thing I respected Dad most for was his humanism. If he asked how you were doing, it was because he was truly interested in you or your family.

Later, benefits continued to improve. There was a trip to Ireland for selected management personnel. I was fortunate to be selected! There were free product samples, maternity leave, full dental benefits, a Christmas party, and celebration dinner for those giving years of service to the company. Eventually, the corporation installed a tuition reimbursement program also.

Honestly, I did not know of any company that did more for its employees than the L. J. Minor Corporation. Many a person and many a family can say today that their life was made better because of their employment at Minor's.

To summarize, my work experience at Minor's was probably one that most people will never have the fortune of experiencing. I can only say thank you to my parents for giving me this wonderful opportunity and livelihood. Thanks to all the great people that I dealt and worked with through the years who helped make this such a rewarding, memorable experience.

Thanks for the memories and God Bless you one and all!

Chapter 31

Happenings in My Life

by Kathleen Minor Swanson

Family	**Education**	**Work History**
Professional Organizations/Honors		**Other Organizations**
Services to Community/Church	**Credits**	**Hobbies**

Quote from Langston Hughes

"Hold fast to dreams. For when dreams go, life is a barren field."

As a proud father of my daughter who dedicated her life to teaching and education, I present as a foreword to her contribution to the text, a list of readings for culinary enrichment. Each reader should build his or her library, as I have done, with a wide variety of books, monographs, and current literature. These will get you well started on your collection.

Readings for Culinary Enrichment
by Dr. Lewis J. Minor

- 1. Blake, Anthony and Quentin Cruse, GREAT CHEFS OF FRANCE, Marshall Editions, Ltd., 71 Eccleston Square, London, 1978.

- 2. Brillat-Savarin, Jean Anthelene, THE PHILOSOPHY OF TASTE, Liveright Publishing Corporation, New York, 1948.

- 3. Carnacina, Luigi, GREAT ITALIAN COOKING, (The Grand Cucina Internazionale), Abradale Press Publishers, New York.

- 4. Cichy, Ronald F., FOODSERVICE MANAGEMENT, Van Nostrand Reinhold Company, New York, 1994.

- 5. Cichy, Ronald F., QUALITY SANITATION MANAGEMENT, Educational Institute of the American Hotel and Motel Association, 1407 South Harrison Road, P. O. Box 1240, East Lansing, Michigan, 1994.

- 6. Diat, Louis, COOKING A LA RITZ, J. P. Lippincott Company, New York, 1941.

- 7. Escoffier, A., ESCOFFIER COOK BOOK (and Guide to the Fine Art of Cooking), Crown Publishers, Inc., 419 Park Ave. South, New York, N. Y., 10016, 1969.

- 8. Frederikson, Karin, THE GREAT SCANDINAVIAN COOK BOOK, Crown Publishers, Inc., 419 Park Ave. South, New York, N. Y., 10016, 1967.

- 9. Gourmet, THE GOURMET COOKBOOK, Vol. I and II, Gourmet Books, Inc., 777 Third Avenue, New York, N. Y., 10017, 1950.

- 10. Guy, Christian, AN ILLUSTRATED HISTORY OF FRENCH CUISINE, Bramhall House, New York, 1962.

- 11. Jackson, Stanley, THE SAVOY (The Romance of a Great Hotel), E. P. Dutton Company, Inc., New York, 1964.

- 12. Jones, Evan, AMERICAN FOOD (The Gastronomic Story), E. P. Dutton Company, Inc., New York, 1975.

- 13. Knight, John B. and Lendal H. Kotschevar, QUANTITY FOOD PRODUCTION, PLANNING, AND MANAGEMENT, 2nd Edition, Van Nostrand Reinhold Company, New York, 1989.

(Editor's Note: When reading this text, please observe the dedication which Dr. Kotschevar and I wrote to Dr. Minor as follows:

"For his love, dedication, and service to God, country, and mankind, and for his contributions to the Hospitality Industry and its students, the authors dedicate this book to Dr. Lewis J. Minor, Chief Executive Officer, L. J. Minor Corporation, Cleveland, Ohio.

By the way, this book is now under revision for its third edition to be available soon.)

- 14. Knight, John B., KNIGHT'S FOODSERVICE DICTIONARY, (Edited by Charles A. Salter), Van Nostrand Reinhold Company, New York, 1987.

- 15. Kotschevar, Lendal H. and Donald Lundberg, UNDERSTANDING COOKING (Programmed), Marcus Printing Company, 206 Appleton Street, Holyoke, MA, 01040, 1965.

- 16. Kotschevar, Lendal H., QUANTITY FOOD PRODUCTION, McCutchen Publishing Corporation, 2256 Grove Street, Berkeley, CA, 1966.

- 17. Kotschevar, Lendal H. and Margaret McWilliams, UNDERSTANDING FOOD, John Wiley and Sons, Inc., New York, 1969.

- 18. Minor, Michael, and Georgia Lockridge, THE GOLDEN TOQUE RECIPE COLLECTION, Van Nostrand Reinhold Company, New York, 1992.

- 19. Montague, Prosper, LAROUSSE GASTRONOMIQUE, (The Encyclopedia of Food Wine, and Cookery, Crown Publishers, Inc., 419 Park Ave. South, New York, N. Y., 10016, 1961.

- 20. Page, E. B. and P. W. Kingsford, THE MASTER CHEFS (A History of Haute Cuisine), Edward Arnold Ltd., 41 Maddox Street, London, 1971.

- 21. Pepin, Jacques, LA METHODE JACQUES PEPIN (An Illustrated Guide to the Fundamental Techniques of Cooking), Times Books, Three Park Avenue, New York, New York, 10010, 1979.

- 22. Ranhofer, Charles, THE EPICUREAN (The Great Classic of Haute Cuisine), Dover Publications, 180 Varick Street, New York, 1971.

- 23. Ronbauer, Gina S., JOY OF COOKING, Bobbs Merrill Company, Inc., New York, 1980.

- 24. Rietz, Carl A., MASTER FOOD GUIDE, AVI Publishing Company, Inc., Westport, Connecticut, 1978.

- 25. Robotti, Peter J., MUCH DEPENDS ON DINNER, Fountainhead Publishers, Inc., 475 Fifth Avenue, New York, 1961.

- 26. Tannahill, Reay, FOOD IN HISTORY, Stein and Day Publishers, 7 East 48th Street, New York, N. Y., 10017, 1973.

- 27. Taussig, Ellen, YOUR HOST PETER GUST, Herman Publishing Company, Inc., Boston, MA, 02116, 1979.

- 28. Trager, James, THE FOODBOOK, Grossman Publishers, New York, 1970.

- 29. Trager, James, THE BELLYBOOK, Grossman Publishers, New York, 1972.

- 30. Watts, Stephen, THE RITZ, The Bodley Head, Ltd., 10 Earlham Street, London, 1963.

- 31. Wechsberg, Joseph, BLUE TROUT & BLACK TRUFFLES, Alfred A. Knopf, Inc., New York, 1953.

- 32. Wechsberg, Joseph, THE BEST THINGS IN LIFE, Little Brown & Company, Boston, Toronto, 1960.

- 33. Wechsberg, Joseph, DINING IN THE PAVILLON, Little Brown & Company, Boston,

- 34. Zaccarelli, Brother Herman, FOOD SERVICE MANAGEMENT CHECKLIST, John Wiley and Sons, Inc., New York, 1991.

Final Note: The reader may wish to use the Reader's Guide to Periodical Literature for further enrichment readings. The period 1960 to 1980 covers writings by Joseph Wechsberg, and the renowned chef, Paul Bocuse. "Cuisine Minceur" articles appear in th 1980-1990 Reader's Guide.

Family

Married 6/16/62 to James V. Swanson. Lived in Alexandria, Virginia while husband was in Basic Training (Army), Ft. Belvoir, Virginia, 6/62 - 9/62.

Relocated to Germany while husband was stationed there, 10/62 - 6/64. Lived off-post in Grobkrotzenburg in an apartment upstairs at the home of Paula and Julian Gay.

Our son, Kevin James, was born while we lived in Germany. He was born May 22, 1963 at the U.S. Army hospital, Frankfurt am Main. He was baptized on the army post when he was two weeks old by Rev. John Patrick Jennings, just a day before the death of Pope John XXIII.

I returned to the States with Kevin in June, 1964, the day Daddy was granted his Ph.D. Due to the loss of an engine in the turbo prop we flew on with Icelandic Airlines, we missed our connection flight in New York which would have taken us to Lansing that morning; we were placed on a later flight. Grandpa and Grandma Minor met us at the

Lansing airport and drove us back to the farm. We switched on the TV in time to see the degree awarded.

Jim came Stateside a couple of weeks later on a troop ship. Ruth Ann cared for Kevin so I could go to New York to meet him.

He planned to work at Owens-Illinois as an engineer, but Tom Ryan persuaded him to go to work for the L. J. Minor Corporation. We settled in Cleveland temporarily at 20877 Fairpark Dr.

During the winter we were able to purchase our first home at 200 Baldwin Dr., Berea. Grandma used to call this our "dollhouse." It was a basic three-bedroom home with garage and patio with a roof. We later added a dormer, so at the time the home was sold, it was a four-bedroom.

Our daughter, Kimberly Jo, was born March 19, 1965 at Fairview Park Hospital. She was baptized at St. Mary's in early April. Carol stayed with Kevin during my hospital stay, and because Kim was only four pounds at birth, she stayed on even after I got home. The day Kim was baptized, a tornado touched down in Strongsville, which tore homes from their foundation. We were fortunate to have been spared. Mother, Rosalie, and Mary were with us.

Kim was three when we moved to our second house at 156 Westbridge Drive. This was a colonial-style two-story three bedroom, 1 1/2 bath home with a dining room and basement, both features which had not been available in the first house.

In 1965, both Jim and I started teaching, he in Medina County and I in Berea City Schools. We were fortunate to have Wilma Tinkey, an octogenarian from the area, come to our home to care for the children. When they reached school age both Kevin and Kim started school at Lechner in Berea.

Jim worked part-time at Kent State and Case-Western Reserve on advanced degrees, with a goal of becoming a college instructor. Finally, he was given a stipend which enabled him to work on the degree full-time, while I continued teaching. He secured a part-time teaching position in the evening program at Cleveland State in their academic centers. The position was eliminated when the academic centers were closed and combined with the downtown campus (1971).

In the winter of 1972, he taught at a high school for delinquents, Cuyahoga Hills, and tried to secure another position to allow us to stay in Cleveland. An opening at the college level did occur, in Frostburg, Maryland. Frostburg State College interviewed and hired him. So that during Hurricane Agnes we headed to Maryland to buy our third house. We bought a place at 236 E. Main Street, four bedrooms, two baths and a nearly vertical backyard.

When Kevin, now ready for grade four, heard we were heading for Appalachia his first question was, "Do they speak English there?" We moved down the first of July, 1972, and enrolled the children in Frost Elementary the following month. When the principal, Mr. Scott, proudly pointed at the array of book covers and titles in the library, Kevin called him down, saying he had long since read all of those and others, and he had! He always loved reading. For Kim, though, the change was a positive one. Things were done at a slower pace.

We settled into a routine with Jim teaching at the college and my painting woodwork and arranging things in the house. Other than part-time contractual work at the college, there was nothing available job-wise for me. I worked with student teachers, doing supervision and teaching Foreign Language Methods and Education courses. Jim and I applied to adopt a child through county social services. Meanwhile, we hosted an AFS student from Germany, Arnold Neuha.

We had such a difficult time trying to help him fit into the family that once he left at the end of the school year, we called the social services to withdraw our application to adopt, at which time we were informed that they had two girls for us, Cathy Diane and Betty Ann, aged 8 and 5. We went to meet them and couldn't say "no." Kevin and Kim, Jim and I all took to them immediately. A new chapter began.

Kim, who was in 7th grade at St. Michael's school, was charged with seeing that Cathy got to and from school. Betty, who only went to school half days, being in kindergarten, spent the other half day with Pat Keating. Kevin was in high school at Bishop Walsh in Cumberland, and I had gone back to full-time language teaching at the high school (and middle school level in Mineral County, West Virginia). Things got complicated, but went well for the most part.

Jim found his work at the college rewarding. I enjoyed my work and everyone got along fairly well in the evening. Once Kim went on to high school, Cathy & Betty began having accountability difficulties. The sisters at St. Michael's agreed to give them after-school tasks, like erasing the boards or working on homework, so they were supervised until someone older would be home.

Kevin graduated from high school in 1981 and went on to Columbia University School of Engineering. The following year Jim's position at the college was cut "due to lack of enrollment in the department." This was a time of crisis. He went back to a one-semester high school math teaching job in Pennsylvania, a dead end. I continued through the school year, keeping my chin up, but panicking inside. As I signed out with my principal for the summer, I broke down and told him the bind we were in. That afternoon another principal in the county called Jim in for an interview. He was hired to teach Spanish and math at Elk Garden the following year. He stayed on there for eight years, until an opening occurred at Westmar High in our home county.

Kim graduated from high school that year and went to study English and Spanish at Seton Hill College in Greensbur, PA. The house next door to ours was becoming very run down, and we worried about its being sold to a "slum lord" for college housing. To avoid the problem, we bought it and made a family project of renovating it with insulation, siding, wiring, plumbing, a kitchen, utility room, walls, ceiling, painting, etc. Before we had finished, a teacher approached us about renting it. We agreed. Until she moved, things worked out well.

Meanwhile, a house became available in LaVale at 711 National Highway. We bought it and moved in just before Thanksgiving, 1987. The following week, Cathy ran away. She said she would never leave Frostburg. She never made it through her junior year of high school, choosing to "hang out" instead.

Betty finished high school and went on to a trade school for the travel industry, located in North Miami. She did all of the written assignments required as prerequisites to the on-campus residency during her high school senior year and in the summer following. She went to Florida for her residency studies in August, and was hired upon completion of the program by the central offices of Alamo Car Rental.

Kevin went to work upon graduation with the firm of Arthur Andersen Consulting, Manhattan office. Kim went back for more education at San Diego State University to earn her teaching credentials in English and ESOL (English for Speakers of Other Languages).

Jim trained in Baltimore at the archdiocese headquarters and was ordained deacon by Bishop Murphy on Kevin's birthday, May 22, 1976. A week later, Kevin and Josephine selected our first dog, Appalachian O'Reilley VIII. She was an Irish Setter who helped raise the children, especially when they were having problems. She died on George Burns's birthday, 1991.

Cathy married Jamie Radcliff in 1990. This proved to be a disaster, as he not only refused to work, but constantly fought with Cathy and threatened her and Kari, her daughter born the previous June. Kari's father was another man, Bill Michael.

Bill returned to the area after Cathy and Jamie had been separated for a while. In 1991, Cathy was again pregnant. She delivered a baby boy in July, 1992, Charles William Michael.

Last summer we bought a "home away from home" in St. Augustine.

Education

1954 - Diploma, Grade 8, St. Angela Merici Fairview Park, Cleveland
1958 - Diploma, High School, Fairview High School
1961 - B.A., French, Spanish, English Education, Michigan
State University, East Lansing, Michigan
1963 - Courses in German, University of Maryland overseas division
1969 - M.Ed., French & Spanish, Kent State University, Kent, Ohio
1976-1986 - Various Courses in Graduate Education, Frostburg State, Frostburg, Maryland
1987 - Basic Computers - West Virginia
1989-90 - Courses in teaching writing, WVCOGS (West Virginia College of Graduate Studies)

Work History

1957-58 - S.S. Kresge Company, Summer 1959 Camp Cardinal for Girls
1959-61 - RA, Gilchrist Hall, MSU
1961 Summer - Counselor, Congress of Strings, MSU

1961-62 2nd Semester - Teacher, Evart Schools
1963-64 - Teacher, U.S. Army GEI Program
1965-68 - Teacher Berea School
1973-76 - Contractual Instructor Supervisor of Student, F.S.C.
1976-present - Teacher and County Curric. Chairman, Mineral County Schools
1990-92 - Part-time contractual instructor, F.S.U.

Professional Organizations/Honors

Pi Delta Phi (French)
Sigma Delta Pi (Spanish)
Phi Delta Kappa (Education)
AATF - Am. Association of Teachers of French
WVFLTA - West Va. Foreign Language Teachers Assn.

Other Organizations

CDA (Catholic Daughters of America)
NEA (National Education Association)
WVEA (West Va. Edn. Assn.)
MCEA (Mineral Co. Edn. Assn.)

Services to Community/Church

1963-71 - Teacher CCD, Germany/Berea
1963-64 - Leader, Girl Scouts
1974-86 - Teacher CCD, Md. Home room mother, as needed while the children were in elementary school. Member of PTA and Home School Assn. while the children were in school.

Credits

Wrote the manual to be used by middle school teachers in our county and trained communication arts teachers to implement the program. West Virginia Department of Education personnel aided in the implementation.

Worked on writing teams twice in conjunction with the W.V. Dept. of Education identification of appropriate learner outcomes at different stages of language study and overall goals.

Sponsored a French Club at our school, as well as a chapter of La Societe Honoraire de Francais, which I started locally, affiliate with the national SHF to give recognition to outstanding students of French.

Listed in <u>Who's Who Among America's Teachers</u>, 1992 edition.

Have traveled to Mexico, Canada, France, Spain, Switzerland, Belgium, Luxembourg, Germany, Italy, Austria, Liechtenstein, Ireland, Puerto Rico, St. Martin and St. Barthelemy.

Worked with the Middle States group to respond to the President Carter's Commission Report of FL Teaching.

Traveled to Columbia, Md., and Washington, D.C., as the West Virginia representative and corresponded with Rep. Paul Simon on behalf of our concerns.

Acted as an evaluator on the North Central team to Hampshire County, WV.

Attended national conference of ACTFL and NE Conference, as well as regional conferences in Youngstown, Pittsburg, Frederick, Maryland, Washington, Fairmont, Morgantown, Charleston and Parkersburg.

Hobbies

Playing the piano, embroidery, translation, poetry, travel, shopping, walking, and eating out, singing with family and visiting, hiding out in St. Augustine, root for the Jaguars, Spartans, Lakers, Tornados, Orioles and Agassi.

Chapter 32

Beyond the Grand Gold Medal

by Michael L. Minor
(1977-1995)

Introduction   Childhood   My Early Career   Working Hard

In Honor of Dad   In Honor of Hermann Rusch by Dad

**Food for Thought
by Brillat-Savarin**
(1841, as published in Physiologie du Gout)

"The discovery of a new dish does more for the happiness of mankind than the discovery of a new star."

"The man who gives dinner for a group of his friends and takes no trouble over what they are to eat is not fit to have any friends."

"An animal swallows its food; a man eats it . . . but only a man of intelligence knows how to dine."

"The creator has imposed on man six great and principal necessities, which are: birth, action, eating, sleep, reproduction, and death."

"An expert cook is a scientific man, in theory and practice, so that his place is between the chemist and the physician."

Introduction

To Dad from Mike Minor: "Thanks, Dad, for sharing everything with me. The following is written for your book. I hope this meets your expectations. I will never be the writer you are, but it does cover my career with the L. J. Minor Corporation focusing mainly on the values you and Mom taught us. Thank you for including me. I know the book will be a great remembrance of a great company!"

My years of service with the L. J. Minor Corporation have impacted my life significantly by teaching important fundamental principles such as honesty, integrity, commitment to quality, respect of fellow employees, teamwork, and perseverance. These principles were instilled in all employees, sales representatives, consultants, and business affiliates by the founder of the company, Dr. Lewis J. Minor, in his written "Business Aims" and through his personal example of business management.

My professional career was impacted by giving me the opportunity to work with and learn from superstars in the food industry. You see, one thing my father believed in was surrounding himself with professionals from all aspects of the food industry, who shared the same fundamentals of running a successful business. Did the L. J. Minor Corporation impact my life and professional career? You bet!

Childhood

Even as children we were involved in my father's business. When he had a new product to evaluate, he would ask the family members to serve as his taste panel. My mother would prepare the samples and then have us taste and evaluate each for flavor. The results of these early taste panels helped to give my father the direction he needed to develop the flavor profile of the product he was developing.

We helped with odds and ends and jobs as needed. I think the most significant contribution was assisting with packing 1 oz. samples of beef and chicken base under the diligent supervision of my older sister Ruth Ann. My father would pay $0.01 per sample. On a good day, you could usually get 300-500 packed and earn what I considered then a lot of money. We also helped from time to time with deboning poultry, loading trucks, packing one pound jars, and other jobs that needed to get done.

When the company moved from West 115th Street to the present location, there was a lot of cleaning, painting, and fixing up to be done. I worked with my mother and the other family members helping mainly with the painting and clean-up on weekends or whenever spare time permitted.

Even though we all helped out as children, my parents never let the company activities interfere with our childhood fun. We always had the time to play with our friends and go places with my mother and father. The company was very demanding of my parents, but somehow they both spent as much time as possible with their eight children.

My father was always active with the Boy Scouts and Explorers. He took us to Cleveland Barons hockey games, the annual bicycle races, the Knights of Columbus track meet, camping every summer, and the one activity I especially remember which was the midnight sled riding at Memphis/Tiedeman hill.

My mother was always busy doing all the things a mother does to make your childhood memorable. No matter how much she had to do she was always there when you needed a little love and encouragement. One of the family traditions I always enjoyed was the Sundays when we would all go out to dinner at Stouffer's at Westgate or downtown to Mills and then out to a movie.

My childhood years in Fairview Park were wonderful years filled with a lot of great memories, memories I will cherish for the rest of my life. So the early years of the company impacted me personally by teaching me the importance of doing a quality job at whatever I did, but more important, the need for quality life at home with my family.

Besides the involvement with family members, I had the opportunity to meet and become very close friends with people working for the Minor Corporation or friends affiliated in some way, all of whom impacted my life by exhibiting dedication, honesty, and integrity in all their business and personal dealings.

The individuals I remember most as a child were people like Mary Mele, Nancy Clancy, Joseph and Mrs. Adams, Herman Taber, Ralph Napletana, Aunt June and Uncle Eddy Morgan, and, of course, Uncle Tom and Aunt Babe Ryan who treated all of us as if we were their children. I will never forget Christmas with Uncle Tom and Aunt Babe Ryan. It was as if Santa and Mrs. Claus really existed, but instead of driving a sleigh pulled by reindeer, they drove a Lincoln Continental. These people were all very special in different ways, but all were good friends to my parents and great role models for us kids.

Following the eighth grade, the family moved to Lansing, Michigan where my father began a new career teaching at Michigan State University. A career that would touch the lives of thousands of students and indirectly lay the foundation for the Minor Corporation's future customer base. During my years in Lansing, I had very little involvement with the Minor Corporation, but I did begin my career in culinary arts working at the Kellogg Center Hotel under Mrs. Evelyn Drake in the bakery. I held this position through four years of high school and two years of college, initiating my career as a professional chef.

Why a professional chef? Because my father told me "To work for the Minor Corporation you have to be a chef for at least 10 years." So, although I had little involvement in my teenage years, my career path was clear for later involvement. I cannot begin to explain how important that advice was in later years as an employee of the company. Because of my training and work as a chef, I had the foundation, knowledge, and experience necessary to be successful with the tasks of the various positions I have held during my years with the Minor Corporation.

My Early Career

My career as a chef began, as I mentioned previously, at the Kellogg Center. Halfway through my second year of college, I realized that becoming a chef was the career path I wanted to follow. To prevent any interruptions in my chef training, I decided to volunteer for two years of service in the Army.

During my tour of duty I was the chef for General Sutherland, Commanding General of Fort Knox. Following my duty with the General, I was assigned to the central pastry kitchen as a baker. After completing my first year of service, I married Edwina and we have been together for over 25 wonderful years now.

Upon returning from our honeymoon, I soon received orders to go to Vietnam. During my tour of duty, I cooked for the Commanding General of the 199th Infantry Brigade and received a medal of commendation for the job I did during my 11 months of service as the General's chef.

Upon returning from Vietnam, I began a four year apprenticeship at the world famous Greenbrier Hotel in White Sulphur Springs, West Virginia, working under the direction of one of the most renowned chefs of the 20th century, Mr. Hermann Rusch. I graduated from the program as class Valedictorian and winner of the Otto Gentsch Gold Medal.

(Editor's Note: As a student at Michigan State, I had an opportunity to invite Chef Rusch, based on Dr. Minor's recommendation, to speak at a Les Gourmet seminar of which I was the organizer. Later, I took a second honeymoon to The Greenbrier to visit Chef Rusch and had the opportunity to see the School from which Mike Minor graduated. I am impressed that he graduated at the top of his class, as Chef Rusch accepted only the finest and the waiting list was years in length. My sincere congratulations to Mike for this distinguished honor, but I know he was just at the beginning of his career, so let's get back to his story!)

The education, work experience, and camaraderie during my years at the Greenbriar gave me the knowledge and credentials to continue my career as a chef. Following graduation, I accepted a position as Sous Chef (Chef Foreman) at the Williamsburg Inn, in Williamsburg, Virginia. After a year in Williamsburg, I took a job as Executive Chef of the Peach Queen Guest House at the Deering Milliken Research Corporation in Spartanburg, South Carolina.

My duties included planning the menu, purchasing ingredients, and preparing the meals for Roger Milliken, President and CEO of the company, and for his department Vice Presidents and their guests including the Governor of South Carolina and the Ambassador from Belgium. During my time there, I entered several culinary art shows. In April, 1976, I won the John Secter Trophy, the top prize of the Culinary Art Salon in Charlotte, North Carolina. This award had special meaning for me in that John Secter was one of the chefs that significantly contributed to the success of the Minor Corporation.

In the fall of 1976, during a visit to the International Culinary Olympics in Frankfurt, Germany, my father said, "Mike, you have completed 13 years as a baker/chef and I think it is time for you to join the Minor Corporation." This was what I had waited for and the reason why I had worked so hard. An opportunity to work for the company that my parents and the many dedicated employees, friends, and affiliates had worked so long to build into one of the most respected companies in the foodservice industry. After 13 years of working in kitchens, it was time for me to bring my years of experience to my mother and father's company. To say that I was excited would be an understatement!

Working Hard

In February, 1977, I joined the L. J. Minor Corporation under my father's direction, "While learning the business, keep your eyes open and your mouth shut." My official career with the Minor Corporation , which had begun unofficially 20 years earlier as a child, had begun. Words cannot describe how proud I was to finally be a part of this great organization.

My first assignment was working with Blanca Nieves in Quality Control (Q. C.). Under her direction she taught me the importance of quality control from the time ingredients enter receiving until the products are loaded on the trucks and shipped to customers. The quality and commitment I learned from Blanca helped me understand the importance of following established procedures at all times and never permitting a sub-standard product to leave the plant.

Following my time in Q. C., I began what ended up being about a two and one-half year training program in all aspects of production. Most of my time was spent working in the cook rooms and batch formulation.

While working in cooking and batch making I was able to observe production procedures, work along with the plant employees, and gain an overall understanding of the ingredients and methods of manufacturing meat, poultry, seafood, and vegetable food bases. After several months of on the job training, I met with my father and told him "Do not take this the wrong way, but the people in your plant do not know how to work."

Because of my experience as a chef, I looked at the plant facility as a type of kitchen facility where ingredients were cooked and mixed together just as they were in all the other kitchens in which I had worked previously. I explained several production procedures that would cut production time and labor without altering the finished product. Gradually, under the direction of Mike Zelski, Jan Williams, and Ruth Ann Fields, the new procedures were implemented and greatly improved the plant's productivity and ability to keep up with the growth of business.

The next step in my training was to work in production scheduling, under my sister, Ruth Ann Fields. Ruth Ann was the most highly regarded person in the plant by all the employees and senior management. Production scheduling was one of the most demanding of any job at Minor's. The coordination between Customer Service and production had to be precise in order to assure the customer would receive the product ordered when they needed it. A complete knowledge of the production process was imperative to be successful at production scheduling.

The most significant thing in production scheduling was the implementation of the Master Production Schedule, a process implemented by Ingolf Nitsch with the help of Ruth Ann and myself. With this new method of scheduling, the company was able to do a better job of long-range production planning. Over time, production scheduling has changed dramatically, but the fundamental task of scheduling, producing, and shipping the products to meet the customer's needs still remains.

Research and Development (R & D) was my next assignment. I think this stage of my career with Minor's was most closely related to what I learned as a chef in a much more technical way. In cooking and baking, I used recipes. In R & D I used 100% formulas. Jan Williams was my primary teacher, although I had the opportunity to work with other professionals in product development; people who were knowledgeable included Chef Carl Richter, Chef Warren LeRuth, Mike Zelski, and, of course, the most knowledgeable of all, Dr. Lewis J. Minor. These people all took the time to teach me the steps of product development from researching and testing raw materials to the final scale up into a production batch and everything in between.

One of the more enjoyable parts of my job was to act in the capacity of judge in local, regional, and national culinary competitions. One such event took place at the Culinary Institute of America. The resulting PR was excellent for the company, as the following press clipping shows:

> WEST LAFAYETTE, INDIANA - The final judging for the "Great Ideas Begin with Handy Fuel Contest" fell to three eminently capable individuals: chef Michael Minor, Corporate Executive Chef, L. J. Minor Corporation, Cleveland, Ohio; Chef Ferdinand Metz, President of the Culinary Institute of America; and Chef Baron Galand, National Vice President of the American Culinary Federation.
>
> "All valid recipes were prepared in the kitchens at the Culinary Institute of America, Hyde Park, New York, with meticulous attention to the submitter's instructions," said Chef Minor. "Each entry was then evaluated on the basis of cost of preparation, convenience, variety of uses, originality, taste, eye appeal, and ease of preparation."

My most memorable challenge came when my father gave me the assignment to develop Fish Base in February and have it ready to see by the National Restaurant Show in May. Wow! I had a total of four months to go through all the steps of developing a new product, a task that seemed virtually impossible.

You guessed it! The product was developed and on the shelf for sale in time for the Show. These were the types of challenges my father would put on people, but because of the quality of the people involved, the tasks were always accomplished.

Some of the other products Jan Williams and I developed included Pasta N'Pizza Base, Sauce/Soup Thickener (Dry Roux), Poultry Glace, Shrimp Base, Crab Base, and New England Clam Chowder Prep.

Besides my involvement in product development, I was also involved with production methods and procedures in the plant. My involvement included researching new equipment and plant layout and design. The present production facility was a result of the planning of Ruth Ann Fields, Ingolf Nitsch, Mike Zelski, Tom Arthur, and me. It resulted in a state-of-the-art manufacturing facility.

Recipe development was also a key area of responsibility in R & D. Minor's products are flavor ingredients and recipes have always been an important tool to demonstrate the products to foodservice operators. Together, Jan Williams and I implemented the recipe development process at the Minor Corporation and with the help of our chef and dietetic consultants, developed over 3,000 recipes, a few of which are featured in the next chapter.

Through the dedication of Jan Williams and others, the foundation was laid for the present R & D department at Minor's. This is a department in which I continue to be involved to develop flavor targets for future products.

While working in R & D, I became more and more involved with product presentations, trade shows, demonstrations at culinary and hotel management schools, and working directly with customers on specific projects. These activities helped gain industry exposure for the Minor Corporation as well as for me personally.

Hans Bueschkens, then Vice President of Sales, Canada, suggested the L. J. Minor Corporation participate in the 1980 International Culinary Olympics. As soon as the idea was presented to my father, the stage was set for an event that would permanently impact my career as a chef and give the Minor Corporation tremendous international exposure.

The original proposal was that Hans and I and maybe one other chef participate with the hope of winning a couple of gold medals. My father's reply was "Why should the Minor Corporation go as a pea shooter, when we can go as a cannon?" The work then began to put together a full team of chefs.

This, again, was a task that at the time seemed close to impossible because we had only nine months from the original proposal until the competition in Frankfurt. Once again, with the help of the super team my father had built, the task was completed. We did not come home with a couple of gold medals; instead we came home with three. One of the medals I won personally and one gold medal was awarded to the Minor Corporation for our superior product quality.

This one event immediately established my credibility as a chef on an international basis and provided the opportunity to introduce our products to the world. The Minor Corporation took another team of chefs to the competition in 1984. The following press release was widely distributed and published in many of the nation's papers as well as in the trade press.

L. J. Minor Corp. Becomes First Official Sponsor of 1984 U.S. Culinary Team

CLEVELAND, OHIO - With a $50,000 commitment, the L. J. Minor Corp. is the first Official Sponsor of the 1984 U.S. Culinary Team to the International Culinary Competition in Frankfurt, Germany.

At a press conference honoring the U.S. Team, Gen. John D. McLaughlin, U.S.A. (Ret.), chairman and president of the Cleveland food base firm, presented a $25,000 check - first half of the $50,000 Official Sponsor donation - to John Dankos, president of the National Restaurant Association.

Gen. McLaughlin praised the U.S. team members: "As first Official Sponsor of the 1984 team, the L. J. Minor Corp. demonstrates its belief in American foodservice leadership. In the past, our chefs have shown the world that Americans can prepare fine cuisine using American ingredients and American know-how, winning 32 gold and two silver medals in 1980.

"I believe the American chefs on this 1984 team will match or improve on this record. As a member of the American food industry, the Minor Corp. salutes the American team, and affirms our belief in their talents with our sponsorship."

Funds to promote the team and its participation at the International Culinary Competition are being raised by the ACF/NRA U.S. Culinary Team Foundation, a non-profit organization jointly sponsored by the American Culinary Federation (ACF), a national organization of professional chefs and culinarians, and the National Restaurant Association (NRA), leading trade association of the foodservice industry.

The L. J. Minor Corp. is the world's leading manufacturer of premium quality natural flavor Food Bases and convenience preparations for soups, sauces and gravies.

Its many products are used by foodservice professionals in restaurants, hotels, institutions, schools, colleges and processing kitchens throughout the U.S., Canada, and overseas.

Under my direction as team manager, with the help of Hans Bueschkens and the team members, we captured in 1984 the highest award ever received by an American food manufacturer, "The Grand Gold Medal." The insight by two great men, Hans Bueschkens and Dr. Lewis J. Minor, brought world recognition to the Minor Corporation, a small family-owned food base manufacturer in Cleveland, Ohio. To this day no other food manufacturer in the United States has achieved that award.

Sales and marketing was the next step in my career at Minor's. Because of my work experience in quality control, production, research and development, and product presentation skills, I now had all the tools to be successful in sales and marketing. I began my involvement in sales by taking over the management of all the trade shows in which the Minor Corporation participated.

At the time we participated in approximately 325 shows per year. These included all the national, regional, and distributor shows. Pat Peters and I together did all the budgeting, logistics, and staffing for all the shows. Thank God we had developed a wonderful team of chef and dietetic consultants over the years to work at the shows or this would have been an impossible task.

314

In 1986 the Minor Corporation was sold to Nestle. The company has continued to grow and prosper since the sale. Nestle has given the Minor Corporation the funds necessary to keep up with the increasing demands for production, research, development, sales, and marketing support.

My present title is Vice President of Culinary Services. As the title indicates my duties are focused on the application of Minor bases in cooking. I continue to work with the sales and marketing side of the business. My duties include:

*Recipe Development

*Training

*Product presentation to present and potential customers

*Product formulation for industrial accounts

*Involvement in professional associations such as the ACF and IFT

*Presentations at hotel and restaurant management schools and culinary schools

*Advisor to senior management on company issues

As with any jobs, my career at Minor's has had a lot of highs and lows, but the highs far outweigh the lows. It has been a wonderful company in which to work, affording a wealth of personal gratification. But most importantly, it has given me the opportunity to work for "The Man, The Legend," Dr. Lewis J. Minor.

In Honor of Dad

Dr. Lewis J. Minor
Founder, President, CEO
Chairman of the Board (retired)
Senior Scientific Consultant
L. J. MINOR CORPORATION

On July 17, 1995, my father, Dr. Lewis J. Minor, was honored at the annual American Culinary Federation Convention. The award presented to him and my mother, Mrs. Minor, was the Hermann Rusch Humanitarian Award for 1995. Other honors and awards received by Dad are presented in the following paragraphs.

On July 17, 1992, Dr. Minor received the prestigious MCCA Outstanding Alumnus Award in Honor and Recognition of Exemplary Leadership to Michigan Community

Colleges.

The Michigan Community College Association is made up of twenty-nine separate colleges in the State of Michigan. The award was presented to Dr. Minor by one of his former students, Robert J. Kent, President MCCA, and Trustee, Kalamazoo Valley Community College. The award was first presented by the Association in 1985 and is based upon achievement in one's professional career, service to humanity, honors received and a strong commitment to the purpose and philosophy of the community college mission.

Two former recipients of national and international prominence were Dr. John A Hannah, President Emeritus, Michigan State University and Alumnus, Grand Rapids Community College who became the first honoree in 1985 and Donald W. Riegle, United States Senator and Alumnus, Mott Community College (Flint), who was honored in 1989.

Mrs. Minor and two of their six daughters, Ruth Ann Egan and Carol Elizabeth Walker, were guests at the ceremony.

Other awards received by Dr. Minor are:

1989 Award for help in upgrading American Chefs to Professional Status. Given in recognition of continuous effort on behalf of this nation's culinary industry and in particular for effective participation in causing the U. S. Department of Labor, in January of 1977, to officially upgrade the American Executive Chef to deserved professional rank and status. Presented at ACF Headquarters in St. Augustine, Florida by Mr. Jack F. Braun, CCC, AAC, President, American Culinary Federation and Dr. William F. McLaughlin, President, L. J. Minor Corporation

1988 Elected to membership in the Culinary Hall of Fame at ACF Headquarters, St. Augustine, Florida, by the American Academy of Chefs

1986 Honorary Award given by the Order of the Golden Toque

1984 Alumnus of the Year of the Hotel, Restaurant, and Institutional Management School, Michigan State University, by Dr. Michael Kasavana and the Faculty Committee

1983 Elected to membership in the National Institute of the Foodservice Industry College of Diplomates, for contributions to the advancement of foodservice education, and service to the United States Army Quartermaster Corps during World War II

1978 Honorary Ph.D. in Business Management, awarded by Dr. Morris Gaebe and the Honors Committee of Johnson and Wales College, Providence, Rhode Island

1977 Honorary Member Pacific Coast's Antonin Careme Society for Professional Chefs

316

1973   United States Army Quartermaster School, in recognition and appreciation of help in improving U. S. Army field foodservice by John D. McLaughlin, Major General, U. S. A. Commandant, Fort Lee, Virginia

1972   Honorary Faculty Member, United States Army Quartermaster School, for contributions to the Army Food Program. Presented by John D. McLaughlin, Major General, U. S. A. Commandant, Fort Lee, Virginia

1968   Honorary Member of The Honorable Order of the Golden Toque Professional Chefs Society

1942   Citation for outstanding civilian contributions to the development and manufacture of K-Rations for the U. S. Army Troops in World War II. Presented by Colonel Roland A. Isker, Commandant, U. S. Army Food Depot, Chicago, IL

In Honor of Hermann Rusch by Dad

On the Occasion of the Dedication
of the New Hermann G. Rusch Science Lab

A Letter from Dean Thomas L. Wright
Johnson & Wales University

Dear Dr. Minor:

    I wish to thank you once again for the donation of the Hermann G. Rusch Science Lab -- I have enclosed photos from the dedication which I am sure will have great meaning to you.

    Also enclosed are copies of two letters that were written by Dr. Rusch in appreciation for what you made possible. I respect Dr. Rusch tremendously, he has been a mentor for so many of us. Through your efforts, this man has been able to receive the greatest honor of his life.

    In closing, thank you for your friendship and sponsorship. Wishing you a world of joy in this new year, I remain

Respectfully yours,

Thomas L. Wright, Dean
Johnson & Wales University
January 5, 1995

(The purpose of the new lab is to test and compare cooking equipment, gas vs. electric. A local electric company donated $250,000 worth of state-of-the-art equipment in addition to Dr. and Mrs. Minor's contribution of $500,000 to Johnson and Wales University.)

Dedication for Dr. Lewis J. Minor
by Hermann G. Rusch

In every generation there are a few men and women who for some attribute such as philanthropic aims or intellectual achievements have won the respect and love of their fellow men. It is these men and women who raise the average of humanity and by their words and deeds brighten the world around them.

Such a man is our distinguished Dr. Lewis J. Minor and his family. The story of his life is well-known. We are familiar with his achievements and the culinary profession has benefited from his generosity. Nevertheless, it will be pleasant to review this evidence of his love for the chef's education.

His huge donation to create the "Hermann Rusch Lab" at this great Johnson & Wales University in my name is greatly appreciated. The memory of Dr. Minor, his sterling qualities and his love for a great profession will always be a reminder of "virtuosity," the master of tolerance, love and amity.

I am very honored by this humanitarian action of Dr. Lewis J. Minor, donating this huge sum to build a new kitchen at this great University in my name. I am indeed very fortunate and pleased and I am sure that many culinarians will learn the art of cooking the right way so as to succeed in a vocation beneficial to mankind.

COOKING IS AN ART
A NOBLE SCIENCE
COOKS ARE LADIES & GENTLEMEN

Hermann G. Rusch
November 24, 1994

Letter to Dr. & Mrs. Lewis J. Minor
by Hermann G. Rusch

Dear Dr. and Mrs. Minor:

Your absence at your Honor-Party given to you at Johnson and Wales University was very regretful and all present hoped that by now you are well again. The performance of the dedication was outstanding and the great honors I received because of your generosity were overwhelming. "Thank you Dr. Minor" - it will always be a reminder of having a great friend who cares - we are very thankful - keep you in high esteem.

318

Your son Mike and Edwina added charm to the Party and his speeches of respect and love for his parents added joy to the gathering. He is a master humanitarian like his Dad. I will send you a full report at a later date of this magnificent dedication ceremony of Dr. Lewis J. Minor Science Lab Kitchen in my name "Hermann G. Rusch."

With Love and Best Wishes and
God's Blessings

Respectfully yours,
Violette & Hermann G. Rusch
November 24, 1994

Chapter 33

Minor Gold Medal Recipes

by Michael L. Minor
(1977-1995)

Beef and Macaroni with Tomatoes		**All-Purpose Meatballs**
Chili Con Carne	**French Onion Soup**	**Minestrone Soup**
Stove Top Beef Stew	**Bacon, Lettuce, and Tomato (BLT) Soup**	
Old-Fashioned Chicken Noodle Soup		**Ham Pasta Salad**
New England Clam Chowder		**She Crab Soup**
Lobster Bisque		**Lobster Newburg**
Country Sausage Gravy	**Shrimp Bisque**	**Shrimp Creole**

I'm Telling Everything, Even My Secrets!
(Irish Humor by Hal Roach)

The little Jewish boy and the Catholic boy were arguing. The Catholic boy said:
"Our Parish Priest knows more than your Rabbi."

The little Jewish boy answered:
"Of course he does. You tell him everything."

Each of the following recipes was contributed by Gold Medal Award Winning Chef Michael L. Minor. They have all been recognized by the L. J. Minor Corporation as being Minor Chef developed and kitchen tested. They are dedicated in this book to the entire Minor family who gave of themselves so that others might enjoy life more.

Beef and Macaroni with Tomatoes

YIELD: 2 qts. + 1 cup (6 to 8 servings)
PREP TIME: 10 minutes
COOKING TIME: 40 minutes

2 cups elbow macaroni, uncooked   1 (28 oz.) can crushed tomatoes in puree*
1 lb. ground chuck or lean beef   1/2 cup onions, chopped
3 cups hot water   2 Tbsp. sugar
2 Tbsp. MINOR'S BEEF BASE

1) Cook macaroni as package directs for 6 to 7 minutes. Drain and set aside.

2) In a heavy 4 qt. sauce pot, cook and stir ground beef over medium heat
   until browned, about 10 minutes. Drain fat.

3) Add water, BEEF BASE, tomatoes, onions, and sugar, mixing well. Heat
   to boiling over medium heat. Reduce heat and gently boil 25 to 30 minutes,
   stirring occasionally.

4) Stir in drained cooked macaroni. Heat to a gentle boil. Reduce heat and gently boil
   5 - 10 minutes, stirring occasionally.

5) Serve hot, garnished with parsley or grated Parmesan cheese.

*The crushed tomatoes in puree may be replaced with 1 (29 oz.) can tomato puree.

All-Purpose Meatballs

YIELD: 30-32 (1 oz.) meatballs (6 to 8 servings)
PREP TIME: 30 minutes
COOKING TIME: 30 minutes

1/2 cup milk, hot   3 Tbsp. onions, finely chopped
1 Tbsp. MINOR'S BEEF BASE   1 Tbsp. parsley flakes
3/4 cup dry bread crumbs   1 tsp. Worcestershire sauce
1 egg, slightly beaten   1 lb. 8 oz. ground chuck or lean beef

1) In a large mixing bowl, combine milk with BEEF BASE, stirring well until BEEF BASE is dissolved.

2) Mix in bread crumbs, egg, onions, parsley flakes, and Worcestershire sauce.

3) Add ground beef and mix only enough to combine thoroughly.

4) Using a tablespoon, shape 30-32 meatballs and arrange in a 9 x 13 baking pan.

5) Bake uncovered at 400°F 20 to 25 minutes until meatballs are lightly browned. Remove from oven and pour off excess fat.

6) Serve hot with gravy or sauce over buttered noodles, rice, or spaghetti.

VARIATION: For cocktail meatballs, shape into 60-64 smaller meatballs. Reduce baking time to 15 to 20 minutes.

Chili Con Carne

YIELD:	1 gal. (12 to 15 servings)
PREP TIME:	15 minutes
COOKING TIME:	45 minutes

3 lbs. ground chuck or lean beef	3 1/2 cups hot water
1 1/2 cups onions, chopped	1/4 cup. MINOR'S BEEF BASE
1/2 cup all-purpose flour	4 (15 oz.) cans kidney beans, drained
2 Tbsp. chili powder	1 Tbsp. sugar
1 (28 oz.) can crushed tomatoes in puree*	

1) In a heavy 8 qt. sauce pot, cook and stir ground beef and onions over medium heat until beef is browned, about 10 to 15 minutes.

2) Stir in flour and chili powder until well blended. Remove from heat.

3) Add crushed tomatoes, water, BEEF BASE, kidney beans, and sugar, mixing well. Heat to boiling. Reduce heat and gently boil 25 to 30 minutes.

4) Serve hot in individual casseroles, garnished with shredded cheddar cheese or chopped onions.

*The crushed tomatoes in puree may be replaced with 1 (29 oz.) can tomato puree.

VARIATIONS: If desired, complete the recipe without adding kidney beans. Separate into 4 portions of approximately 2 1/2 cups when cooled. These portions can be frozen and thawed as needed. When thawed, add 1 can of drained beans to each portion and heat thoroughly.

French Onion Soup

YIELD:	5 1/2 cups (4 to 6 servings)
PREP TIME:	20 minutes
COOKING TIME:	40 minutes

2 Tbsp. margarine or butter
3 cups (4 medium) onions,
   sliced 1/8" x 1"

5 cups hot water
2 Tbsp. + 1 tsp. MINOR'S BEEF BASE

1) In a heavy 3 qt. saucepan, melt margarine over medium heat. Add onions and sauté 25 to 35 minutes or until onions turn a rich brown color, stirring frequently. Be careful not to burn the onions.

2) Add water and BEEF BASE. Heat to boiling, stirring frequently. Reduce heat and gently boil 5 minutes.

3) Serve hot, garnished with toasted French bread topped with melted Gruyere or Swiss cheese.

Minestrone Soup

YIELD: 1 gal. (12 to 16 servings)
PREP TIME: 40 minutes
COOKING TIME: 2 ¾ hours

3/4 cup dried Great Northern Beans
2 qts. cold water
2 1/2 qts. hot water
1 1/2 tsp. salt
6 Tbsp. (3 oz.) margarine or butter
1 3/4 cups onion (1 medium), medium diced
3/4 cup (1 medium) green pepper,
   small diced
3/4 tsp. garlic, finely minced
   (4 medium cloves)
1 cup celery, small diced
3/4 cup (2 medium) carrots, medium diced

1 cup bean broth, drained from cooked beans
3 qts. hot water
1/3 cup MINOR'S BEEF BASE
3/4 cup crushed tomatoes in puree
1/2 cup ditalini (or elbow macaroni)
2 1/4 cups cabbage, medium diced
1 3/4 cups potatoes, pared and cut into
1/2" cubes
1 1/2 tsp. parsley flakes
1/8 tsp. sweet basil, crushed
1/8 tsp. dried thyme leaves, crushed
1 tsp. sugar

1) Sort and rinse beans. Cover with cold water, 2 inches above beans. Either soak beans overnight, or boil beans for 2 minutes, remove from heat and let stand for 1 hour covered. Drain beans and discard water.

2) Combine soaked beans, 2 1/2 qts. of hot water and salt. Heat to boiling. Reduce heat and gently boil for 1 1/2 to 2 hours until beans are tender. Drain beans, saving the broth. Set aside.

3) Melt margarine in an 8 qt. heavy sauce pot. Add onions, green peppers, garlic, celery, and carrots. Sauté over medium heat until almost tender, about 15 to 20 minutes.

4) Add drained cooked beans, measured bean broth, 3 qts. of hot water, BEEF BASE, tomatoes, ditalini, cabbage, potatoes, parsley flakes, sweet basil, thyme, and sugar. Heat to boiling. Reduce heat and gently boil for 20 minutes until ditalini and vegetables are tender. Serve hot.

Stove Top Beef Stew

YIELD: 2 qts. + 1 cup (7 to 8 servings)
PREP TIME: 40 minutes
COOKING TIME: 2 1/2 hours

1 Tbsp. vegetable oil
1 1/2 lbs. boneless beef chuck or
   stew meat, trimmed and cut
   into 1" cubes
1 qt. hot water
2 Tbsp. + 1 tsp. MINOR'S BEEF BASE
2 Tbsp. tomato paste

1/2 tsp. paprika
1 1/4 cups carrots, cut into 1" slices
2 cups potatoes, large diced
1 cup onions, sliced 1/4" x 2"
1/2 cup all-purpose flour
3/4 cup cold water
1/2 pkg. frozen peas

1) In a heavy 4 qt. sauce pot or Dutch oven, heat oil over medium heat. Add beef; sauté 30 to 40 minutes, until brown.

2) Add water, BEEF BASE, tomato paste, and paprika, stirring well. Heat to boiling. Reduce heat; cover and gently boil 1 1/2 hours, stirring occasionally.

3) Add carrots, potatoes, onions. Cover and continue gently boiling 45 minutes.

4) In a small mixing bowl, blend together flour and water using a wire whip. Slowly add slurry to stew, mixing continuously. Add peas; cover and gently boil 10 to 15 minutes, until vegetables are fork tender.

5) Serve hot with crisp French bread and a tossed salad.

Bacon, Lettuce, and Tomato (BLT) Soup

YIELD: 6 cups (4 to 6 servings)
PREP TIME: 20 minutes
COOKING TIME: 25 minutes

4-5 slices regular sliced bacon,
   small diced
2 Tbsp. margarine or butter
3 1/2 cups (1/4 of a large head)
   iceberg lettuce, julienne cut 1 1/2"
   to 2" long
1/2 cup + 2 Tbsp. all-purpose flour
3 1/2 cups hot water

1 Tbsp. + 1 tsp. MINOR'S CHICKEN BASE
1 tsp. MINOR'S HAM BASE
3/4 cup tomatoes (1 medium), medium diced
dash ground nutmeg
dash ground red pepper
1 cup half and half cream

1) In a heavy 2 1/2 or 3 qt. saucepan, cook bacon over medium heat until lightly browned, about 10 minutes. Do not drain fat.

2) Add margarine and heat until melted. Stir in lettuce and sauté 2 minutes.

3) Blend in flour with a wire whisk. Stir over medium heat until well blended and evenly cooked, about 2 to 3 minutes. Remove from heat.

4) Add water, CHICKEN BASE, HAM BASE, tomatoes, nutmeg, and red pepper. Heat to boiling, stirring frequently. Reduce heat and gently boil 6 minutes, stirring occasionally, until thickened.

5) Add cream, mixing well. Heat to a gentle boil, stirring frequently.

6) Serve hot, garnished with crumbled bacon bits, cherry tomato slices, or buttered croutons.

Old-Fashioned Chicken Noodle Soup

YIELD: 2 qts. (8 to 10 servings)
PREP TIME: 20 minutes
COOKING TIME: 15 to 20 minutes

2 Tbsp. margarine or butter   1/4 cup MINOR'S CHICKEN BASE
1 cup onions, small diced   2 cups medium egg noodles, uncooked
1 cup carrots, sliced 1/8" thick   2 cups (8 oz.) cooked chicken,
1/2 cup celery, sliced 1/8" thick   small diced
7 cups hot water

1) In a heavy 4 qt. saucepan, melt margarine over medium heat. Stir in onions, carrots, and celery and sauté 5 minutes.

2) Stir in water, CHICKEN BASE and noodles. Heat to boiling, stirring frequently. Reduce heat and gently boil until noodles are tender, approximately 8 to 10 minutes.

3) Add chicken and continue boiling gently 3 to 5 minutes, stirring occasionally.

4) Serve hot, garnished with chopped fresh parsley.

Ham Pasta Salad

YIELD: 5 1/2 cups (6 to 8 servings)
PREP TIME: 30 minutes
COOKING TIME: 2 hours

1 cup mayonnaise
1/4 cup cultured sour cream
1/4 cup. MINOR'S HAM BASE
1 1/2 tsp. brown sugar
1/4 tsp. chili powder
4 cups cooked rotini*

1/2 cup tomatoes, medium diced
1/2 cup boiled ham, small cubed
1/3 cup celery, small diced
1/3 cup kidney beans, rinsed and drained
1/4 cup green peppers, small diced

1) In a blender or food processor, combine mayonnaise, sour cream, HAM BASE, brown sugar, and chili powder. Mix on medium speed until well blended, about 3 to 4 minutes.

2) In a large mixing bowl, combine blended mixture with remaining ingredients and toss lightly. Chill well.

3) Serve garnished with halved cherry tomatoes.

*1/2 lb. (3 cups) uncooked prepared per package directions.

New England Clam Chowder

YIELD: 4 cups (4 to 5 servings)
PREP TIME: 20 minutes
COOKING TIME: 20 minutes

2 1/2 Tbsp. margarine or butter
1/2 cup onions, small diced
1/4 cup all-purpose flour
1 1/2 cups hot water
1 Tbsp. MINOR'S CLAM BASE

3/4 tsp. MINOR'S PORK BASE
1 (6 1/2 oz.) can chopped or minced
    clams, undrained
1 1/2 cups potatoes, medium diced
1 cup half and half cream, hot

1) In a heavy 2 qt. saucepan, melt margarine over medium heat. Stir in onions
   and sauté 2 minutes.

2) Add flour, stirring until well blended and evenly cooked, about 2 to 3
   minutes. Remove from heat.

3) Stir in water, CLAM BASE, PORK BASE, clams with broth, potatoes, and cream.
   Heat to boiling over medium heat. Reduce heat and gently boil until potatoes
   are tender, about 12 to 15 minutes, stirring occasionally.

4) Serve hot, garnished with oyster crackers or sliced green onions.

She-Crab Soup

YIELD: 4 cups (3 to 4 servings)
PREP TIME: 10 minutes
COOKING TIME: 15 minutes

3 Tbsp. margarine or butter   1/8 tsp. paprika
1/3 cup all-purpose flour   dash ground mace
2 3/4 cups hot water   1 cup half and half cream
2 Tbsp. MINOR'S CRAB BASE   2 Tbsp. pale dry cocktail sherry

1) In a heavy 2 qt. saucepan, melt margarine over medium heat. Blend in flour and stir with a wire whisk until well blended, evenly cooked and bubbly, about 2 to 3 minutes. Remove from heat.

2) Add water, CRAB BASE, paprika, and mace, mixing well. Heat to boiling over medium heat, stirring constantly. Reduce heat and gently boil 7 minutes, stirring frequently.

3) Add cream and wine, mixing well. Heat to a gently boil for 1 minute, stirring frequently.

4) Serve hot, garnished with chopped cooked crab meat or sieved hard cooked egg yolk.

Lobster Bisque

YIELD:	2 qts. (6 to 8 servings)
PREP TIME:	20 minutes
COOKING TIME:	15 minutes

6 Tbsp. (3 oz.) margarine or butter
3/4 cup all-purpose flour
1 1/2 qts. hot water
3 1/2 Tbsp. MINOR'S LOBSTER BASE

dash cayenne pepper
1 1/2 cups half and half cream, hot
1/3 cup pale dry cocktail sherry

1) In a heavy 4 qt. sauce pot, melt margarine over low heat. Blend in flour and stir with a wire whisk until well blended, evenly cooked and bubbly, about 2 to 3 minutes. Remove from heat.

2) Add hot water gradually, mixing well. Stir in LOBSTER BASE and cayenne pepper. Heat to boiling over medium heat, stirring constantly. Reduce heat and gently boil for 10 minutes.

3) Add hot cream and dry sherry, mixing well.

4) Serve hot, garnished with chopped cooked lobster, chopped fresh parsley or chives.

Lobster Newburg

YIELD: 4 cups (3 to 4 servings)
PREP TIME: 45 minutes
COOKING TIME: 15 minutes

3 Tbsp. margarine or butter
1/4 cup + 2 Tbsp. all-purpose flour
1 1/4 cups hot water
1 Tbsp. MINOR'S LOBSTER BASE
dash ground red pepper
1 cup heavy whipping cream, hot

1/2 Tbsp. margarine or butter
8 oz. (2 lobster tails) cooked
   lobster, drained and cut into 1/2" pieces
2 Tbsp. pale dry cocktail sherry

1) In a heavy 3 qt. saucepan, melt margarine over medium heat. Blend in flour and stir with a wire whisk until well blended, evenly cooked and bubbly, about 2 to 3 minutes. Remove from heat.

2) Stir in water, LOBSTER BASE, and red pepper, mixing well. Bring to a boil, stirring constantly. Boil and stir 1 minute, until thickened.

3) Stir in cream, mixing well. Set aside.

4) In a large heavy skillet, melt margarine over medium heat. Add lobster and sauté 2 to 3 minutes until hot.

5) Add sauce and sherry, mixing gently.

6) Serve hot over toast points or butter rice, or in pastry shells.

Country Sausage Gravy

YIELD: 5 1/2 cups
PREP TIME: 15 minutes
COOKING TIME: 20 minutes

1 oz. butter*
1 lb. pork sausage (bulk)
1/2 cup all-purpose flour
2 tsp. MINOR'S PORK BASE
1 cup water
3 cups milk

1) Sauté sausage in butter over medium heat until browned.
2) Add flour to sausage, mix well. Cook 3-4 minutes.
3) Add remaining ingredients, mix very well. Bring to a gentle boil - gently boil 10 minutes.

*Butter added - needed for roux; not enough grease in sausage

Shrimp Bisque

YIELD: 2 qts. (6 to 8 servings)
PREP TIME: 15 minutes
COOKING TIME: 15 minutes

6 Tbsp. (3 oz.) margarine or butter
3/4 cup all-purpose flour
1/2 tsp. paprika
1 qt. 1 1/2 cups hot water

4 Tbsp. & 1 tsp. MINOR'S
        SHRIMP BASE
1 1/2 cups half and half cream, hot
3 Tbsp. Sauterne wine

1) In a heavy 4 qt. sauce pot, melt margarine over low heat. Blend in flour and paprika using a wire whisk. Stir over medium heat until well blended, evenly cooked, and bubbly, about 2 to 3 minutes. Remove from heat.
2) Add hot water gradually, mixing well. Stir in SHRIMP BASE. Heat to boiling over medium heat, stirring constantly. Reduce heat and gently boil for 10 minutes.
3) Add hot cream and wine, mixing well.
4) Serve hot, garnished with chopped cooked shrimp, chopped fresh parsley or watercress..

Shrimp Creole

YIELD:	5 1/2 cups (5 to 6 servings)
PREP TIME:	40 minutes
COOKING TIME:	15 minutes

1 Tbsp. vegetable oil	1 cup hot water
2 Tbsp. margarine or butter	2 Tbsp. MINOR'S SHRIMP BASE
1 cup green pepper, sliced 1/4" x 1"	1 (14 1/2 oz.) can stewed tomatoes, chopped
1 cup celery, sliced 1/4" thick	1 (6 oz.) can tomato paste
2/3 cup onions, sliced 1/4" x 1"	1/2 tsp. hot red pepper sauce
1 lb. shrimp, peeled and deveined	1/4 tsp. garlic powder
1 cup fresh mushrooms, sliced 1/4" thick	1/8 tsp. ground thyme

1) In a heavy 3 qt. saucepan, heat oil and margarine over medium heat. Add green peppers, celery, and onions. Sauté and stir 2 to 3 minutes.

2) Add shrimp and mushrooms. Sauté and stir 2 to 3 minutes.

3) Add remaining ingredients. Heat to a gentle boil over medium heat. Reduce heat and gently boil 5 minutes, stirring occasionally.

4) Serve hot over cooked rice.

Chapter 34

A Family Affair

by Carol Minor Walker
(1953-1963, 1979-1986)

A Tribute to Love   **Ruth Minor's Motto**   **Happiness**

Family Memories   **My Heritage**   **The Company**   **Consulting for Minor's**

A Tribute to Love
by Carol Minor Walker

In this world where we all live
Tributes are made - we receive and give
The tribute today is of a different type
It's a tribute to love to a husband and wife
Love that's endeavored much more than most love could bear
A man and woman walking hand-in-hand and learning to share
The sickness and health, the good with the bad
Many happy moments and many so sad
Raising the children with never a gripe
Showering them with security, strength, patience, and love is proof of the type
Total dedication to their set goals in life
No time for themselves, just living for others
Considering all mankind, sisters and brothers
Two people's lives so completely entwined
Beautiful, unselfish love of this kind
Love that's been growing for so many years
Cannot be destroyed by any earthly fears
Many years ago, on this very special day
Solemn wedding vows were made
For the complete fulfillment of these vows
This tribute to love is now paid

Two human beings that can love so completely
Must have another Being watching and loving them sweetly
It's not success and power that a good marriage consists of
It's the little everyday things, mutual respect, faith in Our Lord, and love
February 11, 1978 love is in the air
Can't you feel it everywhere?
With family and friends so very dear
This wonderful love we can now all share

Ruth Minor's Motto
by Carol Minor Walker

If a job is once begun
Never leave it 'til it's done
Be the labor great or small
Do it well or not at all

Happiness
by Carol Minor Walker

If you sit down at set of sun
And count the acts that you have done
And counting, find one self denying act,
One word most kind
That fell like sunshine where it went
Then you can count that day well spent
But, if through all the live - long day
You've cheered no heart by yea or nay
If through it all You've nothing done that you can trace,
That brought a smile to someone's face
Then you can count that day as worse than lost.

Family Memories
by Carol Minor Walker

Tonight, dear family and friends, may I express
my personal meaning of happiness?

Love has surrounded me all my life
from a father and mother, a husband and wife,
a winning team throughout life's mainstream.
Their virtues are many, too many to name -
through thick and thin, remaining the same,
ambitious and strong, yet loving and caring,
to them success meant helping and sharing.

A love that overflows, not to just a few,
may I now take the time and say thank you,
to my beautiful Mom and wonderful Dad,
thank you so much for all that we've had.
You've built a business and became a success,
but You've never lost sight of humbleness.

Whenever I'm disheartened and feeling blue,
I dream of a childhood that I once knew.
We moved to Cleveland when I was just five,
six children born, two yet not alive.
What courage it took to pack up and leave
that "one-horse town" of Harbor Beach,
bigger and better things hoping to reach
our life was adventure, comparable to none,
there was hard work involved but plenty of fun.
My childhood - always, I remember it well -
those camping trips - gee, tents were swell!

Dad started the business, food bases were perfected,
then a few good salesmen were carefully selected.
It's a mystery to me how Dad and Mom spared
enough of their time so we'd all know they cared.

While Dad was busy with the Minor Base,
Mom was busy running kids all over the place.
One had one lesson, the next another,

338

yet, we wouldn't have had any without our mother.
Every morning they arose at the crack of dawn,
and by the time we children got up, breakfast was on.
From the fresh "squeezed" orange juice in the morning
to the roast beef and gravy at night,
we never ate a thing that wasn't prepared just right.

Mom labored out of love and never complained
practically alone, a household she maintained.
Just raising eight children is quite a chore,
but together, Mom and Dad, You've done so much more.
You've showered happiness and love all over the place
and given us memories that no one can erase.

I've never underestimated what a great life I've had.
I love you so much, my dearest Mom and Dad.

September 2, 1981

My Heritage

Love is not a big enough word to describe my feelings toward my parents, Lewis J. and Ruth E. Minor. I am forever thankful to be their daughter. Having the good fortune to be part of the Minor family, my entire life has been filled with the love and support of my parents. As a child I was given many advantages including a Catholic education and a variety of lessons.

My parents were hard-working, self-sacrificing people who complemented each other perfectly. The Golden Rule has been their philosophy as they have moved through life. Because of integrity, quality, perseverance, loyalty, and many more attributes, the L. J. Minor Corporation, under the direction of my dad, grew into a highly regarded and prosperous business in the food industry.

My affiliation with the Minor family began on the day I was born, June 25, 1946 in Toledo, Ohio. The first memories that I have are from Harbor Beach, Michigan on beautiful Lake Huron. When I was just one year old, we moved there. Our home was a lovely Dutch colonial house. Even though I cannot recall a lot from those days, I can remember a few friends and neighbors. I can remember Daddy singing in a men's chorus and being involved with Scouting.

We left Harbor Beach in the fall of 1951 and relocated in Fairview Park, Ohio, a western suburb of Cleveland. Our new address was 20877 Fairpark Drive. I was five years old and in the first grade.

339

This new house was like a palace to me! It was a large bungalow with a lot of charm and many unusual features. Sharing a bedroom with my sisters Kathleen and Ruth Ann was even tolerable as the room was quite spacious. We had an adjoining dressing room with locker-like closets on three walls and a vanity the length of the fourth. There were two walk-in closets off the dressing room, but the best feature was a porch off our bedroom. Those closets and the porch served as perfect "hide-outs" from my brothers and sisters when I needed peace and quiet.

It is important to say that Ruth Ann and I always had a normal childhood. We had an exceptional home life. Mommy was a dedicated wife, mother, and homemaker. She was up daily before dawn and would have breakfast ready when we arose. Often we had fresh, hand-squeezed orange juice along with breakfast.

The school we attended, St. Angela Merici, was a block from our house which enabled us to go home for lunch everyday. Our lunch consisted of home made soup, sandwiches, fruit, and home-made cookies, brownies, or pudding. After school we had lessons which took a large chunk out of Mommy's days. I took organ, violin, tap dancing, ballet and acrobatics. I was only one of eight who needed chauffeuring at one time or another.

Each one of us had many extra-curricular activities. The most amazing part of the day was our evening meal. We always ate together as a family between 6:00 and 6:30 PM. Dinner was a delicious, full course meal fit for the finest chefs of the world. How did Mommy have time for such extraordinary feasts with all of her other responsibilities? That is the proverbial $64,000 question!

There was more to our childhood than going to school, working, and lessons. In the summer months there were visits to our grandparents. Often times I would spend a week or two in Lansing, Michigan, with my Grandpa and Grandma Angell. They had a farm which offered endless intrigue.

Grandpa and Grandma Minor lived in Detroit, Michigan, and belonged to Western Golf and Country Club. There was nothing greater than spending warm summer days in the Olympic size pool at the club. Each of my grandparents had a knack for making me feel special. Times spent with them are treasures of my heart.

Every summer we had a two-week family vacation. Those were the happiest, most exciting times of my childhood. We always went camping and stayed in an enormous orange tent. Daddy and my older brother, Bryan, would dig a trench after pitching the tent. Some probably could not understand the sport of camping, but living in the wilderness and sleeping on the ground in sleeping bags gave us an appreciation of nature, and bonded our family close together. Our vacations were modest in cost yet priceless in adventure and fun.

In 1960 our vacation was totally different than what we had grown accustomed to previously. We went out west because the Boy Scout Jamboree was being held in Colorado Springs, Colorado. We were gone for six weeks. Riding in a car for several hours per day was not exactly comfortable, but we would sing and eat baked goods as we rode along. Seeing the landscape as we crossed the country was a great geography lesson. At the end of a day we would stay in a motel since there was no camping on that trip.

While in Colorado Springs we stayed in a cottage. At the close of the Jamboree we headed for California. We visited my Uncle Russel, Mommy's brother, and his family in California. We did a lot of sightseeing from San Francisco to Disneyland. It was the trip of a lifetime and an experience that I will never forget.

Holidays were wonderful times at home. Daddy and Mommy went to great lengths to keep the legend of Santa Claus alive. Daddy would take us for an annual Christmas Eve drive to see the lights and sometimes a movie. When we would return home, Santa would have paid a visit. Christmas morning we attended Mass; then my Uncle Tom and Aunt Babe would come bearing gifts. The house was filled with wonderful aromas coming from Mommy's kitchen. Dinner was the highlight of every holiday, prepared to perfection by our very own master chef, Mommy.

The Company

While I was busy being a little kid and having fun, Daddy was establishing a company. I had no idea what he did for a living until the day I visited his work place. The first plant operation was in a warehouse owned by a Mr. Joe Bertman. It was not much, but I was impressed.

Daddy owned a business and made food bases with his name on the labels! There was an aroma in the air which I shall never forget, a very distinctive seasoned smell produced from the ingredients of the bases.

The size of the Hobart mixer really surprised and amazed me. The only mixer I had ever seen was the Sunbeam Mixmaster that my Mommy used for baking. Being a kid, I had no idea that mixers came in jumbo sizes, and here was Daddy with a mixer large enough to hold a person. Wow!

Daddy hired a woman named Audrey Chubbs as his assistant. Audrey was a most competent employee. She was hired on a part-time basis but soon became Daddy's "right arm" at work. Since Audrey was capable of running things at the plant, Daddy could pursue other aspects of the business.

When the L. J. Minor Corporation relocated to West 115th Street in 1953, I became involved. On the weekends, I would go to the plant with my older sisters and brother and help pack one ounce samples.

There was a large stainless steel sink in the production room. Daddy had foot-pedals installed on the sink to turn the water on and off. Sanitation was the purpose for the pedals, but for a short kid like me they were a God-send. Before the foot pedals I would turn a bucket upside down and stand on it to reach the faucet. Life was fun with a boss like Daddy. He would often take me to Clark's Restaurant for lunch on Saturdays. I would have a great lunch and get a toy from a treasure chest.

Daddy hired a couple more women to work full time. Rose Wilson and Helen Crites were the laborers in packaging and labeling. When production was slow the workers were

341

always busy with sanitation and organization.

Working at the plant on the weekends became a way of life for my sister and me. Ruth Ann, who was one and a half years my senior, suddenly became my boss. What a revolting development that was! Seriously, she was a good boss. She taught me how to do a lot and made sure it was done right. Our job was packing and labeling one and four ounce samples. Daddy paid us a penny for every sample packed as I recall.

The method of packing the base was primitive. We used teaspoons. It was not hard work but sometimes seemed tedious. After each jar had the exact amount required, we would wipe the lip with a damp cloth then put the lid on. Every jar was labeled by hand as the jars were too small for the labeling machine. It was imperative to apply the labels evenly. Perfect presentation of the samples was mandatory. This was not always an easy task, yet at the end of the day there was pride in a job well done.

After a few years at the West 115th Street location with the business constantly growing, the space there was no longer adequate for production. Daddy found a building on West 25th Street which he purchased. This building became the new plant. It was 1959-1960 when operations moved to West 25th Street. The new plant was much larger and seemed more sophisticated than the old one.

The first time I went inside it, I thought it resembled a hospital operating room. The production area was very bright and shining clean with huge stainless steel tables. The employees wore white lab coats with aprons and hair nets. As with the two former plants, that distinctive seasoned aroma was ever present.

(Editor's Note: Through the years I always wanted to visit the L. J. Minor Corporation in Cleveland and was never allowed to do so. In editing this book, I have come to realize, as the reader would note also, that no one except inspectors were allowed to see or visit the plant. This past year, though, by special permission from Dr. Minor and the company, I, at long last, toured the plant. While I cannot reveal anything here, due to confidentiality, I do wish to confirm that the distinctive seasoned aroma in the plant is one of the most marvelous smells of one's lifetime. It is the aromas of home cooking, holiday feasts, and freshly baked bread all wrapped into one. What a pleasure to have experienced it!)

The L. J. Minor Corporation had offices in the Bulkley Building downtown in Cleveland. My Uncle Tom Ryan worked at the office with his secretary Mary Mele. The office was unfamiliar to me. In all my years in Cleveland, I only visited the downtown office a handful of times.

Ruth Ann and I began working at the new plant. I was twelve years old and earning 50 cents an hour. Our work load had grown enormously, yet 50 cents an hour was a most generous wage for somebody my age. Instead of using teaspoons to pack the sample, a new more efficient method was put into use. We began using cake decorating tubes which allowed us to pack more quickly. On a daily basis Ruth Ann and I would do hundreds of samples. To this day I can still hear the sound of glass jars jingling on the stainless steel tables.

Audrey and Rose would often work on Saturdays. They were fun-loving, upbeat women and were fond of me. I have always been grateful that I had a good rapport with them. They realized that I was still very young. Periodically they would ask me to do favors for them to break the rigorous routine Ruth Ann had assigned to me.

Looking back, I do not believe those favors were that important, Audrey and Rose just wanted me to have a break every now and then. Sometimes Ruth Ann took her job as my boss a little too seriously!

With the rapid growth in business came constant change. There were new faces at work frequently. The variety of bases and other products had become vast. Employees were happy and proud to be working for the L. J. Minor Corporation.

For years Mom usually provided our transportation to and from work. When Ruth Ann started to drive, our work schedule changed drastically. "The boss" decided to work in the middle of the night so we could finish by mid-afternoon. Back in those days there was a Mass at 2:00 a.m. on Sunday mornings at the Cathedral downtown. After attending Mass we would go and work eight or ten hours depending on the work load. Ruth Ann's rationale was, if we started early we could get home early and still have a social life. This sounded reasonable to me, after all, she was the boss!

My younger brother, Mike, began helping out at times. Some friends from our neighborhood were recruited to work at extremely busy times. With the extra help, production grew to two or three thousand samples daily. Ruth Ann worked along with us but maintained her managerial status at all times.

Working for the company as a child prepared me for adulthood. Not only did I have money in my pocket, but I had a feeling of self-worth. Before leaving the company in 1963, I could perform most every production job. My work performance was not without error, but I learned a lot from my mistakes. Without a doubt it was the best job of my lifetime. Yes, those were the "good old days!"

In 1963 I moved to Lansing, Michigan, ending my employment with the L. J. Minor Corporation. I was sixteen and a junior in high school. Dad and Bryan were both enrolled at Michigan State University. We lived in my Grandpa and Grandma Angell's remodeled farm house. Dad was working on his doctorate.

Shortly after arriving in Lansing I enrolled in beauty college. I attended Eastern High School and Farthing's Beauty College on a co-op program. In June of 1964 I graduated from high school and beauty college. Having obtained my cosmetologist's license, I began working in a beauty shop.

Meanwhile, back in Cleveland, Ruth Ann was a full time employee at the L. J. Minor Corporation. She began that career immediately after her high school graduation in 1962. Besides being sisters, our relationship had evolved into best friends and confidantes. We were in close contact which kept me aware of the progression of the business. My participation at Minor's during its formative years allowed me to maintain an interest in the business.

Consulting for Minor's

After several years, I was hired by the L. J. Minor Corporation in November of 1979 as a consultant. I was to be an extension of the taste panel and the research and development team. Shortly after being hired by Mike Zelski, Jan Williams came to Lansing to give me instruction on my job procedure.

My job was to test randomly selected products, complete scoring sheets, write comments, and return my findings to Jan Williams in an expedient manner. The products were found to be very standard and high in quality at this time. Natural flavors and appearance were the norm. Occasionally, there was a problem with foreign material or a rancid taste and odor in a base. If I felt a problem demanded attention, I would write a letter or make a phone call to Jan Williams.

In 1983 I was informed that my new boss was Sharon Schrader. I began sending my findings to her. In December of 1983, I received a performance letter from John D. McLaughlin. I received another generous bonus in December of 1984. Being involved with the L. J. Minor Corporation from the grassroots level, I feel I have always done a conscientious job and was compensated well.

The L. J. Minor Corporation was sold to a group of investors in 1983. My parents had serious health problems and an opportunity arose to sell the business for a fair market value. Dad always worried about leaving a debt for his children. When I was a child he would often say that he would try to reduce his debts so we would only owe $10,000 apiece when he died. Perhaps he was joking, but he must have had concerns! With the sale of the business came an end to an era. For years the L. J. Minor Corporation's logo read "Always in Good Taste." This logo was appropriate not only because of the excellence of the food bases but also for the excellence of the L. J. Minor Corporation in its entirety.

A new era emerged with the sale of the business. Dr. and Mrs. Minor became full time philanthropists. Over the past several years they have secured the future for their children and grandchildren. Many friends and relatives became the recipients of their generosity. An enormous amount has been given for education, in particular to Dad's alma mater, Michigan State University.

They have lived the American dream. Quality is a key to their success story as it has been a major ingredient in all their endeavors both personal and professional. Their legacy will be passed on from generation to generation by all whose lives they have touched.

Thank you for allowing me to share these thoughts which have been written with love and admiration for Dr. and Mrs. Minor, my parents.

Chapter 35

More on Quality

By Josephine Minor
(1964-1988)

Lew and Ruth Minor
A Couple beyond Compare

Early Employment   **A Position in Quality Control**   **Learning Computers**

Lew and Ruth Minor
A Couple beyond Compare
by Josephine Minor

For fifty plus years, they've been an example of
        two people who truly know how to share
They give each other respect, understanding
        and love
To others, they inspire hope and faith in
        God above
A living legend, due to his opinions and convictions,
        Lew encourages others to be leaders
        in their own field.
Ruth, on the other hand, with wisdom and mild manner, promotes patience and trust,
        her gentility is very real
It's a thrill to join in this golden anniversary
        celebration for Mom and Dad Minor
I'm sure the family will all agree there
        are no parents finer
Silver laughter, golden giving, everything
        worth dreaming of
They shared with us their priceless treasure
Something simple, simply love.

Early Employment

Being the sixth child of Lew and Ruth Minor's eight, I was the "bonus" baby as I arrived July of 1951, the same year as the L. J. Minor Corporation was founded. During those early years, Mom often took me along when she visited our plant on West 115th Street in Cleveland.

My older brothers and sisters usually worked there on Saturdays to insure ready availability of product to our customers. My parents had three faithful employees at this time, besides us children. They were Audrey Chubbs, Rose wilson, and Helen Crites.

There were no job descriptions back then as everyone helped in every task. This plant was adequate for seven or eight years, until manufacturing needs increased and one room would just not do it. My parents then moved production to the current business address on West 25th Street.

Most of the family relocated to Lansing, Michigan, in 1963 when Dad began teaching at Michigan State University. My sister Ruth chose to stay in Cleveland and continue to work at the company. During my summers as a teenager, I would sometimes help out at the plant by labeling or packaging jars.

There were approximately ten employees at this time, with Ruth doing the production scheduling, executing quality control duties, and acting as the sole supervisor. "Ruthie" was definitely a stickler for flawless job performance, but she never hesitated to roll up her sleeves and "dig in" when needed.

Mike Zelski was hired as the plant manager when the company and I were "sweet sixteen." Dad recruited Mike after having him as a student in class at MSU. Not only is Mike an innovative businessman, but, with his amiable temperament, people are usually receptive to his ideas.

Tom Ryan, Dad's cousin and closest friend, was the top manager in Cleveland at that time. He was a polished attorney with candor, wisdom, and a keen sense of humor. Due to "Uncle Tom's" powerful communication skills, he managed the Customer Service Department. He also bargained with purveyors and undertook any financial negotiations that were required.

From time to time, during my summers at the plant, Uncle Tom would call me direct from his downtown office on what we referred to as the "hot line." He would always invite me to lunch for an "uncle-to-niece" chat. These luncheons included food for thought, as Uncle Tom related classic episodes from his life to me.

A Position in Quality Control

It was June of 1980 when Dad and Mike Zelski hired me for Minor's Quality Control (Q. C.) Department. The company was undergoing growing pains, attributed to increasing sales volume. Expansion in several areas was needed to alleviate this problem.

Training for new employees was done by Mike and Ruth. By adjusting her scheduling techniques, Ruth initiated more efficient time/cost methods of packaging and production. Mike saw the importance of acquiring more sophisticated equipment to allow for greater increase in manufacturing. He also had the foresight to locate and secure a spacious shipping facility in Brecksville, Ohio.

The Research & Development Department was directed by Mike Minor and Jan Williams. Their staff worked diligently experimenting with, formulating, and testing new bases. Dry Roux and Fish Base were a couple of Mike's creations. These and several other products that originated at this time are still marketed by the company.

Blanca Nieves was my co-worker in Q. C. Blanca had been working alone for some time and she was very knowledgeable and precise about procedure. Personally, I was more impressed with Blanca's mellow temperament and her cheerful ways. She showed infinite patience while teaching me how to weigh Control Products (C. P.s) our term for special seasonings added to each product. This entailed calculating the ratio of raw materials to be blended together. The exact weight and measure of individual C. P.s was vital to the flavor of each completed batch of base. For many years, Joseph Adams, a friend and business associate of Dad's, supplied the spices and oleoresins I worked with every day.

Blanca and I sampled all raw materials upon receipt, then ran comparison tests against the "specs" we kept on record. After all, if the raw materials were not "up to snuff," the food base would not be up to Mom and Dad's standards.

Before any finished batch could be packaged, it had to be approved by Q. C. Flavor, of course, was the top priority, but testing was done for color, aroma, and consistency also. After we ran these tests, we logged in each batch by corresponding number and date.

Sanitation was another concern of the Q. C. Department. Blanca and I made several walk-through inspections of the entire plant every day. I am happy to say that we seldom found any area needing attention.

Thanks to team leaders, like Margie Stanley in packaging, cleanliness was maintained at each work station. At the end of a shift, our official clean-up crew was on site scrubbing and polishing like a "white tornado." One of the U. S. D. A. inspectors told me that he and his colleagues referred to our plant as "The Hospital" because of its spotless appearance!

Learning Computers

After two years of work, I encountered my first computer terminal in the office of Ingolf Nitsch. Ingolf had taken over the position of production scheduler. In an attempt to keep up with the times, my brother, Mike, and I enrolled in an introductory computer course.

Upon completion of this class, Mike Zelski asked me to work only half of each day in Q. C. and the other half learning data entry the "Ingolf" way. Since the course had been devoted largely to computer theory and history, my "hands-on" experience started at Minor's.

Initially, I was inputting daily production and packaging figures which were calculated by the supervisor. Then I began signing out orders according to the inventory displayed on the Brecksville warehouse screen.

As luck would have it, I had only been working on this schedule for a few weeks when "Ingy" announced that he would be going to Germany for a month! During Ingolf's absence, Norbert Urban, our computer programmer, called regularly to ask if things were running smoothly. Norbert was a brilliant young man who single-handedly wrote the varied programs for our IBM system while he was still in college.

When Ingolf returned, he asked me to work full time on the computer in inventory control. Though I missed my job in Q. C., within a few months I felt comfortable running all the available computer programs, including the time/cost information stored for monthly financial reports.

As plant operations continued to evolve, I felt that modification of some programs could make them more efficient. When I approached Norbert about this, he asked me to outline what I wanted altered. We then met to discuss my ideas and Norbert developed an ingenious way of changing just a segment of a program, rather than rewriting it entirely.

After a few more years, Ingolf was promoted to Assistant Vice President of Manufacturing. He needed someone for the production scheduling position. My nephew Dorsey Fields got the job and became my new supervisor.

My dad gets all the thanks for prompting me to join his employee force before the company was sold. It was during those years that I appreciated the value of two of the principles expressed in Dad's business philosophy. First, he treated all of his employees with respect, honesty, and caring. Secondly, Dad's integrity and commitment to customer satisfaction required that every L. J. Minor product be superior in quality.

Chapter 36

Working in Packaging, Quality Control, and Research & Development

by Mary Minor
(1977-1984)

Introduction   A Day in Packaging   A Day in Quality Control

A Day in Research and Development   A Tour of the Plant   Conclusion

Quote from Aristotle

"Youth has a long time before it and a short past behind it."

Who Lives Longer?
(Irish Humor by Hal Roach)

O'Toole asked the doctor if it were really true that women live longer than men. The doctor replied:
"Yes, particularly widows!"

(Editor's Note: My wife, Whitney, and I were students at Michigan State University when we first met Mary Minor. We were attending a dinner in 1971 with Dr. and Mrs. Minor. As we sat chatting, the subject of piano lessons was discussed. Being only eight or nine, Mary was being encouraged by my future wife, Whitney, who had studied piano when she was that age. Today, Mary and Whitney still remember that conversation and wonder where all the years have gone. She was a beautiful girl back then, and she provides another beautiful story here regarding the L. J. Minor Corporation.)

Introduction

As the youngest of eight children, my experience at the L. J. Minor Corporation began many years after the business was established. I applied for a summer job in 1977

349

and was 15 years of age at the time.

George Hvizd was plant manager and Mike Zelski was Vice President. They interviewed me for a position as packager. George expressed how important it would be for me to display high performance skills, to be punctual, and responsible. He made it very clear that there would be no preferential treatment shown to me on the basis of my being a family member. In fact, he told me that other employees would be watching my performance closely, and thus, I would be scrutinized like a goldfish in a bowl.

Being offered the position, I was to stay with Minor's for seven years. In later years, I was to be exposed to Quality Control and Research & Development as well as packaging. This is a story of what factors helped to make the company a success. It begins with a day in packaging.

A Day in Packaging

There were two packaging shifts at this time. Day shift ran from 7:00 a.m. to 3:30 p.m. and night shift ran from 6:00 p.m. to 2:30 a.m. I worked days. After arriving at the plant and getting clothed in your "garb," which consisted of a white uniform (your choice of a dress or pants/shirt), steel toed shoes, an "OR" cap (this is like a cloth shower cap), and a work apron, you were ready to punch the time clock.

Next you would check the production schedule. This informed you of how to plan your day, what equipment and utensils would be needed, and what type of containers, boxes, lids, labels, and bags would be used that particular day.

The overall orchestration of the production area was run by none other than my sister, Ruth Ann, who was in charge of production scheduling. There were others in the team with whom I had the pleasure of working.

Bart Katuscak overlooked our work and made sure all machinery was running smoothly. There were five packagers, and our team leader, Margie Stanley, was not only a dedicated employee of very long standing, but she was also a lovely person. She demonstrated very good leadership qualities. She knew the ropes and set the pace for the team.

Margo Rivera, Confi Massa, Mary Sealy, and I made up the day shift packaging team. Interestingly enough, packagers were always women. Of course, the guys would help us if we needed it. To be a good packager, you had to be patient, accurate, strong, quality minded, and fast. These women possessed all of these characteristics and one more, possibly the most important. This was a sense of humor.

The work was demanding, but my co-workers were a riot and the time would just seem to fly. The packaging assistants varied, but our "main man" was Victor Quinones. He really respected us and made our work more enjoyable. He was a gentleman and kept things on an even keel in the area. I guess you could say he was our stabilizer.

Others I would like to mention are Rich Hern, Jerry Hord, and Gilbert Cortez. These men were essential to the overall performance of the packaging department. If they were not efficient at setting up equipment needed for the day and having all supplies available for us, such as the cases, containers, etc., all of production would be thrown off.

Smooth production was insured by good communication skills, and everyone doing their part efficiently. Even though we all had our duties, we all helped each other out. None of this "it's not my job" business went on here. We worked together to get the job done.

Having introduced the workers, I would like now to explain how packaging was done. Normally, a different product was packaged each day of the week. Chicken and beef may be done more often, but seafood and mushroom bases were always done on Friday. Yes, my parents are Catholic!

Employees would always say how stray cats would follow them home on Fridays. The aroma from the fish, lobster, clams, and shrimp seemed to penetrate through your skin.

Following is a typical production schedule for the day shift, which was planned, as I said, by Ruth Ann:

450 cases 1 lb. Chicken Base (12 containers to a case)
25-50 lb. Pails Chicken Base
50-25 lb. Pails Chicken Base
110-10 lb. cases Chicken Base (2 containers to a case)
75-5 lb. cases Chicken Base (4 containers to a case)

If we finished our schedule before 3:30 p.m., we could work on these:

20 cases Chicken Gravy Prep
15 cases AuJus
25 cases Samples

One never had to worry about running out of things to pack as Ruth could always find more! Heaven forbid you try to convince Ruth that she may have overdone it on the schedule. She would pile more on. She was the wrong person to go to for sympathy, as far as work goes. She had a favorite saying if you complained to her, she would tell you to "offer it up to the poor souls in purgatory," then she would tell you in so many words to get to work. Yet, Ruth was a "hands-on" supervisor. There were many times we would have large orders to fill, or would be shorthanded and Ruth would put her work aside to lend us a hand.

The employees looked up to Ruth and admired her for her determination, honesty, sincerity, and dedication. I do not believe Ruth had any formal training in management, but as far as I was concerned, she was the best and put to use many of her own managing techniques that were very effective.

Something Ruth displayed always and equally with each employee was respect. She also was excellent at communicating. She was a very good listener, and could sometimes read between the lines. She was very intuitive and loved her work and her employees. This love diffused through the plant and resulted in high employee morale and conscientious output of work. I have heard from many people, that since Ruth has gone, the atmosphere in the plant is just not the same. They say no one is indispensable, but Ruth proves this saying wrong.

Before the days of plastic, the one pound and sample containers of product were packed in glass jars. The bulk containers (10, 25, 50, and 100 pound) were fiber drums lined with a plastic bag. We could fit about 30 cases of glass jars on our one packaging table. However, before using the jars, each and every one of them was labeled on a labeling machine by a remarkable woman, Julia Perez.

She worked in the back of the plant where there was no air conditioning, only a fan, and she used to have to spray the back of each label applied to drums with adhesive before applying it by hand. She also had to manually punch the batch code number on every label. About 1981, self-stick labels became available saving a tremendous amount of time.

The cases of jars would be brought to packaging. After sanitizing the table, we would start to empty jars onto the table and vacuum the inside of each jar out. This procedure was done to assure the sanitation of the jar.

One of the packaging assistants would fill our packaging pump with the base. This entailed using a special machine to lift the 350 pound bowl and empty the product in the funnel shaped pump. One packer would pump the product into the jars. There was a foot pedal for this.

Another one or sometimes two packers would weigh jars. Margie was extremely fast and accurate at this job. She would slide those jars one by one over that scale so quickly. I was in awe!

Another packer would apply the jar lids. This may sound easy enough, but believe me, this took a good strong arm and lots of speed. Margo and Confi were tops at this.

After applying the lid to the top of the jar, a special hand held machine was used to screw the lid on tightly. This machine spun very quickly and really vibrated. It was difficult to hold onto for an extended period of time.

After lids were on tightly, the jars were placed in the cases. Each case was hand-stamped with the name of the product it contained, and the batch code number would have to be visible on all cases.

We would stack the cases three high and send them down the conveyor to shipping, where the cases would be sealed and stacked on pallets. Packing the larger quantities of bases was quite another matter. All drums would have to be labeled and stamped with a batch code number and then lined with the appropriate size plastic bag.

All these drums used to be packed by hand. None of us had to workout in those days, since we had biceps that would put Arnold Schwarzenegger to shame! We used plastic scrapers to lift the product out of the large mixing bowl.

These bowls were very deep, so you can imagine that as you got closer to the bottom, it was more difficult to lean over and lift the product out. Fortunately, we did not have to lift the 100 or 50 pound drums. We would take the scale off with the empty container on it, then fill the pail. The scale would be set up level with the conveyor. The 10 and 25 pound drums were stacked before being sent to shipping.

Different procedures were used for different products. Liquid products such as Consommé and Au Jus used to be filled by hand utilizing quart measuring cups and funnels. Caps were then applied and tightened with the manual machine.

Around 1981, a very large vat was purchased to hold the liquid products. A new packaging technique was put to use. A long metal shelf of sorts was set up under 12 spigots that were attached to the vat. The packers would place 12 bottles on the shelf under the spigots and then depress a lever, which would lower the spigots into bottle necks and fill with product. This also was a great time-saving procedure. We could now pack 12 containers in the time it took to pack one!

There were two drawbacks. Sometimes a bottle would not be lined up just right and the liquid would spill. Also these spigots sometimes leaked. So after the filled bottles were removed, they would need to be washed off before being packed into the cases. Oh well!

Gravies and dry soup mixes required another packaging method. The product was dumped into the pump, as with the bases, but the product was packed in foil-lined bags. These products were extremely hard to weigh because of the consistency of them.

Again, one packer would fill the bags, usually two packers would weigh the product, then another would seal the bags with a small heat-sealing device that was controlled by a foot lever. You could only seal two packages at a time, and would have to hold this heat-sealer down for approximately one minute to get a thorough seal.

This just about completes our day in packaging. As each portion of the packing schedule was completed, the packaging room and table would be sanitized and all equipment and utensils used would be delivered by packaging assistants and/or packers to the pan room for complete cleaning and sanitation.

While in the packaging room, I learned the importance of good communication skills and what the meaning of a team effort is. I was amazed at how consistently hard these people worked on a daily basis, and how efficient they were. For the most part, they all carried a very positive attitude to work with them.

Some of the tools that were used by the company which I believe helped in this efficiency were the use of a very detailed organization chart, excellent team leaders, outstanding planning on the part of the production scheduler and inventory control personnel, open lines of communication between production scheduler and foreman, foreman and packaging assistants, foreman and team leader, and work incentives.

For example, if you were on time for work and present at work every day for three months, you earned a paid day off or $100 cash. Another perk was receiving your choice of a large turkey or ham on holidays, plus boxes of nuts as gifts for everyone. Summer bonuses were also paid in addition to year-end bonuses.

The key motivator I believe was being acknowledged by my mother and father and knowing they truly appreciated and were grateful to each and every employee. They would visit the plant on occasion and would always chat with the employees, not just management. The best reward was seeing them walk through those doors into the packaging area with smiles that lit up the place. To see them personally greeting, thanking, hugging, and caring for their employees was so wonderful. It is so necessary to feel appreciated, and to be seen and heard!

A Day in Quality Control

Quality Control's two main functions were to assure that the highest quality standards were being met for all ingredients as well as the finished product and to monitor the maintenance of proper sanitation of all equipment and work areas within the plant.

Blanca Nieves, a very dedicated, sensitive, and quality minded lady headed up the department. In my opinion, a better candidate could not have been found.

Some qualities that are needed as a quality control staff person include honesty, precision and accuracy, thoroughness, keen senses, especially olfactory and gustatory, for testing products and raw materials, and confidentiality. Blanca possessed all of these qualities. Her interaction with the plant employees was unique.

The quality control staff are sort of like the "game wardens." They must inspect all equipment before it could be used. If the sanitation of this equipment was not up to "snuff," the item would be tagged with a "hold" label, which meant not usable. The equipment would then have to be thoroughly cleaned and sanitized again, then reinspected by quality control before it could be used.

Another function of the Quality Control department was to keep accurate records of all batch weights, formulas, batch code numbers, etc. I would have to say that Q. C. is one of the essential components of a successful foodservice business. The higher the standards, the better the overall functioning of the facility and finished product.

Employees sometimes would take offense if a piece of equipment they had cleaned was tagged. So, of course, their hostility was directed at Q. C. Blanca took the brunt of this resentment, and may I add, in a very graceful way. I always admired her patience and tolerance. I think her motto must have been "Silence is Golden."

(Editor's Note: In support of what Mary is saying, the Bible is very clear regarding why Blanca has been so successful on the job. One verse says, "A gentle answer turns away wrath, but a harsh word stirs up anger" (Proverbs 15:1). Also, another Scripture teaches us how we need to respond when people around us are complaining and criticizing others. It says, " . . . let every one be quick to hear, slow to speak and slow to anger; for the anger of man does not achieve the righteousness of God" (James 1:19-20). As we can see here, Mary's comments regarding "Silence is Golden" are indeed wise.)

There usually were three quality control staff persons. Ms. Vokt, R. D., and Sharon Shrader also worked in Q. C. It was important that staff members were somewhat compatible as their work area was very limited. The room was off limits to other employees and was located off the packaging room.

It would put you in mind of a science lab. It had counters on three walls, and shelves full of test tubes, scales, books, cooking utensils, etc. I would estimate the floor space to be about 10' x 4'. It was small but the job that was performed there was essential.

Looking at what went on there, on certain days of the week, raw materials would be delivered. When I say raw materials, I am talking about some of the product ingredients including sugar, salt, oleoresins, meats, flour, etc.

Our responsibility was to take samples of all of these items and run them through standardized tests to assure that the quality met our specifications. If not, the items would be rejected. Some of the qualities that may be checked for included freshness, date of expiration, color, aroma, flavor, weight, solubility, density, and others.

Each product had its own specific test. After the raw materials were checked, you would document your test results. A log was kept for all materials and batches. Another function of the Q. C. department was to sample all the finished products before they could be packaged. We would take two 2 ounce samples of each batch of product.

These were tested for quality. Some of the characteristics that were checked for included color, aroma, flavor, concentration, consistency, weight, and solubility. All the criteria had to be met before packaging could begin. We inspected all equipment that was cleaned in the pan room and made sure that machines were properly sanitized before use.

If a product failed to meet criteria, as stated previously, a "hold" tag was placed on it until the problem was remedied. Unfortunately, there were times that no remedy could be made, and the product would have to be discarded.

We had to strictly enforce personal hygiene rules, too. Hand washing was a top priority. It was very similar to what you see in a hospital. There were sinks installed near every work area requiring you to wash your hands after eating, returning from the restroom, picking something up off the floor, sneezing or coughing, and before sanitizing anything. Disposable plastic gloves were also available for use.

With the guidance of Mom and Dad, Mike Zelski, and Nancy Clancy, I began my education at Cuyahoga Community College My experience went hand in hand with what I was learning in school about foodservice operations, writing specifications, procurement of food products, sanitation, etc. I feel fortunate to have been exposed to Q. C., as I was studying nutrition in college.

My course on "Nutrition for Consumers" really sparked my interest. I went on to pursue an associate of applied science in dietetic technology. As you probably know, many of the duties of a dietetic technician revolve around food, food procurement, food prep, food handling, food storage, menu planning, nutritional analysis, and therapeutic diets, to name a few.

A Day in Research and Development

When I was offered a position part-time in R & D to receive some hands on experience in some of these areas, I was very excited. R & D was located outside of the plant in a separate building that looked like a regular house. There was a nice simple kitchen located on the first floor, along with a room that resembled a dining room, and , on the other side of this room, there was located an office.

Ruth Engler, Jan Williams, Bev DeLaney, Michael Minor, and others were some of the professionals with whom I had the honor of working. The dietitians here performed administrative duties. They developed new formulas, worked on the nutritional analysis of products, did extensive research, implemented some of the in-services for plant employees, attended numerous dietetic and foodservice seminars and shows, found new sources to procure food items from, wrote specifications for products, helped develop new products, helped write books on menu planning, and developed low-sodium recipes.

Jan, Bev, and I worked together the most. Nothing slipped by these two ladies. They were very conscientious, extremely organized, creative, and quality minded. They seemed to thrive on their work. It was apparent in their attitudes and dedication that this was much more than just a job to them. Jan had a laugh like no other which was music to our ears. These people's love of life was contagious and they were a joy to be around.

If Mike Minor were not walking through the plant, "relating to" the employees, you would usually find him busy in the kitchen in R & D. He seemed to have fun no matter what he was doing. At this time Mike was working on developing fish base and dry roux. What is so neat about Mike, though, is that he is a very humble person. He does not like a lot of recognition and attention.

In the morning, I would sometimes ride to work with Mike. He was up when the "cock" crows, and would arrive to work about 5:30 AM. I would still be half asleep, so he would roll all the windows down and crank up the country music full blast. I was always awake by the time we arrived!

Then, if you had the pleasure of working with Mike in the kitchen, you got to listen to his jokes and songs all day. I remember one in particular that went like this: "Nothin' could be fina 'than to work with Michael Mina' in the Mooo-oor-ning!" What a trip. Needless to say, the atmosphere in R & D was quite relaxed most of the time. It was kind of "homey" at times, and library-like at others.

Because the activities varied so much from day to day, a typical day in R & D is more difficult to describe. The day might start out with testing raw materials that may have been questioned from quality control.

Then you might work on writing some specifications for certain products such as beef, pork, fish, etc. You might make calls to distributors to have information sent regarding their products, so they could be compared with comparable products. Developing recipes for the products was a priority, as was taste-testing the products and recipes.

One of my main functions was to help Maureen Beyer set up the taste panel. There were at least six members of the taste test panel. This testing was done every afternoon. Members of the panel were Ruth Fields, Mike Zelski, George Hvizd, Ruth Engler, Jan Williams, and Bev DeLaney.

The purpose of this panel was to test certain products or newly developed recipes. This was one of my favorite jobs! I especially enjoyed the days we tested lobster bisque, potato leek soup, chili, and cream of mushroom soup! This was not a good place to be if you were watching your weight, believe me!

Evaluation sheets were filled out by each member of the taste panel. Some of the characteristics we judged included appearance, consistency, aroma, color, and taste. Each member of the panel would judge the product, then discuss the results. If improvements needed to be made, suggestions would be offered. This was a tremendous learning experience for me.

A Tour of the Plant

The efficiency of the plant was due in part to the layout of the facility. At the plant's entrance, or the front of the building, was the shipping department. This was run by Mike Whalen. Products to fill orders were kept here as well as samples.

Next, through double stainless steel doors, was the packaging room. This was a large room measuring 30' x 45'. It housed three large Hobart mixers, about twenty very large mixing bowls, the packaging table, machines used in packaging, the conveyor leading to shipping, scales of all sorts, and all packaging equipment.

Just off of the packaging room was the production scheduler's office, quality control (also known as Quality Assurance, or Q. A.), and the ladies' restroom. Heading to the middle of the plant now, you enter a narrow hallway. Along one side were two cooking rooms, where Mario Quinones was our main meat cooker.

Physically, Mario was small in stature, but man was he strong. His job entailed lifting large pans of extremely hot poultry in and out of the steamers. I would estimate that one of these pans weighed 80 pounds or more. He must have had a high tolerance to heat as this room was extremely small with a large oven and large vat. The temperature must have been 110 degrees plus, I am sure. He would stand in the hall when the meat was cooking to be relieved. What amazed me the most was that he did not complain. He made light of situations and enjoyed his work.

On the other side was the chicken picking room and a third cookroom. If I had to say what the worst job at the plant was, I would have to say picking chickens. I have a respect for these women like no others.

There was a large table in this room with some stools around it. After the poultry was cooked, the meat was delivered to the chicken picking room. The meat was then removed from the carcasses, by hand. You wore plastic gloves, but you still burned the heck out of your fingers. Then the juice would be all over, running down your arms. These women, who all spoke Spanish, wore plastic coats over their regular uniforms and were pros

357

at what they did. I remember walking by this room and hearing them speaking and laughing. I always wanted to take Spanish so I could converse, yet, the chicken picking room was always one place I tried to steer clear of!

Meat and other products were weighed out by a husky woman named Anni Fleig. As far as I know, she was the only woman who could handle this job. The pans of meat were extremely heavy. They would be put in plastic tubs, weighed, and then placed on tray carts to be put into the cooler until needed.

Next, you would enter a larger room in a very loud and busy area. This was the pan room. A man named Steve Veres was in charge here. He and his assistant, Larry King, had a very important job. They were responsible for washing all the utensils and equipment within the plant. Some of these items were very heavy, such as cooking pans, large plastic receptacles, mixing bowls, etc. These men wore rubber type boots and plastic coats over their uniforms. The chopper/blender room was in this area opposite the pan room where all meat, seafood, and poultry are chopped.

The batchmaker's room was also off of the premix area. This was where all the ingredients were combined to make the finished product. There were usually three or four batchmakers. My nephew Dorsey Fields had this job at that time. Dorsey was a "Jack of all trades." I think he has done it all. He began work at a young age and has been with the company about 15 years. He looks as if he will follow in his mother's footsteps. The other batchmakers were Bill Hoke, George Rivera, and Rick Perez.

There is a very large warehouse which is where the raw materials were received and stored. Tony Camargo was in charge of receiving. This job required good planning skills and safety was a must here. The materials were stored on pallets, three shelves high, about 20 feet in height. A fork lift was used to transport and store materials. There was a huge walk-in cooler and freezer located in the warehouse. This area also housed all the boxes and containers. Boxes were actually made in the warehouse. This job was done manually by a couple of employees including Jim Wiggins and Dan Hvizd. Each box was folded and then stapled by a manually operated foot pedal apparatus. These guys had some leg muscles on them!

Another job which was carried out in the warehouse was labeling. At the very rear of this building was the foreman's office, the cafeteria, and the inventory control office. The break room as we called it, or lunchroom, had an atmosphere all its own. One of my favorite parts of the day was morning break. At 9:00 a.m., a canteen would arrive at the plant full of junk food. This was truly an experience. Some of the hot sellers were very large breakfast rolls, chips, and packaged sandwiches. It amazed me that these small women could pack away two or three doughnuts and a bag of chips just before a large lunch at 11:30 a.m. Where they put it, I will never know!

We would all congregate in the break room where there was a smoking and a non-smoking room. It was a relaxing time, where we could chat, vent our frustrations, laugh, read, play cards, make plans, etc. Problem was it passed quickly as we only had 15 minutes. At least it was long enough to regroup and prepare for the next two hours prior to lunch.

358

Inventory control was being coordinated by my sister, Josephine, at this time. Josephine was also the plant "comedian." She could get a laugh out of anybody. I still can see her doing the "Southside Shuffle" through the plant. She never was speechless (that has not changed) and would lift others' spirits by her comical expressions. She has a flair for making people laugh.

Another unique part of the plant was the flour building across from shipping. While I was there, the job of toasting the flour was done by an elderly man by the name of Arthur Tubbs. This building gave off an aroma of freshly baked bread, and it was always nice and warm. Art worked alone in this area, and never seemed to mind. He would stand outside the building to get relief, and chat with employees who may be passing by.

Above R & D were the plant secretary and plant manager's office. A conference room was also located here. Our plant secretary Diana Nieves welcomed visitors, salespersons, answered incoming calls, dealt with correspondence, and handled many other aspects of the business. She was a very people oriented person and very sweet. Her disposition and attitude were gentle and kind.

The company secretaries were headed by a wonderful Irish woman, Nancy Clancy. I think she will be proclaimed a saint one day! Her daughters, Bridget Clancy-Bell and Nancy Shramek, daughter-in-law Cheryl Clancy, Mary Ryan, Ceil O'Donnell, Rose Capezzuto, Judy Ward, and Katie Brockmiller comprised the office staff located in the Bulkley Building on Euclid Avenue, Cleveland, Ohio.

These women were very closely knit. They worked, dined and socialized together. There seemed to be an excellent rapport between these ladies, Mike, and the clients. Some of these ladies' duties were payroll, accounts receivable, receiving orders, answering employee questions regarding health or dental insurance, explaining vacation pay, workman's compensation, retirement plans, etc. They were very knowledgeable about many aspects of the company and had outstanding personalities. It was always a joy to talk with any one of them. Whenever you were in a slump, you could pick up the phone and talk with one of these ladies. They were always happy to help solve problems and they had a calming affect on people.

Conclusion

In closing, I would like to express the best way I can what the L. J. Minor Corporation was to me, and list some of the factors that made the business the success that it was. My experience at Minor's was much more that just a means of making a living. This was my first job experience and was a personal growth opportunity.

What I benefited the most from was learning to work as part of a team for a common goal. This has helped me in all of my pursuits such as education and employment. I truly believe that one of the greatest assets the company had was the diversity of culture. Cleveland is known as a "melting pot," and the plant was just that.

Some of the cultures seen within the plant were Puerto Rican, Irish, German, Polish, and African-American. Our differences were complementary as we learned from each other, shared different life experiences, were introduced to a variety of ethnic foods, and learned to respect others' beliefs and values. I feel my life was enriched by these people and their cultures.

There were many family members employed at the plant. Many companies would not allow such a policy. I feel the company benefited from this too. If a study were done, I think that many of the long timers at the plant had relatives also employed there. Margie Stanley, Ruth Fields, Margo Rivera, Julia Perez, Victor Quinones, Blanca Nieves, are examples of this.

There was a cohesiveness between the employees such as I have never seen anywhere else. They not only worked together, but also socialized outside of work on a regular basis. We became like a family. As I said earlier, my parents always displayed an attitude of appreciation and respect. This resulted in high employee morale, which in turn resulted in better work performance.

My parents also encouraged people to further their education. They implemented a program within the company to help foster this love of learning. Any employee interested in attending school would be reimbursed for his or her tuition if it was a related field of study. Employees could choose the school they wanted to attend. The only stipulation was that a 2.0 or higher must be obtained.

Even though my parents are no longer involved in the L. J. Minor Corporation, their outstanding business ethics, values, and love of their fellow man have undoubtedly left an indelible mark on the company, its employees, and all associates and friends of the company. I would like to express my gratitude to my parents, as well as to all employees I encountered along my journey at the L. J. Minor Corporation. My memories are happy ones and my life has truly been enriched by this experience. With love and gratitude, then, I write of these experiences and wish the best for each of you!

Chapter 37

The Good Years Continue

by Dorsey Fields
(1977-1995)

Early Memories   After the Company was Sold   New Responsibilities

Quote from Charles Walgreen

"We believe in courtesy, in kindness, in generosity,
in cheer, in friendship, and in honest competition!"

Shedding Light on The Subject
(Irish Humor by Hal Roach)

Two little boys were traveling on the train for the first time in County Cork. They took out their lunches, and began to eat, just as the train entered a pitch black tunnel.

"Have you eaten your banana yet?"

Asked the first boy.

"No."

Replied the second, and asked:

"Why?"

The first boy said:

"Don't touch it! I took a bite out of mine and went blind!"

Some Advice on Eating
(Irish Humor by Hal Roach)

"It is not the minutes at the table that make you fat, it's the seconds."

Early Memories

My work experience started with the L. J. Minor Corporation in 1977. Little did I know that fifteen plus years later, I would not still be with the Minor's!

When I was very young, around 5 or 6 years old, I remember visiting my mother in the plant. There were so many nice people including "Chubby," who used to cook beef, and several ladies who would be packaging samples and one-pound jars in glass. I grew up listening to conversations my mother had over the phone. She would continue to the late hours giving instructions to supervisors. She was the most dedicated, hard-working person in the company, and she was mother!

The first actual work that I performed was in the area of "box-making." We would come in on Saturday and Sunday for 8-10 hours to stamp and assemble corrugated boxes for the upcoming week's production.

At this time, the company was small. The majority of employees were located at the manufacturing facility with a small corporate office in the Bulkley Building. The boxes were assembled and stored in an old apartment building next to the hardware store, off West 25th Street. Later, a new warehouse was completed and all dry storage was moved there including raw materials, canned goods, some equipment, all corrugated boxes, and chemicals.

Gilbert Cortez was the first employee I worked with and he trained us well. Cases, once assembled, moved from storage on pallets across the parking lot to the packaging area for finished goods. All distribution was done from a small warehouse area adjacent to the packaging area.

From 1978-1982, I worked on weekends in assembly and during the week in case assembly and packaging. Job descriptions were not clearly defined so when we were done with our regular duties, we would assist in other areas including packaging, clean-up, or whatever needed to be done.

Work hours for our group were 3:00 p.m. to 9:00 p.m. I usually worked four days per week after school, but the company was very flexible regarding the schedule for high school activities such as sports.

In the late '70s, we were not highly automated with equipment or computers, as compared with today. However, the company was well managed from a quality and cleanliness standpoint. There was also a strict adherence to standards in all areas of production, packaging, and clean-up. We were all well trained by other employees and supervisors before taking on any new responsibilities.

My first supervisor was Tom Mele, a man I truly loved! He was not only a great

Lewis J. Minor with mother Kathleen, cousin Thomas A. Ryan, father Newell W., and son Bryan, age 8.

Lewis J. and Ruth E. Minor's home, 20877 Fairpark Drive, Fairview Park, OH (moved to in 1951).

Joseph Bertman, General Foods Distributor, Cleveland, OH.

Bertman Foods, E. 76th Street, Cleveland, OH, 1951, General Foods Distributor. Site of original L. J. Minor Corporation (outside of building containing a room approximately 18' x 20').

West 115th Street, Cleveland, OH. Site of second L. J. Minor Corporation processing facility, 1953-1961.

New product development was an ongoing goal at the L. J. Minor Corporation.

Dr. Thomas A. Ryan.

George M. Hvizd, Assistant Plant Manag

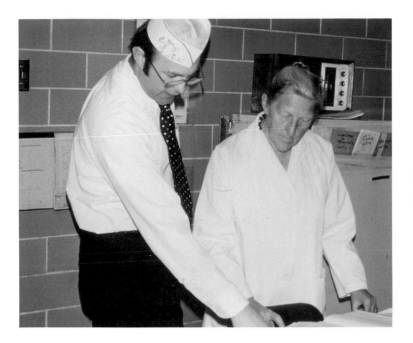

Ruth Engler and Mike Zelski discussing procedure specifications.

Mary A. Mele, Dr. Thomas A. Ryan, and Chef Emil Burgermeister.

Celebrating the move into Suite 436. (Left to right: Beverly DeLaney, Mrs. Ruth E. Minor, and Nancy Clancy).

Bryan G. Minor, age 17, inside West 115th Street plant.

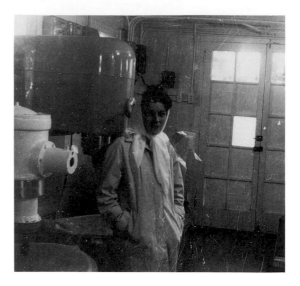

Kathleen M. Minor, age 18, inside West 115th Street plant.

Ralph A. Napletana.

Herman Taber at dinner given in his honor, receiving gift from Nancy A. Clancy.

Don A. Lutz.

2621 West 25th Street, Cleveland, OH. Site of third and present processing facility (outside).

2621 West 25th Street, Cleveland, OH. Site of third and present processing facility (inside).

MSU Agricultural Marketing Clinic, March 1963. Lewis J. Minor, President, L. J. Minor Corporation, William C. Mills, Jr., North Carolina State College Extension Poultry Specialist, Herman Busscher, Busscher's Poultry Company,

Lewis J. Minor, Ph.D. Degree, 1964.

Angell Century Farmhouse, 4023 Turner Street, Lansing, MI; residence of Lewis J. and Ruth E. Minor from 1962-1980.

Group of original chefs affiliated with the Minor Corporation including Lewis J. Minor. (Back row left to right: George Marchand, Herman Breithaupt, Otto Denkinger, Harry Bazan, Michael Palmer, Emil Burger-meister, John C. Secter, Jean Caubet, and Pierre Bach. Front row: Dave Swanson, Ernest Koves, Lewis J. Minor, Thomas A. Ryan, and Newell W. Minor).

Dinner at the Angell Century Farmhouse with Emil Burgermeister, Newell Minor, Eric Swanson, Jean Caubet, Ernest Koves, Lewis and Ruth Minor and others.

Lewis J. Minor, and to his left, Eric Swanson and his wife Hazel.

Michael S. Zelski.

Dr. Lewis J. Minor and Ruth E. Minor with Michael Zelski, Plant Manager.

Group picture of plant employees on break, October 1977.

L. J. Minor Corporation National Sales Conference, Michigan State University, August 31 through September 2, 1981.

L. J. Minor Corporation National Sales Conference, Michigan State University, August 31 through September 2, 1981.

2621 West 25th Street, after renovation of purchased building, with two refrigerated trailers used; one for storing packaged product, setting up orders, and shipping dock, and the other for storing raw materials needing refrigeration.

New receiving warehouse under construction, August, 1977.

New receiving warehouse completed, October, 1977.

Dr. Lewis J. Minor made regular visits to the plant.

Ruth Engler and Joe Thomas checking products
for storage testing.

Dr. Lewis J. and Ruth E. Minor at Cleveland office. (Left to right:
Ingolf Nitsch, Michael L. Minor, Jack Cassidy, Lewis J. Minor,
Michael S. Zelski, Ruth E. Minor, Gen. John D. McLaughlin,
Herman Taber, Dave Swanson, Nancy Clancy, and Ralph Napletana).

Group of original chefs affiliated with the Minor Corporation. (Left to right: George Marchand, Michael Palmer, Herman Breithaupt, Jean Caubet, Otto Denkinger, John C. Secter, Harry Bazan, Emil Burgermeister, and Pierre Bach).

Group of original chefs affiliated with the Minor Corporation. (Front row left to right: Herman Breithaupt, Emil Burgermeister, Ernest Koves, George Marchand, and Walter Wingberg. Back row: Otto Denkinger, John Todd, Harry Bazan, Alec Cline, and Jean Caubet).

Kathleen Minor Swanson.   **Hermann Rusch.**   **Chef Jean Caubet.**

Lewis J. and Ruth E. Minor granted U.S.D.A. Inspection for West 25th Street facility. (Left to right: Chef Emil Burgermeister, Audrey Chubbs, Thomas A. Ryan, Ruth E. Minor, Inspector Emil Kralik, Lewis J. Minor, August Erb, Dr. Romaine, U.S.D.A. District Head, and Ronald (Joe) Gilbert, Plant Manager - 1961).

Dr. Lewis J. Minor making presentation in memory of Chef John Secter at Johnson & Wales University.

Dr. Lewis J. Minor shaking hands with Walter Luftman of the Culinary Institute of America. Photo includes other members of the CIA and General John D. McLaughlin (second from left).

Dr. Lewis J. Minor speaking with Brother Herman E. Zaccarelli with Mrs. Minor to left.

Men responsible for having the status of the executive chef changed from domestic to professional through the U.S. Department of Labor. (Bottom row left to right: Dr. Lewis J. Minor and Louis Szathmary. Top row: Edwin Brown, Richard Bosnjak, Gen. John D. McLaughlin, Jack Braun. Not shown, Ferdinand Metz).

Lewis J. Minor with General John D. McLaughlin, Dr. Ernest Koves, and Dr. Lendal H. Kotschevar.

Nancy Clancy, Director, Customer Service, receiving Key Employee Award. Presented by L. J. Minor Corporation President, William F. McLaughlin.

Dr. Lewis J. Minor accepting Diplomate Award.

Dr. and Mrs. Lewis J. Minor at dedication/opening of the Lewis J. Minor Technical Center at West 25th Street location. Included in photo left to right: Lewis J. and Ruth E. Minor, Cleveland Mayor George Voinovich, General John D. McLaughlin, and Cleveland Councilwoman Helen Smith.

Dr. Lewis J. Minor and General McLaughlin with Officers of the British Army Catering Corps School, Aldershott, England, 1978.

Dr. Lewis J. Minor discussing meal preparation with Instructors at the British Army Catering Corps School.

Dr. Lewis J. Minor and General McLaughlin inspecting food with Instructors at the British Army Catering Corps School.

Dr. Lewis J. and Ruth E. Minor with U.S. Ambassador to Ireland, 1980.

Minor employees and their families on their trip to Ireland at the Cliffs of Moher.

Commendation from Ohio House of Representatives, Office of Mary Rose Oakar.

Jan Papez, representative from office of Congresswoman Mary Rose Oakar.

Ruth Ann Minor Fields.

Inspector Emil Kralik in shipping warehouse checking proper product identification.

Ruth Ann Fields, Operations Manager, with Supervisors Dean Hunt, Daniel Mullen, Ernie Burgess, George Henderson, William Hoke, and William Weinmann.

Nancy Clancy and the Customer Service Team. (Left to right: Rose, Katie Brockmiller, Mary Ryan, Ceil O'Donnell (seated), Nancy Clancy, Judy Ward, and Diana Katuscak).

Dr. Lewis J. Minor giving presentation. Included in
photo: Michael L. Minor, Lavere Vokt, Janet Williams,
and Ruth Engler.

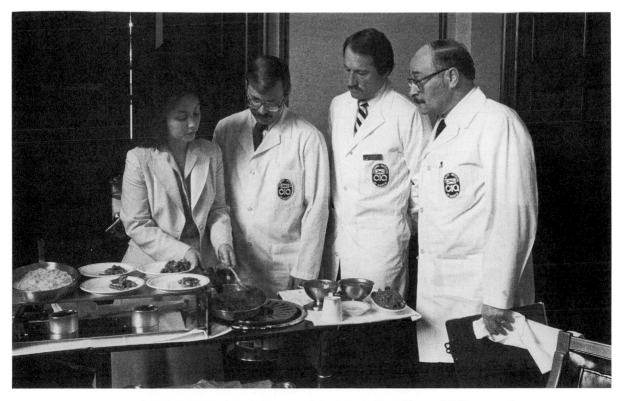

Chef Michael L. Minor with Chefs Ferdinand Metz and
Baron Galand, serving as judges for a competition held
at the Culinary Institute of America, Hyde Park, NY.

Minor's 1980 Culinary Olympics Team. Viktor Baker, Richard Walklete, "Tony" Takashi Murakami, Hans Bueschkens, Mike Minor, Bruno Zuchold, and Richard Tromposch. Not shown: Socrates Inonog.

Dr. Lewis J. Minor receives Gold Medal given to House of Minor by IKA (Internationale Kochung Aus Stellung), sponsor of the Culinary Olympics held in Frankfurt, Germany in 1980. Presenting Dr. Minor with the medal is Hans Bueschkens, Minor Culinary Olympics Team Manager.

L. J. Minor Corporation's 1984 Culinary Olympics Team. Hans Bueschkens, Bernar Urban, Dieter Kiessling, Bill DelaVantura, Ingolf Nitsch - Team Captain, Michael L. Minor - Team Manager, Hans Herzig, Saburo Shibanuma, Paul Ebling, and Milos Cihelka. The Grand Gold Medal is pictured in front of the team.

Michael L. Minor, Minor Culinary Olympics Team Manager, with Hans and Donna Bueschkens and Ingolf Nitsch during the 1984 Culinary Olympics in Frankfurt, Germany.

Carol Minor Walker.

Josephine Minor.

Mary Minor.

Dorsey M. Fields.

Ingolf Nitsch.

person to work for, but he was a friend. Tom gave us instructions prior to each shift and entrusted us to execute the schedule.

After a few months of working alone, Pat Clancy and others joined in box-making. We eventually had a crew of 3-4 workers each weekend. Tom Fisher helped us and worked during the week as well. He was older and seemed to complain a lot. I learned from him how not to treat fellow employees, yet, he was a good quality worker and it was good to be exposed to his demeanor - this was his value.

Larry King worked production during the week and also worked many weekends with us. He was a good person and worker, rarely complained and had a great sense of humor.

Tom Mele and Larry would like to give each other a hard time, so they kept things entertaining. We worked hard and long hours but always had fun. The Clancy boys, including Pat, Terry, Marty, and myself worked as a team. Terry became a good friend; we spent a lot of time together in high school and outside of work in sports and other activities. Terry was the best man at my wedding and will always be a dear friend. Rich Mahon is another friend who kept things "light". He continues to be a leader in manufacturing to this day.

During the weekend, we would prepare 2,000-2,500 cases per shift. Case sizes were many and varied with product names hand-stamped on each of four sides. Today, through new machinery, this is all done automatically.

Mike Zelski, George Hvizd, and Mike Minor were the upper management of the company. Gen. McLaughlin was President. Mike Zelski would always take time to talk with employees as he toured the facility.

Mike knew everyone personally and did a great job of making everyone feel they were a part of the team. He was a great manager, resulting in high employee morale.

Mike Minor is a stalwart manager and was a friend to everyone. Mike inspired employees to give their best quality and hardest effort. He leads by example! Through the years he has been a support and personal consultant. He is one of the most creative people in the company, with great product and service concepts. He, Mike Zelski, and Ruth Ann Minor Fields kept morale high.

Mother (Ruth Ann) was an important manager for the company at that time. she provided great front-line leadership to the supervisors and employees. Her tenacity and high standards for quality and cleanliness were an important driving force that all employees adhered to and upheld.

She had a good rapport with all U. S. D. A. inspectors and their management. They knew her standards were higher than their own. She also was a great friend to many employees who would go to her for counsel and employee assistance. She was the matriarch of the company.

Others who were supportive and effective at this time were Jan Williams, Beverly DeLaney, and Maureen Beyer in R. & D. Together with Ruth, they were important decision makers within the product development process.

I worked day shift during the summers from 1978-1983, usually in packaging under

Bart Katuscak. Most of my time was spent emptying bins, stacking cases, and bringing supplies to packaging.

Packaging was done mostly by hand, utilizing a semi-automated machine, that would place the plastic seal and lids on one-pound cups. This was slow and cumbersome with a much downtime as the machine would malfunction frequently. Anne Mahon, Margie Stanley and Confi Massa could run the machine better than anyone else, packaging 400-500 cases on a good shift.

All bulk packaging was done by hand. The crew consisted of eight people, six women who filled cups and ran the machine, and two men who kept supplies filled, maintained equipment, and emptied bins.

After the Company was Sold

In May of 1983 my mother picked me up from Bowling Green University and informed me that the company had been sold. She explained the reasons were in the best interest of the family. Nonetheless, I thought things would change drastically in terms of morale, but this did not happen.

Large additions to the facility were completed over the following years. Even though the morale and culture of a small, family owned business was still present, for everyone change was difficult.

The realization that change was inevitable and the family business years were over finally struck home. I decided to prove to myself that I could be successful without having the "family ties."

George Hvizd interviewed me in 1983 for a full time operations position paying $7.10 per hour. I decided to transfer to Cleveland State and began in packaging on the first shift. My supervisor was Bart Katuscak and a key working partner was Reynaldo Massa. He could assemble all the packaging equipment and pumps with his "eyes closed". He now works in maintenance and is a great contributor to quality.

Operations consisted of two shifts with the day shift working 5 days, scheduled for 8 hours, and the night shift working 4 days, scheduled for 10 hours. The day shift would set up the pumps, equipment, and packaging supplies at 6:00 a.m. for work to begin at 7:00 a.m..

The production crews started at 5:00 a.m. to set up 3-4 completed batches of base for packaging crews beginning at 7:00 a.m.. Our task in the morning was to assemble the seal and lidder machine for the one pound line, set up the packaging tables, scales, conveyor belts, turntable, bulk packaging lines, and bring in all supplies including cups, lids, cases, etc. At the end of each shift we tore down all equipment and pumps and worked in the pan room to help clean up.

It was important that we accounted for all parts before and after each shift. All tools for equipment assembly were stored, numbered, and locked with only one person per shift having a key. The packaging area was centrally located to the pan room, shipping area, cookrooms, and Quality Assurance.

Major equipment consisted of the buffalo chopper, seven steamers and two ovens for cooking, a seal and lidder for one pound cups, six mixers for dry blend and flour toasting, two kettles, a can opener, pan washer, and other equipment.

From the fall of 1983 for one year, I worked in the cookroom. There were two shifts with three cooks on each shift. I worked the day shift from 5:00 a.m. to 5:00 p.m.. During the next six months I worked a split shift.

A typical work week was 60 hours which was great for overtime pay. The day shift team included Mario Quinones, Bill Weinmann, and myself. Bill was fairly new with the company but was well regarded as one of the best workers. Mario was a veteran employee and a mentor to many.

The cook's position was physically demanding for several reasons including: exposure to high heat and cold temperatures during the same shift, heavy and awkward lifting, long hours, and burns and cuts.

Mario was prone to heat exhaustion and seizures. Room temperature would reach above 110°F with high humidity. We were constantly going from the extreme heat directly to the cooler to pan chicken or to the freezer to pull frozen stocks or meat.

We had real teamwork in the cookroom. Bill and Mario were great leaders and offered their learning experiences to others. Bill and I became friends and he has continued to be a leader and asset within manufacturing as a front-line supervisor. Individuals like Bill Weinmann have made the Minor Corp. successful.

The near catastrophe of 1984 is an interesting story. Fortunately, neither Bill or Mario were in the room chicken was cooked in and the deboning ladies were on break, so they were not in the work area. I was across the hall from the main cookroom in the room beef was cooked in.

A few minutes prior to the accident I had been in the room checking the beef stock reduction. The other kettle had been turned on (normal procedure) to prime for the chicken fat rendering.

The doors to the cookroom were closed and I was back to work when the blast blew open my doors causing me to fall and knock my head against the oven. I stood and I noticed pieces of plastic, metal, wood, and glass on the floor. What a "shock wave! The kettle being primed in the chicken cooking room malfunctioned causing the explosion that rocked the surrounding rooms!

The room was devastated! It was hard to believe the sight. After a few minutes everyone was gathering around the cookroom in disbelief.

Tom Arthur, who was the newly hired manager of engineering, really impressed me in the way he took over the situation with the fire department. Tom had us back in production the next day. The kettle's three steam release valves had all clogged from what the manufacturer thought might have been calcium deposits formed from the water used. We have used purified water inside the kettle jackets since that day.

The jacket had no release and had allowed pressure to build up within the thick, stainless steel walls. The explosion ripped the kettle inside out and lifted it off the floor, hitting the ceiling with such force that it damaged a steel beam across the ceiling. If anyone would have been in the room, they would have been killed. Thank God no one was injured.

Over the years, Tom Arthur has been a good friend. I have a great respect for him as a person and a manager. He is another superstar that separates Minor's from competition.

In the fall of 1984, I accepted a new position as first shift utility. The basic responsibilities were to fill in for all positions as needed and help as back-up/support for main processing areas including cooks, final blend, and dry blend.

It provided great experience with time spent in the following areas:

Distribution: Order picking, unloading and loading trucks, storing finished goods using tow motor, warehouse organization, scheduling trucks, and deliveries, etc.;

Final Blend: Operating the chopper, weighing ingredients including salts, sugar, oils, fats, stocks, meats, set up, and clean-up;

Dry Blend: Operating the mixers, set up, clean-up, weighing ingredients including fats, oils, and dry ingredients;

Cookrooms: Prep product, refer to prior text;

Packaging: Package product, set up, and clean-up;

Pan Room: Equipment clean-up, pan washing, bin washing, equipment storage, and chemical preparation;

Receiving: Unloading of trucks, storage of ingredients and packaging, staging of raw materials and packaging, warehouse organization, Q.C. of certain raw materials;

Flour Toasting: Toasting, grinding, sifting, set up, and clean-up.

The main purpose of this position was to fill in for others while on vacation or out for the day. Much of the time was spent in the main processing areas to relieve bottlenecks in production.

In 1985, the utility position took on added responsibilities of testing new products in production (pilot runs) and closer work with product development. I was responsible for testing new products and documenting the best process methods and formula adjustments.

Learning the different areas was important, but contributing ideas to improve each work area was just as important. I found that the employees who worked everyday within the specific functions were the experts and together we would suggest better methods and ideas to raise productivity and quality.

Employees I considered leaders and experts within their work areas included Mario Quinones, cookrooms; George Rivera, dry blend; Danilo Santana, final blend; Margie Stanley, Anne Mahon, and Confi Massa, packaging; Reynaldo Massa and Rich Mahon, packaging support, Charlie Mills and Chris Dionidis, distribution; George Henderson, sanitation; and Arthur Tubbs, flour toasting.

These people worked well with others within a team. We learned everything about the work functions from these leaders and supervisors. We always worked within the team environment.

In flour toasting, Arthur Tubbs accomplished this in a separate building next to a tire shop off West 25th Street. Pallets of 50 pound bags of flour were unloaded and stored in the back room next to two mixers. Flour was toasted, cooled off, placed in a chopper to chop large flour balls, sifted, and placed in bins. Approximately, 4-5 batches were toasted and completed on a shift.

The heat was unbelievable while the toaster was being emptied. This was the dustiest job with the exception of the dry blend area. Arthur worked alone in this separate building due to the higher risk of a dust explosion from the gas toaster. Later the toasting function was moved to the dry mix area when facility expansion occurred.

Distribution moved to Brecksville in 1984 with the acquisition of the old Oscar Mayer facility. The facility was basically doubled in size in 1992. I worked about two weeks total a year in Brecksville, picking and setting up orders. The great challenge was to see who of the regular crew could complete the most orders error-free.

We would set up 25-40 orders per shift depending on the load. We used two electric (important to use in food industry) forklifts to unload goods from Cleveland and move stock around the warehouse. We also had two electric and three manual pallet jacks. All orders were palletized and stretch wrapped with the exception of orders less than 500 pounds, which needed to be "stamped' with the customer's name and address.

Orders were logged and errors and damages tracked on a monthly basis. It was important to write the day codes for each product on the filed copy of the order in the rare event of a recall or customer complaint. Having the date code would allow Q. A. to check the shift and batch from which the product in question came.

Q. A. kept a sample library from each batch up to one year. Several products had to be put on hold for Q. A. release after seven days. Special red hold tags were placed on each pallet until we received word from Q. A. to release it.

During peak inventory build-up periods, particularly prior to shutdowns and major holidays in July and December, excess finished goods were stored in outside storage. This would fluctuate from 80-200 pallets of finished goods. The inventory build-up for a two or three week shutdown would begin about eight weeks prior and continue to build.

It became evident by 1988 that we had to make changes in the production cycles and overall operational philosophy to better manage finished goods inventory. We actually needed a larger distribution facility in 1987 due to the amount of finished goods inventory on hand but we were able to put this off until late 1992 due to changes made in production scheduling from 1986-1992.

Most people do not stop to think about how important warehousing and distribution are in completing the handling process to your customer. It is this group's ultimate responsibility to make certain the right product is delivered on time, in good condition, with every order. Operations can do everything exactly right, but if warehousing does not keep the case clean, undamaged, and delivered on time, all the effort is lost. This area is a "cost" center that should always be strictly controlled.

Mike Whalen, the distribution supervisor, did a good job of managing the truck lines and organization of the warehouse and logistics. The crew has grown from three on one shift in the early 1980s to two shifts of four employees.

The facility was doubled in size and three more loading docks added in 1992. Much of the paperwork and truck line communication is computerized and systems and software have changed this area of operation greatly over the past five years.

One day in the spring of 1986 I was working in the dry blend area and was requested by my supervisor to report to Dick Zirbel in upper management. The meeting was to discuss three new positions that were going to be available including production supervisor, human resource administrator, and production scheduler.

Ruth, Dick, and Ingolf Nitsch were responsible for providing me with the opportunity to select any of the three positions. I always wanted to be a production supervisor, but the experience and career opportunities gained from scheduling looked more rewarding.

Dick suggested working with Ingolf would be good experience. Ingolf suggested exposure and responsibilities with inventory and computer development were important. My hope was Bill Weinmann would have the opportunity to get the production supervisor position, which he did and has performed exceptionally well for the company. Bill's personality and leadership skills make him the best supervisor we have.

During the first day as production scheduler, I was informed by Ingolf that I would also be Josephine Minor's supervisor. Josephine and I worked well together and she was a great help to me in learning the inventory system and how to get things done with the supervisors.

Josephine is one of the most intelligent people I have ever worked with and was extremely productive. I really enjoyed working with her. As scheduler I was responsible for raw and finished goods inventory management, writing daily and weekly production schedules, assisting with inventory control and packaging schedules, and label programming. We would fill in for each other as needed.

Josephine's responsibilities included signing out all orders, relieving inventory, calculating and inputting production, inputting and updating formulas, inputting information for labor reports, running all production and inventory reports, both monthly and weekly, and calculating everyone's time cards for payroll. We used the main terminal in her office for our computing needs. It was a personal computer with programs written in BASIC.

Scheduling was an exciting position because decisions made needed input from sales and marketing and interfaced with every area of operations. The production schedule drove all aspects of purchasing, packaging, production, labor usage, distribution, and required good communication with Q. A.

Bart Katuscak, another great employee, and I were constantly at odds over changing schedules and lead-times for raw materials. The tough ones to schedule were make-to-order (MTO) items that required exclusive raw materials with long lead-times. At first we employed the philosophy that make to order meant do not do anything until the order shows up and then mandate a 30 day lead-time for shipment or delivery.

This approach worked all right for some customers, but progressively more industrial and chain accounts were moving to just-in-time (JIT) inventory systems and lead-times were being cut drastically. We also incorporated the philosophy of assemble to order (ATO).

In 1987 we began to approach our suppliers differently, requesting shorter lead-times, floor stock arrangements, and smaller minimum order quantities. Ideally, you want as high an inventory turnover as possible to move raw materials in quickly through production, finished goods delivered to customers immediately, payment received to allow for better cash flow, higher and lower interest payments, and return on invested capital (ROIC).

We found a lot of hidden costs in excess inventory that needed to be eliminated. This is still a primary focus today. The old philosophy of high inventory was tolerable to have focus on customer satisfaction and order fulfillment. By performing better sales forecasting and production planning, you can achieve both higher customer satisfaction while reducing variable inventory costs. Cost savings can be passed on to customers and price increases delayed.

We employed several tools and procedures to help better manage the overall manufacturing resources. A wise man, Bob Aherne, once told me "the profit centers of the company reside outside the manufacturing and corporate walls." In other words, every activity we do is cost. Perform only those activities that add value to your customer.

Our manufacturing processes became more complicated as the company was going through huge growth spurts between 1983 and 1993. The number of new products and complexities in formulation added new raw materials. The number of new procedure changes in production were awesome and continue through 1994.

By 1989 it became clear we needed more flexibility within the West 25th Street facility to manufacture smaller batch runs efficiently. We decided to create a "tactical" team with two new positions.

The team would produce and package all small orders from start to finish utilizing smaller equipment while the main plant operations ran the larger, standard productions. The tactical team stayed out of the main stream production and were able to efficiently produce these custom and non-standard products. This was a major competitive advantage for us to reduce inventories, lead-times, costs, and increase customer satisfaction.

As time proceeded, Ingolf picked up more responsibility and he passed more activities to me. Even though Ingolf and I did not always agree, I always respected his authority and great ideas. Ingolf taught me discipline, creativity, and organization. He is a friend and a great teacher of his own skills.

Josephine, Sharon Mullen, and I worked together for nearly a year before Josephine left and we hired Jean Leib to take Josephine's job. It took about three months to fill Josephine's position. It was tough to find the right person for this very important job.

Sharon and I worked eighty hour weeks to keep up with all the planning, inventory control, label programming, and scheduling activities until we hired Jean and got her fully trained.

From 1986-1990 we added a lot of new programs and complexities to the computer system and we were building the shell of a new system requiring us to load all information into the new system and run operations on both for about 12 months. Ingolf is an innovator. Our value was to tactically execute his concepts.

Sharon left in 1988 and we hired Scott Pearsall as the new production scheduler. I knew he would be a great asset to the company right away. I cannot say enough good things about both Scott and Dean Hunt and the great work they continue to do in production planning and scheduling. When the going gets though in a football game - you put the ball in the "warrior's" hands. Dean and Scott are great "ball carriers" for Minor's.

In 1987 I accepted the new position of production planning administrator. In this capacity I spent more time with corporate and technical personnel. It was clear that we needed change at a faster rate in manufacturing to meet the ever changing needs of our customer. For several years we managed in different functional "silos," which led to poor communication. The competitor resides outside your company walls - we forgot this concept at times.

Many new teams were implemented with some success in improving communications between staff and mid-management.

Bill McLaughlin was President at this time. He spent time in each of the different departments across the company to gain a first hand experience of where the "real" decision-making and value-added activities took place. He would see first-hand the dynamics of different groups. Bill is a leader of leaders. Bill is a visionary. I have tremendous respect for Mr. Bill McLaughlin.

A cross functional team was assembled that researched basic philosophies and methods for "World Class Manufacturing." The ultimate goal was to win the Malcom Baldridge Award and become "World Class." But we knew the most important goal was simply to strive for continuous improvement.

The movement brought back a greater awareness of our original "Guiding Business Principles" by our founder, Dr. Minor, and it did help with teamwork. We did not act on enough of the operational tactics quickly and at times there was no teeth behind accountability groups.

Having headed up several task forces within distribution, new product development, sales forecasting, and order entry, I saw the following and more accomplished:

370

Flexible Production Plans:	Added tactical teams and additional utility positions. Eliminated temporary help and moved to a part-time, on call pool to work up to 30 hours per week, among others;
Celina Facility:	Set up and trained all labeling and operations functions scheduling, inventory and production systems;
Systems:	Developed improved computerized label printing and production systems;
Inventory Management:	Increased turns, generating huge cost savings to company.

All of these activities plus more were accomplished as a team. Decision making was made by a "team with a head." Even though we needed the team's input and expertise, the final decisions had to be made by the leader, whether Ingolf, Ruth, Dan Mullen, me or whomever. It doesn't matter whether you are a gazelle or a lion in life - either way, you better be running hard when you wake up in the morning.

New Responsibilities

By 1991 I had received the full national marketing responsibilities and additional sales responsibilities for accounts in Ohio, Michigan, and Indiana for the industrial group. We executed a great customer survey that provided a wealth of information. We set it up to gain real, unbiased information from specific individuals. This helped us design new strategies for the following year that really paid off. My boss was Dr. Sam Lee, who was responsible for the industrial sales and marketing group along with being the head of technology. He is a person with great vision and wisdom. Sam taught me if your competitor wakes up at 6:00 a.m. - you better be up at 5:00 a.m.

New products launched from 1990-1993 included meat base concentrates, meat marinades, cheese bases, economy bases, herb concentrates, au jus concentrates, and a multitude of customized formulations for bases. Customers drove this process.

These flavors were usually based on customer specific needs. We launched the biggest new products at the national Institute of Food Technologists (IFT) Show in July. We would perform tasting demonstrations in application of flavors at the booth, produce new literature, publicize and advertise in trade journals, and do direct mailings to customers to create awareness.

The best way to present the product was and still is in a live demonstration to the customer. We might target certain customers with applications in mind to fit their new product development efforts.

Being involved with long term planning for the business segment was great experience, and by 1992, I was given more responsibility to develop strategic plans and new product development management with our own internal technical group and Nestle's research facilities.

In January of 1992, my new title was Manager of Business Development for Industrial. We needed an administrator and marketing assistant to handle all promotional and advertising duties and I began to work more closely on new product development projects with most large accounts nationally. Another stalwart employee, Denise Reed, took on new marketing responsibilities.

In June of 1991, Dr. Sam Lee was promoted to President of Food Ingredients Development Company (FIDCO) and Hugh Renck was promoted to Vice President of Industrial. Hugh was a good manager who did not know a lot about the industrial business but learned quickly. Hugh is a friend and nice person who has more common sense than most people. Hugh had been the national sales manager for the deli soup business and his position was being eliminated due to Stouffer's taking this business over. We were happy to have Hugh lead our "crusade".

In December of 1992 I was given new responsibilities as Western National Account Manager for Industrial when Bob Aherne retired. This was a good opportunity to manage our industrial brokers and develop value with large industrial customers. Then, in August of 1993, Bob Elliott asked if I would be interested in joining the foodservice group. I thought this would be good experience with the only drawback being a move away from Cleveland. However, this too became a benefit and learning experience.

The foodservice business is managed and operates totally different from the industrial and chain business. After traveling to the markets and meeting the brokers and distributors, I knew there would be a lot to learn and this was exciting to me.

The country is split into six zones. The zone I managed was the South and Central Texas, Arizona, New Mexico, Colorado, Wyoming, Oklahoma, Kansas, Missouri, parts of Nebraska, and Louisiana. Travel was intense, especially before we moved to Dallas, traveling about 70% of the time. A friend and broker told me Dallas is becoming the "center of the universe." I believe him.

The main responsibilities of the zone manager include development of regional sales and marketing plans, management of budgets and spending, management and training of broker sales force, development of key accounts, and interaction and management of key distributors in each market. I really enjoyed the zone manager position because it was fast-paced and there was a lot of responsibility in different management areas. Several great brokers and sales associates included Bill Hookersmith from San Antonio and David Stennes from Southern California. They've each added value.

We did a good job within the zone increasing sales and establishing a foothold for important new products like the newly launched low sodium bases and classic sauce concentrates. We had good relationships with several of the broker management and sales reps. Mike Manista helped sales reach record-setting growth.

After spending so many years at the plant or office, it takes an adjustment to move out on your own. Being out in the field in these types of positions is almost like having your own business without the high personal risk. Brad Alford, another great leader and tactical thinker, was instrumental in advising this career change.

In July of 1994, during a sales meeting in Cleveland, I met with Tracy Thomas, head of chain development. He wanted to make some changes and asked my opinions about some of the national accounts in Dallas. I asked him if he needed help since John Fagan was leaving and he offered me the Western National Account position. Tracy adds a tremendous value in terms of his vision and as a "ball-carrier" for the team.

This was a hard decision to make for two reasons. First, I had only been in the zone manager job a little over a year, and second, I really liked the zone job and was still in a learning mode.

After consulting my wife Cathy, who always provides great support and insight, Mike Minor, and others, I decided to take the job. The opportunity to have experience in three areas of sales and marketing is tremendous. I have found out very quickly, National Account Management takes a great deal of patience and constant follow-up and persistence. The opportunities are few but potential rewards for new business are great.

Project development is usually very customer and menu specific. It helps generate new product and service innovation. Most chain account customers are looking for signature items that can be made consistently in all their units. Most interface is done with the development chef or research and development groups, purchasing group, or food and beverage manager and customer marketing groups. Projects move slowly, usually 3-12 months before business is developed. It doesn't hurt to consult with your customers' upper management.

We are on the cutting edge of new product and system development for these customers. We are definitely a flavor development supplier, no longer just a base company! I have had countless good memories and great learning experiences with this company and all the teams. Our strength lies in differentiation and strong culinary and technical expertise. Our culinary innovation is unmatched.

The opportunity to leave the company has presented itself several times, but thankfully I chose to stay with the Minor team. I want to thank Grandma and Grandpa for starting a great company that has provided my family with a good living and a great many experiences. More importantly, I appreciate their guidance, support, and ideals as people who have influenced me as much as my own mother. I also appreciate the support from several special people during the hard times; including my wife, Cathy, my mother, Ruth, and Mike Minor. The company and the individuals I have been involved with have shaped my career and life. I hope my contribution back to the company and employees has been beneficial to them in return.

Our winning philosophy: "Be the customer company, through hard work, innovation, consideration, love and always provide service with a sense of urgency and fighting spirit!"

PART 3

L. J. MINOR: THE MEMORABLE YEARS

FROM THEN UNTIL NOW

REFLECTIONS AND FAVORITES

Chapter 38

L. J. Minor: The People Company

by Ingolf Nitsch
(1980-1995)

Going to Lunch	**A Position at Minor's!**
Enjoying the Work	**A New Position**

When Computers are Your Life
(Irish Humor by Hal Roach)

Doolin said to his pal Flanagan:
"I don't like to think of myself getting flabby. Let's just say that my hardware is turning into software!"

Getting the Job Done
by Lewis J. Minor

Don't always be seeing green fields - far away!
Don't be a dreamer,
Be a doer!

Going to Lunch

In the fall of 1975, I was in awe one day while sitting in a large lecture hall listening to my professor. It was my first quarter at Michigan State University, pursuing a major based on my dream of opening a restaurant some day. MSU is noted as a premiere school for Hotel, Restaurant, and Institutional Management and Dr. Minor's class was a required course in the program.

His life story, which he told with such conviction on that first day, silenced the audience and filled their minds with inspiration and challenges. He told of his company in

375

Cleveland and how he and his wife started from only an idea and very little money. Through their limitless efforts and with the help of their children and family, they built a successful business and made a good honest living.

Something about Dr. Minor and his story really intrigued me. I wanted to learn more about him. Gathering enough courage, I approached him after class and asked if he could perhaps find the time to share more about his life. Without hesitation, he responded "we'll get together for lunch one day." I remember the pride I felt from his acceptance of my request. Me, a first year student, one of hundreds in the class, was going to have lunch with the professor.

Dr. Minor stopped me as I was leaving class the next week and asked if I was free that day. The afternoon went by very quickly as we dined at a restaurant, Starboard Tack, just off campus. I listened for several hours as he chronicled his life. I was high for days afterwards as I reflected on what he had said and especially on his closing words. He had asked if I would be interested in assisting him with his classes.

My relationship with Dr. Minor, his wife and family grew over the next several years. There were class picnics at their home, class trips and other social and business events. I assisted Dr. Minor, my sophomore through senior years while also working as a student cook at Kellogg Center, an on-campus hotel.

During my senior year Dr. Minor invited me to join his company, but recommended I first attend Johnson and Wales University (J & W), a culinary school in Providence, Rhode Island. He felt the formal culinary education would round out my management degree and prepare me for working with the company's chefs. Having reservations of deviating from what was, until that time, a determined career path, I asked my parents for their opinion. They are traditional hard working European immigrants, who, without giving it a second thought, instructed me to follow my professor's advice. I would find out that fall how important that decision was.

A Position at Minor's!

After accepting an official offer from Mike Zelski, Executive Vice President of the company, I arrived in Cleveland on June 10, 1980. Sharing an office with Mike Minor and at the age of 23, I began my career as food production analyst. George Hvizd, the factory manager at the time, prepared a detailed training program that I was to complete over the next six months.

The hands on experience in the different production departments quickly provided me with a good understanding of the factory and employees. Like most new graduates, I was anxious and got involved in as many things as I could. I began by evaluating the effectiveness of existing processes and made recommendations for improvement.

There were many very impressionable things from those first few weeks. I was addressing everyone by their last name when Mike Zelski told me that he and everyone else could be addressed by their first names. It was tough getting used to but I remember it made me feel welcome and comfortable. The feeling of family was strong. There weren't many salaried employees.

At the time there were 23 factory employees producing approximately 1.5 million pounds of product in 12 basic flavors. Products were available in one pound and net weight (larger volume) containers. The company switched from glass to plastic containers just before my arrival. Samples remained in 4 oz. glass jars.

We all worked out of an old house attached to the factory via a warehouse. Conditions were tight but we didn't mind. The building was approximately 20,000 sq. feet nestled within the center of a city block to where a passer-by would not even know it was there. This was good because our policy was that we didn't allow anyone in unless they were employed in the factory. Not even corporate or sales people were allowed in. On a couple separate occasions Dr. Minor was denied egress by an employee who didn't recognize him. Dr. Minor complimented each of them for their compliance to policies.

Jan Williams, who was in charge of product development, and her staff, including Beverly DeLaney, Maureen Barendt Beyer, and Mrs. Ruth Engler were all wonderful to work with. It didn't take long to feel like part of the family.

While still at J & W, I was informed that the company would send a team to Germany that October. Mike asked me to be the administrative coordinator of the team that he captained. It was a hectic three months preparing for the trip, but we were successful in coming home with 3 gold, 4 silver, and 1 bronze medals.

That summer, I worked with both Mikes in the design of our new dry and final blend rooms. Dr. Minor didn't believe in over extending himself from a financial standpoint, so most of the building projects were done in phases. It was exciting working on this capital project, my first of many to come. We were planning on adding a dry blending room, final blending room, cooler, freezer, and a shell for a future kitchen and additional final blend room. I didn't realize while I was at MSU how valuable my facility design classes would turn out to be. We worked with a local architectural firm that the company had used for it's previous expansions.

The installation of our new final blend machine, which was purchased earlier and put into storage pending this expansion, allowed us to move from small batch sizes of 300 pounds or less up to 700 pound batches, with the entire emulsion made in one step rather than several. We were using three and four high chambered steamers to cook chicken and roasted our meats in ovens.

There was a lot of manual labor involved, from preprep through packaging the product. Many changes have been made since. We still use a conservative approach to the justification of new equipment or any automation. The diversity of our products' consistency does not lend itself well to automation. With the wide range of bulk density, it is difficult to find equipment that will measure within tolerances. Much of our equipment has been purchased overseas and "Minorized".

Quality and consistency were my focus for choosing projects to work on. A major project was the standardization of formulas and process procedures. We computerized formulas and procedures that were previously typed and printed them on 3X5 cards that were laminated and issued to employees. We still mandate that employees work from formulas and procedures in their possession and not from memory. The "Pocket-Sizer" as we referred to them, helped assure consistency. Our next evolution will be to have formulas, procedures, pre and post operations on line, real time.

We are a U. S. D. A. inspected facility and are the flagship for them in the Cleveland area. We're inspected twenty-four hours a day, seven days a week, with the exception of Saturday and Sunday night. Our relationship with them has always been an honest one and one of mutual respect. We're proud to accept recommendations for improvement and welcome their comments as a partner, not an adversary.

The sanitation of the facility and the personal hygiene of the employees were extremely important. Quality Assurance (Q. A.) routinely trained employees on the practice of good handling procedures. Chemicals and sanitizers were custom selected and used to provide the safest possible environment for a food plant. Today we use an aggressive approach in training employees on how vital it is to be in the know when it comes to good manufacturing practices. Each employee is trained in basic sanitation and specially trained on how to clean their own work stations.

In early '83 I focused my attention on our time sharing computer which was a popular service in the late '70's to mid '80's. Cost constraints prevented ownership of a mainframe and forced us to use an outside service. We needed to jump on board with the new PC and software technology available. After hearing from several vendors that they couldn't supply what we were looking for, we decided to strike out on our own.

Mike Zelski's trust in me was admired and appreciated. He approved my recommendation to hire Norbert Urban as our programmer and to design and program our own system. Little did I know what I was getting us into.

Norbert was a recent high-school graduate and a new friend I had made since arriving in Cleveland. He came on board in February and we were off. I designed the system and Norbert wrote the code. Within six months we had accomplished what the software pros said couldn't be done. We had a system that handled materials from receipt through finished goods shipment.

That same basic system with only a few bells and whistles added over the years is only now, ten years later, being replaced. The switch still hasn't been turned off. Though it isn't integrated with the corporate financial system it has taken us a long way in the management of the factory.

Norbert and I spent many long days that ran into the early hours of the next morning during the time we programmed the system. It was a real challenge, one that we all learned a lot from. Josephine Minor, Dr. Minor's daughter, was our first major user of the system. As inventory control coordinator she was the key operator of the system. A wonderful person to work with, Josephine kept the factory and especially our office alive. Her favorite motto, though not reflective of her performance, was "garbage in, garbage out". I have repeated that phrase many times to many individuals since.

When Ruth took over production operations, I moved to production scheduling in 1983. Until that time, we produced beef base on one shift and chicken on the next. Orders were piled high at times waiting for product. And it was worse during certain periods of the year when there was a chronic shortage.

We created our first "master schedule" in hopes of improving the throughput of the factory. Considered a radical change at the time, we introduced an "alternate week" approach. We began producing chicken one week and beef the next. Most functional areas realized significant improvements in efficiency. It would be the first of what has been an annual adaptation by manufacturing to the continuously changing market demands.

Minor's aggressive annual growth beginning in the mid '80's, coupled with new products and changing customer demands, forced us to learn how to quickly adapt our operations. These changes, which at times were quite radical and exciting, were not always at first received with total understanding by the work force. However, commitment, regardless of the level of understanding, was always 100%. Employees were excited over the company's success and they knew decisions were made in everyone's best interest.

Master schedules are determined by balancing factory resources and customer demand. It maximizes the efficiency of the factory while minimizing inventory levels and factory throughput fluctuations. It normally results in employee schedule changes. It is one of the keys to the successful and continuous attainment of new factory efficiencies.

Enjoying the Work

Minor's was a real "people company". All levels of employees were considered as part of the company family. Dr. & Mrs. Minor were very generous and understanding of individual needs. Merit increases, benefits loans, etc. were all done with generosity and feeling. I personally was helped several times in different ways and greatly appreciated it.

Christmas parties with spouses were always enjoyable as were the annual awards banquets. Many of us traveled annually to Chicago for the National Restaurant Show. We had many special dinners with company friends. William Della Ventura whom I met while on our first Olympic trip and is now a close friend, was the executive chef at The 95th. in the John Hancock Building. We had most of our functions there for many years or at the Cleveland Athletic Club. Billy and I entered several culinary competitions at the show. Other trips included ACF conventions which were held in different locations every year.

My wife and I were visiting my parents in Michigan in the Spring of 1983 when I got a call from Mike Zelski requesting that I return immediately to Cleveland for a company meeting. I remember being very troubled by the nature of the request but never expected what would be announced. The room was filled with the key management personnel. Anticipation was high!

Mike Zelski announced that due to health considerations, Dr. Minor was selling the company! Selling the company? My heart sank! What about Mike Minor? I had always thought he would take over the company. Apparently Dr. and Mrs. Minor had their reasons

379

for soliciting outside suitors. Within months we were owned by a handful of investors from the East. The two key players, Walter Luftman and Jim O'Neil, were quite unique individuals. We would become very thankful to them for the hands off approach they used.

Gen. McLaughlin, the man who had taken the company national became President. Mike Zelski left the company shortly thereafter as did George Hvizd, the factory manager. Richard Zirbel, a gentleman with a long history in the food production business joined the company as the Vice President of Operations. I was still in charge of production scheduling at the time and heavily involved in the design of our long overdue cookroom. We had fears that the new owners would not understand how desperately we needed it. We presented our justification and permission was given to proceed.

Given our size, we found it difficult to find equipment manufacturers that could provide equipment with the capacities we required. We eventually decided to use a manufacturer out of Denmark. It was to be a modern facility that allowed us to process poultry in their own juices, dry roast meats, sauté vegetables and seafood, and concentrate juices. There were no comparisons to the old individual chamber steamers we were using before or the old convection oven we used to roast our meats.

Chris Garbers our industrial engineer and Greg Abramovich his technician worked for months adapting formulations and writing new process procedures including sanitation and safety procedures, employee training, and many other details needed to be completed before we could start up. We were successful with our attempt and soon the kitchen was producing very efficiently.

After his first year, Mr. Zirbel told me that in order for me to advance my career, I would need to supervise people. Agreeing, he promoted me to manager, manufacturing services. I was responsible for procurement, production planning, human resources and warehousing and distribution. Ruth continued to manage the operations side of the house. I enjoyed working with the individuals in my new team: Bart Katuscak - purchasing agent; Dorsey Fields - production planner; Lori Foss - human resources and Mike Whalen - warehousing and distribution.

Mr. Zirbel was right, managing people was a different experience. It was exciting and I had a lot to learn. We began a strong focus on team participation and continue that approach to this day. A great deal of my continuing education focuses on leadership.

Dorsey was promoted to production planner, my previous position. He took the challenge and continued heading the factory towards greater flexibility. He's a maverick in his own right and continues the tradition of innovation, motivation, and dedication today in chain sales. Dorsey and I became good friends during those early years and though I don't see him often now, I reflect on those times often.

The company sent another team to the Culinary Olympics in '84. This time I went as a participant and was successful in achieving gold medal status. All together we came back with seven gold medals which allowed us to be awarded the Grand Gold, the first U.S. company ever having done so. It's a real experience sitting in an auditorium filled with participants listening for your name to be read along with the medal status you had won.

It was an emotional high hearing "gold medal" after my name. This was to be the last Olympic competition the company would enter.

Our personnel philosophy has been to promote from within the company as much as possible. All of our supervisors worked as hourly employees before accepting their new positions. They play key roles in the effectiveness and efficiency of the factory. Originally assigned to fixed functional areas, they now rotate between disciplines. This practice wasn't very popular with them or their employees but it has dramatically increased their effectiveness. They now understand what the required relationships need to be between production and packaging.

On December 31, 1986 the company was sold to Nestle Enterprises Inc., part of Nestle S.A., the world's largest food producer. It was a panic situation once announced that the current owners were taking advantage of the tax law changes. They needed to get out before the year ended and we needed to find ourselves a suitable white knight. Time was short! After blitzing the market of potential suitors, the company had to open its files further than was appropriate. Competitors and many others wanted us.

The White Knight turned out to be Jim Biggar of Nestle Enterprises, Inc. Sight unseen, only through his relationship with Dr. Minor, Jim purchased the L. J. Minor Corporation and added it to the Nestle family. NEI has merged with Carnation since then and we are now part of Nestle U.S.A. Though we are one of the smallest companies held by Nestle USA we are still quite independent.

We have our own marketing and sales departments, do our own product development work, and utilize our own warehouses and distribution system. We are currently a very flexible manufacturer of hundreds of customized formulas for the foodservice, chain and industrial markets. The factory itself is over 100,000 sq. feet and has over a hundred employees.

Paste bases are still the primary product along with dry gravies and sauces. Several of the original employees from when I joined have recently retired but there are still many that continue to contribute as they have all along.

A New Position

In 1987 I was promoted to Vice President, Manufacturing and assumed responsibility for the entire factory. After Ruth's retirement in '89, I decided not to fill her position but have the supervisors report directly to me. Dan Mullen became lead supervisor, and was responsible for coordinating operations. Dan's talents and dedication served the company well as they still do today. He is currently the manager of process control which includes the responsibility for daily production and developing commercially reproducible formulas.

Flavor additions were the largest part of our new growth. Contrary to today we did very little customization during the '80's. Though we did have some industrial customers, the product they purchased was only a slightly modified standard product. Today, the largest part of our growth is in the custom formulation work for chain and industrial customers. We currently have several hundred formulas including paste bases, dry gravies, and liquid sauces.

Employees are still at the top of my priority list. We implemented a comprehensive program that allows for employees to receive 80 hours of training annually in team process solving, fundamental or advanced education, safety, sanitation, operations, and job learning. Employees are paid to attend their classes which are scheduled during a normal working day.

Establishing an environment conducive to the promotion of creativity and professionalism is critical. Too rigid, and you dampen creativeness; too relaxed, and you create contentment. In interviewing new employees, I always ask if they've ever seen the TV series, Mash? That's how I would describe the people within our Manufacturing Group. These men and women are as professional as they come. They have the drive and commitment of personal sacrifice to get the job done and done right. They do all of this, and they enjoy it! They laugh, joke around, and at times can get pretty abusive with each other, but in the end they always respect each other. I wouldn't trade it or them for anything. The factory efficiencies gained and our ability to quickly adapt to new market demands is a result of the superior staff at the factory. It takes a team of hard working, intelligent people to be successful and we are blessed with a great many! I'm listing several groups of individuals and the year they started at Minor's as recognition for their loyal dedication.

My senior management team includes Bart Katuscak, Procurement Manager - '75; Dan Mullen, Process Control Manager - '78; Mike Whalen, Manufacturing Logistics Manager - '77; Ron Gasper, Value Engineering Manager - '90; Lori Foss, Manager Employee Services - '86; Elsie Harmody, Staff Assistant - '86.

Our top notch junior officers that continue to drive improvements include Steve Warner, Associate Buyer - '89; Michelle Matun, Administrator Process Development - '90; Scott Pearsall, Administrator - Production Planning - '89; Dean Hunt, Assistant Administrator Production Scheduling - '81; Dan Hoy, Warehousing Supervisor - '87; Tim Thomas, Sanitation Technologist - '87 and our superstars that have moved up from the hourly ranks include: John Petro, Operations Training Technician - '85; Richard Hearn, Loss Prevention Technician - '79; and Moses Cruz, Personnel Coordinator - '93.

Our floor supervisors include Bill Hoke - '83, Bill Weinmann - '82, Jerry Hord - '81, Wes Janke - '89, Wanda Cortes - '86, Greg Abramovich - '80 and Carl Horn - '87.

Our diehard support staff includes Barbara Schanz, Receptionist - '79; Beverly DeLaney - Manufacturing Services Coordinator - '76; Barbara Krupar, Inventory Control Coordinator - '94; Drema Meeks, Process Development Coordinator - '86, Kenny Bockmiller, Process Development Technician - '84, Janet Kelly, Purchasing Coordinator - '90 and Jean Witherspoon - Manufacturing Administrative Coordinator - '92.

Others include Tom Arthur and his Engineering and Maintenance Staff and Linda Kahle and her Quality Assurance Staff.

The people and I always look forward to visits from Dr. and Mrs. Minor. I'm very proud to show them all of the progress we've made from a capital, business, and people standpoint. We all love and respect Dr. and Mrs. Minor for all of the wonderful opportunities they bestowed upon us. Thank you!

Chapter 39

Research and Development

by Janet H. Williams
(1975-1986)

Serving on The Taste Panel
(Irish Humor by Hal Roach)

The newly wed Mrs. O'Brian said to her husband:
"I have a piece of cod for you that will melt in your mouth."

Mr. O'Brian said:
"I told you before, you have to let it thaw out first."

An Invitation

During a sunny day in early May 1975, my home phone rang. On the other end of the line was Mrs. Ruth Engler, consultant with The L. J. Minor Corporation. I had worked with Mrs. Engler in the early '70s during my employment with Stouffer's Management Food Service and Restaurants - Inns Divisions. She was Director of Quality Control for both Divisions. I first met her in her role of conducting Quality Control Checks in my MFS unit of operation at the First National Bank of Chicago. Later she was my supervisor for three years while I was working as Administrator-Staffing and Training for Stouffer's Restaurants -

Inns Division.

She asked if I was interested in a part-time research & development job working with her at Minor's during the summer and fall months. I always admired Mrs. Engler's high quality standards and her many contributions to the Stouffer Corporation. I missed working with her both professionally and personally. I jumped at the chance. I soon met Mr. Michael Zelski in the corporate office at the Bulkley Building in the Playhouse Square area of Cleveland, Ohio.

The interview quickly turned into an induction into The L. J. Minor Corporation. Mike was very proud of working for Dr. and Mrs. Lewis J. Minor and enthusiastic about the future opportunities with the Minor company. He gave me directions to the employees' "Coffee House" next to the Minor's manufacturing plant on West 25th Street where I was to meet with Mrs. Engler.

When I arrived, Mrs. Engler greeted me and showed me through an apartment-size kitchen, two employee dining rooms, and into an office having a large desk, book shelves, and a filing cabinet.

Mrs. Engler described the six month consulting work she performed from early May through late October each year for Minor's. In 1974 she worked on developing a soup mix-- Split Pea Soup Mix with Ham using a modified smoky ham base. This year, 1975, they were continuing development of the special ham base and starting the development of Potato Soup Mix with Leeks. She assigned test kitchen work for me to perform with these products. Thus began my 11 year career with Minor's.

During the next several weeks I conducted test kitchen work under Mrs. Engler's direction. We prepared finished soups with experimental formulations and variations of reconstituting directions. I prepared variations of dairy products with water for determining the best flavor and consistency of Potato Leek Soup. Soon we initiated a program of reconstituting all the Minor's manufactured products for evaluating ease of kitchen preparation and quality attributes of the prepared products for flavor and product consistency.

Taste testing evaluations were performed by the Minor's staff. A key employee who contributed much to the quality standards process was Ruth Ann Minor Fields, daughter of Dr. and Mrs. Minor. Ruth has keen sensitive taste buds and can identify flavors of the ingredients used in manufacturing the Minor's products. Ruth was so very helpful to me during the eleven years that I worked in R & D at Minor's. I'll always be grateful to Ruth for her patience, guidance and support.

My Work Begins

My knowledge of the functions of foodservice ingredients was the bridge for learning the functions of food processing ingredients (raw materials). My background experiences and training with Stouffer's and my MSU graduate work, especially my master's thesis of "Standardization and Production Control in Quantity Food Service", became invaluable resources for me at Minor's.

The information we gained from these quality attribute evaluations performed by our in-house staff, was used by Mrs. Ruth Engler for developing written descriptions of the Minor's Bases, Preps, and Mixes and for the corresponding finished products. I used the knowledge we gained for improving the product direction copy of each manufactured product.

Next we developed and organized a test kitchen program for preparing and evaluating the quality functions and attributes of the raw materials used in the manufacturing of the Minor's products. Later this program was expanded to include incoming raw material test samples from our current and new ingredient suppliers.

Anyone assigned to work in R & D was expected to participate in the program for learning the flavor, aroma and other quality characteristics of each raw material. Gradually we all became familiar with the ingredient qualities of each raw material that provided the flavor profiles of the Minor's products. Eventually we developed a quality assurance program for evaluating the incoming raw materials purchased from our suppliers.

With the exception of Dr. Minor, none of us were food scientists. We quickly learned that we could count on the leadership of Dr. Lewis J. Minor, Chairman of The L. J. Minor Corporation, to provide the technical direction we needed for product development work.

I first met Dr. and Mrs. Minor in June of 1975 when they came to visit the manufacturing plant and meet the new R & D assistant working with Mrs. Engler. We invited Dr. and Mrs. Minor to join our product evaluation taste panel. During our discussion we reviewed our current work and R & D goals. They gave us excellent feedback of our work and directions for future R & D projects.

My familiarity with the Minor's Food Bases had first started during my employment at Stouffer's, as these were the bases used in the Stouffer's Standardized Recipes. There I had developed confidence in the Minor's Bases and enjoyed working with them. The Food Bases always gave us excellent flavor results in the Stouffer finished products served in the Restaurants and Management Food Service units.

Dr. Minor's "Business Aims" from the start of his company were selling "quality products that are consistently controlled to insure uniformity" and giving " the customer exactly the product that he specifies". I was thrilled that I had the opportunity to become better acquainted with Dr. and Mrs. Minor and to learn firsthand about their business goals and how the business had developed from its beginning.

Taste evaluations of the Minor's reconstituted products were important activities to the members of the Minor family, for the parents as well as the children, and later the grandchildren. Many members of the family were involved in determining the flavor qualities of the manufactured products.

Taste Panels

After my orientation to all the Minor's manufactured products, Mrs. Engler directed me to initiate a working taste panel for getting input to our R & D assignments. As a start, Mrs. Engler contributed a score sheet that she had developed during her Stouffer employment as Director of Quality Control. The quality attributes for the Minor's products evaluated included flavor, aroma, consistency, color, and appearance and was based on a nine point scale ranging from "like extremely" to "neither like nor dislike" to "dislike extremely".

The employees who participated at the regular working taste panels represented quality control, production scheduling, manufacturing, and research & development functions of Minor's and were expected to be regular members. A quorum of five members was the requirement for conducting panels three times per week. Those people whose schedules did not allow them to be available that often were asked to be alternates for the regular members when they had days off.

Responsibilities of the regular working taste panel included: 1) to consistently evaluate experimental testing of new and/or improved product prototypes for further product development work; 2) to evaluate test samples of new raw materials for using in product development; 3) to recommend product development ready for the Finished Product Approval process; and 4) to evaluate recipe development products for Minor's labels.

The Finished Product Approval process involved two evaluation groups titled, the Preview Approval Group and the Final Approval Panel. The members of the Preview Approval Group were Mike Zelski, Executive Vice President, Mike Minor, Corporate Executive Chef, Ruth Minor Fields, Production Manager, Mrs. Engler, when she was in Cleveland, and myself. We would select the best two to three experimental prototypes for approval consideration. Duplicate test samples would then be sent to Dr. and Mrs. Minor.

The test samples were accompanied with a concise memo of explanation and sensory scoring forms. Dr. and Mrs. Minor would promptly complete the sensory evaluations and return the forms along with a memo giving their approval or rejection of the test products.

When the products were rejected, Dr. Minor always sent a written memo giving us direction for further product development work. Oftentimes they would ask other family members to participate in these evaluations and would also send us their sensory scores and comments. I always found these comments of value in performing the follow-up work from the Product Approval processes. The next steps for the approved products were developing the manufacturing formulas and the label copy for the packaging.

Raw Material Research

In the summer of 1976, Mrs. Engler recruited the second former Stouffer employee for research and development work at Minor's. Mike Zelski interviewed and hired Beverly DeLaney to join our part time R & D effort. Beverly started working with Mrs. Engler learning the Minor's products. Shortly after Mrs. Engler completed her six month consulting assignment for the year, Mike Zelski appointed me R & D team leader. Beverly and I started working together part-time on product development.

It soon became apparent to us that the raw materials were the building blocks of the Minor's products and that the flavor quality of the finished product was only going to be as good as the quality of the raw materials in the product. If we were to develop new products for the Minor's customers and prospects, then we needed to initiate a program for Raw Material Research in R & D

Many of Beverly's talents and skills were a match for this assignment. I knew we could depend on Beverly's keen attention to detail and her dedication to accuracy in her work. Beverly began her research by investigating new raw materials from our current suppliers. The following program developed:

1) Requesting test samples and written specifications of raw materials;
2) Preparing test sample cutting tests for bench tasting evaluations;
3) Selecting the raw material samples passing our tasting for product testing;
4) Preparing small batch formulations of products using the selected raw materials;
5) Conducting taste panels and shelf-life studies of these experimental products.

One of the current suppliers was the Joseph Adams Company in Valley City, Ohio, manufacturer of oleoresins of spices, herbs and vegetables. The late Joe Adams and his son Pat were very helpful to us in setting up our cutting tests for evaluating test samples of these very concentrated ingredients. With their guidance we designed our starch-water tests for taste evaluations. The first step is preparing a cooked sauce of flour and water; next making a blend of salt with a gram of the oleoresin. The final step is mixing the cooked sauce with the oleoresin-salt blend for tasting.

Product Development

In 1976, Beverly and I completed the R & D work for Potato Soup Mix (with Leeks) and two custom food bases of turkey and chicken for Teddy's Frosted Foods company which later was bought out by Weight Watcher's, Inc. In 1977 we developed two additional custom food bases of beef and lobster for the same food processing company.

Also, in 1977, Dr. Minor sent us an experimental formulation for Vegetarian Consommé Base, Chicken Style. We made a small batch and evaluated it at our taste panel. We all felt that the product was great and needed no further development work. The R & D work was completed for the product and sent to manufacturing. I was amazed that anyone could sit down and write a perfect formula without testing it...and was now convinced that Dr. Minor was a genius!

We completed the R & D work for Shrimp Base in June of 1977. This product development work became our prototype for the development of natural flavors in the

Minor's Food Bases. As we developed the Shrimp Base we focused our efforts on predominance of the natural shrimp flavor. Freshly cooked raw shrimp was served to our regular taste panel for evaluating the quality attributes.

Some of the members were more experienced with the flavor of freshly cooked shrimp than others. Panel discussions also helped the members identify the ideal quality characteristics. As we received shrimp test samples we evaluated these as well during our taste panels. When all the members had developed their taste acuity for shrimp, we evaluated the shrimp base prototypes.

During the development, raw materials were selected that enhanced and complemented or were bland enough to blend well with the freshly cooked shrimp flavor. We rejected any raw materials that would mask and overpower the natural flavor of shrimp. For taste-testing, the base prototypes were reconstituted with boiling water making shrimp stock. After we determined the preferred dilution level of 1 lb. to 4 gallons of water, we began our recipe development of Shrimp Bisque. Recipes were always chosen that highlighted the base flavors for the product label copy and our customer sales demonstrations.

Besides developing new products, we performed product improvement projects of the manufactured products. Often product improvement projects are not customer driven. I can vividly remember the improvement project for the LeChef Brand Gravy Preps! The Plant Manager, George Hvizd, told me that the sales representative from a large company supplier had just informed him they were no longer going to manufacture the modified food starch that we purchased from them. That future shipments would be stopped within two weeks. Minor's was using this food starch in several of their manufactured products. George wanted to know how soon R & D could recommend a replacement starch for purchasing.

It was fortunate that Beverly and I were working on the right raw material research project at the time. We had investigated food starches from several suppliers and evaluated the quality attributes of each test sample with the members of the taste panel. We had just finished selecting the best food starch samples and were in the process of making experimental Gravy Preps for evaluating the starch samples in gravies made from the Gravy Preps with the taste panel that very week! We concentrated our product development efforts on finding the preferred starch replacement and met our two week deadline for purchasing. I was especially pleased with the results of our work when I learned from Mike Zelski that Dr. Minor had not only approved the starch replacement, but had decided to change the Gravy Prep product line from the LeChef brand to the Minor's brand, because product quality had been improved.

In the late '70s industrial sales began, and a new product line was started for meeting the needs of the industrial customers and prospects. The current formulations of the Minor's Food Bases were modified to meet individual industrial customer needs; e.g. replacing an animal fat with a vegetable oil and the removal of MSG, etc.,

Our R & D activities now involved developing new products, reformulating for improving products, and modifying products to customer specifications. We needed a system for reviewing and determining the product development steps required for each product. A concern I had was that the employees in R & D, including myself, had limited knowledge and training of the steps required to develop a product ready for manufacturing.

To keep us on track and not allow any required work from falling through the cracks, I designed a product development chart and steps listing; a short version to use as a product development check off and a longer version to use as a training/communication tool with the R & D employees.

During the time I was research and development director, I used these tools faithfully in my work. A listing of the product development accomplished from 1976 through 1985.

Shelf-Life Testing

In late 1977 Maureen Barendt Beyer, a full time employee, started working fifteen hours a week in R & D. Her remaining work time was usually assigned to quality control work activities. After her initial training with Beverly DeLaney and me, she performed test kitchen and taste panel work assignments. The three of us worked together as a team in R & D and began to think of ways we could use our current facilities and equipment to initiate shelf-life testing.

We had an outside local micro biological laboratory where we sent product samples for analytical results, but we didn't have an incubator available to us for accelerated shelf-testing. Why not think about the shelf-life testing from the foodservice operator-customer point of view? If we could locate an ambient storage area that was typical of many foodservice storerooms, then we could start shelf-life testing with the Minor's Food Bases. We checked the room temperature of several storage areas and found the 80 degrees plus temperatures we were seeking on shelving near the ceiling area in the R & D storage/cloak room.

The design for the shelf-life test consisted of requesting a large enough quantity of a Food Base from the same manufacturing batch to place base samples in the refrigerator, freezer, and the ambient storage areas after the initial taste panel of the Base. Taste panels were then scheduled and conducted after intervals of 30 days, 3 months, 6 months, and 1 year. We evaluated the flavors and other quality attributes each time, comparing the control sample from the freezer with the refrigerator and the ambient temperature samples for any noticeable differences. Also micro biological testing by the local laboratory was coordinated for the same time intervals for each sample.

Tests were done for the standard plate counts, coliforms, coagulase positive staphylococcus, yeast, and mold counts. We never had problems on the shelf-life tests with the microorganism counts of the Food Bases. Our taste panel evaluation ratings did show some flavor changes over time with the ambient temperature samples. That's why we always recommended that the product labels state "Refrigerate Upon Receipt" for protecting the freshly cooked natural flavor of the Food Base.

As the base sales increased, the Food Bases were frequently shipped by truck to the Southwest and West Coast areas of the country. The warm temperatures and the trucking vibration seem to cause the bases to separate occasionally. So we designed a vibration shelf-life test to find out at what temperatures the bases would separate. Since I drove over 50 miles each way to work, and over some rough road, we decided to put the test pails in my car trunk for getting the vibration and ambient temperatures needed.

Design variables included tests for six months of warm and cold temperature weather periods, and for the more and less dense bases, representative of the base product line. We evaluated the quality attributes before and at the end of the six month test periods with the taste panel. If a base showed signs of separation, we designed experimental formulations modifying raw materials and/or processing methods to reduce/eliminate base separation.

The R & D Product Development Team

Maureen Beyer soon became a valuable member of the R & D effort. Two of Maureen's talents were her abilities to coordinate with others and to think and apply what she learned quickly. During the next five years, Maureen conducted the test kitchen and taste panel work.

While Beverly DeLaney performed the Raw Material Investigation of acquiring test samples and specifications, planning and scheduling the product shelf-life testing, and overseeing the evaluation results of the taste panels, I functioned as the R & D team leader and executed the product development work of new products, improving manufactured products when needed, and designing experimental products for industrial sales.

The product development work included doing all the copy for sample size, 1 lb. size, and net weight labels of each product as well as overseeing the label application process for getting U. S. D. A. approval of the meat and poultry products. We all wore many "hats" doing our product and recipe development work. It was a fun and exciting time during this period of company growth!

As business increased and more work was needed, we added man-hours to the R & D effort. Maureen gradually became full time in R & D, while Beverly and I began working four days per week. To make us more productive we hired another part-time employee. Gaynell Layton began working with us in early 1980 as the R & D attendant.   H e r responsibilities were housekeeping, grocery shopping for ingredients needed, setting up and serving taste panels, keeping equipment cleaned, storing samples and ingredients properly, and assisting preparation in the test kitchen. The late Gaynell Layton had high standards of cleanliness, was easy to get along with, and performed her work assignments well. She was an asset to our team.

Another person who started in R & D in 1981, working with us one day a week, was Marcia Fazio, a neighbor of Ruth Ann Minor Fields. We were fortunate to have Marcia, an experienced typist and office worker, perform the R & D typing of request letters for raw material test samples and specifications, copy for product labels, test kitchen forms, and testing how-to-instructions for foodservice and home size recipes. We looked forward to Marcia's arrival every Wednesday, when she performed the typing for completing our work.

Recipe Development

In early 1977, Chef Mike Minor started in manufacturing on a year long company training program that was developed for him by Mike Zelski. The first day that Mike Minor began working in Cleveland, he became a member of the taste panel. .We soon became well acquainted with Mike, as he also shared office space with us in the R & D area.

When the foodservice sales forces learned that a chef was working at the plant, they started requesting recipes for using Minor's products. The finished products of the Minor's Food Bases are ingredients to the foodservice operator/chef for use in their food preparations that are served to their customers. The primary value of the Food Base is enhancing the natural food flavors for increasing the tasting enjoyment of the prepared food dishes.

When food tastes good, customers will come back again. Foodservice sales needed recipes for sales demonstrations and competitive selling. Although Chef Mike Minor was working in his training program in manufacturing, he started using his creative talents and skills to begin a continuous recipe development process for selling the Minor's products.

When we had finished our first team efforts of recipe development, we had completed over 60 "Chef Developed and Kitchen Tested" standardized written recipes ready for printing. The two sales literature handouts included foodservice recipes for soups, sauces, gravies, entrees, and specialty menu items using 18 of the Minor's products. We had also provided input for four basic product applications for using the Minor's Food Bases:

1) As a complete stock or broth
2) As a seasoning and flavor booster
3) As a replacement for salt seasoning
4) As a baste for roasted, baked or grilled meats, poultry or seafood

Later we showed how to use the Food Bases for reducing the amount of salt, while adding natural flavor, in finished food dishes.

Minor's Training

We had been working with several of the Minor's chef consultants, designing glace concentrate prototypes for making a fish stock. These experimental glaces were similar to the product formula for Minor's Glace de Viande, a concentrated beef and vegetable stock. We had tried several different fish species, but were not achieving the clean taste of freshly cooked fish using this method. I decided to try making a Fish Base, rather than a Glace, and using a steam method for cooking the fish to get the flavor quality we were seeking.

392

At that point Chef Mike Minor expressed an interest in developing this product as a part of fulfilling his R & D assignment for his year's training program. Since Mike Minor already had experience in the manufacturing cook room, he decided to use the cookroom steamers. He cooked several fish varieties and made experimental fish base prototypes of each.

The taste panel evaluated the flavor and the other quality attributes both as a stock and in application as a sauce for each prototype. We selected one species of fish that we all agreed had the Minor's flavor quality. I coached Mike through the remaining product development steps, following our product development chart. In 1980, Minor's Fish Base, along with several "Chef Developed and Kitchen Tested" foodservice recipes, were introduced to the foodservice market. We all were very excited about the product feedback we received from the sales forces.

While doing his R & D training, Mike became interested in another experimental product we had put on hold. We referred to it as "White Sauce Prep." The product concept was a dry replacement for the traditional roux of cooked butter and flour used by chefs and cooks for thickening soups, sauces, and gravies. Mike, with his usual enthusiasm and speed, developed the final prototype after only four trials for the Minor's White Sauce and Cream Soup Prep (Dry Roux).

Because the product concept was unique, we needed to develop many foodservice recipes and product applications for demonstrating how to use the product. The recipes and applications took longer than the development of the product! All of us in R & D and Mike were very proud of this NEW product introduction.

Under Dr. Minor's leadership, learning was a way of life. He encouraged us to seek out what we needed to know not only from himself, but from the Minor's food industry consultants. Dr. Minor hired consultants on retainers, who were scientific experts in the food industry and recently retired from full time positions.

Having technical experts available for consultation was of great benefit for me. One of these people was Dr. Joseph Rakosky, an authority on soybean technology, from Morton Grove, IL. We had many phone conversations about vegetable proteins that helped me with my product development work. I am grateful to Dr. Rakosky for patiently answering my many questions.

Whenever there was a technical area of knowledge that I needed to know more about, I was encouraged by both Dr. Minor and Mike Zelski to take a seminar or short course in the subject. Over the years I attended many of these, such as:

Hydrocolloid Technology
Flavor and Color Technology
Intermediate Moisture Foods
Sensory Evaluation Methods for the Practicing Food Technologist
Ingredient Technology
Food Science in the Foodservice Industry

Successful Interaction of Technology and Marketing
Accelerated Shelf-Life Testing of Foods and Biologics
Water Activity: Theory and Applications

Dr. Minor often asked career people from the foodservice and food processing industries, who he believed would contribute to the knowledge and understanding of his students, to speak in his classes and share their experiences. When Dr. Minor asked me to be a guest lecturer at his Flavor class offered by the School of Hotel, Restaurant, and Institutional Management in the College of Business at Michigan State University, I felt very honored.

He requested that I cover three of the company's responsibilities and our standards for achievement: (1) good manufacturing practices (GMP); (2) quality control/assurance (QA/QC); and (3) new product development, in my presentation to his class.

We were given special permission for taking pictures in making the slide presentations of the manufacturing, quality control, and R & D processes for illustrating each of the three topics. The manufacturing facility was off limits to anyone not employed by Minor's or U. S. D. A. at the plant location, or a member of the Minor family. The primary reason for the tight security of the operations and product formulations was that there were so many competitors in the marketplace making similar products.

Minor's had unique high quality products and needed to keep them that way. With the photography skills of Maureen Beyer and the cooperation of the Production Manager, Ruth Ann Minor Fields, we completed two slide programs. The first was a Minor's product induction and walk through of the manufacturing processes covering the GMP and QC/QA practices. The second program showed how we did the product development steps following the Product Development Chart.

As the years progressed, I was invited several times to give the slide presentations to Dr. Minor's classes at MSU. On one occasion in June, 1982, I received a certificate from Dr. Minor designating me as an honorary faculty member in the School of Hotel, Restaurant, and Institutional Management. I was extremely pleased with this recognition.

As the company sales increased, new sales representatives were hired by the brokers who needed to learn quickly about the Minor's product line and customer sales applications. Soon we were asked by Mike Zelski to develop and conduct product orientation programs for these new people. With these new salespeople we conducted product tastings of the reconstituted Food Bases, Sauce and Gravy Preps and Soup Mixes, performed recipe preparations for demonstrating the use of the products, and reviewed the key product information in the sales literature.

We also taste-evaluated with them the primary competitor products found in their sales area, comparing them to Minor's. In response to their request to tour the manufacturing facility, I presented the slide program of the Minor's product induction and plant walk through that we used for Dr. Minor's classes. Actually this was the best way to see and understand the processing of the Minor's products. They would not have seen many of the products being made had they just toured the plant during the time spent.

The New R & D Technicians, 6/83 - 1/86

Another part of the Minor's training was on-the-job training which we relied on heavily in R & D for getting reliable and productive work performances. As industrial sales placed more work demands on R & D, we hired a summer employee in June, 1983 from Michigan State University who was majoring in Foods and Nutrition.

Peggy Spink Nordman was energetic, very helpful to others, and performed her assignments well and on time. We offered her a full time position as product development technician upon her graduation in December of that year. She also helped R & D with the training on the new technical equipment we had purchased for learning more about the Minor's products being sampled to industrial customers.

Technical information requested by industrial customers included percent of salt, sodium, fat, protein and moisture, pH, and water activity of the products. The equipment we initially purchased was for testing water activity and percent of sodium of products in our test kitchen. Space limitations prohibited us from buying any more technical equipment.

We sent product samples for testing to the local outside laboratory. They provided some of the data needed, but they too had limitrf technical equipment for performing all the tests that we required. We searched for testing laboratories outside the Cleveland area and found several. Pursuing this activity was taking a lot of time from the product development work...and foodservice sales also continued with their requests for more and more nutritional information of the Minor's products.

Kathleen McGowan, a recent graduate from the University of Akron in Foods and Nutrition, started in June 1984. Kathleen was trained and assigned to coordinate the testing with the outside laboratories for getting the technical and nutritional information, and handling the requests for the industrial and foodservice customers. This newly created position was in good hands with Kathleen's love of a challenge and willingness to persevere.

Late in 1984 the entire R & D staff became involved with the design and planning of a new R & D facility to be built with the next manufacturing plant expansion in 1986. The new plans for R & D included a large new test kitchen, a technical laboratory, a sensory evaluation room and R & D office areas. This was an exciting time as we all looked forward to more working space for performing our work.

In 1985 we had our first termination in R & D, Maureen Beyer decided to stay home, after the birth of her second child, to care for her family. She was a valued member, as both test kitchen supervisor and product technician, before the birth of her first child, and then, as R & D systems specialist in her last position with the department.

The second termination was Peggy Nordman whose husband was transferred to Columbus, OH. Peggy's last assignment with us was test kitchen supervisor and product technician. Her excellent performance in product development was greatly missed!

We were fortunate to interview and select two people for filling the position openings in a short time period. Margaret Rauch started in R & D as test kitchen and taste panel supervisor in late May, 1985; Suzanne Lesko Gubics began her employment in June, 1985, as product & applications technician.

Both Margaret and Suzanne are college graduates in foods and nutrition and have several years of work experience in hospital foodservice in the Cleveland area. I was delighted having two employees with kitchen food production experience in R & D who would be working on product applications for foodservice as part of their job assignments.

Several times per week I met with each one, for on-the-job training discussion and feedback. Margaret liked planning work activities and was patient and methodical in her work. We set weekly goals to accomplish. Suzanne was thorough and strived for accuracy in her work. She was always willing to do the research needed to get the information required for moving ahead in her product development projects.

After the company was sold by Dr. and Mrs. Minor to private investors in April, 1983, the organizational structure changed. Dr. Minor, however, continued with the company as the scientific consultant. Over the next two-and-a-half years, Dr. Minor's involvement in overseeing the R & D activities, as he did in the past, gradually became diminished due to the changes in the organizational reporting relationships.

During this same time period, industrial sales began requesting several new product concepts for showing to their prospective customers. Many of these product concepts involved technical knowledge we did not have yet within the R & D staff.

As a result, a new R & D position was created and fulfilled when Joellen Ionni started in December 1985. Joellen was the first experienced Food Technologist employed in Minor's R & D. During the short time I worked with Joellen, I found her to be very capable, and I regretted I was not able to work with her longer before other organizational changes occurred.

At the beginning of 1986, I believe we realized that an end to an era had arrived within the company we knew. We were on the threshold of a new beginning in January, 1986, not knowing where it would go. Many personnel changes occurred throughout 1986, along with several new hirings in sales and marketing. At year end, the biggest change was the sale of the company by the private investors to the Nestle company.

Overall, my work those eleven years in R & D for the L. J. Minor Corporation was very satisfying. Working relationships with others, within R & D and the company, were enjoyable and rewarding. The opportunities to learn and grow were extraordinary. Every day was different and exciting! It was both fun and challenging to develop and organize the standards for the many new work activities as they were needed and then to follow through with the training of the employees for accomplishing the R & D assignments. I loved the atmosphere of a small, family owned company, and greatly admire the outstanding achievements of Dr. and Mrs. Lewis J. Minor!

The following pages depict some of the guidelines implemented by L. J. Minor Corporation during the '70's and beyond for sanitation and product development.

Plant Sanitation Guidelines

To Minor Corp. Plant Employees, Supervisors and Managers:

We are fortunate to work for a company whose name today is a proud synonym for quality in the marketplace, whose products are natural and wholesome and contribute to human health and pleasure; a company whose founders initiated generous employment policies that share the good fortune of the firm with its employees.

We have an exceptional product-quality reputation to maintain and an excellent company to perpetuate in the competitive arena.

Many firms manufacture products that to some extent make allowance for human error; slight off-tolerances in almost any manufactured consumer product will not harm the user. Even significant errors can occur occasionally in large, manufactured items - automobiles, for example - without disaster. We read of hundreds of thousands of cars being recalled for replacement or correction of a single part.

But our product - food that is consumed by humans - is unique. There is no room for error. Even a single small incident of contamination is an event worthy of national attention, and the unfortunate manufacturer can face ruin for one, isolated event.

Therefore, dedicated workmanship is required if we are to continue to make a quality product, maintain an enviable corporate reputation and enjoy individual success and prosperity. Personal cleanliness and sanitation are the foundations of fine workmanship.

This instructional handbook is provided as a comprehensive reference for all plant personnel. These guidelines will assist in restraining the growth of bacteria that could harm our customers and destroy overnight our fine product line and excellent reputation. Dangerous bacterial growth can be controlled by conscientiously practicing a strict program of personal hygiene and sanitation.

Two factors have a major impact in curbing bacterial growth:

1. Good sanitation and personal hygiene procedures minimize the amount of bacteria that can get into the product.

2. Maintaining all product ingredients under ideal conditions prevents bacterial growth and provides an unfavorable atmosphere for bacteria to multiply.

The guidelines contained in this booklet are for the protection of everyone. Your compliance guarantees you a major role in the company's future success.

398

To Each L. J. Minor Employee:

YOU are the important person who assists in accomplishing the goal of the L. J. Minor Corporation for high quality, clean and wholesome products. In order to maintain our standards of excellence, we ask that you strictly observe the following health and sanitation regulations. They have been established to:

1. Keep our products clean, wholesome and of the highest quality.

2. Make proper sanitation a daily habit.

3. Protect you from accidents.

I. HAND CARE

    A. You must wash your hands with germicidal soap:

        1. When you come to work

        2. After every break

        3. After you eat or smoke

        4. After you pick up any object from the floor

        5. After you cough or cover your mouth with your hand

        6. After you blow your nose

        7. After you use the toilet

        8. After you come from outside the plant

        9. After you touch contaminated equipment or containers

    B. Your fingernails must be short and clean, with no polish.

II. HAIR COVERINGS

    A. Your hair should be washed frequently and always be clean.

399

B. All plant employees must wear an operating room style cap while in uniform. This cap must completely cover your hair and prevent your hair from touching the collar of your uniform.

III. UNIFORMS - ALL EMPLOYEES

A. Wear a clean uniform provided, according to schedule. DO NOT WEAR IT OUTSIDE THE PLANT AREA. Do not use pins to fasten any part of your uniform, as pins may come loose and fall into the product.

1. FEMALE EMPLOYEES: Your uniforms are to be buttoned, except top button, and worn with a clean apron. Blouse or dress sleeves must be short when worn under the uniform so as not to extend below the sleeves of the uniform.

2. MALE EMPLOYEES: Your shirt is to be buttoned, except top button, and tucked inside the trousers for safety. To prevent body hair from getting into food, you must wear a T-shirt under your uniform shirt.

B. Remove apron and/or lab coat before going to the lunchroom, leaving the plant, going to the restroom, or while performing any cleaning function. Hang the apron or lab coat on the special hook provided.

C. Stockings or socks must be worn while working.

D. All employees must wear fresh, clean, appropriate underwear under the uniform.

E. All plant personnel must wear steel-toe safety shoes and keep shoestrings tied at all times.

F. Only white, washable (not fuzzy) sweaters or knit turtleneck shirts are allowed. They must fit snugly and must be worn under the lab coat.

IV. PERSONAL BELONGINGS

A. For reasons of safety and government regulations, rings, jewelry, watches and earrings - including all pierced earrings - may not be worn in the plant. A religious medal must be pinned with a safety pin to an undergarment and covered with outer clothing. Plain gold wedding bands are permitted.

B. Do not carry objects behind your ears or in shirt pockets; for example, cigarettes, pencils, pen knives, etc.

V. PERSONAL HYGIENE AND HEALTH

A. Take a bath daily.

B. Use deodorant.

C. Do not wear perfume. Use cosmetics and aftershave sparingly.

D. Keep hair clean and free of dandruff.

E. Men must be clean-shaven and well groomed without beards. A mustache must be neat and closely trimmed.

F. Brush your teeth daily.

G. Throat cultures may be taken at the plant when deemed necessary.

H. Any cut, bruise, lesion or open wound must be properly bandaged and your hands must be covered with disposable plastic gloves.

I. If you have a respiratory infection - cold, bronchitis, etc. - notify your supervisor immediately and wear a mask.

J. Cover your mouth with your hands or a tissue when coughing or sneezing, then wash your hands immediately.

K. Spitting is prohibited.

L. SMOKING IS PROHIBITED IN THE PLANT. Smoking is permitted in the Smoking Room. Cigarette butts must be placed in the cans provided.

M. Do not eat food or candy or chew gum or tobacco in the plant.

N. USE OF ALCOHOLIC BEVERAGES OR DRUGS IS PROHIBITED DURING WORKING HOURS, INCLUDING LUNCH TIME. NO ONE WILL BE PERMITTED TO WORK UNDER THE INFLUENCE OF ALCOHOL OR DRUGS.

O. No personal radios are authorized without permission.

P. All clothing must be stored in your locker, and lockers must be kept clean and neat.

VI. PERSONAL WORK HABITS

A. Keep hands and fingers out of food. Use proper utensils and always wear plastic disposable gloves.

B. Wash and sanitize small utensils after every use.

C. Do not wipe hands on uniforms or aprons.

D. Do not handle the inside of lids, containers or plastic bags.

E. Cover foods and utensils when not in actual use, at break and lunchtime, and during cleanups.

F. Place rubbish in proper containers.

G. Wipe up any spills immediately.

H. Always keep all doors throughout the plant closed.

I. Do not sample food being processed. Only authorized personnel may sample food.

VII. PERSONAL FOOD

A. Store personal food in the employees' lunchroom refrigerator. Eat only in the lunchroom.

It is obvious that rules and regulations guiding the daily activities in a food-processing plant are numerous and require very strict compliance.

This is necessary to protect the public who consumes our products, as well as to insure our own health and safety.

Please observe and obey each of these regulations so that the plant of the L. J. Minor Corporation will continue to be a safe, sanitary and wholesome place in which we can all continue to work and prosper.

_____ DEVELOPMENT CHART

(Check one): ____ New or ____ Improved Product.   Date: _____

Priority Rating (#1, 2, 3, or 4): _____ Request by _____

Directions: Check (✓) the Step of current work and fill in date when completed.
Write in N A, when the Step is <u>not</u> appropriate to the project.

<u>STEPS:</u>

____ (A)   ESTABLISH THE PRODUCT STANDARD.

____ (B)   RESEARCH FORMULA BACKGROUND OF EXPERIMENTAL PRODUCT.

____ (C)   INVESTIGATE RAW MATERIALS.

____ (D)   DESIGN EXPERIMENTAL FORMULA(S).

____ (E)   PREPARE EXPERIMENTAL TK PRODUCT(S).

____ (F)   EVALUATE TK PRODUCT(S) AT TASTE PANEL.

____ (G)   RE-FORMULATE AND CONTINUE TO EVALUATE ATE

____ (H)   REQUEST MICROBIOLOGICAL TESTS OF TK EXPERIMENT.

____ (I)   DO PRODUCT YIELDS OF TK EXPERIMENTAL PRODUCT(S).

____ (J)   AS REQUIRED, REQUEST NEW PACKAGING FOR EXPERIMENTAL PRODUCT.

____ (K)   BEGIN DEVELOPMENT OF LABEL DIRECTIONS AND RECIPES USING TK EXPERIMENTAL PRODUCT.

____ (L)   ORDER NEW RAW MATERIAL(S) REQUIRED FOR MAKING EXPERIMENTAL PRODUCTION BATCHES OF PRODUCT.

____ (M)   ORGANIZE A FORMULA FOR AN EXPERIMENTAL 1/2 PRODUCTION BATCH OF THE PRODUCT.

____ (N) REQUEST TEST RUN OF EXPERIMENTAL 1/2 PRODUCTION BATCH OF PRODUCT.

____ (O) COST EXPERIMENTAL FORMULA AND PACKAGING, AND CALCULATE ESTIMATED PRICE OF PRODUCT.

____ (P) REQUEST RECOMMENDED APPROVAL BY TASTE PANEL.

____ (Q) REQUEST PANEL OF FINISHED PRODUCT PREVIEW APPROVAL.

____ (R) FOR A NEW PRODUCT REQUESTED BY A CUSTOMER, REQUEST CUSTOMER EVALUATION.

____ (S) REQUEST FINAL APPROVAL OF FINISHED PRODUCT BY DR. AND MRS. MINOR.

____ (T) REQUEST FINISHED PRODUCT EVALUATION BY GENERAL MCLAUGHLIN.

____ (U) FINAL APPROVAL OF NEW PACKAGING/MATERIAL BY MANAGEMENT CAN BE COMPLETED.

____ (V) DESIGN AND INITIATE SHELF-LIFE STUDY OF PRODUCT AND PACKAGING FOR YEAR'S STORAGE UNDER BOTH REFRIGERATION AND ROOM TEMPERATURE CONDITIONS.

____ (W) COMPLETE DEVELOPMENT OF LABEL DIRECTIONS AND RECIPES USING EXPERIMENTAL 1/2 PRODUCTION BATCH OF PRODUCT.

____ (X) ORGANIZE A FORMULA DRAFT FOR A FULL PRODUCTION BATCH OF THE APPROVED PRODUCT.

____ (Y) REQUEST TEST RUN OF EXPERIMENTAL FULL PRODUCTION BATCH OF APPROVED PRODUCT.

____ (Z) PREPARE AND CALCULATE IN LBS. AND %'S FORMULA BREAKDOWN OF RAW MATERIALS USING THE "COORDINATING FORMULA FORM".

____ (AA) UPON INGREDIENT STATEMENT APPROVAL, PREPARE LABEL

COPY DRAFTS FOR 1 LB. (OR ITS EQUIVALENT), NET WT. AND SAMPLE SIZE LABELS.

____ (AB) REQUEST USDA (LABEL APPLICATIONS) TRANSMITTALS FOR MEAT AND POULTRY PRODUCT FOR 1 LB., NET WT. AND SAMPLE SIZE LABELS.

____ (AC) CALCULATE ACTUAL PRODUCT PRICE AND SEND TO MANAGEMENT.

____ (AD) RESEARCH AND PREPARE DESCRIPTIVE COPY FOR ADVERTISING'S REFERENCE IN PREPARING A PRODUCT PROMOTIONAL FLYER.

____ (AE) COMPLETE COMPUTER WORK.

____ (AF) NEW PRODUCT IS READY FOR PLANT PRODUCTION AND MARKETING.

____ (AG) AFTER PRODUCT IS ESTABLISHED IN PRODUCTION, COLLECT SAMPLES FOR NUTRITIONAL ANALYSIS WORK.

____ (AH) REQUEST PRODUCT SPECIFICATIONS TO BE EVALUATED AND WRITTEN.

____ (AI) REQUEST PROFILE DATA OF PRODUCT TO BE WRITTEN.

8/6/80

PRODUCT DEVELOPMENT STEPS
OF NEW AND IMPROVED PRODUCTS

____ (A)   ESTABLISH THE PRODUCT STANDARD.

    ____ (1)   Research literature and professional sources listing references.

    ____ (2)   Prepare selected recipes which produce a quality Standard product, and evaluate at Taste Panel.

    ____ (3)   Review competitor products, both retail and institutional, and evaluate at Taste Panel.

____ (B)   RESEARCH FORMULA BACKGROUND OF EXPERIMENTAL PRODUCT.

    ____ (1)   Study related manufactured product formulated

    ____ (2)   List flavor-contributing ingredients from

    ____ (3)   List possible raw materials to try in the
Consider raw materials used in manufacturing and sensory evaluation reports of test samples tray evaluations.

____ (C)   INVESTIGATE RAW MATERIALS

    ____ (1)   Review R & D files of Raw Materials, Suppliers, and Test Sample Catalog.

    ____ (2)   Review I F T Directory and others.

    ____ (3)   Call or write companies requesting test samples -- find out:
a) local distributor or direct buying
b) minimum order size
c) price per unit
d) product availability--year around or seasonal
e) request technical information and suggested directions for use.

    ____ (4)   Do Test Sample Tray Sensory Evaluations of new raw materials with members of the taste panel.

____ (5)   Do yield studies of test samples being considered for possible use in experimental formulations, taking both weights and measurements, such as, can weight, drained weight and measure, cleaned weight and measure, etc...Also do time and temperature studies as required.

____ (6)   If microbiological specifications are not available for a new raw material, send a sample for microbiological testing, requesting initial study only.

____ (7)   Record and file above information in the appropriate Raw Material File with a cross reference note in the Supplier's File.

____ (D)   DESIGN EXPERIMENTAL FORMULA(S)

____ (1)   Organize a trial formula for a Test Kitchen batch size of the experimental product. Carefully note raw, cooked, cleaned and drained weights. Calculate amounts as raw material percentages, totaling 100%.

____ (2)   Convert raw material percentages to gram weights. (For best blending results, calculate a 2 to 3 lb. TK batch size.)

____ (3)   Write procedures for an experimental TK formula, using the plant formulas as procedure reference guides.

____ (E)   PREPARE EXPERIMENTAL TK PRODUCT(S)

____ (1)   If working on product improvement, prepare a TK Standard to use as a reference Standard at the Taste Panel evaluations. (The first evaluation is to validate the TK Standard compared to a current manufactured Standard.)

____ (2)   Allow experimental products to stand under their proper storage conditions for 4 to 5 days to assimilate minimum shipping time to customers, before doing sensory evaluation testing with the Taste Panel. (This gives a more valid evaluation of the product.)

____ (F)   EVALUATE TK PRODUCT(S) AT TASTE PANEL.

____ (1)   For New Products: Evaluate product quality characteristics and compare to astandard recipe made from scratch.

____ (2)   For Product Improvement: Evaluate product quality comparing to a current Standard product.

____ (G)   RE-FORMULATE AND CONTINUE TO EVALUATE AT TASTE PANEL.

    ____ (1)   Study previous Taste Panel and TK test results. Organize a new trial formula (TK batch size) of the experimental product.

    ____ (2)   Refine formula calculations to improve flavor characteristics based on Taste Panel test summary.

    ____ (3)   Revise and improve formula procedures based on TK recommendations.

    ____ (4)   Use yield results from previous TK tests. Request additional yield trials to obtain average TK yield statistics for using as reference guides in production batch formulations.

    ____ (5)   Compare and evaluate at Taste Panel new TK experimental products to the TK experimental product most preferred by the Taste Panel thus far. (For Product Improvement projects -- continue to use a current Standard product, either a Standard TK or manufactured product depending on purpose of each test, as needed for sensory progress, and a product reference guide.)

    ____ (6)   Keep accurate notes and records, including background calculations, of product development.

    ____ (7)   Repeat Steps G(1) through G(6) until the Taste Panel results show a definite preference for one of the experimental formulated products.

____ (H)   REQUEST MICROBIOLOGICAL TEST OF TK EXPERIMENTAL PRODUCT.

    ____ (1)   Request both initial and 30 day shelf-life standard tests of coliforms, standard plate count, staph., yeasts and molds.

____ (2)   Study results and adjust formulations as necessary.

____ (I)   DO PRODUCT YIELDS OF TK EXPERIMENTAL PRODUCT.

    ____ (1)   Weigh level tsp. and Tbsp. of product at least 5 times each and record on product yield cards.

    ____ (2)   Pack and weigh product in various packaging containers currently being used for manufactured products. Evaluate trial packaging at Taste Panel for product appearance and packaging material acceptability.

    ____ (3)   When manufactured product packaging is not acceptable for the experimental product, list packaging specifications needed.

____ (J)   AS REQUIRED, REQUEST NEW PACKAGING FOR EXPERIMENTAL PRODUCT.

    ____ (1)   Request new packaging samples (containers and/or materials) for trial packaging testing and Taste Panel evaluations. Repeat Step 1(2).

    ____ (2)   When the Taste Panel recommends a preference for one kind of packaging, request:
        a)   a copy of the suppliers USDA/FDA letter stating approval of packaging for food use.
        b)   the supplier's packaging specifications and technical data.
        c)   the cost per a complete packaging container.

    ____ (3)   Summarize and report to Management the results of packaging testing and recommendations of Taste Panel.

____ (K)   BEGIN DEVELOPMENT OF LABEL DIRECTIONS AND RECIPES USING TK EXPERIMENTAL PRODUCT.

    ____ (1)   Test reconstituting yields and procedures. Evaluate at Taste Panel.

    ____ (2)   List suggested uses of experimental product. Discuss with Taste Panel.

    ____ (3)   Develop 1 or 2 popular recipes for label copy. Have Taste Panel evaluate and approve each recipe. Record yields, temperatures and times.

____ (L) ORDER NEW RAW MATERIAL(S) REQUIRED FOR MAKING EXPERIMENTAL PRODUCTION BATCHES OF PRODUCT.

    ____ (1) Before ordering, estimate raw material(s) amount needed for annual usage, checking with Management.

    ____ (2) Order new raw material(s) from suppliers. Prepare a Test Sample Delivery Info. form.

    ____ (3) Prepare "R.M./Supplier Updating Memo" giving purchasing details of the new raw material(s).

____ (M) ORGANIZE A FORMULA FOR AN EXPERIMENTAL (1/2) PRODUCTION BATCH OF THE PRODUCT.

    ____ (1) Estimate size of a full production batch comparing density of the experimental product to related manufactured products. Consult with Plant Management and Methods Research before estimating full production batch size.

    ____ (2) Calculate raw material amounts for 1/2 production batch size.

    ____ (3) Write procedure for 1/2 production batch noting times, temperatures, mixing speeds, etc.

    ____ (4) Consult with Plant Management and Methods Research about equipment needs. New equipment requests must be approved by Management.

____ (N) REQUEST TEST RUN OF EXPERIMENTAL 1/2 PRODUCTION BATCH OF PRODUCT.

    ____ (1) Prepare "Request for Experimental Production Batch Memo" and send to plant staff involved in making the experimental batch.

    ____ (2) Request microbiological testing of 2 samples of the experimental product for both initial and 30 day shelf-life studies.

____ (3)   Request experimental product sample for sensory evaluation testing.

____ (4)   Request weight of batch, and related details of times, temperatures and yields.

____ (5)   Record data for improving procedure of the next trial test run.

____ (6)   As necessary, readjust batch size calculations to fit equipment better.

____ (O)   COST EXPERIMENTAL FORMULA AND PACKAGING, AND CALCULATE ESTIMATED PRICE OF PRODUCT.

    ____ (1)   Calculate amounts needed for an estimated full production batch.

    ____ (2)   Calculate in lbs. and %'s formula breakdown of raw materials using the "Coordinating Formula Form".

____ (P)   REQUEST RECOMMENDED APPROVAL BY TASTE PANEL.

    ____ (1)   Compare the experimental 1/2 production batch with the experimental TK batch preferred, and evaluate at Taste Panel.

    ____ (2)   When the Taste Panel recommends approval of the experimental 1/2 production batch product, it is ready for the two Finished Product Approval Groups.

    ____ (3)   The Taste Panel evaluates and approves food service recipes and recommends approval of label recipes.

____ (Q)   REQUEST PANEL OF FINISHED PRODUCT PREVIEW APPROVAL.

    ____ (1)   For a new product: Evaluate new product only.

    ____ (2)   For an improved product: Compare and evaluate the (old) Standard product to the (new) Standard product.

    ____ (3)   When the Finished Product Preview Group recommends final product approval, it is ready for customer request (when appropriate) and Final Approval by Dr. and Mrs. Minor.

_____ (4)   Finished Product Preview Group evaluates and approves label recipes.

_____ (5)   Finished Product Preview Group evaluates and recommends approval of product packaging.

_____ (R)   FOR A NEW PRODUCT REQUESTED BY A CUSTOMER, REQUEST CUSTOMER EVALUATION.

_____ (1)   Plan and type experimental labels.

_____ (2)   Pack experimental product samples in approved packaging.

_____ (3)   Prepare "Shipping of Samples Request Memo".

_____ (4)   Contact customer by phone or letter (as appropriate).

_____ (S)   REQUEST FINAL APPROVAL OF FINISHED PRODUCT BY DR. AND MRS. MINOR.

_____ (1)   Prepare memo with a brief explanation and reconstituting directions of product.

_____ (2)   Pack samples, repeating Steps Q(1) and Q(2). Prepare "Shipping of Samples Request Memo".

_____ (3)   When finished product is given Final Approval, request product evaluation from Marketing.

_____ (T)   REQUEST FINISHED PRODUCT EVALUATION BY GENERAL McLAUGHLIN.

_____ (1)   Prepare memo with a brief explanation and reconstituting directions of product.

_____ (2)   Pack samples, repeating Steps Q(1) or Q(2). Prepare "Shipping of Samples Request Memo".

_____ (U)   FINAL APPROVAL OF NEW PACKAGING/MATERIAL BY MANAGEMENT CAN BE COMPLETED.

____ (1) Upon approval, designing and printing of packaging and cartons can be requested by Operations Manager.

____ (2) Packaging contract assignment can be initiated and approved by Management.

____ (V) DESIGN AND INITIATE SHELF-LIFE STUDY OF PRODUCT AND PACKAGING FOR YEAR'S STORAGE UNDER BOTH REFRIGERATION AND ROOM TEMPERATURE CONDITIONS.

____ (1) Request the number needed of approved packaging containers for study.

____ (2) Do initial approval evaluation by Taste Panel of the product.

____ (3) Pack product in packaging container and arrange storage conditions.

____ (4) Request microbiological testing of product in the approved packaging containers at the beginning of shelf-life study.

____ (5) Evaluate storage products at the Taste Panel after 30 days, 90 days, 6 months and 1 year.

____ (6) Request microbiological testing of product in approved packaging containers at the end of the year's shelf-life study.

____ (7) Prepare report of Storage Shelf-life Test Results

____ (W) COMPLETE DEVELOPMENT OF LABEL DIRECTIONS AND RECIPES USING EXPERIMENTAL 1/2 PRODUCTION BATCH OF PRODUCT.

____ (1) Repeat yield studies of I(1) through I(4).

____ (2) Prepare 1 gal. amount (or its equivalent) of approved label recipe checking yield accuracy. Evaluate by Taste Panel.

____ (X) ORGANIZE A FORMULA DRAFT FOR A FULL PRODUCTION BATCH OF THE APPROVED PRODUCT.

____ (1) Coordinate formula work with R. H. who oversees final drafts of plant formulas.

____ (2)   Calculate raw material amounts, checking math carefully.

____ (3)   Update formula procedure from last trial.

____ (4)   Edit formula, reviewing trial and yield data.

____ (Y)   REQUEST TEST RUN OF EXPERIMENTAL FULL PRODUCTION BATCH OF APPROVED PRODUCT.

____ (1)   Repeat Steps N(1) through N(4).

____ (2)   Compare and evaluate the experimental full production batch to the experimental 1/2 production batch to the experimental TK batch at Taste Panel. When Taste Panel recommends approval at this Step, the product formula is ready for finalizing Steps that follow.

____ (Z)   PREPARE AND CALCULATE IN LBS. and %'S FORMULA BREAKDOWN OF RAW MATERIALS USING THE "COORDINATING FORMULA FORM".

____ (1)   Update the product costing.

____ (2)   Prepare proposed ingredient statements in descending order, and request approval selection by Management.

____ (3)   Prepare computer calculations.

____ (AA)   UPON INGREDIENT STATEMENT APPROVAL, PREPARE LABEL COPY DRAFTS FOR 1 LB. (OR ITS EQUIVALENT), NET WT. AND SAMPLE SIZE LABELS.

____ (1)   Send label copy drafts to Management.

____ (2)   Proofread label brown proof's for accuracy.

____ (AB)   REQUEST USDA (LABEL APPLICATIONS) TRANSMITTALS FOR MEAT AND POULTRY PRODUCTS FOR 1 LB., NET WT. AND SAMPLE LABELS.

_____ (AC) CALCULATE ACTUAL PRODUCT PRICE AND SEND TO MANAGEMENT.

_____ (AD) RESEARCH AND PREPARE DESCRIPTIVE COPY FOR ADVERTISING'S REFERENCE IN PREPARING A PRODUCT PROMOTIONAL FLYER.

_____ (AE) COMPLETE COMPUTER WORK.

     _____ (1) Prepare and calculate "finished goods forms".

     _____ (2) Complete computer forms for
a) 100 lb. batch formula
b) finished goods quantities.

     _____ (3) Proofread computer runs for accuracy.

_____ (AF) NEW PRODUCT IS READY FOR PLANT PRODUCTION AND MARKETING.

_____ (AG) AFTER PRODUCT IS ESTABLISHED IN PRODUCTION, COLLECT SAMPLES FOR NUTRITIONAL ANALYSIS WORK.

     _____ (1) Collect 6 samples from each batch. Collect from 3 different production batches made 3 different days to obtain random sampling of product.

     _____ (2) Calculate nutrient assessment probability.

     _____ (3) Write letter selecting nutrients to be analyzed.

     _____ (4) When nutrition information returns, prepare product drafts of Nutritional Analysis.

_____ (AH) REQUEST PRODUCT SPECIFICATIONS TO BE EVALUATED AND WRITTEN.

_____ (AI) REQUEST PROFILE DATA OF PRODUCT TO BE WRITTEN.

8-13-80

Chapter 40

A Decade of Memories

by Beverly V. DeLaney
(1976-1986)

| A Phone Call | I Accept! | A Big Surprise |

My Colleagues, The Minor Clan   My Job and Various Projects

Both Happy and Sad Days

Quote from Michael E. DeBalsey

"Do not shorten the morning by getting up late;
look upon it as the quintessence of life, as to a certain extent sacred."

"I Always Asked You To Break It to Me Gently"
(Irish Humor by Hal Roach)

Doolin had a cat that he loved very much. He had to go to Dublin for a few days and he called his brother Mike to ask him to watch his cat. Mike said that he would. After two days, he called to ask Mike how his cat was doing. Mike says:
"The cat is dead."

Doolin says:
"Why did you have to tell me like that? I am all distraught. Couldn't you have told me some other way?"

Mike says:
"What way could I have told you?"

Doolin says:
"You could have said the cat is up on the roof of the barn. The next time I

called you could have said the fire brigade came and tried to get the cat off the roof of the barn, but the cat fell. The next time I called, you could have said, the vet came and he tried to save the cat, but it was no use. The cat died. You see, if you had told me that way, it would not have been such a shock. By the way, how is mother?"

Mike responds:
   "She is on the roof."

A Phone Call

The phone rang shortly after I returned home from class on July 1, 1976. I immediately recognized the voice at the other end of the line. It was Mrs. Engler, my former boss at Stouffer's Frozen Foods, calling to learn if I'd now be interested in returning to work.

It was Stouffer's policy to call people by their last name, so she has always been Mrs. Engler to me. She had retired from Stouffer's and was now a part-time food consultant at the L. J. Minor Corporation where she helped formalize a quality control program and started the research and development department. Mrs. Engler also wrote job classifications for all the plant workers. If I decided to return to work, she wanted to interest me in working at Minor's rather than possibly returning to Stouffer's.

Ever since I moved to Cleveland in 1958, I had known her. Before arriving, I had obtained a *Home Economists In Business* directory to get the names of prospective employers. How pleased I was to learn that Stouffer's was not only headquartered in Cleveland but also had a frozen foods plant there. I wrote to Mrs. Ruth Engler to learn if a position for a home economist might be available. Her reply suggested I call her for an interview appointment upon my arrival.

Except for seeing many landlords, Mrs. Engler was the first person I met in Cleveland. She hired me as manager of the test kitchen and I worked for this exceptional woman for three years until I resigned on August 15, 1961, to have my first child.

During the following years, she offered me three part-time jobs at Stouffer's. But I was happy being a mother of two sons, a housewife, and an active community volunteer and leader, such as PTA president, and had no desire to return to the business world. I had, however, enjoyed occasional consulting jobs for several major food corporations.

By 1976, my time requirements for mothering were decreasing. Would there be a change in my life next year when my younger son would enter junior high school, or would I happily continue what I was doing? To help determine this, I took a course at Cuyahoga Community College titled, "Opportunities In A Changing Life Style." It was designed to assist the student in deciding one's place in the changing world by exploring and making choices in work, career, home, and volunteerism and how to find available opportunities.

417

Thus, her call came a year earlier than I would have liked. However, as this was the fourth call from her regarding a job, if I turned her down again, perhaps she wouldn't call about a fifth opening. Since she was offering me a fine opportunity, it seemed wise to investigate further. I told her that I would not be available until school started in September, but she felt that would be all right.

A few days later, she invited me to have lunch with her and Jan Williams at The Rusty Scupper, a downtown restaurant owned by Stouffer's. Mrs. Engler had introduced Jan, an ex-Stouffer employee who had worked in the management foodservice and the restaurant divisions, to Minor's. Jan had a master's degree and was a registered dietitian, so with this experienced background, she joined Minor's in 1975 as director of research and development. They now wanted to add a part-time person to the department. Jan would be my supervisor.

At lunch they told me about Dr. Lewis J. Minor and how he developed food bases and started a company with Mrs. Minor's assistance in 1951. They spoke of these ambitious people with great respect. High quality products and good customer service were the emphasis at this small growing company. They explained the main objectives of the R & D department including to improve manufactured products, to develop new products, to test prospective new and improved ingredients, and to develop product information. As a research and development assistant, most of my work would be done in the test kitchen and would include detailed record keeping. After lunch we drove to the plant located on West 25th Street near Auburn Avenue.

Dr. Minor had purchased a run-down carwash and a nearby house at this site in 1959. Now the plant included the manufacturing facility and warehouse, a flour processing building, several garage-type storage buildings, and the "Coffee House," so-named because employees took their coffee breaks there. The first floor of this converted house, located across an alley from the flour building, had an employees' lunchroom, kitchenette, and a smoking room. It also housed the R & D department.

The only office was occupied by Jan and Mrs. Engler, but it had enough space for a third desk. The lunchroom doubled as the taste panel room when plant employees were working. There was also a small test kitchen, a cloakroom with storage shelves, and a bathroom with a tub which proved to be a useful ice bath for chilling foods some years later! After a tour of the first floor and more discussion of my prospective job, which would be similar in many ways to the work I enjoyed so much at Stouffer's, I was informed that the next step would be to meet Mike Zelski, vice president of operations.

The appointment was set for 10:00 a.m., August 5 at his main office at Minor's corporate headquarters, 436 Bulkley Building at 1501 Euclid Avenue. The office door was down a long corridor on the fourth floor. A friendly woman with a wonderful, warm smile, who introduced herself as Nancy Clancy, greeted me and showed me to Mike's office.

He spoke very highly of Dr. and Mrs. Minor and this company, a leader in manufacturing and marketing premium quality food bases, while showing me a display of products in small bottles in a wooden case. He explained Minor's was looking for a person with a basic knowledge of cooking principles and quality food preparatio; one who was particular with details. As we spoke, I became more excited about this opportunity and challenge. It almost seemed too good to be true, as I realized there weren't many food industry jobs in the Cleveland area.

Since my father was an executive with a major food corporation and my mother was a nutritionist, I was surrounded by food talk since a young child. Since I was interested in a career in foods, I selected a college which offered a foods and nutrition major. Unlike most classmates, I was fortunate to be able to start planning a course of study for my major as early as freshman year. My hope and goal in life was to be a well-rounded person, combining a part-time career in the food industry with time for my family and community. This just seemed perfect!

I Accept!

Within a few days, Mike called and offered me the position. I was very excited! Realizing this was a fine opportunity, I accepted and agreed to start work the first of September. I felt a little uneasy because the boys wouldn't be returning to school until the eighth. However, I was certainly appreciative that Mike, Jan, and Mrs. Engler were willing to wait for me.

My older son Jimmy would be at school all day. My greatest concern regarding the boys was that David, my younger son entering sixth grade, wanted to continue to come home for lunch. "I won't be alone. Sisi will be here," he said with such youthful honesty. Sisi, the dog, was his constant companion. What a blow to a mother's ego!

September 1, 1976, came quickly and I was back in the business world! My first day was memorable. Mrs. Engler took me on a plant tour, now permitted since I was an employee. Tours were usually not given to non-employees because ingredients and processes used were proprietary. It was on this occasion that I was introduced to Ruth Fields, supervisor of production and packaging, and one of Dr. and Mrs. Minor's daughters. She made me feel very welcome.

We returned to our office shared with Jan, and I was given three typed pages to study. The objectives and the responsibilities of the R & D department were listed on page 1. My duties were briefly described on the second page and five steps of the experimental procedure were listed with some detail on the last page.

"TAKE TIME TO BE ACCURATE" in capital letters was underlined at the top of page three. I was glad to read that, as I felt it was important to work carefully, taking the time to pay attention to details and to do the job right the first time.

To become familiar with Minor's product line, I made small batches of manufactured products used as standards in comparison tests for R & D and quality assurance. I shall always remember my first trip to the plant to get an ingredient for a base I was going to make. As I opened the door, the loud clanging of glass jars hitting each other and the loud clanking of metal lids from the packaging line were almost deafening. I probably looked

419

confused as, no doubt, I didn't have any idea where to find the ingredient.

Within moments, a man who introduced himself as George Henderson, came over to ask if he could help. I was stunned but so pleasantly surprised because at my former employer's, most plant personnel turned their backs to R & D people. We were looked upon as nuisances who were in their way. George kindly assisted me in my mission. How nice to experience this helpful attitude. This incident confirmed my feeling that I was glad I decided to work here. Many thanks, George!

Soon I was recording ingredient information about test samples, sometimes yielding poultry and seafood samples, and writing directions for making experimental and standard batches. While making the products, cooking times, temperatures, observations, and comments were written on the work sheets. Again, it was critical to take the time to be observant and accurate. I also wrote the directions for reconstituting products and prepared them for taste panels. Bottled spring water was used for all cooking, as well as the same type and size of pan for each set of tests. Each pan was carefully coded with marked masking tape which identified the contents.

Setting up a tray for each panel member, I would serve the samples. The tray had a folded paper towel, one spoon for each sample, a product evaluation sheet for each set of samples, and a paper cup of water from the cooler. The panelist who initialed his or her sheet, gave a numerical rating (4 excellent, 3 good, 2 fair, 1 poor, 0 unacceptable) to the following attributes of each sample in randomly letter coded cups: appearance, color, texture/consistency, odor, and flavor/taste. I then recorded the taste panel results by averaging the numerical scores and copying panelists' comments. Jan reviewed the summaries and determined what action was to follow, which I communicated to other departments.

Panels were held three times per week. Most of the tests were for raw material testing, improving the manufactured products, and new product development. The first recipes using Minor's bases that I remember being evaluated, were those using Lobster Base. These recipes were for a booklet which was later reprinted in 1977. We recognized the importance of being familiar with competitors' products, so on occasion, these were also scored. Results were presented at sales meetings. After a time, I was asked to join the panel.

Two special projects early on are remembered. One was to perform experimental work with a new marinade product on imported steaks. It was to tenderize and flavor the less expensive cut of meat being purchased by a restaurant chain. All the samples were cooked on an electric grill I brought from home. When we were finally ready to demonstrate the new product, we went to one of the restaurants where the marinated steaks were grilled and taste tested by restaurant personnel, our sales and marketing people, and Jan.

The other project was to assist Chef Emil Burgermeister who experimented with different species of fish, herbs, and spices for a fish base. I felt honored to be working with this prominent man. For many years, the L. J. Minor Corporation supported culinary education by contributing to chef training and apprenticeship programs and by establishing student loan funds at culinary schools and colleges. Dr. Minor was instrumental in developing the chef status as a professional. By 1981, Minor's employed more than 20 master executive chefs who were in sales and also provided customer education.

Benefits are an important part of the work-reward system. Their value is a welcome premium to the basic paycheck. Many are provided by most employers including holiday and vacation pay, medical, dental and life insurances, and pension and profit sharing contributions. But as with so many other things, Minor's went above and beyond the norm. Those of less monetary value are just as memorable.

What a big surprise to learn of the holiday food gifts when my first Thanksgiving at Minor's approached. We were offered the choice of a ham or a turkey! This occurred again before Christmas and hams were given out for Easter. Everybody looked forward to the annual delicious Christmas dinners at the plant as well. But this wasn't all. Over the years, Christmas gifts to the employees included nuts, fruitcakes, preserves, and the marvelous Greenbrier Cookbook. Again, imagine my surprise when I received a two-year service gift in the fall of 1978, a lovely Hamilton watch which I still wear.

The first and second annual Plant and Corporate Office Staff New Years Dinners were held at the Cleveland Athletic Club in January 1982 and 1983, given as stated on the 1983 invitation: "In appreciation of all your efforts contributing to the continued success of the L. J. Minor Corporation during the past year." It was The General, formally Lt. Gen. John D. McLaughlin, U.S. Army (Retired), who was president and chairman of the board, who initiated the First Annual Awards and Appreciation Dinner for all employees in March 1985. My five years of service was recognized that evening by a lovely gold charm, the Minor's emblem enhanced with a ruby. How nice to work for a company which shows it appreciates the efforts of its employees in so many ways.

At last, the long awaited important day finally arrived in January 1977, when I had the honor and privilege of meeting Dr. and Mrs. Minor. Their embraces caught me by surprise and I could immediately understand why employees spoke of them with such fondness and respect. They united the employees, so that we could all work toward the uncompromising high standards and goals they established for the company.

Being nervous before panelists was not unusual, as they had come to taste products and I knew the taste session had to go smoothly with no last-minute hitches. Their warmth and friendliness eased my anxiety and, fortunately, they were mostly pleased with the products so carefully planned and prepared. This brought back many memories of when Vernon Stouffer used to come to the test kitchen at Stouffer's to taste.

From time to time, Dr. and Mrs. Minor stopped by for scheduled meetings and taste panels or visited to observe the growth of the company. They must have been very proud after each addition to the plant was completed, usually necessitating the hiring of more employees. On St. Patrick's Day 1982, they surprised us with decorations for our desks. Each white bud vase had an Irish flag and scented wood fiber roses handmade by a friend. How thoughtful! Mine decorated my desk for many subsequent Marches.

421

A Big Surprise

One of the biggest surprises of my life occurred in early April 1983. I entered the cloakroom to hang up my coat and put on my lab coat. Ruth was there and handed me an envelope while smiling a big grin as she often did. Inside were two very generous checks, one from Ruth E. Minor, the other from Lewis J. Minor, with a card noting, "This tax-free gift is in appreciation for services rendered to the L. J. Minor Corp." Awe-struck, I couldn't hold back the tears. I was so very deeply touched.

After all, they had a large family and many grandchildren. It was hard to understand why they would even think of me, a regular employee who was just doing her job. It was like manna from heaven to a single, financially struggling mother. Most of it was spent on tuition bills for my sons. I did feel guilty after buying a Canon camera to take on a special scout trip. I had wanted to replace my old one for years. Thank you! Thank you again, Dr. and Mrs. Minor from the bottom of my heart! I didn't know at the time that they were in the process of selling the company.

What a shock when it was later announced that on April 28, 1983, the company was under new ownership, a private investment group. It was almost impossible to realize that Dr. and Mrs. Minor no longer owned the company. Dr. Minor became chairman of the board emeritus and senior scientific consultant. Gen. John D. McLaughlin, who had been president of the company since 1979, was elected chairman of the board, chief executive officer, and president. All other officers' positions remained unchanged.

We hoped that business would continue as usual, and that no major changes would occur. We also very much wanted the company to continue its past success. It had to be especially difficult on Ruth since she had grown up with the company and had contributed so much to its growth by being an important part of the day-to-day operation for so many years. It also had to be hard on her brother, Mike Minor, to realize he was no longer working directly for his parents.

It has been wonderful to be able to work and get acquainted with some of Dr. and Mrs. Minor's family: three daughters, Ruth, Josephine, and Mary, their son Mike, granddaughter Sallie Fields, and grandson Dorsey Fields. The men are still at Minor's. At the time of this writing in 1994, Mike is Vice President of Culinary Services and Dorsey is National Account Manager, Chain Development. Some memories about each follow.

My Colleagues, The Minor Clan

Only a month after I met Dr. and Mrs. Minor, Mike joined the company in February 1977. He came after earning credentials and gaining experience as a chef. This was wise and admirable on his part. Yet, he had grown up with Minor's products, so he was familiar with them.

The first part of his long training program was spent in the plant, but since his desk was in our department, we quickly came to know him as an easygoing but hard-working, likable fellow. We even got a little acquainted with his lovely wife, Eddie, who'd bring their three cute daughters Andrea, Amy, and Ann to visit Daddy at work. Then he would take them out to lunch. This brought back memories of when I visited my father at work.

Mike is also remembered for his stories and jokes. We were amused many times by his true and not-so-true tales of when he was growing up, school stories, and experiences in Vietnam. (Remember the general's canary?) I once told him he should write a sequel to Cheaper By The Dozen about the adventures of the Minor clan!

It was fun working with him, assisting in developing beef base recipes for a booklet. Over the years, he developed many foodservice recipes featuring Minor's products. One example was a French bread recipe. The bread was so delicious when topped with cheese and toasted for garnishing French onion soup made from Minor's prep or from Minor's Beef Base.

Mike never had a failure, even though he improved recipes several times before he got the results he wanted. I can still smell the wonderful aroma of the bread baking. Yes, I'm convinced that the story about real estate agents suggesting their clients bake bread just before open houses has lots of merit. We always teased Mike about how terrible his bread was, that he would just have to make more for us to taste! The same occurred when he experimented with fruit pie fillings using the new Soup/Sauce Thickener (Dry Roux) which he had developed. "Make some more, Mike," I'd tell him.

When we were developing a nutritional soup, Mike brought in a sample from Canada which he claimed might be a terrific ingredient for it. He gave me cooking directions and asked that it be evaluated at taste panel. While serving the unappetizing purple samples, several panelists exclaimed, "What is this?" "For our nutritional soup," Mike replied in all seriousness. Everyone proceeded with much hesitation and filled out their score cards. Before the panel ended, Mike confessed that the mysterious ingredient was seaweed! Oh, Mike, the joke was on us!

After much planning, Mike practiced his food layouts for two weeks in July 1980 in preparation for the Fifteenth International Culinary Olympics to be held in Frankfurt, Germany in October. More than forty nations were to participate in this international cooking exhibition. He was the captain for Minor's International Team of nine chefs. We were the only American food manufacturer represented. All recipes entered used Minor's bases and preps.

Ingolf Nitsch, a former student of Dr. Minor's at Michigan State and a graduate of Johnson and Wales College, joined Minor's that July. Being a bright young man, fluent in German and having a culinary background, he provided valuable support to the team. We were thrilled that each team member won a medal including three gold, four silver, and two bronze. We were ecstatic that Mike won a gold!

At work an announcement was made on the PA system as soon as the exciting news from Germany was received. All the employees were so very happy for Mike. We also realized that having such a successful team was great for the company. Maureen Barendt Beyer and I had fun decorating Mike's and Ingolf's office for their homecoming. We were so proud of them!

The gold medal was as beautiful as any of us imagined it might be. The immediate problem was that it needed to be put on a ribbon to hang around Mike's neck. He selected a handsome 1 1/2" wide red, white, and navy blue ribbon. My friend Pat Harris, an expert seamstress and her husband Al, an engineer, designed the pattern which Mike approved. Voila! How distinguished he looked wearing that gorgeous gold medal!

Mike, Ingolf, and the company were still so excited about the competition that several years later, the decision was made to return in 1984 for the Sixteenth Culinary Olympics. But this time, they had their hearts set on the Grand Prize. Mike didn't compete, but was the team manager for the eight chefs. Ingolf, the team captain, did enter the competition. Again, Minor's products were used by each chef.

After much planning, much practice, much attention to each minute detail, much stress and strain, the team successfully reached its goal by winning seven gold medals and one silver. It was awarded the Grand Prize in Gold! Our team was the best of the best! It was the first American company sponsored team to win this prestigious award in the eighty-eight year history of the Culinary Olympics. We were thrilled that Ingolf won a gold medal and we were so very proud of him! Ask him for his Roast Loin of Rabbit in Herbed Cream Sauce recipe! The panel of distinguished judges thought it was extra special.

Josephine Minor worked for a number of years in the inventory control department, typing information into the computer. I got to know her better when we attended the Institute of Food Technologists (IFT) convention in New Orleans in June, 1983. We walked miles in the gigantic Superdome visiting hundreds of booths, where we met and talked with others in the food industry, tasted samples, and collected too much literature which got mighty heavy as the day progressed. It was a lot of fun to be with her.

The Minor's booth, which featured several chefs in their checkered pants, white coats, and toques serving delicious soups, was always crowded. We also attended several informative lectures with Jan. One evening, Josephine and I were the guests of Mr. and Mrs. Joseph Adams and their son Pat, longtime friends of Dr. and Mrs. Minor. They took us on a boat trip on the Mississippi River, followed by a pleasant carriage ride pulled by a horse named Jackson. Josephine and I still reminisce about this trip.

Mary Minor worked on and off in the plant for several years while attending school, including the summer of 1977. I shall always remember the little green velvet stockings she passed out one Christmas. They were filled with trial sizes of beauty aides and candies. How thoughtful! My stocking is hung on our tree each year, and with it, a memory of Mary.

Ruth and I became special friends when we discovered our birthdays are only one day apart. I have known her the longest, since my first day at work. She completely surprised me with a gorgeous mum plant, a lovely calendar, and a card signed by the employees for my birthday in 1977. I'll never forget that unexpected thoughtfulness! Thanks again, Ruth! This shows how much she cared about the employees. That was Ruth, always doing nice things for others. She had a marvelous sense of humor and a big laugh to go with it.

The company was truly a family business in its early days, with the Minor children helping on weekends. Ruth's leadership skills were apparent then. How nice that she was able to develop them over her career. She worked at the plant during summers when in high school and became a full-time employee after graduation. Over the years, she worked in all areas of the plant, becoming familiar with all job details.

She worked her way up to eventually become supervisor of production and packaging and received another well-deserved promotion in 1984 to manager of operations. Ruth had a wealth of knowledge about the products and their development. She was an invaluable consultant on all aspects of them. She also had a keen sense of taste, being able to distinguish any minute desirable or undesirable variation. Her taste panel scores and comments were especially noted.

My first work with her was on packaging tests, when I would give her test containers and lids for production to fill and package using their equipment. She was very cooperative in assisting the R & D department in all projects involving production. How nice that such a team effort existed.

Although these memories are to cover through 1986, I feel compelled to add that Ruth took early retirement in August, 1989 after more than 29 years of dedicated service. The company was her life. She cared so deeply about it, its products, its customers, and its employees. We almost couldn't imagine the plant without Ruth. We were stunned and saddened. Certainly the place would never be the same. Yet, we were very happy that this longtime widow who raised her family alone would be remarrying and starting another career. Ruth was honored in an emotional tribute the day before her last day of work, when she was named the first Key Employee. She has been greatly missed, but we remember her with much fondness.

Sallie Fields, Ruth's daughter and Dr. and Mrs. Minor's granddaughter, worked at the plant for a while. She usually worked on second shift, so I was not able to get to know her very well. However, I got well acquainted with her brother, Dorsey, who started working for the company in 1978 as a part-time employee while attending high school. Soon he was married and later became a father. He realized his responsibility and continued his education to help meet it. I remember him studying for a test one day during his lunch hour. He was a utility man at the time.

Dorsey told me that he did not want to do that kind of work the rest of his life. He had a dream of something better and was working toward it. After gaining more experience in the plant and when the opportunity came along, he applied for the production planning administrator's position which was also responsible for inventory control. The well-deserved promotion was granted and I am happy that he has received several subsequent promotions. Mother, Grandma, and Grandpa must be very proud of him. I am, too!

My Job and Various Projects

One of my early responsibilities was to design, plan, and schedule shelf life tests, and record and report the results. Product and package testing were started in 1977. Product tests involved formula or ingredient variations which were compared to standard products, as well as new products. They were stored in glass jars, the same type of containers as used in production, and later, in polypropylene cups.

Package tests involved standard products stored in glass jars, later in cups, which were compared to the same products from the same batches stored in test containers. These included cups made from different resins (polypropylene and high density polyethylene), several types of seals versus no seals, polypropylene jars with metal screw caps with and without liners, and poly or foil-lined bags. One standard set and one experimental set were stored in the shipping cooler for the refrigerated samples. One set of each was stored in the cloakroom for the room temperature samples. Usually, the control was the product in the glass jar stored in the cooler. I recorded the temperatures of these areas each month for many years.

Broths made from the bases were tasted and scored for appearance, color, consistency, odor, and flavor at the beginning of the test to verify that the bases were acceptable. It was important to check standards to be certain they met Minor's specifications. Taste panelists later evaluated broths after one, three, six months, and one year in storage. Each time, scores were given for each attribute, and appearances of the bases were recorded. Microbiological testing was performed at the beginning of the test and one year later, at the end of the test. After several years of testing this way, we started using an incubator which provided much quicker results.

It was fun to design several unique tests. We needed to learn how much abuse the container in which our first frozen product, Glace de Viande, could withstand during shipping and handling. A stress test was developed by dropping frozen containers of product from different heights. We also wanted to substantiate what effect cold and hot weather had on our bases during shipping.

Starting in October 1981, one pail of Chicken Base and one of Beef Base were stored in the shipping cooler, and one pail of each from the same batches was put in the trunk of Jan's car for six months to simulate shipping conditions. She drove about 50 miles each way to work, so mileage added up quickly. Taste panel evaluations were set up similarly to other shelf life tests. A hot weather transportation test was started the following May using Fish Base and Lobster Base. Quality deterioration was evident after only one month, so the necessity of shipping and storing these products under refrigeration was soon determined. It is interesting that we had to prove what should be done, which we now do automatically without giving it a second thought!

Since photography is my hobby, I was especially excited to work on numerous food photo projects. I have always enjoyed the fun and challenge of special projects. Fortunately, I'd had experience at Stouffer's and later did some freelance work for food photographer Ed Nano. In late 1977, pictures were needed for product profile sheets and publicity releases for food editors. Gene Walker came to photograph one layout of four foods I prepared using Chicken Supreme Sauce including a soup, a sauce for vegetables, an economy dish, and an entree.

A last-minute decision was made in April 1979 to have nine photos taken of foods prepared with Minor's products to display at the annual National Restaurant Association Show in Chicago in May. I looked forward to working again with Ed at Studio Associates. I was also pleased that Jan appointed me chairman of a committee of Chef Emil Burgermeister, Mike, Jan, and me to plan this immense undertaking.

We also worked with Walt Nicholes from the ad agency. Realizing that studio time is an expensive investment, detailed and organized planning was critical for successful results. We had many decisions to make including what Minor's products to use, foods to be prepared, recipes, equipment needed, grocery lists, as well as backgrounds, dishes, utensils, and props used to create certain moods. We scheduled practice sessions, studio dates, and made assignments.

It was fun selecting different backgrounds, props, and dishes of various sizes, shapes, colors, and textures from Ed's big collection. I took them back to work for use in our practice sessions. I also took an inventory of his kitchen equipment to determine what to bring from ours. Mike did a wonderful job in preparing most of the foods which were picture-perfect. Mike, Jan, Maureen, and I worked with great concentration at the studio.

A grand total of 60 products in nine layouts were photographed in both black-and-white and color in only 1 1/2 days of studio time. Ed was very pleased and Walt was ecstatic, as we all were! In addition to displaying the photos at the show, they were used in advertisements, product publicity, new product literature, and also used by sales reps.

Sometime afterwards, I wrote "General Procedures for Food Photography" listing all the details that must be decided and acted upon before the studio date. The last photography project involving R & D personnel occurred in August 1982. Mike determined what foods were to be photographed and then prepared them. I selected the backgrounds and dishes for the five layouts including pork dishes, breakfast, lunch, munch, and dinner.

Jean Hunter, a Minor's broker from Chicago who had experience in food photography, was a great asset at the studio. There is an energizing excitement about the lights, camera, action, and the click of the shutter when many eyes are focused on the subject of the moment. It was always rewarding to see the photos, at which time you felt all the hard work and attention to each minute detail made it worthwhile.

Another special project lasted four months, starting in December, 1982. I was thrilled that Dr. Minor asked me to obtain photographs for review for use in a textbook he was writing titled, Volume 1: NUTRITIONAL STANDARDS of the L. J. Minor Foodservice Standards Series. I worked from an outline which listed the subjects and how many pictures were needed for each chapter. He wanted 60 to 70 photos in the book. I phoned about 300 people at food companies and commodity promotion groups across the nation.

At last, over 200 pictures , organized according to categories, were put in thirty-six large envelopes which were packed and shipped to the managing editor. Their receipt was acknowledged with enthusiasm, but unfortunately, I later learned they arrived too late for use. I was disappointed, but the experience of talking with so many interesting people and making those contacts was useful in subsequent work. I was delighted to later receive an autographed copy of the book as well as an autographed copy of Volume 2: SANITATION, SAFETY & ENVIRONMENTAL STANDARDS from Dr. Minor. These gifts will always be cherished and they are a marvelous addition to my personal library.

A third special project was working about one Friday a month for Mike Zelski at the corporate office, starting in April 1982 and continuing for about 1 1/2 years. This experience broadened my outlook on the company, and I enjoyed getting acquainted with the women in the office.

One assignment was to make a chart of the houses near the plant that were purchased by Minor's in anticipation of future expansions, and to keep track of business pertaining to these rental properties. For instance, when houses were demolished, I requested that the insurance for them be canceled. Mike was active in numerous professional organizations, being president of one and an officer of another, so I took care of some of his business for these.

Mike, the L. J. Minor Corporation, and co-workers added much joy to one of the most memorable days of my life, November 19, 1981. How completely surprised I was to receive a letter of congratulations from him, with a check from the company to pay for my family's tickets (two Eagle Scout sons, my parents, and me) when I was honored with others as recipients of the Silver Beaver Award at the annual Boy Scouts of America awards dinner held in Stouffer's grand ballroom. I was embarrassed that Minor's had been notified, for I felt there were other scouts more deserving. Word spread fast as many cards and notes were received, as well as two beautiful bouquets, one from the women at Minor's whom I hardly knew. I was overwhelmed!

A second incident regarding Mike and scouting occurred in early 1983. Friends had invited me to drive with them to New Mexico in July to attend a week's training session at the Philmont Scout Ranch. This was a once-in-a-lifetime invitation! I did not have enough vacation days, but hoped I could possibly work something out with the company. Jan suggested I see Mike, who informed me that I had two personal days available. Great! Now I needed one more day. Back to Jan who was willing to let me work a makeup day. Our trip was so tightly scheduled, my friends picked me up after work and we headed west from the plant. I shall always be indebted to Mike and Jan, as the Philmont experience was one of the highlights of my scouting career!

Another project was different because I dreaded it as I planned it. It was not fun. By October, 1986, Ingolf decided we should switch from the old filing cabinets with drawers to the new style open slant Jeter file cabinets. This was the appropriate time to tackle the monumental task of reorganizing three files including the active raw material files, the historical raw material files, and company files. My new system would provide a more efficient way to obtain information. Duplicate and outdated papers and those no longer needed were discarded. Over 120 hours of overtime were dedicated to this project lasting six weeks. It was tedious and time-consuming. What a happy day when the last file was reviewed and transferred!

It is amazing how much the physical plant has grown since 1976. A new warehouse was built in 1977 where packaging was stored. It had previously been kept in several garage-type storage buildings which were dismantled by Jan's husband, David, who was happy to get them for his farm. Parking spaces had been at a premium, usually necessitating double parking, which at times proved very inconvenient. We were all delighted with the additional room!

We kept growing, so old houses on Pearl Court were demolished two years later for a new 27 car parking lot! Additional warehouse and processing areas were built in 1980, and a new warehouse was added in 1982. Numerous rental properties including the "Taylor" and Durkee Buildings on West 25th Street were torn down in 1983, which expanded the parking area along the south wall of Kredo Hardware.

The distribution center in Brecksville was purchased that same year, and an open house was held in November so employees could visit our newest facility. A new entrance and parking lot off Auburn Avenue, as well as new locker rooms and restrooms, a lunchroom, offices, and an equipment storage area, all very much needed were added in 1984. Corporate headquarters in The Bulkley Building were expanded to the fifth floor that same year. How fortunate to be part of a thriving company when many others were downsizing!

The construction which affected our department occurred mostly in 1979. Our third filing cabinet was full, we were bursting at the seams, and desperately needed space for more personnel and equipment because improved and new product development work was increasing. We were excited when approval was given to remodel our first floor of the "Coffee House" and to build a breezeway to connect our building with the plant.

The biggest job for Jan was to plan the new expanded test kitchen which combined our old one and the employees' kitchenette. She selected new appliances and equipment and got a big black monster commercial stove Mike wanted. Jan, turned interior decorator, did a marvelous job at coordinating linoleum, carpeting, wallpaper, window blinds, and new furnishings. I purchased Farberware cookware, small equipment, tools, and gadgets for the new kitchen.

Just as important, Jan had to make plans for our move to temporary quarters, the front apartment on the first floor of the Durkee Building, proudly identified by its name in big letters over the main entrance. Owned by Minor's, its attractive Tudor architecture was out of character in the neighborhood. The apartment consisted of a living room/bedroom, a small kitchen, and a bathroom.

It had to be quite a job to plan the logistics of running the department in an even smaller space. Office and kitchen items not critical to the daily operation (we hoped) were packed and stored. The kitchen had an apartment-sized stove and refrigerator, and a small sink. A table with two chairs and a utility cart filled the room. Maureen served taste panelists in shifts! Three desks for Jan, Mike, and me were squeezed into the living room/bedroom, identified by the Murphy bed folded into a cabinet. Jan's desk was against the wall in front of the window facing West 25th Street. Mike's desk and mine were abutted so we faced each other when we were sitting at them. There was hardly enough space to move around, but knowing this was temporary, we made the best of it and eagerly looked forward to returning to our remodeled department.

Mr. and Mrs. Krislipp, the building superintendents, welcomed us and were accommodating as much as possible. It took a while to adjust to the heavy and noisy West 25th Street traffic and to become convinced we were in a safe place. There was only a sidewalk between the street and our building, which was protected by a banged-up guardrail hit by too many drivers unable to negotiate the curve in the road.

One day Mike noticed a police car parked outside. In dead seriousness he said, "Bev, they're coming after you. They think you're running an abortion clinic in here!" A passerby who might have seen us going from the apartment building to the plant in our white lab coats and Mike in his white uniform may have concluded that!

The few months passed quickly and soon we left our cozy quarters for our much appreciated remodeled department. The employees' lunchroom and smoking room were relocated in the plant, so we gained an extra room and the all day use of the taste panel room where Mike and Jan put their desks. The improved lighting made a big difference in there. It was nice at last to see all of Jan's plans in place. The new test kitchen was quite a showplace! Hurrah! After we got settled, we had an open house in December to show off our new place. We were pleased that several women from corporate came out for this special occasion.

We also welcomed the new breezeway, so we no longer needed to go outside in the rain or snow to get to the plant. Some years later, it was carpeted and furnished with two chairs to make a reception area where I met with many sales reps.

Three years later in 1982, Jan and Mike started to plan a much larger test kitchen, a chef's kitchen, a taste panel room, and offices. My assignment was to collect information and do research on equipment such as coolers, freezers, ice makers, steam tables, cooking units, mixers, and so forth. Construction of this facility would be on the second floor of a new wing with an estimated completion date around June 1985. However, this did not become reality until 1986.

As the company grew, it was not surprising that our job responsibilities changed. In August 1980, Jan informed me that Maureen, who had worked a lot with me since November 1977, would be taking over my test kitchen duties. I knew I'd miss them, but looked forward to changes and new opportunities. I was glad that she was a competent person and very conscientious about her job. However, scheduling her daily assignments, I still had close ties with the kitchen.

This change gave me time to read food industry journals and meet with sales reps from many food companies to learn of new developments and ingredients which might be used in Minor's products or products being developed. I had already started meeting with reps in May, Will Dixson of Hercules and Rick Share of Food Masters being the first two. I learned a lot from such people, but we also realized the importance of the company developing relationships with current and prospective suppliers.

This led to my becoming in charge of test samples which were catalogued by category and manufacturer, stored in the cloakroom, shipping cooler, or freezer and scheduled for testing. The samples or solutions were prepared for bench tests, which taste panelists evaluated at their convenience between certain hours, three or four sets each week. Test dates and results, "K" for keep and "R" for reject, were recorded. The "keeps," which seemed possible prospects, were rescheduled, and "rejects," as well as old samples, were discarded. It was a big job to keep track of the hundreds of samples. In addition, later on, product technologists requested samples through me.

At the same time I learned about my new job responsibilities, Jan also told me about the new structure for taste panels. "The Regular Working Taste Panel" would require five people, usually Ruth Fields, George Hvizd, Lavere Vokt, Jan Williams, and me. If one was not available, I would ask for one of the alternates being Ruth Engler, Mike Minor, Ingolf Nitsch, or Mike Zelski.

This panel would evaluate experimental products and products made from recipes developed for Minor's literature. Improved and new products would be evaluated by the "Preview Approval Group" being Ruth Engler, Ruth Fields, Mike Minor, Jan Williams, and Mike Zelski. Four would be required for that panel. If the products were approved, samples would be sent to Dr. and Mrs. Minor, the "Final Approval Group."

Both Happy and Sad Days

One of my happiest days was when George Hvizd ordered the first truckload of frozen beef stock, over 1 1/2 years after my initial call to the prospective supplier. Our longtime current supplier of this critical raw material used in one of our best selling bases, unexpectedly decided to close the plant where it was processed because they had developed a powdered beef stock as a replacement.

Our taste panel rejected this new product many times. The surprised salesman informed me that all his other customers were switching to the powder. "That's fine if it's fine with them, but it's not fine with us," I said, continuing a mini-lecture on the high quality standards of the L. J. Minor Corporation, and that we were not willing to compromise the flavor of our products. I remembered Dr. Minor had written in a memo: "Flavor is the business of the L. J. Minor Corp."

My top priority quickly became finding an acceptable frozen beef stock. Countless calls were made until a company, learning of our volume requirement, became interested enough to change their processing to meet our specifications. One year later, after many samples, many batches of base, many taste panels, and several name changes (until agreeable to us, the supplier, and U. S. D. A.), and packaging changes (one being a heavier mil plastic bag to prevent leaking), the taste panel approved the beef stock. Thus, it authorized me to write a "Raw Material Supplier Update" memo to George Hvizd on September 29, 1983. He could now purchase this frozen beef stock! A gentle reminder was typed at the bottom of the last revised supplier's spec.: "We hope that regular production of this item will commence soon."

In the meantime, Mike Zelski and maybe George visited the old supplier and convinced them to continue manufacturing the stock a while longer so we could build up a substantial inventory. This was done, but every once in a while, I'd remind George about the new supplier who occasionally called me, anxiously waiting for our orders.

In early 1984, the man who worked so diligently with me, informed me that he would be retiring in the spring and hoped we would place a truckload order before then. The entire situation was embarrassing to me, and again I spoke to George. What a happy day when I arrived at work on April 3, and there on my desk was a copy of the purchase order for the first truckload of beef stock! The long awaited day had finally arrived! With great relief and much excitement, I immediately called the man and teased him that this was his retirement gift from the L. J. Minor Corporation and me! His company had worked above and beyond for this order and it was well deserved and way overdue!

Another happy day was December 27, 1983. I told Jan of my engagement to Bill DeLaney, and assured her that I would continue working. She wouldn't even have to change the routing slips because my initials would remain B.D.!

A couple of very sad days occurred in 1985. October 2 was my younger son's twentieth birthday, a special occasion to make it a happy day. It turned out to be memorable for another reason, a sad reason. Jan announced to the department that Mike Zelski and George Hvizd were "on administrative leave." She assured us that no further changes were anticipated. Everybody was shocked.

It seemed impossible. We couldn't imagine the company without them. For a long time, they had been dedicated to Minor's and deserved much credit for its growth and success. Dr. Minor had hired Mike, a former student at Michigan State. They had worked up through the ranks with well-deserved promotions. At the time, Mike was senior vice president, marketing and George was assistant vice president, logistics-support manufacturing.

After Mike's and George's offices on the second floor of the "Coffee House" were vacated, R & D personnel were able to move into them. We were very grateful for the badly needed office space. Kathleen McGowan, Maribeth Hackney, and I occupied Mike's old office, Jan went into George's, and Babi Scott moved to the receptionist's area. The only copier at the plant was located here. How very convenient, in contrast to the days when the only one in the company was at corporate. All material to be copied had to be sent there! I marvel at how so many people worked in such cramped quarters on the first floor, for the department had greatly expanded under Jan's successful leadership. Remember that even Mike and Ingolf had desks there. By June 1986, the following people had worked or were still working in R & D. I hope to include everybody with their starting dates.

Beverly (Daigle) DeLaney in September 1976
Maureen (Barendt) Beyer in November 1977, left May 1985
Gaynell Layton in January 1980, left April 1986

432

Marcia Fazio in February 1980, left June 1984
Peggy (Spink) Nordman in June 1983, left December 1985
Ellen Smith in April 1984
Kathleen McGowan in June 1984
Babi Scott in August 1984
Marcie Schneider in March 1985, left April 1985
Margaret Rauch in May 1985
Suzanne Lesko in June 1985
Joellen Ionni in December 1985
Christine (Bodnar)Sola in February 1986
Maribeth (Hackney) Meluch in March 1986
Janice Guarnera in May 1986

Another sad day occurred when Mrs. Engler retired and moved to Florida, at about the same time Mike and George left. For some years, she and her husband had wintered there and spent summers at their Bath, Ohio home when she worked at Minor's. She was my mentor and special friend. We corresponded, and as we had done since 1958, exchanged birthday and Christmas cards. I enjoyed calling her for her birthday the past several years. I was deeply saddened at this year's call in May 1994, when Mr. Engler told me she was critically ill. Only in March had I written her a long letter and included at Dr. Minor's request, his invitation to her to contribute to this book. A verse whose author is unknown comes to mind:

> "When we asunder part
> It gives me inward pain
> But we shall still be joined in heart
> And hope to meet again."

On the afternoon of May 14, 1986, Jan suddenly announced an unscheduled department meeting. We quickly gathered around the table in the taste panel room. She shocked us with the news which the General had told her that morning. The research and development department would be disbanded and a technical services department would be formed effective the first of June. She would no longer be vice president of research and development, but become vice president of market development, a newly created position. We would all be reassigned. She, Kathleen, and Babi would go downtown to the corporate office. (Plans later changed and Kathleen remained at the plant.)

The product development and applications group and the test kitchen personnel would become the technical services department under Dick Zirbel who was being promoted to senior vice president and general manager of manufacturing. Maribeth would be transferred to the quality control department and I would join the procurement department. We all sat motionless. We were too stunned to speak. Never before had this group been speechless.

After what seemed to be an eternity, but was no doubt only a minute or two, I said, "I guess we all need something to get us up and out of our chairs." That broke the ice and people slowly started to get up and leave the room in dead silence. I had a heavy heart for Jan. She had done an outstanding job of building the department from when there was only her and Mrs. Engler, who was part-time, to ten people. Many new products were developed under her guidance and the department had broadened its scope of responsibilities in many new areas. She had put so much effort in the plans for the new facility which was almost completed.

At this time, my title was R & D Source Specialist which had changed from R & D assistant in 1984. Maribeth and I were the members of the ingredient and product research group with Kathleen McGowan as manager. Before we went in our different directions, we honored her at a party and presented her with a framed certificate, written in calligraphy, which read:

Congratulations and best wishes, Jan
L. J. Minor R & D Team

Christine Bodnar	Suzanne Lesko
Beverly DeLaney	Kathleen McGowan
Janice Guarnera	Margaret Rauch
Maribeth Hackney	Babi Scott
Joellen Ionni	Ellen Smith

After the initial shock wore off, it became clear that this was a logical move for me. I had been doing a lot of work for the procurement department for many years. After I started getting test samples in 1980 and later on when product technologists were hired, my work became less involved with products and more focused on raw material research.

For a long time, I had already been sending out "Raw Material Supplier Update" memos, usually regarding newly approved raw materials and their suppliers. As I gathered information, the need for an approved supplier list for these ingredients seemed vital, so I wrote the first one. As new or alternate suppliers were approved or when a raw material was no longer used, a revised list was issued.

How it has grown and changed over the years! I had searched for alternate suppliers for critical ingredients. When the last U. S. manufacturer stopped making MSG, I had to find a foreign source. I also searched for suppliers for new ingredients for new products. Individually quick frozen (I.Q.F.) lamb for Lamb Base was one of the hardest to find. I was already obtaining and filing manufacturer's specs, labels, letters of guarantee, and material safety data sheets for ingredients we were purchasing, and sending copies to Bart Katuscak, procurement specialist.

Purchasing information for raw materials was also obtained for Bart including availability, costs, units of purchase, minimum order quantities, and so forth. Raw materials were often approved from specific plants. For example, chicken fat processed at two plants owned by the same company might be different. Thus, if Bart wanted to order from either plant, fat had to be approved from both. In 1985 and 1986, I wrote L. J. Minor specifications for meat, poultry, seafood, and dairy raw materials, which were used as guidelines for purchasing.

While finishing up work in R & D, I became more and more excited about my new assignment and looked forward to working for Bart, another longtime Minor's employee, and his boss, Ingolf Nitsch, manager of manufacturing services. But as exciting as anything else, I must confess, I was thrilled to finally have my own office after ten years! I had always shared one with two other people. No more somebody else's desk abutted to mine. No more disturbing others because I did so much business on the phone.

A new title came with my new office. I was raw material research coordinator. I recall Bart taking me on a tour of the brand new engineering/maintenance wing, not quite completed, and showing me our offices, as he was also glad to be relocating. In fact, at one time when we were so short of space, his office was a table in the lunchroom from where he called in all his orders! Afterwards, he occupied several real offices!

The new technical center was dedicated in December, 1986. It included test and development kitchens, a sensory evaluation room, a microbiological lab, and offices. The expanded technical capability would allow the company to respond even faster to the increasing demands of our customers.

In the fall of 1986, the employees were informed that the owners, the private investment group, had put the company up for sale, that representatives from numerous major food companies would be visiting, and that it would probably be sold before the end of the year. We usually knew in advance who was coming. Many hummed the familiar Campbell Soup tune "M-m-m good, m-m-m good" the day that Campbell personnel visited.

Many were concerned about what would happen to us if we were swallowed up by a major food company. How secure were our jobs? What about layoffs? Even though our processing was unique, would this plant be closed? Some of these questions were answered in a letter dated December 29, 1986, from Bill McLaughlin, the General's son, and now our president and chief operating officer. It announced "the formal acquisition of the L. J. Minor Corporation by Nestle Enterprises, Inc. on December 29, 1986."

It was sent to our homes with the 1985 annual report of Nestle Enterprises, so that we would gain some insight into "the challenges and opportunities" that lay ahead. Stouffer Foods Corporation was already owned by Nestle Enterprises, so I had come full circle and was back to where I started in 1958! In fact, Jim Biggar, president of Nestle Enterprises, was not only an ex-Stouffer employee, but married Margie Stouffer, Vernon's daughter. We were also glad to learn that Dr. Minor would continue to serve as senior scientific consultant and still be a part of the new organization. Thus, another era in the history of the L. J. Minor Corporation began.

In closing, I feel very honored to have been invited by Dr. Minor to contribute to this book. It has given me the opportunity to reminisce about many valued memories, and to reflect on the growth and success of the L. J. Minor Corporation, which has been overwhelming.

The strong foundation and high standards for premium quality products and for outstanding customer service established by Dr. and Mrs. Minor in 1951 have been the building blocks of this flourishing company. I am indebted to Mrs. Engler for her perseverance and for recommending me, and to Mike Zelski for his confidence in me to do the job and thus for hiring me.

There have been opportunities and challenges, and even frustrations, but how fortunate I have been to be a part of the L. J. Minor team. My career has been very enjoyable and rewarding. How grateful I am that it has been personally satisfying. Through the company, Dr. and Mrs. Minor have made a difference in my life and in the lives of countless others. You have touched our hearts in so many ways. Bless you!

Chapter 41

Further Insight into Quality:

Quality Assurance

by Blanca Nieves
(1972-1995)

Quality Control

by Maureen Beyer
(1977-1985)

My Introduction to Minor's   **Sample Department**

Quality Control Department   **Research and Development Department**

A Quality Life
by Lewis J. Minor

"Life is like a cup of tea,
 It's how you make it."

On Specifying Quality
(Irish Humor by Hal Roach)

Danaher went into the hardware to buy some nails. The hardware man says to him:
"How long do you want them?"

Danaher says:
"Well, I'd like to keep them."

Quality Assurance
by Blanca Nieves

I started working for the L. J. Minor Corp. on January 12, 1972, as a cleaning person. I was taken through the plant and told to clean all walls, doors, hinges, tops of bowls, floors, etc. Basically, I had to do all general sanitation throughout the plant. When I finished with my regular duties I was told to continue looking for more places to clean, even if it wasn't my responsibility.

About three days later, the person in charge of the quality assurance department at that time came to me and gave me a toothbrush to clean the grouting and the grills of the air conditioning units. I went to Mike Zelski and said to him that I was going to quit. I was so mad because I felt that giving me the toothbrush to clean with was an insult. I was told that Dr. Minor's daughter worked at the company, but I did not know who she was.

There was a lady who used to pack samples, Helen Crites, who seemed bossy and I thought that she was the daughter of Dr. Minor. Little did I know that the person I had been confiding in with my problems was Ruth Fields, Dr. Minor's daughter. By noon of that day I realized that I really needed this job and I went back to Mike Zelski and asked for my job back. After work I went to the store and bought a big brush and used this along with a pail and a cloth to continue my cleaning duties throughout the plant.

When needed in packaging, I used to help . Everything used to be packaged by hand. For instance, the gravies. The bags had to be opened, filled by hand, weighed, folded, and heat sealed, then boxed so that the label on the bags all faced in one direction.

The one-pound containers were packaged in glass jars. In order to package product in glass jars, we first had to sanitize the table, then place the glass jars on the table upside down. They were passed through a vacuum. The glass jars were then taken to the food pump; food base was placed into the jars, and we then hand-weighed each and sealed them with a metal screw type lid. The products were packaged back into the boxes and then placed on the conveyor and sealed.

The boxes were taken and placed in a trailer located in the front of the building, which was kept refrigerated. The trailer was where we kept the product before it was sold to a customer. We did our shipping of orders from here. Samples of our products were placed in 1 oz. glass jars. We packaged these containers by hand using a pastry bag. Eventually we started packaging samples in 4 oz. glass jars. The larger size containers, including 100 lb., 50 lb., 25 lb., and 10 lb., were packaged in plastic bags inside a fiber drum.

Some of the brands of bases which we packaged when I first started included Select Beef, Select Chicken, Caterer Chicken, Caterer Beef, Choice Chicken, Godfrey Chicken, Godfrey Beef, Minor's Turtle, Lobster, Clam, Beef, Chicken, Ham, Pork, and Brown Sauce (Espagnole) bases. Other products included Beef Consommé, Au Jus, and Chicken, Beef, Pork, and Turkey Gravies.

In 1974 I was weighing control products half a day and cleaning half a day under the direction of Joe Thomas who was in charge of quality assurance at that time. The formulas were type-written and clipped together. I was told how careful I needed to be with the oleoresins because one little mistake could alter the taste of the product. For me this job was fun because I didn't need to clean all the time and it was like following recipes, and I had always enjoyed cooking and mixing ingredients together.

Premixes were made in a small room located in the back of the plant near the small warehouse. There were three Hobart mixers in the packaging room where the products were finished. There was a pan room located in the center of the plant, where all the utensils were washed and cleaned. There was a cookroom with five steamers used to cook the chickens. Across the hall from the cookrooms was a room for deboning chickens.

The ladies in charge of chicken picking would take the veins, skin, and bones out and discard them. They would then separate the dark meat from the white meat and place the meat into lugs which were taken to the cooler until it was ready to be used. This room was also used for picking veins and shells from clams used to make Clam Base. This procedure was also done for the lobster meat used to make Lobster Base.

All meats that were cooked were used that same day to make the bases. No left-over meats were kept. Then they had a room located next to the grinding area where they roasted beef for Beef Base or pork tenderloins for Pork Base or lobster for Lobster Base. We had a small grinding room where an employee named Pearl would grind these meats to be used in their appropriate bases.

One wintry, blizzard day in 1978, all the lights in the plant went out. This was our day for manufacturing Chicken Base. We had all this chicken on the table that needed to be picked or it would become spoiled. All the employees from management on down banded together and picked chickens by candlelight. The chicken meat was used after the lights came back on. In those days and still today we are only allowed to make seafood on designated days and other meat and poultry products on the other days.

For cleaning the plant we used to hire high school students to work after school to do cleaning and then they would also help with the packaging. On weekends they would do a thorough cleaning, using hand scrubbers for the floors, cleaning the walls and ceilings, etc. The plant was always kept thoroughly clean. Two of my sons had a chance to work after school at the company. I believe that some of those who worked after school are among our best employees today.

In 1975, I started working in the quality assurance department full time. That is when they made up the Formula Books, one for Premixes or Plant Products (PP's), one for Control Products (CP's), and one for Manufactured Products (MP's). I was trained by Ruth how to taste the products, how to keep records of the batch weights, how to test products, and how to figure errors, if any, in batches. I was taught about the various temperatures product should be kept at by Ruth and Mike Zelski and how critical these temperatures are in order to prevent bacteria from growing.

We collected samples on all batches made and kept a library of refrigerated and room temperature products as references. These samples were used to check on product complaints or as standards to compare as new batches were made. We would also send

439

samples to an outside laboratory for microbiological testing.

We would do swabs and airplates on equipment and the plant areas to make sure that everything was thoroughly clean and bacteria free. This was one of many critical procedures that Dr. Minor required in order to maintain the integrity of our products. New products developed were sent to Dr. Minor and various chefs for their approval.

In 1976 my daughter, Diana, started working for the company after she graduated from high school. She worked in filling the sample order requests. Eventually, she met and married Bart Katuscak who was already working for the L. J. Minor Corp. I now have two beautiful grandchildren from them and they are both happy and still working for the L. J. Minor Corp.

Dr. and Mrs. Minor, and their children including Ruth Fields, Michael Minor, Josephine Minor, Mary Minor, and the other children with whom we had the pleasure of working, always made the employees feel as if we were part of their family. They always treated us well, not only by the salary and good benefits they provided us, but by their friendship which I will always treasure.

I'm still working in the quality assurance department and I still practice and believe in the principles and practices that Dr. Minor implemented and had taught to me. I know that I have been appreciated by the Key Employee Award I was presented in 1990.

Dr. Minor, I would like to thank you for enriching my personal and family life. All I have are good memories of the many years I worked for you. I take pride in having played a part in making the L. J. Minor Corporation a successful company for you and your family.

God Bless You!

Quality Control
by Maureen Beyer

My Introduction to Minor's

One nice summer day, I was taking care of some children. A car unexpectedly pulled into the driveway. The children got extremely excited. They screamed and ran out of the house to meet this visitor. I learned this was the children's grandfather. As he visited and talked to each one of them, it was obvious that he loved them very much.

Anyone could tell what a caring person he was by his actions with these children. In future years I came to know that this man was not only the children's grandfather, but he was also Dr. Lewis J. Minor. I also learned that he cared about his employees as much as he did for his family.

My experience at the L. J. Minor Corporation began in 1977. I applied for a job as a secretary. I went for an interview. The interview must have gone well. I was hired, but not as a secretary. My position had the title of "sample person," and I was to work with each product and sample.

Sample Department

The job of a sample person encompassed many things. The final goal was the shipping of the samples of the Minor products to prospective customers and sales representatives. I learned how to label the product jars with the hot glue labeler. It was tricky to get the glue to the right temperature and to get the label on straight. Learning how to make and stamp (label) boxes was also part of the job, and this included using a large foot operated stapler.

The packaging of samples was a slow job. One had to accurately weigh the product into a 4 oz. glass jar. We filled a pastry bag with the product and squeezed it into the jar. Then came the tedious part of adjusting the weight through the small jar opening. French Onion Soup was the real time consumer as you first weighed the Beef Base, then you forcefully packed the toasted onions on top, while checking again for the proper weight of the total product. The accurate weight was very important with all products. But on such a small package it was even more critical to the final reconstituted prepared product. Neatness of the jars, labels, and packaging were also very important.

(Editor's Note: How I remember the great years of receiving the Minor Food Bases at my office prior to a Minor chef demonstration to the students. As I learn of the tedious job of packaging the French Onion Soup, one of my favorites, how much more I appreciate the quality of the entire product line. Those little bottles, as Ms. Beyer has noted here, neatly filled with base and then topped with toasted onions. Prior to this product being available, I rarely prepared this time consuming delight at home. After the product was introduced, I would simply bring water to a simmer, add the product, top it with melted cheese on toasted croutons, and I had one delicious meal. Thanks, Ms. Beyer, Dr. Minor, and all of you who worked on this great Minor product!)

The sample orders came from the downtown office. Most orders could be filled and shipped soon after arrival. Others had to be coordinated with the production scheduler in order to save some of the product to be packaged as samples. I picked out the requested samples, and carefully packed them in the appropriate box. I weighed the box and prepared it to be shipped by U. P. S. Product sample requests for food shows were usually large and required one or two of every product.

This initial position at Minor's was a real learning experience. The company saw to it that I was properly trained and knew my job before the previous "sample person" moved on in the company.

Another large responsibility of the "sample person" was to pack and ship all the

Christmas gift boxes that were sent. Thankfully, production scheduled some Saturdays to help do this. We always sent out well over 100 gift boxes each year.

At this point, Minor's was a small company and very employee oriented. The benefits were an outward sign that the employee was very important to Dr. and Mrs. Minor. It could also be seen when Dr. and Mrs. Minor came in the plant many times throughout the year.

On their "walk-thru" they would stop and talk to each employee -- this was usually on a first name basis. They were always interested in you. They were very caring and did not come across as superior. They came in as one of us -- one of the family. They were happy. Dr. Minor would joke with the employees. It was reassuring to see owners so interested in the employees that they interacted with everyone in the plant.

As time permitted, I helped out in many areas of production. This was very interesting, as I got to see and learn a lot about packaging and production. It was also interesting to see how the products were made. Later, as the plant grew, so did the need for a new position which would eventually be called "utility person."

One of the first places I helped in was packaging. This was a fast-paced place to be. The glass jars were filled and weighed. The lids were put on and then tightly turned with the lid tightener. The filled jars were then placed in boxes, sealed, and counted before going to the shipping department. In later years a more automated packaging system was installed. Then the packaging room was much quieter because of the switch from glass to plastic packaging material.

Another area that I helped in was in "chicken picking." When I started with Minor's, I thought this job name was a joke. It turned out to be accurate. People stood by the hot cooked chicken and removed the skin, bones, cartilage and veins. Only the "picked through chicken" could be used in making the Chicken Base. As I learned more about the product, I learned this was an important job. In later years, when I worked in R & D, many people tried to get us to buy frozen, already machine picked, chicken. We tested many samples. The flavor was not the same, nor was the quality. Frequently, we found gristle and pieces of bone..

One accident I remember very well. A batch of finished Lobster Base was being pushed up front for final weighing and testing, when the wheel of the dolly caught on something, and the contents spilled all over the floor. What a sight! All 350 or so pounds of red Lobster Base everywhere. Of course, we had to immediately throw it all away. What amazed me to this day is the fact that the supervisor didn't yell and get mad. He said it was an accident, so just clean it up and get on with the rest of production. (Actually I think this was Mike Minor.)

Sometimes I also helped in the grinding room. This was where the freshly cooked meat, picked through chicken, and seafood were ground to the proper coarseness. The ground product was then weighed to be mixed in the final blending stage.

Over the years to keep up with the production demands, the plant kept growing and growing. It was done in many phases, and it was interesting to see the progress. Every addition seemed too large, but in time we always outgrew the "new" addition.

Quality Control Department

As time went on, there developed a need for an assistant in the quality control department (Q. C.). I was fortunate enough to get this job. I was trained by Blanca Nieves, who through the years has upheld the standards Dr. Minor had set. Being trained for Q. C. was a real eye opener into an interesting and detailed department. Our job in Q. C. was to see to it that the product was made in a sanitary facility, with quality raw materials, with proper processing methods (no short cuts), in order to finish up with a high quality product.

In order to do all this, there were numerous checks and tests. We began each morning with our daily walk through the plant. We had a list of rooms and equipment to check BEFORE production could begin for the day. We inspected for cleanliness from receiving to production to shipping and even the outdoor property. Every room and cooler were checked.

We went over all pieces of equipment to see that they were properly cleaned. We checked the cooler and freezer for the right temperatures. We made sure all products were correctly labeled -- no matter what phase of production they were in. We checked filters, floors, proper raw material rotation as well as product rotation.

We routinely monitored the scales for accuracy as well as the professional scale checks and maintenance records. Anything not up to standard, or that required attention was tagged "HOLD." The supervisor was notified as to all "HOLDS." After the supervisor had corrected the problem to meet our standard, we would release it for use. All this was recorded in a daily log. Now production could begin.

We always kept boiling water available for the many tests to be completed throughout the day. We would look at the production schedule to see what the agenda was for that day. The Formulas were also kept locked up in Q.C. We were responsible for letting the designated employees check them out and making sure they were all returned.

All raw materials were examined as they arrived or soon afterwards. We looked to confirm that the raw material's label and ingredients statement matched the approved raw material list. We made certain that the packages were all sealed, clean, and coded. If the raw material was refrigerated or frozen, we would check for the proper temperature. We would then take a sample of the raw material to be tested in the Q. C. lab.

All the receiving information, as well as test results, were recorded. There were a variety of tests depending on the raw material -- we referred to our files for the required tests. All tests were done in comparison to a standard. First we observed the overall appearance of the raw material. Then we performed the following test(s) including a starch test, a sugar test, a dissolving test, a specific gravity test, a cooking test, percent fat test, sodium test, and a spectrometer test.

In time we developed more advanced methods. We tested for the total quality that was needed to go into the product. We tasted for freshness, to be certain that there were no "off flavors." We checked for color, consistency, and proper texture. Some raw materials were sent out for bacterial analysis.

We had an interesting experience with butter as we kept receiving sour butter. We could never detect the sourness upon arrival with our test. And the product was always in code and used soon after arrival. Dr. Minor advised us to melt the butter and smell it to see if it was going sour or not. This proved to be a very important test.

If a raw material came in from an unapproved manufacturer for that specific raw material, we would put it on "HOLD." We would then notify R & D, which would then test it. The usual R & D testing steps were 1) taste test the raw material, 2) make an R & D experimental batch (a 5 lb. or so batch) and test it, 3) make a full size experimental batch and test it. The raw material would then be approved or rejected and added to the appropriate list. Of course if it were rejected, the full size batch was then disposed of as well. Communication with purchasing was important because they always had to be up to date on the approved and rejected manufacturers of each raw material.

Once we got in a shipment of salt, a routine and standard material, and let it go into production, only later to find out it would not work in the products. The crystal size was inconsistent, so it was totally unacceptable. This is when we fine tuned the raw material testing procedures for new suppliers with R & D

Many times we did not make the receiving or production departments happy when we rejected or put a raw material on "HOLD". We had to do our job of upholding the quality standard set, even if it meant numerous headaches for the other departments.

The formulas to make the products were in three or more parts. This was to insure confidentiality of the formulas. No one person had access to all the parts. It was a finely tuned system that worked very well. There was a Controlled Product (CP) which was controlled and dispensed by Q. C. The CP was usually special spices, seasonings, or minute amounts of ingredients. The Plant Products (PP) was a special mix which was made in our plant, usually in the Premix Room. The final product or the Manufactured Products (MP) was the final mixing and processing to be done "up- front". In later years with the new equipment, these formulas had to be adjusted, but the three part formula was kept intact.

Since it was a Q. C. job to be in charge of the Control Product, we checked the daily schedule to know what Control Product we would be handing out or putting directly into the Plant Product or Manufacturers Product. We had to see that every batch had the proper Control Product. We also kept in close contact with production scheduling to know what the long term schedule was, as we needed some time to properly weigh, mix and label Control Products.

Oleoresins went into many of the Control Products. This was an extremely difficult product to clean up after, so you learned quickly to be as neat as possible. We purchased our oleoresins from the Joseph Adams Company. Mr. Adams, the owner, was another very caring and wonderful person. It was another family run business that cared about its customer. I find it very rare to get the customer service one should have in the world today. The Minor Corporation and the Joseph Adams Company were two businesses that knew this was important. When I was in R & D, we took a trip to Mr. Adams' plant. He took us on a tour and explained how the oleoresins were made. This helped us in our work of developing new products.

We did some spot checking of manufacturing procedures and weight checks of the PP's We kept standard samples of PP's to do taste tests. These helped if there was an error. If an error was made, we could often identify the missing or extra ingredient and correct the mistake. One of the plant products was the caramelized sugar. This process required constant monitoring. We needed the sugar to be caramelized (not burned), and with a deep brown color. We tested the sugar often on our spectrometer to assure the color would be in the right range.

The other controlled items monitored by Q. C. were the soap for cleaning and sanitizing. These substances required proper dilution to do the best job. So we pre-measured and distributed them. We also checked again after the equipment was cleaned to be sure it was also sanitized.

During the numerous production stages, the processing procedures and products were tested. We checked the temperatures of cooked items, the specific gravity, the grinding and mixing procedures, the thawing procedures, the can opening procedures, and that all liquid raw material, PP's, and MP's were properly stirred.

One product that required close monitoring throughout the cooking procedure was the Glace de Viande. We took many samples and checked the specific gravity until it was within set guidelines. Then it was allowed to go to the next phase of processing.

The product was tested at numerous stages with the final testing done "up-front." Each batch of product was weighed, checked for consistency, and appearance. Samples were then taken and labeled. We took numerous samples. One was put in the cooler, one in room temperature storage, and one for testing.

We routinely sent samples to the lab for bacterial analysis, and also to a consultant to taste test, as a double check. Our Q. C. taste test was conducted immediately, preparing it as the package directions would call for. We would test the reconstituted product for its appearance, color, texture, consistency, odor, overall flavor.

We had to have unanimous approval to let the product be packaged. If we had any questions, we would notify Ruth Ann Minor Fields, Mike Minor, Mike Zelski, and Jan Williams. If there was any question as to the quality of the final product, it was put on "hold" for further testing. Of course this did not make packaging or shipping very happy. But it was again the quality standard we were after. If it was approved, we would put an approval tag on the label, and it could then be packaged.

We kept a daily log of the products made, along with their weight and product code. This was important if we needed to backtrack, in case we received a complaint of any type. We had the history and a sample or two in reserve for testing.

The Q. C. department also monitored the T. B. tests and kept accurate records. We performed a strep test monthly on all employees as well as a swab test of the equipment, and room "plate counts." All new employees were required to have a physical examination and a chest X-ray before being allowed to begin work.

Again, the thorough training for this job was excellent. It was interesting work, and

I enjoyed it. We all worked together, took breaks together, and were made to feel important.

Through the years of my employment with the L. J. Minor Corporation, the one key person to the whole plant operation was Ruth Ann Minor Fields. She had total knowledge in every aspect of production, packaging, raw materials, quality control, formulas, procedures, scheduling, and taste testing to see to the making of a high quality product. If anyone had a question or problem, he or she always relied on Ruth, since she knew the history and reasons why certain things were done in certain ways.

Research and Development Department

With the constant growth of Minor's, R & D's scope of responsibilities increased. When a part-time R & D kitchen assistant position became available, Jan Williams requested that I fill it. Eventually, I became a full time R & D assistant. As I received further training, I became the research assistant. Then as our staff grew, I became the test kitchen supervisor and product technician. My final position with the corporation was an R & D system specialist.

Beverly DeLaney trained me well in the test kitchen. Our main job was to prepare, serve, and clean-up from the taste panel. We evaluated our bases, gravies, soup mixes, competitors products (these never had a chance against the Minor's product), raw material, new and experimental batches, and recipe development.

We began the day by labeling the "taste cups." This was done only with a ball-point pen as marker odor was distracting to the panelists during sensory evaluation. Next was the advanced prep, which was the measuring of all the ingredients that would be prepared for the panel. We then prepared the product as the consumer would.

We would record any problems in mixing or cooking as well as in the final yield. The prepared broth, gravy, or soup was then placed in a hot water bath. The panelist were called, and the panel was served. We always began with the mildest flavor products and worked up to the more seasoned ones. As an example, first a white sauce would be served, then a chicken broth, then a beef broth, and finally a pasta and pizza sauce (with spaghetti).

The taste panel was made up of R & D staff, production, and purchasing management, all of whom had to have a very acute sense of taste. It was actually an honor to be able to be part of the panel. You had to be very sensitive to the flavor, odor, color, and texture of every item.

Thankfully I was not one on the taste panel when all of the caviar was screened. The items served were all coded, and no one saw the code until after everything was evaluated. The panelists would score the items served, usually against a standard. When finished, Jan would lead the discussion, reveal the codes, and all would share in ideas as to what the next step would be. We would record all of the taste panelist score sheets and average them.

Numerous tests were done on raw material and test samples to screen out the bad and keep the good. The best test samples went on to further testing. Daily we set up one tray of test samples or raw material to be evaluated as time permitted. Numerous times we tested butter flavors for our Dry Roux. The one ingredient we chose was far superior to any butter flavor tested as of 1985.

When we were notified of the plans to enlarge and improve the R & D department, Jan did a lot of research and had consultants come in to evaluate our taste panel and discuss our needs. From these discussions two main improvement were to be made: 1) proper airflow across the taste panel area, 2) special lighting with which to best evaluate the product.

While our kitchen and office were under refurbishing, we had the pleasure of moving to an apartment directly facing West 25th Street. This was an experience! It was a challenge to prepare, serve, and evaluate the product in the temporary quarters which were cramped. I was sure a truck or car was going to come right through the front window. Somehow we managed and really came to appreciate our newly refurbished department. Actually we enjoyed working in our new kitchen and office.

This gave us room to accommodate another body in the kitchen. We often had the honor of working with (or in the way of) our chef, Mike Minor. We were able to enjoy some of his fine creations. We especially enjoyed the era when he was making the "perfect French Bread."

We helped him in preparation for food shows by weighing items in advance or even cooking woups and chili, "cryovacing" them for shelf life stability, with the help of Mike. Assisting Mike in packing food ingredients and equipment for the food shows was done routinely. We all saw his sample plates before the Culinary Olympics and were all very happy for him when he won his Gold Medals.

He did receive unusual food samples. Once he was visiting some chicken processing plants and returned with a product for us to cook up and taste test. Thankfully we never did have to prepare it. It was chicken testicles! He told us they were a delicacy when fried. I wonder what ever happened to those samples in the R & D freezer?

The test kitchen staff was responsible for the grocery shopping for the ingredients we needed to prepare our taste panel. This list grew as Mike wanted some recipes tested. Then when R & D got into the recipe development full swing, we had major shopping to do.

Recipe development was done as directed by Jan. She did the research and sketched up a recipe to try. Sometimes we would do a quick test on a Friday and see how close we were before bringing it to a taste panel. The yield of the cooked product was very important. We developed both home sized and foodservice size recipes. After the recipe was approved by the panel, we did a "freeze-thaw" test on the cooked product. To many of our customers this was important as to the versatility of the recipe. We proofread the brownproof as well as the final copy of all recipes before they could go out to customers.

We did run some technical tests in the test kitchen. Some of these included percent salt, percent sodium, pH, percent moisture, percent fat, water activity, and specific gravity. The nutritional analysis was sent to an outside lab for evaluation.

We made experimental batches of products in our test kitchen. This began by calculating the formula, to the .00000 % of each ingredient. This required a lot of math! We scheduled our making of the batch to coincide with the production schedule. We used our equipment in the test kitchen for chopping and mixing. We tried to simulate plant processing as much as possible. If the base was acceptable from the taste evaluations, we would then work up the full size experimental production batch.

Some experimental batches took a lot of tinkering to get them just right. I am told that the Vegetarian Consommé, Chicken Style was requested at a meeting. Dr. Minor then suggested to Jan which ingredients to use and at what percentages. We made an experimental batch (and many more). After many trials we ended up using a formula very close to the original one suggested.

During my years, I was able to see quite a few products come through the developmental pipeline through R & D including Crab Base, Fish Base, Dry Roux, Vegetarian Consommé, Chicken Style, Pasta and Pizza Sauce, Poultry Glace, and N. E. Clam Chowder to name a few.

Working with the coordinator, Ruth Ann, I worked with the formulas, keeping them updated as to ingredient amounts and processing changes. Being the production supervisor, she kept us informed as to possible future changes. With the larger equipment we had two types of formulas around. One was the original, and the other was a pocket-sized version.

These were laminated and could be carried around by the employees. It was eventually my job to see that our files had copies of all size formulas, and keeping a history of all the formulas used.

All label changes were coordinated with R & D. The brownproof as well as the final label, cup, or pail, were all proofread in R & D. After we made sure there were no mistakes, these would then be released for use.

The most difficult of these was the U. S. D. A. label changes. If we made any change, we had to submit the label for the U. S. D. A.'s approval. This required filling out a transmittal form which included the formula change. We listed the percentage of the ingredients and attached the new label. This also required a lot of record keeping. We kept the original approval from the U. S. D. A. as well as the final approval transmittal.

We kept many files. A time came when we needed more filing cabinets and someone was concerned about the formulas and their confidentiality. So new fireproof filing cabinets were ordered. They came complete with combination locks. Actually, I think we finally had four or more and I never heard of the floor caving in.

We had numerous customer service requests, and most of these were easy to accommodate. Many customers wanted our products with a slight processing or ingredient change. These products kept the manufacturers product number and just had a letter added onto it to signify the variation in the formula.

The plant was kept off limits to those not employed by the company. The outside doors were locked, and you had to have a key to enter. Keys to everything! The doors the upstairs office were also locked, as was the door to R & D. Our desk was always kept locked with instructions to not leave any papers around. The cloakroom which had test samples in it was kept locked. The filing cabinets had combination locks, as did the files in the basement.

When the packaging material was to be changed, we had to be involved. We tested all new packaging materials to see if the flavor was affected and how well it held up. We tested each material for a year, checking at different intervals. One sample was kept at room temperature, one in the cooler of the standard material as well as the new packaging material. These were all evaluated at the taste panel.

In this department you always had to develop new tests. One interesting test included the trunk of Jan's car. We had complaints that the product was "settling out." Most of these complaints came from the western side of our country and in the summertime. So we developed a new test. A pail of the product was put in our storeroom, one in the cooler, and one in Jan's car. She recorded how many miles it traveled at each testing stage. This was done during the winter and summer, and the results of this test led us to do this on a regular basis.

Food photography was also included in our job descriptions. This was a real experience. We took all of our products and ingredients to a food photography studio. Each dish was carefully selected. The dish was then washed with a vinegar/water solution to make it shine. The food was prepared and carefully placed on the dish by Mike, who would then garnish it. We found this to be a very time consuming project. I do appreciate the work that goes into good food photography.

The numerous laboratory results were received in R & D. We made sure that, if needed, any immediate action was taken. We then routed the reports to Q. C., plant manger, production supervisor, and other necessary personnel.

Jan and I worked together on getting some of the formulas into the personal computer for ease of calculating. When I left there was still much work that could be made easier with a computer.

Picture taking of the inside of the plant was not allowed. This was to preserve the confidentiality of the equipment and processing of the product. Near the end of my employment, we were asked to take pictures for slide presentations. I began taking select pictures for this assignment. Jan eventually was able to put together a very nice slide show.

Toward the end of my working at the company, many changes were going on to make the whole company and atmosphere stressful and uneasy. The shifts in owners caused turmoil even though it was denied. It was a sad day when the Minor's sold the company, as we knew nothing would ever be the same as it had been when they were the owners. But we were also very happy for the Minors. They could enjoy life and not have the worry of the company.

The benefits we had as employees of this company were outstanding! They included an excellent vacation package, medical coverage, holiday turkey and ham, and a yearly Christmas gift. We had bonuses, profit-sharing, and a 401(k) plan. Come to think of it, I wonder why Dr. Minor did not give us a paid holiday on St. Patrick's Day?

My overall experience at the Minor Corporation was very positive. I learned a lot and I think the "on-the-job" training I received was very valuable. In fact, it was a big factor in my advancement within the company. I enjoyed my job and it raised my self-confidence level. I have fond memories of the years I spent there.

Having left Minor's to be with my young family, I felt, along with my husband, that it was important for me to be home and to lovingly raise our children. Our children are our first priority as they are only young once. Yes, I do miss the job (and the money), but my family is all important. I am sure that Dr. and Mrs. Minor would agree. If I ever go back into the work force full time, I hope that I can find as wonderful an employer as I had at the Minor Corporation.

Chapter 42

Living the Vision:

For Over 25 Years

by George Henderson
(1964-1995)

For Nearly 20 Years

by Bart Katuscak
(1975-1995)

Family Influence   My Work Begins   Responsibilities Expand

Through the Years

by Diana Katuscak
(1976-1995)

As One Big Family

by Bridget Clancy-Bell
(1979-1995)

Speaking of One Big Family
(Irish Humor by Hal Roach)

Casey was asked by the priest to prove from the scriptures that it was unlawful to have more than one wife. Casey quoted the verse:
"No man can serve two masters."

Quote from William Lawrence Sullivan

"It is ages that are transient; it is moments that are everlasting."

Quote from Hugh Downs

"Random purposeless activity is the restorative
that balances other activities in life."

For Over 25 Years
by George Henderson

The date that I was first hired by the L. J. Minor Corporation was October 26, 1964. I had heard the company was looking for a shipping, receiving, and inventory clerk through my late uncle Jimmy Hyster who worked for the company at the time.

He recommended that I talk with Joe Gilbert who was the plant foreman. After my interview, Joe hired me. In those days, if we were "short-handed," I would be asked to work in areas like premix, cooking, making sauces, etc. Thus, I learned quickly several different jobs!

After being with the company only three and one-half months, I accepted the position in premix that was available. At that time, the beef was cooked in two small ovens that were on legs, and the chicken was cooked in steamers.

Once chickens were cooked, they were moved to another work area where they were placed on a table and a couple of people would remove meat from the bone and skin and veins from the meat. This operation was called deboning. I remember in 1965, a new chopper was added. In 1966 the first pan washer was installed, and in 1968, the first addition was completed. It was in this area that the pan washing was moved as well as the premix weighing area.

Prior to that the pan washing was done in a small room in the front of the facility off of the final blend and packaging area. On either side of that room were the restrooms and an office area which was occupied by the U. S. D. A. and management as time progressed.

The first "titled" Quality Assurance (QA) employee was Pat Hamilton. She was hired to make and weigh up Control Products (CP), sample and taste test all products made as well as incoming raw materials, and fill out "batch cards" and logs to accompany all products tested. Prior to her employment, for a short while, some of the CP's were measured out by the premix department.

In 1968 I left Minor's for a position with another company. After being there for six months, I was asked to return to Minor's as a part-time employee in January, 1969.

One of my fondest memories while employed at the Minor Corporation was during the earlier '60s when Dr. Minor was teaching at Michigan State University. He would periodically take time to come to the plant and personally teach us proper food handling and personal hygiene procedures.

He taught with heartfelt dedication which made his presentations educational and enjoyable. It also reinforced the pride and commitment the company stood for, particularly when someone like the CEO would make time to interact with his staff at all levels! This is unheard of in the '90s!

Mike Zelski, who was a former student of Dr. Minor, was assigned the plant manager position in 1968. In 1974 he offered me a supervisory position. Also that year a new shipping cooler was added to the southwest corner of the existing plant. This cooler had two and one-half times the capacity of the refrigerated trailers that we were using to store packaged manufactured products and set up outgoing orders.

When Mike Minor came with the company in June of 1977, he helped develop the Fish Base, which had been in the development stages for a long time. He also found easier, less strenuous, and less time consuming ways to do certain methods, including, but not limited to, sautéing mushrooms.

In 1979 a receiving warehouse was added to the northeast end of the facility, and in 1981 the new chopper room was added. From the very beginning, I realized that Ruth Ann was the backbone of the Minor Company. When she spoke everyone would listen. She was one of the important keys in the success of the Minor Corporation.

In addition, I have always felt like I was a part of the Minor Corporation because I was there when the original building was only a five-room plant. After the sale of the business, Dr. Minor would still have a "walk through" the plant and talk with me as well as with the other employees of the plant.

On September 10, 1994, I received an award for 25 years of service. Unofficially, I have been working for the company for 30 years!

For Nearly 20 Years
by Bart Katuscak

I am currently the Manager of Procurement for the L. J. Minor Foodservice Division of Food Ingredient Specialties. I began working for the L. J. Minor Corp. in 1975, but my association and familiarity with the company began long before I was first employed by them.

Family Influence

While I was growing up, I first became acquainted with the L. J. Minor Corp. through my father. He was employed by a local plumbing contractor and would often be sent to the small company on W. 25th Street in Cleveland to do work. He would tell us how amazingly clean this facility was and how everyone was required to wear white uniforms and hairnets.

He would go on talking about how all the employees would wear plastic gloves when handling the food and packaging, and that the employees routinely washed their hands when exiting or entering a processing area. My father could not help being impressed with this factory in spite of his dislike of having to wear one of the hairnets himself, constantly being hounded to wash his hands when he went in and out of the building, and the fact that they disallowed his cigar smoking in the factory.

Little did I know back then that this little company would become the focal point of my life professionally and be a major factor in my personal life.

The L. J. Minor Corp. became a more regular part of my family's life when in 1970 my mother went to work for the company. She took a job working the evening shift as part of the packaging crew. Over the next few years I would become very familiar with the company through work related conversations with my mother.

She loved working for the L. J. Minor Corp. because of the people associated with the company. Many of the friendships she developed during those years exist today despite the fact that my mother retired in 1987.

Since her retirement my mother has anxiously awaited the annual Award Banquet Dinners. They allow her to get together with many of her former co-workers who still work for the company or who may have also retired over the years. The banquet also gives her an opportunity to see how the company has grown and prospered over the years. It is an event she looks forward to each year.

My Work Begins

As I stated, my employment with the L. J. Minor Corp. began in 1975 when I took a job with the company during my summer and Christmas breaks from Ohio Wesleyan University. I was immediately impressed by what I saw.

In the business and marketing classes I had taken in school, I was taught the complexities of running a business and the various approaches to taking products to market. What I saw in reality with the L. J. Minor Corporation was a very simple philosophy. This philosophy I was told at the time was the cornerstone of the company and one upon which the owner and founder Dr. Minor had built the company. In simplest terms it was to develop and provide high quality products and service at fair market price and recognize the employees of the company as its greatest asset.

This philosophy was not just a bunch of words written down and hung on the wall as is the case with many great thoughts and ideas. From the very first moment I walked into the plant, I saw Dr. Minor's philosophy being practiced and adhered to. I became part of a work force whose primary goal was to provide the finest product possible, a product in which the quality would never be compromised or questioned.

This dedication to quality was evident with a simple walk through the plant. It was

454

now obvious to me why my father, years before, had been so impressed by the plant. Cleaning and sanitation standards for the facility and processing equipment were the starting point for building high quality Minor Bases.

From my first day of work, cleaning, sanitation, and proper food handling procedures were taught and stressed over and over. Much of my time during those early years was spent sweeping, mopping, and scrubbing. It was continually preached to us that no matter how busy we were or how heavy a work load we had, sanitation and food safety were our number one priorities.

Quality was also evident by looking at the ingredients used to make Minor bases. Only the finest ingredients were used. Fresh wholesome chickens for the Chicken Base, fresh lean beef for the Beef Base, pork tenderloins for the Pork Base, North Atlantic lobster meat for the Lobster base, and so on.

Each base would be formulated using the finest meat, poultry, seafood, and vegetable products available. It may sound corny, but I firmly believe that the employees took extra pride in making the bases knowing that only the finest ingredients were being used. They saw a commitment to quality in the raw materials being used and felt the need to assure that this dedication to quality be carried throughout the processing and packaging of the products.

The dedication of the employees to the company was tremendous, but so too were the dedication and commitment of the Minor family and the management team to the employees. There was a genuine concern by the company for the welfare and development of its employees and their families.

This commitment to the employees by the company was shown not only through fair wages, great benefits, and bonuses to all employees, but also through a work environment which fostered an openness between management and employees which made us all feel a part of a team. The feeling prevailed that there was no great difference between management and employees. We were all team members working to better the company and ourselves.

It became obvious to me during that first summer that Dr. Minor's philosophy of quality, service and employee well being was not only being preached but practiced by every employee within the company. I was very fortunate to be part of such a company so it was a very easy decision for me when I got out of school in May of 1976 to seek full time employment with the L. J. Minor Corp. It is a decision I have never regretted and one that changed my life forever.

Much has transpired since my initial years with the L. J. Minor Corporation, but the memories are still very vivid and ones I look back on with fondness. Even today I reminisce about the "good old days," and the people with whom I shared those moments.

- I can still see little Julia Perez as she applied paper labels to each of the glass jars in the back room.

455

- I walk out of the back storeroom to see a material warehouse limited to housing about two dozen pallets of materials. The dock worker is complaining, as his lift truck gets stuck on the bump outside the receiving door.

- I open the swinging doors opposite the receiving door and see Tony Caraballo weighing up dry ingredients in our premix room as the sound of the Hobart mixers fills the air.

- As I walk toward the processing area Steve Verez, "Uncle Steve", as he is known to everyone, talks to Lucille as they scrub pans in the equipment clean-up room.

- As I go through the swinging doors into the processing area I am immediately hit with the smell of the chickens in the cookroom to my left, as they are being removed from the steamers by Mario Quinones.

- To my right, I can hear Anna Caraballo, Virginia Serrano and the other chicken pickers gabbing away in Spanish as they sit around a stainless steel table piled high with cooked chicken. They carefully separate the meat from the bones.

- I walk forward a few more feet and hear the high pitched whine of the small 40 quart VCM Chopper as Anni Fleig looks through the small opening on top to see if the product has been chopped fine enough.

- Just then Clarence Smith bursts from Cookroom II carrying a pan of cooked beef complaining how hot it is in the cookroom. Anni tells him to shut up and go back to work.

- As I leave this area I enter our final blend/ packaging room. To my right I see Danny Marzan attending to the four Hobart mixers lined against the wall used for final blend.

- Ruth Fields, Dr. Minor's daughter, sits at her desk which is situated at the entrance to the room. Ruth diligently goes about the task of signing out orders which just arrived via delivery service from our Corporate Headquarters in the Bulkley Building in downtown Cleveland. It's a wonder she can concentrate on the task before her because the room is filled with the unending clanking of glass jars as they are set on the large stainless steel table in the center of the room.

- Margie Stanley directs the other packaging ladies in the cleaning, filling, weighing and lidding of these jars.

- Gilbert Cortez stands atop a small ladder and scoops base from mixing bowls into the funnel which sits atop and feeds our food pump.

- Gaye Taylor stands below tapping a foot pedal which activates an auger filler. As each jar fills she slides it across the table where Margarita Rivera sets it upon a scale and check weighs it.

- The jar is once again slid across the table where Confi Massa awaits to lid it. The jars are then placed back into the original boxes and slid via a conveyor through a tunnel into our shipping cooler.

- Exiting a small office which sits off the front of the packaging room is Emil Kralik, our U. S. D. A. inspector. He is on his way to make his rounds.

- Observing his moves from the small Q. A. lab next to Emil's office is Blanca Nieves. She is probably wondering what kind of mood Emil is in today. Blanca was in charge of making sure the quality of each batch of product made was up to product specification. She was also responsible for maintaining the strict standards of sanitation throughout the plant.

- As I go through the double doors at the front end of the packaging room I bump into Tom Mele. He's on his way to see Ruth about the production schedule he will be responsible for tonight. He mumbles something about the schedules being impossible to finish lately, but, I know somehow, some way he'll find a way to get it done.

- The shipping dock lies ahead. As I enter the dock area the sliding doors leading to the shipping cooler glide open with a rumble. Out walks Charlie Mills. He's upset that no one has come to help him clear the conveyor line leading from the packaging room. The line is piled high with cases of base waiting to be sealed. Lining the aisles of the small cooler are orders that Charlie has picked and are waiting for the arrival of the truck lines.

- I walk through the cooler and into the dry storage area separated from the cooler by a large metal door. Along the one wall is a long table at which a lovely young lady by the name of Diana Nieves goes about the job of setting-up and shipping sample orders. As I walk by she looks up and smiles at me. Her dark brown eyes seem to be smiling at me also. As I walk on I get the feeling that she likes me and it makes me feel good.

- I exit the building through a small door at the rear of the dry storage area. Before me lies a large old, but well maintained house.

- Before going into the house I decide to stop and see Arthur Tubbs who works in a small building opposite the house. This is where Arthur toasts the flour used to make our gravies. The aroma of the flour being toasted could be smelled outside. As I go

457

through the door Arthur sits atop his stool against the wall as the flour toaster he attends turns before him. As I walk closer I see that his eyes are closed and I hear the ticking of his egg timer which will alert him to the end of the cooking cycle. I leave being careful not to disturb him.

- I enter the house which is home to our product development department and doubles during the noon hour as the employee lunch room. The tantalizing aroma of numerous herbs and spices and the sizzling sound of frying foods strike me as I walk in.

- I immediately surmise that Mike Minor is once again in the midst of one of his base creations. Sure enough Mike is diligently at work while telling anyone within hearing range about his round of golf the day before.

- Maureen Beyer is one step behind him trying to clean up the mess he leaves behind.

- In the other room a taste panel is in process. Sitting around the table critiquing Mike Minor's creation are Jan Williams, Beverly DeLaney, and Ruth Engler of our product development department.

- George Hvizd is also seated, but the expression on his face tells me that he'd much rather be somewhere else.

- Mike Zelski is also present, which surprises me since Mike spends the majority of his time overseeing matters at our corporate offices.

- In Mike's absence, however, the fate of corporate rested in the able hands of Nancy Clancy. Nancy without question is one of the finest individuals I have ever had the pleasure of knowing.

- Supporting Nancy in her role of servicing our customers is Mary Ryan, Judy Ward, Ceil O'Donnell, Rose Capezutto, and Nancy Jr., Nancy's daughter.

The factory was very small when I first began working for the L. J. Minor Corp., with the work being very manual and labor intensive as my trip down memory lane might attest. Many things have changed in the 19 years I've been with the company, with perhaps the greatest change being the continual physical growth of the facility and the emphasis on automation whenever possible.

- The individually labeled glass jars have been replaced with preprinted plastic tubs. The small material warehouse was replaced with several new material warehouses capable of housing in excess of 500 pallets of materials.

- The Hobart mixers which were used to produce about 100 lbs. of premix at a time have given way to mixers capable of producing 10 times that amount.

- Instead of cooking individual pans of chicken, beef, pork, etc., we can now cook thousands of pounds of each at a time.

- We can now chop and mix our ingredients into a finished product in a single step as opposed to the multiple steps required years ago.

- In packaging, the manual filling, weighing, lidding and boxing have been totally automated.

- The shipping operation has been relocated to our Brecksville Distribution Center which, like the plant, has undertaken several expansions over the years.

- The physical growth of the plant and conversion to automation in our processing and packaging areas would not have been possible without the tremendous growth in our sales and marketing areas under the guidance of Gen. John D. McLaughlin.

Dr. Minor's insistence on the highest product quality and finest service levels possible built a foundation of loyal Minor Base customers that continued to grow over the years. Fortunately, as the company grew so did my position within the organization. My first three years were spent running our shipping department.

Responsibilities Expand

In 1979 I was promoted to materials foreman. As materials foreman, I was responsible for supervising several departments within operations. Those departments included shipping, receiving, packaging, housekeeping and maintenance. I was also responsible for ordering many of the raw materials and packaging items used in production. These years were extremely challenging. The continual plant expansions we were undertaking created many opportunities as well as problems over the years.

We knew that we had to expand in order to grow as a company. We had to build in a way that not only satisfied our immediate needs, but would allow us to expand in other areas in the future which we knew were inevitable given the company's history to that point. The questions of what areas to expand, how much, what equipment to purchase, and how to staff these areas were ours to answer.

In 1984, because of the substantial growth in the business, it became obvious to management that my duties of supervising at times up to 19 employees as well as ordering most of our raw material and packaging needed to be divided up. I was given the option of staying on as the supervisor or going into purchasing full time. I chose the latter.

459

It was a tremendous opportunity for me. The company at this time did not have what I would call a formal purchasing department. The purchasing responsibilities up to this point had been split between myself and George Hvizd whose primary job was that of operations manager.

From that point on my main responsibilities have been purchasing related. Over the years I have developed and implemented the policies and procedures which have established and formalized the purchasing department as the professional department it is today.

Major accomplishments for the department include establishing and implementing a formal purchase order system. We have set up and maintained a supplier base that wants to be part of our growth by supplying top quality materials at fair prices. We have made servicing the needs of production our number one priority, and have developed and maintained the systems needed to accomplish this goal. Most importantly, we have conducted business in a professional and ethical manner at all times. I will never accept less.

Over the last ten years, the task of purchasing the raw materials, packaging and supplies for the W. 25th plant has been challenging and rewarding. As the company has grown so have our needs. When I first began ordering the materials, our needs were small and I often had difficulty finding suppliers willing to service us. Many suppliers felt that our material volumes just were not large enough for them to bother with. Others were willing to gamble that these small volumes would grow over the years. Many of the suppliers who were willing to work with us back then are still supplying us today. Their commitment to the L. J. Minor Corporation back then is being rewarded with our loyalty today.

Purchasing for a company like the L. J. Minor Corp. can be very difficult. Because our line of products includes meat, seafood, poultry, and vegetable bases as well as dry and liquid products, I am required to purchase a wide variety of materials. This requires me to be as knowledgeable as possible about each of the market items I am trying to purchase and what factors may influence the price and availability of each of them. To keep abreast of what is happening with chicken, turkey, beef, pork, ham, lobster, clam, crab, fish, corn, onion, spice, and other items is very difficult and time consuming.

The job has been very rewarding, however. It has given me the opportunity to meet hundreds of people over the years who may have come to call on me or I have met while traveling.

My 19 years with the company have been extremely rewarding professionally. As stated earlier. The L. J. Minor Corp. has also had a great affect on my personal life. Remember Diana Nieves, the lovely brown eyed young lady who smiled at me as I passed her in the Dry Storage area several pages ago? We married in 1980. Diana continues to work for the company as a chain development customer service representative in our Solon, OH headquarters. Her mother, Blanca, still works in our quality assurance department. Diana had two brothers who also worked for the company for short periods of time some years ago.

Since my father's first encounter with the L. J. Minor Corporation back in the mid

1960's, the company has served as employer to my mother, for 19 years until her retirement, and to two of my brother-in-laws. My mother-in-law, my wife, and I are still employed here after 23, 19 and 18 years respectively.

To say I owe a lot to the L. J. Minor Corporation and to the vision of its founder Dr. Minor is an understatement.

Through the Years
by Diana Katuscak

I have worked with the L. J. Minor Corp. for the past 18 years. I started with the L. J. Minor Corp. in August 1976. My maiden name at that time was Diana Nieves. I had just finished high school and I was looking for a job so that I could continue my studies.

My mother, Blanca Nieves, was already employed at the company working in the quality assurance department. She knew of a position in the sample area that was opening up and recommended that I place an application. My mother always spoke highly of the L. J. Minor Corporation and the people with whom she worked. It was an easy choice to make and one I never regretted. The L. J Minor Corporation has greatly affected my personal and professional life.

George Hvizd was the plant manager at that time. He interviewed me and hired me to process and ship sample order requests. We were a small company. At that time there were probably only about 50 employees.

I worked in the sample area for two years. In those days we packaged the samples in 4 oz. and 1 oz. glass jars. Each jar was hand-labeled by Julia Perez or myself.

Packaging of these samples was done by hand. Margie Stanley showed me how to pack the Lobster Base into a pastry bag and fill each container by hand. She was so neat and clean about the way she did it and she made it look so easy. I thought this was going to be fun.

When it was my turn I ended up having Lobster Base all over me, and my hands were sore from squeezing the pastry bag. With experience I became better, but never as good as Margie. I was responsible for packaging, maintaining an inventory of bases, and shipping sample order requests to our chefs and sales people.

We had a dry storage area in which I processed and shipped the sample orders. We would package the request in 12 x 4 oz. or 6 x 4 oz. boxes to ship them out. For larger requests, such as samples for shows, I would package them in a 100 lb. drum. Carefully, we would pack the containers with enough padding inside to assure no damage would happen to them while in shipment. We did a lot of our shipping of samples by United Parcel Service.

Next to this area was our shipping cooler. Charlie Mills, Mike Whalen, and Bart Katuscak were in charge of shipping the larger orders out from this area. The men were always helpful to me and we all had a good friendship.

The sample orders originated from our corporate headquarters located downtown in the Bulkley Building on Euclid Avenue. Nancy Clancy and her staff would take the requests, type them, and send them down to our W. 25th St. plant location by mail service for me to process.

Nancy was always pleasant and helpful when I needed assistance on a sample request they would send. I looked forward to the day I could meet her. Little did I know that some day in the future I would be working with her.

During the holidays Dr. and Mrs. Minor would send gift packages of bases to many of their customers and friends. We would send a gift box containing six individual bases of their choosing. Ruth Fields taught me how to gift wrap each one and place holiday stickers on each end, then send them out to the respective customers.

During this busy time, Mary Minor, would come in from Michigan and help me set up the many boxes I had to get ready. There were times Ruth would bring in Sallie and Kristin her daughters to help me. We used to do at least 200 - 300 gift boxes. As the company grew so did the list of people receiving Christmas Gift boxes.

Whenever I would be caught up with my orders I would help the ladies on the packaging table. I can remember one day helping them package our Glace de Viande. Ruth and Mike Zelski helped. We would clean the table, then place the glass jars upside down on the table and pass them through a vacuum to clean them.

Glace de Viande had to be packaged at a certain hot temperature and sealed with a screw type lid. You had to be very careful not to burn yourself when pouring the product into the jars. I left that job up to the experts such as Margie Stanley and the other packaging ladies. I helped in placing the glass jars into the boxes. The glass jars were so hot I thought I would have blisters on my fingers when we were through. The managers at that time would always pitch in and help when needed. We all worked well as a team to get the job done.

In 1978 I went to work with George Hvizd, our operations manager, as his secretary and receptionist for the plant facility. I was so happy to have this opportunity but I really was going to miss working with Charlie, Mike, and especially Bart. I really enjoyed working for George and it let me apply the skills I learned during my business courses in high school.

At this time I was attending night classes at Tri-C West Campus. The L. J. Minor Corporation believed in continuing your education and provided the means for an employee to pursue this. Unfortunately, I did not complete my studies, but I hope to someday pick up where I left off and get a degree.

In 1980 Bart and I married. We had a great reception and the majority of the guests were the Minor's employees whom we were happy to have share this moment with us. We now have two beautiful children, Matthew and Danielle. They are growing up eating a lot of Chicken Soup made with Minor Chicken Base and using a lot of Michael Minor's wonderful recipes. You might say that Minor's Bases helped keep my family healthy and happy.

In 1984 I was asked to work in helping implement a retail program at our Brecksville facility. This program enabled consumers to purchase our product in 8 oz. containers for home use. Gen. John D. McLaughlin felt a need for this to be done. I worked together with Nancy Shramek and Liz Adler to put the program together. We did this for a few years. Now, we have two outside distributors handling the consumer mail order program for the L. J. Minor Corporation.

It's amazing the responses we received from loyal Minor users. Once a customer is hooked on using the Minor Bases they do not want to use anything else. Of all the jobs I was involved with in the company this was the one that I enjoyed the most. I felt good being able to help someone. I felt confident in the integrity and quality of the products we were offering to the consumers and we would convey this knowledge to the consumers when we would talk with them. Dr. Minor instilled his philosophy of quality in all his employees. That's why I feel we are so successful today.

From 1986 - 1994 I worked with Nancy Clancy in foodservice customer service and for a couple of years maintained the consumer mail order business on my own. Nancy was a wonderful supervisor to work for. She is very knowledgeable about the business and acted as a special friend when we needed her. She is a very unique person and one the company can never replace.

For the last few months I have worked with our chain development department as their customer service representative forecasting our custom products.

You really have to work hard and believe that what you are doing will benefit others. The core of a successful company is its employees and how they have been treated. That's why I feel it's so easy for myself, my husband, my mother, and all the other employees who have worked with Dr. Minor and his family members to continue to make the L. J. Minor Corporation - Food Ingredients Specialties successful.

The friendships I have made personally with the members of the Minor family will last forever. Thank you.

As One Big Family
by Bridget Clancy-Bell

"Honesty, integrity, accuracy, punctuality, courtesy, kindness, friendliness, helpfulness, and cleanliness" is a phrase from Dr. Minor's Business Aims, established in 1952. This phrase has been my guide throughout my career at the L. J. Minor Corporation.

Two years prior to my official hire date of July 13, 1979, I worked during summer breaks and after school. At that time, the L. J. Minor Corporation had five full-time employees and three part-time employees at corporate headquarters in downtown Cleveland, Ohio. Job responsibilities were shared by everyone.

In 1982, when William F. McLaughlin joined the L. J. Minor Corporation, job responsibilities were put into perspective to align the continuous rapid growth of the L. J.

Minor Corporation. The L. J. Minor Corporation now has over seventy employees within ten structured departments at corporate headquarters in Solon, Ohio.

The L. J. Minor Corporation manufacturing facilities have been located at W. 25th in Cleveland, Ohio, for over thirty years. Construction phases progress continuously to meet the demanding production volume. This immaculate facility has over one hundred and sixty skilled dedicated employees, of which eight work at the Brecksville Distribution Center.

During my years of employment, the L. J. Minor Corporation has been through many challenging periods with successful changes in management, acquisitions, and consolidation.

Although the L. J. Minor Corporation consistently moves forward, the company still provides its employees with a generous compensation package, including profit sharing, attendance bonus, educational assistance, 401(k) with company match, paid vacation, job advancement, etc.

Extracurricular company activities are also a given at the L. J. Minor Corporation. Each year the employees and their guest are hosted with an awards ceremony in appreciation of their committed service. Service awards are distributed to employees with a gift selection. A summer family picnic is scheduled each year with a fun-filled day of swimming, adult and children games, dunk tank for charity, favors, and raffle prizes. Tickets for employees and immediate family members are distributed each year to watch the Cleveland Indians, the professional baseball club of Cleveland, Ohio

The L. J. Minor Corporation also sponsors employee sports such as softball, volleyball, basketball, bowling, etc. The consideration and compensation offered allows employees to be loyal, responsible, and respected individuals.

Dr. L. J. Minor founded the L. J. Minor Corporation in 1951, with the support of Mrs. Ruth Minor and their children. Various generations of extended families still continue to make their livelihood at the L. J. Minor Corporation.

My family members currently employed at the L. J. Minor Corporation include my mother, Nancy Clancy, who has officially retired after thirty-five years, but is continuing employment temporarily during the L. J. Minor Corporation and Fidco consolidation. My sister, Nancy Shramek, sales analyst, foodservice division, and my sister-in-law, Cheryl Clancy, sales administrator, chain development, are still with the company.

Other family members employed were my father, Terrence Clancy, a full-time Cleveland Police Officer working part-time in the sixties at the L. J. Minor Corporation to supplement income to raise seven children. My three brothers worked during summer breaks and after school, and include, Pat, engineer specialist, MetroHealth Hospital; Terry, director of business operation, Communication One; and Marty, Manager, Asset Management, Mellon Bank. My two sisters who have not been employed by the company are Coletta, executive secretary, TransUnion Credit Bureau; and Charlotte, social worker, Cuyahoga County.

Hiring family was common during the seventies, including, to name a few, the families of Camargo, Katuscak, Mahon, Massa, Nieves, Perez, and Quinones. After all, the L. J. Minor Corporation has always been one big happy family to me!

Chapter 43

More about Operations: My Experience

by Dan Mullen
(1978-1995)

Working with Minor's

by Dean Hunt
(1981-1995)

Lead by Example

by Bill Weinmann
(1982-1995)

Dedicated Employees

by Bill Hoke
(1983-1995)

No One Is Perfect
by Lewis J. Minor

Never judge an Indian before you've
    walked several miles in his moccasins.
Always try to put yourself in the other fellow's place
    before judging him.

Doing Time
(Irish Humor by Hal Roach)

Mrs. O'Brian said to her friend Mrs. O'Leary:
"My husband Pat never did a day's worth of work in his life when he was alive. But he is working now."

Mrs. O'Leary said:
"How do you mean?"

Mrs. O'Brian said:
"I had him cremated and his ashes put in the egg timer."

My Experience
by Dan Mullen

Before I begin my story, Dr. Minor, I would like to express the impact of your recent visit to the plant for all us "old timers." You have been a father and a family to us all. We have "grown up" with you and your family. You have taught us and have had a great impact on us. You have made all of our lives better and made us all better people.

One night when things were going bad in the plant and we did not think we would ever get done, my wife, Sharon and I reflected; Each employee has different talents ... a true melting pot of individuals. But, God brought us all together here to learn that by working together we are a great team. Dr. Minor must be doing something right. Minor's is blessed. We know you are no longer associated with the business, but you, Mrs. Minor, and your entire family are engraved in our hearts and souls. Your visit brought back all these emotions and memories. Most of all, it told us that Dad and Mom still care about their kids.

My experience with Minor's began on the day before my nineteenth birthday in 1978. After going to college in the morning one day, I came home from working at McDonald's where I was a floor supervisor at the time. I sat down to dinner with my parents. My father, a Cleveland policeman, started to tell me that the wife of one of his partners, Mr. Clancy, works at this place on West 25th Street and they need a beef cook.

Mrs. Clancy had been working there about 10 years and said the company is growing. Mr. Clancy told Dad they pay $4.25 per hour with full benefits, profit sharing, pension, and an attendance bonus. Also, if you do a good job you get a $.25 raise in 30 days.

At first, I was a little skeptical about West 25th, but for all the above mentioned, I would go anywhere. I was only making $3.25 per hour with no benefits. I told him I would be interested. He gave me George Hvizd's number and said all you have to do is make an appointment for an orientation. He said to let George know you know the Clancys and the

466

job will be yours. I called George and he said the job was mine if I wanted it after he gave me some details.

He said anyone recommended by the Clancys was good enough for him. I made the appointment for the next day, my birthday. George gave an excellent orientation. He gave a lot of detail about the company and its history. I wanted to start right away. He reminded me I should not burn my bridges behind me. I should give McDonald's a two week notice. I did and I started my new job on February 8, 1978. It's incredible, I remember all this like it was yesterday!

My first day left some questions in my head. I started in the beef room. Needless to say it was a lot harder than George made it out to be. Being 5 feet 10 inches tall and 120 pounds, I used muscles I did not know existed. Rick Perez was "training" me, but was recovering from his wedding which took place over the weekend. Everyone seemed nice, except for the lady who was throwing around 60 pound pails of ingredients like they were feathers. Take note, do not get her mad!!

Some of the Puerto Ricans were talking about me in Spanish, nothing malicious. I wondered how long I should wait before I let them know I speak and understand Spanish. The rest of the week I was on my own as Rick called in sick.

My body is so sore from the new work. I do not know if these new muscles I have found can do the job again. There has to be another way. There is a lot of double handling. There has to be someone who I can talk to about making some changes.

The sugar in that monster of a machine they call the sugar cooker is boiling over. Where is the hose? I cannot see as the smoke is so thick and my eyes are burning. I clean up the mess and the buzzer goes off for the oven. The beef is ready. Time to separate the meat from the juice. Will my new muscles be able to do it? I had this same challenge yesterday.

Suddenly, I hear someone screaming, "I need chuice!" What is "chuice?" The door opens and it is Anni Fleig, the lady who had been throwing around 60 pound pails of ingredients like they were feathers. She looks mad and yells, "I need my chuice!" Oh no, my second day and she is mad at me already, and what is "chuice?"

Well, I figure out what "chuice" (juice) is. Anni is actually a nice lady, just a little hyper. I meet the owner's son Mike and talk to him about my ideas. He likes all my ideas and tells me to try them out tomorrow. I think I am going to like it here. I think Mike and I are going to get along just great.

Needless to say, Mike and I got along very well. He and I made a lot of changes to improve the efficiency and the product. He was like a big brother to me. He offered me a supervisory position 6 months after I started. I trained in every area of the plant under Mike's close observation for almost 2 years before becoming the first shift supervisor.

It was one of the best planned programs in which I have ever been involved. It not only exposed me to the workload and work area itself, but also to the people and their personalities, and them to mine. We still use this program today with any new management hires.

One of my favorite times was with Mike working almost 36 hours straight preparing the soups and sauces for the annual Notre Dame alumni dinner. It was a lot of work. It was a lot of fun. Mike was plain crazy!

As part of my training, I had to learn scheduling and inventory control. This was not as easy as it is today. Everything was done with paper, pencils and, if you were lucky to find one, a calculator. This is where I really got to know Ruth, the owner's daughter. She was a big sister to me. I learned scheduling, planning, and inventory control well from Ruth.

As the years passed, we continued to plan together, with the input of the employees, as the company grew at rates around 15%. Some radical changes took place in scheduling, the building, and the equipment. One of these changes was inventory control being computerized by Ingolf Nitsch. Others included:

- Going from meat products on days and poultry products on nights to meat products one week and poultry products on the other;

- Changing to chicken on the first three shifts of the week, followed by pork or turkey for one shift, beef for two shifts; lobster, shrimp, crab, fish, or clam for one shift; mushroom and vegetable base for one shift, and finally three shifts of liquid, dry or gravy products;

- Going from the 60-quart Schnell chopper to the chopper mixers;

- Going from the Hobart mixers to the large blender;

- Going from the old beef room, chicken room, and deboning room to the new state of the art cookroom and deboning room.

More importantly, I learned friendship, love, understanding, humility, the "do whatever it takes" attitude, and I guess I will call it maturity from Ruth. These are the just some of the keys to the success of the L. J. Minor Company.

One of my most memorable and frightening experiences occurred shortly after I completed my training as a supervisor. We had recently purchased the new chopper/mixer. It was a beautiful new machine in a new room. It replaced at least 4 pieces of equipment, three Hobart mixers and a 60-quart Hobart chopper.

468

On this day Dave Jacobs and Gary Pasko were running the machine. It was near the end of the shift. Gary and Dave were beginning to disassemble the machine and preparing to clean it when I entered the room. Dave left the room to take the baffle and the gasket to the equipment clean up room. Gary closed the hood and was filling the bowl with water. Dave brought the detergent back from the equipment clean up room and poured it into the bowl as I left the room. I was just going to enter the premix room when I heard the machine turn on, but this time something was different.

Loud "chinging" sounds were coming from the room. I ran back to the room and opened the door. There on the floor were Gary and Dave as pieces of the metal blades ricocheted off the bowl into the facing wall. I thought they were dead, they were not moving.

After what seemed to be an eternity, but actually was only seconds, I saw Gary's arm move and his hand try to hit the emergency stop button. He could not hit it at the right angle. I went on all fours and crawled along the wall like a scared rat to the main breaker. I finally reached it and turned it off. I ran to Gary and Dave. They both jumped to their feet and ran out of the room. I ran after them to see if they were all right. They were, thank God!

They were white as ghosts. Mike Minor, Dave, Gary, and myself went back into the room. We found that Dave had left the large wrench in the bowl after removing the baffle. One had thought the other had removed it. Upon examining the room, we found there were six inch pieces of the blades imbedded all the way into the plaster wall. Then Mike asked where Gary and Dave were standing when they started the machine.

Gary was right in front of the control panel and Dave was just to his left in front of the nylon deflector shield. Gary asked why and Mike picked up the nylon deflector shield and flipped it over. Imbedded in the shield was an eight by four inch piece of blade that would have split Dave's head in half. Dave turned even whiter and ran out of the room. Pieces of the blades were imbedded in the bowl and had pierced the hollow hood. It was the most incredible and devastating destruction I have ever seen by a piece of equipment.

Another of my very memorable experiences was working with Dorsey and Josephine. Dorsey, Dr. Minor's grandson, was the production scheduler and in charge of all of inventory control. As with all of the family, he had to work his way up through the plant before being considered for promotion. Dorsey was and still is great fun, but very conscientious when it comes to his job.

Josephine, Dr. Minor's daughter, did the inputting of all the information for inventory control. She was responsible for accurate inventory counts. Josephine has a laugh that would bring a smile to anyone's face. Well, I am not sure how I got drafted, but Josephine was not getting accurate counts that matched what the computer calculated we should have after production from the stores areas.

Dorsey and Josephine asked for my help and I began to "investigate" for them. Nearly all of the time I would come back with an answer. Either someone counted wrong, the receivings were incorrect, poor yields or incorrect production was reported. I guess because of my investigating, nearly always finding an answer (getting my man), my non-excitable nature, and my appearance, I reminded Josephine of Deputy Dog. Dorsey thought it was hilarious. The nickname stuck. Anytime Josephine or Dorsey needed help or investigating they called for Deputy Dog.

There are so many stories, so many memories, and so many wonderful people at Minor's. People here before I started are still working here or just now retiring. People who started about the time I started, also in their late teens or early twenties, are still working here. That is what the L. J. Minor Company is and was about, PEOPLE.

People who cared about quality from the product planning stage to the time the customer used the product. We had "Total Quality" before any of us heard of that key word. The "family," all the employees, were always asked for suggestions in planning, scheduling, methods, equipment purchases, and plant expansions. The key word for that is "Employee Involvement," I think.

We wrote down which batches went into which containers and what lot numbers from purchased processed materials went into what batches. "Lot Traceability" is the new key word for this operation. We took temperatures at important stages of the processes or checked the quality of incoming raw materials. They call these "Critical Control Points" or a "Hazard Analysis Critical Control Points Program".

We have (and had) the attitude and the saying to "do whatever it takes." The Nike Company has taken our attitude and saying and paraphrased it into a multibillion dollar advertising campaign and company logo, "Just do it." Well, I guess it is and was more than just PEOPLE who CARED, it was and is PEOPLE with VISION and PEOPLE with COMMITMENT. The L. J. Minor Company was a large family of children trying to repay their parents, Dr. and Mrs. Minor, for their gifts which included unconditional love and a comfortable and better way of life. These children became prepared for life and became just like them, PEOPLE WHO CARE.

Working with Minor's
by Dean Hunt

In late January of 1981, I received a call from Dan Mullen, whom I had known since high school. He asked me if I would be interested in applying at his place of employment, a great company called the L. J. Minor Corporation.

He explained to me that it was a super place to work, had terrific people, and prepared the highest quality meat, poultry, seafood, and vegetable bases that chefs would use to save time in preparing meals. This call was a blessing to me as I was just out of high school and my wife Tesa was pregnant. I jumped at the chance to come down and apply.

One of my most vivid memories of all time is the day that I applied, and in particular, taking a tour of the facility after indicating that I would be willing to work there.

Mike Minor gave me this tour and I remember thinking how genuine and "down to earth" this man seemed.

Mike explained the various operations inside the company and showed me the pieces of equipment that were used to prepare the product. I also remember that "Ham Base" was being prepared that day, and as I walked through the plant on my tour, there was this delicious aroma of ham and spices wafting through the air.

Even today, whenever we prepare Ham Base, it reminds me of that first day I was at the company. Both Tesa and I were elated and thankful the day that we were notified that I had been hired officially.

My first job was on second shift working between 4:30 p.m. and 2:30 a.m. I started melting sugar, placing raw rooster halves in metal pans for cooking, melting chicken fat, helping to roast beef, steam cooking chicken and fish, sautéing mushrooms, lobster, and crab, and doing clean-up.

From my first day at the company, there were certain things that really stood out including:

1.   The respect and love that all the employees had for the Minor/Fields families;

2.   Everyone that I met or was introduced to had great things to say about the company - what a great place of employment it was, and what wonderful people owned and operated it;

3.   From the first minute I stepped through the doors at the L. J. Minor Corporation sanitation and cleanliness were continuously stressed and repeatedly reinforced as "a way of life." We were given a booklet containing good sanitation, cleanliness, and grooming rules that must be followed while on the premises and should be followed and practiced in your own home. Dr. Minor had written this material as he realized that without proper sanitation and cleaning, he would not have a high quality business in the food preparation industry. As mentioned, sanitation and cleanliness were continuously stressed and everyone had to follow the correct cleaning practices in their areas from cleaning equipment to cleaning rooms. Today, sanitation is still considered essential to the success of the business, and is given the highest of priorities. Much credit must be given to Dr. Minor, Ruth, and others for instilling this priority in the very fiber of the manufacturing operation.

In October of 1983, Ruth and Mike chose me to be a packaging supervisor on second shift. I felt honored to be chosen to be on their management team, partially due to the fact that I was only 21 years old. I realized what a wonderful opportunity this was for me and my family, and even to this day, I cannot fully express my gratitude towards them in choosing me for this responsibility. Because of the trust and confidence they showed in me, I was determined not to let them down and that I would do everything I could to help the company succeed and grow.

When I first started supervising, much of the packaging operation was done by hand or manually, and was not fully automated. Certain products were placed into glass jars with screw on lids. Most of the packaging was done with the entire packaging crew gathered around a large stainless steel table, where each individual container was measured and weighed out, some as small as 1 oz. We still measure some things out this way!

We did all of the packaging in one small room, and stored the finished packaged goods in one small, adjoining warehouse/storeroom. The products were shipped directly from the plant to our customers.

Not long after I became a supervisor, the company started to invest in automated pumps and packaging equipment, and this greatly propelled the entire packaging operation. We were now able to handle the increasing volume that was expected of us. Some random thoughts on the challenges of supervising are:

- There are conflicts between employees due to their differing personalities and amount of time spent together. I had my share of "putting out fires";

- Convincing people of the need for change and getting them to accept new ways of doing things, new ideas, and higher expectations;

- Getting a group of people to work together as a team with one common goal;

- Being a good listener;

- One final note on supervising is that I really enjoyed the friendship and camaraderie with the other supervisors who developed over the years. We had some great times together!

Today, I am the production scheduler for the company. It is a position that is extremely challenging and is full of responsibility. A few closing thoughts are:

- I looked forward to coming to work every day. Working with nice people such as Ruth, Mike Minor, and many others. You wanted to do anything you could that would help the company;

- As an employee, you were so proud to be working for this great company. Knowing that you were making *the best* food products in the business and that you were part of its success was quite a thrill;

- The generosity of the Minor family was great: a bonus for coming to work every day; hams or turkeys for our families at Thanksgiving, Christmas, and Easter; generous pay increases; overtime pay when there was extra work that needed to be done; a clean environment to work in every day; and the love and respect you felt from them;

• The Minor family was like a second family to me. I could identify them with many in my own family. Dr. and Mrs. Minor reminded me of my own grandparents. Mike, Dorsey, Edwina, Josephine, and Mary all seemed like various uncles, brothers, aunts, and sisters;

• Then there was Ruth. She was like a mother to me and to many other people. She was a deeply caring person who was always willing to listen to your joys and sorrows. She provided great leadership and led by example. Most of all, all of these people were and are friends.

Lead by Example
by Bill Weinmann

In April of 1982, I was working in a shop making conveyers. Grease and oil was everywhere. The smell of the petroleum would sicken me each morning and into the day. There was a break in one of the hydraulic lines directly over my head. Oil would rain on me throughout the day.

One day I asked the vice president of the company, who happened to be the owner's son, that the oil leaks be repaired or at least channeled to another area. I asked him this after I had slipped on the greasy floor hurting my pride! He just laughed after witnessing this hilarious event.

In 1982 there was a recession. I had just lost my job at Stahl Metal Products which I had held for nine years. The company had decided to move to Valdesta, Georgia, for strictly monetary reasons. I had a wife and two sons to support. I needed a job. Not only was there a recession going on, but there was also a gasoline shortage. The car I drove was a 1973 Chevy Impala, which is a boat and is in no way fuel efficient.

At long last I took a position with a conveyer company, but it was 37 miles from my home. I really hated to go to this job. Yet I did not quit because I owed it to my family to support them.

It is hard to fill out applications when you are working a full time job. I told my friends that I was looking, and if anyone could give me a tip on who was hiring I would appreciate it. My uncle, Steve Veres, (who is not really my uncle but has known me since birth), told me about the L. J. Minor Corp.

Steve had been with the company for probably 15 years. When I mentioned to him that I was looking for other work, he told me if I shaved off my beard he could set up an appointment for me to come in and fill out an application. I asked him what Minor's did and he said, "You ever heard of Campbell's soup?" I replied, "Yeah." He said, "Well, we make products that go into their soup". I was totally confused. I asked Steve what kind of work he did and he told me he was responsible for cleaning all of the production equipment.

Uncle Steve lived in an apartment over what was once Westown Tire. This building was right in front of the Minor Corp. If Steve would oversleep in the morning, someone from the company would walk up to his suite and wake him up to come to work.

The opportunity had to be investigated, so I shaved. I went to fill out the application. I remember that there was a house built up against the factory. The main plant was built right against this house. It was the nicest house on Auburn Avenue. I had to enter the house through the shipping department.

The upstairs of the house was the personnel office. The downstairs was for the R. & D. department. I had to take the day off in order to keep my 9:00 a.m. appointment. I was greeted by Diana Katuscak who was a secretary. Diana is now with customer service. She is married to Bart, whom she met while working at Minor's. He is now the procurement manager.

After filling out all of the vital information on the application, I had to meet with George Hvizd. He was the personnel manager at the time. He told me of how stable the company was and that it had been around since 1951. He also told me about the Culinary Olympics and how Mike Minor's team won four gold medals a year or so ago. This had a direct impact on the business which was probably one of the reasons why they were looking for help.

George said he would give me a call in a couple of weeks. I really felt good when I left his office because he had given me a warm, sincere feeling that he was truly going to give me a call in a couple of weeks. I honestly felt that he was not just blowing me off.

Two weeks passed and my wife, Barbara, gave me a call at work. She told me George Hvizd was trying to get a hold of me. I called him immediately. He wanted to give me an interview for a job in equipment clean-up. I would be working with Uncle Steve!

The next day I took off to go to talk to George. Diana greeted me with a friendly smile. She asked me to have a seat and instructed me that George would be with me in a few minutes. George welcomed me into his office. I remember talking about the Cleveland Indians and how I got the impression he was a great fan. He had gone to about every opener since he was a kid. He offered me the job making twenty five cents an hour less than my current job. This was no big deal since I was spending forty to fifty dollars a week on gasoline.

He also told me about the attendance bonus. If I worked three months without missing a day or was not late, I would receive $150. Six hundred dollars a year just to show up to work! Boy, what an incentive! Boy, what a company! I accepted the job but told him I owed it to the other company to give them two week's notice. George replied by saying something like, "Fine." I was on a high!

Imagine, I was to have a new job in a small, family run organization less than two miles from my house. This was great!! When I was having dinner, Barbara said she had some news for me. She told me she was pregnant. This really made my day. I was happy, but could not afford to have another kid. I did have hospitalization with the conveyer company. At Minor, benefits would not start until ninety days after my start date.

Things were so bad for me that I was three months behind on my house mortgage. I was so financially strapped that I decided to call George back the next day and tell him, "Thanks, but no thanks." I had lunch. It was tuna fish on rye bread. I called George Hvizd back to tell him of my situation. I said, "My wife is expecting another child and I really cannot quit my job at the present time because of the hospitalization. I really did not want to waste your time. I am still interested in your company."

George told me to give him a call after the baby was born. I figured he was just being courteous and professional. I hung up the phone and went back to work. While I was at lunch, my foreman welded a piece of quarter inch angle iron to the machine I was running. This piece moved up and down about a foot off of the floor. My foreman neglected to tell me of this new option on my machine. Naturally, it came down on my left foot.

Because my foot was lodged under the machine, the machine shut off with this piece of heavy equipment on my foot. I screamed and hollered. I was off in a corner where no one could see me. When my foreman saw there was no production from my area, he instinctively investigated. The machine was lifted from my foot and my bloody shoe was removed. An ambulance was called and I was off to Medina County Hospital. I remember thinking in the ambulance I would not have been able to start at Minor in this condition anyhow. I had a couple of broken toes, some contusions, bruises, and was in lot of pain! I missed a whole week of work.

Three days after my accident, a plumber friend of mine gave me a call. He needed someone to give him a hand putting in a new water line to an apartment building from the vault in the tree lawn. I threw away my crutches and walked with a cane. Honestly, I actually needed the extra cash. Barbara had talked with the bank about making house payments on the principal only. (We did get caught up on our payments and eventually sold the house. We purchased a roomier home that is often referred to as "the house that Minor's built.")

We finished the water line and were putting the cover over the manhole. This 150 pound cover fell directly on my left foot. I tried to play it off like it did not hurt. I could not fool my plumber friend. He gave me an open bottle of Four Roses and within 10 minutes, I was feeling no pain.

On October 25th, Jennifer was born. I was still at the conveyer company greasier than ever. I decided to give George a call to see if I still had a shot. He remembered me and said he would keep me in mind.

Some time in the end of November he called me back. This time, he offered me a job as a beef cook. I accepted the position over the phone and had to go in for an interview with Ruth Fields, Dr. Minor's daughter. She was also the plant manager. I showed up on time for the plant tour and interview with Ruth. She was wearing all white. White slacks, dress and a lab coat. She also had on a blue turban. Everyone else wore a white hair net. I figured that the blue turban symbolized that she was a boss.

Ruth took me through the plant showing me all areas of production and packaging. The warehouse was only a couple of years old at the time as were the cooler and the freezer. One of my jobs was to empty the cooler every Friday and clean it from top to bottom. The freezer had to be swept out on Friday. The floor was scrubbed once a month with a chemical that would not freeze.

The cookroom was a room approximately 10' x 10'. It had two convection ovens in it. The other side of the hall had seven steamers for cooking chicken. Mario was the chicken cook. That side of the cookroom had two 100 gallon kettles as well as an 80 gallon kettle. Another room in the same area had a table loaded with cooked chicken, which four ladies would hand debone.

There was also a premix room and a chopper room. The premix room had three Hobart mixers in it. The chopper room had a giant blender for making the bases. Packaging was all done in glass jars. What a noise this made!! The vibration of the equipment on the table was really nerve racking. The lids were screwed on by hand.

Last on our tour was the pan room. This is where Uncle Steve worked. Most of the cleaning meant picking the equipment up by hand. This was a hot area with no ventilation. There was quite a bit of lifting to do too.

Ruth explained the importance of sanitation. "Hot water never cleaned anything." She informed me this by going into a classic speech about using soaps and elbow grease. Oftentimes a question would arise about a sanitation problem and someone would reply with the old answer of "hosing it down." Ruth would always go into the spiel of "Hot water never cleaned anything."

Anyway, each person was responsible for their own work area. If powder would spill on the floor in packaging, one of the packagers would grab a broom and sweep it up right away. No use in walking through it and tracking it through the plant all day. The philosophy behind each person cleaning up after himself is that if you have to do the clean up, you will work neater. This made sense to me.

Wash your hands after you use the bathroom. Wash your hands after sneezing or coughing. If you drop a utensil on the floor, wash it off and sanitize it. Wash your hands after washing the utensil because the utensil is dirty and now so are your hands.

No gum chewing or spitting allowed! It all sounded logical to me, after all, I was to be working with food. I gave my present employer two week's notice. They tried to get me to stay by offering me $1.00 more per hour. I explained the attendance bonus policy to my former boss and he more or less laughed at me and told me that was impossible.

Before I could start work at Minor's, I needed to get a TB test. This test was required for food handlers every two years. On December 13, 1982, I experienced my first day on the job at L. J. Minor. I was to meet Dan Mullen at 5:00 a.m. I showed up at 4:30!

In 1982, you entered the building from West 25th Street. The building sat in the back of two apartment buildings as well as Westown Tire. I parked my car in the gravel lot next to Pearl Court. (Houses were still standing then. Now all the homes are torn down and the maintenance shop stands there.) I was the first one there. Because there was not

476

much parking, we had to park three deep. At the end of the shift when I would go home, I would have to see who was parked behind me and go back in the building and ask them to move.

Dan showed up and let me in. He gave me a key to a locker where we kept our clean uniforms. We would take our clean uniforms and put them in another locker with our street clothes. Our soiled uniforms would go back into the first locker at the end of the shift.

The front door is now replaced by two loading docks. When entering the building, we passed through a room with two hydraulic pumps. This room is still there with the pumps having been replaced through the years. Next came the packaging room. This is where the time clock was. The main entrance is now down the side street (Auburn Ave.), with the time clock on the same end of the building.

The men's locker and restroom were through packaging, down the hall from the cookroom, through the panroom, and to the right. The women's facilities were on the other side of the packaging room. They were even smaller then the men's room. I was ready to start. Dan was just a kid. I had a feeling that he knew his stuff just by the way he explained how to do things. He, just like Ruth, expressed the importance of sanitation.

We washed our hands before starting. We took seven boxes of "Keebko" beef. Each box had four 16 pound bags in them. We got the pans for the ovens from equipment storage. There were also these wires that looked like shelves out of an old refrigerator.

First we had to wipe the pans down with Fri Free. This was a Minor product that was something like Pam. Next we dumped a bag of beef into an oven bag and placed it into a pan. A wire (refrigerator shelf) was placed on top of the bag. The wire got hot and helped cook the beef. The whole pan was placed in an oven rack. The oven rack held 13 pans. With two ovens going, we cooked 26 pans of beef.

While one run was cooking, I had to take my empty trash (boxes) to the compactor, clean my area, and get 26 more pans of beef ready to go. This was a continuous cycle. I can't recall if I was cooking five, six or seven runs on a shift.

When the beef was done, the cooked meat was pulled out and the raw meat placed into the oven. The cooked was dumped through a strainer and the meat and juice separated. Three pans of beef were strained at a time. These were put into a lug. When six lugs were full, the beef and cylinder full of juice were taken to the chopper room where beef base was made. Now that the pans were empty, raw beef had to be panned up and the process started over again.

Mario came in later in the morning. He was the chicken cook. At the time, we produced beef on the day shift and chicken on nights. The chicken was steam cooked and hand deboned. The cooked, deboned chicken was held in the cooler packed with dry ice until it was needed.

One of the best memories I have is when Ruth would come by each morning and say "Good morning, Bill." She always had a smile on her face and she called me by my name. She, as well as Mike Minor, Mike Zelski, and other members of management, would always go out of their way to make you feel at ease. They treated you like a person, never demanding, always asking.

Sometime during the next week, Bart Katuscak came into my room and gave me a ham and wished me a Merry Christmas. This really shocked me. I was not expecting this. "What a great place this is," I remember thinking to myself. Later on in the day, Ruth gave me a box of Christmas nuts. She told me to share them with Barbara and the kids. She was not a boss to me but more of a neighbor. I even got a Christmas bonus from the company, too. A Christmas bonus after only working two weeks for the company!

At the factory there were probably about 35 people working when I first started. Now there are a little over 100. This was a growing company when I started and continues to grow.

My next task with the company was to become part of a three member team. As I said before, we packaged beef on day shift and chicken on the night shift. We were now going to produce chicken one week and beef the next. Mario Quinones, Dorsey Fields, and myself were asked to start at 5:00 in the evening and work until 5:00 a.m. the next morning. This was a four day work week.

The only catch was that if we did not get all of our work done on Thursday by 5:00 a.m., we had to stay and finish. I did put in some 15, 16, and 17 hour work days then.

For the most part, the end of the shift was primarily clean up. We had to hand scrub the steamers as well as the rest of the kettles and room. As we became busier, we had to add a second three member team of cooks. My hours, as well as Mario's and Dorsey's, were bumped back to 11:00 p.m. Sunday until 11:00 next morning. We were doing basically the same thing, only a little more of it.

Dorsey moved on to be a utility worker on day shift so he could further his education. Mario's brother, Victor replaced him. Dorsey eventually moved on to become the scheduler. He replaced Ingolf Nitsch who moved on to become the vice president of operations, the position he currently holds today.

Dan Mullen was now the first shift production supervisor. George Henderson was on second shift. Dean Hunt and Bill Hoke were the packaging supervisors. We were becoming more diverse and needed another production supervisor. I applied for the job.

Ruth made me a supervisor on third shift. I used to start around 10:00 p.m. and stay until Dan and myself got things started in the morning. Ruth taught me that communication was a very important part of any job. If there was something that had to be completed or even started for me, I would leave not only Dan a note, but Ruth and George, too. This way, I was sure it would be carried out.

When I was on third shift, I had to open the building on Sunday night. One time there was a storm. Lightning must have hit the building and caused all the fire alarms to go off. It was so nerve racking that I got a ladder and removed all of the bells.

Another time ADT must have got a distress call from our alarm. While in the locker room changing my clothes, two armed officers stormed in and asked what I was doing there. I explained I had to open the plant so we could get started with production. After taking

478

my name and ADT security code they left.

One Sunday night there was a snow storm. Ingolf called the plant to see if we were working. I said I was here so we would be working. He said okay and hung up.

Two people had the misfortune of losing their lives from traffic accidents near the plant. One involved a Porsche that hit an old Pontiac. The driver of the Porsche crossed the center line and hit the Pontiac. The passenger in the Porsche was killed. I remember the sun roof of the Porsche landed some 50 yards away from the wreck. It was in our parking lot.

The other was an unlucky fellow who could not negotiate the curve on West 25th. He hit the pole in front of Westown Tire. Then the fence we had installed after we had the apartment buildings tore down on West 25th. It was on a Thursday. The fence company finished the job at around 9:30 at night. It was a hot, sweaty, summer night. I heard the door bell ringing. I went to answer it and it was Uncle Steve.

He was mumbling something about something hitting his car. I walked up front and sure enough another reckless driver. This guy was drunk. He was trying to start his car. I knew it would not start because the hood was up to his dashboard. Antifreeze was leaking out of his radiator which was along side of his left front fender. How did his car get smashed? What was against Uncle Steve's car? You guessed it, the new fence. This guy also failed to make the curve and hit the fence. He tore down a good 150 feet. He smacked down two upright I-beams.

This was no ordinary fence. It was designed to keep people out. It was probably 15 feet high. The top I beam came down and landed on Steve's car. The drunk's momentum kept him moving such that he hit the beam and pushed it through Steve's door and pinned his car against Westown Tire. When this guy realized what was going on, he tried to walk away. I grabbed him by the shirt collar and made him sit in his demolished car until the police arrived.

The company was developing into a large organization. George Henderson had moved on to the stores position. I took the second shift production position. I also had a general clean up crew. My responsibilities also included a complete plant clean up on Friday nights.

Dean was still the second shift packaging supervisor. We would sit down the night before and decide on what order I would have the product made so Dean could have it packed. If I went out of order, product may have sat in the bins until he was ready to pack it. I did not want this to happen because we would run out of bins in which to keep the product .

Lavere Vokt was the quality assurance person assigned to the night shift position. She only worked until midnight. After she left, it was up to Dean and me to check the product. I believe working nights without any technical support from Q. A., scheduling, or any of the other departments involved, really had an impact on my development as a supervisor. There was no one there to ask, so Dean and I had to make decisions on our own. Fortunately things always seemed to work out for the better.

We had bought a larger machine. This allowed us to make more premixes at one time. A good example is the beef gravy we used to make one batch at a time in the Hobart mixers. We now could make 15 batches at once! Another larger chopper was also purchased. Batches of finished base could be doubled in this new equipment. We also added a metal detector. We metal detected products that were purchased in cans. The first time we used it we found a can lid. I still hear Mike Minor boasting to everyone about how it had just paid for itself.

Informal company meetings were held often. It was frequently a safety or sanitation meeting. Sometimes it was a state of the company session. We even had a third bonus at one time. It was an energy conservation bonus. Anytime the company saved some money, lets say by making sure the lights were turned off when no one was in a room, dollars were kicked into a pool. This was only given one time that I know of. I think it was a real paper work trail for management to keep up with.

The group of investors who had purchased the company from Dr. Minor in 1983 eventually sold the business to Nestle's. Ruth called me at home. I was sound asleep. She had me come in to tell me some news. Actually, Mr. Zirbel told me the news. We were all excited because of the capital we could acquire from a large organization. Not to mention the clout we could have being a Nestle's organization with purchasing power.

When I started, the lunchroom was at the far end of the plant to the left of the premix room. An addition was added to the building as was a new lunchroom. The old one became the supervisors' office. The locker rooms were also moved to that end of the facility. Another addition was put on to the building and an even bigger lunchroom was put up. Again the supervisors' office was relocated to the second lunchroom. Before I started, the lunchroom was above the hydraulic room. This was really crammed quarters. I could not stand up in there. My head would hit the ceiling.

After a couple of years, we had the need to add another shift. We had worked five eight-hour shifts except for second shift packaging. They worked four ten-hour days. Most of the other employees thought this was a great idea. Other shifts were reorganized to fit this schedule. This was what turned out to be a first class move. Now we had Friday, Saturday and Sunday free. Our gravy business was about to explode into new areas. We purchased a form fill and seal machine. This weighed and formed a bag of gravy.

Ruth kept me informed of our new adventures, along with Tom Arthur. Tom was in charge of maintenance. He also purchased the small machinery. We set up the new gravy crew to work on Friday, Saturday and Sunday. We not only packaged it on the weekends, but we made it as well. Can you guess what responsibilities were added to my job description? Jerry Hord was my team leader. He filled in for me and actually did my job when I was not there. He is a good guy with a great sense of humor.

As the company grew, I had the opportunity to go on day shift. I would give up all my sanitation duties and move on to the stores department. This includes receiving, transfer of finished goods to the Brecksville Distribution Center, and the sample department. I recommended Jerry to Ingolf to take over my second shift job. The weekend has its own supervisor and George Henderson got the sanitation part of my job. My kids Billy, Steve, and Jenny wanted to know what time I would be home. I told them probably by six. Why? They wanted to know how much time they actually had to get their rooms cleaned.

While I am not implying that it took this many people to do what I had done, the sanitation job got a lot more complex with many different chemicals. We added many more people to the department too. The building itself was growing in size. Sanitation work sheets had to be created and updated which would be a job in itself.

On the weekend, we are running more than just the form, fill and seal machine. We are packing liquid product using a liquid filler machine which packs the product directly from the kettle in which it was made.

Another thing that Ruth instilled in me was to further my education. L. J. Minor Corporation pays the cost of tuition and books to go further on in school, as long as it is not, let's say, going to learn how to fix televisions, unless you are planning to fix TV's for the company!

These are just a few of the fond memories I have about some of the fine friends and episodes I have experienced with the company. It was a "mom and pop" organization that is growing into a large corporation. I hope that as a supervisor I can keep the tradition of making the employees feel as if they are part of a family. I will treat people the way I want to be treated. Lead by example.

Dedicated Employees
by Bill Hoke

My work experience with L. J. Minor began in March of 1983. At that time I was hired as a formula batchmaker. My first impression of the company was my interview and walk through with Mike Minor. Little did I realize at the time that he was Dr. Minor's son.

The first thing I noticed was the friendly environment that was present at the plant. No one was too good to say a simple "Hello" or "Good Morning." This went for even the Vice President, Mike Zelski, who would always say hello and know you by name!

Then when this older fellow came through and stopped to say hello, I later found out that he was the founder of the company, Dr. Minor. I was really impressed!

After working for a couple of weeks, I got a call on a Saturday morning from Ruth that she needed help on a rush order. I said I would be right there. I got to the plant and Ruth said she needed me in final blend first, then in packaging.

Another employee and I did the batches in final blend and cleaned up. Then both of us proceeded to the packaging room. There I was introduced to Bridget Clancy-Bell who was helping out at the plant this particular weekend while during the week she worked in the main office located in the Bulkley Building downtown.

Also working with us in packaging were Mike Minor and Ruth Fields. I thought to myself, this is where I want to work . . . where there is this type of dedication! In December of 1989 the first shift employees teamed up with several ladies from corporate to complete orders for the Christmas rush. It was impressive to see the office staff working hand-in-hand with the factory workers to get the job done!

In 1984 I was promoted to packaging supervisor on the day shift. Prior to filling this position, I was trained for six months in all departments in operations. This was done so I could, if necessary, assume the processing supervisors responsibilities.

My duties as packaging supervisor included all of packaging, shipping, and sample packaging. Also, as an on-going trainee, I attended many seminars (company funded) to help enhance the overall performance of my department.

With the help and training I was given by Ruth Fields, I was able to do the task the company expected of me and make the people assigned to my department feel needed and appreciated. This is the feeling Dr. Minor showed to each of us. Likewise, this is the way each employee was to be treated.

This "task," I might add, took little or no effort as I was surrounded by the best of work crews. My crew ranged from 13-15 employees on a regular basis, and many more when added help was needed.

Since I had been cross-trained in all work areas, I was familiar with each of the employees, which made things easier when they were asked to work in my department as well as when I needed to assume the processing supervisor's position temporarily. I might add that this cross-training gave me a greater appreciation of each position in operations, of what was expected of every individual, and what their needs are.

Currently, I am furthering my education by attending Cuyahoga Community College with the hope of bettering myself to meet future demands of the Minor Corporation. Each of the supervisors rotate every six months into a different supervisory position and time slot, including weekends. This was established so we each have a better understanding of the overall operation.

At this time, I am also working with a team of individuals who develop the master schedule for the year. This team is comprised of people from scheduling, managers of packaging and processing, the Vice President of Operations, and a supervisor.

Earlier this year, another team was made up to evaluate the hourly positions at the West 25th Street plant. This team consisted of the packaging and processing managers, human resource, technical, maintenance, and two supervisors (myself being one).

We are looking at each of the jobs, reevaluating and regrouping them, and will put the new classifications into effect at the end of August, 1994.

The job I accepted back in 1983 has turned into a career (hopefully life long) and I attribute my success to Dr. Minor and his business ethics. My statement to Dr. Minor is:

> "The L. J. Minor Corporation was built on your view, Dr. Minor, of the way the product should be made. Also, the way you treated people and gave them respect really impressed me and I will try to always treat my fellow workers with this type of respect. Thanks for being that Leader!"

Chapter 44

My Life and Times at L. J. Minor

by Tom Arthur
(1969 plus, 1984-1995)

The Initial Years   **Enjoying Full Time at Minor's**

Cookroom Kettles
(Irish Humor by Hal Roach)

Enos ran into Murphy in the cookroom full of steam jacketed kettles and asked:
    "What's the difference between a collision and an explosion?"

Murphy said:
        "If you're in a collision, there you are. But if you're in an explosion, where are you?"

Building Minor's
by Lewis J. Minor

There are two main classes of people in society
        "builders" and "wreckers."
Minor's retained the "builders.

The Initial Years

I first became associated with Minor's when I was still an apprentice electrician. I was transferred to a company called G&B Electric back in January of 1969. The owners were Roy Gair, the senior partner, and Henry Kondrat, the son of an insurance man who sold insurance to Minor's. I had assumed that is how G&B became associated with The L. J. Minor Corporation.

The first project I can remember working on at Minor's was an addition for a new cleanup area, small warehouse, and new men's restrooms/locker rooms. The general contractor was Roper Construction, which was basically a masonry contractor that was skilled in glazed tile work. Other contractors were Lossman Plumbing and Tyler Refrigeration.

My first impression of Minor's was that of a small company that was making some products that I had very little understanding of, but were made under very strict quality regulations. The reason I thought of quality was that very few projects that I had worked on used glazed tile because of the expense. Something else that struck me as strange was that they kept their garbage in a refrigerated room. We also had to wear special hats and always had to wash up before we went into the building.

The next couple of years I found myself working on various projects for G&B and I completed my apprenticeship with them and decided to stay on with the shop because it was a good shop to work for and did quality work.

During this couple of years span, we would go back to Minor's to handle any electrical problems that would develop, since they had no maintenance department. It was during this time that I came to know some of the people who worked for Minor's, directly as employees and indirectly as contractors.

My first contact was Mike Zelski, I believe. Mike was a true gentleman and always very pleasant. He would usually be the one to call us if work needed to be done. Things went on like this for sometime and over this period we got to know more of the employees including Tom Mele, George Henderson, Ruth Ann, and George Hvizd as well as the people who worked for the regular contractors.

We saw Minor's continue to grow. It seemed like we were there more and more installing new equipment, adding refrigerator trailers for more storage, increasing the size of the electrical service, and the like. Sometime during this period we started to work in the buildings and houses around the plant as Dr. Minor continued to purchase them.

Things were pretty good for me. I had gotten married, had my first child and become a foreman for a good company when my boss, Henry Kondrat, took a trip to Hawaii with his father-in-law, who was a fairly famous polka band leader in the Cleveland area. When he returned from the trip, he seemed very different. We got to talking about a week later, and he told me that he and his family loved Hawaii and had decided to move there.

Henry at the time was pretty much running the company, since Roy was up in years and had more interest in his boating than the business and he wanted to retire to Florida.

At this time I knew I had to find a new shop to work for or perhaps purchase the business. Things happened pretty fast; Henry made plans to leave within about six weeks and Roy was already talking about closing the doors.

Things were pretty slow in the construction industry at the time. In fact, so slow that my oldest brother was working as an electrician in New York City because there was no work here. I thought about it and approached my brother about us going into the electrical contracting business together. We decided to purchase G&B Electric and see how things went.

Minor's was one of our better accounts along with some other food processors, bakeries, and dairies where we gained experience in the food industry. By this time, Dr. Minor had a fellow named Don Lutz purchasing and managing the properties for him. Besides the work at the plant and at the flour toasting operation on Fruitland Ave., we were also doing some house wiring repairs for Don Lutz, as well as converting some of the other houses and buildings into labs and product development facilities; areas that were very much needed by this rapidly expanding business.

The next major addition occurred in about 1974 and was built primarily as a finished product warehouse. It was an approximately 2,000 square foot building made of prefabricated insulated panels.

Building this structure required us to move and expand the electric service to the building. While trying to design this, we questioned Mike Zelski as to future plans for development at this site and designed the switch gear for future expansions. I believe that this was the second promise we made to Minor's that we would never have to increase the size of this service again!

The way this addition was planned, there was a contractor hired to do the concrete, structural steel, and the insulated panel work. Lossman Plumbing, Tyler Refrigeration, and G&B Electric all had separate contracts and were working directly for Minor's. The contractor doing the structure ran into financial difficulties during the project and this created some problems in trying to get this project completed.

It was at this time that we talked to Mike and George about getting a professional architect as well as a quality general contractor to oversee any future projects and try to develop a master plan. Our advice was taken, and contacts were made for the future.

We also, at the time, talked to Minor's about the importance of proper maintenance in the facility. A preventive maintenance schedule was set up and Minor's hired a handy man to handle some of the simpler repairs.

For the next several years, there were many smaller projects: more houses turned into labs and offices, moving the flour toasting operation from Fruitland to West 25th Street in another converted building, a new lunch room, and a lot of new equipment.

The business was really growing at this time and over the next few years many people were added. Mike was spending more and more time in other areas of the business and George Hvizd was pretty much handling operations in the plant.

One of the new people coming to work at Minor's was Mike Minor, who had been honing his skills as a chef. Mike was working in various areas of the plant, learning the operations, when I first met him. The first thing anyone would notice about Mike was his enthusiasm for the business. Before long we were working more and more with Mike because he was the person who ordered the new equipment.

During this time a master plan for the growth of the factory was developed with the architect and general contractor. The next major addition was the new dry goods warehouse, which nearly doubled the square footage of the plant. The new master plan was in place and as part of it we were once again increasing the size of the electrical service.

We <u>again</u> assured Minor's that this would be the last time we had to do this.

It was only a short time after this addition was completed that Mike Zelski and Mike Minor called and told us that they bought a new piece of equipment that would streamline the way they processed the product. The machine specifications were given to the engineers and architects and a small room addition was planned to house this new equipment. The new equipment had a 100 hp motor on it and when the calculations were completed, we again had to increase the electrical service to handle this equipment. This equipment added a lot of capacity to the total output of the plant and was a major step in the company's growth.

A receiving cooler and freezer were added along with the building shell for a new cookroom and other mixing and weighing areas. Don Lutz had been busy purchasing houses and buildings adjacent to the plant property so that the master building plan could come to fruition.

It was about this time, while Minor's business was growing and prospering and our contracting business was flat, that I first considered doing other things. We would have some good months and some bad months, but could not seem to get it to the size that would support the overhead that we had.

My brother purchased my interest in the business allowing me to take some time off to spend with my family and decide what I wanted to do. By this time I had three children, and wanted to enjoy them while they were still young. I returned to work for my brother as a mechanic and was enjoying not having as much responsibility and having to put in so much time to the business.

It was at this time that a new packaging room, welfare facilities, equipment storage, a small maintenance area, and the second floor shell for a new office and technical center was being bid out by the general contractor that was then doing the work for Minor's.

My brother's company was not the successful bidder on this project, but we were still doing the service and electrical maintenance work at Minor's. I was surprised to hear that Minor's had purchased the old Oscar Mayer facility in Brecksville, and I was to go there to get the building in shape for conversion to a distribution center. It was while I was working out there that I was first approached to come to work directly for Minor's.

Enjoying Full Time at Minor's

So, how did I come to officially work for Minor's? It was early February, 1984, when the phone rang at my home at about 4:45 in the morning. It was Mike Minor on the line calling from the plant, stating that the chopper was down. I asked him why he didn't call my brother, and he said that he wanted to make sure that it was me who was coming to work on it. I got dressed and made it to the plant as quickly as I could.

By the time I arrived, they were running the chopper. Mike told me not to worry about it at the moment and that he needed to talk to me. It was then that he asked me what it would take to hire me to run the maintenance for Minor's. I was quite surprised and asked Mike if he were serious. He said he was. I told him that I would have to think about it and let him know.

To be truthful, I had just begun to really like the fact that my time was now my own, and that I was no longer in the contracting business with my brother. I knew that this position would require a lot of time and effort if it was going to be done properly.

In talking to my wife Gloria about what transpired, I told her I didn't know if I should take the position or not, but, as always she was very positive about things and said that things happen for a reason and that I should seriously consider it.

A few days later I talked to Mike and told him what I needed monetarily to take the position. It was about a week later that I met with Mike Zelski and George Hvizd about the position. My starting date was established as March 3, 1984.

My first couple of days were pretty uneventful, and I was just getting my feet wet. There were quite a few recurring problems that came to light after talking to the employees. It was a little scary because I didn't know where to start or what to work on first.

Even at this stage of my relationship with Minor's, I didn't know Ruth Ann too well, but was impressed with the hands on knowledge she had about things and how she and the other supervisors all pitched in to get things done.

It was Wednesday of my first week, and I was meeting with a salesman in the new lunchroom when several of us who were there heard this noise that sounded like a muffled explosion.

We went running into the plant to find a pile of rubble where the cookrooms once were. The first thing that entered my mind was that we had people hurt or killed. Everyone just sort of stood there looking at the damage.

Raw gas could be smelled and was coming from somewhere. I asked if the supervisors could get the buildings evacuated. There was some remodeling work done in conjunction with the new addition and no one knew where the gas shutoffs for the cookroom were. We had to shut the main at the street to get the gas off. We didn't know at this time what the cause of the explosion was. Everyone was just relieved that no one was seriously hurt or killed.

After clearing things out of the way, we could see that one of the kettles had exploded with a tremendous force. It had taken down two walls of the cookroom and damaged the others. There was damage to the equipment and possible structural damage to an I-beam that was directly above the kettle.

The bottom line was we had to have cooking capabilities as soon as possible or we couldn't produce. We got in contact with some of our contractors and figured if we worked around the clock we could be back in production by Monday. I can remember back to that Sunday night and thinking to myself, why did you take this job?

My baptism of fire did accomplish some things though. It helped me to make my mind up on which project I would like to start first. It made me determined that something like this would never happen again, and it gave my associates some confidence in my abilities to perform.

After the smoke cleared from this experience, it was time to get a department developed that had the technical expertise to handle the more and more complex equipment that we had and were contemplating buying, as well as having the in-house capability to maintain this rapidly growing facility.

At the time I had one maintenance person and one handyman who reported to me. We were already working two shifts and weekends packaging gravy, and had no one to cover the maintenance needs for these shifts. We were called in on a regular basis to get equipment running at night and on weekends.

Things at this time were changing rapidly. The new addition was just being completed. Bart, Ingolf, Ruth, George Hvizd and Mike were all given new responsibilities. We got our first computer and people were moving into new offices.

The company had just been sold to a group of investors and Gen. McLaughlin was the President. I had just met Bill McLaughlin and some of the investors and I was asked to develop a plan for the maintenance department along with budgets. I did that as best I could with the information that I had and developed the plans.

The first person I requested that we hire was someone to help me in getting the information that was needed to properly maintain things. We had a lot of information to acquire and this person had to be very detailed and tenacious. I knew just such a person.

Speaking with George Hvizd, I requested that we hire Nancy Grad. She had been working for my brother's company and was looking for something else. George knew her from his dealings with my brother's company. The necessary approvals were obtained, with the stipulation that she would only spend half of her time working in maintenance and the other half performing duties for manufacturing.

The company was continuing to grow at astounding rates. I was very impressed with all of the talented people who worked there and tried to learn as much about the business as I could. Things were still moving quite quickly. We moved into the new maintenance room, got a computer of our own, were working on new offices in the second floor shell as well as planning a new addition for an added chopper room and premix area. A new thaw box and new supervisor's area were added as the growth continued.

The time had arrived to hire an added maintenance person. We couldn't keep up the pace of trying to cover the needs of the second shift by continuing to come in when they had problems. I was previously approached by a mechanic who also worked for my brother. The needed approvals were obtained, and Pat Halligan started working as a second shift maintenance technician.

We were all cramped into an area that was approximately 240 square feet. In this area, we had our inventory, work benches, tools, equipment, two desks, and a computer. It was time we got proper facilities to perform our duties.

Approaching management, I asked to build a two story addition that would be a maintenance shop on the first floor and office building on the second floor. This addition was to also include our first shipping and receiving dock that would be at grade level. No one could understand why we needed so much room, but I knew it was essential if we were to grow into a department that had the internal capabilities to support our continued expansion.

Bart, Ingolf, and Josephine were all sharing a single office at the time and Bart was considering an assistant to help him with his duties. A decision was also made to reassign Beverly, who was doing research work, from the R & D department to purchasing. We approached management with the proposition of utilizing the second floor as an engineering/purchasing office complex. The project was approved and constructed within six months.

We were already in the design stages for a new cookroom and also talking about completing the second floor shell for the R & D department when the engineering addition was being completed. We had hired another maintenance person, George Young, and I hired an old friend of mine, Rod Williams, to install some ceilings and cabinets for us.

We were working with a new engineering firm that specialized in U. S. D. A. facilities and they were located in Cincinnati. I was putting in a lot of time and just keeping my head above water. I knew Rod was very knowledgeable about construction and would be a great asset for the company. I hired him as a consultant and said we would see what happened from there.

When I had just been promoted to engineering manager, Pat was promoted to maintenance supervisor. George Young was working as second shift maintenance technician and had a good background in equipment design. The designs of the tech center and cookrooms were completed, and construction started. We had purchased our second computer and decided on a computerized maintenance system as well as a computer aided drafting (CAD) system. These systems made us much more productive and helped us in doing our jobs.

The technical center was dedicated to Dr. Minor in December of 1986 and Walt Nicholes wanted our assistance in installing a plaque for this dedication. This was the first time I saw Dr. Minor's original business philosophy. I was very impressed. The statement was just plain common sense and yet included every value that was needed to run an exceptional, quality business.

Nestle had now purchased the company and things continued to change. The cookroom was completed in early 1987. I was able to hire Rod on permanently, additional talented maintenance people were added, and George was promoted to project engineer for equipment.

Since then, the growth has continued with more additions and, <u>yes</u>, more promises that we will never have to increase the size of the electrical service again (until next time). I feel that I have been very fortunate to be associated with so many talented and dedicated people. I guess it is just like any recipe: if you use quality ingredients, prepare them just right, and use the right amounts, you can't miss with the end product!

Chapter 45

On Advertising and Public Relations

by Walter S. Nicholes
(1975-1989)

An Opportunity with Minor's   **The First Ad Campaign**

Product Publicity Expands   **Working In-House**

Speak Out and Say Something
(Irish Humor by Hal Roach)

Shawn calls his mother in County Cork and asks:
"What do you think of the bird I had sent to you?"

His mother says:
"Lovely. It had a kind of nice salty taste."

Shawn says:
"Oh, no, you cooked it? That was a rare South American parrot! It spoke
five languages."

His mother said:
"Why didn't it say something?"

Do Something--
Let the Word Get Out!
by Lewis J. Minor

Do something. It's better to do something,
whether it's right or wrong.
It's better than doing nothing!

An Opportunity with Minor's

Producing advertising and public relations for the L. J. Minor Corporation -- from November 1975 to December 1989 -- was more than just a good job. During that time I was able to apply all the skills I had learned in my several previous employment opportunities which included writing, teaching, managing and selling. The Minor years were most gratifying, and working with the company helped to fill important needs in my life.

Early into my first project, I knew I was involved with people who were committed to top quality performance on a daily basis. Minor's was then a small production and service family business. To each manager and employee, the belief that Minor's products should be the best they could possibly make came as naturally as breathing: *top quality was simply how it should be!*

Soon enough I was accepted as a working member of this community, with enough shared information and freedom, along with requisite responsibility and budget, to recommend effective advertising and public relations projects and make them work. Here was a refreshing, invigorating client!

After coming to Cleveland with my family of five in 1958, and working for several years in sales and sales management, I again focused on writing, specifically writing advertising copy for Hauser-King-Marford, one of the city's biggest direct mail firms.

A year later, I opened my own one-man ad agency. Two years after that I helped create a five-partner agency which lasted another two years before the partners began to be dangerous to each other. The day I heard about L. J. Minor, I was a partner handling eleven diverse clients in a small four-person suburban agency named AD/MARK.

Jerry Stiegler, an advertising space salesman, stopped by to introduce himself. Months later, he told me our agency was his first official sales call in his new capacity as account executive for *Restaurants & Institutions*, one of the foodservice industry's most prestigious publications. He confessed that he wanted to practice on a small prospect before trying to sell the big ones. Early on, both Jerry and his editors at "R&I" came to appreciate the special quality of the Minor Corporation and helped in various effective ways to convey our message to their readers.

After our affable meeting, Jerry said he wanted to do a favor for my agency, for himself, and for a "nice little downtown Cleveland company with a great product but no national advertising and they really need help. "One problem," he said, "Is that you have to impress a retired U. S. Army general."

Since leaving my previous agency, I had discarded all my neckties except two for weddings and funerals, allowed my hair and beard to grow, and worn beads to a couple of parties. In our small shop, we dressed and worked informally. I had also mentioned earlier to Jerry that my past included U.S. Navy duty as communication officer and navigator of a large auxiliary vessel and that I still had flashbacks of my conflicts with standard issue, orthodox, unimaginative, totally inflexible U. S. military minds.

But I did make the contact. From my file copy of a November 12, 1975 letter to

Mike Zelski, Minor's general manager, I quote in part: "We are a compact agency, remarkably efficient, and versatile. I'm confident you'll find us capable of any kind of advertising or promotional work required for your company." I also named some of our Cleveland foodservice clients, and asked for an introductory meeting.

In early February, I finally met Mike with Gen. McLaughlin present. I'd learned that prior to joining Minor's in 1974 as Vice President of International Sales, Gen. McLaughlin headed the U.S. Army Support Command in Europe with 70,000 people reporting, directly or indirectly, to him. He had also commanded the U.S. Army Quartermaster Center at Fort Lee, Virginia. Joining the Army first at 16, discovered underage, kicked out, joining again at 18, he rose through the ranks to permanent three-star rank at retirement.

With no necktie, but a trimmed beard, neat slacks, clean turtleneck shirt and no beads, I was apparently presentable. Mike was cheerful and friendly. Gen. McLaughlin was instantly unlike any high ranking military mind I had ever met. He put me instantly at ease with a humorous greeting, cleared some desk space, sat back, appraised me briefly and said: "OK, Walter, if you're such a hot-shot ad man, tell us how to sell our new Lobster Base."

I replied, "Gentlemen, I've read as much as I could about the Minor Corporation. I'm impressed by the quality claims culinary professionals make for Minor's products and their many benefits. There's certainly an enormous potential market. But to work right, I have to know more about your marketing objectives that only you can tell. Who are your present customers? Who do you want for your new buyers? Tell me about this new product? What are its benefits, drawbacks? Right now I don't know exactly how I'd go about advertising Lobster Base. But if you want some evidence that I really can sell foodservice products, I'll be happy to show you."

They assented and I presented a few ads we had created for local clients and which were then appearing in national foodservice publications. Then Gen. McLaughlin reached behind him and produced a large red plastic lobster. He tossed it over and said, "Walter, let's meet again in whatever time it takes you to come up with a presentation, along with costs, to get this Lobster Base off the ground. And keep this as a reminder." I still have the lobster, one claw slightly damaged, otherwise intact.

He also gave me a large manila envelope of ads and product literature produced by the small print shop that also made labels for Minor's product containers. Most impressive for me was an editorial feature reprinted from *The Culinarian*, the official publication of the American Culinary Federation, the national organization of professional chefs. It detailed Dr. Minor's foodservice teaching and research career and his deep respect for and use of retired professional chefs as Minor's sales force. It also acclaimed the unmatched quality of Minor's products since the company's founding in 1951.

The First Ad Campaign

So impressed was I by this remarkable unsolicited praise for one man and his company's products by the most prestigious association of professional chefs in America that I began immediately to work up a presentation.

There were two ways I might go. One was a brief, low cost proposal promoting only the new Lobster Base. This involved designing an ad, recommending its insertion in some effective publications, and also producing a basic information brochure or flier to show chefs benefits of using the new base. Cost of this package at that time: $3500.

But the right way to sell this product, and also herald the L. J. Minor name to thousands upon thousands of potential customers now wholly unaware of Minor's or its products, was something else. The right way was an honest-to-goodness full scale marketing program which, for starters, would include space advertising, product information releases, corporate public relations, and a cohesive "family" label design. Also a new logo design to visually impress America's commercial foodservice industry with Minor's corporate values of *quality, service, optimism and patriotism!*

Deciding to spend some speculative time and money, I went for the right way. In three weeks, I had draft copy and layout ready for an attractive full line brochure that included vital company history, the endorsement of the American Culinary Federation, six incontestable advantages of using Minor's bases, and practical menu applications for Minor's 32 products, logically categorized into Meat Bases & Sauces, Poultry Bases & Sauces, Seafood Bases, Vegetable Bases, Complete Soups, and Specialties.

Because product application photos didn't exist, we used artists' renderings to show the appealing, delicious soups, sauces, and entrees that chefs could make *"quickly, easily, and economically"* with Minor's Bases. We also made finished art for a half-page ad showing a triumphant lobster, wearing a three corner hat and holding an American flag, climbing out of a jar labeled Lobster Base. The top headline proclaimed "Let Them Eat Lobster!" The subhead below stated: "Minor's revolutionary Lobster Base brings the noble flavor of North Atlantic lobster to the people!"

The ad would appear in early 1976 issues of foodservice publications. And 1976, recall, was the 200th anniversary of America's Declaration of Independence, with overtones of the French Revolution and Marie Antoinette's memorable phrase, real or attributed to her: "Let them eat cake!"

The ad copy advised chefs they could now add many *profitable* new lobster dishes to their menus at affordable prices because previously expensive sauces and entrees could be made at far less cost, and often with richer natural lobster flavor, simply by using Minor's new Lobster Base in the recipe. As this was the truth, it was easy copy to write. The ad concluded with this bold offer: **"Share lobster with the people! Free Lobster Base recipe booklet shows many ways to popularize delicious lobster flavor."**

Since the ad promised a Lobster Base recipe booklet, we had to include costs for its design and production. I also recommended a series of new product information releases to about 50 publications, several in-depth editorial features detailing the "L. J. Minor Story" for placement in prominent foodservice journals, and recommendations for a comprehensive

493

corporate marketing plan. Cost would be about $35,000 for starters. If Minor's agreed that ongoing advertising, public relations, and sales promotional materials were essential for growing a business, then a percentage of annual gross sales was to be budgeted for these and other marketing expenses annually.

Again through Mike Zelski, I arranged for my presentation. I opened by stating I wanted to show two options: one to sell Lobster Base to restaurant chefs only; the other to sell Lobster Base as well as Minor's entire product line not only to restaurant cooks and chefs but to other fast growing foodservice segments such as hotel and restaurant chains, commercial food processors, student feeding, and so on. Gen. McLaughlin said, "Let's see the big plan." I showed him what I had prepared. When I ended, he asked, "How much?"

"I don't know exactly," I said. "We work differently from most agencies who charge monthly or annual retaining fees plus hourly rates and out-of-pocket expense. We work on a project basis and charge only for work performed. For example, we'll give the Lobster Base ad a numbered project file, a complete accessible record of every cost in creating the ad. It holds invoices to us from artists, typesetters, photographers, everybody involved. Plus the record of my time -- to the quarter of an hour -- for meetings and copy writing. So we have an exact record of every cost when it comes to sending you the bill. If you think it's too much, we review the file. Now I don't know exactly what the overall project will cost. I think you should budget at least $35,000 for the work I've outlined here, and for the balance of the year."

Then and now for me, $35,000 represents a lot of money. I grew up poor and the feeling never entirely left. Gen. McLaughlin picked up the proposed colorful full line brochure, studied it a few moments more and looked over at Mike who nodded. Then he said, simply: "OK, let's get started. But you've got to change that flag in the ad. We can't have the American flag trivialized, even unintentionally." Later we replaced the American flag in the ad with a tattered nondescript banner and that was the beginning of my professional relationship with the L. J. Minor Corporation.

The first paragraph of a letter dated April 20, 1976, addressed to Michael Zelski, Gen. Manager, reads: "Dear Mike, I want to thank you and Gen. McLaughlin for the trust and confidence you have both shown by electing to have Ad/Mark, Inc. represent the L. J. Minor Corporation as your advertising agency of record."

By 1976, Minor's had established a basic national sales organization, most of whom were retired professional chefs. Minor's bases then represented a remarkable challenge to the traditional culinary practice of preparing the many different meat stocks used to make soups, sauces, and entrees. The claim was made, and could be demonstrated, that Minor's seasoned meat concentrates -- or "food bases" as Dr. Minor named them -- when simply mixed with boiling water would reconstitute into instant, wholesome meat stocks equal to or better than those made by the traditional, expensive, labor intensive method taught in classical culinary schools!

That is to say to a professional chef, "By using Minor's bases you can make, in a few

494

seconds, a stock as good or better than you used to make with all your expensive ingredients and hours of professional time and skill. And it costs less, too!"

Of course no professional chef in his right mind would believe such a statement, especially if he saw it in an advertisement. But if another professional chef made the same claim, possibly a brother chef known by reputation or chef association membership, then the prospective chef customer had to listen!

This is what Dr. Minor already knew, and it was on this premise that Tom Ryan -- the company's first sales manager and close personal friend of Dr. Minor -- had built the foundation of the company's present and future sales force: chefs selling to chefs; prestigious American Culinary Federation chefs educating other chefs and cooks to use Minor's bases as professional culinary tools. Customer education was the benchmark and bottom line of every Minor's marketing program. The more a chef knew about using Minor's products to his best advantage, the more he would be likely to buy more and also recommend them to his apprentices and others within his influence.

Already, even with inadequate advertising and promotional literature, Minor's sales had been building, forcing plant and personnel expansion, and requiring major capital expenditure. Tom Ryan realized the company had to grow. Prior to his death in January of 1975, he, with Dr. Minor's approval, brought Gen. McLaughlin on board to organize the inevitable expansion in the form of a modern, cost-accountable business.

Mike Zelski then was deeply occupied with new personnel and product development. Gen. McLaughlin was assigned broader management responsibilities by Dr. Minor as implied by this excerpt from my letter to Gen. McLaughlin dated May 27, 1976: "Dear General, I appreciate your letter of May 19. I understand advertising and public relations programs for L. J. Minor Corporation are under your control and will, of course, submit any proposal or material to you for approval before release or production."

From then, I reported primarily to Gen. McLaughlin. Of course, there were periodic operation review conferences that included Dr. Minor, Mike, and others involved with advertising and marketing projects. We became an efficient team with a single objective: to promote the enduring image of the L. J. Minor Corporation as the highest level of product quality and customer service which human effort might hope to attain.

We were unusual in another aspect in that Minor's management shared several common principles regarding the human relationship. I recall a marketing review meeting in the later years with Dr. Minor, Gen. McLaughlin, and myself. As we began, I observed, "I'll bet no place else in the universe is there another for-profit business meeting in session right now where all the participants were Eagle Scouts." We had each been active teachers in our lives as well.

Through the early years, I worked with lean-to-modest budgets. But getting maximum sales exposure from lean budgets was my specialty. I was a master of product publicity, able to gain the maximum number of new sales leads for Minor's chef-salesmen at the lowest cost per lead.

Product Publicity Expands

The commercial foodservice industry is enormous and varied. Dozens of professional publications vie for the attention of a vast readership. These magazines are invariably mailed free to foodservice personnel known to have purchasing power. For their entire income, the publications depend on paid advertisements of foodservice manufacturers wanting to sell products to readers who are "qualified buyers". With so much competition for advertising dollars, it was possible to work mutual back-scratching deals with publications that reached the culinary professionals who we wanted to buy Minor's Bases.

My message to each such publication was essentially the same: "My client's advertising budget is small. Right now, we can afford a few small black-and-white ads. But we have a remarkable product. Truthfully, it helps chefs work easier, makes restaurants more profitable and customers happier. Your publication mission is to inform the industry about new products and services that help achieve essentially these ends. So your readers *should* know about Minor's bases whether we can afford to advertise or not.

"It's your obligation to help the industry! That's why the post office lets you mail thousands of your bulky magazines every month practically at taxpayer expense. So how about your printing for free some of our newsworthy -- and for a change, true -- product information releases? In return, we'll place one or two of our available ads with your publication.

"This way we can really test your readership claims. We'll see which readers respond. And if they're the executive chefs, working cooks, and institutional dietitians we're looking for, then we'll certainly consider placing more and larger ads."

What I already knew and had verified in all professional magazines, whether read by hog farmers or nuclear engineers, was that few readers believed *anything* that advertisers promised in conventional ads. But leaders gave some credibility to benefits claimed in new product information stories because these appeared to be written by the publication editors who, they must reason, have less causes to lie than the advertiser.

In fact, response to published product releases was consistently higher than from ads. On average we would draw around 40 valid responses the first month a small ad appeared. A product release describing the same product in half the space in the same publication invariably attracted 100 or more.

So Minor's product publicity spread over the dozens of competing foodservice publications, along with a modest schedule of carefully-placed small ads, plus a couple of in-depth editorial features in prestigious journals, produced thousands upon thousands of sales leads in the late 70's and early 80's from potential customers in every American city that boasted at least one restaurant managed by a professional chef.

Another early marketing strategy was to continue to nurture and extend Dr. Minor's past and present invaluable relationship with America's professional chefs. Dr. Minor's professional history and scholarly association with America's culinary industry is described elsewhere in this book. Our job, where advertising and promotional dollars could help, was to continue to expand this supportive relationship.

Rather than quickly spend our available advertising budget on a few very expensive ads in the major foodservice magazines, our primary ad program consisted of many inexpensive "good will" advertisements in local ACF chapter newsletters. None of these paid agency commissions and they consumed a lot of working time because almost every newsletter was a different size or shape and had different printing specifications. Each little publication with its perhaps 50 or so readers required the same production time and paperwork as a national publication ad reaching 50,000 readers.

Also, these newsletter editors were often temperamental executive chefs, not media professionals. Chefs, I quickly learned, were often averse to formal correspondence or record keeping other than their recipe files. But while placing these many ads was sometimes vexing and rarely profitable for the agency, the project had a valuable payoff.

Each of these small newsletters lived a precarious existence, depending on members' dues for publication. When our ads began appearing on a regular, frequent basis in principal city ACF chapter newsletters, Minor's was soon correctly perceived by the brotherhood: (and growing sisterhood!) of professional chefs as we wished it to be: *the intentional, significant supporter -- nationwide! -- of the American chef*

Many chef-editors wrote their own editorials praising Minor's products. They wrote these from the heart since most were users of Minor's Bases. They printed my product releases verbatim and always gave our ads preferred viewing positions, often on the front or back cover or inside the front cover. This extremely low cost campaign of numerous specialized ads and product releases specifically directed to ACF chapter newsletters paid off remarkably in continuing good will for the company. It was bread cast on the water.

At this point, to continue describing advertising's specific role in Minor's sales success becomes more difficult. New owner directives, many new managers, and new market forces all had come into play as the company sold more product and became more visible to competitors as well as customers in the marketplace.

Some months after Ad/Mark, Inc. had acquired the Minor's account, Mike Zelski asked me one day whether our agency was having financial problems. The company that previously printed Minor's labels, and whom we still used to print our new designs, had called Mike to say they had not been paid for work invoiced to our agency. I said I thought the agency was in good financial shape. I knew, for a fact, that Minor's always paid our agency invoice the day it was received. It turned out my partner was using agency income, including Minor's always-prompt payments, to underwrite personal investments, and was stalling our creditors. I said he must desist or I would resign.

He did not desist so I advised each of my accounts that I was resigning from Ad/Mark as of a given date. No more than that. A few days later, I contacted each previous client, advising that I would put together a new agency and asked them to sign on. Each did and thereafter our agency was named *Walter Nicholes & Associates*.

A key person in our new agency was a remarkable young woman, Stephanie Howard, later to become a full partner. Stephanie was the most affable, honest, and efficient office manager one could possibly imagine. She quickly organized the office with simple efficiency, kept meticulous records, and charmed our suppliers and clients. She also insisted that all of our suppliers, as well as the publications, be paid on time. Ahead of time if a discount was available, but never a day late!

This was exceptional for a small ad agency in Cleveland at that time. It was common practice for bigger agencies to delay paying their small creditors -- often the same individual artists, photographers, and typesetters used by Nicholes & Associates (these people were our associates) up to two or three months. If a small business protested over much, the message came down: "Well, if you can't wait a little for your money, I guess we'll have to look elsewhere." Of course there always was someone else who could do the work. Competition for the advertising dollar between graphic arts suppliers as well as between publications was always present and intense.

Stephanie paid our employees and small suppliers first. Then the remaining creditors and finally us if anything was left. She also set protocol for how the agency should be approached for our business to suppliers, especially publication space salesmen. "We don't give away anything to get our clients' business and we shouldn't take gifts from people who want our business." was how she put it. In those days, no ad agency owner or media buyer ever had to buy lunch. He could simply phone a publication in which one or more of his clients advertised and implicitly order an account exec there to lunch him free in Cleveland's finest restaurants.

Instead of this, we occasionally took favored suppliers and publication account executives to lunch and *we* paid the bill. We developed close relationships with our regular suppliers. They knew we demanded their best and we got it. We would also get emergency service if needed with little or no protest, and could always depend on their making our deadlines.

Foodservice publications were also regularly stiffed by some of the big agencies who habitually paid space bills two or three months in arrears and still took the two percent discount offered by the publication for payment within 10 days of invoice. Stephanie always paid our publications within 10 days and took her two percent which was good for us and good for the publication. In return for our consistent prompt payment record, publications often gave our ads preferred positions without the usual added cost. They also usually printed Minor's new product releases just as I wrote them.

By 1983, Minor's remarkable growth mandated substantial new capital expenditure while Dr. Minor looked forward to a debt-free retirement after his long career in business and university education. In April, he sold his company to a small investor group experienced in the commercial foodservice industry and committed to maintaining Minor's standard of "Only the best!" Gen. McLaughlin, who had been President since 1979, now became Board Chairman, President, and CEO. Dr. Minor continued as Chairman Emeritus and Senior Scientific Consultant.

By then, the Minor's account represented 60% of our agency income and accounted for about 75% of my working time. Our clients making nuclear power plant motors and oil drill gauges had left and I had become active in world peace and anti-nuclear movements. The Minor's corporate communications budget was nearing a million dollars and I was handling this practically free of oversight, although my programs were always presented for corporate overview and approved by Gen. McLaughlin.

Also, as larger, colorful Minor's ads appeared more often in major trade publications, larger Cleveland agencies began to solicit what would now be for them a profitable account. Gen. McLaughlin asked me to prepare a report comparing the merits of Minor's using an outside agency -- as we were at the time -- to an inside agency, that is, an advertising department of company employees.

My report showed each had benefits and drawbacks. All factors equal, two basic differences stood out: 1) inside agencies were usually far less expensive; and 2) outside agencies hypothetically had the broad experience and financial independence permitting them to challenge, if necessary, certain destined-for-failure projects that might be championed, say, by the client CEO or board chairman.

The report was concluded with something like this: "As an inside agency, I can continue to save Minor's money without decrease in program quality because the people doing the present good work will also do the future work. What I must know is, as a Minor's employee, can I still say 'No' to you and Dr. Minor when we disagree regarding aspects of the advertising program? Possibly brush some egos? How can I know this won't cost me my job? I've been able to say 'No' in the past when I thought necessary because without the Minor's account, though I value it above all others, I can still pay our bills and survive."

Working In-House

The assurance I needed was given, and in December, 1983, Minor's purchased the assets of Walter Nicholes & Associates and took our agency "in-house." I became vice president of advertising and public relations and Stephanie became my assistant. Mary Supplee continued her role as secretary and receptionist, now greeting callers with "L. J. Minor!" instead of "Nicholes Advertising." Our art director chose instead to work as a free-lance artist for the local advertising community. I directed my previous clients to the local agencies that I thought could help them best, and thereafter devoted my full energy as a new employee to Minor's corporate advertising and public relations programs.

As the company steadily gained major market visibility, it also reaped the problems which swift corporate growth generates along with the benefits. In the face of stiffening price competition from business rivals who saw their once secure "soup base" customers now converting in droves to Minor's "food bases," Gen. McLaughlin continued to organize and grow the company along modern business lines, staffing new departments with experienced career-trained sales and marketing managers supported by computerized information systems.

The advertising/marketing program also grew apace. By July, 1985, I was unable to do all the required creative direction and copy writing myself. Seeking professional help, I found Don Windfield, a veteran of New York City's advertising community and owner of a medium size agency there. Having recently moved to Ohio with his wife, Karen, also a graphic arts professional, Don worked out of the Hanna Building directly across the avenue from Minor's headquarters in Cleveland's downtown Playhouse Square.

We connected well and quickly. Don was better informed with more experience handling large accounts. He helped evolve the image of our advertising from "Growing Family Company" into "Arrived Important Corporation." He was educated and widely read, a proficient pianist, knew jazz and classical music, was honest and had a droll wit. He could be wildly funny whenever he chose and make me helpless with laughter. He was rare, too, in being a gifted advertising professional without the frequent insufferable ego, so we had no problem sharing either praise or blame when subsequent ad projects deserved either. In January, 1986, Buyers & Windfield became Minor's agency-of-record and we worked together until my responsibilities changed again in 1988.

In December, 1986, the L. J. Minor Corporation agreed to be acquired by Nestle Holdings, Inc., parent company of eight U.S. food-related companies owned by Nestle, S.A., based in Vevey, Switzerland. Minor's continued to be operated as a subsidiary of Nestle Holdings, Inc., with a management team headed by Bill McLaughlin, president; Dick Kennedy, senior vice president, sales and marketing; and Dick Zirbel, senior vice president, manufacturing and technical. Gen. McLaughlin continued as a special consultant and president of L. J. Minor, International.

Paul Hamerly was later named vice president of marketing and, as corporate advertising is properly contained within the corporate marketing program, Don reported to Paul. My title became vice president of corporate communications and from then until my retirement at age 65 in December, 1989, I worked on special corporate public relations projects, reporting to Gen. McLaughlin or Bill McLaughlin, depending on the project.

This about concludes my sense of individual input into the L. J. Minor Corporation. As a subsidiary of Nestle, the company continues to develop new products and new markets. I hope subsequent Minor's brand products will persist in setting the quality standard wherever they compete for sales. It's certainly a bigger company today than anyone I knew in 1975 thought possible. Except, perhaps, Dr. Minor and Gen. McLaughlin. And whether *bigger is better*, of course, is the on-going question.

Certainly many more persons are employed and that's good. Dozens of varietal new food concentrates -- *culinary tools*, Dr. Minor used to call them -- now exist to benefit America's culinary industry. New cooks and chefs who never knew of Minor's until the wide-ranging marketing programs executed during the later Nestle years now are regular customers. Perhaps the sizable corporate profits created will be generously dispersed. So these are benefits to be regarded.

500

Due either to retirement, restructuring or dismissal, most of the managers I worked with are no longer with the present company. Gen. McLaughlin died on January 3, 1992, and I thought some of my own life went out with this remarkable man whom I loved and who was so guiding and caring of me during my years at the L. J. Minor Corporation.

Possibly only because Minor's was a very small company, with perhaps 80 full- time employees when the singular combinations of destiny first brought me to its door, could it relate to its workers, suppliers, customers, and competitors according to those "Business Aims" which Dr. Minor first stated for publication in 1952, and practiced unfailingly during the years he owned the company:

"I believe that honesty, integrity, accuracy, punctuality, courtesy, kindness, friendliness, helpfulness, and cleanliness are the tenets upon which my business shall be built.

I will endeavor always to be fair and helpful, not only to employees, my management team, and stockholders, but also to customers, government agencies, and competitors.

My experience in the food industry indicates there will always be room for a company that will sell quality products that are constantly controlled to insure uniformity at a fair price that will result in a normal profit.

Service will be the keynote of our business and every effort will be put forth to give the customer exactly the product that he specifies."

When Nestle, General Motors, Ameritech, Bank America, Exxon and other such multi-national corporate conglomerates can operate according to these standards, perhaps then *bigger* will be unqualifiedly *better*. Unlike these essentially inhumane organizations as they now exist, the L. J. Minor Corporation that I knew was a rare example of ethical, humanistic, modest, ambitious capitalism and I was honored to have been able to play even a small part in its success.

Chapter 46

The Golden Age of Merchandising

by Howard L. Schatz
(1967-1988)

Customer Service
by Nancy Clancy
(1959 - 1994)

Quote from Aristotle

"Live by memory rather than by hope."

A Willing Spirit
(Irish Humor by Hal Roach)

Murphy spent his entire life researching ghosts. He was finally delighted to meet one that was friendly and asked if he would be able to take its picture. The ghost agreed. Unfortunately, the flash did not work, which just goes to show you:
"The Spirit was Willing, but The Flash was Weak."

Introduction

July 25, 1994

Dr. Minor:

This writing has two beginnings. The first is my earliest recollection of what seemed to me to be important events or incidents that remain clear in my mind and shaped my life, the way I think, judge people, and react to external forces that may have a positive or negative influence on my family or business.

The second could be more appropriate to the needs of this book, that is, my introduction to the Minor product line and subsequent steps leading to our brokerage and some of the key points in its rise to success.

The research documentation upon which I based my writing required much study. The following paragraphs include documents to support my writing. The reader will receive a general sense of the activities within HLS, Inc. and its relationship to Minor. Now for my story!

Howard

Throughout history, men have planned their careers only to discover that invisible forces which some call "fate" or "destiny" deal a different hand and an unexpected outcome.

There is an old Russian folk tale that says "Men sit and plan. God sits and laughs." Destiny can weave a strange pattern of life, and so it was with my many careers. Things happen and an unseen force moves you along its path.

My Minor career is no exception. Dr. Minor requested I write a narrative of these years and they are here recorded. Documentation, in support of the experiences and events, are now the property of Dr. Minor.

A review of my years with the Minor company required study of records long forgotten. Mental cobwebs had to be cleared and events in the long journey placed in perspective.

To understand my record, it is necessary to know the background and standards which guide me. I have a strong belief in a solid foundation of moral values and personal integrity. I prefer the handshake of a man of good faith than formal contracts with persons of dubious character.

Contracts are, by their very nature, adversary producing documents. You are not on the same side or the same team. It is a vehicle where one party gains dominance over another for personal or corporate gain.

Contracts provide a "corporate veil" for unscrupulous persons to hide behind, to protect them from personal liability for their words, deeds, or actions. During Dr. Minor's corporate ownership, contracts between brokers and the company did not exist. They were not necessary. The successors to Dr. Minor's ownership, on the other hand, did indeed need contracts due to a difference in management philosophy.

My 15 years with the Minor company rested, quite comfortably, on a handshake agreement with Dr. Minor. It may be an old-fashioned virtue, but his word is his bond. This is priceless without reservation.

The Minor Culture

Each business entity is a mirror reflection of the management and leadership style of its founder. Dr. Minor set reasonable goals for the company and organized a lean top level management staff to provide support and a commitment to quality food products. A rich culture was in place which bore his indelible stamp and his philosophy of ethics and service in business. It was a culture benevolently infectious with a sense of mission, a management obsessed with quality of product and an atmosphere that created enthusiasm that those outside the company could never understand or appreciate. The environment encouraged taking full personal responsibility for one's actions and by our performance stand out, but at the same time be a conforming member of a winning team. We, in effect, were the extended Minor family.

My odyssey could be viewed as a paradox. The journey began in my formative years where a foundation of values and ethics were instilled in me by my parents. We lived in a small country town of less than 2500 people and eight churches. A part of the fabric of our community was the welcomed sound of church bells on Sunday to call parishioners to services. The folks in our town had a mutual respect for each others' religious beliefs.

In my early years I worked in my father's butcher shop. The country was in a depression, not long after the Crash of '29. My father was a stern, no nonsense taskmaster who believed that hard work was the answer to all needs. I can never recall when he ever made more than a living wage. His basic philosophy was, "If you want something, you will have to work for it. Nobody will hand you anything without sweat equity."

A bit of family history. My grandfather on my father's side was an itinerant carpenter, in Byelorussia, building and repairing farm equipment. He came to America to better feed his family and perhaps find a more humane way of life. My father was born in

New York City. My mother was an orphan, her parents were murdered by the Cossacks in the Pogroms of 1903 in Odessa. At five years of age, cousins brought her to Philadelphia and she was unofficially adopted by her mother's sister, whom I knew as my "grandmother." My mother's adopted "father" and his eight sons were all in the meat business. It was not until the second generation of either family that a child entered high school. Knowledge of one's family history instills a sense of being and importance to daily living.

Our Meat Store

In our store, service to the customer was paramount. It meant extending credit for food until the next payday or if the customer was unemployed, extending credit until he obtained a job. Most paid their obligations; some did not.

Our town was surrounded by farms. Farmers would come into town to shop for supplies for the coming week for their live-in employees. Out of respect to the community, the farmers shopped mostly on Saturday night because their clothing and shoes bore the barnyard odors and smells. They did not wish to offend anyone.

Pre-cut meat or poultry was unacceptable. It had to be cut, on the block, in front of them, to their satisfaction. We were the only store in town that stocked sides of beef, on the rail, along with whole hogs, lambs, and calves. The farmers took great pride in selecting the carcass or quarter of beef we would cut into handy pieces for cooking.

These hard working people of many ethnic backgrounds were mostly first generation immigrants. In those days, people worked to satisfy needs for survival. "Wants" would have to wait for better days.

On Saturdays, I rode with my uncle making deliveries. Just outside of town was Campbell's Farm. My father supplied meat and groceries to the "main house." It was there that I met Dr. Dorrance, president of the Campbell Soup Co. Dr. Dorrance would arrive in a limousine, driven by a uniformed chauffeur, the first I had ever seen, with his hunting dogs in the back seat to hunt for rabbits and pheasants in what was locally known as Campbell's Woods. I was only about 12 or 13 at the time. After my first meeting with Dr. Dorrance, whenever he visited, he never failed to call me by my first name. I thought that was just great, and an early lesson in the importance of remembering a person's name and the effect it can have on him.

As Charles Dickens wrote, "It was the best of times and the worst of times." Hard work was expected and accepted as necessary for economic survival. President Roosevelt closed the banks; money ceased to exist. People survived on faith, trust, and credit. The barter system enabled many small business operations to continue. My father would give the local German baker lard to make his bread, cakes, and donuts. In return the baker would give us donuts and bread to sell to recover the cost of the lard. Everyone worked together. There was not time for ethnic, race or religious differences: we were all equal. Perhaps it was the best of times.

We lived adjacent to the Baptist Church. The preacher's son and I were great friends. Getting into trouble was easy. To earn a little money, we trapped muskrats in the local swamps, skinned them in the basement of the church, and sold the pelts which were later made into ladies coats. It was when we shot a chicken hawk and hung it from the rafters in the cellar of the church that trouble began. Seems that the hawk was loaded with lice when the good Reverend Moss discovered our enterprise. He did not appreciate our entrepreneurship. That was the end of the trapping business.

In retrospect, it was just as well. Perhaps it was the hand of fate. The preacher's son and I were working the traps in a swamp bordering Campbell's Woods. It was winter with thick ice on top of the marsh. We were tired and decided to take a short cut home instead of following the streams. Half way across we both crashed through and nearly drowned. How we ever got out of the freezing mud alive, I do not know. Another lesson was learned. Short cuts can be very dangerous to one's health.

Father Ryan, our local Catholic Priest taught me the value of charity and humility and how to give to those less fortunate so those on the receiving end could retain their personal dignity. During the depression jobs were rare; and vast unemployment was the norm. Welfare and unemployment checks did not exist. Many families were hungry, without money to buy food or fuel.

Father Ryan would come into our store and give my father a list of persons in dire need. He would say how much money he had to buy food. He and my father would then make up orders, pack the food in boxes and give them to me to deliver on my bike. Father Ryan instructed me to deliver the food with respect and never tell the recipient who provided the gift. He said it was an answer to a need. If he was short of funds, my father filled the boxes without thought of payment. He said it was our duty to help where possible. Another facet of my foundation of values.

In June of '41, I graduated high school . Pearl Harbor in December changed the world. I was working during the day and attending Wharton School at night. I enlisted in the Army in July and was called up in November. I was part of a large group of volunteers sworn in before Independence Hall in Philadelphia at 11:00 a.m., November 11, 1942.

A week later I was in the Army Air Force training center, Miami Beach, Florida for basic training and assignment. I was assigned to the training center butcher shop on Normandy Isle. The shop was a confiscated supermarket taken for Army Mess Support Service. Later, I was transferred to the Surf Club at 92nd and Collins. The Club had been transformed into a mess hall feeding four thousand plus G.I. personnel per meal. This new assignment opened the door to another facet: foodservice. I served my apprenticeship in the retail/wholesale meat business. I quickly learned that food preparation, baking, and cooking is an entirely different world. I liked it. Every day was a learning experience and my feeding masses of troops provided personal satisfaction in the knowledge that our jobs were important.

Thus, I began a career in foodservice, but not before Uncle Sam provided six months of combat training. The balance of my military life was spent working as a cook or meat cutter. I served in the South Pacific and the China-Burma-India theater and returned home

506

four years later.

Destiny stepped in again. I enrolled at Temple University. The week classes were to begin, my father took ill, was hospitalized, and I had to take over the family business. Duty and obligation to family had priority over personal wants and needs.

New technology developed for the war effort changed the meat business forever. Prior to the war, frozen foods were an expensive novelty. Blast freezers began to appear, and boneless beef once shunned by "real butchers" was beginning to be accepted. Packaging technology soon developed plastic for meat wrapping and in the process eliminated thousand of jobs in food markets. Displayed, hand cut meat, sold by men behind the refrigerated meat case was replaced by self-service. The customer's individual identity disappeared. He became a nameless, faceless buyer. Personal relationship with his or her favorite "butcher" ceased. Trained meat cutters were replaced by the band saw.

The invention of new plastics and equipment changed the foodservice business. The Cry-O-Vac system provided bone-in and bone-less primal meat cuts and individual portion cuts in precise weight and sizes, fresh and frozen. A new industry was thus created. Shipping cattle to the Eastern packing houses became obsolete due to transport costs and the unavailability of good cattle. Sources of fresh and frozen meat were now in the mid-west. Personal quality selection of rail meat, once the pride of the professional buyer was gone. Box meat was now the product of choice.

Prior to the war, our store always provided meat supplies to restaurants, so it was natural for us to begin to process control meat items. We were forced to buy large freezers, special equipment for cutting and packaging. The business grew, but expansion was impossible without Federal Inspection. Our property was too small and funds for a new facility were not available. We could not expand our sales base to cover the new added expenses of processing, so my father chose to close rather than assume massive debt. The depression years inflected a deep psychological effect upon those who survived, that being fear, insecurity, and loss of dignity. The risk was too great.

Sherry's Restaurant

In 1950, my wife and I opened Sherry's Restaurant and Pastry Shop. It was a successful venture for some ten years until two giant malls opened within a short driving distance from town. This competition effectively killed traditional small town business. Small stores closed, offices moved to new "business parks," and our customer base was destroyed. The town never recovered its former vibrant business district. We found a buyer for the restaurant and I began my career in hospital foodservice.

In 1962, I became Director of Food Services for Metropolitan Hospital in Philadelphia. In the early '60s many hospitals employed managers that were trained in commercial foodservice or in military feeding services. College level educational programs designed for hospital management were needed but were not available in the Philadelphia area. In response to this need, Rutgers University in New Brunswick, New Jersey, offered a two year program in Hospital Management at their Extension Division, Camden, New Jersey with night classes. I graduated in 1966.

The same year, Rutgers University and the New Jersey Department of Health, Veterinary Division united to offer a one-year program of education and training for meat inspectors. Classes were conducted by Dr. Oscar Sussman, DVM, Ph.D. and Chief Veterinarian of the state. At the time, New Jersey maintained meat inspection service for retail and slaughterhouse facilities.

Dr. Sussman taught practical meat and food inspection procedures as well as animal hygiene. We were focused on ante-mortem and post-mortem services designed to eliminate diseased meat and processed foods from reaching the public. We were instilled with a sense of urgency to make immediate decisions. Equivocation was unacceptable. I am certified by Rutgers University in Slaughtering, Packing, and Processing of meat and poultry. I have been a licensed and Registered meat inspector since 1966 by the New Jersey Department of Health, Division of EPA. This training as a food inspector has proved to be of great value in my representation of the Minor product line.

Minor Introduction

My introduction to the L. J. Minor Corporation began in 1964. During my tenure as food director of Metropolitan Hospital, a food salesman visited my hospital with a chef from the Minor company. This was my first meeting with Dr. Ernest Koves.

He presented to me one ounce samples of product and gave a very brief verbal instruction on application, a few recipes, and "profile cards" describing the base line. I later requested more information as to proper usage of the bases from the local salesperson, but not being a chef, he could not help us. I was told that Dr. Koves would stop in on his next visit, next year!

In 1966, Dr. Koves, at a monthly meeting of the Hospital Food Directors Association of which I was a founding member, presented a two hour working demonstration of Minor products to a capacity audience of chefs and food directors in the kitchen of the Atlantic City Hospital. It was there that I learned the practical value of bases. I became an ardent convert and supporter as well as buyer.

In 1968, I became foodservice director and member of a team designing and building a new kitchen and cafeteria for the Helene Fuld Hospital in Trenton, N.J. The new facility became reality and my five years at Fuld were very enjoyable and productive; however the dark cloud of labor strikes was a negative. We had three violent strikes in my five years, the last being ten weeks long. I was ready for a change to a calmer environment.

In 1967, my daughter Sharon, the recipient of several academic scholarships, entered Cornell University. My son, Kevin, was in high school and would soon enter college.

My financial position needed improvement to support the children's education. How best to achieve this? My thought was, why not return to food sales as a method of raising funds? To this purpose I visited Dr. Koves in New York City with the idea of becoming a

Minor distributor. Dr. Koves was receptive to gaining a new distributor. He explained financial arrangements and shipping procedures. Shipping small orders would solve my distribution problem and keep expenses low.

With approval from the Minor Corporation, I could begin selling Minor Base products. I then met with my hospital administrator and explained the need to increase my financial status. Wage increases of any substance were not possible as President Nixon had imposed a Federal Price/Wage freeze limiting salary increases to 5.5% per year. I told him of my plan for food distribution and was given permission to pursue my new business venture, providing it was not a conflict of interest and did not interfere with my hospital duties.

Initial progress was slow. I selected the health care market because I knew and understood dietary requirements and cost containment problems. The Minor products were priced to reflect quality and value, but purchasing personnel could not justify the cost because they did not know how to define quality. Many chefs and food directors were unaware of the superior quality of our product. I quickly realized the first priority would be one of education. Buyers and end-users had to be taught the benefits to be derived from our products.

A desire to buy had to be created. Product education and cooking demonstrations increased sales. Hospital accounts receivable increased beyond reasonable limits. Hospitals were notorious for slow payment of obligations.

Our small company was self-financed, every dime earned went back into the business. Extraction of funds for personal use was out of the question for several years. Banks refused to loan on hospital accounts-receivable saying that they were poor risks. In truth, in over 20 years I never lost a dime on any hospital account.

Tartan Foods

A week after the last strike settlement, I received a call from Tartan Foods, the largest food distributor in the Philadelphia area. The caller simply said that Mr. Earl Perloff, President of Tartan, wished to meet me at 7:00 a.m. that coming Friday morning. I knew him to be Chairman of the Board of Directors of Philadelphia General Hospital and Chairman of the Presidential Committee on Re-Organization of Hospitals in the United States. I accepted the invitation.

He opened the meeting by stating that he did not believe any meeting should ever take longer than one hour. For 50 minutes the conversation was limited to hospital management. The last 10 minutes were spent on his thoughts of converting Tartan into a one-stop shopping foodservice experience, a new concept at that time. The meeting adjourned and I returned to work. At 8:00 a.m. the following Monday morning, he called me, personally, and without preamble said the job was mine at double my present salary. When could I begin? I remember clearly saying, "I appreciate your faith in my ability, but no position was ever discussed!"

Without hesitation, he said he would give me authority to plan, organize, and direct a new meat division for Tartan. I would be the buyer of meat and dairy products. I would operate autonomously within the existing Tartan organization structure. I accepted.

That evening, I met with the general manager of Tartan and explained my small distribution activities. I offered to transfer the accounts to Tartan. I did not wish any conflict of interest. He was not interested. He said my business would die on the vine. His prophecy proved false.

Because we were at a financial impasse, I accepted the position . Growth was not possible without additional capital, all of our funds were in accounts receivable. I preferred to stay "independent" but had to face reality. It is regrettable that Minor sales were placed on the back-burner for nearly five years.

My position entailed teaching meat knowledge to the grocery sales force. I visited their customers and did meat cutting and yield tests to sell the new boxed meat program. The very program that put the small meat market out of business. Fate travels in strange circles.

Selling box meat to chefs, who by custom and tradition preferred buying rail meat, was like trying to move a brick wall. The belief was that box meat was inferior in quality. Boxed meat was widely accepted by supermarkets, but not by chefs. A series of unusual events prompted my resignation from Tartan.

The Minor office in Cleveland called to inform me that Dr. Koves had died on June 8, 1976. My wife and I attended the funeral in New York City. It was there that we met Dr. & Mrs. Minor, Gen. McLaughlin, and Mr. Eric Swanson, the Detroit Minor broker.

After the funeral, Mr. Swanson invited me to attend a seminar at Princeton University where Chefs Caubet & Breithaupt would be presenting cooking demonstrations on June 17, 1976. I attended the seminar and enjoyed seeing those marvelous chefs in action. Mr. Eric Swanson was the moderator.

Once again the mysterious hand of destiny beckoned. Mr. Eric Swanson died, July 21, 1976. I was invited to attend his funeral in Dearborn, Michigan. After services, the Minor brokers and friends joined the Swanson and Minor families for a luncheon at the Dearborn Inn.

At the luncheon, Gen. McLaughlin spoke to me concerning my position at Tartan. He inquired as to how I was able to achieve a personal sales record of $100 thousand per year in Minor bases and simultaneously hold a full time job. I explained in detail. On the first day of active employment, I made a second attempt to turn over the accounts, without cost, but the Tartan general manager was completely uninterested. So, I continued selling, but not to their accounts. I avoided any conflict on this point.

After the luncheon and prior to departing, Gen. McLaughlin offered to me Dr. Koves' New Jersey and Eastern Pennsylvania broker areas. He laid it out in a few words. Remuneration would be on commission from paid sales. Expenses and sales costs were my personal responsibility. The position required opening new distributor accounts, and developing end-user accounts for the distributors. I would receive a map of assigned area, samples, price sheets, and a copy of my predecessors accounts. This constituted my complete orientation and training program. This was on Saturday. I would reply by Monday morning.

A Puzzlement

This indeed was a pleasant puzzlement to evaluate. My position with Tartan was secure, salary good, life and health insurance fully paid by the company, pension fully funded, auto supplied, and I enjoyed the freedom to operate my department without corporate micro-management.

My relationship and knowledge of the Minor Corporation was limited to that of a manufacturer selling to a distributor. Dr. Koves was my company contact. My conversations with him were brief. Midnight calls from him were the norm. The script was always the same: "What are you doing? Why are you not in the kitchens when the chefs are working at night? I want you to get off your behind and get me more business. Good Night!" It must be understood that Dr. Koves was charismatic and irascible and an excellent chef in the European style. One had to know him to appreciate his manner and philosophy. He was a joy to know.

My decision to join the company and give up the comfort of a steady pay check was made on the basis of two factors. First, the reputation of Dr. Minor as a "mensch," which is an accolade to a person of integrity and honor. I knew of his obsession with "quality" and his meticulous attention to product safety, years before it became fashionable.

Dr. Minor's one price policy, of selling his products to all distributors at the same price, exasperated the large buyer but delighted the small entrepreneur. Economic fairness prevailed. The position offered opportunity and potential security. Potential was a key word; an untapped market existed for quality base products.

In my youth, my father told me about a lecture he attended given by Dr. Russell Conwell, founder of Temple University in Philadelphia. It changed his life. In later years I purchased the short story Dr. Conwell used in his lectures. It was entitled "Acres of Diamonds." This is a beautiful story packed with insight, thought, and motivation. One line in the story said "The opportunity was never greater for achievement than right here in Philadelphia". For me these words were a prophesy come true. I accepted the position and became a member of the Minor family. Destiny was kind to me and opened the door to be the best I could be.

Metaphorically speaking, acres of diamonds do exist if you but dig for them in your own backyard. Our record is solid proof. As promised, the sales records arrived. Annual sales for Southern New Jersey and Eastern Pennsylvania totaled $92,000. Philadelphia ARA was assigned to a broker in Massachusetts. Improved focus and attention to ARA was needed, so I purchased the account from the broker.

Dr. Minor's policy of eliminating bureaucratic constraints gave the green light for meaningful sales development. In place was a positive attitude that was diametrically

511

opposite my experience in a typical hospital organization. Obstacles to progress were non-existent. Absent was the traditional hierarchy and charts with departments isolated in little boxes. The company did not have broker job descriptions, policy manuals, rules on client management, intrusive management types, or impossible quotas. The company was poised for growth.

How To Begin?

Without a mentor, my venture would require definite direction, a method to acquire distributors and users of our products. A blueprint for goal achievement had to be identified and implemented. The keystone to the plan was "Niche Merchandising."

In 1975, I met a gentleman by the name of Bud Wilson. It is from him that I learned that merchandising is a very special, separate and distinct component of marketing. Bud wrote a primer on the subject that provides clarity of reason and substance.

In the world of business, marketing is the over-all function of moving merchandise. Merchandising is a sub-function of marketing dealing with strategy to move products. It is the manipulation of merchandise and tactics to make the flow of products more rapid and effective. In a capsule, merchandising is market strategy to get the Right Product to the Right Place in the Right Quantity at the Right Price at the Right Time in the Right Light.

This became my blueprint for action. Finely tuned, niche merchandising is simply specialization within a small market. This definition and focus was a perfect evaluation. Minor advertising stated: "Less than 1% of the foodservice dollar was used in the purchase of food bases." I was determined not to share my piece of the market pie!

In my bake shop days, I knew that making a pie crust was as easy as 1-2-3. One part water, two parts shortening and three parts pastry flour. Our niche merchandising had to be reduced to a similar formula. My hospital experience taught me that before a doctor can treat a patient, he must first identify and document the problem through diagnosis; therefore, accurate diagnosis of the niche market was needed to develop plans and strategy.

Our goal was to bake a new market pie, to create a new quality base category not to be confused with commodity products being sold in the marketplace. We emphasized an easily remembered theme in seminars, cooking presentations, and selling: "Dr. Minor set the Standards or Control in food bases for other manufacturer to emulate." Quality in other bases was to be judged against Minor products. When the competition used the phrase "Our bases are almost as good as Minor's, but cheaper," I knew we had established a new quality level. We were now perceived as the leaders and our pricing policy was justified.

Guided by the blueprint, I had to identify what class of buyer buys. The buyer could be a chef in a restaurant or diner, an institutional buyer for a hospital or university, but each of these has special needs. What were the needs? Could our products fit all needs? Were they reasonable in cost for the commodity buyer as well as the specialty buyer? How best to sell, by the pound or by yield, by the serving? Was the end product, i.e. soups, gravies etc. for direct resale to a restaurant customer or to be bulk packed and sold as a finished ready-to-eat item?

Was the product being purchased as a necessity or a luxury? Was it a convenience item or to be used only in an emergency? Were sales or purchases made routinely or by impulse? Where was the level of satisfaction? Each of these questions could apply to a hospital foodservice department. Bases were purchased as a necessity to feed patients. The level of satisfaction came from knowing the right product to use. Our standard product would be incorrect for a low salt, low fat broth, but correct for regular patient or cafeteria usage. Sales were made on a regular basis depending on patient census and employee needs in the cafeteria or coffee shop.

Where and when could you most effectively make a sale? When did the buyer buy? At what time of the day? Was it a weekly or a monthly schedule? Did selection of types of bases differ with the time of the month or year or season? This information was vital. In the Army I was taught to be an expert marksman with the rifle. If I used a shot-gun and scatter shot, I never would have reached the target. So it is with selling. One must focus on the target and confine sales energy to a narrow range of interest. Mass marketing techniques were not conducive to niche specialized products.

To sell our products it was important to know if they were right for the customer. The products had to feel right, taste right, smell right and have the proper nutritional values. Our bases had to be packed in sizes usable to each food production need. One-pound containers were correct for the average restaurant kitchen, but a 50-pound container was correct for the industrial chef.

Variety was important. We could offer bases to fit every culinary need. A wide variety of bases provided product for special needs, but beef and chicken base always were the most requested items. Most importantly was differentiation of Minor products from the commodity bases being sold. This could not be stressed too much.

Stories/Facts/Myths

Through the years, I have always used stories to make a point, emphasize a fact, or describe an event. People remember stories because they often turn cold facts into a warm, human experience. It provides a comfortable level of understanding. It makes it easier for the recipient to understand a concept and picture in his mind the message you are sending.

Stories from personal experience are always best. I have freely used stories, based upon fact and truth involving Dr. Minor, the family company, how and why our products are differentiated from competing products. I was proud to speak of Dr. Minor's support to culinary education and the many scholarships he had provided to worthy students. In essence, I created a plausible positive culture giving a halo effect, but one justifiably earned. I found this to be a very effective low profile selling technique. High pressure sales efforts were not appropriate to our needs.

Sales Perception

Distributors viewed Minor products as specialty items and products within this classification historically produced small sales. My view was that small sales would grow and establish a good foundation for growth. If a restaurant purchased one case of beef and chicken base per week, we had a 100 case per year user. Using our blueprints, we sold benefits, not features. We wanted to produce a customer that would re-order on a constant weekly basis. Sales could be increased by selling one item at a time. Repeated end-user calls are expensive, but it proved to be the correct path for us to take. It was our policy to spend at least 90% of our time with the end-users, the chefs and food production people. The results speak for themselves.

A product or package may win prizes, but not customers. Advertising may attract readers, but a reader may not buy. A salesman may be making calls, but not obtaining sales. The products standards may be high, but buyer acceptance low. The missing ingredient is merchandising to accomplish the expected sales results. Sales are made through a buyer's eyes. Quality is defined in terms of a customer's perception.

It was obvious that we needed increased exposure. We were not in this for ephemeral result, but rather for the long run. This could only be accomplished by reaching people. What better way than to become part of seminars and educational presentations? It was then that I embarked on a series of cooking demonstrations and presentations at culinary meetings, colleges, distributor sales meetings, and teaching soup and sauce techniques using bases at local culinary schools.

Product Seminars & Demonstrations

Throughout my foodservice career, I had been active in trade organizations. I reasoned that these groups would now provide a viable platform to present my niche merchandising story to people engaged in food production and management.

My activities included being President of both the South Jersey Restaurant Association and in later years the Hospital Food Directors Association . I was elected a life member, with full voting rights, to the Hospital Food Directors Association, being one of five members so honored in its 30 years of existence. I was also a member of the American Hospital Association, the Foodservice Executives Association, and the National Association of Meat Purveyors. In 1975 I became a chef member of the American Culinary Association Professional Chefs of Atlantic City, N.J.

In October of 1979, at the request of Gen. McLaughlin, I represented the Minor Corporation in a U.S. Air Force Open Mess Workshop held at McGuire Air Force Base in New Jersey. Present were some 150 Officers and Non-Commissioned officers. These gentlemen were in charge of Officer Clubs and NCO Clubs at Air Force Bases around the world. For most of them, it was their introduction to bases. During my 90 minute presentation and question and answer session, I learned that the Air Force still employed

514

the same methods and techniques of food preparation I had used 35 years previously when I served as a cook. Complete lists of all attendees, their stations, and sources of supply were turned over to Gen. McLaughlin to be followed-up by Minor brokers and distributors for potential sales.

Beginning in 1980, I annually was a featured educational speaker for the Professional Chefs Association . In 1985, at the request of Chapter President Gustav Mahler, Executive Chef of Trump Castle Casino, one entire evening session was devoted to evaluation of meat quality, primal meat cut identification, and cutting yields. Our audience numbered 315 culinary members which was the largest turnout for a monthly meeting. As was our custom at presentations, we spent the entire day in the hotel kitchens preparing six soups for the soup bar and preparing hot entree items for the buffet table showcasing Minor products.

The evening was a great success, without a doubt our finest culinary presentation. It was judgment time from our peers. The chefs cleaned up the entire buffet and Chef Mahler had his staff prepare additional food. The evening was also a vote of confidence and a tribute by the chefs to Dr. Minor and perhaps myself.

Chef Minor

In January '85 Chef Michael Minor offered support services to the brokers by offering to pay $200 per working day to dietitians and chefs for sales work and cooking demonstration seminars. For those brokers incapable of performing these duties, it was a good offer and valid to accept. However, it was our policy of not requesting either payment or professional assistance, as my son Kevin and I were capable, individually or together, of conducting a speaking engagement or food production exhibition regardless of size of audience. If there was a scheduling conflict, perhaps, two or more such events in a day, we hired, on a per diem basis, a C.I.A. or Johnson & Wales graduate to do the honors.

Unlike company chefs and teams that hop, skip and jump from meeting to meeting or one trade show to another across the country, we limited our activities to our geographic area. The company chefs are strangers without a linking relationship to those attending a presentation. It was our experience that, for the average food production staff of a hospital or restaurant group, a very formal professional chef, complete with his medals, was an intimidating presence. The message was never completely understood. Workers believed that only a professional chef could use our bases and it was beyond their ability to use the products. It was for that very reason that we always spoke to them on their level of understanding. The company intent was good, but a starched, bemedaled professional chef was a negative.

In my retail meat market days, we were taught to sell in depth, sell related food items and know our customer. A customer buying eggs was a candidate for bacon, bread, butter, and even tea or coffee. When we were selling restaurants, one of my father's salesmen once boasted of how many stops he had. I remember my father saying "I prefer customers to stops; sell in depth; increase your sales with related items; slow down; mileage does not indicate sales performance."

With that in mind, we always planned to "work the area" after each presentation. We had several of our salespersons accompany us for the express purpose of meeting the attendees, face to face, make appointments, then spend the next few days in visitation. The barriers were removed and we were not strangers entering their establishments. It was an effective method of selling.

Chef responses to shows vary according to region, ethnic background, and culture. I remember doing an ACF show in Carlisle, Pennsylvania, a good four hours from home. I checked into the hotel where we were to perform, planning to stay over-night as we were scheduled to begin at 9:30 p.m. I prepared a creditable food preparation.

The chefs tasted, ate everything in sight; the plates came back clean and empty. However, they sat there like the Sphinx in Egypt. Not a smile, not a comment. They were totally devoid of expression. Asked for questions, I could not get a response. I finished at 11:30 p.m. and was defeated in expectation by their reactions. I checked out of the hotel and drove home, arriving about 4:00 a.m.

In the next few weeks our sales in the area enjoyed a very substantial increase and we gained eight to ten new Minor customers. So I figure that some things are beyond explanation.

We did several ACF shows in the Harrisburg/Reading area. Not long after one of these shows, my distributor in Reading, Pennsylvania asked me to bring my pots and pans and join him for a demonstration at the Hershey Country Club presided over by an exceptionally fine master chef, Walter Schefhauser. I was greeted by a drill-sergeant authoritarian commanding question, "What do you think you are going to do in my kitchen?" With tongue in cheek, I replied, eyeing the very stern chef, "I came here to teach you how to cook." A very long, silent few moments...and then he began with a jovial laughter. "I have seen your lousy demonstrations. Promise not to cook in my kitchen, and I will buy your Minor bases!"

Walter and I became good friends and subsequently performed several ACF meetings together, I with the bases and Walter with expert ice carving. I learned that it is fatal to take oneself too seriously; a sense of humor can be infectious and remove barriers where a formal approach would fail.

A sampling of the many cooking demonstrations and cost containment events for foodservice personnel were conducted at the University of Pennsylvania, Penn State University, Fairleigh-Dickinson University, Rutgers University, Jefferson University and Hospital, Elizabeth-Town College, Princeton University, Lady of Lourdes Hospital, Lawrenceville School, over 125 ARA management accounts and some 40 hospitals in our area--casinos, hotels, and restaurants too numerous to mention.

On culinary management, I gave lectures at the University of Pennsylvania, the ARA series of seminars, and was a featured speaker at a management conference at Rutgers University for the National Association of College & University Food Administrators.

Working with students was always a joy. At Fairleigh-Dickinson two classes were

516

combined for a double-time session. We also had superb support from the administration at the Hershey Foundation Training School, Hershey, Pennsylvania. The Atlantic City ACF chapter sponsors the School of Culinary Arts at the Atlantic County Community College where we annually enjoyed the pleasure of working with future chefs. I might add that the L. J. Minor Corporation donated $10,000 to this fine school for a soup and sauce kitchen. This was duly appreciated.

TV And Me

The most exciting and challenging project Kevin and I ever presented was a full one-hour TV show for the Hospital Television Networks and the New Jersey Hospital Educational Trust. This program was beamed via the SMATV or "Satellite Master Antenna Television," which was a private cable television system serving some 4000 hospitals across the country with medical advances and management news.

The script was titled, "Relationship of Food Bases to Quality Food Standards in the Health Care Industry." Actual running time was 48 minutes without a break in continuity. Due to a tight budget, we were required to do the show without a rehearsal. The TelePrompTer was not available due to a malfunction that occurred minutes before our show. There was no time to make cue cards. It was a one shot, what-you-see-is-what-you-get show. On this snowy February day, I had the flu and 102 degree fever, but the show must go on. Without Kevin's support and assistance, it would never have taken place. The master copy of the tape was sent to the advertising department of the company and was shown once in the board room at a sales conference.

ARA Food Management

When a good working relationship and rapport can be established and management knows you are working on their behalf, miracles can happen. ARA is a prime example. Today this company is a five billion dollar sales powerhouse.

When I assumed responsibility for ARA, their annual purchases of Minor products was $17,000. At the end of our tenure in 1988, ARA purchased $1.3 million of Minor products from me for their Woodhaven Foods distribution center in Philadelphia. Nationally, the purchases exceeded $3 million.

How was this accomplished? All one needs is twelve years of patience and persistence, making points one by one. Acceptance is not easily awarded, it must be earned.

Gen. McLaughlin joined the firm in 1976 as sales manager. He suggested to me that I make an appointment and see an old friend of his, who was National Purchasing Director for ARA. An appointment was made with Mr. Robert Dick. Mr. Dick was courteous and business-like in manner. I presented my credentials, a short overview of Minor products and included our price lists. It was then that I quickly learned that he and the General were not good friends, but casual acquaintances.

After reading the literature, he inquired how we expected to do business on a national scale, to a major buyer, when we were charging the identical prices for a buyer of 10 cases of product as one buying 500 cases? We did not offer discounts, promotions, or allowances. The General suggested that I avoid discussing these subjects if they came up in conversation.

How could they be avoided? I listened for the next 30 minutes to a very forceful lecture on effective marketing to a national account. It was probably the summation of an entire college course in marketing.

For a finale, he told me that the General had personally visited him on a sales expedition and had bombed out due to a lack of any meaningful programs and demonstration of service to sales. He said that he thought I had been set-up for a fall. To his credit, Mr. Dick said the door would be open to me and that I should continue service to the Woodhaven account to the best of my ability and given time to evaluate my performance, would support me accordingly. It was instruction not easily forgotten.

Thus the door was opened a crack. That was progress, so I continued to service the Woodhaven account. They provided excellent support by extending courtesy and access to the management accounts. We were invited to ride with their sales staff, visiting customers, introducing our products, and making appointments to return at a later date for demonstrations to their production personnel.

Our programs featured not only a cooking demonstration, but also nutritional analysis and cost containment suggestions for a staff of two cooks in a small nursing home with the same attention and energy as we would give the staff of the Pentagon. In time, many nursing home food managers moved up to a larger institution and did not forget the attention we had supplied in their smaller facility. Many sales managers believe that they must always reach for the brass ring and the larger account. While they were chasing rainbows, we were making sales; small, but dependable re-orders of products.

My performances were being monitored by ARA management. As a result, in the early '80s ARA Headquarters requested that I become a speaker, as part of a series of management seminars to present the assigned topic "Achieving Culinary Efficiency & Excellence in Food Management." The seminars were conducted at McNeill Pharmaceutical headquarters, Fort Washington, Pennsylvania. The second was held at the C & P Telephone Co., Hunt Valley, Maryland, and the last at the U.S. Postal Training Center, Potomac, Maryland. The seminars were given about a week apart and were attended by some 125 managers at each session.

An era of exceptional co-operation between ARA National and the Minor Corporation began to flower as a direct result of the seminars. I must give Dale Carnegie credit for my public speaking effectiveness. At the end of my lecture at the Postal Training Center, the manager of ARA Pentagon requested that we visit his operation and conduct a series of hands-on cooking sessions for his production staff.

My son, Kevin, and I were pleased to travel to Washington and work at the Pentagon. We provided six separate full day teaching sessions, about ten days apart. We

518

worked side by side with their chefs to prepare complete meals for thousands of military and civilian staff. Production was in volumes of 100 to 125 gallons of soup, sauces, gravies, chili, stews, and center of the plate items. It was a joy to convert the Pentagon into an enthusiastic user of our products. From then on, the welcome mat was always extended and we made many friends on the production staff. When management and staff were transferred to other properties, they specified our bases. Like the pebble in the pond, the circles widen and our sales increased.

Shortly after the Pentagon series, the regional manager of ARA Baltimore-Washington requested that I assist in a blind-tasting of bases to be conducted at the George Meany Labor Center, Towson, Maryland. Each attendee was to bring a pound of chicken and beef base, in a plain container. Each was marked by a number, no trade name. The names of the products were sealed in envelopes and were to be opened at the end of the session to identify bases used. The bases were diluted, as per manufacturer's instructions, into a broth or stock and were tested for taste, flavor, salt level, fat level, mouth feel, clarity of stock. Cost of products was not a consideration and not presented. It was an even playing field for evaluation.

By secret ballot and over-whelming votes, Minor was the winner. The ballots and test results were sent to ARA Quality Standards in Philadelphia for their information and research files.

In Philadelphia, ARA allowed me free access to their research and quality standards laboratories where chefs test products for inclusion to recipe formulations. Years of persistence and continuous visitation were needed to develop a good working relationship with this unit. We did get the brass ring when the final results were in. Our bases provided all the qualities they were seeking. The doors opened on the national level to all Minor brokers, when our bases, by brand name, were included on proprietary recipe cards to be followed by all ARA chefs. We became the product of choice. Our products were the first endorsement of a brand name on approved recipe specifications. This was voluntary and without cost to L. J. Minor Corporation.

During this period I worked with Carol Carlson, Administrative Dietitian, ARA Headquarters on a low fat, low salt stock base, our Glace de Viande. This product was approved for use in ARA Health Care units. On September 24, 1986 an agreement was signed whereby H.L.S. INC. (our brokerage name) would conduct certain services for ARA Healthcare Nutrition Services in the area of soup and sauce preparation. We provided about 35 presentations from New York to Washington, D.C. in a variety of health care facilities ranging from a small nursing home to large hospitals. These services continued for two years. Our sales increased and we gained entry into many new accounts.

Wining & Dining

Several times each year we would host a diversified group of Minor product buyers, potential buyers, and distributor groups to a pleasant evening of relaxed dining. This is an effective public relations and goodwill enhancement policy. We often had mixed groups of hospital food directors and University food directors at the same affair with good results. New friendships were gained and participants exchanged "shop talk", learning from each other.

We were always selective in choice of site and style of the restaurant for our affairs. We entertained on a high service, food preparation, and presentation level. We enjoyed 100% acceptance when extending invitations to The Fountain Room at the Four Seasons Hotel or Le Bec Fin Restaurant in Philadelphia. Both are highly rated in a variety of national polls on fine dining. On some events we reserved a private room or rooms as needed. On one evening we reserved the entire Le Bec Fin Restaurant. In South Jersey our best responses were at Chef Robert and the Famous Rams Head in Absecon. I might add that Chef Robert made a delightful sauce for his famous steaks from our Espagnole and Glace de Viande. The chef added some special touches and a good splash of fine wine.

All of our selected restaurants gave us meticulous professional service and exquisite food presentations. We never offered a preset menu; guests could always choose their favorite food and wine. Whatever the cost, it was beneficial to our sales efforts.

Distributor sales persons were entertained as a contiguous group of one company. On these occasions, we would introduce new items, new uses for our standard items, or sales promotions. Unlike other hosts, we did not hustle or pressure distributor sales persons. We offered the same high level of white glove service. Our guests were treated with respect and dignity. Our sales always increased following the "catered affair."

Our first reservation of an entire restaurant came by fate. Chef Michael Minor called and requested that I select the finest restaurant in Philadelphia to entertain 35 to 40 of the nation's best chefs attending the American Culinary Federation Convention in our fair city. This was an easy decision, the Le Bec Fin, operated by Master Chef George Perrier. I made the reservation for his first sitting 6:00 to 9:00 PM.

A week before the event, Chef Minor called to cancel saying that he was advised to entertain the chefs at a highly publicized 200-year-old seafood operation. I had done demonstrations using our seafood bases in their kitchens several times and knew it for what it was...a tourist type, kitchy decorated restaurant. The food would never take a blue ribbon at the county fair.

Rather than cancel Le Bec Fin, I invited some 35 foodservice people. The purchasing director of ARA and the new sales manager, several University food directors and their wives, several hospital food directors and their wives, and some leading food distributors and their wives. Don Jacobs of the University of Pennsylvania did the honors of wine selection. Gen. McLaughlin welcomed our guests. We had no speeches and the event was a huge success.

It was our practice, when doing distributor sales meetings, to move the meeting to a restaurant/customer of that distributor. We would prepare the soups and sauces and let the restaurant staff serve or assist the chef in preparation of the entire meal, always serving items containing Minor bases.

In late 1987, I introduced Jane McKinney, Minor dietitian, to Carol Carlson with the purpose of having the Minor Corporation extend the work we were doing in health care to ARA accounts in other parts of the country. I was pleased to open the door to Minor staff to provide educational programs to ARA Nutritional Services.

ARA Sales

Reaching our level of sales was not simple or without obstacles. Until 1985, we never had a promotion program of any substance. Our price base was rock solid. Gen. McLaughlin asked me to develop a promotion based upon base purchases. I wrote it, as requested, he approved it, and I put it into place signing ARA executives. It was an incentive, but not really that important to our progress. I informed him that if we did it for ARA, Robinson/Patman regulations said we had to offer it to other distributors as well on the same basis. Thus the door was opened. I would have preferred to remain with Dr. Minor's original policy of pricing. Incentive cash programs to distributors are commercial welfare hand-outs. They are counter-productive to sales performance and never end.

We faced formidable competition from CPC/Knorr, Lipton and LeGout. I must admit, I have employed what might be considered unorthodox methods to defend our niche position.

In a meeting with the President/General Manager of ARA Woodhaven, I half jokingly said it would be mutually beneficial if there were fewer competing brands in his inventory. His response was immediate. "What did you have in mind?" I replied, grabbing a thought out of thin air, "You could eliminate CPC/Knorr for starters." Unexpectedly he said, "Buy out their inventory and see what you can do to increase our revenue and profits with Minor products." I agreed, not knowing the implication or size of the undertaking.

Arrangements were quickly made, on the spot. I had 10 days to remove the inventory. The total cost charged to me, personally, was $62,000. Payment due in 30 days.

While I was pleased to have one less competitor in this account I was ambivalent because the CPC representative was a good friend. I contacted him immediately and was surprised by his response. He said that if it were possible and the opportunity had presented itself, CPC would have enjoyed to take the same action. I had just gotten there first!

He inquired as to what I was going to do with the Knorr products. He knew I had to unload it somewhere, somehow. Knorr did not wish me to flood the market with price cutting or devaluing the products. So he took the whole load at my cost less 10%. The net cost to me was $6,000 and we remained good friends for years. In fact, we helped each other with new accounts when it was possible and did not damage Minor sales. The home office in Cleveland was never informed of this transaction. With a million dollar account to protect, did the end results justify the means?

Merchandise Exchange Program

There were times when a distributor would be short an item or two to complete orders. Rather than have him substitute, we would borrow the item from a stocking distributor and deliver it to the distributor needing the items. Credits and charge transactions were handled by the Cleveland office. When monthly transfers reached $10,000 a month I decided that it could not continue.

A policy change was developed which provided compensation to the stocking distributor to pay for his warehousing and accounting costs. I did not want this charge to be a negative factor toward our sales as substituting a competitor's product was more profitable than paying transfer costs. I discussed the problem with Gen. McLaughlin. I wanted to transfer product without an up-charge for costs. I knew that some Minor brokers provided this service, but the company was placing inventory at the broker's office facility for this purpose. I did not request this courtesy.

With the General's permission, I incorporated QE2 Foodservice Co. to service this need. Our sales office building had sufficient space to install walk-in coolers and a freezer. We purchased and paid for an inventory of Minor bases. When transfers were made, the Minor home office credited QE2, and charged the receiving distributor. There was no up-charge for our expenses. We absorbed the costs.

When Minor was sold to Nestle, the new management severely criticized us for providing this service with the admonition that we should discipline distributors to either order more products or do without until the next delivery. Simultaneously, we were instructed to dissolve QE2 as being an illegal enterprise.

This circumstance was given the importance of a heated face-to-face meeting with the national sales manager who made the out-right charges that we were conducting a clandestine operation. These allegations were untrue.

The meeting was followed up with a letter with the instruction to destroy QE2 and unless this was accomplished, there was the open threat of a lawsuit from Nestle to force the issue. Upon receipt of the letter, I had our legal firm review our complete records. Our CPA firm did a search and audit to make sure the inventory was balanced with purchases and credits. Not one cash or charge sale was ever made to a customer except through the Cleveland office. There was never a conflict of our contract or conflict of interest. The records documented that there was never a profit to QE2; in fact we encountered losses to our profit structure.

HLS Inc.
Manufacturers Representatives
651 S. Evergreen Ave.
Woodbury, NJ   08097

July 1, 1987

To: All Minor Distributors
Subject: Charges for product stocking through exchanges
From: Howard L. Schatz

Effective immediately, in order to effectuate a fair and even-handed sales policy, the following policy concerning exchanges of Minor products is suggested:

1.   A charge of 10% based upon distributors cost, can be made on all product picked-up by a Minor Rep to a requesting distributor. Example:
       Turkey Base 12x1 lb. Distributors Cost: $48.00
       A transfer charge of $4.80 will be added.

2.   100% of this service charge will be paid to the distributor who provides the product to compensate for accounting and warehouse expenses.

3.   The policy of no compensation for time, travel or other expenses, in these transactions for the Minor Rep, will continue.

4.   Requests for one or several cases of product can also be provided by the Minor Corp. through U.P.S. shipment, provided that the distributor will pay for additional U.P.S. freight charges.

RATIONALE: It is impractical to assume that each distributor will maintain a fully stocked and well balanced inventory of Minor Natural Food Bases to satisfy all customer needs. Out of stock items may be requested. However; as with all good things, our policy of exchanging product between distributors has been abused. Numerically, the requests have been soaring. We are delighted that Minor sales are at an all time high and increasingly the Public does Appreciate Quality, but it is unfair to the distributor who maintains an adequate inventory, enough to supply others who do not, to absorb extra operational costs without compensation.

Our minimum order of 500 pounds is probably a low for the industry. There are distributors who are substituting exchanges for placing orders on a regular basis. There are questions whether they should be carried as a qualified Minor distributor.

Lastly, product sales (exchanges), without compensation for expenses, places the stocking distributor in an unfair competitive position. He is bearing additional investment and expenses not incurred by non-stocking distributors and yet is expected to sell product based upon the same cost factor.

Legal opinion concurred that all transactions were not in any violation with our contracts or with any existing FTC or Robinson/Patman/Clayton Federal Regulations. We did not dissolve QE2 and continued to service our distributors with Minor products and sales continued to increase.

On another matter, a U.S.D.A. Inspected meat processor/Minor distributor said he was experiencing a problem with ground meat products sold to schools as meat balls and meat patties. I inspected his processing procedures and there was nothing to indicate a problem would later develop when the products were cooked.

About the same time, the newsletter of the National Association of Meat Purveyors, of which I was a member, requested from the membership a possible solution to this perennial problem on a national level. The meat processors could not find a solution to this vexing problem.

Many times when ground meat products are prepared into meat balls, meat loaf, Salisbury steak, etc., after cooking the centers remain with a reddish color, indicating uncooked product. The meat items were thoroughly cooked, but perception is reality.

After I researched my meat hygiene textbooks and class material from my meat inspection classes at Rutgers and also reviewed Dr. Kotschevar's book on quantity food production which documented the theory of vegetables dehydrated in a nitrogen gas, I wrote the letter on the following page, which the National Association of Meat Purveyors published.

This provided a service to my Minor customer, to my fellow members of the meat association, and obtained a bit of publicity for Minor products.

Support to the Company

We enjoyed a good rapport with other Minor brokers and assisted them when possible at their trade shows. I worked many shows in the Baltimore-Washington, D.C. area as well as the Harrisburg/Hershey/Pocono Mountain trade shows. I was chef for a product demonstration at the Washington Airport for United Airlines.

Traveling to San Francisco, I assisted the broker at the NACUFS convention, greeting many of the eastern university food directors, making contacts, and following up at a later date. The Minor company requested my assistance at three national conventions of the American Dietetic Association. These were held in Atlanta, San Antonio and Anaheim. Annually, Kevin and I manned the company booth at the Chicago Restaurant Show and we often had as many as five of our people present staffing the Minor booth at the New York Hotel Show. Contacts made at these shows were important and furnished many good prospective customers. All of this was voluntary. It was our policy never to submit a request for expenses or travel costs. It was just the right thing to do.

During the 1980 Christmas season my wife and I took a cruise on the famous QE2 to the Caribbean. I carried several cases of base samples aboard ship, and having previously become friends with the executive chef, Mr. Bainbridge, he allowed and assisted me in conducting soup and sauce demonstrations for his production staff. Our products were new to them as they did not exist in England. The ship's photographer recorded the events in the kitchens of the QE2. Original photos were given to Gen. McLaughlin for placement in the company records.

Attached to the photos were letters from Mr. Bainbridge and Mr. Victor Coward, sous chef, endorsing the quality of our bases and the suggestion that we contact Cunard Lines food purchasing office in New York for possible inclusion of our bases to the inventory aboard ship.

Two positive results were suggested. The first, of course, was the inclusion of bases aboard the QE2 and secondly, a tie-in for advertising and publicity might have been developed with a cooperative effort between Minor and Cunard Lines. The opportunity was ripe for action. With all good intent, I told Mr. Bainbridge that Minor would be more than pleased to send their master chefs to demonstrate the value of bases for the production staff of each Cunard Ship. He welcomed the idea and potential training for his chefs. No other company had ever made such an offer.

Sales Calls

There is no more difficult way to earn a living than by making "cold calls" in an attempt to sell product or services. There is an invisible wall between the prospect and the sales person. This wall must be penetrated and a friendly rapport developed before a sale can be consummated.

Many sales persons do not understand that chefs will not or cannot stop their activities of food preparation, production, or kitchen supervision to listen to a sales talk. Sales are made under extreme conditions of high heat, poor ventilation, and greasy atmosphere that will cause one's clothing to stink from oil vapors resulting from over-heated fryers and worn out grease. Only in institutional environments or buying offices of chain accounts, will one find nice, clean, air conditioned offices.

Foodservice kitchens are staffed with a polyglot of many races and languages. For example, a very successful operation and a good Minor account is a local 250-seat restaurant/diner that is staffed with men from Turkey, Egypt, Greece, Bangladesh, and Mexico. The owners are Greek. Most of the staff does not speak English, but to their credit they work well together. Nick is the head chef. He is no-nonsense and hard-working, understands very little English, consistently produces volumes of substantial tasty, well-prepared meals. I have learned over the years to approach Nick first with quality, second, with benefits, and last, and only when asked, the cost of a particular product. He is known on the street as a "tough" customer.

Nick has no time for trivia, will not accept substitutions of product, or allow salespeople in his kitchen. I felt privileged to be an exception to his rule. Why? Because on many visits I have taken off my jacket, put on an apron, and spent an hour or more assisting him in cutting and preparing meat for production. It is a labor of love for me and service to sales.

The institutional buyer or the dietitian in a health care facility is totally different by education, training, and priorities. These buyers insist on making appointments for their time. Interviews are granted at their convenience. However it has been our sad experience that these same professionals have no compunction or remorse in breaking and not keeping appointments without notice even if the appointment may have been confirmed the day before or with the knowledge that the salesperson might travel a hundred miles to keep his commitment. Some buyers will refuse to see you, even after they personally have given the appointment, with no explanation. Buyers do not respect the Golden Rule.

Buyers vary in personality, approach to their jobs, and time is needed to learn their real priorities for purchasing. Is it quality? Is it service? Is it rebates and discounts? Perhaps volume purchases can result in trips to the Bahamas or weekends at Atlantic City Casinos. This information must be known to sell successfully.

There are buyers who consistently set appointments just in time for a "sponsor" to take him to lunch. Others look for tickets to a ball game or tickets for a Broadway show. With many it is expected and freely accepted. With no guarantees of sales.

To protect his or her company, a salesperson must watch out for the overly-friendly and solicitous buyer, particularly in opening a new account. The potential customer may be looking for a new source of credit, the product being of secondary interest. When you open a "new" account, you are taking business away from another distributor or manufacturer. Be prudent and learn the real reason for the switch. Extreme caution must be taken in credit extension.

In all of our years, I am proud of the fact that the Minor Corporation never lost a dime on any account, I approved for credit, due to non-payment. If a company failed, and there were several, we automatically assumed complete responsibility and personally paid the invoices. I have sued companies when I believed Minor could have been paid, but they chose not to honor their obligations. The home office was never informed of our actions. It was for us, a personal obligation to keep faith with the folks who had confidence and trust in us. My approval of credit was a guarantee that Minor would be paid for products shipped.

We have learned that when a salesperson enters the "private space" of the chef, you are on his turf. He is defensive. The chef understands that the salesperson standing in front of him is in the transfer business. His purpose is to transfer money from the buyer's pocket to his own. This he will try to prevent by whatever means is at his disposal unless he is convinced it is in his best interest. Care must be taken, because cold calls and even regular repeat calls can easily become adversarial encounters.

Bottom line, you must know your accounts, their needs and wants. Each customer is an individual and must be treated with respect, courtesy, and deference to his position regardless of his ethnic origin or language spoken.

Over time, I have employed socially polished, well-mannered college graduates, some with a Masters Degree in Business Administration, and I've seen them "crack" under the strain, pressure, and tension of selling to rude, crude, could-care-less buyers. Many believe that selling is a demeaning experience. These university-trained people cannot stand rejection or being treated as "just salespersons" from what they believe to be uneducated kitchen help or buyers beneath their own social status or educational level. Many feel that they are management types and should be telling people on the "front lines" how sales should be made and pontificate their expertise from a distance.

Remembrances

Remembrance, contemplation, and review of the Minor chapter in our life awakened special memories created by destiny. As the records were studied, events, people, places, good times, and some incomplete successes became clear as if they happened only yesterday.

We have been enriched, beyond measure, by our friendship with Dr. and Mrs. Minor, unique, wonderful people who conducted business and lived by principles, ethics, and integrity sadly absent in today's world. The Minors are generous to a fault, giving back to humanity their life's treasure that they worked and struggled so long and hard to earn.

Our success in Minor sales was enhanced by preparation, motivation, and tenacity. The foundation of our sales success was the unfailing support given by Dr. and Mrs. Minor. While it is true that a corporate structure existed to run the company, the unseen presence of the Minors was there.

Our sales record had its rewards, financially, to be sure, but beyond that, and perhaps more importantly, is the psychic income, the satisfaction of accomplishment. I freely admit of my enjoyment when giving a cooking demonstration or doing a public speaking management presentation. Presentation of the Minor story to an audience of 250 persons is nothing short of euphoria. I presented the story to high-ranking military officers, as well as professional management groups representing the best there is in American commerce, and never failed to communicate a level of understanding that enhanced the cost/value relationship of Minor products to their individual needs.

Our sales success required a working knowledge of our products, an understanding of human psychology, not in the academic sense, but that gained from a lifetime of experience which includes many mistakes and failures, especially failures to understand human nature. I am indebted to a law professor from the University of Miami who taught me the value of using props in a public speaking engagement. The appropriate use of props can make a show come alive.

When doing cost/value studies between Minor bases and other products on the market, I always stressed that it is necessary to use real chicken to get a rich, nutritious, flavorful chicken stock. Chemicals and artificial flavors will not accomplish the job. For this purpose, I always used a large live chicken, placed in on the stage or near the podium and proceeded with the Minor story. Naturally, the audience was focused upon the chicken.

Many times I have been identified as the "Minor man with the Live Chicken" even years after the actual event. I knew then that our message was understood and well

527

received. We sold a lot, no, tons of chicken base by not taking ourselves too seriously. A sense of humor, properly applied, is important in sales work.

The demographics of food distribution has changed dramatically in the past few years. The demise of the small distributor is to be mourned because he built food distribution as we know it today. The rise of mega-giant distributors is the result of buying, trading, or exchanging a multitude of small distribution companies.

It is now a game of numbers, of market share, of predatory practices and the individual broker is the only link between the manufacturer and the end-user and his days are numbered with direct computer links between buyer and seller. Who will tell the stories? Who will introduce the products? Who will sell the benefits and convince the buyer to buy a specific product? The Minor Chapter in our lives was the Golden Age of Merchandising.

Customer Service

by Nancy Clancy
(1959 - 1994)

The year was 1959 -- what a memory! I was introduced to the L. J. Minor Corp. via Manpower, Inc., a temporary placement service. Because the assignment was only a half day, no one wanted to take it. But before I get too far into my story, I want to say what a privilege it is to share some of my experiences during those early years.

My daughter Nancy was born in 1956, and Patrick came in 1959. They were at home with my husband, Terrence, who had the day off, so I did not mind going in for the half day. I was to report to Mary A. Mele, the office manager.

As soon as I walked through the door of Room 432 in the Bulkley Building, Mary said, "Stop, don't take off your coat . . ." I thought oh, oh, I'm through before I start, but she continued, ". . . I want you to go to the bank and post office." Yes, I am back in business!

Under the watchful eye of Mary, I learned order processing, invoicing, tracking shipment, ordering raw materials, accounts payable, accounts receivable and payroll. After three months, Mary said Thomas A. Ryan wanted to speak with me.

Tom was a fine gentleman, but a bit intimidating, surrounded by three walls of mostly law books. His large frame sat behind a huge, cherry wood desk with a glass top and behind him was a long credenza and a large picture of "Dutchman" hanging above it.

Tom Ryan asked me to work permanently for the L. J. Minor Corp. and I accepted. We talked and I found him to be very congenial, laughing easily with a few good jokes. When I left his office, I thought to myself, now that wasn't so bad. In fact, it was good as I had been recognized for my contributions. Little did I know that this would be the start of 35 great years with fine people.

Mary A. Mele, our office manager, was a wonderful teacher. She was demanding and expected 110%. Any action, rule or procedure was for the greater good of the company. she was a perfectionist, dedicated and a professional. Even through her illness, Mary showed strength and courage and we all learned from her strong convictions. Her love for the L. J. Minor Corp. showed in everything she did. She had "taken care of business" very well. Mary succumbed to cancer in 1974.

Tom Ryan said every person needed a new wallet every year, so at Christmas wallets were a gift for representatives and customers. We also had assorted gifts of appliances, cutlery sets, watches, pens, etc. Green ties made by Mrs. Brennan were sent whether you were Irish or not. It was a lot of fun and good spirit. I don't know who was more excited - Tom Ryan and Dr. Minor sending or the people receiving. The gifts were always chosen very carefully for quality and usefulness.

Recognition was ongoing at the L. J. Minor Corp. We were often given a "pat on the back" and "atta boy or girl." Yes, we received generous bonuses that were wonderful, but it was also nice to hear those thank you's as well. I did not see Dr. Minor too often during the first few years. He was attending Michigan State University where he would receive his Ph.D. and go on to teach in their School of Hotel, Restaurant and Institutional Management. When I did see him, it was always a pleasure. He assumed the role of friend rather than employer. Dr. Minor was always very solicitous and inquired about the family. He took the time to talk to his employees. His time has always been a precious commodity, a gift itself.

"The customer is always right" is rather patronizing. We gave our customers more credit than that. They were smart, informed people who had our respect. Information regarding arrival time and carrier were given up front and late shipments or damage were dealt with immediately. We had direct contact with the customer, distributor or representative. We tried to know our customer and they knew we were there to handle concerns. A commitment to the customer was a commitment to the L. J. Minor Corp,

In 1963, as we grew, we moved right around the corner to Room 436. Lynda Kelch, Melissa Daily, Kathy Weiss and Virginia Schmid were early employees who had worked several years between 1963 and 1969. Here were the stalwarts of the customer service department (including accounts payable, accounts receivable, payroll and collection along with customer service functions):

1969	Judy Ward --	gentle, considerate
1974	Cecile O'Donnell --	easy laugh, sincere
1975	Mary Ryan --	ready smile, concerned
1978	Rose Capezzuto --	caring, candid
1980	Katie Bockmiller --	serious, thoughtful

Each brought their unique expertise to the department and were aggressive, dedicated and committed to exceeding customer expectations.

We expanded our offices in 1963, the plant in 1963 and 1964, the cookroom in 1969, and added a new warehouse and distribution center in 1977. For 25 years, everything was fine. In fact, too fine, because in 1984, our company was purchased by investors headed by Messrs. James O'Neil and Walter Luftman.

With the sale came change and, as nice as the two gentlemen were and as cautiously as they tried to handle the sale, change is difficult. The smallest change came when the company name changed from L. J. Minor Corp. to L. J. Minor *Corporation*. More difficult were the loss of Michael S. Zelski (the "S" was for SUPER), Herman Taber and Ralph Napletana, two mentors who had brought me along after Mary Mele's death. No longer would I hear Dave Swanson, the Boston accent of Frank Aicardi, the fun loving jokes of Bob Krump, the happy voice of Jack Cassidy and others. They say change is good and yes it is, but change is also very difficult.

My time with the L. J. Minor Corp. would not have been possible without the support of my husband, Terrence, a Cleveland Police officer for 30 years. I thank God for my husband and our seven children who helped make work and home a family affair. It seems like only yesterday that I walked through the hallowed doors of the L. J. Minor Corp. - an organization that was a family with the highest work ethics, having caring owners, executives and management that bolstered morale by working with the employees. My precious years are memorable and have enhanced my life. I was extremely fortunate to have had an active part until 1994 when I retired. Change is a constant in our business life, but life after the L. J. Minor Corp. has been GOOD!

Chapter 47

More on Marketing: With International Flair

by Hans J. Bueschkens
(1979-1995)

In the Industrial Division

by John G. Cassidy
(Late 1980s)

Through TQM

by Paul Hamerly
(1986-1992)

Employee's First	**Industry Experts as Low Cost Consultants**
Try Them Out on a Consulting Basis	**Leadership**
Public Relations **Quality**	**A New Parent**

A Great Sales Job
(Irish Humor by Hal Roach)

Mary Kate bought herself a hat and told her husband:
> "Don't worry, I didn't spend any money on it. It was on sale, regularly for 20 pounds and I got it for 10. So I bought it with the 10 pounds I saved!"

Expanding Service to New Markets
(Irish Humor by Hal Roach)

Flanagan had a dog he was very fond of. He went to see Father Murphy and he said:
"The dog died and money is no object because I have lots of money. I would like to have a nice burial service for my dog."

Father Murphy replied:
"I am sorry that we do not have Mass or burial services for animals, but there is a new denomination down the road, and God knows what they are up to, but why don't you go and see them."

Flanagan replied:
"I will and do you think sixty thousand pounds will be enough?"

Father Murphy said:
"Why didn't you tell me that your dog was a Catholic? You must tell me these things."

Selling Takes Persistence
by Lewis J. Minor

Don't expect to get a hit
    every time you come up to bat.
There has never been a .500 hitter in the majors!

With International Flair
by Hans J. Bueschkens

It was January 1, 1979, the official date when the Bueschkens International Consultants Ltd. joined culinary forces with the L. J. Minor Corporation on a full time basis.

Having the pleasure of meeting Dr. Lewis J. Minor and Lt. General John D. McLaughlin several years earlier during the American Culinary Federation (ACF) annual National Convention and the National Restaurant Association (NRA) trade show in Chicago, I accepted the invitation to represent the L. J. Minor Corporation worldwide in the new Export Division of L. J. Minor.

The last 15 years have been without a doubt the most rewarding years of my career in the culinary arts. The L. J. Minor Corporation was very chef-oriented and a great supporter of the American chefs. After 34 years in kitchens and as a food and beverage

532

director, I entered the world of foodservice and the manufacturing world.

Since I always believe that we must return something to our beautiful world for what we have received, I thought it would be of interest to L. J. Minor to enter the IKA, World Culinary Olympics, in 1980, in order to prove to the world of culinary arts that the culinarians of Minor's were worth their weight in Gold, literally!

At that time the only Gold Medal winner from a manufacturing company in the U. S. was, to my knowledge, Sara Lee, and their outstanding pastry chef, Casey Sinkeldam, had won it. Minor's chefs won three Gold Medals, four Silver Medals, and one Bronze Medal, plus the coveted Gold Medal for the HOUSE OF MINOR. The Gold Medal winners were Chef Michael Minor, CEC, USA, Chef Takashi Murakami, CCC, Canada, and Chef Hans Bueschkens, CCC, Canada.

In 1984 the chefs of the L. J. Minor Corporation competed in the IKA '84 for the second time under the leadership of Michael L. Minor and the results were so outstanding that it stunned the culinary world of foodservice.

Eight Minor chefs brought back to America seven Gold Medals, one Silver Medal, and the coveted GRAND GOLD of the IKA, a feat and record which still stands today as no other foodservice company has achieved such a distinction! These culinarians returned to L. J. Minor, in their humble way, a little of that which they had received while being members of the Minor culinary family.

During these years, Hans Bueschkens was promoted to vice president, international operations in the L. J. Minor Export Division. Also, in 1980, Hans Bueschkens was elected to the leadership of the World Association of Cooks Society (WACS) in Milano, Italy, as World President., a position he held until 1988, thus being the only World President of WACS to be elected twice.

During that time the following piece appeared in the *Hospitality Educator*, Sept/Oct 1983, page 3, and is indicative of the type of great press President Bueschkens accomplished while serving WACS.

Specified For Flavor and Value: Minor's Food Bases & Preps!

By Chef Hans J. Bueschkens, President
World Association of Cooks Societies

L. J. Minor products are specified by quality-conscious restaurants, institutions, caterers, central kitchens and food processors. Superior flavor is one part of our package. Value is the other.

We combine natural food flavor with ease of use, and help you cut costs for fresh ingredients, energy, storage and equipment. Minor's natural flavor Food Bases and sauce and gravy prep are available throughout the U.S., Canada, and overseas.

For more information, recipes, or product demonstrations, call us or your foodservice distributor.

Minor's products are authorized to bear the "Seal of Culinary Merit" awarded by the American Culinary Federation, Inc.

L. J. Minor Corp. is an Official Sponsor of the U.S. Culinary Team, 1984 International Culinary Competition, Frankfurt, Germany.

L. J. Minor Corp.
436 Bulkley Building - Cleveland, Ohio 44115

It was the L. J. Minor Corporation and their support, both time and dollar wise, that made these eight years in WACS such a success. During President Bueschken's eight years of travel, 20 new nations did join WACS, the largest increase in its membership history during an eight year time period.

But these years of travel were also to benefit the L. J. Minor Corporation. Our excellent products were exported throughout the world including Europe, Asia, Australia, Africa, and Canada in the Americas. Our international friends did visit us in the head office in Cleveland, Ohio, and also during the largest trade show in the U. S., the NRA Show in Chicago.

We always did represent Dr. Lewis J. Minor's motto "ALWAYS IN GOOD TASTE." People were always very important to the L. J. Minor Corporation.

In the states, Chefs Minor and Bueschkens looked at other ways to promote the Minor image. A National Recipes Contest was a great success. The follow-up was the National Chefs Calendar, using the twelve winners of the former contest.

In 1989 the L. J. Minor Corporation launched the ACF/LJM Chefs Professional Award, an award which even today is one of the outstanding presentations -- a black tie affair -- at the annual National ACF Convention.

The Award is to commemorate the 1977 elevation of American culinarians from the title DOMESTIC to PROFESSIONAL, made possible on the request of the ACF's Chef Jack Braun, Richard Bosnjak, and L. Edwin Brown, Secretary General, and the support of Dr. Lewis J. Minor, Lt. General John D. McLaughlin, and Dr. Louis Szathmary. This must be considered the greatest contribution ever made to the American culinarians by a food manufacturing company in the United States of America!

The L. J. Minor Corporation is also one of the official sponsors of TEAM U. S. A. since 1980. Minor chefs have been very active in their support of the American Team abroad and in their support of ACF activities and culinary salons in the U. S. A.

Dr. Lewis J. Minor always was and is a firm believer in the contributions a chef can make. As a matter of fact, one of Minor's first culinary salespeople was the great chef Jean Caubet of Detroit, Michigan.

Even today in the year 1994, Minor -- FIDCO, a member of the Nestle family, still has the largest culinary division in Nestle U. S. A., with six chefs and vice president Michael

L. Minor, CEC. as support team for national sales and customer services.

Dr. Minor also believes strongly in the support of future culinarians as they enter their chosen field of our noble profession. Large scholarship donations to the major culinary schools in the U. S. A., such as the Culinary Institute of America, Johnson & Wales University, and Michigan State University (MSU), will ensure future culinarians the help needed.

The latest program for the hospitality industry will be the the Michael L. Minor Master of Science in Foodservice Management at MSU in Lansing, Michigan. Young men and women will be invited from around the globe to join this program which is to provide a practical, flexible, and dynamic culinary executive education program, for leaders of our hospitality industry.

The circle of the L. J. Minor culinary family is coming full turn. The many Minor chefs over the years, from 1951, the founding date of the company, through the Culinary Olympics of 1980 and 1984, to the present time, assure through the humble support of Dr. Minor, that thousands of young culinarians are prepared to take their positions for years to come in our truly wonderful world.

As mentioned at the outset, the 15 years with the Minor culinary family has been without doubt the most rewarding years in my professional career of 48 years. Minor's is a great company of wonderful people that did care for their fellow men, provided the world with one of the finest food bases, and re-invested in the future of culinarians of tomorrow.

God bless the Minor family and our sincere thank you for giving us the privilege to share these 15 years with you.

In the Industrial Division
by John G. Cassidy

First and foremost, the industrial division at Minor's was, if my memory is correct, started by Dr. L. J. Minor. The first real industrial account was Stouffer's in Cleveland and the first product was Beef Base, made in Mrs. Minor's kitchen. Dr. Minor made a presentation to Stouffer's after saying a few prayers as he walked around the block in downtown Cleveland waiting for his appointment.

The R & D staff including Ruth, Mike Zelski, Jan Williams, and Mike Minor concurred with the marketing people in Minor's in believing that there was indeed a place for Minor quality products at the manufacturing level. Most of the top ten food companies in the U. S. are now or have through the years used L. J. Minor products to improve the flavor of their national brand products. L. J. Minor was and is a silent partner in many famous food products.

To accomplish the above, L. J. Minor put together a technical/marketing team to work with food manufacturing firms to help them solve both their flavoring and nutritional problems. The team approach worked and L. J. Minor was rewarded with business from industry. Eventually, 20% of the overall business at L. J. Minor was from food manufacturing sources with several food companies purchasing in excess of a million dollars annually.

The good people at Minor's -- and there were many -- led by an owner dedicated to presenting a quality product to the industry at a fair price (in Ireland a good value), made L. J. Minor great in a great food industry. The rest is history!

A good firm run by a good leader -- God Bless -- and realize that all of this, of course, would not have been possible if Dr. Minor had not married an angel!

Through TQM
by Paul Hamerly

Great companies, like great religions and institutions, have underlying strengths that make them successful. Sometimes it is a grand vision or strategy, sometimes it is the practical means of getting things done, and sometimes it is just ways of treating people. At the L. J. Minor Corporation, I had the pleasure of observing all three.

In early 1986, I joined the Minor Corporation as director of marketing, subsequently holding the position of vice president of marketing until the end of my service at the end of 1992. Having graduated from a top ten MBA program and worked for a large, Fortune 500 company (SmithKline Beecham and H. J. Heinz), I did not know exactly what to expect in a $30 million privately owned *family based* company like Minor's.

Family company is emphasized because there were plenty of not only Minors, but also McLaughlins, Clancys, and Cassidys in the management and work force. The Irish stereotypes (I mean no malice for I am partially Irish myself) of a big Irish family held true. These people could argue until they were red in the face, then walk arm in arm to dinner telling jokes all the while. No grudges held, just a way of life among family.

During my seven-year tenure, the company grew almost twofold to $60 million while undergoing substantial changes in ownership and management. Nestle bought the company and we hired a lot of people from larger food companies along the way. We were able to maintain enviable profitability in spite of these changes. This success was born out of not just an endearing Irish culture, but some underlying secrets that gave Minor's an enduring advantage in the market.

Employees First

Haven't we all learned that the customer comes first? Peter Drucker, the great management teacher, says the "purpose of business is to create a customer." But I learned an important caveat for senior management while at Minor's. Dr. Minor prepared his credo on December 12, 1952 in his "Business Aims" . . .

L. J. Minor Corporation Business Aims

I believe that honesty, integrity, accuracy, punctuality, courtesy, kindness, friendliness, helpfulness, and cleanliness are the tenets upon which my business shall be built.

- I will always endeavor to be fair and helpful, not only to employees, my management team, and stockholders, but also to customers, government agencies, and competitors.

- My experience in the food industry indicates there will always be room for a company that will sell quality products that are constantly controlled to insure uniformity at a fair price that will result in a normal profit.

- Service will be the keynote of our business and every effort will be put forth to give the customer exactly the product that he specifies.

There is a great deal in this credo, and the way that employees are brought up might lead you to question where they fit within all the constituencies mentioned. But Dr. Minor's actions left little doubt about the priority. He and virtually all future management of the company constantly showed that they were concerned about the welfare of the employees. What do the employees think? How will this decision affect them? How do we keep pride and morale high?

Of course customers are important, and no one can deny that the stockholder is important. But if management takes care of employees, employees will take care of customers, and customer's actions will benefit the stockholders.

Your priority just depends on where you are in the company. "On the front lines (which is usually at lower levels of the company) you need to constantly focus on the external customer. But as one progresses up the organization, one needs to provide the support, training, compensation, and feedback to lower levels in order to keep them focused on the customer.

Many companies prioritize their constituencies in their credo or mission. A comparison of several will show that most are different, and perhaps there is no one right answer. But putting the employee first for senior managers has worked at Minor's, and I believe it will work just about everywhere else.

Industry Experts as Low Cost Consultants

It might seem ironic that a company with high employee retention and length of service would believe and practice the use of consultants to such a degree. But this was one of the hallmarks of Minor's.

From the early years, and perhaps out of necessity, the company would hire chefs and food technologists as consultants, paying them on a per diem or monthly retainer basis. Most of the chefs were in a semi-retirement stage in which they had great skills, great contacts, and a desire to be productive, but did not want to work 60 hour weeks any longer.

These independent agents of the company were extremely loyal. While only paid for one to several days per week, their minds were thinking about ways to help the company around the clock, even on weekends. Substantial business and enduring goodwill was generated through this approach. Most chefs considered it a mark of distinction to carry a Minor's calling card "chef consultant."

Often I think of the vast number of industries in which this same idea could result in similar results. I think it would work particularly well where know-how is involved -- engineers, computer programmers, operations people, scientists, etc.

Try Them Out on a Consulting Basis

This practice of using consultants was extended to many other areas of the company, but in a different way. When looking for an area of specialization that the company did not have experience with, they would often bring someone in on a consulting assignment first. This gave the company and candidate an opportunity to try each other out at reduced risk. If both were pleased with the direction, an offer for full time employment would be made.

My employment is a case in point. While employed at H. J. Heinz, I was called in for a few days (vacation days on my part) to provide a point of view on the company getting into the consumer market. I provided a five-page, well-thought-thorough recommendation that resulted in a full time offer to join the company. I was able to join the company with a little more stature and viewed as an expert in something, not just a cold, new hire.

Leadership

During the 1970's and 1980's, we went through a period where the productivity of the United States increased at slower rates than other "up and coming" countries including Japan, Germany, Korea, Singapore, to name a few. Labor unions were on the decline and most everyone questioned the work ethic of the common laborer and skilled worker in the United States.

Finally, in the 1990's, we are beginning to understand the impact that leadership has -- both positive and negative -- on the performance and prosperity of an organization. Highly paid CEO's like Lee Iacocca at Chrysler and Jack Welch at GE have made a difference over a sustained time and are worth what they are paid. Albeit on a smaller scale, we have been blessed with top notch leadership at Minor's for decades.

We had four leaders from 1951 to 1992. Dr. Lewis J. Minor, Mr. Tom Ryan (whom I did not know, but heard much about), General John D. McLaughlin, and Bill McLaughlin were very different people with very different approaches to leadership, but they had two things in common -- treatment of people and direction of the organization.

If you had the privilege of working for any of these men, you could count on them knowing you well, including work styles, personal interests, and even family members. Dr. Minor set the standard for all of the others to follow, particularly in his way of caring about everyone in his employ.

Your opinion was asked for and heard. Decisions were made at the appropriate level, but the information gathering process was almost always democratic. We met around a table, spoke our piece, and a decision was made. Positive feedback was given publicly; criticism was given privately.

Production workers were valued. Company plans were communicated using formal and informal means to everyone in manufacturing. Top management knew almost all workers on a first name basis. Even when that was not the case, what a morale boost for the CEO to shake hands and say a simple hello to everyone, thanks for your work.

The direction of the organization was always set by the CEO and it was set simple enough for everyone to understand. One common thread to our leadership from the 1950s until today was a commitment to the chef, the principle user of our bases. Dr. Minor understood that these people were trained to make food taste and look appealing, and they make the ultimate decision of which flavors to buy and use.

Each leader also had a focus on what would make the organization successful given its challenge at the time. With Dr. Minor, I believe it was commitment to quality and values -- not an easy combination for a start up enterprise just trying to get by. With General McLaughlin, it was single minded commitment to the Minor brand and prompting greater performance on a geographic basis equal to the top market. With Bill McLaughlin, it was establishment of a custom products capability and a total quality management program.

One of the most interesting aspects of our leadership was the often limited interaction we had with the CEO. Several examples will help make the point. After establishing the roots of the company, Dr. Minor left the Cleveland area to pursue his doctorate and teach at Michigan State University. For many years, he traveled to Cleveland with Mrs. Minor only once a month or as needed for Board meetings or special issues. General McLaughlin maintained his residence in Virginia for almost ten years while running Minor's. He would be in Cleveland at Minor's only 2 to 3 days per week.

While Bill McLaughlin lived in Cleveland and got to know the company intimately from the inside for 5 years prior to his presidency, he was president of the trade association IFMA (International Food Service Manufacturer's Association) in 1989 and also was president of Minor's sister company FIDCO from 1990 to 1992, both of which allowed him very limited time in Cleveland. In fact, from January to August 1992, Bill relocated to Glendale as executive vice president of Nestle Brands, so we were entirely without a president for eight months. Profits in 1992 still exceeded our goal.

Public Relations

The L. J. Minor Corporation set a standard for the entire food industry (and perhaps all industries) in the area of public relations. Of course the name Minor's means nothing to the average consumer, so we are talking about public relations to the food industry. This program took many forms, but it centered on the chefs and research and development personnel within the industry.

While the total public relations effort would be too lengthy to detail, highlights include:

American Culinary Federation:

1. Financial support to keep the organization growing through its early years;

2. Advertising in the national magazine "The National Culinary Review" on the back cover;

3. Assisting with getting the federal government to recognize the chef as a professional by the U. S. Department of Labor in 1977, thus raising the chef from domestic to professional status. This gave the chef a much needed starting point for the esteem needed to make the culinary field a profession in the United States as it is in other parts of the world, particularly in Europe;

4. Advertising in regional publications and local donations;

5. Establishment of the Chef Professionalism Award in 1990 to honor the four regional and one national chef each year who best demonstrate professionalism in their career. Awards include a medal, plaque, black tie dinner at the national convention with over 1500 in attendance, $2,500 scholarship to the culinary or hotel school of the winner's choice and news releases.

Culinary Competitions:

1. Founding and on-going sponsor of the U. S. Culinary Olympic Team during the Culinary Olympics held in Germany every four years from 1972 forward. This included financial support, product donations, and professional assistance (from experienced judges) as needed;

2. Minor's sent its own team in 1980 and 1984, winning the "Grand Prize in Gold" in 1984, the only corporate team to ever win such an award;

3. Sponsorship of other national and regional competitions as well as providing judges as needed.

Education:

1. Financial support to culinary schools to include The Culinary Institute of America, Johnson and Wales University, and many other national and regional schools;

2. Financial support to hotel schools to include Michigan State, Cornell, and many other top schools in the U. S. and Canada;

3. Product donations and speaking engagements at both of the above to plant the Minor's name with future culinarians and managers early in their career.

Food Processing:

1. Technical articles to help R & D personnel flavor their foods;

2. Customer seminars with major customers such as Kraft, etc.

(The net effect of all PR for Minor's including these and other programs was an awareness level of somewhere in the 70-80% range among food-service and food processing industry professionals.)

Quality

There is no question that quality was a fundamental aspect of Minor's from its inception, as evident in Dr. Minor's Business Aims. But the definition of quality changed.

Although I was not part of the company from 1951 to 1986, my impression is that quality was originally defined at Minor's by what the customer wanted. Over time, we learned that using premium ingredients and premium processing methods resulted in a demonstrably superior product that met the customer's need and delivered good profitability.

The company needed to adapt to rapidly increasing demand during the 1980s, which necessitated changes in production methods and even suppliers. The challenge is to hold onto quality while growing.

Add on top the ownership changes of 1983 (Dr. Minor's sale to private investors) and 1987 (the Nestle acquisition) as well as a rapid influx of middle and senior management and you have a real challenge maintaining quality. How can the average employee produce consistent quality when he or she is worried about his or her job?

Complacency may have also set in. The tremendous success of the Minor's brand product line (at prices 20% premium to our nearest competitor, LeGout) gave the company an air of invincibility. soon we began to define quality as using top quality ingredients, an idea mis-appropriately placed on the process rather than the customer benefits.

As part of Bill McLaughlin's vision in 1988, we re-committed the company to a full fledged Total Quality Management (TQM) process from top to bottom. This TQM process, in our view, was kicked off in just the right ways:

1. We initiated the effort not out of desperation or short-term need, but to improve the long term competitiveness of the company;

2. Senior management was committed to the program. We read a number of books and went to various seminars long before the formal effort started;

3. A total quality manager with experience was hired, reporting directly to the president. With a title of manager (instead of vice president), he was positioned to be more accessible to the full employee base;

4. We emphasized heavy training from top to bottom, a custom designed approach for our company, and the fact that this was an on-going, never-ending process and not a one time program.

The heart or essence of quality was re-invigorated into Minor's. We again defined quality by what the customer wanted, but expanded the idea more formally and rigorously to internal as well as external customers. This effort led to better performance by the company over a five-year period, even though it is difficult to accurately isolate and measure the net effect.

There were other benefits that perhaps we did not originally envision. An immediate benefit was the provision of a common terminology for discussing ideas and change, something that had been sorely missing (since many of us were from different backgrounds and companies).

A second benefit was the freeing up of management time to work on the future instead of the past. Specifically, problems and their solutions became the responsibility of the people involved in the process, not senior management. Senior management would support the improvement effort, participate in it, and reward its participants, but we would no longer need to shoulder complete responsibility for working out the problem. What a difference!

A New Parent

In late 1986, concurrent with the tax reform act of 1986, we were sold to and became part of the world's largest food company, Nestle. While Nestle was judged to be a good fit for Minor's, we still had a lot of trepidation over how we would be managed and what the expectations of our new owner would be.

Fortunately, we were put under the direction of Jim Biggar, Chairman of Nestle Enterprises, Inc., the operating arm of Nestle in the United States. Jim had grown up with and helped lead the Stouffer's organization through its many changes of ownership (family owned -- sold to Litton -- then sold to Nestle), so he understood a bit about where we were coming from.

Jim allowed us a great deal of autonomy and provided assistance and support where needed. This is very unusual in a large corporation, where the organization structure is largely driven to simplify life for senior management, not the employee or customer base.

Due to a consolidation of Nestle on a worldwide basis and particularly in the United States, Jim Biggar resigned in 1992 and Nestle U. S. was re-organized under the direction of Timm Crull (former Carnation president) out of Glendale, California. Again, this led to a great deal of uncertainty for our division, certainly the smallest of the "Nestle family." For many months, we did not have a solidified reporting relationship within Nestle.

In 1992, the company became a part of the foodservice arm of Nestle (called Nestle Brands) and Brad Alford of Carnation was named president. Then in 1993, the Minor Corporation was merged with a sister company, FIDCO, that supplies flavor ingredients to the food processing industry. The name has been formally changed to Food Ingredient Specialties, and it is now run by Dr. Sam Lee. This new entity should be stronger in the marketplace due to a sharing of technological resources, manufacturing capability, and sales contacts.

Certainly the company has been through a lot of changes induced by our parent company and many of those changes have been very positive. At the same time, let us hope the many strengths of Minor's developed over so many years by so many inspired people carry forward and do not get forgotten within the mammoth size and scope of Nestle's worldwide operations.

In closing, and in order to assure some sense of balance to my account, I need to add that our company had its fair share of problems, struggles, and weaknesses. I am not so naive or senile (yet) to forget the more challenging aspects of helping direct the Minor Corporation.

Yet, at the same time, I have many memories of the friends made, the goodwill generated and wisdom earned while working at Minor's. In the way of employee emphasis, use of consultants, leadership, public relations, and quality, I cannot wait to apply what I have learned to the "next Minor's," and I can only hope that we will be half as successful as the L. J. Minor Corporation has been.

Chapter 48

Chefs Contribute:

Treasured Memories

**by Robert H. Nelson
(1969-1995)**

Professionalism

**by L. Edwin Brown
(1974-1995)**

Culinary Team U. S. A. and the L. J. Minor Corporation

The ACF Chef Professionalism Award and the L. J. Minor Corporation

Award Objectives   **Winner's Prizes**

Testimonials

**by Jean Richter
for Carl Richter
(1976-1985)**

(Editor's Note: As a way of introduction to this chapter, the following announcement was typical of the type of press given to chefs as they joined the L. J. Minor Corporation. Dr. Minor always did what he could to raise the image of each chef and his continual public relations campaign has succeeded as demonstrated by the stature the chef has in society today. Once again, thank you Dr. Minor!)

Chef C. Arthur Jones Named
Minor Corporate Chef Advisor

Appointment of C. Arthur Jones, CEC., CCE., as Corporate Chef Advisor to the L. J. Minor Corporation was announced today by Michael L. Minor, Vice President and Corporate Executive Chef. Chef Jones is one of 34 prominent American chefs who work for the Minor Corp. in various capacities involving sales, customer relations, and new product application and development.

Chef Jones began his culinary career 54 years ago as a kitchen boy in the Sands Point Yacht Club in Great Neck, New York. Since then, he has combined extensive executive chef responsibility for prestigious American hotels, restaurants and private clubs, with active involvement in professional culinary training and education.

He is one of few American chefs to win recognition by the American Culinary Federation both as Certified Executive Chef (CEC) and Certified Culinary Educator (CCE).

Chef Jones was an instructor at the Culinary Institute of America from 1961 until his retirement in 1979 when he was presented the Escoffier Award. He was inducted into the Honorable Order of the Golden Toque in May, 1982, and is active in the San Diego chapter of the American Culinary Federation.

Chef Jones' work with the Minor Corp. includes sales and product application seminars, as well as consultation and demonstrations for the hospitality, institutional, and processing foodservice industries.

Quote from Jonathan Swift

"Every man desireth to live long but no man would be old!"

Chefs Debate Strong Drink
(Irish Humor by Hal Roach)

Two chefs were in an Irish pub arguing about which kind of whiskey is stronger, Irish whiskey or Scotch whisky. The first chef said that Scotch whisky is much stronger than Irish whiskey. The other chef said no way--Irish whiskey is stronger than Scotch whisky and I can prove it to you. The first says:

"How are you going to prove it?"

The other says:

> "Well, last Saturday night, my wife and I were having a bottle of Irish whiskey and we drank the whole thing and the next morning we got up and went to Mass."

The first chef says:

> "That does not prove anything! I'm sure there are lots of people that drink a bottle of Irish whiskey and get up and go to Mass the next morning."

The other says:

> "Yes, but we are Jewish!"

Quote from Pat Norman

"Strength of purpose surmounts overwhelming odds."

Treasured Memories
by Robert H. Nelson

As I look back over the years and recall all the events and all the culinary shows that I have attended and the great chefs that I have met and learned so much from, I consider myself very lucky. I have to especially thank the L. J. Minor Corporation for many treasured memories.

My first meeting with Dr. Lewis J. Minor was at a founding chefs meeting of the Capital Professional Chefs ACF Chapter in Lansing, Michigan, in the winter of 1969. It has to rank as one of my most memorable occasions. As a new chef to the area, I was made to feel by Dr. Minor like I had been with the ranks for years.

At that time I was already aware of the high quality of the L. J. Minor Food Bases. From this very moment on, I would have the good fortune to have both Dr. and Mrs. L. J. Minor for what would become lifetime mentors. I learned so much so quickly from Dr. Minor.

To sum it up, he taught me to be a consummate professional at all times. He would say, "Dress well and look like you do not need the job even when you go to the grocery store." Before I knew it, I was a guest presenter for Dr. Minor's Quantity Foods class. Yes, I demonstrated the old world way of producing stock, sauces, and soups, and the modern method of using his already famous food bases.

In a few short years, I would have the honor and privilege to teach one of the classes Dr. Minor had at Michigan State University and become the first "chef hands-on lecturer" of any university in the world. Dr. Minor introduced me to chefs in the immediate area. He invited me to wonderful dinners at their beautiful farm house. Mrs. Minor would prepare the most marvelous food for visiting chefs.

Dr. Minor had his ever watchful eyes on me. To be sure I dressed and acted professional at all times. He was preparing me for bigger and better things to come. Whatever I did was right as this was my real start with the company. I was hired to do shows on a part-time basis.

The greatest of all shows for me was Chicago's National Restaurant Show. Here I would work with the greatest chefs in the world. The L. J. Minor Corporation chefs helped me in every way and called me "the baby," after all I was only in my late forties and they in their sixties and seventies. Everyone came to the L. J. Minor Corporation booth as it was a gathering place for all foodservice people. All the good things started here and my new career got a jump start here too!

Two times I was sent to the Culinary Olympics in Frankfurt, Germany. My job was to oversee the preparation and production of the L. J. Minor soup and sauce samples. The L. J. Minor Corporation won gold and silver medals and a special gold medal was presented to Dr. and Mrs. Minor in 1984 for their Food Bases. It was a proud moment and I was a part of this.

(Editor's Note: In 1984 while serving as an associate professor in Cornell University's School of Hotel Administration, I, too, was to be a part of the Culinary Olympics and had finalized all arrangements for my travel.

Unfortunately, working in the foods area of the School, the democratic process came into play a few weeks prior to my departure and my colleagues voted to send one of the teaching assistants in my place. I was crushed, but never said anything, as I had traveled the world doing seminars and others were not so fortunate.

Knowing of my situation, Dr. Minor and Gen. McLaughlin were kind enough to send to me a two-hour 16 mm film documenting the festivities of the 1984 Culinary Olympics. I shall never forget their generosity and neither shall the hundreds of hospitality students who have viewed this film in my food classes since 1984! The time was truly one of great celebration and I encourage anyone able to attend a future Culinary Olympics to do so. I am still looking forward to going for the first time myself, possibly in 1996, where it will be held in Berlin, Germany for the first time.)

For five years, I was the ACF Central Region apprentice coordinator. At the end of the ACF apprentice contract, Dr. Minor called me to have lunch with him. I will never forget his words: "There are two people who want you to work full time for the company." There was silence, I asked who, and he said, "My son, Michael, and me." I then joined the ranks of the great Minor group of chefs. Just to name a few:

Richard Benson, CEC, AAC

James Kosec, CCE, CEC, AAC

Clark Bernier, CEC, AAC

George Marchand

Wolfgang Bierer, CEC, AAC

Herman Breithaupt

Hans Bueschkens

Emil Burgermeister

Jean Caubet

Mike Minor, CEC, AAC

Willy Rossel, AAC

Hans K. Roth, CEC, AAC

Frank Scherer

Poncho Valez

One late afternoon in August of 1980, Dr. Minor called me to have lunch with him at Walnut Hills Country Club. What would it be? Because of his wisdom and wise tutelage, I was doing very well with the company.

With business on his mind, Dr. Minor came straight to the point. He said there was an opportunity for a chef in the HRIM program at Michigan State University. But there would be some hitches since it would be a joint appointment with Housing and Food Services and it would be teaching Quantity Food Production.

Dr. Minor said, "Chef Nelson, I want you to do this. If they do not want you in one hour, a week, 6 months, or 6 years, you are back with the Company." When Dean Lewis heard this, he said, "He has got a better deal than I have!" In short I was made an honorary faculty member and after 12 years of successful teaching, all has worked out well.

After several years, in fact, the Director of HRIM, Don Smith, who at first did not really appreciate chefs, in my opinion, hired me full time. How could I let Dr. and Mrs. Minor down after all they did for me and my family?

In 1990 came the biggest moment in my chef career, when my position was endowed for $1 million by Dr. and Mrs. L. J. Minor and my title became: **Robert H. Nelson, CEC, CCE, CFBE.**

Never ever did I hear or get a complaint on Minor's Food Bases. Even to this day, people in a decade of my evening school Gourmet Cooking Classes ask me over and over again where they can be purchased.

At the Culinary Olympics in 1980 we could hardly handle the crowds who wanted to sample our Food Bases. Robert Morley, the star of "Who's Killing the Great Chefs of Europe," came to the booth and tried our Lobster Base. He called me a "faker" and said "How could something this grand come from a base?" As always, the product spoke for itself.

In conclusion, no one will ever know just how many people Dr. and Mrs. Minor have helped throughout the years including students, chefs, culinary schools, the American Culinary Federation, and humanity in general. I know that I am the luckiest chef in the world and all because of a great man and his wife, who worked hard to build a great company and have shared their success with chefs and culinarians all over the world.

Professionalism
by L. Edwin Brown

My first convention of the American Culinary Federation was in 1974 at the Sheraton in Cleveland, Ohio. It was very appropriate that this meeting was the one in which Louis I. Szathmary, Ph.D., Chef/Owner of the Bakery Restaurant in Chicago, made his very famous speech which went as follows:

"Mr. President, Distinguished Head Table, Fellow Domestics, I feel that we should concentrate on only one single issue. We should try to find somebody who could lobby for us in Washington to change our designated status from domestics to what we are -- professionals.

When I said exactly the same sentence in Dallas ten years ago, I received the same lukewarm applause that I received now, but nobody really did anything about it to my knowledge. And I think the time is coming closer and closer that if we do not do it, somebody will make the change. And if we don't work for this change, we will all be 'Outside looking in.'

I closed a speech in Dallas some 14 years ago with a story which was carried in the *Saturday Review*, the *New York Times*, and in the *Readers Digest*, but it was not mentioned in any of the chefs publications in the U. S. A. That time I talked about the era of the Holy Roman Emperors -- when the chef of the Emperor sat and ate with the Emperor at the head table, while the German Princes and Counts and Spanish Princes and Barons sat down there where you sit now. And, while the chef sat with the Emperor, his personal physician could not live inside the city walls -- he had to live outside with the gypsies and the dog walkers and other domestics, and he could not look at the Emperor's face because they said 'A man who sticks his finger for money in somebody's behind cannot look at the face of the Emperor.' That was the status of the doctor who took care of him. And what happened then. The doctors went on to lobby and make their profession the strongest.

And what do chefs do? Every one of them kept their own secret. They didn't want to set up schools. They didn't want to spend a penny on lobbying. And now the chef is permitted to enter the club where he works only through the back door. He has to kiss the behind of the guy who cuts his calluses for $10 because he is a 'doctor of podiatry sciences.' You cannot buy a pair of glasses from a guy who does not have a doctor's degree. You cannot get an enema in a hospital from somebody who doesn't have a degree, who doesn't have a professional standing, but we, chefs, are domestics. It is up to us. Nobody will change our status if we don't work on it. I, as a little man, so help me God, always tried everything possible. I'm a chef. I'm proud of it. And I can outdo anybody, anytime, in front of anybody. This is my chosen profession. This is what I want to be, even if I am called a domestic. But I'm fighting it. And nobody will fight for us if we don't fight for ourselves. Now, what can we do? We have to start the war. The greatest strategic mind in human history, Montecucoli, said, 'Only three things are necessary to win: money, money, and money!' That is what we need, so we can put a man in Washington: MONEY. We have a man in this room who is retiring this month, and is well known in Washington. I don't think we could get a better man than Gen. John D. McLaughlin, and I didn't ask his permission to mention his name, but I bet, if he would have an office, we could really get some results.

The first problem we have to solve -- not to be classed as domestics nevermore. As soon as we have a professional standing, we can talk to the restaurant owners. I'm a restaurant owner myself and I know what a restaurant can do for the workers if the owner wants to do it. My assistant chef probably makes only $5,000 more than that street cleaner in New York, but I send him every year on a fully-paid study-vacation trip with his wife. Because when he learns something, he learns also for me. I also benefit from it. If I can do it, how come the big restaurants cannot do it?

What have we been doing for years and years -- playing ping-pong with nobody at the other end of the table? Let's wake up, and before we do anything else, we must find out what we are: domestics, dog walkers, chamber maids, or chefs? Are we members of a profession or not? And, after stabilizing our status, we can start to educate the youngsters. Then we have the power to close a restaurant if they hire an untrained somebody else for the kitchen, instead of one of us. Please don't applaud. I would rather you think of how you can, as an individual, not wait until others will do it and start to get the

550

needed money. We need it for one single purpose: to set up a professional lobbyist in Washington who would lobby for our professional interests. Believe me, this is the only way to do it. How can you personally help? Very simple. Offer to an organization in your community a gala dinner; or present a demonstration for $150, $200, $300 and give that money to your national treasury for a lobbyist fund only. It is easy to talk. I'm writing out, after lunch, a personal check for $500 to start the special collection for this purpose. And may God help me and encourage every one of you do do likewise.

Fellow culinarians, I started my speech addressing you as fellow domestics, and I bid you good-bye as fellow professionals.

May God help us to achieve this goal. Thank you." (This is reprinted from the June, 1986 *National Culinary Review*.)

Following this fiery speech, Chef Louis wrote out a check for $500. Otto Nasser, of the Pink Pig in Los Angeles and Chef Raymond Marshall, owner of the Acapulco Restaurants, and many other chefs also gave moneys which became the Washington Fund, a fund which was designed to lobby Washington in order to be able to elevate the status of the executive chef out of the Dictionary of Occupational Titles in the domestic categories into Category I for professional, technical, and managerial occupations category.

After Dr. Minor heard of this speech and activity, he contacted Gen. John D. McLaughlin because he knew his way around Washington very well. He advised the General that he should help us in every way that he could and that the American Culinary Federation should not spend any of the money for raising the status of the American chef to the appropriate level.

Gen. McLaughlin worked very diligently with the American Culinary Federation, having attended his first convention in 1972 and never missing one up until the time of his death in 1992. He was always there to help the ACF when we needed help and advice.

In the late summer of 1976 the Bureau of Apprenticeship and Training of the United States Department of Labor contacted Chef Jack Braun of the Lemon Tree Restaurant in Pittsburgh and myself. They invited us to submit a proposal to take the apprenticeship program, which had been developed by the Chefs and Cooks Association of Pittsburgh and the Community College of Allegheny County, and establish it as a model for a National Culinary Apprenticeship Program for Cooks under their program titled, "New Initiatives in Apprenticeship Training."

Jack and I worked with Richard Bosnjak, CEC, who was the president of ACF and with Ferdinand Metz, who was the president of the Pittsburgh Chapter, ACF. We worked diligently to prepare a proposal as we were accustomed to working with very little money (the ACF had at this point in our history total assets of $60,000). We submitted a proposal for a one-year contract with the Bureau of Apprenticeship and Training for $250,000.

They came back and said the proposal was excellent but we needed more staff to implement what we wanted to do in order to establish a national program. We recalculated the steps and submitted a proposal in excess of $600,000.

In March of 1977, I signed a contract with the Department of Labor with Secretary of Labor Ray Marshall to register 1,500 apprentices in a one-year period. During these negotiations, Jack, Ferdinand, Richard, and I learned to know many of the people who were working in the Department of Labor at that time and especially the people who were involved with the Dictionary of Occupational Titles.

We were able to edit and amend the titles which had been written. The one factor which helped us a great deal was the fact that the executive chef was responsible for the training of apprentices. This was one aspect that enabled us to achieve our goal of having the executive chef assigned to No. I, the professional, technical, and managerial occupations category rather than the domestics one. We were able to achieve that goal without expending any money from the Washington Fund due to assistance from the L. J. Minor Corporation and Gen. McLaughlin's efforts working with us.

At the convention in Honolulu in 1977, President Bosnjak proposed to the board that the Washington Fund, which had a little over $8,000, be converted to the ACF Building Fund. It was time for the ACF to think about investing in a building to house the headquarters for their organization. Upon hearing what had happened, Dr. and Mrs. Minor were the first donors to the Building Fund, giving $10,000 after having invested nearly $50,000 from their company on the reclassification of chefs.

In November of 1982 we dedicated the library board room of the ACF to Dr. and Mrs. Minor. On October 23, 1989, Dr. and Mrs. Minor, Chef and Mrs. Louis Szathmary, Gen. McLaughlin, as well as Richard Bosnjak, Jack Braun, Ferdinand Metz, and I were at the ACF national headquarters in St. Augustine, Florida to dedicate a beautiful bronze plaque honoring those who helped gain professional status for the American executive chefs.

This was the first time that Dr. Minor and Chef Szathmary had seen the building in which they had invested. This plaque now hangs at the entrance to the national library and board room commemorating this significant event.

Culinary Team U. S. A. and the L. J. Minor Corporation

In 1978, ACF President Ferdinand Metz met with Walter Conti of Doylestown, Pennsylvania, immediate past president of the National Restaurant Association, and Mr. John Dankos, of Richmond, Virginia, president of the National Restaurant Association, to explore the idea of developing a foundation between the ACF and the National Restaurant Association to fund the International Culinary Competition Team.

Kraft Food Service had been the sole sponsor for many years and they had advised us that they could no longer shoulder this financial burden and that they were looking for some help to be able to accomplish these goals. The National Restaurant Association's responsibility was to help solicit funds from corporations to support the foundation. The ACF was to select and manage the Culinary Competition Team.

The L. J. Minor Corporation and Kraft Food Service were the founding sponsors in this new venture. The L. J. Minor Corporation has maintained their sponsorship to this day. Gen. McLaughlin served as president of the Foundation until his death in 1992.

The ACF Chef Professionalism Award and the L. J. Minor Corporation

In 1988, Gen. John D. McLaughlin came to me and the ACF with a proposal to establish the American Culinary Federation Chef Professionalism Award sponsored by the L. J. Minor Corporation.

This was a document which was negotiated with Paul Williamson and myself from our national office and Gen. McLaughlin, Paul Hamerly, and Hans Bueschkens of the L. J. Minor Corporation. It was an award to be given to active ACF members who had demonstrated professionalism.

Other qualities for the award included being recognized as an outstanding leader by the community, outstanding chef for culinary competency, involved chef with apprentices and students. Nominations could come from any ACF chapter for this prestigious award.

Award Objectives

1. To recognize each year an active member of the ACF who has demonstrated an outstanding level of achievement in contribution to cuisine in America. The nominee must be a member of the ACF for the past five years and not be a consultant to or employed by the L. J. Minor Corporation.

2. To promote chef professionalism to the foodservice industry and to the public at large.

3. To encourage active ACF members to advance their own professional status.

4. To commemorate the efforts of three outstanding individuals: Lewis J. Minor, Ph.D., food scientist/entrepreneur/philanthropist; Chef Louis Szathmary, Ph.D., chef/restaurant owner; and Lieutenant Gen. John D. McLaughlin, U. S. Army, retired.

Their combined vision and effort helped to attain a long-sought goal for American chefs: official U. S. government recognition of ACF Executive Chefs as professionals.

Today, the U. S. Department of Labor's "Dictionary of Occupational Titles" assigns the description of the Executive Chef to the No. 1 "Professional, Technical, and Managerial

Occupations" category.

In order to complete their application the chef must write an essay between 750 and 1,000 words describing their philosophy of culinary professionalism.

Since 1990 the following individuals have been honored as winners of the American Culinary Federation Chef Professionalism Award:

1990

Lisa Brefere, CEC, New York	Northeast
Robert J. Lippert, CCE, CWC, AAC, Michigan	Central
Kenneth G. Wade, CEC, AAC, Florida	Southeast
*Roland G. Henin, CMC, CCE, AAC, Oregon	Western

1991

*Roland Schaeffer, CEC, AAC, Pennsylvania	Northeast
Roland Zwerger, CCE, AAC, Illinois	Central
Reimund Pitz, CEC, CCE, AAC, Florida	Southeast
Michael Ty, CEC, AAC, Nevada	Western

1992

*Hartmut Handke, CMC, AAC, Ohio	Northeast
Victor Gielisse, CMC, AAC, Texas	Central
Hans Schadler, CEC, AAC, Virginia	Southeast
Walter Leible, CMC, AAC, Arizona	Western

1993

Nickolas Zakharoff, CEC, Maryland	Northeast
Louis Jesowshek, CEC, AAC, Louisiana	Central
*Walter Rhea, CMPC, CEC, CCE, AAC, Kentucky	Southeast
Stafford DeCambra, CCE, AAC, Hawaii	Western

1994

Edward G. Leonard, CEC, AAC, New York	Northeast
Nick P. Marino, CEC, AAC, Michigan	Central
*Johnny Rivers, CEC, AAC, Florida	Southeast
Werner Zefferer, CEC, AAC, Nevada	Western

Winner's Prizes

To the four Regional Winners:

A silver medal and silver plaque in the theme of the award program. The Silver Medal will be presented to the Regional Winners at the Regional Conference, and the Silver Plaque will be presented at the National Convention;
Paid trip-for-two to the award-year National ACF Convention. Includes standard fare transportation, lodging, and ACF Convention registration fees for two.

To the National Winner in addition to all Prizes Awarded to Regional Winners:

A gold medal and gold plaque in the theme of the award program;
Name inscribed on a separate, permanent plaque at ACF headquarters;

L. J. Minor Corporation grant of $2,500 as an honorarium to the national winner;

L. J. Minor Corporation will donate $2,500 as a student aid scholarship, in the name of the National winner, to an institution offering a culinary program accredited by the American Culinary Federation Educational Institute (ACFEI) selected by the National Winner.

Gen. McLaughlin designed the plaques and medals and they were produced in London, England by the official jeweler of the Royal Family.
Annually the awards are presented at the ACF National Convention at a dinner sponsored by the L. J. Minor Corporation. The regional winners are recognized at the ACF conferences at a dinner where they are introduced.
In conclusion, the American Culinary Federation and its Educational Institute are indebted to the generosity of two individuals, Dr. Lewis J. and Mrs. Ruth E. Minor, who have followed the culinarian's code to the utmost by passing on their worldly assets to those who are to follow to enhance our profession!

Testimonials
by Jean Richter
for Carl Richter

When Carl retired in 1976, he received word from the L. J. Minor Corporation asking if he would like to work with other retired chefs, sharing their experiences and knowledge with people in the food business. At the time, Minor Bases were not an unknown product to Carl as he had used them for many years.

In his previous employment, he had control of the foodservice at over 150 colleges, universities, and cafeterias. When he was first introduced to the Minor Bases, he realized they were the best method to do away with the "stock pots" in these kitchens. So often, some of the cooks used the stock broth as a "garbage" pot, putting in unwashed peelings, etc. He proved over and over again to clients that it may cost them a penny more, but with Minor Bases they would have a high quality and pure broth, far superior to any other on the market.

Carl was also a consultant for major companies on behalf of the L. J. Minor Corporation, and created many recipes for their particular needs. Very often he used our kitchen for research and development of new recipes.

Carl was an early riser and enjoyed working in the peace and quiet of the house at four or five o'clock in the morning. I must say it was so pleasant to awaken to those wonderful aromas that drifted through our home.

Working for the L. J. Minor Corporation started off as a job and in a very short time we realized that we were accepted into a family of warm, caring, and fun-loving people. It was a camaraderie that made one feel dedicated and loyal to the company and to each other.

At every business function, Minor's always had time set aside for a private reunion of their colleagues. They arranged for wonderful dinners and a time to just "let your hair down" and relax with the family.

One such occasion that is so memorable to me was the 1984 Culinary Olympics in Frankfurt, Germany. We met at a typical German restaurant called "Grey Beck," located in the old Frankfurt area. We sat at long wooden booths and out came huge platters of pork, family-style bowls of sauerkraut, and mashed potatoes.

After this delicious feast, the steins of beer and apple wine came, along with the lovely sounds of German music. We all linked arms and swayed from left to right singing along with everyone, including the waiters. What a wonderful time was had by all!

This is just one of many exciting memories of our association with the L. J. Minor Corporation. I reiterate what Carl has said numerous times, "On three continents, I have never worked for more decent and fine people."

(Editor's Note: At the end of this text is found Appendix 1 which provides "More From Chefs".)

Chapter 49

Minor Blessings

by Dr. Ronald F. Cichy

Two Nuns at an Away Game
(Irish Humor by Hal Roach)

Two nuns with their headdresses on went to an away MSU football game in Ireland, and the fellows sitting behind them started complaining. One fellow said:
"I think I'm moving to Canada. There aren't as many Catholics there."

The other one said:
"I think I'm moving to Scotland. There aren't any Catholics there."

Then one of the nuns turned around and said:
"Why don't you both go to hell. There aren't any Catholics there!"

On Having Children
(Irish Humor by Hal Roach)

A man told me that he and his wife had three children named Eenie, Meaney, Miney and we don't want any MO!

Speaking of Children
(Irish Humor by Hal Roach)

An Irish child was standing up on a tall wall and his mother says:
"Come down off of there. If you fall down and break both legs, don't you come running to me!"

Quote from Goethe

"We can respect a man only if he doesn't always look out for himself."

Those First Years

Our School of Hotel, Restaurant and Institutional Management at Michigan State University (MSU-HRIM, and now called the School of Hospitality Business) was blessed in 1964 when Dr. Lewis J. Minor decided to join the faculty. When Dr. Minor completed his Ph.D. in food science at MSU in 1964, MSU-HRIM Food Professor Dr. Lendal Kotschevar urged him to sign on as a visiting professor to bring his vast knowledge of food science to undergraduate and graduate MSU-HRIM students. Our School was blessed for the next two decades as Dr. Minor taught thousands of students food science and, more importantly, life's secrets of success.

Dr. Minor's appointment recommendation, dated October, 1964, shows that he was appointed to teach HRI 245 -- Food Production Technology -- described as a "course of the physical and chemical properties of food; an integral part of the revised curriculum which, with the prerequisite of one year of high school chemistry, replaces Chemistry 101, 102, and 103 in the undergraduate curriculum." That was a tall order for a new professor who was paid the princely sum of $4,000 to teach the course. The course met in Room 110 Anthony Hall, its site for over a decade.

In addition to MSU-HRIM students, Dr. Minor often had students from other majors at MSU take his HRI 245 course. One such student, Kenneth Fox, a graduate research assistant and Ph.D. candidate in the Department of Food Science at MSU, took HRI 245 as part of his language substitution. After completing HRI 245 in December of 1968, this Ph.D. candidate wrote to Dr. Minor to let him know his feelings about the course. "I believe that HRI 245 is one of the best courses I have had concerning introductory food science," he wrote. "In this one course I feel that more of the principles of food chemistry have been taught than in any single introductory course that I have had. The material covered in HRI 245 was current, timely, well presented, simplified... and pertinent to the objectives of the course." He went on to write "... I think it would be a much greater contribution to the Food Science Department and its undergraduate curriculum than it is to HRI... This course is much needed in the Food Science Program. I would hope that someday this course could be offered as a Food Science course or as a joint FS/HRI course." The student told Dr. B.S. Schweigert, then chairman of the Food Science Department at MSU. According to Dr. Minor, Dr. Schweigert was not totally pleased with these accolades.

Dr. Minor regularly took students on field trips to learn applications of principles presented in his class in a real-world environment. In 1965, he sponsored a group of 37 *Les Gourmets* students on a field trip to "observe the technical aspects in the operation of restaurants, hotels, and hospitals in the Chicago area." The group visited Ivanhoe Restaurant, Continental Coffee Company, Henrici's Restaurant, the O'Hare Inn, the Statler Hilton, and St. Anne's Hospital. Henry Ogden Barbour, then director of MSU-HRIM, approved the request which also included MSU-HRIM Instructor William Stafford. Since travel funds were short in those days in the School, Dr. Minor's company paid for all expenses associated with the trip.

In 1967, and regularly throughout his years at MSU-HRIM, Dr. Minor was invited to present a Food Flavor Seminar at Cornell University's School of Hotel Administration. Dr. Jeremiah J. Wanderstock, the professor in-charge of the seminars, extended the invitations on behalf of Robert A. Beck, dean of Cornell's Hotel School.

When Dr. Kotschevar left MSU-HRIM and Dr. Blomstrom replaced Professor Barbour as director, the MSU-HRIM faculty met. After the meeting, Dr. Blomstrom informed Dr. Minor: "The faculty decided that you should teach Dr. Kotschevar's Quantity Food Production course." Later, when Gary Shingler was his lab assistant, Dr. Minor urged Dr. Frank Borsenik, then acting director of MSU-HRIM, to hire Don Bell to teach Quantity Food Production.

In the fall of 1968, I began my undergraduate studies in MSU-HRIM. This was a time on campus of protests against the military draft and the Vietnam war and the military-industrial complex. It was the time of the SDS (The Students for a Democratic Society), "Blowin' In The Wind," regular student take-overs of the MSU Administration Building, and teargassing of MSU students marching in protest on Grand River Avenue. It was the era of musicians such as the Rolling Stones, Sly and The Family Stone, Joe Cocker, Leon Russell, The Who, and others who encouraged us to not conform to the values of our parents, teachers, or leaders. For me, the late 1960s were characterized by an introduction to wine (Boone's Farm Apple, Pagan Pink, MD 20-20) via upper-class students who would buy the contraband product on Friday night (with a small surcharge added) for our weekend enjoyment. My friends and I enjoyed Memorial Day get-togethers at Lake Brownwood in Paw Paw, and open air concerts (a la mini-Woodstocks) on campus.

In the summer of 1968, I met a lifelong friend on campus during MSU's new student orientation. We attended orientation together, discovered that we were both declared HRIM majors, and left after three days believing that we would probably not see each other again soon. His name is W. Bradley Gonsalves, a native of Kalamazoo, Michigan. To our pleasant surprise, when we arrived on campus to begin Fall Semester 1968, we were both assigned to live on 3S Floor of Holden Hall. In many ways we were unique, particularly since we had declared HRIM as our majors and completed the HRIM degree four years later, without ever changing our majors. After spending a decade in the hospitality industry, Brad is now a very successful special agent for Northwestern Mutual Life Insurance Company and he lives in Columbus, Indiana. He is the living testament of the flexibility inherent in an MSU-HRIM degree.

On many occasions, we have discussed Dr. Minor's positive influence on us even in the 1960s age of "shut it down" protests. One of Dr. Minor's basic principles is "Aim for the eagle, don't shoot for the rat." When I was appointed as the director of MSU-HRIM in 1988, Brad sent me a brass plate for my office wall that had inscribed on it: "You have hit the eagle, rather than shooting for the rat." I treasure that advice from Dr. Minor and that plaque from Brother Bill to this day.

My Initial Contact

Indicative of his lifetime commitment to quality, Dr. Minor wrote Dr. Blomstrom a letter in June of 1970 stating that "we failed to give the students what they need in the HRI 435 lab." HRI 435, in those days, was the capstone food production systems course. Dr. Minor noted that for five years (beginning in 1965), he had tried to have a chef appointed to the MSU-HRIM staff. He went on to write that the "lab program certainly does not fulfill the need for quantity food production training" and Dr. Minor recommended to Director Blomstrom that "A chef who is experienced in teaching, specifically Chef George Marchand, should be appointed." Dr. Minor also wrote: "I believe that unless we move in this direction, we're failing the School and students." Despite his ongoing urging, that appointment of a full-time chef faculty member was not to occur in MSU-HRIM until the early 1980s.

But I am getting ahead of myself and the chronology of Minor blessings in our School. As an undergraduate student, my first contact with Dr. Minor was when I enrolled for his HRI 245 course during Spring Term 1971. In those days, HRI 245 was called Food Production Technology and it was 5 credits, the same number of credits as College Algebra and Principles of Accounting at MSU; most courses were 4 credits. At the start of Spring Semester 1971, Brad Gonsalves and I and about 150 other HRIM students reported to Room 110 Anthony Hall for a 3:00 to 5:00 p.m. HRI 245 class. The class met on Wednesdays and Fridays.

As we sat in the room in anxious anticipation at a few minutes before 3:00 p.m., what could be described as an "army" of graduate assistants marched to the front of the room. Each carried what appeared to be a 10 foot stack of mimeographed materials. Then the legend... Dr. Minor... entered the room and it was so quiet that you could hear a pin drop in this vast lecture hall.

(Editor's Note: My congratulations for a best paragraph award to Dr. Cichy. I, too, was

in the class that day to meet Dr. Minor for the first time and can honestly verify that what he has just said is totally true!)

He began his lecture with his often repeated principle: "Aim for the eagle, don't shoot for the rat." Then with commander-like efficiency, he ordered his graduate assistants to distribute to each of us a foot-tall stack of mimeographed papers. This was the manuscript from his seminal book, <u>Food Service Science</u>, published later in the 1970s, as we were all to learn. Dr. Minor additionally assigned two of Dr. Kotschevar's books as required reading. He told us about his expectations of us in the course, including keeping a detailed notebook of notes from the guest speakers that he had invited. He informed us that the completeness of the notebooks would be part of our final grade in the course. He told us that before a guest speaker entered the room, some of us students (on a rotating basis) would be expected to sweep the floor and remove the trash with brooms and dust pans provided by Dr. Minor. Dr. Minor said that his mother had taught him long ago to "put your best foot forward."

Then the master launched into a lecture on the topic of food science and chemistry. Having had chemistry for two years in high school, I was barely able to keep up. I felt sorry for the others who had not had such background. At the close of the first class session, Dr. Minor lectured us on the ill effects of smoking. This topic was to be reinforced several times throughout the course. In those days, students and some professors even smoked during classes, but not in Dr. Minor's class. Two specific incidents will serve to illustrate his lifetime hatred for smoking.

During one class session in HRI 245, a campus instructional media student employee was operating a slide projector for a guest speaker. The student was obviously not an HRIM major and casually lit a cigarette during the guest speaker's presentation. We all thought to ourselves, "As soon as Dr. Minor sees the violator in the back of the room, he is in big trouble." Sure enough, Dr. Minor smelled the smoke, rose in his traditional seat in the front of the room, and lectured the student employee and all of us on the ill effects of smoking.

The other story is one about an MSU-HRIM professor who enjoyed smoking cigars. Dr. Minor was overheard on more than one occasion telling this colleague that a cigar has "a flame at one end and a fool at the other." The anti-smoking advice was regularly a part of Dr. Minor's lectures even before the U.S. Surgeon General had the courage to publicly proclaim the ill effects of smoking. While in the 1990s, with its focus on health and growth in popularity of smoke-free environments, it may be difficult to relate, Dr. Minor was decades ahead of his time in his preaching about the rights of non-smokers.

Brad Gonsalves and I and the other students in HRI 245 during Spring Term 1971 survived the rigors of Dr. Minor's high standards. But more importantly, we learned a great deal from Dr. Minor and his line-up of dedicated guest speakers. Even though we suspected that he knew more about the subject matter than his guest speakers would address or that Dr. Minor would admit, his philosophy was to bring in the experts. These experts added a diverse richness to our education as future hospitality leaders. We were also treated to Dr. Minor's personal philosophies, in addition to his extensive knowledge of food science and technology, in his classes. He explained how he operated the L. J. Minor Corporation by telling us the following, besides his often quoted "Business Aims":

> •   "A six thousand dollar investment had little to do with the ultimate success of the L. J. Minor Corporation. Money wasn't the deciding factor, faith was. Faith, Hope, and Charity, with God's help, with professional management, dedicated employees, great chefs, loyal customers, dependable suppliers, and with help and cooperation from the U. S. Government's Meat Inspection Department;"

Dr. Minor has always been an advocate for the important role that a qualified chef plays in the success of a place of hospitality. Two of his timeless lessons that he taught us in HRI 245 were the following:

> •   "An executive chef teaches students how to serve a good meal and make a profit at the same time. Students learn to respect the chef's knowledge. They come to recognize that to know about food production, you have to cook and have hands-on knowledge about food and people. They learn that the chef must have control - in buying, for example -- or the customer suffers;"

> •   "A chef also teaches how to work in limited kitchens. Architects, not chefs, design kitchens. A professional chef demonstrates the advantages and limitations of fresh, frozen, and convenience foods, how to control waste and run a clean operation, while focusing on quality."

And the lessons from Dr. Minor continued beyond the walls of the classroom. Often, I would visit him in his Eppley Center office during his office hours to ask his help in clarifying a confusing point in the reading material or lecture. While he would spend the first minutes of our meeting explaining in simple terms what I did not understand about the course material, he would spend much more time sharing his philosophies of business and life, in general. For example, I learned in his office the following:

> •   "The customer is smarter than you are;"
> •   "Quality is remembered long after the price is forgotten;"
> •   "Accuracy is the key to success;"

- "Be well heeled."

The last bit of wisdom was taught to Dr. Minor by his Irish mother. He explained that you should never appear in public wearing shoes that are worn in the heels. This tenet has served me well through the years. So has "You should go to work dressed like you don't need the job." Dr. Minor, always the impeccable dresser, showed us this lesson in both word and example. Personally, I have used these lessons in all phases of my personal life and professional career. And I also "survived" Dr. Minor's HRI 245 and earned a 4.0/4.0 in this 5 credit course.

Graduation, Work, and School

In June of 1972, I graduated from MSU-HRIM and accepted a position as the food and beverage manager at a small Northern Michigan hotel called the Chippewa Hotel. With only 50 guest rooms, the hotel did 80 percent of its annual gross revenues in food and beverage, consisting of an *a la carte* dining room, several banquet rooms, catering, and a show bar with live entertainment. Within 6 months, the hotel manager left and I was appointed the hotel manager at the young age of 22. During the next two years, I practiced what I learned from Dr. Minor and other professors at MSU, and successfully built a profitable place of hospitality. One of our basic operating principles was "The guest is smarter than we are. We must meet the guests' needs and exceed the guests' expectations." This was particularly important since much of our food and beverage business came from guests in the local community. During staff meetings, I would often hear Dr. Minor's words coming from my mouth as we continuously tried to improve quality and value.

While I was off managing a hotel, Dr. Minor continued teaching at MSU-HRIM. Typically, he taught two courses during both Fall and Spring Quarters. In addition to HRI 245, HRI 265 -- Food Production Standards -- was added to his course load. This course covered the necessary topics of nutrition and sanitation. He continued to also support the School financially. Even though he was an alumnus of MSU's Department of Food Science, he and Mrs. Minor joined the MSU Presidents Club (a $10,000 commitment) in 1974 with all donations designated for MSU-HRIM.

In July of 1976, Dr. Minor wrote a letter to Dr. Blomstrom, director of MSU-HRIM, to "pay tribute to my graduate assistants Mr. Brian Michelson and Mrs. Debbie Block who were both outstanding." He also wrote: "Mr. Joseph Koppel's contribution to the success of HRI 265 is also noteworthy. However, the entire effort would not have been fruitful without the constant help of my experienced secretary, Mrs. Todd. ...with your continued interest and help we'll be able to further improve the professional training of our growing student body." Dr. Minor has always been one to recognize the initiative and support of others.

In the fall of 1975, I returned to MSU to begin my MBA program in HRIM. One of the first professors that I met with was Dr. Minor. I mentioned that I thought I would like to explore college teaching as a career and he suggested that perhaps I could try teaching in the Hotel, Motel, and Food Program at Lansing Community College. He also suggested that I contact John Farris, a professor at L.C.C., and a former student of Dr. Minor. John Farris was most helpful and I taught HMF classes at L.C.C. for two years.

When developing my MBA course plan, I was permitted to take one 400 (senior) level course, in addition to the 800 level MBA courses. The course that I selected was HRI 455A, Food Flavor Evaluation, taught by Dr. Minor. I selected this 4-credit course because I knew that it had received rave reviews from the students who had taken it, because my teaching interest at that time was food courses and I felt the need to acquire as much knowledge in that area as possible, and because it was being taught by my favorite professor and one of my favorite human beings.

In the spring of 1976, I enrolled for HRI 455A and it was a challenging course, initially developed by Dr. Minor at the urging of Dr. Kotschevar. While Henry Barbour was the director of MSU-HRIM, a national conference was scheduled at MSU as a joint venture between MSU-HRIM and Food Science faculty. Attendees were from the foodservice field and speakers included Dr. Trout and others from the food science department as well as Dr. Minor. The flavor course, as we called it, had a unique blend of chemistry, food science, practical applications, guest speakers, and the Annual Minor Spring Picnic. I earned a 4.0/4.0 in Dr. Minor's Food Flavor Evaluation course.

Beginning in the mid-70s, Dr. and Mrs. Minor hosted an annual picnic at their farm home on Turner Street. After they moved to their Westchester address, the picnic was held at Francis Park. The picnic and all the details were coordinated by the students in HRI 455A. The menu was an outdoor barbecue, including hamburgers cooked on Dr. Minor's own invention, the vertical rotating broiler. The vertical rotating broiler was designed such that no drippings from the hamburgers came into contact with the cooking charcoal; this design avoided the formation of dangerous carcinogens. The vertical rotating broiler was a topic of conversation at each picnic. The guests realized that Dr. Minor practiced what he preached.

Guests at the annual picnic included faculty and staff members from MSU-HRIM, the Department of Food Science, chefs in Michigan, and various personal and professional friends of Dr. and Mrs. Minor. Volleyball, baseball, and horseshoes were always a part of the picnic. The Minors encouraged their guests to bring their children and the children enjoyed the festivities. Mrs. Minor seemed to delight in the presence of the children. As a former teacher and a current mother and grandmother, Mrs. Minor always seemed happiest when she was with the children. I noticed that she never referred to them as kids, but always called them children and treated them with the respect and dignity that they deserve. Mrs. Minor, in so many ways, is the quintessential parent and a fine example and role model for what is required of a loving, nurturing, and caring parent.

The picnic was a great deal of work, a fine learning experience in planning and delivering a special event, and fun as well. As a reward, Dr. Minor took all of us in the class on a rented MSU bus to the Detroit Athletic Club for lunch at his expense. We enjoyed cuisine that was out of this world, met the chef, and met the Executive Manager Mic Bossler, an alumnus of our School. That field trip was a most unique learning experience, since we were introduced to the requirements of a traditional, center city private club that many of us had read about but few had visited.

During my two-year MBA program, I regularly visited with Dr. Minor in his HRIM office. The discussion topics ranged from food production to personal topics. He continued to share his personal philosophies with me. One such philosophy was "eaten bread is soon forgotten," a principle that his mother had taught him. The point of the principle was that people soon forget what you do for them. I understood how important it was to frequently recognize and thank those who help and support you.

Also I heard the story of Dr. Minor's family and how his mother traveled alone via ship to the United States from Ireland when she was 16 years old. She started in the hospitality industry at the Mather Inn in Ishpeming, Michigan. I also heard about his father's love for fishing. Both of these facts, I am sure, influenced Dr. Minor's later interest in both the hospitality industry as a career and fishing as a hobby.

Dr. Minor also shared his grandfather's philosophies with me. One that I shall never forget is: "Since man to man is so unjust, I hardly know which one to trust. I've trusted many to my sorrow, so pay today and I'll trust tomorrow." I also heard many stories about Dr. Minor's undergraduate and graduate studies as well as his positions with Atlas Drop Forge, Kewpee's Cafeteria, LaChoy Chinese Foods Company, Owens-Illinois, McKay-Davis Company, and, of course, the L. J. Minor Corporation.

Dr. Minor was always keenly interested in my future. He regularly asked how my MBA studies were progressing, how my teaching position at L.C.C. was going, and how my position as a graduate academic advisor for undergraduate HRIM students in the College of Business Advisement Center was developing. When he saw that I needed a lift, he was always able to tell me a joke or two to lift my spirits before I left his office.

In the fall of 1976, I met with Dr. Minor to tell him that I had decided that, after I completed my MBA, I would pursue a Ph.D. at the University of Tennessee, since I had some success with teaching hospitality courses at L.C.C. and felt that an academic career was one I wanted to pursue. As soon as he heard about my plans, he said, "What's the matter with MSU, do we have fleas?" He suggested that I visit with Don Bell, visiting lecturer in MSU-HRIM who was pursuing his Ph.D. in MSU's Department of Food Science. Dr. Minor also suggested that I visit with the administration in Food Science to see what Ph.D. options were available for me at MSU.

Don Bell was a very popular teacher in MSU-HRIM and I knew him since I had taken the capstone course in Food Production Systems from him when I was an undergraduate HRIM student. He explained that he was able to tailor a Ph.D. program in food science and human nutrition with the help of Dr. Mary Zabik. He suggested that I talk with her. I met with Dr. Zabik, a professor of food science and human nutrition, and explained my interest in acquiring more knowledge in food science and human nutrition so that I could apply the information to teaching and research in hospitality management.

Together, with the input of Dr. Minor and the support of his friend Dr. Larry Dawson who was then the chairman of the Department of Food Science, we built a custom-designed Ph.D. program consisting of selected courses from both food science and human nutrition.

This customer-friendly approach to a Ph.D. program made me feel very good until I realized that I was to finish my MBA in spring of 1977 and immediately begin a sequence of courses for my Ph.D. program during Summer Term 1977. The sequence started with the CEM 130 - Introduction to Chemistry. Dr. Zabik strongly recommended that I take a chemistry sequence because I had not had a chemistry course since Dr. Minor's HRI 245 course in Spring of 1971.

Enrolling in CEM 130 during the summer of 1977, I discovered that the course was structured such that it never met. Instead, students learned the course in an independent learning format utilizing a text, a workbook, and a series of cassette audio tapes. Since I was commuting from Brighton, Michigan, each day and was on the road approximately one hour each way, I studied while driving by listening to the tapes. I earned a 3.5/4.0 in CEM 130.

During Fall Quarter 1977, I enrolled for CEM 131, the follow-up inorganic chemistry course which was taught using the same format. I earned a 4.0/4.0, largely due to my daily commuting/study time and Dr. Minor's encouragement. His main message to me during our office visits that quarter was "pace yourself. A Ph.D. program is a major commitment. Don't burn yourself out before completing the Ph.D." He also told me countless stories about his experiences as a graduate student at MSU.

In mentioning to Dr. Minor that I felt it was in my best interest to leave my teaching position at L.C.C., I said I still needed a source of income since I was largely self-supported. He said that he would talk to Dr. Blomstrom, the director of HRIM, and Don Bell, the HRIM faculty member who taught the food production courses in HRIM. During our next visit, Dr. Minor asked me to visit with Dr. Blomstrom. Dr. Blomstrom offered me a graduate assistantship with Don Bell in the food production course, which regularly planned and prepared specialty theme dinners for targeted groups. Another Minor blessing.

During Winter Quarter 1978, I took CEM 241 -- Organic Chemistry -- in a course at MSU with a live professor and a group of almost 300 students in a large lecture hall. In preparation for this course, during the Christmas break, I reread Dr. Minor's Food Service Science book. That strategy served me well since I earned a 3.0/4.0 in CEM 241. During the spring of 1978, I enrolled for BCH 401 -- a course called Basic Biochemistry at MSU. The class was huge, consisting mostly of pre-med and pre-vet senior students who had many chemistry courses as background. The course was taught via prerecorded video lectures on a large screen TV in a lecture hall in the Veterinary Medicine building that seated in excess of 500 students. That course was a major hurdle in my Ph.D. coursework, since my two previous degrees were in business with an HRIM major, and since I did not have the same extensive college-level chemistry background that the other students had. Additionally, I was not competing for the best grade in that course as a prerequisite to entering medical or veterinary school. BCH 401 was a struggle for me. I studied, made my own audio tapes that I listened to during my daily commute, prayed, and was able to "escape" that course by earning a 2.5/4.0. When I went to the Biochemistry building to learn my final grade, I was so pleased that I had passed the course that I literally kissed the building. I realized that I would never have to take another biochemistry course and that my grade trend line in chemistry courses since 1977 -- 3.5 - 4.0 - 3.0 - 2.5 -- indicated clearly that I should quit taking chemistry courses while I was still ahead.

Over the next two years, I finished my coursework for my Ph.D. degree and passed my Ph.D. comprehensive exams in Winter Quarter 1979. In the spring of 1980, I began my Ph.D. dissertation research by first visiting with Dr. Minor in his Eppley Center office. We discussed possible topics and I expressed my interest in researching the area of quality assurance. Dr. Minor suggested that I consider identifying a Food Science professor as the chair of my dissertation committee. He suggested that Dr. Nick Nicholas, whose area of expertise was quality assurance and statistical quality control, would be a good choice. I had already had two Ph.D. courses with Dr. Nicholas and felt that we could work together. It was a marvelous marriage in the sense that Dr. Nicholas had the expertise in quality assurance and statistical quality control while I had a keen interest in the application of those principles to the hospitality industry, and specifically a food and beverage organization. The challenge was to identify a company where we could do the research. Again, Dr. Minor came to the rescue.

Dr. Minor suggested that I contact Bill Morgan, a senior VP for the Elias Brothers organization and an alumnus of MSU-HRIM, and ask him if we could do the research in the Elias Brothers Company. The company was ideally suited for the research since it had a centralized company-owned commissary and over 150 individual restaurants. Bill Morgan agreed to help and we began researching an application of quality assurance principles in a commissary foodservice system during Spring Quarter 1980. The on-site research continued throughout both Summer Quarter 1980 and Fall Quarter 1980.

In tandem, I undertook a library search and literature review of quality assurance literature. This proved to be very time consuming. I was spending hundreds of hours in the library. It was fortuitous that one day I dropped by Dr. Minor's office and he asked me how my research was progressing. I explained my frustration with the library research and the sheer amount of time involved in the process since I had to spend hours in the library reading the literature and taking notes. Time was at a premium because by this point I had moved to Bellville, Michigan and was commuting a total of three hours each day. I said that being able to photocopy the articles and read them later would help tremendously. He asked: "What do you need? And how can I help?" I told him that I could use a small amount of money to buy nickels to use in the library's photocopying machine. He said that Nancy Clancy would send me a check for $50 from the L. J. Minor Corporation. Remembering the adage that "eaten bread is soon forgotten," I thanked Dr. Minor after receiving the first check. These checks, $50 per month, were mailed to me over the next year and helped tremendously in funding my Ph.D. research as well as typing the various drafts of my Ph.D. dissertation.

After I completed my Ph.D. coursework and dissertation research, it was time for my Ph.D. defense. My Ph.D. oral defense took place on April 28, 1981. All of my committee members were present, including Dr. Minor. A few days prior to my defense, Dr. Minor summoned me to his office to discuss my strategy during the defense. He started by sharing what had happened during his Ph.D. defense. He told me how he prayed before his defense. Dr. Minor said that, in many ways, a Ph.D. defense is a humbling experience. He suggested that if I did not know the answer to a question, I should simply say so, rather than trying to fake the answer. He advised that I should try to encourage interaction between my committee members during my defense as a way to deflect the pressure from me. Dr. Minor told me that after his Ph.D. defense, his major professor remarked: "Lew, you took longer to answer fewer questions than anyone that I know." Prior to my dissertation defense which began at 9:00 a.m. on April 28, 1981, I visited St. John's Catholic Student Parish and silently prayed for courage, wisdom, and perseverance. During my defense, which lasted almost two and one-half hours, I used Dr. Minor's strategies.

Then the moment of truth came when my major professor, Dr. Mary Zabik, asked me to leave the conference room so that the committee could determine my fate: pass, pass contingent on substantial revisions, or fail. This was the moment of truth in my mind. As I waited in the hallway for what seemed like hours (actually it was less than 15 minutes), I became more anxious to learn my fate. Then Dr. Zabik emerged from the conference room, extended her right hand to me, and said: "Congratulations, Dr. Cichy, you have passed your defense." I returned to the room, received a congratulatory handshake from each committee member, and asked them to sign the paperwork to indicate my successful completion of the defense and all requirements of the Ph.D. degree. The committee only asked me to correct four minor typographical errors in my dissertation prior to submitting the final copy.

When I left that meeting, I was flying high on Cloud Nine. All of the pain, work, and sacrifice over the past four years had paid off and I had completed my goal. That afternoon, I stopped by Dr. Minor's office for a debriefing. He greeted me with a warm "Dr. Cichy" and a handshake. I asked him what had taken the committee so long to discuss after I left the room and before Dr. Zabik emerged and congratulated me. He said: "We weren't discussing whether or not you had passed the defense. We dispensed with that topic in the first few minutes. Rather, I was telling a few jokes to the committee members while you waited in the hallway." I thought to myself: "Well, he told me in advance that this was in many ways a humbling experience. I'm almost certain that he wanted to make sure that was a lesson that I never forgot." I went through the graduate commencement exercises in June of 1981 and, afterwards, Dr. and Mrs. Minor hosted a luncheon at MSU's University Club for me and my family, HRIM faculty members, and friends. My mother created her famous chocolate cake with white icing and decorated it with a graduation theme. At the luncheon, Dr. Minor sang "My Mom" to my mother and it brought tears to her eyes and the eyes of many others in the room. The moment brought to mind the poem Dr. Minor had written about his own mother which went as follows:

My Mom
by Lewis J. Minor

Who ran to get me when I fell,
    and did some pretty story tell,
    and kissed the spot to make it well?
My Mom!

New Opportunities as Dr. Cichy

Dr. Blomstrom offered me an assistant professor's position in MSU-HRIM beginning Summer Quarter 1981 and I accepted. I was hired to teach HRI 245 -- Food Production Technology and HRI 265 -- Food Production Standards in the quarters that Dr. Minor was not on campus, as well as quantity food production, cost controls, and maintenance and engineering during other quarters. For a variety of reasons, both personal and professional, I left MSU-HRIM in the Summer of 1982 and accepted a position at the University of Denver's School of Hotel and Restaurant Management beginning Fall Quarter 1982. I also had offers from the University of New Orleans and Florida State University. Although he was saddened to see me leave MSU, Dr. Minor put me in touch with the Denver broker for the L. J. Minor Corporation, Bob Krump, and an L. J. Minor Corporation Chef, Jim Kosec, in Denver. The plan was to meet with these two gentlemen and have them help me get acquainted with other industry leaders in the Mile High City. The plan worked beautifully. Within a few short weeks of my arrival in Denver, I had met the key players in both the Chef's Association and the Restaurant Association, thanks to the help of Jim Kosec and Bob Krump. These two men turned out to be lifelong personal friends.

During my two-year position at the University of Denver, we successfully launched the HRM Masters of Business Administration degree and strengthened the undergraduate HRM degree by bringing a number of hospitality industry chefs and executives into my classes. For example, our purchasing class was largely made up of guest speakers addressing the various commodity groups, often with product samples that they brought in to share with students. I adapted the "guest speaker model" from Dr. Minor's MSU-HRIM classes to DU's HRM courses that I taught and the students applauded the change. Regularly, during each Fall and Spring Quarter when Dr. Minor was teaching HRI 265 at MSU, he would invite me to fly in for an expense paid (by the L. J. Minor Corporation) trip, including a lecture for his students on the topic of foodservice sanitation. It was a unique thrill to return to my alma mater in that capacity twice each year and it also gave me a chance to visit with Dr. and Mrs. Minor and my family. During these visits, Dr. Minor would usually ask me if I had long-term goals and if I had thought about what I wanted to do in the future. I told him that after spending time in both the Rocky Mountains and San Juan Mountains thinking about the future, I had decided that my goal was to be the director of a major (top 5) school of hospitality management by 1995. He suggested that I should be putting in place, right now, strategies to make that dream become a reality.

On December 1, 1982, I signed a contract with the Educational Institute of the American Hotel and Motel Association to write a book entitled <u>Sanitation Management: Strategies for Success.</u> I had researched the topic over the past six years and had taught a course several times on the topic, so I felt qualified to write this book. The contract called for the completed manuscript to be delivered by April 1983. When the book was published in early 1984, it contained the following dedication:

> "<u>Sanitation Management: Strategies for Success</u> is dedicated to Dr. Lewis J. Minor, founder of the L. J. Minor Corporation, Cleveland, Ohio, and Distinguished Visiting Professor in the School of Hotel, Restaurant and Institutional Management, Michigan State University. Dr. Minor has been my role model, teacher, mentor, and coach."

When the book was revised and published as <u>Sanitation Management</u>, Second Edition, in 1993, it contained the following dedication:

> "<u>Sanitation Management</u> is dedicated to Dr. Lewis J. and Mrs. Ruth E. Minor, founders of the L. J. Minor Corporation. Dr. Minor is Professor Emeritus of the School of Hotel, Restaurant and Institutional Management at Michigan State University. He taught the author and thousands of today's hospitality industry and education leaders the value of high standards with his classic statement: "Aim for the eagle, don't shoot for the rat.""

On July 13, 1983, Dr. Minor and I signed a contract with AVI Publishing Company, Inc. in Westport, Connecticut, to co-author a book titled <u>Foodservice Systems Management</u>. Almost in tandem, Brother Herman Zaccarelli, then director of the Purdue University Restaurant, Hotel, and Institutional Management Institute adopted the pre-published manuscript for the Institute's new professional cooking course. Because of delays in editing and production by the publisher, this book -- actually the first of mine to be prepared in manuscript form -- was my second book published in late 1984. The book was dedicated to "The future leaders of the hospitality industry -- apprentice chefs and students majoring in hotel and restaurant management." Considered a classic, our book is still on the market a decade after it was originally published.

In 1983, Dr. Minor was one of four industry leaders elected to the National Institute for the Foodservice Industry's College of Diplomates. I attended a champagne brunch with more than 400 industry leaders on May 22, 1983 to witness the induction at the Chicago Palmer House. Dr. Minor was recognized for his "extensive record of accomplishment in foodservice education." The program went on to note that "through his various activities and efforts, he has assisted students and restaurant operators for many years. Dr. Minor generously has provided scholarships and loan funds for students of foodservice education at colleges and culinary schools. A visiting professor at the School of Hotel, Restaurant and Institutional Management, Michigan State University, he has emphasized the need for and benefits of high standards of quality and service. As the author of numerous articles in scientific journals and through research and active participation in industry conferences, he has enlarged the product knowledge of restauranteurs. Dr. Minor also rendered important service to the U.S. Army Quartermaster Corps during World War II."

At this tenth annual ceremony, Dr. Minor was presented by Warren W. Rosenthal, president of the National Restaurant Association. When it was time for his response, after the induction, Dr. Minor told the audience an abbreviated story of his life and sang several Irish songs. There literally was not a dry eye in the audience when he completed his remarks and songs.

During the ceremony, as I sat in the audience with members of Dr. Minor's family, I reflected on the relationship that I had with this great man over the past dozen years. I felt blessed and fortunate indeed to have gotten to know Dr. Minor, both as a professor and as a person. In many ways, he was a friend and confidant, but also a role model. I came to the realization that few people go through life and have the opportunity to develop a relationship with another person such as my relationship with Lew. The relationship existed on many levels and planes of interaction. It was mutually beneficial and supportive. It is a relationship that is unique and one to be treasured.

Time Moves On with Rich Rewards

During the next year, several major changes took place in both Dr. Minor's and my lives. For health reasons, he decided to resign from his position at MSU-HRIM at the end of Spring Quarter 1984. Dr. Minor wrote to Dr. John Henderson, then acting director of MSU-HRIM, to inform him of his decision. Dr. Henderson wrote back to him on May 7, 1984 and the letter said: "The faculty at its meeting on April 30 voted unanimously that we postpone any decision regarding your intended resignation. Your value to HRIM, the University, and particularly the students, is so great that we would hope you would reconsider after you take off the academic year 1984-85. If after that time out for a rest, you could return in the 1985-86 academic year, the faculty and students would once again be the beneficiaries of your great talent and dedication to higher education."

Dr. Minor wrote to Acting Director Henderson on June 14, 1984 and said: "After receiving the faculty request, I've decided to take a year's leave and then return to teach again. My participation in the cardiac rehabilitation at Lansing General is producing satisfactory results. I'm feeling better now, and my heart is much stronger." In July 1984, College of Business Dean Richard Lewis wrote to Dr. Minor and said: "In reading the SIRS (Student Instructional Rating System) forms for Spring Term, we found the students in your 455A class so positive and enthusiastic... They were a pleasure to read. ...Congratulations, and thanks for doing such a good job with this class!"

But it was not meant to be... Spring Quarter 1984 marked the end of an era in our School. Dr. Minor had completed twenty years of teaching two courses each in Fall and Spring Quarters. His positive impact on today's hospitality industry and education leaders is still felt as hundreds of his former students occupy positions of prominence in both hospitality academia and the hospitality industry.

As was mentioned earlier, Dr. Minor was paid $4,000 to teach in 1964. By 1984, his salary from MSU-HRIM was slightly over $40,000 per year. I once told him that rumor had it that he taught his courses for $1 per year. He said that, in his view, he should be paid the same as a qualified tenured professor and to do less would lower the salaries for all.

But Dr. Minor gave away all of this salary and more to the MSU-HRIM School and other sources. For example, on September 16, 1983, he wrote to Don Smith, then director of MSU-HRIM: "Ruth and I are able to make this grant to HRIM as an expression of our appreciation of your commitment to improving the quality of the HRIM program... and hope to repeat this grant annually." The letter was accompanied by a check for $25,000 from Dr. Minor and a check for $25,000 from Mrs. Minor to be used for support of the HRIM professional Chef Robert Nelson's teaching initiatives. In addition to providing financial support for MSU-HRIM, Dr. and Mrs. Minor also contributed to the following organizations, associations, foundations, and institutions:

- American Culinary Federation
- American Culinary Federation Educational Institute
- Cornell University's School of Hotel Administration
- The Colonial Williamsburg Foundation
- Culinary Institute of America
- Indiana University
- Indiana University and Purdue University at Fort Wayne
- Johnson & Wales University
- The Margaret Kotschevar Memorial Fund
- Michigan Restaurant Association
- The National Institute for the Foodservice Industry (NIFI) Educational Fund
- The Order of The Golden Toque
- Purdue University Restaurant, Hotel, Institutional, and Tourism Management
- Rochester Institute of Technology
- Ryerson Institute
- Sullivan County Community College
- The William F. Harrah College of Hotel Administration at the University of Nevada-Las Vegas
- WKAR Educational Radio
- WKAR Educational Television
- And others

The impact of these two benefactors has been felt for decades throughout the hospitality industry and hospitality education.

In 1984, I interviewed at University of Massachusetts-Amherst, University of New Hampshire, and Boston University and had offers from all three hospitality programs. In 1984, I left DU's School of HRM and originally planned to move to Boston to accept an associate professor position at Boston University in their Hotel and Restaurant program in BU's Metro College. After careful consideration and a number of long conversations with Bob Krump, Jim Kosec, and, of course, Dr. Minor, I decided that for both personal and professional reasons I could not move to Boston. Instead, I drove to East Lansing via a circuitous route that took me from Denver to Tulsa, Oklahoma, to Lubbock, Texas, to Columbus, Indiana, to West Lafayette, Indiana, to East Lansing. Upon arrival in East Lansing, I visited with the publisher of my Sanitation Management: Strategies for Success book and was offered a position as the director of seminars and conferences. Before saying yes or no, I went up north to Manistee, Michigan, to visit my parents and think carefully about my next move while sitting on the shores of Lake Michigan.

After a period of soul searching, keeping in mind my goal of being the director of a major hospitality school by 1995, I decided it was advantageous to accept the offer of the Educational Institute of the American Hotel and Motel Association, located on MSU's campus. Beyond the pure positive energy level and excitement of the people in this organization, I believed that the move would help strengthen my portfolio of skills and contacts on the hotel side of the hospitality industry. Prior to leaving the University of Denver, my strengths (both academically and the majority of my work experiences) were on the foodservice side of the industry. Over the next four years at the Educational Institute, I was responsible for seminars and conferences, professional development, and the development of the award-winning Spirit of Hospitality guest services training program. I traveled hundreds of thousands of miles planning and delivering seminars and conferences in the United States, Canada, and Europe. I also regularly taught HRI 265 during Fall and Spring Quarters at MSU. And I came to know many hospitality industry executives in all segments of the industry. Of course, I stayed in touch with Dr. and Mrs. Minor.

My Job as Director

In the Fall of 1987, I was invited to apply for the director's position in the MSU-HRIM School. Even though my 1995 (then 7 years in the future based on my planning time line) goal was to be in such a position, I again found it necessary to do some soul searching. One of the individuals whom I asked for advice was Dr. Minor. He told me to apply and actively encouraged me to do so because he believed that I could do some good at the School. Then I spoke with Bob Krump, my dear friend in Denver, and he advised: "Be careful when you go after something that you think you want... you just might get it." I discussed the opportunity with many friends and family members, both inside and outside of the hospitality industry. My fiancee, Shelley Grange, and I had many conversations about this topic and what it would mean to us personally, given our September 10, 1988 wedding date.

One of the attractions of the MSU-HRIM position was that I would be more in control of my travel schedule. Another major factor was the opportunity help put the School back on track, given that it had experienced a great deal of controversy in the early and mid-1980s. I knew the MSU-HRIM faculty members from my past and current affiliations with them and sincerely believed that, together, we could make a positive difference in MSU-HRIM.

My decision to pursue the position and accept the nomination to apply was cemented during a conversation with Dr. and Mrs. Minor over lunch at the University Club. He said that it was his sincere belief that I could make a positive difference at MSU-HRIM. He also told me, as he has on several occasions, that he believed the faculty in the School were geniuses and were dedicated to helping reposition the School as a leader. Mrs. Minor agreed that my current travel schedule would not be conducive to sustaining and building a strong marriage and family. Following this luncheon, Shelley and I had a conversation and we decided to "go for it" and that I would apply for the MSU-HRIM director's position. From an initial field of over a dozen applicants, and after several interviews and months of waiting, I was offered the position and accepted it. My position as the director of and a full professor with tenure in the School of Hotel, Restaurant and Institutional Management at Michigan State University began in August of 1988.

In the first month, the MSU-HRIM faculty met, refocused the School's mission, developed a strategic plan, and brainstormed and prioritized five fund raising goals totaling $5 million over the next five years. The mission of the School of Hotel, Restaurant and Institutional Management, as defined by the faculty in August 1988, is to be the leader in hospitality education through teaching, research, and service. The mission, strategic plan, and prioritized fund raising goals were formally adopted by the MSU-HRIM faculty during the September 1988 faculty meeting. They were also endorsed by the MSU-HRIM Alumni Association Board of Directors during its Fall 1988 meeting.

(Editor's Note: As an alumni of MSU-HRIM, I must commend Dr. Cichy for accomplishing the many goals he has identified for our School. As the reader will learn in the next few pages, he, along with the excellent HRIM faculty, has repositioned the School to become the "leader in hospitality education through teaching, research, and service." We are all so proud of him and the job he has done!)

Our priority #1 fund raising goal was to open the MSU-HRIM state-of-the-art Food Production and Management Education Facility (FP&MEF) in Kellogg Center. That 8,200 square foot laboratory (triple the size of the original laboratory space) was talked about for many years, planned over a several year period, and was under construction in the Fall of 1988. While some advised that we could take another year or two to open the laboratory, it was my personal belief that we needed to open the labs as soon as possible to have a tangible and visible statement that our School was back on track and positioned again to become a leader. With a great deal of work, support from MSU's Provost and MSU-HRIM Alumni who make Presidents Club pledges to cover the $80,000 needed to complete the FP&MEF project, we opened the multi-million dollar Food Production and Management Education Facility on tax day, April 15, 1989. With the opening of this facility, which included a senior-level food production kitchen, a junior-level quantity food production kitchen, a 90-seat dining room, an executive conference room, and a 90-seat amphitheater classroom/demonstration kitchen, our first fund raising goal had been achieved in just eight short months after I joined the School as the director.

The second fund raising priority was to permanently endow the *Chef de Cuisine* faculty position in MSU-HRIM. Even though Chef Nelson had been a member of the MSU-HRIM faculty since 1981 when Dr. Minor brought him to our School, his salary was funded with "soft" money, not State of Michigan General Fund dollars. We all realized that if we expected a chef position to be permanent in the MSU-HRIM faculty, our only choice was to raise a $1,000,000 endowment, the interest of which would be used to fund the annual salary and benefits of the position. This goal was explained to Dr. and Mrs. Minor, MSU-HRIM Alumni and Faculty, and our School's distinguished industry friends. In the Fall of 1988, Dr. and Mrs. Minor pledged $250,000 to begin the endowment and delivered a check for $100,000 to the School.[1]

The check was presented to me; MSU-HRIM Professors Dr. Michael Kasavana, Chef Robert Nelson, Dr. Jack Ninemeier, Dr. Ray Schmidgall; and College of Business Dean Richard Lewis at a luncheon at the University Club. I made the statement that the $250,000 commitment was just one of the special contributions that the Minors have made to HRIM. Their ongoing financial support and their personal commitment to bringing world-renowned chefs and other experts to campus have been deeply appreciated. Our plan was to solicit the remaining $750,000 to complete the chef's position endowment from industry corporations, MSU-HRIM Alumni, and friends of our School. Dr. Minor put us in contact with several organizations who were beneficiaries of the talents of MSU graduates and were likely targets for solicitation.

Over the next three years, Dr. and Mrs. Minor paid the remaining $150,000 of the $250,000 pledge; the last payment was made in October of 1991. During the three-year period of the original pledge, we tried several strategies to complete the endowment. Because of the poor financial state of the hospitality industry in the late 1980s and early 1990s, we were unable to obtain commitments to complete the endowment of the chef's position. I traveled around the country and even to Vevey, Switzerland, to meet with the head of the Nestle Foundation but had no success. Times were tight both for MSU-HRIM Alumni and their companies and even though everyone that I spoke with acknowledged the high priority need for a permanent chef faculty position in our School, no one would step up and make the financial commitment. Alumni who were supporting MSU-HRIM were largely engaged in helping to pay back the FP&MEF labs loan.

In the spring of 1991, our School launched the MSU-HRIM Visiting Distinguished

Chefs Series, under the guidance of our chef faculty member Robert Nelson. The series was designed to bring prominent chefs to campus for a culinary demonstration as well as working side-by-side with HRI 345, <u>Quantity Food Production</u>, students in the FP&MEF laboratories. The first two chefs to participate in the series were Chef Michael L. Minor, Vice President - Professional Services, and Chef Frank A. Scherer, Executive Chef for the L. J. Minor Corporation. In his introductory remarks to the HRI 345 students, Chef Nelson said, "The L. J. Minor Corporation has had a strong relationship with the School for nearly three decades. It was Dr. Minor's leadership that first brought chefs to MSU." Chef Nelson went on to praise the link between business and education that Dr. Minor had fostered.[2] Throughout the years, many outstanding chefs have been invited to MSU and have brought their extensive culinary knowledge to campus in the MSU-HRIM Visiting Distinguished Chefs Series.

In the summer of 1991, Dr. and Mrs. Minor visited our home in Okemos, Michigan. We had just built and moved into this home and they joined us one evening for dessert. While Mrs. Minor and Shelley entertained and were entertained by our one-year old daughter Grace, Dr. Minor and I worked out the preliminary details for completion of the chef's endowment. He and Mrs. Minor offered to pledge an additional $750,000 over the next three years to complete the chef's position endowment. The next day, I met with the MSU Development Fund and the Dean of the College of Business to work out the details of the gift. It was Dr. and Mrs. Minor's request to keep the announcement of the gift confidential until January 10, 1992. Since Dr. and Mrs. Minor were making a pledge to complete the $1 million endowment after personally paying the initial $250,000 in the endowment, we formally named the position to be endowed: "The Dr. Lewis J. and Mrs. Ruth E. Minor School of HRIM *Chef de Cuisine*." Dr. and Mrs. Minor said they planned to present two checks -- each $125,000 -- to the School on January 10, 1992, and pay the remaining $500,000 to complete the endowment in installments of $250,000 per year. After many meetings with development, the dean, and Dr. and Mrs. Minor's attorney, we signed the agreement and began to plan the January 10, 1992 luncheon to announce the endowment.

The announcement of the endowment of the Dr. Lewis J. and Mrs. Ruth E. Minor School of HRIM *Chef de Cuisine* was made at a luncheon at the MSU University Club on January 10, 1992. Special guests included Dr. and Mrs. Minor, members of the Minor family, MSU-HRIM faculty members, executives and chefs from the L. J. Minor Corporation, the MSU-HRIM Hospitality Association student president, Brother Herman E. Zaccarelli, a representative from the American Culinary Federation, and MSU administrators including the MSU provost, College of Business dean, MSU housing and food services executives, and MSU development fund representatives. After an invocation by Brother Herman, the luncheon was served. Then Provost David Scott and College of Business Dean Richard Lewis thanked Dr. and Mrs. Minor. Provost Scott said that the endowment is "an outstanding gift to the University, which builds on a long tradition of outstanding gifts from Dr. and Mrs. Minor." Dean Lewis remarked: "If the road to excellence is a journey that's sometimes long and difficult, then thanks to the Minors that journey seems more like a rocket ride to the moon."[3]

Dr. Minor delivered an eloquent history of the L. J. Minor Corporation during his part of the program.[4] He reminded the audience that "Eaten bread is soon forgotten. We always know what's happening to our gifts here (MSU-HRIM). They keep us fully informed." I chose to highlight three reasons why the gift from Dr. and Mrs. Minor was important. I said: "The first is because it will help our School not simply move -- but rather leap toward achieving its mission. This endowment will establish our School as the first hospitality education school in the world that has faculty talent with a strong foundation in business, applications in hospitality management, and hands-on food production education by an endowed chef. The service component (of our mission) will also be addressed through lifelong education, Evening College, and community outreach programs presented by the chef. The second benefit will be for our students -- the future of this great industry called hospitality.

These students will understand "Who is the Chef?" as eloquently penned (November 4, 1979) by Dr. Minor and as practiced, internalized, and lived by the Dr. Lewis J. and Mrs. Ruth E. Minor School of HRIM *Chef de Cuisine* forever."

WHO IS THE CHEF?

Who is the chef and what are his goals?
A person of qualities rare and unique
Attuned to the kitchen - who works and controls
A myriad of functions of which we now speak.

Whose kitchen is clean with a sparkle and glow
For cleanliness holds first place in their hearts
The health of their patrons and safety they know
Transcends kitchen science and culinary arts.

They patiently tutor and train every cook
To be clean, safe and fast in preparing each meal
With the hands-on skills not learned from a book
But by practice, diligence, dedication and zeal.

They select each ingredient with caution and care
So that what they combine will result in the best
Although cost and production ideas are shared
Insuring that they may compete with the rest.

Preparation and garnish for them is the art
Focusing in on the final presentation
So their well-traveled guests may set them apart
As one of the best culinarians in the nation.

"Chef Nelson presents these principles in his food production classes. Additionally, as the faculty advisor of *Les Gourmets*, our annual dinner for parents, alumni, industry, and the community, he showcases the talents of our young people. As a faculty advisor of the student International Association of Culinary Professionals, he furthers the basic tenets of "Who Is The Chef?" And through his position as our School's Special Events Coordinator, he has hand-picked our elite corps of HRIM students called the Green Team who prepare and serve special events -- all with a focus on hospitality education. Chef Nelson's bottom-line emphasis complements other faculty members in our School.

"The third impact is on the global hospitality industry through the 6,000 distinguished alumni of our School who are in hospitality leadership positions around the world. With a firm foundation in food production management, our graduates will have many of the tools necessary to meet the pressing challenges of the rapidly evolving and diverse international hospitality industry. As future leaders, they will be prepared to solve today's problems and position their hospitality businesses with a vision for the future. On behalf of the MSU-HRIM Alumni Association and its Board of Directors, as well as the many hospitality companies that competitively recruit our students for internships and our graduates -- I express my appreciation to Dr. Lewis J. and Mrs. Ruth E. Minor."

The First Dr. Lewis J. and Mrs. Ruth E. Minor School of HRIM *Chef de Cuisine*

After my presentation, I officially announced the name of the endowment and appointed Chef Robert Nelson as the first Dr. Lewis J. and Mrs. Ruth E. Minor School of HRIM *Chef de Cuisine*. I also presented him with a monogrammed chef's coat with his name and title as well as new business cards. We gave Dr. and Mrs. Minor a framed hand-calligraphy of "Who Is The Chef?" We also videotaped the event to record it for posterity.

The Spring/Summer 1992 issue of the <u>MSU-HRIM Hospitality Leader</u>, a newsletter published semi-annually for the distinguished alumni and friends of MSU-HRIM, had six articles about this historic gift. The cover article featured Dr. and Mrs. Minor. "A Tradition of Giving" recorded Dr. and Mrs. Minor's history of philanthropy.[5] In "From Chemistry to Food Service Science," several MSU-HRIM Alumni, all former students of Dr. Minor, expressed their appreciation for the Minors.[6] An excerpt from that story follows:

In fact, a lot of HRIM graduates know what they're talking about thanks to Dr. Minor. His 20 years of teaching in the School of HRIM gave him the opportunity to influence the lives of many. "More than 1,000 present leaders in the international hospitality industry have been deeply touched by this great professor and view him as a role model, preacher of high standards, and a mentor," says Dr. Ron Cichy, director of the MSU School of HRIM.

Richard Brooks, Vice President of Rooms Management for Stouffer Hotels & Resorts, recalled how Dr. Minor brought "a high standard of excellence to the classroom. Perhaps most important, he had a sense of identification with his students which was communicated every day. He brought reality to the classroom and shared his experiences freely." Houston Striggow, managing director of United Restaurant Services, Inc., said that by bringing chefs into the classroom, Dr. Minor "provided his students with an appreciation for food and the foodservice industry."

Michael Zelski, Director of Technical Development for FEARN International, remembered how Dr. Minor "taught with a mix of theory and real-world experience that led to better understanding." Bennett Schwartz, Vice President of Harper & Associates, said that Dr. Minor "did not have to teach - he taught because he enjoyed it, and I enjoyed learning because of him." M.A. "Mic" Bossler, Executive Manager of the Detroit Athletic Club, summed up the feelings of Dr. Minor's former students when he said that, "I learned from Dr. Minor that in life great deeds are never done alone...there is always someone to thank. Thank you, Dr. Minor."

In another article, "Taking Stock of a Life," Dr. Minor recalled his personal and professional accomplishments.[7] He was pictured with Mrs. Minor and the L. J. Minor Corporation chefs in one photo and the L. J. Minor Corporation executives in another. In "Ruth Minor - A Partner in Every Sense," Dr. and Mrs. Minor were pictured with family members.[8] In this article, I remembered chefs visits to campus and the annual spring picnic and Mrs. Minor's role:

> Ruth's dedication extends beyond her husband and family, too. Dr. Ron Cichy, HRIM director, recalls how when Dr. Minor brought chefs to campus, Ruth was always there to host them. "At the annual picnic held at their house for many years, Ruth was more than hostess. She shepherded the students along, making sure they staged a successful event. And Ruth's unconditional support of her family has made her a model care-giver for people like me who are new parents ourselves."

In another article, "Chef Nelson -- Linking Industry with Academia," we reported the accomplishments of Chef Robert Nelson, the first Dr. Lewis J. and Mrs. Ruth E. Minor School of HRIM *Chef de Cuisine*.[9]

In this same issue of the newsletter, the president of the MSU-HRIM Alumni Association, John R. Weeman Jr. (MBA'79), thanked Dr. and Mrs. Minor in his column

579

titled, "Two Kinds of Opportunities" in the following way:[10]

> This has been quite a year. From my perspective, two events stand out - one that saw the realization of a major goal and another that opened up a whole vista of new, challenging goals.
>
> Few would doubt the significance of the first - Dr. Lewis J. and Mrs. Ruth E. Minor's gift of $1 million to endow the *Chef de Cuisine* position in the School of HRIM. You have been quick to recognize the importance of this event to the students of the School. Dan Mathews, Jr. (BA'66) called it "an extremely critical part of developing our industry's future leaders." Ray Dault (BA'50) called the Minors special people who have given "thousands of us a helping hand" and who now extend that "helping hand" to future generations of hospitality leaders.
>
> The generosity of the Minors will give future School of HRIM students the opportunity for a complete, well-rounded education. Their example inspires each of us to examine our own contributions. And that's where the second opportunity of this year comes in.

President John Weeman went on to describe the second opportunity as a way for MSU-HRIM Alumni to get involved with the MSU-HRIM Alumni Association's strategic plan and committee activities.

My column called <u>Future Vision</u> in this same issue was devoted to Dr. and Mrs. Minor; it was titled "Salute to the Supreme Benefactors."[11] It was written as follows:

> Once in a lifetime, a person has the good fortune to meet another person who epitomizes a genuine human being. The genuine human being is caring, empathetic, responsible, dependable, self-confident, loyal, helpful, courageous, and honest. Rarely are you blessed with meeting two genuine human beings in a lifetime. Our School and I, personally, are indeed fortunate and blessed to know two: Dr. Lewis J. and Mrs. Ruth E. Minor.
>
> They are living examples of the four foundations of leadership consistently identified in our research of leadership qualities of CEOs/presidents in the hospitality industry.
>
> They exemplify vision in a leader. They have brought professional chefs to our campus classrooms since the mid-60s. Many of us were students when Dr. Minor introduced chefs with names such as Burgermeister, Breithaupt, Caubet, and Marchand in our classes. They introduced us to these and other professional culinarians who taught us quality standards of food production. It was their goal to help our School be the first hospitality business major to have a full-time certified executive chef on our faculty. More than a decade ago, they willingly furnished financial assistance to bring

Chef Nelson to our faculty from the Minor Corporation.

They exemplify communication. Both Dr. and Mrs. Minor are first and foremost teachers. To be effective, a teacher must communicate believing that knowledge is to be shared, not hoarded. Dr. Minor invited industry experts into his classes to communicate the best and latest thinking about their individual topics of expertise. On many occasions, Dr. Minor has communicated with a song or a humorous anecdote about Murphy or O'Shea.

They exemplify trust. Both have tremendous character, integrity, and sensitivity for their fellow human beings. Our School's Supreme Benefactors have been honest, supportive, and freely giving of their emotional and financial support over the past 28 years. Dr. and Mrs. Minor and the Minor Family have trusted in and believed in our School.

They exemplify perseverance. They have been with us from the beginning of the focus on chefs at MSU. Our hospitality business graduates are better future industry leaders because of this focus. And Dr. and Mrs. Minor will be with us forever now that the School has a permanent endowed Dr. Lewis J. and Mrs. Ruth E. Minor School of HRIM *Chef de Cuisine*. Dr. Minor's philosophy of 'Aim for the Eagle, don't shoot for the Rat' has encouraged us to persevere in our leadership quest.

For all time, our School, its students and faculty, its 6,000 distinguished alumni, and its prominent industry friends will recognize these two leaders. Chef Nelson and those who follow in his footprints as the *Chef de Cuisine* are challenged to carry the name, philosophies, and exemplary leadership message of Dr. and Mrs. Minor forward forever. Here's to the future!

You realize that I compared the results of my leadership research with the many gifts from Dr. and Mrs. Minor. Once the $1,000,000 endowment gift from Dr. and Mrs. Minor was announced, they received several letters of appreciation from MSU administrators, MSU-HRIM distinguished friends, and MSU-HRIM Alumni. MSU President John DiBiaggio wrote: "Your generosity in fully endowing the Chef's position means a great deal to us and I know will immeasurably strengthen the School's educational programs. We share your pride in Chef Nelson and are especially proud that his position will now, and forever, be known as the 'Dr. Lewis J. and Mrs. Ruth E. Minor School of HRIM *Chef de Cuisine*.' This is a fitting tribute to you both for all you have done for the culinary arts and we are thankful that you have chosen to simultaneously honor MSU with your gift... on behalf of our faculty and students, you have my heartfelt thanks." James F. Rainey, Associate Dean for Academic Programs in the College of Business, wrote: "...thank you for your continuing strong support for our academic programs and students... I treasure your friendship... I hope that you continue to experience good health and prosperity for many years to come."

Dr. Robert W. McIntosh, MSU-HRIM Professor Emeritus of Tourism, wrote to me:

"This must be the largest gift ever given to a hotel school. And, certainly the largest ever by a faculty member! Such good news. Wonderful, generous, unselfish..." Dr. William Lazer, MSU Professor Emeritus of Marketing, wrote to the Minors: "You both have always been most supportive. That, to me, is your hallmark. Your continuing assistance, and that of other friends like you, has kept MSU's HRIM School at the forefront of university education for the hospitality industry. Your significant donation will help sustain the School's leadership role and further advance its commitment to maintaining excellence. As someone who has long admired your contributions to MSU's HRIM programs, I wanted to share my feelings on your signal gift." William F. McLaughlin, President of the L. J. Minor Corporation, wrote to me: "January 10th will be a great day for the university and we are very proud of Dr. Minor's generosity."

Several MSU-HRIM Alumni also wrote to Dr. and Mrs. Minor. Following are excerpts from some of their letters. John Anderson (BA'80), Manager of Compensation for Hyatt Hotels & Resorts, wrote: "As a graduate of the HRIM School and as a member of the MSU-HRIM Alumni Association, I would like to once again thank you for your generosity. Our School will continue to be the best as a result of your commitment." Richard Brooks (BA'69, MBA'72), Vice President of Rooms Management for Stouffer Hotels & Resorts, wrote: "For those who know you, the gift is not a surprise... While teaching, you brought a high standard of excellence to the classroom. You held high expectations for each of your students. When we completed your class, we had information which was useful and added to our professional skills... You brought reality to the classroom and shared your experiences freely... Your commitment to the School sets an example for us to follow..."

Dan Mathews, Jr. (BA'66), vice president of the MSU-HRIM Alumni Association and ARA Services, Inc. Vice President-Western Area, wrote: "It is your foresight that has allowed the HRIM School to continuously improve its programs. I want you to know I consider it an honor to know both of you..." John Mueller (BA'50), Director of Food Services for Carter Hawley Hale, wrote: "What a pleasure to learn of your faith in the continuation and strengthening of our wonderful Hotel, Restaurant and Institutional Management School at MSU... This effort will help buoy those of us out spreading the word and trying to reach our many alumni for their support... You two are an inspiration to all of us..." Alex Nicodemi (BA'73), Vice President-Food Services for Variety Vending & Foodservice, wrote: "How fortunate we are to have such generous and dedicated friends at MSU. As a former student of Dr. Minor's, I can also say that we are lucky to have such a warm individual in our company; you have always been there for us... Our students and industry will benefit by this cornerstone endowment." John O'Donnell (BA'69), General Manager of the Locust Club, wrote: "Your exceptional generosity is an unselfish manifestation of your belief in our profession and the goals of Michigan State's School of HRIM. As one of your former students, I'm not surprised!"

Don Payne (BA'65), owner of the Family Buggy Restaurants, Inc., wrote: "As a dedicated alumnus, Presidents Club member, and *Homo sapien* with green blood, I want you to know how appreciative and excited I am. It is a great day for the School." Ben Schwartz (BA'72), Vice President of Harper Associates, wrote: "Your endless contributions to the School have undoubtedly allowed MSU to move progressively toward the mission of being the leader of education in the hospitality industry. It has been almost 20 years since I attended your classes on campus at Michigan State, yet I still have fond memories." John R. Weeman, Jr. (MBA'79), President of the MSU-HRIM Alumni Association and Vice President of Hilton Hotels Corporation, wrote: "After all you've given over the years to MSU, not only of your financial resources, but of yourselves, this most recent commitment certainly exemplifies superior Spartan Spirit!... I never had the opportunity to take your course as an MBA-HRIM candidate, but the contribution you have made to thousands of students is part of MSU's heritage."

On March 12, 1992, our School hosted a tribute dinner for Dr. Lewis J. and Mrs. Ruth E. Minor in the MSU-HRIM Food Production and Management Education Facility dining room. The guests included former students and spouses, Minor family members, chefs, Minor Corporation executives, MSU-HRIM student leaders, MSU administrators, MSU-HRIM faculty members, friends of the Minor family, and Monsignor James Murray, pastor of St. Mary's Cathedral. After Monsignor Murray's inspirational invocation, I made the following opening remarks: "The Minor family has had a relationship with our School for over three decades. I have been blessed with a personal and professional relationship with this family for 22 years. Our School has had a mutually-beneficial relationship with the Minor Corporation since 1964 when Dr. Minor joined the School's faculty. Tonight, the alumni, faculty, students, and distinguished friends of our School gather to pay tribute to MSU-HRIM's first couple of hospitality ... Dr. Lewis J. and Mrs. Ruth E. Minor. Alumni around the globe tonight are pausing and remembering the contributions of this generous couple and family. A number of our distinguished alumni are with us in spirit and others are here tonight to say thank you to these two guardian angels -- The Supreme Benefactors of MSU-HRIM."

A number of letters were read from friends and former students who could not attend the tribute, including Dr. Lendal H. Kotschevar, Dan Mathews, Jr. (BA'66), Raymond A. Dault (BA'50), Dr. John Knight (BA'72), Dr. Robert Brymer (BA'72), John Anderson (BA'80), and Hugh A. Andrews (BA'71, MBA'72). Speakers who paid tribute to Dr. and Mrs. Minor in person that evening included Michael Zelski (BA'67), John Zehnder (BA'69), Michael Rooney (BA'71), R. Houston Striggow (BA'75), Professor Warren Sackler (BA'73), Richard Brooks (BA'69, MBA'72), and Dr. Ray Schmidgall.

The following story about the endowment was shared by myself with the audience:

It took us several months to discuss the details of the endowment of the Dr. Lewis J. and Mrs. Ruth E. Minor School of HRIM *Chef de Cuisine*. During that period, Dr. and Mrs. Minor and I met several times for lunch--at the University Club and at Sirko's Restaurant, had discussions over coffee at their dining room table in their home, and even discussed the gift when they visited our new home. It was hilarious. Our daughter, Grace, wanted to talk and play with these two new 'grandparents' and did play with Mrs. Minor-- while Dr. Minor and I discussed the gift to our School.

Through it all, I tried to figure out why Dr. and Mrs. Minor wanted to give a million dollars to our School. I discovered that it was not because of the recognition--for they have been recognized as industry leaders by many distinguished hospitality organizations and individuals worldwide. It was not for the need to financially support the School, the College, or the University--because they had been and are the supreme benefactors of our School, in their financial and emotional support over the past 28 years. It was not for any reasons other than two. The first reason, which was foremost in their minds-- both having been teachers and teachers, I might add, in the true sense of caring, sharing, and mentoring both to family as well as students. Their first reason for the million dollar endowment was for the MSU-HRIM students. For you see, the students are the primary reason why we are here. The students are the focus of our School's mission: to be the leader in hospitality education through teaching, research, and service.

The students are the living example of the Hospitality Association's mission to provide opportunity, guidance, and responsibility for future hospitality leaders. And the students are the reason for the MSU-HRIM Alumni Association's recently refocused mission: to provide active leadership in support of the mission of the School through membership participation, image enhancement, financial commitment, and promotion of interaction among students, faculty, alumni, and friends. The first reason behind their generosity was the MSU-HRIM students--the future of this great hospitality industry. In our book entitled - Foodservice Systems Management, published in 1984 by AVI Publishing Company, and authored by Dr. Minor and me, the dedication reads:

> "To the future leaders of the hospitality industry -
> apprentice chefs and students majoring in hotel
> and restaurant management."

The second reason for making this unselfish and nonselfserving gift was to stimulate others to follow their example. And it's working.

Dr. and Mrs. Minor... it's working! We are all very proud of your leadership by example and are forever indebted to you two and the Minor family for your tireless energy, unmatched commitment, and deep abiding faith and love. Where there is faith and love, there is hope. Hope that one day our School will achieve this noble mission which guides our course and is kept alive by generosity such as yours.

Next, we unveiled a special wall display in our dining room that is permanently present in our Food Production and Management Education Facility for all to see. The philosophy was penned by Dr. Minor on November 4, 1979. This philosophy is a tribute to chefs everywhere. Then I read "Who Is The Chef?" to all present. I told them that each had a copy of the philosophy on the cover of tonight's menu. I promised that the philosophy will be on display in our two FP&MEF kitchens and amphitheater classroom, as well as the School's Eppley Center offices.

Then I called Dr. and Mrs. Minor to the podium and presented a copy of the menu for the evening, matted in Irish Green and Spartan White for their home library. It had been signed by all guests and students present at this tribute dinner. All of us also signed additional copies of the menu from the tribute dinner which were later matted and framed and hung in the FP&MEF dining room. The evening closed with remarks from the first Dr. Lewis J. and Mrs. Ruth E. Minor School of HRIM *Chef de Cuisine* Robert Nelson and an introduction of the HRIM student management team and student staff members who planned, produced, and served the tribute dinner. As with the January 10, 1992 luncheon, the dinner and remarks were videotaped. After the dinner, I received separate warm thank you letters from both Dr. Minor and Mrs. Minor.

Over the next year, we continued to receive additional financial support from Dr. and Mrs. Minor. As they had for over a decade, they sent a donation each semester (MSU had now changed from the quarter to the semester system) so that we could purchase food supplies to use in the hands-on laboratory sessions of HRI 345, Quantity Food Production. Without this generous support, Chef Nelson would have been relegated to simply discussing food production with students. With the support, Chef Nelson was able to buy materials for his demonstrations, as well as the hands-on laboratory sessions for the students. Because of a regulation at MSU, we were not permitted to charge students a lab fee in this course, even though we had formally requested approval to charge a lab fee on several occasions from MSU's provost. These contributions made the difference in a quality food education for our students and Chef Nelson judiciously spent the funds to enhance their education in our School.

In the 1992-93 School year, our Visiting Distinguished Chefs Series really began to function at top speed. Chef Phyllis Flaherty Bologna, Executive Chef/National Account Development for General Foods USA Foodservice Division and a former Culinary Institute of America chef instructor, joined us on campus for three days.[12] Chef Denis F. Ellis, Executive Chef at the University of Notre Dame, also stayed for three days sharing his cruise ship, hotel, and college foodservice experiences.[13] We were impressed with the uncanny physical resemblance between Chef Ellis and the famous Chef Auguste Escoffier. Chef Clarke Bernier, Corporate Executive Chef for the L. J. Minor Corporation, shared his expertise in and techniques of sauce and soup making.[14] Chef Nelson also invited representatives of the MEISEL/SYSCO organization each semester to HRI 345 to do a can cutting and illustrate the distinction between real and perceived value and the role of value in customer satisfaction.[15]

On September 10, 1993, Dr. Minor was named the 1993 Departmental Outstanding Alumnus by the Department of Food Science at MSU.[16] He received the award in the Hannah Administration Building conference room and members of his family, friends, and faculty members were present to witness the presentation. It was an inspirational tribute for this 1964 Ph.D. in Food Science Alumnus. I was pleased to attend the ceremony as a alumnus of the same department at MSU.

In the early summer of 1993, Dr. John B Knight (BA'72) visited our School after accepting his position as the Director of the Hotel, Restaurant, and Tourism Management program at Indiana University and Purdue University at Fort Wayne, Indiana. John and I knew each other since 1971 when we were classmates in Dr. Minor's HRI 245. We discussed the need for an article about Dr. Minor and both expressed an interest in co-authoring the article. While we were together on campus, we assembled the research for the article and discussed how, ideally, we would like to have it published in The Cornell H.R.A. Quarterly. After many drafts and rewrites, the article titled "Lewis J. Minor: The Man, The Legend" was published in the February 1994 issue of The Cornell H.R.A. Quarterly,[17] and is reprinted in full in this text.

The Michael L. Minor Master of Science in Foodservice Management

In the summer of 1993, Lew and Ruth expressed an interest in possibly giving another major gift to MSU-HRIM. After a series of meetings and conversations with them, their attorney, the MSU provost and College of Business dean, MSU's development officer Paul Osterhout, and the MSU-HRIM faculty, we convened on November 4, 1993 for a luncheon in the FP&MEF dining room. Present for this historic occasion were MSU President Peter McPherson, MSU Provost Lou Anna Simon, MSU College of Business deans, MSU-HRIM faculty, MSU Development office executives, members of the Minor family, and faculty members and administrators from the Department of Food Science at MSU.

Prior to the luncheon, Dr. and Mrs. Minor told me that they were considering a dozen sources for this major gift, including MSU-HRIM. The gift was by no means a "given" for MSU-HRIM at that time; rather, we were competing with other organizations. Dr. Minor's vision was a culinary arts two-year degree program, supported by the endowment gift. I investigated the possibility of such an arrangement at MSU but was told by MSU's provost that a two-year degree was out of the question at MSU. The alternative that we members of the MSU-HRIM faculty, in consultation with several MSU-HRIM Alumni, proposed was an executive education culinary program with a bachelor's degree as a prerequisite for admission. This arrangement would meet Dr. Minor's "earn while you learn" criterion and would position the School in a market different from the two-year culinary arts degree-granting institutions. Negotiations for this new program took countless hours and meetings.

In my introductory remarks on November 4,1993, I said: "Thank you and welcome to a day that will go down in the history of the School of Hotel, Restaurant and Institutional Management, The Broad College, and Michigan State University as a day of celebration." Next I introduced MSU-HRIM Alumni Association President Jerry McVety (BA'67) and he led a toast for Dr. and Mrs. Minor with Dom Perignon, furnished by the MSU-HRIM Alumni Association of Southeastern Michigan.[18]

Continuing with my remarks, I said: "We are celebrating today because we have surpassed our goal of raising $5 million in 5 years for our School. When we as a faculty established that goal in the Fall of 1988, skeptics said 'No Way.' I am here to report to you today that as of November 1, 1993, we have raised $5.1 million in cash, in-kind, and additional commitments for the School of HRIM." I told the audience that 80 percent of the amount was raised for program and faculty endowments, the principal of which will be in our School forever. I also reminded them of the four priority fund raising goals.

- 1# priority - Completing the payoff ($80,000) on our multi-million dollar FP&MEF.

- #2 priority - Endowment of the Dr. Lewis J. and Mrs. Ruth E. Minor School of HRIM *Chef de Cuisine* - $1 million.

- #3 priority - Endowment of one or more named professors. The first, the Hilton Hotels Professor of Hospitality Financial Management, a position held by Dr. Ray Schmidgall resulted from a $500,000 gift.

- #4 priority - Complete endowment of the Student and Industry Resource Center. As of the end of October 1993, we have $552,943 in pledges (including $388,538 in cash received) toward the $1 million endowment. We need less than $450,000 to complete SIRC's essential endowment.

Continuing, I said: "And today, our School is announcing another historic event. Thanks to a $2 million gift from Dr. and Mrs. Minor, we will launch the Chef Michael L. Minor Culinary Professional Program during Fall 1994 Semester. This Culinary Professional Program will provide individuals with solid foundations of business-focused culinary management, techniques, and knowledge. The foundation is provided, in part, by two culinary internships, along with courses of study in executive education in the School of HRIM. The Chef Michael L. Minor Culinary Professional Program is designed to attract individuals who have completed their baccalaureate degrees in hospitality management or in other disciplines and are searching for additional education to move their careers on a fast track. Graduates of this post-baccalaureate program will find opportunities in positions leading to careers as executive chefs, foodservice entrepreneurs, foodservice executives, two-year hospitality educators, and corporate executive chefs. The program will be marketed as a fifth year program that enhances the School's image as the leader in hospitality education with a specific business management focus."

Then I introduced MSU Provost Lou Anna Simon who made remarks, including "Endowments can be measured in lifetimes." She pointed out that this gift will "provide a lasting commitment to HRIM excellence."

Before introducing MSU's 19th President - Peter McPherson, I said: "All of our accomplishments and many more were possible because of our School's mission: to be the leader in hospitality education through teaching, research, and service. Today, we again say thank you to Dr. and Mrs. Lewis J. Minor for their unmatched love and psychic and financial support for our School. Once again, Dr. and Mrs. Minor have unselfishly helped position our School as a leader...today and in the future. We are most grateful and appreciative of our Supreme Benefactors. It is with a great deal of gratitude and realization of the challenges before us that we accept this generous gift of $2,000,000 -- the largest single gift in our School's 66-year history. Thank you, Supreme Benefactors."

MSU President Peter McPherson praised the insight of the Minors, saying "this gift is in the true Spartan spirit of the School of HRIM - the School values excellence, and with the Minor's financial support the School can do something truly helpful for people so that they may be truly helpful to others."[19] After President McPherson's remarks, Dr. Minor was invited to the podium for his comments.

The MSU-HRIM Chef Michael L. Minor Culinary Professional Program was officially announced to all MSU-HRIM Alumni and distinguished friends in a special December 1993 issue of the <u>MSU-HRIM Hospitality Leader</u> newsletter. In this issue, we featured an article titled "New Program is Icing on MSU-HRIM Cake" and pictured Dr. and Mrs. Minor with their son, Chef Michael Minor, and Chef Robert Nelson, and several of our MSU-HRIM Green Team student chefs.[20] The article appears next in its entirety:

> The School of Hotel, Restaurant and Institutional Management advanced its position as a leader in hospitality education this past fall with the announcement of The MSU-HRIM Chef Michael L. Minor Culinary Professional Program. This "fifth year" executive education program provides professional, business-focused culinary management training for individuals with baccalaureate degrees seeking a competitive edge for their foodservice careers.
>
> At the request of Dr. and Mrs. Minor, the program is offered in tribute to Mrs. Evelyn Drake, former manager of the Kellogg Center Food Services; Mr. Robert Emerson, former general manager of the Kellogg Center; Dr.

Lendal Kotschevar, Professor Emeritus of MSU-HRIM, and Mrs. Margaret Kotschevar; Chef Michael L. Minor, Vice President of Professional Services for the L. J. Corporation; Chef Robert Nelson, the Dr. Lewis J. and Mrs. Ruth E. Minor School of HRIM *Chef de Cuisine*; Thomas Aloysius Ryan, former CEO of the L. J. Minor Corporation; and Dr. Ronald Cichy, Director and Professor of MSU-HRIM.

The School of Hotel, Restaurant and Institutional Management (HRIM) Chef Michael L. Minor Culinary Professional Program (CPP) is designed to provide professional experience in conjunction with executive education courses in culinary management for individuals with baccalaureate degrees in hospitality management and other disciplines. It is unique in its combination of hands-on training and intense, business-oriented foodservice instruction.

The focus of the program will be three-part, including instruction in business-oriented culinary professional management skills, techniques, and knowledge, to provide individuals with a solid and balanced educational foundation.

This foundation will be realized, in part, through the completion of two internships with cooperating hospitality businesses, providing a minimum of 800 hours of on-the-job training for participants - the opportunity, as Dr. Lewis J. Minor says, to "earn while you learn."

Internships are administered and monitored by the School of HRIM's Student and Industry Resource Center (SIRC). SIRC already serves as the School's unique network to bring students, alumni, and industry together.

The educational portion of the program consists of extensive study in specially-designed culinary-management courses in the School of HRIM. Participants will complete six MSU-HRIM executive education courses, including areas of study in advanced food and beverage management, menu planning and purchasing, food and beverage service, and culinary professional skills.

Applications for the first Culinary Professional Program will be accepted through July 1994, for the 1994 Fall Semester, which begins in August. All in all, participants will get the competitive edge they need to enter career paths as executive chefs, foodservice executives, foodservice entrepreneurs, two-year foodservice program educators, and corporate executives.

In order to ensure that The MSU-HRIM Chef Michael L. Minor Culinary Professional Program provides its participants the finest in culinary management training, the program will be reviewed and monitored by the CPP Program Advisory Council. The council consists of professional chefs and foodservice executives, MSU-HRIM Alumni and distinguished friends, and MSU-HRIM faculty. Council members are chosen on the basis of their professional experience and life-long commitment to the foodservice industry.

Chief among the advisory council's members is Chef Michael L. Minor, the Vice President of Professional Services for the L. J. Minor Corporation. Chef Minor has committed himself to providing participants the best professional culinary management training possible. Chef Minor will help the council to establish operating guidelines for the program, review curricular offerings, and monitor the internship opportunities made available to participants.

Other Council members include Chef Robert Nelson, The Dr. Lewis J. and Mrs. Ruth E. Minor School of HRIM *Chef de Cuisine*; H. Michael Rice (BA'76), Coordinator of Food Services for MSU; and Stephen Thompson (BA'87), Director of Catering for Inter-Continental Hotels. In addition, David R. Hatch (BA'72), vice president of Marketing for Restaura, Inc.; and Dr. Ron Cichy (BA'72, MBA'77), Director of the School, will help monitor the program's curriculum and placements.

A primary goal of the Culinary Professional Program is to create leaders in the culinary field. "It's been a great profession for me," says Chef Minor, "and I hope my involvement in this program will help me repay a portion of what I have received."

According to the U.S. Bureau of Labor Statistics, the opportunity to excel should exist for many. In the United States in 1990 there were more than 3 million positions for chefs, cooks, and kitchen workers, and an additional half million positions for restaurant and food service managers. The number of positions, coupled with a projected growth of 25% to 34% in the next twelve years, makes culinary foodservice one of the most potentially rewarding and secure career paths today.

With this in mind, the MSU School of HRIM seeks to provide talented and motivated individuals the professional training they need to realize their full potential. As Dr. Lewis J. Minor points out, "the Program is intended to help our graduates achieve jobs and happiness for many years to come."

The special edition of the newsletter also highlighted the career achievements of Chef Michael L. Minor, after whom the endowment was named, in an article titled "Who Is The Chef?". What follows is that article in its entirety:[21]

Few chefs today come with the glowing credentials of Chef Michael L. Minor, CEC. His glow because they are solid gold. When he graduated from the Greenbrier's Culinary Program, after a four and one-half year apprenticeship, Chef Minor received the Otto Gentsch gold medal awarded to the outstanding graduating apprentice.

Twice, Chef Minor has returned from the World Culinary Olympics bearing the fruits of victory. During the 1984 competition held in Frankfurt, Germany, Chef Minor managed the L. J. Minor Corporation team which won seven gold medals and one silver, making Minor's the first American food products company to win the Grand Gold Medal in the competition's 88-year history.

Chef Minor has been with the L. J. Minor Corporation since 1977. Today, he serves as the Vice President of Professional Services, and manages a team of three corporate chefs and 25 chef consultants in support of foodservice sales and marketing.

Prior to joining the Minor Corporation, Chef Minor served as *sous chef* of the Williamsburg Inn in Virginia, and was executive chef of the Deering-Milliken Research Corporation Guest House in South Carolina.

He completed his internship with the American Culinary Federation at the Greenbrier Hotel in White Springs, West Virginia, graduating as Class Valedictorian.

Chef Minor committed his full support to the Culinary Professional Program at its recent public announcement. "I promise you that the Program will be a great addition to the MSU-School of HRIM," he said. "As a member of the Advisory Council, I will be sure we all work hard to make the CPP successful."

Like the two previous special events (January 10, 1992 and March 12, 1992), this luncheon was videotaped. We were in the habit by then of sending copies of the videotape to members of the Minor family and selected chefs and chef organizations (e.g. American Culinary Federation), as well as retaining copies in our School.

After the announcement luncheon, we began the mountains of work required to launch the new program. The Chef Michael L. Minor Culinary Professional Program (CPP) Advisory Council (PAC) met during Spring 1994 to define the curriculum. One PAC meeting took place in January 1994 on campus; a second meeting took place during the National Restaurant Association Show in Chicago in May of 1994. We added members to the PAC and discussed ways to market the CPP, given the relatively short lead time to officially launch the CPP in August of 1994.

On January 15, 1994, the Board of Directors of the Honorable Order of the Golden Toque met on our campus. We hosted a dinner for this distinguished group and, in my opening remarks, I said: "On behalf of the School of Hotel, Restaurant and Institutional Management, faculty, students and our more than 7,000 alumni worldwide, welcome to Michigan State University. We extend our hospitality to the members of the Board of Directors of The Honorable Order of The Golden Toque -- an organization that stands for high standards of culinary professionalism. Your members have made outstanding

591

contributions to the culinary profession in education and culinary arts.

In short, it is fitting that we unveil this evening the permanent recognition of a program dedicated - like The Honorable Order of The Golden Toque is dedicated - to pursuit of excellence in culinary arts and sciences. The program that I am referring to is The MSU-HRIM Chef Michael L. Minor Culinary Professional Program. On November 4, 1993, after months of discussions, our School announced a $2 million gift -- the largest in its 67-year history -- by Dr. Lewis J. and Mrs. Ruth E. Minor. The endowment is designed to launch The MSU-HRIM Chef Michael L. Minor Culinary Professional Program. The goal is, as Dr. Minor has professed: "to help our graduates achieve jobs and happiness for many years to come." Unlike the more than 425 culinary arts programs in the United States and 22 other countries, The MSU-HRIM Chef Michael L. Minor Culinary Professional Program is unique. Our program is a post baccalaureate "fifth year" executive education course of study. It provides professional business-focused culinary management training for individuals seeking a competitive edge for their foodservice careers.

The program includes instruction in business-oriented culinary professional management skills, techniques, and knowledge - to provide individuals with a solid and balanced educational foundation. This foundation will be realized, in part, through the completion of two internships with cooperating hospitality businesses, providing a minimum of 800 hours of on-the-job training for participants - the opportunity, as Dr. Minor says, to "earn while you learn."

Internships are administered and monitored by the School of HRIM's Student and Industry Resource Center (SIRC). SIRC already serves as the School's unique network to bring students, alumni, and industry together. The educational portion of the program consists of extensive study in specially designed culinary-management courses in the School of HRIM. Participants will complete six MSU-HRIM executive education courses, including areas of study in advanced food and beverage management, menu planning and purchasing, food and beverage service, and culinary professional skills.

In order to ensure that The MSU-HRIM Chef Michael L. Minor Culinary Professional Program provides its participants the finest in culinary management training, the program will be reviewed and monitored by the Program Advisory Council. The council consists of professional chefs and foodservice executives, MSU-HRIM Alumni and distinguished friends, and MSU-HRIM faculty. Council members are chosen on the basis of their professional experience and life-long commitment to the foodservice industry. Chief among the advisory board's members is Chef Michael L. Minor, Vice President of Professional Services for the L. J. Minor Corporation. Chef Minor has committed himself to providing participants the best professional culinary management training possible."

Then I introduced Dr. Chef John Bandera, Grand Commander of The Honorable Order of The Golden Toque. Dr. Bandera announced that, during a Board of Directors meeting earlier in the day, the Board unanimously endorsed the new CPP.[22] What a thrill it was to hear those words from the leader of the Board of such a distinguished organization of chefs.

After thanking Dr. Bandera and the Board Members present, I continued with my remarks: "A vital ingredient of this new program is Chef Michael L. Minor. A primary goal of the Culinary Professional Program is to create leaders in the culinary field". "It's been a great profession for me," Chef Minor has said, "And I hope my involvement in this program will help me repay a portion of what I have received."

Chef Minor's comments centered around his career experiences in the culinary profession as well as the new CPP. After his remarks, I asked his help in unveiling a permanent recognition of the generosity of our Supreme Benefactors -- Dr. and Mrs. Minor, his parents. After we removed the green silk covering from the wall plaque, I officially dedicated the plaque and read the inscription: "The MSU-HRIM Chef Michael L. Minor Culinary Professional Program. Dr. Lewis J. Minor, Chef Michael L. Minor, Mrs. Ruth E. Minor. The program was established in November 1993 due to the generous contribution of $2 million from Dr. and Mrs. Minor. The executive education program provides professional, business-focused culinary management training. The program is established to pay tribute to the hospitality professionals listed below.

Mrs. Evelyn Drake, former manager, Kellogg Center Food Services. Mr. Robert Emerson, former general manager, Kellogg Center (present in the audience). Dr. Lendal Kotschevar, professor emeritus, MSU-HRIM, and Mrs. Margaret Kotschevar. Chef Robert Nelson, The Dr. Lewis J. and Mrs. Ruth E. Minor School of HRIM *Chef de Cuisine*. Dr. Thomas Aloysius Ryan, former CEO of the L. J. Minor Corporation. Chef Michael Minor, Vice President of Professional Services, L. J. Minor Corporation, and Dr. Ronald F. Cichy, Director and Professor, School of Hotel, Restaurant and Institutional Management - Michigan State University." I concluded by saying: "This plaque will stand as a permanent reminder of the intentions of our Supreme Benefactors -- Dr. and Mrs. Minor." Then I invited Dr. Minor to the podium to share with us some words of Irish wisdom. The special dinner ended with comments from Chef Nelson. As in previous such events, the entire evening's program was videotaped and widely distributed.

We also published three stories about the CPP in the Spring/Summer 1994 issue of the MSU-HRIM Hospitality Leader. One, titled "Toque of Excellence" highlighted The Honorable Order of The Golden Toque Board's meeting on our campus.[22] The second, titled "CPP Plaque Recognizes Minor Honorees," pictured the eight food service professionals who Dr. and Mrs. Minor had chosen to honor with the CPP.[23] The third, titled "God, Chefs, Michigan State" further explained the CPP.[24] A portion of this article was printed as follows:

The Minor's hope to inspire others to aspire to the philosophy expressed by Theodore M. Hesburgh, C.S.C., in his book God, Country, Notre Dame. Hesburgh wrote, "I believe that with faith in God, and in our fellow humans, we can aim for the heights of human endeavor, and that we can reach them, too. Optimism is often thwarted, hopes dashed, and faith threatened, but we will never know what heights we can achieve unless we try." In keeping with this spirit of optimism, the CPP's purpose is to create leaders in the culinary business by providing professional, business-oriented, technology-centered culinary management training for college graduates seeking a competitive edge for their foodservice careers.

The mission of the MSU-HRIM Chef Michael L. Minor Culinary Professional Program is to provide a practical, flexible, and dynamic culinary executive education program that integrates hospitality business management, culinary knowledge, and foodservice technology to create broadened career opportunities for its graduates.

In the Summer 1994 issue of Transacta, a College of Business publication, two stories were printed about the new CPP. In the first, titled "The Next Frontier in Culinary Education," I was correctly quoted as saying: "The present structure of the program is not etched in stone. We'll undoubtedly make changes in the years ahead. It's an evolutionary process. But the concept is sound -- and integration of the culinary, business, and technology aspects of the kitchen, exposing students to the innovations, the cutting edge. This concept, I believe, will substantially upgrade the foodservice industry both here and internationally."[25] In the second article, Chef Michael Minor was extensively profiled, the first time a chef had been featured in this publication for College of Business alumni.[26] We had finally arrived in the view of our colleagues in MSU's College of Business.

At the urging of Dr. and Mrs. Minor, the original CPP was transformed into a Master of Science in Foodservice Management. This change required a number of formal reviews and approvals at the School, the College and the University levels. These reviews and approvals were now required since the CPP (a non-degree, no credit executive program) was changed to a Master of Science in Foodservice Management (a degree, for-credit program).

In The School, the initial reviews took place after the draft curriculum was developed. The curriculum consisted of 30 credits of graduate coursework, including six credits of masters degree coursework from a selected list of Eli Broad Graduate School of Management courses, 12 credits of required masters degree coursework from The School's graduate courses, an additional six credits of independent study/work experience coursework from The School's graduate courses and six credits of electives, which may include three credits of The School's current topics course options.

The philosophy of our School has long been that hospitality is, first and foremost, a business and, secondly, a special type of business. With this philosophy in mind, The School's faculty developed the Masters Degree in Foodservice Management by integrating a strong business course core with a hospitality specialty course core. The concept was designed to provide students with advanced critical thinking, strong analytical and problem-solving skills, a macro approach to management and the opportunity to customize their academic pursuit, based on individual career goals.

The M.S. degree offers students the flexibility and opportunity to choose from

L. J. Minor Corporation, first official sponsor of the 1984 U.S. Culinary Olympics Team to the International Culinary Competition in Frankfurt, Germany.

Michael L. Minor with Jan Williams, Beverly DeLaney, and Ingolf Nitsch, September, 1980.

Current operating plant location of the L. J. Minor Corporation (reception area), 2621 West 25th Street, Cleveland, OH.

Janet H. Williams, Director of Research and Development and Quality Control Manager.

Outside laboratory testing (Accra Lab).

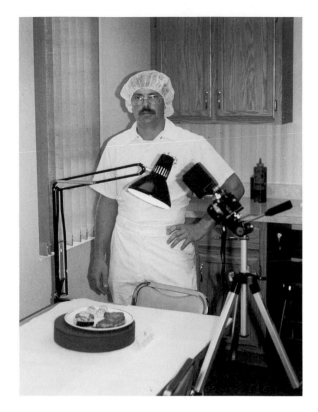

Beverly V. DeLaney.

Michael L. Minor practices for Culinary Olympics, September, 1980.

Durkee, Pearl Bedding, and "Taylor" Buildings, October, 1977.

Ruth Ann Fields, Operations Manager, receiving Key Employee Award with Michael L. Minor (brother) and Dorsey M. Fields (son).

Dr. and Mrs. Lewis J. Minor, opening of new offices at 436 Bulkley Building.

Durkee Building, used by R & D during remodeling of department.

Plant and office employees attending Research and Development (R & D) open house, December, 1979.

Blanca Nieves.

Blanca Nieves in Quality Control lab preparing product for taste-testing.

Blanca Nieves receiving Key Employee Award with William F. McLaughlin.

Quality Control lab with stored, measured control products; also products prepared for taste-testing.

Maureen Beyer.

Group of employees on break, October, 1978.

George Henderson.

Bart Katuscak.

Diana Katuscak.

Bridget Clancy-Bell

Dan Mullen.

Bill Weinmann.

Dean Hunt.

Bill Hoke.

Pan washer, with employee "Uncle Steve" pulling out clean stainless steel mixing bowl.

Tom Arthur.

Walter S. Nicholes.

**General John D. McLaughlin, President of L. J. Minor Corp-
oration, and Walter Nicholes, Advertising Manager, 1980.**

Hans J. Bueschkens.

Howard L. Schatz.

"House of Minor" wins Gold in 1980.

Michael L. Minor with Hans Bueschkens and other team members as winning presentations are being announced at the 1984 Culinary Olympics.

John G. Cassidy.

Paul Hamerly.

Dr. Lewis J. and Ruth E. Minor with Chef Robert H. Nelson and Dr. Ronald F. Cichy. Behind them are Provost David Scott and Dean Richard Lewis, January 10, 1992.

L. Edwin Brown.

Robert H. Nelson.

Chef Carl Richter.   **Dr. Ronald F. Cichy.**   **William F. McLaughlin.**

**Dr. Lewis J. and Ruth E. Minor with Chef Bill Lyman in HRIM
Food Demonstration Lab.**

Dr. Lewis J. and Ruth E. Minor $1,000,000 Outright Gift to Endow Chef's Position in School of HRIM at MSU, January 10, 1992. Included in photo, left to right: Edwina and Michael Minor, Rosalie Pontz, Lewis J. Minor, Josephine E. Minor, Ruth E. Minor, Carol Walker, Ruth Ann Minor Fields, Dorsey Fields, Brother Herman E. Zaccarelli.

Dr. Lewis J. and Ruth E, Minor Tribute Dinner, March, 1992. Pictured with the Minors are numerous HRIM alumni.

Dr. Sam Lee.

Dr. Lewis J. Minor at Tribute Dinner for Dr. Lewis J. and
Ruth E. Minor given by HRIM at Michigan State University,
March, 1992.

Dr. Lewis J. and Ruth E. Minor with Chef Michael L. Minor, November 4, 1993.
Taken in front of a portrait of Chef Auguste Escoffier in the HRIM/MSU
Food Lab Dining Facility.

Dr. Lewis J. and Ruth E. Minor with Chef Michael L. Minor, Chef Robert H.
Nelson, and the HRIM Green Team Students.

education and career tracks such as corporate foodservice management, entrepreneurial foodservice management, training, education, research and consulting. The flexibility of the M.S. is such that the program of study can be tailored to the individual student's needs.

Applicants must have an earned bachelor's degree from a recognized college or university, prior to admission. Areas of academic strength and scholastic performance are reviewed, particularly the last two years of undergraduate study. All M.S. candidates are required to take the Graduate Record Examinations Test (GRE). Test scores should reflect general verbal, quantitative and analytical aptitude, which are indicators of success in graduate school.

Work and experiences that demonstrate dedication and commitment are essential. These experiences should reflect the applicant's career goals and provide the applicant with the ability to relate to today's hospitality business issues and challenges. Employment history, record of activities, community services and letters of recommendation are all considered indicators of future promise. International students must take the Test of English as a Foreign Language (TOEFL).

The Master of Science in Foodservice Management is a very attractive program of graduate study because of the following:

- The foodservice industry now captures about 44 cents out of every dollar spent on food. The Bureau of Labor Statistics predicts that by 2005, jobs in foodservice management will jump by 44 percent.

- An advanced degree in foodservice management could lead to greater employment opportunities and faster foodservice industry advancement.

- The M.S. degree can be completed in one year on a full-time basis or in less than two years on a part-time basis.

- An advanced degree in foodservice management could advance the graduate's competitive edge over others entering the work force with bachelors degrees.

- The strong business focus of the M.S. is what many industry executives have identified as important in an M.S. degree.

- The M.S. degree program offers the opportunity to build a customized education program that is pertinent to the student's own professional goals.

- The faculty are world-renowned experts who conduct cutting-edge research and have authored leading hospitality textbooks and journal articles.

- The M.S. program offers flexibility in both study and career pursuits.

- The M.S. program can provide entry into industry training or college teaching.

After a great deal of study, discussion and planning, the Master of Science in Foodservice Management was unanimously approved by HRIM Faculty and Educational Policies Committees on March 27, 1995. Once approved, the next hurdle was The Broad College of Business faculty. On April 12, 1995, the M.S. was approved unanimously by the Broad College of Business Masters Programs Committee. Following that review and approval, on April 28, 1995, the M.S. in Foodservice Management received a unanimous vote of approval by the Broad College of Business and Graduate School of Management faculty. We were on a fast-track approval process, by comparison with other degree program approval timelines, due to the dedicated commitment of The School's faculty and Jim Henry, the Dean of The Eli Broad College.

The next set of approvals for the M.S. program was at the University level. The required forms were submitted during late Spring 1995 semester. Unfortunately, the University-level committees -- Subcommittee C of the University Curriculum Committee and the University Graduate Council -- were not scheduled to meet during the Summer 1995 semester. This delay frustrated all of us who had worked so diligently at such a fast pace to move the approval process along.

At the beginning of the Fall 1995 semester, significant changes were underway in our School. After forty years as the School of Hotel, Restaurant and Institutional Management, the faculty and alumni unanimously requested that our name be changed to The School of Hospitality Business. The new name was the unanimous choice of the faculty and alumni board of directors. On October 4, 1995, Provost Lou Anna K. Simon informed us that MSU President Peter McPherson had signed the approval to change our name.

In the meantime, due to a backlog of other graduate programs and the fact that the University-level committee met only once each month, there was no progress on the M.S. in Foodservice Management approval at the University level. By late Fall semester, the M.S. had not even been discussed by the required committees. The slow-paced process continued to frustrate us. We were reassured by The Broad College's Associate Dean for Academic Affairs, Jim Rainey, that we should continue with the development of curriculum and marketing materials for our intended M.S. launch in the Fall 1996 semester.

To honor a request by Dr. and Mrs. Minor, the M.S. in Foodservice Management officially became The Michael L. Minor Master of Science in Foodservice Management on February 27, 1996, after being approved by Dean Jim Henry, Director of Investments & Trusts, Nancy Elliott Craig, Provost Lou Anna K. Simon and me. With a mere three-day notice, we were asked to appear before the University's Graduate Council on March 11, 1996. Since I was in Colorado Springs for a Council on Hotel and Restaurant Training (CHART) meeting, Dr. Michael L. Kasavana of our faculty eloquently stated our case before the group of 20 University-level graduate faculty. When I received in my room at the Broadmoor Hotel the message that The Michael L. Minor Master of Science in Foodservice Management had won the unanimous approval of the University's Graduate

Council, I was elated.

The approval has been forwarded to the University Curriculum Committee and the Academic Council. Final approval took place on April 23, 1996, almost one year to the date after the program received unanimous Broad College Faculty approval.

The plan now calls for the launch of the program during Fall 1996 semester. Chef Michael L. Minor, whose name is now officially associated with the M.S., has had input into the program. Dr. Carl Borchgrevink, a faculty member in The School with an unmatched international foodservice background, has agreed to serve as the program director of The Michael L. Minor Master of Science in Foodservice Management. He is ideally suited for this position given his professional work experience, academic background and current areas of research interests.

In this chapter, I have attempted to highlight some of the many blessings that Dr. and Mrs. Lewis J. Minor have bestowed on our School since 1964. In the three decades from 1964 to 1994, these two have become the Guardian Angels and Supreme Benefactors of our School of Hospitality Business, in particular, and hospitality education, in general. We thank them, we applaud them, and we wish them many more years of health and happiness. The videotape of the January 15, 1994 program ended with the Irish song, "An Irishman's Dream" and this old Irish blessing:

> "May green be the grass you walk on,
> May blue be the skies above you,
> May pure be the joys that surround you,
> May true be the hearts that love you."

For all of the blessings that they have given to the School of Hospitality Business at Michigan State University, in the past and forever with the endowments they have established, our continued sincere prayers and best wishes are for them to experience their kind generosity returned in blessings that multiply many fold.

[1]   "Minors Honored," <u>MSU-HRIM Hospitality Leader</u>, (Fall/Winter 1988), p. 1.

[2]   "L. J. Minor Corporation Distinguished Chefs," <u>MSU-HRIM Hospitality Leader</u>, (Spring/Summer 1991), p. 6.

[3]   "Dr. Lewis J. and Mrs. Ruth E. Minor School of HRIM *Chef de Cuisine*, <u>MSU-HRIM Hospitality Leader</u>, (Spring/Summer 1992), p. 1.

[4]   "Lewis Minor: HRIM's Giant of Industry, Education, and Philanthropy," <u>Transacta</u>, (Winter/Spring 1992), pp. 6, 7.

[5]   "A Tradition of Giving," <u>MSU-HRIM Hospitality Leader</u>, (Spring/Summer 1992), p. 10.

[6]   "From Chemistry to Food Service Science," <u>MSU-HRIM Hospitality Leader</u>, (Spring/Summer 1992), p. 10.

[7]   "Taking Stock of a Life," <u>MSU-HRIM Hospitality Leader</u>, (Spring/Summer 1992), p. 11.

[8]   "Ruth Minor - A Partner in Every Sense," <u>MSU-HRIM Hospitality Leader</u>, (Spring/Summer 1992), p. 11.

[9]   "Chef Nelson -- Linking Industry With Academia," <u>MSU-HRIM Hospitality Leader</u>, (Spring/Summer 1992), p. 9.

[10]   John R. Weeman, "Two Kinds of Opportunities," <u>MSU-HRIM Hospitality Leader</u>, (Spring/Summer 1992), p. 2.

[11]   Ronald F. Cichy, "Future Vision: Salute to the Supreme Benefactors," <u>MSU-HRIM Hospitality Leader</u>, (Spring/Summer 1992), p. 2.

[12]   "Chef Bologna...First and Foremost a Teacher," <u>MSU-HRIM Hospitality Leader</u>, (Spring/Summer 1993), p. 13.

[13]   "Fighting Irish Chef Lends English Flavor," <u>MSU-HRIM Hospitality Leader</u>, (Spring/Summer 1993), p. 13.

[14]   "L. J. Minor Chef Demonstrates Soups and Sauces," <u>MSU-HRIM Hospitality Leader</u>, (Spring/Summer 1993), p. 14.

[15]   "Canny Performance Ensures MIESEL/SYSCO Quality," <u>MSU-HRIM Hospitality Leader</u>, (Spring/Summer 1993), p. 14.

[16]   "Minor Receives Major Recognition," <u>MSU-HRIM Hospitality Leader</u>, (Fall/Winter 1993), p. 18.

[17]   John B. Knight and Ronald F. Cichy, "Lewis J. Minor: The Man, The Legend," <u>The Cornell H.R.A. Quarterly</u>, (February 1994), pp. 90, 91, 92, 93, 94, 95.

[18]   "MSU-HRIM Exceeds $5 Million in 5 Years," <u>MSU-HRIM Hospitality Leader</u>, Special Edition, (December 1993), p. 1.

[19]   "A Legacy of Service," <u>MSU-HRIM Hospitality Leader</u>, Special Edition, (December 1993), p. 3.

[20]   "New Program is Icing on MSU-HRIM Cake," <u>MSU-HRIM Hospitality Leader</u>, Special Edition, (December 1993), p. 2.

[21]   "Who Is The Chef?" <u>MSU-HRIM Hospitality Leader</u>, Special Edition, (December 1993), p. 3.

[22]   "Toque of Excellence," <u>MSU-HRIM Hospitality Leader</u>, (Spring/Summer 1994), p. 13.

[23]   "CPP Plaque Recognizes Minor Honorees," <u>MSU-HRIM Hospitality Leader</u>, (Spring/Summer 1994), p. 13.

[24]   "God, Chefs, Michigan State," <u>MSU-HRIM Hospitality Leader</u>, (Spring/Summer 1994), p. 12.

   "The Next Frontier in Culinary Education," <u>Transacta</u>, (Summer 1994), pp. 11, 12, 13.

   "Chef Minor," <u>Transacta</u>, (Summer 1994), pp. 14, 15.

Chapter 50

Leadership In Reflection:

William F. McLaughlin

Dr. Sam Lee

A Letter from Dr. Sam H. Lee   **Comments by Dr. Sam H. Lee**

The Minor Corporation Plant Today

Conclusions

Time And Tide Waits For No Man   **The Best Things in Life**

(To begin this chapter, I am proud to present a Signature Article by Dr. Lewis J. Minor written for this book on November 23, 1994.)

Food Bases Replace Stock Pots
by Dr. Lewis J. Minor

Food Bases were introduced by the L. J. Minor Corporation in the 1950s, forty years ago, and since then have replaced the stock pot. What made this possible was the introduction to the chefs of America of Food Bases with flavor quality that matched the standard for "stock" that was set by the great French chef, Auguste Escoffier, who stated that "Stock is everything in cooking, at least in all good and well-flavored cooking. When one's stock is good the rest of the work is easy, when it is not, nothing worthwhile can be accomplished."

This standard was set 100 years ago. Today, with

Minor's Food Bases, chefs save space, energy, time, and labor by using these Bases to prepare Escoffier standard sauces by simply adding 5 gallons of boiling water to each pound of Food Base, whether it is Chicken, Beef, Fish, Lobster, or whatever.

The Tax Collector
(Irish Humor by Hal Roach)

The definition of a tax collector: "A person who has what it takes to take what you have."

Quote from Vernon Jarrett

"The health of the nation is periled if one man be oppressed."

Saving vs. Spending
by Lewis J. Minor

Always taking out of your account,
and never putting in,
You soon come to the bottom!

In 1982, Gen. McLaughlin negotiated a half million dollar loan that Mrs. Minor and I took from Central National Bank, Cleveland. Thus, after 31 consecutive years of manufacturing without using our business as collateral for a loan, we were forced to do it. We didn't like borrowing. My mother told me when I was a boy, "He who goes a-borrowing goes a-sorrowing."

Although John told us at a board meeting that getting this loan was a historic advance for our business, I didn't like our employees, or the business, or us to be burdened with paying the money back, and paying 12 percent interest annually for using it. This was $60,000 down the drain so far as I was concerned. Of course the government, our 50/50 business partner had to pay half of it.

Amicable relations seemed to come naturally between John and me. We were, in truth, Irish brothers. He kept the Irish flag beside the American flag in his office. John's patriotism was indisputable. He loved our country, and enjoyed his years of military service. He loved the L. J. Minor Corporation and wanted to fulfill Tom Ryan's prophecy that the location on West 25th Street, with the purchase of houses and businesses, and an apartment

601

which were contiguous to the existing plant, made this an ideal spot for a big company someday. Twenty years later, Tom's prediction had come true. Now the plant covers most of a city block with the employee parking lots included.

One time, when our business was in its infancy, Ray Beerend of Basic Seasonings Company in Cleveland said to me, "We'll buy your business from you when you run out of gas." After 31 years, with Mrs. Minor's and my health failing, I had to admit that I was running out of gas. I told John to sell the company to a reputable firm that would take care of our employees, and guard the quality "charisma" of the L. J. Minor products in the trade. In other words, find someone who will keep up and safeguard the quality.

We had some big companies anxious to make a deal with us. Walter Luftman, who was my old friend and Culinary Institute Board Chairman, was in the business of buying and selling companies. He told me he bought and sold Bally Corporation, a refrigeration equipment manufacturer serving foodservice clients.

When we sold the company in 1983 to an investment group from Connecticut, headed by Walter, sales had grown to $18 million per year. We received $13 million according to my secretary, Mrs. Minor. She said, "We gave $2 million to our employees, and paid the IRS $3 million in taxes. That left $8 million for us to invest. An interesting fact is that, since 1974, Mrs. Minor and I have paid about $10 million in taxes, in total. Like the man said, "You can only be sure of two things in life, death and taxes."

The "Peter Principle" had caught me in its trap. After I became a professor in the HRIM School at Michigan State University, and only gave one-half of my time to the business, my contribution to the business diminished, while others took over. I found myself doing less and less, but earning more and more.

The last couple of years that we owned the business my salary reached the phenomenal level of $150,000. Gen. McLaughlin complained that three or four sales people were getting $250,000 per year. He said that was wrong because I was the Chief Executive Officer of the company. He always said that, "The United States Government should honor me with a Distinguished Service Medal for the taxes we were paying."

In the same time period I had received a couple of very nice letters from those guest speakers who were effective in sharing their industry knowledge with the students in my classes. Two of those letters follow.

30 Sept. 1983

Dr. L. J. Minor
3018 Westchester Road
Lansing, MI 48906

Dear Lew:

Just wanted to report I think you have a great class. They were very attentive and took notes throughout the lecture. Miss McMillan and a second young lady were very helpful, please thank them for me. I had a most pleasant surprise when she handed me the two volumes of your books. I spent Thursday night looking them over, and replaced two books on my reference library shelf with those written by Lewis J. Minor. I thought you did an excellent job on Volume 2, many things in this volume will be of great help to me in the field. I thank you for my credits which appeared in Volume 1, sort of scary to see things and ideas on paper one has talked about. My father received such recognition in Tracy's book on ice cream and it was nice to feel I now stand beside him.

I will be very interested in what you found out at the Cleveland Clinic regarding Mrs. Minor. I have a great respect for this institution and have had friends who have been there and feel the same way. I mentioned my very dear friend Dr. Donald Effler who has been written up in several publications regarding his work with heart surgery. I sincerely hope the clinic proved to be helpful. Give Mrs. Minor our best regards.

Sincerely,

Worth Weed

National Sanitation Foundation

October 19, 1983

Dear Dr. Minor:

It was certainly a pleasure to meet with your HRI 265 group yesterday. I felt the presentation went well.

It was a distinct disappointment not to be able to visit with you as we had discussed. Dr. Ninemeier was very helpful.

I want to express my appreciation for the copies of the book. These will be treasured forever.

I certainly hope everything in Cleveland works to your advantage. Thank you and best regards. God bless.

Yours very truly,

D. L. Lancaster

After forming the investment group, buying L. J. Minor Corporation, and selling it four years later to Nestle, Walter Luftman said, "The L. J. Minor Corporation deal was the best I ever made." Luftman, McLaughlin, and James O'Neill were the Board of Directors for the investment group who purchased our business.

When we sold the company in 1983, Herman Taber dealt with Luftman's group to consummate the deal. John McLaughlin didn't want a finder's fee. He told me he would be taken care of by the purchasers.

They appointed him president. After about three years, the board elected Bill McLaughlin, the General's son, president, and he took over financial direction of the company from Ralph Napletana. Herman was dismissed from the new owners employ within six months. Ralph was retained longer so that Bill McLaughlin could learn all that he could from Ralph's great wisdom and knowledge of the company.

William F. McLaughlin, 42, joined the L. J. Minor Corporation in 1982 as vice president and controller, and was named president at the company's regular board meeting on October 30, 1986.

Mr. McLaughlin graduated from the United State Military Academy at West Point, New York, in 1972 and was commissioned in the Infantry. He served for five years with the 82nd Airborne Division at Fort Bragg, North Carolina, holding a variety of command and staff positions.

After completing advanced military schooling at Fort Benning, Georgia, Mr. McLaughlin completed his MBA degree at Syracuse University in 1979. He served his final years in the Army as an instructor in the Army Finance School, with the rank of major.

Soon after Mr. McLaughlin joined the Minor Corporation, he was given additional responsibilities of finance, administration, and manufacturing operations. Early in 1986, he assumed the broader role of executive vice president and chief operating officer.

In January, 1986, Mr. McLaughlin was first elected to the board of directors of the International Foodservice Manufacturers Association (IFMA). In January, 1987, he became a member of the Executive Committee and in 1990 served as IFMA Chairman.

He has also served as a member of the Advisory Board of the American Dietetic Association Foundation, as well as on the Board of the National Restaurant Association Educational Foundation. On May 28, 1988, he was awarded the honorary Doctor of Culinary Arts degree by Johnson & Wales University.

In August, 1989, he was awarded the prestigious Antonin Careme Medal by the Antonin Careme Society of the Chefs Association of the Pacific Coast, for his contribution and support to American culinary professionals.

Mr. McLaughlin lived with his wife, Diana, and their two sons, Eric and Brad, in Solon, Ohio, until recently, when he resigned from Nestle USA and joined Sweetheart Cup in Chicago. After we sold the company to our investment group headed by Walter Luftman, President of the Board of the Culinary Institute of America, we immediately gave two million to our key employees and plant personnel who had been with us more than ten years. Lawyers handling the sale said that no one they had ever dealt with before gave anything to their employees when they sold their business.

We wanted to do this. We felt that they helped us build our business, and deserved a reward for their years of faithful service above and beyond what their retirement benefits would give them. Some families bought homes. This made Mrs. Minor and me happy.

We have also been able to give, as the reader now knows, three million dollars to Michigan State's Hotel, Restaurant and Institutional Management School honoring several people. One million dollars as an outright gift and two million dollars were given as a Charitable Gift Annuity, which pays us interest until we both die.

We also gave one-half million to Johnson and Wales University, one-quarter million to Michigan State University's School of Food Science and Nutrition, which I graduated from, and one-quarter million to the Cleveland Clinic Foundation as Charitable Gift Annuities. This makes a total of four million. We estimate that we have given between one-half million and one million dollars to other charities.

In 1988 O'Neill, from the investment group that purchased the company from me, decided that he would ask Nestle if they'd like to buy the L. J. Minor Corporation. At his own expense he went to Switzerland and opened negotiations with Nestle's officers.

They had recently purchased Stouffer's. They appointed Jim Biggar, President of Stouffer's. He advised Nestle to purchase L. J. Minor Corporation.

Plant expansion has been tremendous since 1983. Just prior to the sale of the company we purchased a shipping plant that had been a bottling plant in Brecksville, Ohio. About 15 acres of land surrounding it went with it.

We had given Mike Zelski the assignment of finding us a suitable facility, and the one he found has been ideal. Several millions have been spent enlarging and equipping the plant on West 25th Street with new machinery and buildings.

In 1993, Nestle merged the Minor Corporation with FIDCO (Food Industry Development Company) to form FIS (Food Ingredient Specialties), a seasoning manufacturer which serves industrial customers. The Minor Corporation's total sales were about $68 million that year. Joining the separate divisions appeared to be a logical move for Nestle, but it was the end of the L. J. Minor Corporation's independence as a member of the Nestle USA Foodservice Division.

FIDCO moved to Cleveland, the Minor plants in Cleveland and Brecksville were expanded in a multi-million dollar building expansion. New laboratory and plant facilities were built to accommodate the FIDCO needs. Now, our son Michael, and grandson, Dorsey Fields, work under FIS management and its president, Dr. Sam Lee.

In 1987 John and Bill McLaughlin hired Dr. Sam Lee, food technologist, from Dole Pineapple Company to be in charge of research and development for the Minor Corporation.

Dr. Lee became president of FIDCO in 1992. Dr. Lee's letter and commentary, which follow, explain the merger of the L. J. Minor Corporation and FIDCO. Minor's industrial sales have been taken over by the new firm called Food Ingredient Specialties (FIS). Dr. Lee is president of this new company.

Connecticut based FIDCO's personnel have all been moved to Cleveland. Plant expansion will follow. Now, all that remains of the L. J. Minor Corporation is the foodservice business. Industrial sales have been transferred to the new company.

This merger is designed to strengthen both companies by adding a pure flavor research capability that L. J. Minor lacked, and an improved industrial sales opportunity that FIDCO needed. Change is the one constant with which we live. Thus, we can be sure not only of death and taxes, but change as well.

Our son, Michael Lewis Minor, is vice president in charge of professional services. He will travel away from home about 180 days in 1994. Dorsey Michael Fields, our grandson, is with FIDCO and is the Dallas-based district sales manager. He will travel an equal number of days this year. They are both making a good living with Nestle.

Both Michael and Dorsey are highly motivated, enthusiastic, and optimistic. With them, God comes first, the family second, and business third, just as it was with me. They are fine, talented, and dedicated human beings of whom we are very proud.

Here then are the items sent to me from Dr. Sam Lee, President of FIS, the company formed by merging the L. J. Minor Corporation and FIDCO.

A Letter from Dr. Sam H. Lee

March 31, 1994

Dr. L. J. Minor
3018 Westchester Road
Lansing, Michigan 48910

Dear Dr. Minor:

I am very glad to be back in the Cleveland area. It is good to be back with old friends even though I enjoyed my two year stay in Connecticut. I suppose that a corporate man should be ready for a next move with short notice.

As you probably know, Nestle, USA is going through many changes to stay competitive. As a part of the changes, The L. J. Minor Corporation and FIDCO merged into a new operating company named Food Ingredient Specialties, Inc. in early 1994. However, we are retaining the Minor Brand name for the foodservice market. The change is to maximize various business synergies between the two successful companies, while reducing business costs. I have been assigned this challenging responsibility. Both companies delivered good financial performances and bring unique capabilities.

Any change is difficult. We will do our best to keep the fine heritages of each company, and yet we have to break from the past to meet new business challenges.

Our business has been good so far. We just completed our strategic long term plan. Nestle is putting many millions of capital infusion to grow the company. The plan is full of exciting new initiatives to bring the company to a higher level. We also have many challenges - customers are increasingly sensitive to price increases; distributors are aggressive in pushing their own labels, and competition is getting more capable. Our management must keep morale and productivity high in the midst of changes. I realize this is easier said than done.

Dr. Minor, I will do my best to keep the tremendous heritage and image you and your team created at Minor's. We still have many fine employees who understand your business philosophy and foresight.

I hope you enjoy the early spring, and I hope to see you and your wife in good health sometime.

Wishing you a happy Easter!

Sam H. Lee
President

Comments by Dr. Sam H. Lee

In early 1987, I joined the L. J. Minor Corporation. At that time the company was making the transition from a small private company to a part of the world's largest food company, Nestle.

Naturally, employees were concerned whether the change would be for better or worse. Looking back, we can proudly say that the results speak for themselves. Over the years, we have grown steadily in sales and profits. With Nestle's support, Minor's invested over $20 MM into modernizing and expanding the Cleveland factory.

Nestle also benefited from the acquisition of the L. J. Minor Corporation. Besides the financial performance, Minor's has been the front-runner of total quality commitment and measurements, employee involvement, and empowerment, continuous process improvement, and customer satisfaction. In February, 1995, Nestle launched "1Nestle" which is a quality initiative that involves all business, all locations, all functions, all levels and all employees. Minor's rich foodservice culinary heritage has also influenced Nestle's use of chefs in their foodservice marketing programs.

How grateful I am for Dr. Minor's creativity and vision. The late Gen. John D. McLaughlin and his son, William McLaughlin, continued to build upon and strengthen Dr. Minor's vision. Brad Alford's tenure brought operational discipline to the company. The company will forever be grateful to these gentlemen, who preceded me as president, for

607

building and nurturing Minor's. They have created and fostered a legacy that has not only set the foundation for the L. J. Minor Corporation, but made an indelible mark in the culinary industry.

When I first walked into the company, I did not fully appreciate the intricate combination of art and science in making food flavor bases. Having had a technical background without much exposure to the culinary industry, I thought that all the employees were doing was simply cooking some meat, concentrating juices, and adding some seasonings before packaging. Additionally, I thought that chefs were opinionated and picky tasters. As I got to know more about our products, people, customers, and the importance of our culinary heritage, I was humbled every day. I began to understand the fine differences in flavor quality in certain cuts of meat, the impact of some proprietary ingredients on the overall flavor, and the importance of the ratios of ingredients. I came to realize that our products were a result of painstaking experimentation and enormous experience. These products are well balanced and carefully prepared to provide consistent quality products to our customers.

Dr. Minor's vision covers more than providing superior quality products. Minor's has built the business around culinary services which provide solutions to foodservice operators. Minor's bases have become synonymous with quality products and services in the industry. It is rewarding to hear from many culinary professionals about how our culinary support has helped them and improved their business.

The culinary industry is also thankful to Dr. Minor and other Minor's managers for their generous contribution to the culinary profession. I have heard countless stories from customers about Minor's determined work ethic, speed of customization, and depth of customer understanding. In short, customers are passionate about the L. J. Minor Corporation.

The corporate transition from a small private company has been a success story. Not only have we fulfilled Nestle's expectation for business growth and performance, but Nestle also has kept its promise to invest in growing the L. J. Minor Corporation. This has allowed us to continue to be the leader in the premium food base category. Our employees also enjoy the security of Nestle's financial umbrella. Being a part of the Nestle family has opened doors for our employees to a multitude of career opportunities for Minor employees within Nestle. My years at the L. J. Minor Corporation have allowed me to grow both professionally and personally.

My biggest challenge is to respect and continue to build upon the company's rich heritage while we move into a new era. We want to provide the best specialty food flavoring systems to solve our customers' problems. I believe that we are well prepared to take on the challenge with our heritage and business philosophies. We will work tirelessly to fulfill our customers' expectations of us.

The Minor Corporation Plant Today

The plant today is light years ahead of what we had. Invested millions have made the plant grow to occupy nearly a city block. Everything is computerized. The processing, labeling, packaging, and even the electricity - all are computerized. Plant and employee sanitation are "state of the art" and beyond. It has to be seen to be believed.

Besides the production facility, which is still located at 2621 West 25th Street, Cleveland, there is a shipping plant, which Mike Zelski originated, in Brecksville, Ohio, and offices located with Stouffer's at Solon, Ohio.

Today's Minor Corporation is a big company with several hundred employees. The future looks bright for these new partners in food seasoning development, manufacturing and sales.

Tom Ryan, Herman Taber, Ralph Napletana, Mike Zelski and I set the table for Gen. McLaughlin, who put together a highly efficient team in production and sales that carried the business to its current annual sales which are expected to reach seventy million plus this year.

L. J. Minor family members who helped build the business include Michael Minor, Ruth Ann Minor Fields, Josephine Minor, Mary Minor, and Carol Minor Walker our son and daughters. Grandson Dorsey Fields is a regional sales manager located in Dallas.

Bill McLaughlin skillfully guided the company's growth and profitability for 10 years from 1983 to 1993 with his father, Gen. McLaughlin's help and guidance. His corporate management team consisted of many people I barely knew. I'll list some of them from memory including Dick Zirbel, food scientist and plant manager; Scott Gundlak, finance director; Michael Minor, professional services director; Tom Hawley, personnel director; Nick Turk, quality assurance director; Sam Lee, food scientist and president; Tom Esposito, food scientist; Jan Williams, home economist and product description specialist; Walt Nicholes, advertising director; Dick Kennedy, sales manager; Paul Hamerly, marketing manager; Ingolf Nitsch, plant manager; Tom Arthur, engineering director; Ruth Ann, plant supervisor; Beverly DeLaney, raw material control manager and plant management assistant; Nancy Clancy, public relations and office manager, plus others, I do not know.

When Bill was moved to the main office of Nestle USA to become Fred Hall's assistant in charge of Nestle's Foodservice group of companies, Nestle made Brad Alford, a business manager, president of the Minor Corporation, a job he held, and did well at for one year. Now he has been moved to another Nestle company, and Dr. Sam Lee is President of FIS (Food Ingredient Systems), the management of Minor Corporation and FIDCO group.

Conclusions

My goal was to secure a lifetime estate for our family. With God's help we were able to get our health back, and now twelve years after selling the business we have accomplished that goal. In addition we have helped the chefs of American to whom we owe so much, plus schools, health foundations, and charities that we have set up memorials with for our parents, benefactors, and associates.

We're happy, and owe a debt of gratitude to Tom Ryan, Mike Zelski, Mike Minor, Herman Taber, Ralph Napletana, Ruth Ann Fields, General John D. McLaughlin, our loyal employees, our doctors who have kept us alive, our estate planner, Alan Claypool, and our Pastor, Monsignor James Murray of St. Mary's Cathedral, Lansing.

Doctors who treated us include: our family doctor, Thomas K. Jamieson; Doctors Frank, Lyne, DeLinn, and Tilden of Lansing General Hospital; Doctors Weakley and Falk of Cleveland Clinic; and Dr. Mercer of Lansing General, who put my pacemaker in. Others at the Cleveland Clinic who operated on my right-carotid artery and stomach in 1995 are Dr. Severn and Dr. Tom Rice.

We thank them and the children in five grade schools, the teens at Gilmour Academy, Cleveland and the priests and brothers at King's College.

Mr. James O'Neill of the Luftman Connecticut Investment Group, who bought the company, advised us to contact Scudder Investment Company, and we did. Herman Tabor went with us. Ruth and I each deposited funds in a dividend account and $2 million in a reinvestment account.

As the reader well knows, we have given $1 million to Michigan State's Hotel, Restaurant and Institutional Management School as an outright gift. We've also made outright gifts of $1 1/2 million for education, health, welfare, and other purposes.

In November, 1993, we each gave $1 1/2 million from our reinvestment accounts for Charitable Gift Annuities. These pay 8% interest until we both die. Two of these $3 million were used to establish The Michael L. Minor Master of Science in Foodservice Management at Michigan State's School of Hospitality Management. We also gave $250,000 to the Michigan State University Food Science Department. My dividend is given back to the Dean's Fund of the Hospitality School.

Time And Tide Wait For No Man

As my mother would say, "Time and tide wait for no man." This has become a truism in America of the '90s. Everything changes in life. We had car service then that gave jobs to young men and women. Now, you are trained by the large petroleum companies to do it yourself. Self-service is what we have now.

Today, we had a nine-inch deep snowfall here in Lansing where we maintain our home. This brought back childhood memories of Highland Park, Michigan, where I was raised. Back in the '20s, we had streets, sidewalks, and alleys that were paved with cement. The city tractors with large rotating brushes kept the sidewalks cleared of snow. When I reminisce, comparing what our way of living has become to what it was like when I was a boy, I wonder if the pell mell way of life we now lead is as good as the life we American people led then.

610

The public buildings, movie theaters, playgrounds, street safety, law enforcement, and police protection were better then. Nearly everyone could afford entertainment. There were free band concerts. Many of the beautiful churches built at that time have since been closed. The beautiful movie theaters are now taken over by "rinky dink" multiple screen movie houses that lack class and comfort.

The moral fiber of our people has been torn apart by drugs, the press, movies, magazines, TV and stage shows that promote depravity and violence. Corruption is rampant in government, schools, and even in so-called religion where infamous sects spring up all over our nation. The "rap" music and TV shows, as well as movies, are destructive of morals. AIDS is spreading like wildfire. Illegitimate births occur at an ever-increasing rate. Prisons are full. Justice favors the criminal more than the homeless.

Maybe Kruschév was right when he said, "We do not need to conquer the Americans; they are going to destroy themselves." Our chef, Ernst Koves, predicted that the crazy people would be running our country. Perhaps he was right.

Politicians have been responsible for lowering the quality standards of our society. Today, we are paying more and more for less and less. They are supposed to serve the people, but today we have let them make us their servants.

Our nation's debt is growing rapidly. We will soon be owned by other countries if this continues. Deficit spending today has become a way of life. We have gone from a debt free society to a debtor nation in less than twenty years. Congress did it. We need a "line item veto" by the President to control useless "Pork Barrel" spending.

Every year we allow 3-1/2 million legal immigrants into our country, who work to become citizens. Every year, some 13 million illegal immigrants have been arriving into our great country. We now have 30 million of these people with illegal Social Security cards, driver's licenses, birth certificates, etc., which they can buy from forgers for less than $100. They make them up quickly for they sell like hotcakes.

These immigrants, who now total about 50 million, steal jobs, welfare money, food stamps, housing, fuel and clothing. All given to them by our government. Tom Ryan would say, "Steal my purse or my wife, but do not steal my vote." With illegal aliens invading our country, voting, getting social security, welfare, and the whole works, how long can we bear these crosses? God only knows!

Politicians campaign on platforms of "creating jobs." They create no jobs, but are letting Political Action Committees buy their votes in order to send more jobs to the foreign workers in Asia, Mexico, the Orient, Israel (to whom we give most of our money each year). With our National Debt growing at a rate of more than one billion dollars per day, the amount of interest we must pay on our debt is growing rapidly.

The bottom line is higher and higher taxes and Social Security payments for our productive workers. This is extra money that is stolen every year from the Social Security Fund. Congress is selling out our jobs, stealing from our retirement fund, and levying higher and higher taxes. Now, nearly 50% of our workers work directly for the government at city, state, county, and federal levels!

We are forgetting that George Washington warned us: "Every government employee that you allow adds another mouth at your table to be fed, housed and clothed." This warning is being ignored.

Buildings in the downtown areas of our cities today are blasé and lack character and beauty when compared to the Golden Tower of the Fisher Building and its setting in Detroit, the Terminal Tower Building in Cleveland, the Chrysler Building, St. Patrick's Cathedral, and Rockefeller Center in New York City. Tom Ryan and I loved all of these and others including many of Cleveland's public buildings such as the library, post office, court house, terminal arcade, and Federal Reserve Building. We also liked the Wrigley Building, Chicago.

We must all pray for our nation. We must involve ourselves in the political process. The time has come to speak out and let our politicians know how we feel. Only as each of us accepts our public responsibility, and returns to the heritage that our forefathers left us in God, will this country once again be great. We must save the family.

The Best Things in Life

During the Great Depression, every Sunday we would listen to the famous radio priest, Father James A. Coughlin, Pastor, Shrine of the Little Flower in Royal Oak, Michigan. One Sunday, Father Coughlin said, "To live, man needs food, fuel, clothing, and shelter." These are the basic necessities, but like most men and women, I need much more than this. Now I'll try to list the things I need to function properly besides the fundamentals of food, fuel, clothing and shelter.

Religion, belief in a Supreme Being, freedom with discipline, law and order, love and friendship. To me a husband and wife must be best friends. I needed ducation, all through my existence. Family, children, grandchildren, and great grandchildren can make a man and woman proud and happy if they are good.

Sports, mainly baseball, golf, tennis, and track are a few of my favorites. I feel that boxing should be banned and athletes who deliberately injure competitors should be disqualified, fined, and barred from competing for all time. Football, next to boxing, is the worst.

Swimming is a great exercise. I like to swim in the Caribbean sea. It's the right temperature in February, about 76 degrees, and is usually not too rough. I like good entertainment, the big bands, Nat King Cole, Bing Crosby, Fred Astaire, Sammy Davis, Judy Garland, Mickey Rooney, John Wayne, Maureen O'Hara, Victor McLaughlin, Anthony Quinn, Irene Dunn, Walter Pidgeon, Cary Grant, Doris Day, Rock Hudson, Haley Mills, Frederic March, James Cagney, Edward G. Robinson, Walter Huston, Lionel Barrymore, Katherine Hepburn, and Spencer Tracy.

Memories are great, especially happy memories, like those of my Mother, Dad, brothers, sister, friends, and some relations like Aunt Winnie who has written to our family, now and then, letters like this one I received back in 1988:

March 17, 1988

Mesa, AZ
82 degrees and sunny but windy

Dear folks:

Have a lovely "Patty's Day." Hope and pray you are all fine, but it worried me when Kathleen (Fargo) mentioned that Lewis was ill. Hope she was mistaken and if he is ill, I shall storm Heaven with my prayers for him for a complete recovery. Seems only yesterday in Harbor Beach, MI where Lewis was born in his grandfather's spacious house where his mom and dad were living at the time and the hustle and bustle at the house at the time of his birth! My mother, Kathleen, was there (his grandmother) and they sent me upstairs as my sister Kathleen was in the first floor bedroom and they wanted me out of the way. I can still hear sister Kathleen's cries of pain while my mother Kathleen was saying her rosary at the top of her voice, while the Dr. and midwife were doing all they could and at long last when Lewis finally arrived, their fears all turned to joy and laughter as they were "cleaning up." Then my mother came up to tell me that it was a dear little baby boy and I could come down now to see him. Wasn't that all just <u>yesterday</u>??

Alas - how time does fly and we wake up one morning and find out that we are old and frail and where has life gone?

Kathleen Beeson calls me every week from Fargo. Thank God for her, but what a cross to have to carry with her husband Bill in a wheelchair since 1985. She had 7 kids all loving and caring, so she is blessed. Her mother Elizabeth (called Lill) has been in a nursing home for years now and she must be 96 or 97 - and just a vegetable. Why, oh, why, does God let her hang on so long? Only He knows.

Larry and I are ill and weak, but we keep on going anyway. God has been very good to us always - and we do thank Him.

A friend from Texas will fly in and drive us home to St. Paul, Minnesota. He drove us down last fall. We both must have surgery on our eyes in May. Hope and pray that all is well with you folks. Would love to hear from you anytime. We leave here April 9 to arrive home April 12th. God Bless dears and be real good to yourselves.

Fondly - Winnie & Larry

Looking back on my life, I thank my father and mother; my wonderful mate, my wife Ruth; my teachers who helped inspire and encourage me; Pat Ryan who gave me my first job; French Jenkins of LaChoy Chinese Food Company; Dr. Olin Ball, Owens Illinois Can Company; Tom and John Donofrio of McKay-Davis Company; George Ross, George Jenks, Jerry Jenks, Al Redfield and Jack Scranton of Huron Milling Company; my second cousin and partner, Tom Ryan; Mary Mele, Nancy Clancy, Mike Zelski, Mike Minor, our daughters, Kathleen, Ruth Ann, Josephine, Mary, and Carol who worked for L. J. Minor Corporation, and Rosalie who didn't get the chance; our dear son Bryan who passed away;

All of the loyal employees who worked in the plant and office for us; my graduate assistants at school, John Graffmeyer, Ingolf Nitsch, Dante Lavelli, Gary Shingler, Bob Brymer, Julie Kotschevar; my colleagues who taught at MSU's HRIM school when I did, Dr. Lendal Kotschevar, Dr. Ronald F. Cichy, Dr. Michael Kasavana, Dr. Raymond Schmidgall, Dr. John Birchfield and Dr. Jack Ninemeier; Chef Robert Nelson, Robert McIntosh and Ed Kazerian; Deans Barbour, Blomstrom, Borsenik, and Smith.

Also my colleagues, Dr. Frederick Fabian, Dr. Malcolm G. Trout, Dr. Bernard Schweigert, Dr. Charles M. Stine, Dr. A.M. Pearson, Dr. Robert Brunner, Dr. Lawrence Dawson, Dr. Leroy Dugan, and Dr. Vincent Hegerty of MSU's Food Science Department.

Chefs Jean Caubet, August Erb, John Secter, Ernest Koves, Carl Richter, Hans Bueschkens, George Marchand, Romeo Lupinacci, Charles Camerano, Sylvino Trompetto, Victor Ceserani, Louis Szathmary, Richard Bosnjak, Jack Sullivan, Pierre Bacque, Herman Breithaupt, Eugene Blumenschein, Emil Burgermeister, James Edwards, Hermann Rusch, Roberto Geaometta, James Kosec, William Lyman, Joseph Amendola, Jean Solomon, Wolfgang Bierer, Frank Scherer, Walter Herman, Clark Bernier, Socrates Inonog, Christian Inden, Ferdinand Metz, Edwin Brown, Arthur Jones, Walter Heller, Warren LeRuth, Jean Cleary, Henry Frank, Milos Cihelka, Richard Benson, Donald Benson, Robert Nelson, William Nelson, Amato Ferrero, Alec Cline, Rene Roncari, Willy Rossel, Otto Denkinger, Louis Bartenbach, Harry Bazan, Herman Leis, Fritz Sonnenschmidt, Oliver Sommer, Roland Swerger, Richard Tromposch, Bruno Zuchold, Joe Vislocky, Thomas Wright, John Yena, Morris Gaebe, Bernard Urban, Johnny Rivers Sr., Hans Roth, Thomas Hickey, Paul Goebel, Edward Gerstung, Robert Lippert, John Ferris, John Kempf, Jon Greenwalt, Robert Werth, John Bandera, Noel Cullen, Nicholas Colletti, John Folse, John Carroll, Robert Ehlers, Michael Minor, Ingolf Nitsch, John Zhender, James Muir, John Stewart, Al Marcello, Baron Galand, Alfred Saarne, Pancho Valez, Michael Palmer, Joseph Pawlitsch, Hans Roth, John Todd, Walter Wingberg, Charles Altorfer, John DeJohn, Al Mahlke, Viktor Baker, Richard Walklete, "Tony" Takashi Murakani, Christina Bayer, Dieter Kiessling, Bill Dela Vantura, Hans Herzig, Saburo Shibonuna, and Paul Ebling are some of our multitudinous friends among the chefs of America and the world. The Minor Corporation probably would not have been successful in sales had it not been for the chefs who helped us through the years.

Now, 45 years later, Michael Minor's professional group of chefs and chef consultants are carrying on that same tradition today. The following is a list of current chefs associated with Minors: Scott Gilbert, Michael Manista, Mario Reyes, William Franklin, Major

Jarmon, Chuck Brower, Marilyn Murphy, Jack Braun, Maurice Fitzgerald, Jim Miller, John Blaze, John Ricci, Claude Lambertz, Mike Howard, and Robert Nograd.

We enjoy living with our children, grandchildren, great grandchildren, friends and neighbors. We are people who need people and value our friends. Life is a game of helping others. Tom Ryan used to tell me when I was teaching, "Man cannot stand defeat." He was so right. I was just lucky to have two great men in business with me. Our young team of Mike Zelski, Mike Minor, Tom Arthur, Ruth Ann, Dorsey Fields, and Ingolf Nitsch were great too -- all of them.

> Fairy tales do come true,
> It can happen to you,
> If you're young at heart.

We cast our little bit of bread on the waters of business, and by hard work, dedication to purpose, and mainly with faith, it came back sandwiches. We gave the world the best we had and the best came back to us.

I'd like to make one thing clear to those who read and, I hope, enjoy this book. While you have a business you may be rich in assets such as property, buildings and equipment. Your net worth may be more than a million dollars, but your personal bank account will be small and ready to be used for growth and expansion. You won't have any real money until after you sell the business. But, first you must build it up with a label and distributor franchise that's valuable to the purchaser; otherwise you have nothing to sell.

Until we sold the company we had only limited funds. For example, the FAA (Federal Aviation Agency) confiscated our home, the Angell Centennial farm house, that we had made into a three-family dwelling. We were forced to sell it, and find another home to move to within two weeks.

With a realtor's help we found the right house. We paid the asking price, made a sizable down payment, and had an agreement that the owners could remain there while they were building their new home. Our money from the sale of the farmhouse would not be paid to us for 60 days.

This was agreed to by the owners. Their sales agent called us to a meeting. She said, "We'd like you to pay my clients the $100,000 you owe now so they can avoid borrowing from the bank to build. You can get the money from your company." I said, "That's not possible, the U.S. Government owns half of our business. We need money for inventory, payroll, manufacturing, and shipping costs. You can't take money needed for the business and use it for personal purchases. Your clients will have to wait for the 60 days agreed on. That's it. Good-bye."

They waited and got the money, on time, after we received it from the Michigan State Highway Department which the FAA appointed as their agent for these forced purchases. Appraisals and settlements were made by the State Highway Department.

We were indeed fortunate to find a house that could allow us to keep the furniture, books, cars, antiques, and leaded glass lamps we had collected over the past ten years. After living in this house for fifteen years, we enjoy the comfort we have built into it for a clean, comfortable, healthy atmosphere, winter and summer. The living area, kitchen, bathrooms, bedrooms and hall stairway, and the recreation room and library in the basement give us all the room we need.

We have a regulation size Brunswick pool table in the recreation room. All the floors are carpeted, even the furnace room. We have two large screen TV's. The one in the family room is a gift from our chefs. Another in the living room, on which we watch videos, sports, the news, and Lawrence Welk, I am able to view while working out on our economy model Nordic Track. The lighting is excellent throughout our home, and is embellished with a collection of several beautiful Tiffany leaded-glass shades.

We're comfortable and have three extra bedrooms for guests. There are three full tile bathrooms and a toilet-wash room. There is a large porch at the back of the house. We have a two-and-a-half car garage with overhead door (automatic), and a large play-room (carpeted), and storage area above the garage and family room. Our front porches are lighted, but not covered. We prefer the family room to the living room, consequently we use that door rather than the main doors at the living room.

Our driveway and walks are cement. Our front and back yards are landscaped. Mrs. Minor has roses, daisies, pansies, geraniums, and other flowers in bloom during the spring and summer and fall months. We have an assortment of nice trees including Colorado Spruce, White Pine, Scotch Pine, Jeffrey Pine, Pin Oak, Black Oak, Red Oak, Maple (both Sugar and Silver), and Shagbark Hickory. Our backyard and our neighbor's backyard are not fenced. This gives one the impression of looking at a park, not a yard. Squirrels, rabbits, and Blue Jays, Cardinals, Sparrows, Chick-a-Dees, Doves, Robins, and occasionally a flock of Cedar Wax Wings come in the fall to feed on the red berries that grow on the huge evergreen bush that hangs over our back porch.

Our street is lined with Oak, Spruce, Maple and Birch trees. Streets in our neighborhood don't have much traffic. This makes walking and bike riding safe and pleasant. Every day -- winter, spring, summer, or fall -- I try to walk. There's a beautiful park with a rose garden, children's playgrounds, baseball and soccer fields, and woods that overlook the Grand River. Every day I walk along the river banks, talk to the fishermen, and cut through the park to get back home. The streets are curved, not straight, and the homes and lawns are well kept. Our neighbors are all friendly.

We are in close proximity to schools, shopping, golf courses, tennis courts, parks and churches. Taxes are high. Michigan's taxes are higher than in most neighboring states. Still, we are willing to pay for the enjoyment we get from living on this beautiful peninsula. Michigan State University and Lansing Community College are nearby.

We love to go to hockey games. There's no smoking, and Ron Mason turns out consistently good teams with the players he recruits. George Perles' football teams, Jud Heathcote's basketball teams, and MSU's baseball, soccer, wrestling, and track teams are excellent, too. Women's sports are also improving rapidly, especially baseball, gymnastics and basketball. We also have a good lacrosse team. This is similar to hockey, but played on a field with a hard ball and nets with long handles in which the ball is caught and thrown. The American Indian invented lacrosse.

Handball and racquet ball are played in the intramural building which has an inside football practice area, tennis courts, a wrestling room and weight lifting room. Our son, Bryan, and his partner won the doubles championship for men in racquet ball in 1963.

Considering everything, General McLaughlin saved our lives, and did us a great favor when he got Walter Luftman to buy the business in May, 1983. Our retirement years have been pleasant. We meet annually with the chefs and their wives of The Golden Toque Society and attend the National Restaurant Association Show in Chicago. We vacation for the month of February on St. Martin's Island in the Caribbean and two weeks in the summer at Oqueoc Lake, in northern Michigan, with our children, grandchildren, and great grandchildren. Mrs. Minor and I also enjoy one-week trips in the spring and fall to Copper Harbor at the tip of the Kewanaw Peninsula, the most northerly boundary in Michigan. We're content and hope to grow old gracefully with God. Without Him we would have nothing. We have followed in His Ways and encourage you to do the same to insure a long and prosperous life, for the Bible says in Proverbs 4:10-27:

> Hear, my son, and accept my sayings,
> And the years of your life will be many.
> I have directed you in the way of wisdom;
> I have led you in upright paths.
> When you walk, your steps will not be impeded;
> And if you run, you will not stumble.
> Take hold of instruction; do not let go.
> Guard her, for she is your life.
> Do not enter the path of the wicked,
> And do not proceed in the way of evil men.
> Avoid it, do not pass by it;
> Turn from it and pass on.
> For they cannot sleep unless they do evil;
> And they are robbed of sleep unless they make someone stumble.
> For they eat the bread of wickedness,
> And drink the wine of violence.
> But the path of the righteous is like the light of dawn,
> That shines brighter and brighter until the full day.
> The way of the wicked is like darkness;
> They do not know over what they stumble.
>
> My son, give attention to my words;
> Incline your ear to my sayings.

Do not let them depart from your sight;
Keep them in the midst of your heart.
For they are life to those who find them.
And health to all their whole body.
Watch over your heart with all diligence,
For from it *flow* the springs of life.
Put away from you a deceitful mouth,
And put devious lips far from you.
Let your eyes look directly ahead,
And let your gaze be fixed straight in front of you.
Watch the path of your feet,
And all your ways will be established.
Do not turn to the right nor to the left;
Turn your foot from evil.

Just don't smoke, drink or use drugs, including alcohol.

Appendix 1

More from Chefs:

Their Responses to a Historic Letter

by

Pierre Bacque

Jean Caubet

Paul Debes

Henry Haller

Ernest Koves

Paul Laesecke

Hermann Rusch

Quote from Robert Peterson

"The years after forty are what life is all about."

Quote from Robert Frost

"I guess I would rather be famous than infamous."

(Editor's Note: This Appendix affords the reader more information about the great chefs of the L. J. Minor Corporation as well as insight into chefs in general. The following is what Dr. Minor told me when presenting this material.)

"This is information on chefs, their training, and their interrelationships with managers, dietitians, maître d's and their personnel. Few people understand the training requirements to become a cook, much less an executive chef. The U. S. Department of Labor requires 6,000 certified kitchen hours, plus other requirements, for cook certification. An executive chef or master chef require 10 years experience or more! This vital information includes first a sample of the historic letter to the chefs followed by their replies."

Thomas A Ryan
Attorney at Law
436 Bulkley Building
Cleveland, Ohio

October 13, 1969

Chef Henry Haller
White House Kitchens
The White House
1600 Pennsylvania Avenue
Washington, D. C.

Dear Chef:

This matter has been previously discussed with you on the telephone.

Dr. Lewis J. Minor of Michigan State University, together with three Professors from Cornell University -

Dr. L. L. Smith
Dr. J. J. Wanderstock
Commander L. E. Bond

are writing a book on foodservice science, which will be published by The AVI Publishing Co., a well-known publisher of textbooks and books on science.

The main and principal objective of the work will be its use as a text for students attending colleges, trade schools and high schools in the hospitality field.

Our present day food scientists are the product of our classical educational system but long years before the use of the test tube, the Bunsen Burner, microscopic lens, and sophisticated measuring devices, there were food scientists -- the professional chef -- who laid the foundation.

The chef was not only a food scientist but an artisan, a technician, flavor expert, nutritionist, and sanitarian.

Every scientific breakthrough, or revolutionary technical advance in the making, processing, or preservation of food has been a challenge to the ingenuity of the professional chef. It is agreed that it is not the nutritional value but how pleasing to the palate is the basic major problem, and that is in the chef's domain.

The authors are very conscious of the importance of the professional chef to food. To emphasize their appreciation of the chef, it is their intention that in the introduction of the book there shall be some paragraphs by celebrated chefs.

Each paragraph would be accompanied by a photograph of the respective chef and a brief biographical sketch.

The subject matter of the paragraphs must be the PROFESSIONAL CHEF. Not to confine, narrow or to influence in any way the thinking of the chef, but simply as a matter of suggestion, the chef might write a:

Paragraph - Historical Portrait - showing the place in society, contribution to civilization and principal function of the professional chef from Escoffier to Apollo 11, or man's landing on the moon.

Paragraph - Protest - against the understanding and appreciation that the American public has for the professional chef.

Paragraph - Declaration - of principles and objectives of the professional chefs as enunciated by their associations, such as, the Academy of Chefs, American Culinary Federation, Epicurean Clubs, Associations of Professional Chefs.

Paragraph - Present day problems and future problems confronting the culinarian worked and the food industry.

Paragraph - Of appeal - appealing to governmental agencies, educators and executives in the food and hospitality industry for greater recognition.

Among the names of those eminent chefs invited to cooperate are the following:

Pierre Bacque   Retired - Former Executive Chef of the
Miami, Florida   Fontainebleau and the Eden Roc Hotels

Jean Caubet Dearborn, Michigan	Retired - Executive Chef President of Chef's Association, Michigan
Paul Debes San Francisco, CA	Former Executive Chef of St. Francis Hotel; Wine Institute; Captain of the U. S. Culinary Olympic Team
Roger Fesaguet New York, N. Y.	President, Vatel Club, 349 W. 48th St. New York City
Henry Haller Washington, D. C.	Executive Chef at the White House
Paul Laesecke Pittsburgh, PA	Master Chef of H. J. Heinz Co. Captain of U. S. Culinary Olympic Team
Hermann G. Rusch White Sulphur Springs, West Virginia	Executive Food Director The Greenbrier

Professor Helen J. Recknagel, Associate Editor of *The Cornell Quarterly*, who has been most helpful in making suggestions to the authors, has agreed to reedit any paragraphs submitted by chefs if they desire to do so. No paragraphs would be published without being fully approved by the contributing chef.

After you give this letter some study, I would appreciate your phoning me, either at the office or my home, reversing the charges. My home phone is: 216-333-0657.

Yours truly,

Thomas A. Ryan

Pierre Bacque

It is indeed a privilege to be able to express one's opinion on a book, The Cuisine from Escoffier to Apollo 11, which so eminent a group are about to write.

In 1847, Auguste Escoffier was born in a very small town called Villeneuve-Loubet in the Maritime Alps. Due to Escoffier and so many others after him in Europe, cuisine not only in the restaurants but in the home, became a recognized art, a status never quite achieved in the United States. Escoffier was a great cook and a master chef. He organized the various stations: Hors d'Oeuvres, Potagers (soup), Sauciers (sauce, stew, braised meats),

Poissoniers (fish), Rôtisseurs (roast meat, game, fowl), Broilers, Fried Cooks, Entremetiers, Garde Mangers, Bouchers (butchers), Patissiers, Bakers, Ice Cream Makers, etc. Heretofore, the stations were divided into First Cook, Second Cook, Third Cook, etc. When an order arrived from the dining room, there was bedlam. Each of the various cooks rushed in to take a hand in making the order.

Mr. Escoffier especially distinguished himself in England at the Savoy Hotel and at the Carlton Hotel. He was responsible for a great part of the prestige that French cuisine held all over the world. President Raymond Poincare purposely went to England to bestow Mr. Escoffier with the title of Chevalier de la Legion d'Honneur. He was further honored in 1928 by President Herriot with the higher rank of Officier de la Legion d'Honneur. Escoffier made many fine chefs, initiating a system of apprenticeship. He served as an inspiration to many cooks and chefs who hoped to continue the tradition that he had established. Cooking, however, deteriorated when hotel owners, concerned with eliminating costly kitchen operations, reduced the number of cooks and stations. Potential cooks and chefs were discouraged by the longer hours, and the hard work. With the exception of a few hotels, apprentices were no longer trained. Since World War II and the prosperity which followed, the trend of dining out has increased tremendously. Therefore, restaurants and hotel dining have become more popular. The supply of cooks and chefs has become scarcer due to the diminished appeal of the profession for reasons mentioned above.

It is particularly unfortunate in this land of plenty where five million farm workers produce enough food and fiber for over 200 million Americans and 60 million foreign consumers that there is such a lack of interest in the preparation of fine foods. Through the unparalleled efficiency of American agricultural producers, ninety-five percent of the United States population is free to dream, study, indulge in other wants and fancies and launch men and rockets to the moon. Yet we continue to neglect this vital area of food preparation which provides so much enjoyment to the simple pleasures of life. There is a lack of desire among young people to enter the field of professional cuisine, although the demand for cooks and chefs certainly is apparent everywhere, and now at interesting salaries. A good chef today command wages equal or better than a business executive or a college professor. It seems to me that hotel and restaurant owners and public relations experts on government levels should provide the necessary encouragement to stimulate interest in the art of cuisine and should introduce training such as is being offered by some universities, to fulfill the many job openings which already exist. Let me emphasize that it is easier today than in the past to be a cook and a chef. We have prefabricated meats and fish, better seasoning and concentrates for making soups and sauces, stews and pot roasts. Other areas of modern life, such as transportation by air cargo, facilitate the restaurateur. Fresh vegetables and fruit can be served almost all year round, a convenience unknown in history. Self-roasting ovens of tremendous capacities and electrical machinery have given us the means of mass production. Standards of quality comparable to the cooking of past masters could easily be maintained if dedicated individuals are trained and willing to offer fine cuisine. We have the best of everything, and we should have the best cooking.

Again let me state that the public must be interested and educated in the art of fine cuisine such as the establishments of yesteryear, which delighted those who patronized them, recalling that Escoffier and his early disciples were France's best ambassadors.

I have been executive chef in the following establishments:

Coin Dore Restaurant in New York City - French Cuisine (3 years)
Hotel Lafayette and Vendome Hotel in Boston, MA - French and Continental
    (7 years)
Seabright Beach Club, Rumson Country Club and Tennis Club (4 years) in
    New Jersey
The Surf Club in Miami Beach, Florida (2 years)
Maxim's Restaurant in Miami Beach (5 years)
Opened the Algiers Hotel in Miami Beach, Florida (5 years)
Opened the Eden Roc Hotel, Miami Beach, Florida (10 years)
Mount Washington Hotel in Bretton Woods, New Hampshire (one season)
The Fontainebleau Hotel in Miami Beach, Florida (3 years)

Member of the Vatel Club for the past 45 years.

A founder of the Epicurean Club of Greater Miami.

Awarded for fine preparation and presentation of food in the Mona Lisa Room at the Eden Roc by the Escoffier Society of Montreal, Canada.

Jean Caubet

Having spent a half century in gastronomics, I have had a chance to realize the changes that have been made in the Culinary field through technology and science.
    Chefs of today will have to consider and adapt themselves to these new techniques if they wish to stay abreast of the trade. With this new revolution of foods and modern equipment, the Chef no longer will have to spend longer hours and days to bring his bill of fare up in time to satisfy the public, providing he is using the best available foods. The days of plucking chickens, cutting carcasses, scaling fish, and cleaning vegetables are gone forever.
    I feel sorry for some of us who were born a half century too soon.

Paul Debes

Though the foodservice industry has moved on to processed foods and standardized procedures, cooking is still thought of by many as a medieval craft.

Today, however, change is in the air. Creativity is in demand. Several optimistic chefs have noticed that people are learning to taste, and to complain - a good sign. Younger restaurant patrons are demanding more natural foods, fun foods, unusual foods. And the recipes for them can't be found in cookbooks written a hundred years ago. The modern chef who can apply the basics of fine cookery to the development of new food presentations is worth his weight in truffles.

Of course, the progressive chef needs an environment of permissiveness in order to be creative. Management must be aware of food trends and encourage the chef to use his ability.

With today's rising costs, allowing the chef to be creative is a matter of economics. The more aggressive restaurant businessmen are expressing interest in the development of exciting new dishes so long as they produce an acceptable profit.

Most American chefs have at least opened their minds to partially prepared or convenience foods. And they have every reason to. It was the great Escoffier who dared to use canned tomatoes at The Savoy in London, some 85 years ago. Although he was severely criticized by his peers, he, nevertheless, found a way to successfully utilize the technology of his day.

In a recent survey of chefs employed in quality restaurants, clubs and hotels, conducted by DINING Magazine, nearly every respondent indicated that he did his own food purchasing. More than sixty percent of those interviewed stated that they were presently using prepared foods in one form or another.

Still, a number of chefs continue to regard processed foods as a threat, if not a downright insult to their profession. But those who have embraced convenience foods indicate that these products afford an excellent opportunity to use one's imagination.

One prominent chef feels that processed foods are the best thing that has happened in the restaurant industry and to the professional chef.

He explains, "The more this country becomes convenience food oriented, the greater the need for the chef. His imagination, skill and creativity can turn these foods into unique dishes at a considerable savings in time and labor. And one is still able to offer the public originality in dining."

Whether aficionados of processed foods or not, most chefs have faith in their art. Maurice Chantreau, head chef at The Four Seasons in New York, summed up the feelings of his colleagues when he said, "I would like to gather all the leaders -- Nixon, Kosygin, Golda Meir, Sadat, Pompidou -- in the private dining room here and give them a good meal. Afterwards they would talk. They would be too happy to fight."

Although today's chef is beginning to express his dissatisfaction, his life is still spent in slavish devotion to his craft. He works a six-day week, usually coming in around 10 a.m. and finishing at 11:30 p.m., with only a brief mid-afternoon break. Family life is a series of snatched moments.

Arno Schmidt, executive chef at The Waldorf Astoria in New York, blames the chef's lack of social status on the hours and work schedules necessary to practice his profession.

He explains, "I can afford to join a country club if I so choose, but I wouldn't have the time to go to it. When you work six days a week and come home every night at 11:00 o'clock, there isn't much time left for private life."

The number one complaint expressed by chefs is long, long hours. There is definite resentment in having to work both days and nights, holidays and weekends, and from nine to twelve hours a day. Several chefs indicated that they work as many as eighteen hours a day. And one chap, who still manages to retain his sense of humor, says that he works sixty-five hours a day.

Besides work schedules, there are many other conditions which prevent the chef from achieving social and professional status.

The European restaurant industry still maintains strict traditions and rigid programs of training and apprenticeships, all of which have helped the chef to carve his place in European society.

This is not the case in the United States. Many Americans, including restaurateurs and some chefs, do not consider cooking to be a high status profession.

Roger Fesaguet, chef at LaCaravelle in New York, contends that, "In this country, people don't make any distinction between a short order cook and a real chef."

Although many chefs are members of local and national organizations, they are not united as are their European counterparts.

The oldest culinary association, The Societe Culinaire Philanthropique, counts many of America's foremost chefs among its membership. Its aim, however, is to help its members in case of sickness or distress, and in case of death, to provide for their burial.

John Spurgeon, chef at David's, Inc., Chicago, and a member of the American Culinary Federation and the Chefs de Cuisine, feels that there is little to be gained from these organizations.

"About the only advantage of belonging," says Chef Spurgeon, "is the prestige in displaying my membership plaques."

Chefs are classified by the United States Department of Labor as service personnel, in the same category as domestic help. This condition is hardly beneficial to the chef's image or personal and professional stature.

But the problems go deeper than the Labor Department's classification system. With the exception of the Culinary Institute of America, which offers a two-year course covering all aspects of culinary education, and a few other under financed schools, chef training is practically non-existent in the United States. Consequently most American chefs are self-taught.

Today's young people, of course, refuse to do it the hard way. Although the ultimate rewards of chefdom are financially appealing, a newcomer to a restaurant kitchen can hardly expect to earn more than $80 a week for the first year. During this time the fledgling chef must remain in a lowly capacity.

The lack of educational facilities and professional training programs; the personal sacrifices the profession demands; and the tightened immigration laws cutting off the flow of European trained chefs are serious problems, causing a great shortage of qualified chefs in this country. Consequently, the kitchen of the future might be far different from those of today.

Pierre Franey, the chef who once reigned over the ranges of LePavillon and is now vice president and executive chef of Howard Johnson's, believes that "In the future, French restaurants will depart radically from the grand pathway of current tradition. I can see a very bright future for a small, very good restaurant where the owner is also the chef and can operate with the help of a very small staff."

To compensate for the current and future shortage of trained chefs, the various chef organizations have suggested a culinary apprenticeship program under which cooks would be recruited from the ranks of kitchen employees and undergo formal training. Many restaurants, hotels and clubs have agreed to hire apprentices and provide them with practical experience under the direct supervision of their chefs. But to make a program of this type an industry-wide reality takes time and self sacrifice of those who are willing to devote their energies to it. Apparently, there just aren't enough of these people around.

A very few dedicated individuals, industry and private organizations, and even several corporations are seriously concerned about the current and future status of the chef and the advancement of the profession. These people and groups support several programs designed to earn recognition for the chef as well as the art of cookery.

The Kiwanis Club of the Peninsula, Inc., headquartered in Hewlett, New York, for example, sponsors a culinary show and presents awards and scholarships to Nassau County schools, apprenticeship programs and student cooks. The Societe Culinaire Philanthropique presents the annual Salon of Culinary Arts, which has been held every year for more than a hundred years.

Perhaps the most prestigious of these programs is the Culinary Olympics, sponsored by Kraft Foods. This event is much more than a food competition between nations. The success of the United States team not only helps to promote the image of the American professional chef, but the entire foodservice industry.

This year, on October 12th in Frankfurt, Germany, the United States team, led by manager Jack Sullivan, president of the American Culinary Federation and executive chef at the Disneyland Hotel in Anaheim, California, will compete with teams of chefs from thirty-five countries to prove that American cuisine ranks with the best in the world.

Still another ambitious program designed to improve the status of the chef is one in which qualified chefs would be licensed or certified. Although the American Culinary Federation endorses such a system, the likelihood of its becoming a reality in the near future is dim. So far, no one has adequately defined the word "qualified." In fact most chefs' organizations have little basis for membership, nor have they come up with a way of distinguishing between the various classifications of chefs.

Still the ACF and other aggressive organizations appear to be moving in the right direction. Perhaps, through their efforts, the chef will achieve the social and business status he so richly deserves.

But first, the chefs of America must organize. That, however, is easier said than done. It's rare to find two chefs who fully agree with each other on any issue. Maybe there's some truth to the legend after all.

Henry Haller

The challenge for the professional chef today is greater than at anytime in history. More and more people are dining out in restaurants and hotels, and interest in international cuisine is at an all-time high. World travel on a scale unsurpassed in history is making the palate of the average American more sophisticated.

Now, with the greater variety of fresh products readily available, and kitchens better equipped to cope with an increasing demand, the food industry faces a tremendous challenge -- the matter of training.

A greater number of young Americans must be encouraged to enter the culinary field, to take over the openings for cooks and chefs and other service personnel which will develop in the near future. We can no longer count on a steady flow of trained chefs from Europe. Every professional chef has the obligation and responsibility to do all he can do to help encourage and train young Americans in our field.

The cuisine of Carême and Escoffier is still very much admired today. Those restaurants in the United States that produce fine French cuisine are a tremendous success. It has been my observation that classical cuisine still has an important place. Any chef who is able to recreate these classical dishes is, and will be, successful.

But the professional chef is no longer just a culinary artist; he must also be a good manager of his kitchens. His food cost and payroll must be such that the kitchen operation yields a profit to his organization. Unprofitable food operations, no matter how exquisite the cuisine, don't stay in business long.

To Dr. Minor, Dr. Smith, Dr. Wanderstock and Commander Bond, I wish great success with their book. I hope a large number of people will benefit from their contribution to the wonderful world of gastronomy, which is after all, the art of good living.

Paul Laesecke

"The only way to save classic cuisine is to can it," says Paul Laesecke, Master Chef for H. J. Heinz Co. "I don't mean that canning is the only way but I do believe that preprocessing or prepreparation of basic soups, sauces, and other fundamental ingredients used by institutional cooking is the solution to the uniformly high quality of commercially prepared food." Paul Laesecke further explains that the best cuisine has always been prepared according to a certain sequence. "In the old days preparatory kitchens supplied the main kitchen with all basic soups, stocks, processed fish, meats and vegetables requested by the various kitchen department heads. Then as now, the roast chef or fish chef or soup chef did not prepare the daily menu from scratch. Each used preprepared ingredients or semi-finished products. The trays of parboiled vegetables from the refrigerator were the equivalent of today's fresh-frozen packages. The stock pots, or more refined white and brown sauces in bainmaris or on the side of the range, were the equivalent of today's condensed products. In the production of fine soups one always found that daily menu selections consisted of an assembly of preprepared, semi-finished ingredients such as veloute and chicken stock, broth and granitures, vegetable purees and meat stock.

"These preprepared products were produced in a different place and at a different time from the actual order by the customer which triggered the mechanism of final assembly. Then as now, most dishes were given a last heating or browning under the broiler or salamander before serving in the dining room. The ability to transform preprepared foods into gourmet dishes differentiates the work of a head-chef or department chef from the work of a short order cook or counterman because, without prepreparation, the chef of yesterday as well as the chef of today could not serve fine dishes. He would be reduced to the service of French fries and hamburgers; and even then, he might not be able to keep up with the volume of business required by the modern standard of efficiency if the potatoes were not fryer-ready and the hamburgers portion size.

"Aside from lack of time, the modern executive chef is faced with lack of skill in the staff. Very often he cannot delegate the prepreparation of basic products to his staff and assume the responsibility of controlling the quality of the finished products. If the executive chef is fortunate enough to have skilled assistants, the increase in labor cost is such that the required profit ratio may force economies affecting the quality of the food. It is difficult today for the executive chef to afford both a highly skilled staff and a generous food cost allowance. Under present circumstances it is only logical to magnify the productive capacity of the head-chef with the resources which industry and modern technology can provide.

"Prepreparation at the factory level enables the factory chef to supply all major kitchens with the products formerly supplied by individual preparatory kitchens. These products are essentially the fundamental sauces, stocks, and other components that go into the preparation of classical dishes. The array of new products supplied by master chefs who work in the gigantic kitchens of institutional food manufacturers is designed to fit the needs of chefs in charge of any food service outlet. From luxury restaurants to cafeterias, all chefs can ask for basic products prepared for them in modern plants. The selection of new products or convenience foods is patterned after the types of ingredients and the flow of production which prevailed in kitchens of the classical style. By using these new products the chef is able to reconstitute what seemed to be hopelessly lost. He is able to control the quality of the food as served to the customer and to vary the number and type of assistants on his staff.

"This is why prepreparation and processing are essential to save classical cuisine. Without them gourmet recipes at the institutional level would become collectors' items rather than standard American fare as we know it today."

The reasons for using processed foods as basic supplies have been expressed by many leading chefs in no uncertain terms, but Paul Laesecke gives this view more emphasis in scientific and technical language. As a research chef he can substantiate his opinion with documentation from industrial kitchens and from the kitchens of luxury restaurants and hotels where he received his early training. His qualifications as an expert in the field of culinary sciences is unchallenged. In addition, constant research and travel make it possible for Laesecke to know both the latest culinary trends in various countries and the latest methods to process the finest preprepared foods. In 1963 he traveled more than 60,000 miles. He established the recipes and basic formulae in many new factories abroad. He also set the pattern for new production lines. He visited major kitchens in many foreign capitals and studied the work and requirements of commissary kitchens on international airlines, such as Lufthansa, KLM and Qantas, in every continent. Laesecke believes in changing basic recipes to please the taste of the various markets served by H. J. Heinz Company. Blind testing of different samples is, of course, the basic method used to determine taste preferences. Sometimes the results are surprising. In Venezuela, for instance, it was expected that a spicy variation of a vegetable soup would be preferred. Testing, however, indicated that the rather bland Canadian style was by far the winner. Also obvious was the majority vote for the addition of the famous green banana or platana, as an ingredient of the soup recipe. Although platana, after cooking, colors into an objectionable pink in terms of American taste, it was found that pink food was quite acceptable in the Venezuelan market. The final recipe was therefore soup with the addition of pink platanas.

In the factories of Heinz operations abroad, Laesecke lets the local market determine the taste of products, but he insists on strict buying specifications and grading according to the highest U. S. standards. He also trains foreign cooks and staff assistants according to American methods and procedures.

He has achieved an almost unparalleled renown as a top medalist in culinary contests here and abroad.

He is a recipient of the two highest awards in the culinary field - an annual medal bestowed by the French government for his entry in the Culinary Arts Exhibit at the National Hotel Show in 1950 in New York City, and a medal from the American Culinary Federation two years later during a similar program. In 1956 he captained the four-man American Culinary Team which swept eight major awards in the Culinary Olympics in Frankfurt, Germany.

This year he is celebrating his 30th year as research chef for H. J. Heinz Company. His influence in food styling has reached international fame and consumers throughout the world praise the universal acceptance of his creations.

Ernest Koves

Today's chef is the manager of all types of foodservice operations. His influence in menu-styling is controlling the American menu more effectively than in the past because equipment and packaging innovation have magnified his productive capacity. As a result, the American public enjoys gourmet style foods everywhere.

Very few, however, qualify for the title of Chef. To succeed, a chef must know the fundamentals of classical cuisine. He must also have an encyclopedic knowledge of garnitures and variations so that a minor addition or change may transform a basic recipe into a classical dish.

The chef must also be a leader. He must apply his leadership to organize his staff as an efficient team which will work in close cooperation with dining room service or with the staff in charge of food and beverage sales.

To control the quality and the styling of the menu, the chef must be able to specify the type of ingredients and the brand which are most likely to fit the requirements of his menu. This privilege is also key to his food cost ratio. As a ratio to food sales, this percentage is not the only control imposed by management over a chef's function in foodservice.

The enormous responsibility entrusted to the chef has often caused the industry to call him a food director or a director of food and beverage operation. Whatever the title, the functions are still those of a chef as defined by Auguste Escoffier and contemporary leaders in the profession. And these functions will always be the most important in the foodservice industry.

Hermann Rusch

In the long history of cookery there has never been a period even remotely approaching the present and God only knows what the future holds in store. No multi-millionaire of even 50 years ago could command for his table - no matter what he spent - the variety of delicious and satisfying food that today's patrons take almost for granted. Today, through refrigeration and rapid transportation, the fruits, vegetables, seafood, and meats of distant areas are available year-round. Today, the 'affluent society' with its millions of well-to-do from all lands, has led to a general knowledge of, and desire for the best foods, the popular dishes of many countries. All this has placed greater responsibility upon those who direct the cuisine, "kitchens" of the great hotels of the world's capitals and resort areas, and of the far-flung national and international transportation companies.

For instance, there are today over 70 foreign countries, spending millions through their travel promotion offices in this country to win a larger share of the U. S. travel dollars. While it is true that many of these countries can offer attractions of a scenic or historic character, it is also true that outside of Western Europe few of the younger nations provide tourist facilities or food comparable to that desired and expected by the experienced American or European traveler. This means that the world over, city and resort hotels are being rushed to completion. And with this comes a new, far wider and more intensive international demand for capable, experienced chefs, especially for Chefs Who Are More Than Chefs. What do we mean by that? Just this, that whereas a generation or so ago, the province of the chef was customarily limited to the actual kitchen itself, today management is searching for the commanding officer type of chef. The man sought is one who not only has served his apprenticeship in every station of the kitchen, but understands and can supervise the procurement of food and its storage as well as its preparation and service. He must know the mathematics of food, not only in determining the quantities of each ingredient needed to produce anywhere from one to 5,000 portions, but to keep a constant, dependable control of portion and meal cost. And he must be a student of the well-orchestrated menus as they change from day to day. He must be a good Organization Man, fair and appreciative of his own staff; frank, reliable and a money-maker for his employer. Thus we have the new concept of the Chef of tomorrow, the Executive Food Director.

The Universities sponsoring Hotel Administration Schools have done an outstanding job producing managerial prospects. The field has been flooded with future managers, every young man and young lady going through these schools dream of the day when he or she will be heading his or her own operation. All this is wonderful and more power to them. But something is very much missing some place along the way. The coordination between the Manager and the Chef is the most important element. To accomplish this one thing is indispensable; the understanding and appreciation of the values of the Chef by the Manger. The wise Manager will recognize and capitalize on these values.

It is a fact that where a good coordination exists between the Manager and Chef, the operation has always been a success, but where it does not exist, most of the time the operation has been a failure.

The person behind the counter filling the plate, the cook, the pantry person, the dishwasher, all of them, responsible to the back of the house key man. The man responsible for the food cost. The man making the money for the house, in other words:

THE CHEF --

What is the Chef?

A chef is a top notch cook with managerial abilities, a man who know all the departments of the kitchen from the purchasing to the storage, to the preparation, to the serving. The man who can buy good merchandise at a reasonable price. Fashion it into very tasty and attractive looking meals, charge a reasonable price for it, please everyone and make a good food cost.

This man is responsible for the success or failure of the operation. He is a miracle man because often he has to accomplish this with poor quality and poor help, still he is expected to serve Gourmet Meals.

He is referred to as the vanishing man of the food business. But don't fool yourself. He is here to stay and will grow bigger than ever in stature. Our business needs his knowledge of Food Artistry and Food Chemistry.

I have sensed a desire to extinguish him, but the desire is only present in persons who do not understand the value of the man or resent his ability because, today, too many operators have come up the fast road to success and have by-passed the trip through the back of the house. So, not understanding its values, not being able to talk intelligently about it they are lost and want to by-pass the Chef, substitute him with someone they can boss or push around.

Had this operator been through a good basic training of the back of the house, the production corner, the money making department, he would be able to talk to the chef on even terms, keep good relations with him and get the best profitable advantages from this hidden, forgotten man.

The best food operation is no more successful than is permitted by the ability of the cook preparing the food and dressing it on the plate for the customer at the table.

The best Manager =

The best Chef =

is no better than the man at the range, but the man at the range is not better than the Chef guiding him, coaching him, and from all this derives success or failure.

So, go teach your young potential managers the basics of the culinary arts, a good basic of cooking fundamentals, so that he in turn will appreciate the values of his chef and allow him to teach and produce and make money for him. Many Chefs have made the success of the Manager, many have carried the Manager, so to speak. So be smart and use him to his fullest.

The curriculum of any hotel school, should cover the Chef's functions so that the graduates of tomorrow will go into the field with the knowledge and understanding of the Chef's job, and will collaborate closer with him for a more harmonious and profitable enterprise.

Some say the Chef is no more and that convenience foods are taking over so that you no longer need a prima donna chef and a pantry is all you will need. This may be so in some instances, but the food will have to be prepared someplace, and wherever it will be prepared, a Chef will be needed to put the taste in, to create the varieties and to put in the finishing touch, appearance, etc. and control the whole application, not forgetting that this will be sometime before reaching its climax and that there also will always be the specialty place, because when convenience reaches its peak, it will create a greater demand for the specialty house and they will be able to make an even greater profit. <u>Always remember that there is nothing new in cookery, only new applications.</u>

The so called "convenience food" is really nothing new. We have had convenience foods for many many years, but today it is at such a level that it can only be a boost to our industry . . .

My most sincere and best wishes to:

Dr. L. J. MINOR

Commander L. E. BOND

Professor HELEN RECKNAGEL

and all others for a well needed Guide Manual.

Appendix 2

Always in Good Taste:
The L. J. Minor Story

The L. J. Minor Corporation History - A people business built with quality products

The Backdrop

February 11, 1939 - Married Ruth E. Angell of Lansing, Michigan

June, 1939 - Graduated from Michigan State University with a Bachelor of Science degree in Organic Chemistry

September, 1939 - Graduate Assistantship in Organic Chemistry at M.S.U.

November, 1939 - Joined staff of La Choy Food Products Co., Detroit, Michigan as Technical Director. Developed and improved the bean sprouting process and a new soy sauce process. Formulated seasonings and Vegemato Juice Cocktail. Left in 1942 due to WWII shortage of tin containers.

November 30, 1940 - Daughter, Kathleen Mary, born. Now teaching French in high schools in Maryland.

January 25, 1942 - Son, Bryan Gabriel, born. Became Captain in U.S. Army - Anesthesiologist. Died on August 3, 1978.

April, 1942 - Joined research group in the metal container division of Owens-Illinois Co., Toledo, Ohio. Tested substitute containers to replace tin including bonderized black iron plate and lighter weight electrolyte tinplate with various protective enamel coatings. Left in 1945 due to phase out of metal container division.

January, 1945 - Joined McKay Davis Co. as Vice President of the Food Division. Supervised plant manufacturing bouillon for Army "K" rations. Received citation from Col. Roland Isker for contributing to the war effort. Established $300,000/year post-war business in seasonings. Left in 1947 to join the Huron Milling Company.

March, 1947 - Joined the Huron Milling Co. of Harbor Beach, Michigan as Technical

Director in charge of developing new applications for Monosodium Glutamate, Hydrolyzed Vegetable Proteins and edible wheat starch.

March, 1949 - While Vice President and Program Chairman of the Great Lakes Section of the Institute of Food Technologies, invited Dr. Thomas A. Ryan as guest speaker for the spring meeting held at the St. Clair Inn in St. Clair, Michigan.

Tom visited us at our house in Harbor Beach after the meeting. He asked, "What are you going to do when you retire - sit on your porch and throw stones at the natives? Why don't you come to Cleveland and start a business?"

Resigned from the Huron Milling Company. Coincidentally, Mr. Toby Bishop, President of Accent Division of International Minerals & Chemicals Co. asked me to join their research group. When I told him of my plan to start my own business, he hired me as a consultant. For the next two years, he paid me $500.00 a month which helped us to get started in the Minor Corp.

October, 1951 - Moved to Cleveland and began development work on the bases in an office adjoining Dr. Ryan's law office.

During the interim from Bryan's birth in 1942, Ruth Ann was born September 22, 1944, and she is the Production Supervisor and quality controller in production at the Minor Corp.

Daughter, Carol Elizabeth, born June 25, 1946.

Son, Michael Lewis, born January 6, 1948. Now Corporate Executive Chef for the L. J. Minor Corporation. Trained under Hermann Rusch at the Greenbrier for 3-1/2 years; Sous Chef at Williamsburg Inn, and Executive Chef at Deering-Milliken. Joined the L. J. Minor Corp. in 1977.

December 1, 1951 - The L. J. Minor Corporation was formed with Lewis J. Minor, Joseph Bertman and Thomas A. Ryan as co-partners - each with an investment of $2,500.00. Manufacturing was done at Bertman Foods Distributors on East 76th Street in Cleveland in an air-conditioned room 18 x 20 feet using a Hobart Mixer purchased for $85.00 and repaired by the Hobart Division in Cleveland for $180.00. Bertman was the first distributor.

The Challenge

We live in a marketing society. You may have the best product, but if you can't sell it, what good does it do?

The Plan

Labels were named by brands for important foodservice occupations:

> No. 1 - Minor's Dietitian brand
> No. 2 - Minor's Maitre'd brand
> No. 3 - Minor's LeChef brand

These were all <u>food bases</u>, and Minor's (name) was in a ribbon on the label.

The <u>soup bases</u> were labeled Caterer brand and Supo or private labels, e.g., Bertman's, Meisel's, 7990 and others.

Beef and Chicken only at the start.

The Aim

Build the Minor Label

The Chefs

Until we recruited Chef August Erb in Cleveland, retired executive chef of the Hollenden Hotel in Cleveland, sales progress was very slow. August introduced the Minor Dietitian brand to the chefs. Imagine! We were selling the chefs the Dietitian brand. Our sales in 1951 were $30,000.00.

Dr. Ryan and Mr. Bertman did not participate in the operation at this time. However, Dr. Ryan joined the company in 1953.

1952 - Tom Ryan, Joe Bertman and I held weekly meetings on Saturday afternoon in Dr. Ryan's offices in the National City Bank Building at 6th Avenue and Euclid. At one of the meetings, I requested that the company purchase a Ford station wagon for business. Joe Bertman insisted that I wanted to use it in my Boy Scout activity as troop committee man. A big argument ensued with two results: 1) I got the station wagon; and 2) I purchased Bertman's 1/3 interest in the company by giving him a substantial gain on his investment. Six months later, I purchased Dr. Ryan's 1/3 interest with a profit to him and became the sole owner of the L. J. Minor Corporation.

Mary Mele, Dr. Ryan's legal secretary, served as the first accountant, purchasing agent and general office supervisor for the company and carried on these tasks while also serving as Dr. Ryan's secretary. She was very efficient and trustworthy and carried this responsibility until her death in 1974. In 1960, she hired Nancy Clancy as an assistant, and Nancy succeeded Mary. Meanwhile, the company records were audited by Ralph Napeltana. Herman Taber, Ralph's associate, was tax consultant to the company. They joined us as consultants in the early 60's.

Sales by Chefs

An important point to emphasize is that our food base sales began and grew not through the medium of salesmen, but through the chefs. The most successful chef-broker was Jean Caubet in Detroit.

The Sales Program

Began when Dr. Thomas A. Ryan gave up his law practice and joined Minor's in January, 1953. He worked on sales promotion and acted as a talent scout for chefs and sales personnel.

The First Salesman

Frank Sigmund, Buffalo, New York, a fancy grocery salesman with Midwestern accounts in Minneapolis, St. Paul and Wisconsin and points in between. His sales of Dietitian brand soon reached $50,000.00/year. The Buffalo Park Lane Hotel was one of Sigmund's biggest accounts. Here we met the fabulous foodservice personage Peter Gust Economou who was trained by the great Statler. Peter Gust loves the Minor Corp. and is one of our biggest boosters. He is now 90 years old. Sigmund gave us the slogan, "The quality is remembered long after the price is forgotten."

July 31, 1951 - A daughter, Josephine Eva, was born. She now works in the computer control department at the plant coordinating production and distribution of Minor products.

1954 The First Broker

With distribution established in Cleveland and Detroit, I appointed our first food broker on a commission basis -- Mr. Johnny Hayes of New York City. He was an Olympic marathon champion in London in 1913. He sold soup bases to a national distributor.

The Second Broker

Robert Buntin of Boston was our second broker. I made calls with him. He sold food bases to the Conway Import Sales Co., and gave us the slogan, "Minor's Bases - Always in good taste." We first used this slogan on our give-away pencils. It now appears on the containers.

1995 The Third Broker

Eric Swanson sold his partnership in Delsoy and joined Minor's as a broker in out-state Michigan. He later got Jean Caubet to split the Wayne-Oakland County income 50/50, and together they built the sales to multi-million dollars a year.

On October 7, 1956, daughter Rosalie Clara was born. Now in the payroll department of the Farm Bureau in Lansing, Michigan. Works on payroll, accounting and computer control.

First New York City Distributor

Tom Ryan and I traveled to New York City and opened up our first distributor there -- a meat packer.

1958 The Stouffer Account

We called on Stouffer's for years with no results. Then one day a Durkee salesman, a Mr. Boswell, told us Stouffer's was having trouble with a new beef tenderloin product re: the gravy. We gave him Mrs. Minor's basting procedure. He passed it on to Mrs. Margaret Mitchell, Stouffer's Vice President in charge of all foodservice operations, through her husband who also worked for Durkee's, Mr. Curtin Mitchell. She tried it, and it worked for them.

Later she tried our Chicken base and purchased it. Orders also came for the Ham base and Clam base. Then she asked for a Mushroom base and a Turkey base. These were developed and sold to them. As a result, our sales increased dramatically.

Another Great Chef

Dr. (Chef) Ernest Koves joined the company after serving at the Astor and several other large New York City hotels. We called him the Dynamo as he could and usually did dominate anyone. He got us distributors in California, Milwaukee, Philadelphia, and New York City.

1960 - Nancy Clancy joined the company as Mary Mele's assistant. She became assistant manager of sales through close association with Dr. Ryan besides handling orders, keeping records and working with Taber and Napeltana on taxes.

1960 The First Cooking School

Chadsey High School - Commercial Foods Department, Detroit, Michigan
Chef Herman Breithaupt, Founder and Head Chef
Chef Richard Schneider, Baking Instructor
Chef George Marchand, Sous Chef

Chadsey High School purchased and used Minor's Dietitian brand bases in training their students. Chef Breithaupt helped Eric, and later Eric's son Dave Swanson, to introduce food bases to former Chadsey students who were then working in Michigan, Iowa, Colorado, and other locations. Chef George Marchand, "The Charmer," joined Minor's in 1968 when he resigned from Chadsey. He kissed the ladies hands and cheeks and demonstrated with a charming personality.

1960 - Emile Bergermeister, Master Chef in Cleveland, retired from Thompson-Ramo-Woolridge Co., and joined L. J. Minor. We called Emile "the fundamentalist." He was a stickler for exactness in every detail when we developed the Clam and Lobster bases. Emile's "fundamentalist" approach kept the seasoning correct as he worked with us on product applications. Later, he joined John Secter and George Marchand in travelling to schools including Michigan State's Hotel School, the Hotel School at Cornell U., Johnson & Wales College, The Culinary Institute, a myriad of junior college programs throughout the U.S. and the school at Strasbourg in his hometown Alscace Lorraine, France.

September 14, 1961 - a daughter, Mary Margaret, is born. Mary is trained in nutrition; presently a sanitation consultant.

1961 The Colonel Sanders Experience

Eric Swanson requested that we develop a gravy that Colonel Sanders wanted. We did, and visited him at his headquarters in Louisville, Kentucky to run tests. He ordered 50,000 cans with his picture on, and we packed a liquid gravy in them. After that first order, he asked for a 20% reduction, and we quit him. No profit at that price. This experience led to development of the Gravy Preps.

1961 - 1964 The Ph.D. Degree

A decision was reached for me to get a Ph.D. degree in chicken flavor. In 1961, I enrolled in the Food Science Department of the School of Agriculture at Michigan State University, East Lansing, Michigan. My thesis was completed, and I received my degree in 1964. My thesis was on the difference in flavor between young and old chickens. Gas, liquid and thin layer chromatography together with infra-red spectroscopy and other analytical methods were used in the research. The investigation showed that older birds have more flavor.

An important letter follows:

June 9, 1964

Dr. L. J. Minor
Department of Food Science
Campus

Dear Lew:

I would like to take this opportunity to congratulate you on successfully completing your Ph.D. degree in this department as well as the excellent research you have completed with Prof. Pearson. From both a personal and professional standpoint, I am impressed with your accomplishment, perseverance and dedication to achieving this objective. I am sure that Prof. Pearson and our entire staff join me in expressing these thoughts and wishing you every success in your continuing professional career.

I am well aware that such an accomplishment is not achieved without real support from your family and your associates at the L. J. Minor Corp. I feel, too, that your standards have been inspiring to the young men and women in our graduate group.

We will be following your continuing contributions with great interest and will be looking forward to close associations in the years ahead.

Sincerely yours,

B. S. Schweigert, Chairman
Department of Food Science
Michigan State University
College of Agriculture

1963 The Hotel School at Cornell University, Ithaca, New York

Dr. Ryan and I succeeded in establishing a liaison between Cornell's Hotel School and the Minor Corp. This lasted for 15 years with Minor chefs demonstrating in their food classes, my articles being published in The Cornell Quarterly, and recipes in color using Minor's bases in the Cornell Quarterly and in their Quantity Food Recipe book. A tableside service brochure featuring Minor's bases together with other commercial products was published and authored by Joseph Durocher. Contacts at Cornell's Hotel School included Dean Robert Beck, Associate Dean Gerald Latti, Dr. Helen Ricknagel, editor of the Cornell Quarterly, Professor Commander Bond, Prof. Vance Christian, Prof. Jerry Wanderstock and others. Most of them are now gone or retired.

1965 Another Great Chef

Chef John Secter, "The Scoop." Chef Secter traveled wherever Dr. Ryan sent him in his big station wagon. He kept filing cabinets in his car with him. He opened many distributors in the East, South and Midwest and got the ARA account.

Chef Secter trained the army chefs to compete in culinary shows. He helped the army chefs to win many honors.

1965 A Star Salesman

Brother Herman Zaccarelli is another star in the Minor galaxy. He made the college-university connection for us by introducing our food bases into the Ivy League schools including Harvard, Yale, Brown, Fordham, Brandeis, Colgate, Princeton and Cornell. He also introduced them at Notre Dame, Illinois, Indiana, Purdue and other Big 10 Schools. He did this through the Association of College and University Foodservices.

Brother Herman reported that on a visit to the White House, the Presidential chef, Henry Haller, told him that he uses Minor's food bases every day and on special occasions.

1964 - 1984

The teaching years in Michigan State University's Department of Hotel, Restaurant and Institutional Management in the School of Business. About 3,000 students attended my classes in Foodservice Science, Foodservice Standards, Food Production Methods and Food Flavor Evaluation.

1968 The Best Plant Manager

My former student, Mr. Michael Zelski, joined Minor's after graduating from MSU's Hotel School. Michael's ability to handle personnel and improve production methods is legendary. He is now marketing manager for Cres-Cor.

1968 - Dr. Ryan planned and held the first company sales meeting. We met at our home in Lansing. The following persons attended, and it is evident what an overpowering influence the chefs had on our sales progress at this time. Attending were:

1.   Dr. Thomas A. Ryan, General Manager
2.   My father, Newell N. Minor, who worked for our broker the Eric Swanson Company as a sales rep in the Detroit area. Dad's most famous quote addressing me - "You wouldn't have a business if it wasn't for the chefs!" A statement whose truth I'll never forget.
3.   L. J. Minor, President
4.   Dr. Ernest Koves, Vice President
5.   Mr. David Swanson, Eric Swanson Sales Co.
6.   Chef George Marchand, Detroit, Michigan
7.   Chef Herman Breithaupt, Detroit, Michigan
8.   Chef Otto Denkinger, Seattle, Washington - "The Explorer" - Otto's son was an executive at Northwest Airlines. Otto introduced Minor food bases in Alaska and Hawaii in the 60's as well as in the Seattle area.
9.   Chef Harry Bazaan, Los Angeles, California - "The Articulator" - Harry was a friend to the chefs in the Disneyland area and was great at writing and talking. He first sold Minor's to the chefs in Los Angeles.
10.   Chef Michael Palmer, Cincinnati, Ohio - Michael was a pastry chef who found uses for our bases in breads and cookies.
11.   Chef Emile Burgermeister, Cleveland, Ohio
12.   Chef John Secter, Fort Thomas, Kentucky
13.   Chef Jean Caubet, Detroit, Michigan
14.   Chef Pierre Bacque, Miami, Florida - Pierre was called "King of the Beach." He opened the Americana and Fountainbleu Hotels and could have any job on the beach.

1970 - Mrs. Jan Williams, home economist, formerly with Stouffer's Foods, was hired by consultant Ruth Engler, who also joined Minor's after leaving Stouffer's through Dr. Ryan's influence. Together they improved quality control and developed specs for raw materials. They also worked together on product development and improvement.

Jan Williams later hired Bev Daigle, another former Stouffer's employee, who worked on developing new raw materials and finding new sources of raw materials.

Mrs. Engler also developed job descriptions for all plant occupations.

The late 60's and early 70's - More salesmen and more chefs:

Mr. Howard Schatz, Hospital Food Specialist, joined the company and has built sales in excess of $2 million per year in the Philadelphia area.

643

Mr. Neil Stoddard developed the St. Louis-Kansas City area.

Tom Calhoun and his brother sold Minor's bases in the Southern California area together with Bud Murphy, Chef A. Cline and Chef Art Jones.

Chef Charles Altorfer, Portland, Oregon.

Mrs. Rosemary Secter, Chef John Secter's widow, in Kentucky and West Virginia. Maurice Fitzgerald in New Orleans.

Chef and Maitre'd John DeJohn in Winston-Salem, North Carolina.

Mr. Dan Ambrosio, salesman in Florida. Worked with Eric Swanson there and Chef Jean Salomon, formerly with the CIA, in the Jacksonville area.

Chef Al Mahlke in St. Paul.

Chef Jim Kosec in Colorado.

Mr. Robert Krump, sales in Colorado.

Chef Henry Frank in Arizona.

Chef Harry Bazaan in Southern California (LA area).

Mr. David Belzer (sales) in Chicago area.

Mr. Dave Swanson and Mr. Ernie Kelly, sales in Detroit.

This was the sales organization that Dr. Ryan build, but the best was yet to come when he recruited General John D. McLaughlin in 1974. Another coup in 1976 was securing the help of Walter Nicholes' agency in advertising Minor's bases. Sales increases soon reflected the favorable influence of Walter's efforts.

In 1977, Colonels Ernie Wilson and Jim Durham, through the Tom Ryan/John McLaughlin influence, started to sell in Virginia, North and South Carolina, and later in Texas.

Corporate Executive Chef Michael Lewis Minor, CEC (Certified Executive Chef), and a member of the American Academy of Chefs, the honorary society of the American Culinary Federation, joined Minor's. He served his apprenticeship for 3-1/2 years with the greatest culinarian of our time, Mr. Hermann Rusch, at the Greenbrier Hotel. He was Sous

Chef at the famous Williamsburg Inn, and Executive Chef for more than two years at the Deering-Milliken Company in South Carolina.

When Michael started at Minor's he worked at every production job in the plant. Later, with Michael Zelski, he worked on improving production efficiency and helped Jan Williams with research, product development and product improvement.

1978 - George Hvizd - The Sanitarian and Packaging Specialist - George was also in purchasing, and for several years did an outstanding job in production. He is no longer with Minor's.

1980 the McLaughlin Sales Strategy

Three sales divisions:
1.   Institutional
2.   Industrial
3.   Export
Now expanding to forth with
4.   Retail

1980 - Industrial Sales Specialist Jack Cassidy joined Minor's giving us a big boost in sales potential.

1980 - John McLaughlin, Jr. (sales) - John Jr. became Jack Cassidy's assistant in industrial sales and has been successful in developing several key industrial accounts.

Plant History

1951 - First Plant at Bertman's

An air-conditioned room 18 x 20 feet in Bertman Foods on East 76th in Cleveland. The first mixer purchased from an equipment distributor for $85.00. I asked, "Does it run?" He answered, "I don't know." We sent it to Hobart's Cleveland service department, and they reconditioned it for $180.00.

1953 - Second Plant at West 116th Street

Our second plant was in what used to be a horse barn for a coal yard. It is a block building that we improved sufficiently to qualify for U.S. Federal Inspection in 1957. Dr. Willie of the Poultry Inspection Division of the United States Department of Agriculture approved our plant for federal inspection in 1957. The plant area was 1500 sq. ft. on two floor levels.

1961 - Third Plant at 2621 West 25th Street

Present location. The building was used as a car wash. We installed an inspector's office, men's and women's lavatories, and a quality control room, together with a processing room all of concrete block within enameled sheet rock ceilings (taped to exclude cracks) and green tile walls with adequate lighting. Plant expansion in 1960 followed in 1963, again in 1970 and again in 1975 and later.

Appendix 3

"THAD EURE" TALK

Follow your dreams, for dreamers are visionaries. Be the best you can be. Keep strong, healthy and happy of body, mind and soul. Be a quality person. Be well-spoken, well-dressed and have the best manners.

Knowledge is power that comes from work, study and vicariously from others. Work and earn while you learn by working in the best places. When training and teaching your employees be kind, courteous and patient. Praise and take a personal interest in them and they'll lift you up. Remember, "Man cannot stand defeat." Have faith, hope and love.

When planning for the future, consider Murphy's Law, "That anything that can happen will happen." Remember Confucius' philosophy, "All things are difficult before they are easy." Perseverance always pays off.

Knowledge brings new opportunities. At age 50 I received my Ph.D. in Food Science from Michigan State University. Another opportunity came with my Ph.D. degree. Dr. Kotschevar asked me to teach Food Chemistry to his students in MSU's Hospitality Business School. After consulting with Dr. Ryan, who managed the L. J. Minor Corp., we agreed that I could teach half-time and spend the rest of the year working with him in building our business.

This resulted in a new course entitled <u>Food Service Science</u> and publication of a text authored by Dr. Laura Lee Smith of Cornell's Hotel School, with contributions by some of my guest lecturers and me. The text has 600 pages of information that can be useful to Hospitality and Foodservice managers. Later, I taught courses in Food Production Systems, Food Production Standards and Food Flavor Evaluation; published textbooks on <u>Nutrition and Flavor and Sanitation, Safety and Environmental Standards,</u> edited texts on <u>University Foodservice Standards</u> by Peter Eccles, <u>Fat and Oil Standards</u> by Harry Lawson, <u>Resort Foodservice Standards</u> by John Knight and Charles Salter, <u>Basic Accounting Standards</u> by Ninemier and Schmidgall, and numerous articles published in <u>The Cornell Quarterly</u>. About 3000 Hospitality Business students took one or more courses that I taught. Meanwhile, by teaching half-time, I still spent 6 months a year helping Dr. Ryan and General McLaughlin in our business of making food bases.

In 1968 we hired a G.I. Bill graduate named Michael Zelski, who was one of my students. He did an outstanding job for the Minor Corp. for 18 years as plant manager.

In 1983, for health reasons, I told Don Smith I had to retire after teaching half-time for 20 years. Mrs. Minor and I also gave our permission to General McLaughlin, on the advice of our attorney, Herman Taber, to sell our company to a small group of investors from Connecticut. Ours was a family business. Five of our children worked for the company. Our daughter Ruth Ann was a plant supervisor, our daughter Carol was a Quality Control checker, our daughter Josephine worked on Quality Control and operated the plant computer, a fourth daughter Mary Margaret worked in packaging and Quality Control. Our son Michael worked with Michael Zelski improving manufacturing methods and equipment. He joined the company as a professional chef in 1977. Today, Michael works for the L. J. Minor Foodservice Division of Food Ingredient Specialties and is Vice President in charge of Professional Services - a team of professional chefs who help key accounts. Another of my former students, Ingolf Nitsch, is now the plant manager for this division of Nestle, U.S.A.

We started making bases in a room measuring 18 x 20 feet in Bertman's warehouse on East 276th Street in Cleveland. Today's manufacturing of bases is done at 2621 West 25th Street, Cleveland, in a plant covering almost a city block, and is owned by Nestle, U.S.A.

Mrs Minor, our children and I are happy to be sharing the fruits of our labors by helping Foodservice Educators who are the backbone and the future of our great Foodservice and Hospitality Industry.

So follow your dreams, for as Langston Hughes, in 1932, says in his poem:

> Hold fast to dreams,
> For if dreams die
> Life is like a broken-winged bird
> Than cannot fly.
>
> Hold fast to dreams,
> For life is a barren field
> Frozen with snow
> When dreams go.

Remember Yul Brynner's last words, "Just don't smoke."

Vince Hegarty (1996) in his book Nutrition, Food and the Environment, states:

> Smoking is the single most preventable cause of illness in the
> United States. More deaths are attributed to it than to alcohol,
> all other addictive drugs, accidents and suicides, combined.

Control you alcohol intake, too. For the line of demarcation between recreation and dissipation rapidly becomes indistinct.

Follow your dreams. Never stop learning. Be all that you can be. Keep up with progress in your field by reading periodicals and attending meetings that are Foodservice and Hospitality oriented.

An Irish Blessing

May the road rise to meet you.
May the wind be always at your back.
May the sun shine warm upon your face,
The rains fall soft upon your fields.
And 'til we meet again,
May God hold you in the palm of His hand.

Index

654